CHRISTIAN *writers'* MARKET GUIDE

SALLY E. STUART

P.284

JOY PUBLISHING
PO BOX 827
SAN JUAN CAPISTRANO, CA 92675

Printed in the United States of America

Library of Congress Catalog Card Number 85-72779
International Standard Serial Number 0891-8279

ISBN # 0-939513-94-3

Joy Publishing
P.O. Box 827
San Juan Capistrano, CA 92675

CONTENTS

I. ABOUT THIS BOOK

Introduction

II. BOOK PUBLISHERS

1. Topical/Subject Listings of Book Publishers

** Indicates a new topic this year*

III. PERIODICALS

** Indicates a new topic this year*

Introduction

The business of writing, like almost any other business, requires specialized tools to do the job right. This market guide is one of the most important of those tools. In some ways it is like other market guides; in other ways it is unique.

First, it deals specifically with Christian markets. Every effort has been made to include as much information as possible on as many different markets as possible. In this ninth edition you will find 84 periodicals, 28 book publishers, and 12 greeting card publishers that were not in the '93-94 edition. In the alphabetical listings, new additions are marked with a (+) plus sign before the title.

In addition, there are five new periodical topics and two new book topics. Those are marked with an asterisk in the table of contents and the topical listings.

In the primary listings for both book and periodical publishers, I have tried to expand the descriptive information and tips to help you better understand the slant of each publisher. For the first time, the periodical section includes the number of pages and the subscription rate. All sections include the Fax numbers, if available.

Book publishers were asked if they publish ethnic books, and their listings reflect that. You will also find some ethnic listings in the periodical section, and it will be expanded for next year. Ethnic markets are included as a topic for both books and periodicals.

This year we have expanded the list of Christian newspapers to over 40, and those are listed under "Newspapers" in the periodical topics.

This year I sent out over 1,700 questionnaires and received responses from about 675; an additional 250 markets were contacted by phone to verify information. Following each of the primary listings is a list of publishers who have been dropped for various reasons, often at their request.

The list of literary agents has grown, as has the list of secular newspapers, with religion editor's names.

I do want to thank those who have offered suggestions for additions or improvements in the past, and encourage all of you to send ideas that might improve content or format in the future.

As with any new reference book, I suggest you spend some quality time becoming familiar with its contents and structure. Discover the supplementary lists available throughout the book. Read through the glossary and spend a few minutes learning terms you are not familiar with. Review the lists of writers' groups and conferences and mark those you might be interested in pursuing during the coming months. The denominational listing will help you start making the important connection between periodicals and book publishers associated with different denominations.

All this time will be well spent as you become more aware of how this market book can help you in the year ahead, as well as simply becoming more familiar with the special needs of Christian/religious publishers.

The most unique feature of this market guide is the extensive topical or subject listings included for both periodicals and book publishers. They will give you clear indications of which publishers are interested in articles or books on which topics. That is a feature you will not find to this extent in any other market guide.

Be sure to carefully study the "How to Use This Book" section. It will save you a lot of time and frustration in trying to understand the meaning of all the notations in the primary listings. Also send for sample copies (or catalog) and guidelines for any of these publishers or periodicals you are not familiar with. Then study those carefully before submitting anything to that publisher. One of the biggest complaints I am still getting from publishers is that the material they receive routinely is not appropriate for their needs. I have tried to assure them that with this guide you will be making more appropriate submissions, but it will take some time and effort on your part to make that a reality. I have given you as much help as possible, but it is still up to you to take the necessary steps to distinguish yourself as a professional. I can't encourage you enough to do that.

Editors tell me repeatedly that they are looking for writers who understand them, their periodical or publishing house, and most of all, their unique approach to the marketplace. With a little time and effort, you can fulfill all their expectations and sell what you write.

I wish you well as you embark on this exciting road to publication, whether for the first time or as a long-time veteran. Each of us has been given a specific mission in the field of writing. We often feel inadequate to the task, but I learned a long time ago that the writing assignments God has given me cannot be written quite as well by anyone else. Unfortunately God has often had to settle for second best when one of us has failed to fulfill His assignment.

Sally E. Stuart
17768 SW Pointe Forest Ct.
Aloha OR 97006
(503)642-9844

HOW TO USE THIS BOOK

This ninth edition of the Christian Writers' Market Guide continues the growth, change, and improvements seen in previous editions. The lists of topics for both books and periodicals is the feature that makes this book most valuable. In the topical sections you will find a letter "R" following each publisher that accepts reprints. (Reprints are pieces that have been printed in other publications, but you retain the rights to.)

In the Book Section last year, I replaced the list of publishers in order by the number of books they publish each year, with a list of only the top 25 publishers, but this year I am including both of those lists. Again this year, those listings are followed by several additional sections of valuable marketing analysis and information.

In the Periodical Section, a comparable list gives the top periodicals (by circulation) in each category and the complete list again, followed by information to help you better understand the periodicals market.

The purpose of this market guide is to make your marketing job easier and more targeted. However, it will serve you well only if you put some time and effort into studying its contents and using it as a springboard for discovering and becoming an expert on those publishers best suited to your writing topics and style.

Below you will find information on its general set-up and instructions for its use. In order to help you become more of an expert on marketing, I am including an explanation of each entry in the alphabetical listings for both the book section and the periodical section. Be sure to study these before trying to use this book.

GENERAL SET-UP AND INSTRUCTIONS

1. Spend some time initially getting acquainted with the contents and set-up of this resource book. You cannot make the best use of it until you know exactly what it has to offer.

2. Study the Contents pages, where you will find listings of all the periodical and book topics. When selecting a topic, be sure to check related topics as well. Some cross-referencing will often be helpful.

3. The Primary/Alphabetical Listings for book and periodical publishers contain those publishers who answered the questionnaire and those who did not. The listings preceded by an asterisk (*) or number symbol (#) are those publishers who didn't respond to a request for information. Since the information in those is a repeat of last year's listing, came from my existing files or available resources, we cannot guarantee its accuracy. For that reason you are encouraged to send for sample copies or catalogs and writers' guidelines before submitting to any of them.

4. In each book-publisher listing you will find the following information (as available), in this format:

a) Name of publisher

b) Address, phone number, and Fax #.

c) Denomination or affiliation

d) Name of editor - This may include the editor's name, followed by the name of another editor to whom submissions should be sent. In a few cases a number of editors is named with the type of books each is responsible for. Address to appropriate editor.

e) Number of inspirational/religious titles published per year.

f) Number of submissions received annually.

g) Percentage of books from first-time authors.

h) Whether or not they will accept books through agents.

i) The percentage of books they subsidy publish from freelance authors (if any).

j) Whether they reprint out-of-print books from other publishers.

k) Preferred manuscript length in words or pages.

l) Average amount of royalty, if provided. If royalty is a percentage of wholesale or net, it is based on price paid by bookstores or distributors. If it is on retail price, it is based on cover price of the book (preferable).

m) Average amount paid for advances -Whether a publisher pays an advance or not is noted in the listing; if they did not answer the question, there is no mention of it.

n) Whether they make any outright purchases and amount paid.

o) Average first printing is number of books usually printed for a first-time author.

p) Average length of time between acceptance of a manuscript and publication of the work.

q) Whether they consider simultaneous submissions. This means you can send a query or complete manuscript simultaneously to more than one publisher, as long as you advise everyone involved that you are doing so.

r) Length of time it should take them to respond to a query/proposal or to a complete manuscript (when two lengths of time are given, the first generally refers to a query and the latter to a complete manuscript). Give them a 1 month grace period beyond that and then send a polite follow-up letter if you haven't heard from them.

s) Availability and cost for writers' guidelines and book catalogs - If the listing says "Guidelines," it means they are available for a #10 (business-sized) SASE with 1 first-class stamp. The cost of the catalog (if any), the size of envelope, and amount of postage are given, if specified (affix stamps to envelope, don't send loose). Tip: If postage required is more than $1.05, I suggest you put $1.05 in postage on the envelope and clearly mark it "Special 4th Class Rate." (That is enough for up to 1#). If the listing says "free catalog," it means you need only request it, they do not ask for payment or SASE. Note: If sending for both guidelines and catalog, it is not necessary to send both envelopes. Guidelines will be sent with catalog.

t) Nonfiction Section - Preference for query letter, book proposal, or complete manuscript. (If they want a query letter, send just a letter describing your project. If they want a query letter/proposal, you can add a chapter-by-chapter synopsis and the number of sample chapters indicated. If not specified, send one to three chapters.) This is often followed by a quote from them about their needs, or what they don't want to see. There is also an indication of whether or not they will accept phone queries.

u) Fiction Section - Same information as nonfiction section.

v) Special Needs - If they have specific topics they need that are not included in the subject listings, they are indicated here.

w) Ethnic Books: Usually specifies which ethnic groups they target or any particular needs.

x) Tips - Specific tips provided by the editor/publisher.

Note: No information is included on acceptance of books on computer disk. Most publishers now do accept or even require that books be sent on a computer disk (usually along with a hard copy), but since each publisher`s needs is different, that information will be supplied to you by the publisher who is interested in your book or manuscript.

5. In each periodical listing you will find the following information (as available), in this format:

a) Name of periodical

b) Address, phone number and Fax #.

c) Denomination or affiliation

d) Name of editor and editor to submit to (if different).

e) Theme of publication - This will help you understand their particular slant.

f) Format of publication, frequency of publication, number of pages and size of circulation - Tells whether magazine, newsletter, journal, tabloid, or take-home paper. Frequency of publication indicates

quantity of material needed. Number of pages usually indicates how much material they can use. Circulation indicates the amount of exposure your material will receive, and often indicates how well they might pay or probability that they will stay in business.

g) Subscription rate - Amount given is for a one-year subscription in the country of origin. I suggest you subscribe to at least one of your primary markets every year to become better acquainted with its specific focus.

h) Date established - Included only if 1990 or later.

i) Openness to freelance; percentage freelance written. If they buy only a small percentage, it often means they are open but receive little that is appropriate. The percentage freelance written indicates how great your changes are of selling to them. When you have a choice, choose those with the higher percentage, but only if you have done your homework and know they are an appropriate market for your material.

j) Preference for query or complete manuscript, whether they want a cover letter with complete manuscripts, and whether they will accept phone queries.

k) Payment schedule; payment on acceptance or publication; and rights purchased.

l) If a publication does not pay, or pays in copies or subscription, that is indicated in bold, capital letters.

m) If a publication is not copyrighted, it is indicated. That means that you should ask for your copyright notice to appear on your piece when they publish it, so your rights will be protected.

n) Preferred word lengths and average number of manuscripts purchased per year (in parentheses).

o) Reporting time - The time they usually take to respond to your query or manuscript submission (add mail time).

p) Seasonal material (also refers to holiday) - If sending holiday or seasonal material it should reach them the specified length of time in advance.

q) Average amount of kill fee, if they pay one.

r) Acceptance of simultaneous submissions and previously published material - If they accept simultaneous submissions, it means they will look at submissions (usually timely topic or holiday material) sent simultaneously to several publishers. Best to send to non-overlapping markets (such as denominational), and be sure to indicate that it is a simultaneous submission.

s) Availability and cost for writer's guidelines, theme list, and sample copies - If the listing says "Guidelines," it means they are available for a #10 SASE (business-sized) with 1 first-class stamp. The cost for a sample copy, the size of envelope, and number of stamps required are given, if specified (affix stamps to envelope, don't send loose). Tip: If postage required is more than $1.05, I suggest you put $1.05 in postage on the envelope and clearly mark it "Special 4th Class Rate." (That is enough for up to 1#). If the listing says "Free sample copy" it means you need only to request them, they do not ask for payment or SASE. Note: If sending for both guidelines and sample copy, it is not necessary to send both envelopes. Guidelines will be sent with sample copy.

t) Poetry: Name of poetry editor (if different). Average number of poems bought each year. Types of poetry; number of lines. Payment rate. Maximum number of poems you may submit at one time.

u) Fillers: Name of fillers editor (if different). Types of fillers accepted; word length. Payment rate.

w) Columns/Departments: Name of column editor. Names of columns in the periodical; word length requirements; payment. Be sure to see sample before sending manuscript or query. Most columns require a query.

v) Special Issues or Needs: Indicates topics of special issues they have planned for the year, or unique topics not included in regular subject listings.

w) Tips: Tips from the editor on how to break into this market or how to be successful as an author.

x) Ethnic: Any involvement they have in the ethnic market.

6. It is important that you adhere closely to the guidelines set out in these listings. If a publisher asks for a query only, do not send a complete manuscript. Following these guidelines will mark you as a professional.

7. If your manuscript is completed, select the proper topical listing and target audience, and make up a list of possible publishers. Check first to see which ones will accept a complete manuscript (if you want to send it to those that require a query, you will have to write a query letter or book proposal to send first). Please do not assume that your manuscript will be appropriate for all those on the list. Read the primary listing for each and if you are not familiar with a publisher, read their writers' guidelines and study one or more sample copies or book catalog. (The primary listings contain information on how to get these.) Be sure the slant of your manuscript fits the slant of the publisher.

8. If you have an idea for an article, short story, or book but you have not written it yet, a reading of the appropriate topical listing will help you decide on a possible slant or approach. Select some publishers to whom you might send a query about your idea. If your idea is for an article, do not overlook the possibility of writing on the same topic for a number of different periodicals listed under that topic, either with the same target audience, or another from the list that indicates an interest. For example you

could write on money management for a general adult magazine, a teen magazine, women's publication, or for pastors. Each would require a different slant, but you would get a lot more mileage from that idea.

9. If you do not have an idea, simply start reading through the topical listings or the primary listings. They are sure to trigger any number of book or magazine ideas you could go to work on.

10. If you run into words or terms you are not familiar with, check the glossary at the back of the book for definitions.

11. ALWAYS SEND AN SASE WITH EVERY QUERY OR MANUSCRIPT.

12. DO NOT RELY SOLELY ON THE INFORMATION PROVIDED IN THIS MARKET GUIDE. It is just that—a guide—and is not intended to be complete in itself. It is important to your success as a freelance writer that you learn how to use writers' guides and study book catalogs or sample copies before submitting to any publisher. Be a professional!

TOPICAL/SUBJECT LISTINGS OF BOOK PUBLISHERS

One of the most difficult aspects of marketing is trying to determine which publishers might be interested in the book you want to write. This topical listing was designed to help you do just that.

First, look up your topic of interest in the following lists. If you don't find the specific topic, check the list of topics in the table of contents and find any related topics. Once you have discovered which publishers are interested in a particular topic, the next step is to secure writers' guidelines and book catalogs from those publishers. Don't assume that just because a particular publisher is listed under your topic that it would automatically be interested in your book. It is your job to determine whether your approach to the subject will fit within the unique scope of that publisher's catalog. It is also helpful to visit a Christian bookstore to actually see some of the books produced by each publisher you are interested in pursuing.

Note, too, that the primary listings for each publisher indicate what the publisher prefers to see in the way of a query, book proposal, or complete manuscript.

R - Indicates which publishers reprint out-of-print books from other publishers.

APOLOGETICS

Baker Book House - R
Brentwood - R
Bridge Publishing - R
Broadman & Holman
Christian Classics - R
College Press - R
Companion Press - R
Concordia - R
Crossway
Eerdmans Publishing
Franciscan Press - R
Franciscan Univ Press - R
Friends United Press - R
HarperSanFrancisco - R
Harvest House - R
Hensley, Virgil W. - R
Huntington House - R
InterVarsity Press
Kregel - R
Liguori Publications
Loyola Univ Press - R
Morehouse Publishing - R
Nazarene Publishing House
Nelson, Thomas - R
Our Sunday Visitor
Oxford University
Pillar Books - R
Presbyterian/Reformed - R
PROBE Ministries - R
Proclaim Publishing - R
Revell, Fleming H.
Review & Herald
St. Bede's Publications - R
Servant Publications - R
Scarecrow Press
Son-Rise
Star Song - R
Still Waters Revival - R
Trinity Foundation - R
Tyler Press - R
Tyndale House - R
Victor Books
Victory House - R
Welch Publishing - R
World Bible - R
Zondervan - R
Zondervan/Academic

ARCHAEOLOGY

Baker Book House - R
Bob Jones - R
Brentwood - R
Broadman & Holman
Christopher Publishing Hs
Companion Press - R
Concordia - R
Didaskon Publishing - R
Eerdmans Publishing
HarperSanFrancisco - R
Franciscan Press - R
Hendrickson Publishers - R
InterVarsity Press
Kregel - R
Morning Star Press - R
Nelson, Thomas - R

Oxford University
Proclaim Publishing - R
Review & Herald
Scarecrow Press
TEACH Services - R
Trinity Press Intl. - R
Tyler Press - R
University Press/
America - R
Welch Publishing - R
Westminster Press
World Bible - R
Yale - R
Zondervan - R
Zondervan/Academic

AUTOBIOGRAPHY

Bantam Books
Brentwood - R
Bridge Publishing - R
Christopher Publishing Hs
Companion Press - R
Creation House - R
CREDO
DaBaR Services - R
Didaskon Publishing - R
Eerdmans Publishing
Fairway Press - R
Friends United Press - R
HarperSanFrancisco - R
Huntington House - R
Kindred Press
Living Flame Press
Living Sacrifice - R
LuraMedia
Nelson, Thomas - R
New Leaf Press - R
OMF Books
Prescott Press - R
Proclaim Publishing - R
Promise Publishing
Rainbow Books (FL)
Son-Rise
Southern Baptist Press - R
Still Waters Revival - R
TEACH Services - R
Trinity Press Intl. - R
Triumph Books - R
Tyler Press - R
Tyndale House - R
University Press/America - R
Upper Room Books
VESTA
Victory House - R
Welch Publishing - R
Westminster Press
Zondervan - R

BIBLE/BIBLICAL STUDIES

Aglow
Alba House - R
AMG Publishers - R
Augsburg Fortress - R
Baker Book House - R
Bible Discovery
Brentwood - R
Bridge Publishing - R
Brown-ROA
Center for Learning
Chalice Press
Christian Classics - R
Christian Ed. Publishers
Christopher Publishing Hs
College Press - R
Collier/Macmillan
Companion Press - R
Concordia - R
Contemporary Drama
Cornell Univ Press - R
Creation House - R
Crossway
CSS Publishing
DaBaR Services - R
Didaskon Publishing - R
Discipleship Resources
Eerdmans Publishing
Fairway Press - R
Forward Movement - R
Franciscan Press - R
Franciscan Univ Press - R
Good Book
Group Publishing
HarperSanFrancisco - R
Harrison House - R
Harvest House - R
Hendrickson Publishers - R
Hensley, Virgil W. - R
Herald Press - R
Honor Books
InterVarsity Press
Kindred Press
Kregel - R
Liguori Publications
Liturgical Press
Living Flame Press
LuraMedia
Morehouse Publishing - R
Morning Star Press - R
Morris, Joshua (kids)
Nazarene Publishing House
Nelson, Thomas - R
New Hope - R
New Leaf Press - R
Novalis
Our Sunday Visitor
Oxford University
Paraclete Press - R
Pastoral Press
Pillar Books - R
Presbyterian/Reformed - R
Proclaim Publishing - R
Promise Publishing
Resource Publications
Revell, Fleming H.
Review & Herald
Roper Press - R
St. Anthony Messenger - R
St. Bede's Publications - R
Shaw Publishers, Harold - R
Sheed & Ward - R
Shining Star
Son-Rise
Southern Baptist Press - R
TEACH Services - R
Trinity Foundation - R
Trinity Press Intl. - R
Tyndale House - R
United Church Press
United Church Publishing
University Press/America - R
Upper Room Books
VESTA
Victor Books
Victory House - R
Warner Press
Welch Publishing - R
Westminster Press
Women's Miss. Union - R
World Bible - R
Yale - R

Zondervan - R
Zondervan/Academic

BIOGRAPHY

Alba House - R
Bantam Books
Bob Jones - R
Bosco Multimedia, Don
Brentwood - R
Bridge Publishing - R
Broadman & Holman
Christian Classics - R
Christian Liter. Crusade - R
Christopher Publishing Hs
Companion Press - R
Cornell Univ Press - R
Creation House - R
CREDO
Crossway
CSS Publishing
Eerdmans Publishing
Fairway Press - R
Forward Movement - R
Franciscan Press - R
Friends United Press - R
HarperSanFrancisco - R
Huntington House - R
ICS Publications - R
Kindred Press
Kregel - R
Living Sacrifice - R
Loyola Univ Press - R
Morrow and Co., William
Nelson, Thomas - R
New Leaf Press - R
OMF Books
Oxford University
Pilgrim Press
Proclaim Publishing - R
Questar - R
Rainbow Books (FL)
Review & Herald
St. Bede's Publications - R
Scarecrow Press
Servant Publications - R
Son-Rise
Southern Baptist Press - R
Starburst Publishers
Star Song - R
Still Waters Revival - R
TEACH Services - R
Trinity Foundation - R
Trinity Press Intl. - R
Triumph Books - R
Tyler Press - R
Tyndale House - R
United Church Press
University Press/America - R
Upper Room Books
VESTA
Victory House - R
Warner Press
Welch Publishing - R
Westminster Press
Women's Miss. Union - R
Yale - R
Zondervan - R

CELEBRITY PROFILES

Christopher Publishing Hs
Collier/Macmillan
Companion Press - R
Eerdmans Publishing
Huntington House - R
Lifetime Books
Morning Star Press - R
Nelson, Thomas - R
New Leaf Press - R
Prescott Press - R
Proclaim Publishing - R
Servant Publications - R
Shaw Publishers, Harold - R
Starburst Publishers
Star Song - R
Tyler Press - R
Tyndale House - R
Victor Books
Victory House - R
Welch Publishing - R
WRS Publishing - R
Zondervan - R

CHILDREN'S PICTURE BOOKS

Alba House - R
Augsburg Fortress - R
Barbour & Co. - R
Bay Publications, Mel - R
Bridge Publishing - R
Brownlow Publishing
Concordia - R
CREDO
Eerdmans Publishing
Emerald Books - R
Fairway Press - R
Friends United Press - R
Forward Movement - R
Gibson, C.R. - R
Gold'N'Honey
Harvest House - R
Herald Press - R
Huntington House - R
Kindred Press
Living Flame Press
Meriwether Publishing - R
Morehouse Publishing - R
Morris, Joshua
National Baptist - R
Nelson, Thomas - R
Our Sunday Visitor
Pacific Press
Pelican Publishing - R
Prescott Press - R
Proclaim Publishing - R
Questar - R
Regina Press
Roper Press - R
Son-Rise
Standard - R
Starburst Publishers
Tyler Press - R
United Methodist
Upper Room Books
Victor Books
Victory House - R
Welch Publishing - R
Zondervan - R

CHRISTIAN EDUCATION

Accent
Augsburg Fortress - R
Baker Book House - R
Bantam Books
Bosco Multimedia, Don
Brentwood - R
Bridge Publishing - R
Bristol House - R
Broadman & Holman
Brown-ROA
Center for Learning
Chalice Press

Christian Classics - R
Christian Publications - R
Christopher Publishing Hs
Concordia - R
Contemporary Drama Service
CSS Publishing
Didaskon Publishing - R
Discipleship Resources
Educational Ministries
Eerdmans Publishing
Fairway Press - R
Friends United Press - R
Group Publishing
Harrison House - R
Harvest House - R
Hensley, Virgil W. - R
Herald Press - R
Honor Books
Huntington House - R
Judson Press - R
Kindred Press
Kregel - R
Liguori Publications
Liturgical Press
Loyola Univ Press - R
Master Books - R
Moody Press
Morehouse Publishing - R
Morning Star Press - R
Morris, Joshua
National Baptist - R
Nazarene Publishing House
Nelson, Thomas - R
New Leaf Press - R
Omega Publications
Our Sunday Visitor
Presbyterian/Reformed - R
Prescott Press - R
PROBE Ministries - R
Proclaim Publishing - R
Questar - R
Rainbow Books (CA)
Religious Education Press
Resource Publications
Review & Herald
St. Paul Books - R
Scripture Press
Shining Star
Southern Baptist Press - R
Standard - R
Starburst Publishers
Still Waters Revival - R
Tabor Publishing
TEACH Services - R
Trinity Foundation - R
United Church Press
United Church Publishing
United Methodist
VESTA
Victor Books
Warner Press
Welch Publishing - R
Westminster Press
Women's Miss. Union - R
Zondervan - R

CHRISTIAN HOME SCHOOLING

AMG Publishers - R
Augsburg Fortress - R
Bantam Books
Bay Publications, Mel - R
Brentwood - R
Brown-ROA
Center for Learning
Christopher Publishing Hs
Crossway
CSS Publishing
Didaskon Publishing - R
Eerdmans Publishing
Fairway Press - R
Focus on the Family - R
Hensley, Virgil W. - R
Huntington House - R
Master Books - R
Morris, Joshua
Nelson, Thomas - R
New Leaf Press - R
Prescott Press - R
Proclaim Publishing - R
Questar - R
Review & Herald
Son-Rise
Still Waters Revival - R
TEACH Services - R
Trinity Foundation - R
Tyler Press - R
Tyndale House - R
Victor Books
Victory House - R
Welch Publishing - R

CHRISTIAN LIVING

Aglow
Alba House - R
AMG Publishers - R
Augsburg Fortress - R
Ave Maria Press
Baker Book House - R
Bantam Books
Barclay Press - R
Bethel Publishing - R
Brentwood - R
Bridge Publishing - R
Bristol House - R
Broadman & Holman
Brownlow Publishing
Chalice Press
Chosen Books
Christian Classics - R
Christian Publications - R
Christopher Publishing Hs
Cistercian Publications - R
College Press - R
Collier/Macmillan
Companion Press - R
Concordia - R
Covenant Publishers
Creation House - R
CREDO
Crossway
DaBaR Services - R
Discipleship Resources
Eerdmans Publishing
Emerald Books - R
Fairway Press - R
Focus on the Family - R
Forward Movement - R
Friends United Press - R
HarperSanFrancisco - R
Harrison House - R
Harvest House - R
Haworth Press - R
Hensley, Virgil W. - R
Herald Press - R
Horizon House - R
Huntington House - R
InterVarsity Press
Judson Press - R
Kregel - R
Life Cycle Books - R
LifeJourney - R
Liguori Publications

Liturgical Press
Living Flame Press
Loyola Univ Press - R
LuraMedia
Moody Press
Morehouse Publishing - R
Morning Star Press - R
Nazarene Publishing House
Nelson, Thomas - R
New Hope - R
New Leaf Press - R
Omega Publications
Our Sunday Visitor
Pacific Press
Paraclete Press - R
Pillar Books - R
Presbyterian/Reformed - R
Prescott Press - R
Proclaim Publishing - R
Promise Publishing
Questar - R
Resurrection Press - R
Revell, Fleming H.
Review & Herald
Roper Press - R
St. Bede's Publications - R
St. Paul Books - R
Servant Publications - R
Shaw Publishers, Harold - R
Sheed & Ward - R
Son-Rise
Starburst Publishers
Star Song - R
Still Waters Revival - R
TEACH Services - R
Triumph Books - R
Tyler Press - R
Tyndale House - R
United Church Press
Upper Room Books
VESTA
Victor Books
Victory House - R
Warner Press
Welch Publishing - R
Wellness
Westminster Press
Women's Miss. Union - R
Zondervan - R

CHRISTIAN SCHOOL BOOKS

Center for Learning
Christopher Publishing Hs
Concordia - R
Eerdmans Publishing
Fairway Press - R
Hensley, Virgil W. - R
Huntington House - R
Morehouse Publishing - R
Morris, Joshua
Proclaim Publishing - R
Son-Rise
Southern Baptist Press - R
TEACH Services - R
Trinity Foundation - R
Victory House - R
Welch Publishing - R

CHURCH LIFE

Alban Institute
Augsburg Fortress - R
Baker Book House - R
Bethel Publishing - R
Brentwood - R
Bristol House - R
Broadman & Holman
Center for Learning
Chalice Press
Christian Publications - R
Christopher Publishing Hs
Companion Press - R
Concordia - R
College Press - R
Creation House - R
Crossway
CSS Publishing
Discipleship Resources
Eerdmans Publishing
Fairway Press - R
Franciscan Press - R
Friends United Press - R
HarperSanFrancisco - R
Harrison House - R
Hensley, Virgil W. - R
Herald Press - R
InterVarsity Press
Judson Press - R
Kindred Press
Kregel - R
Liguori Publications
Living Flame Press
Loyola Univ Press - R
Morehouse Publishing - R
Nazarene Publishing House
Nelson, Thomas - R
New Leaf Press - R
Our Sunday Visitor
Pillar Books - R
Presbyterian/Reformed - R
Proclaim Publishing - R
Promise Publishing
Questar - R
Review & Herald
Sheed & Ward - R
TEACH Services - R
Triumph Books - R
Tyler Press - R
Tyndale House - R
United Church Press
United Methodist
Upper Room Books
VESTA
Victor Books
Victory House - R
Warner Press
Welch Publishing - R
Women's Miss. Union - R
Zondervan - R

CHURCH RENEWAL

Alban Institute
Ave Maria Press
Baker Book House - R
Barclay Press - R
Bethel Publishing - R
Brentwood - R
Bridge Publishing - R
Bristol House - R
Broadman & Holman
Center for Learning
Chalice Press
Christian Classics - R
Christian Publications - R
Christopher Publishing Hs
Companion Press - R
Concordia - R
Creation House - R
DaBaR Services - R
Dimension Books - R
Discipleship Resources
Eerdmans Publishing

Fairway Press - R
Franciscan Press - R
Franciscan Univ Press - R
HarperSanFrancisco - R
Harrison House - R
Herald Press - R
InterVarsity Press
Judson Press - R
Kregel - R
Liguori Publications
Living Flame Press
Loyola Univ Press - R
LuraMedia
Morehouse Publishing - R
Morning Star Press - R
Nazarene Publishing House
Nelson, Thomas - R
New Leaf Press - R
Omega Publications
Pastoral Press
Pastor's Choice Press
Presbyterian/Reformed - R
Proclaim Publishing - R
Promise Publishers
Questar - R
Renewal Press
Resurrection Press - R
Review & Herald
Servant Publications - R
Sheed & Ward - R
Southern Baptist Press - R
Star Song - R
TEACH Services - R
Trinity Foundation - R
Triumph Books - R
Tyler Press - R
Tyndale House - R
United Church Press
VESTA
Victory House - R
Welch Publishing - R
Westminster Press
Zondervan - R
Zondervan/Academic

CONTROVERSIAL ISSUES

ACTA Publications
Baker Book House - R
Bantam Books
Brentwood - R
Chalice Press
Chosen Books
Companion Press - R
Franciscan Univ Press - R
HarperSanFrancisco - R
Harvest House - R
Lifetime Books
LuraMedia
Moody Press
Morehouse Publishing - R
Nelson, Thomas - R
New Society Publishers - R
Paulist Press
Pilgrim Press
Pillar Books - R
Prescott Press - R
PROBE Ministries - R
Proclaim Publishing - R
Questar - R
Review & Herald
Still Waters Revival - R
Starburst Publishers
Trinity Foundation - R
Triumph Books - R
Tyler Press - R
Victory House - R

COOKBOOKS

Bantam Books
Brentwood - R
Fairway Press - R
Herald Press - R
(Mennonite/Amish)
Lifetime Books
New Leaf Press - R
Prescott Press - R
Proclaim Publishing - R
Son-Rise
Southern Baptist Press - R
Starburst Publishers
TEACH Services - R
Univ of NC Press
Victor Books
Victory House - R
Welch Publishing - R

COUNSELING AIDS

Accent
Aglow
Augsburg Fortress - R
Baker Book House - R
Bethel Publishing - R
Brentwood - R
Brown-ROA
Center for Learning - R
Chosen Books
Christopher Publishing Hs
Concordia - R
Creation House - R
Dimension Books - R
Eerdmans Publishing
Emerald Books - R
Fairway Press - R
Forward Movement - R
Franciscan Press - R
Friends United Press - R
Group Publishing
HarperSanFrancisco - R
Harvest House - R
Haworth Press - R
Herald Press - R
InterVarsity Press
Judson Press - R
Kregel - R
Life Cycle Books - R
Liguori Publications
Living Flame Press
Loyola Univ Press - R
LuraMedia
Morehouse Publishing - R
Nazarene Publishing House
Neibauer Press - R
Nelson, Thomas - R
New Leaf Press - R
Pastor's Choice Press
Pillar Books - R
Presbyterian/Reformed - R
Prescott Press - R
Proclaim Publishing - R
Questar - R
Rainbow's End
Resource Publications
Resurrection Press - R
Review & Herald
Servant Publications - R
Shining Star
Son-Rise
Southern Baptist Press - R
TEACH Services - R
Trinity Press Intl. - R
Triumph Books - R
Tyndale House - R

VESTA
Victor Books
Victory House - R
Warner Press
Welch Publishing - R
Westminster Press
WRS Publishing - R
Zondervan - R
Zondervan/Academic

CULTS/OCCULT

AMG Publishers - R
Baker Book House - R
Bantam Books
Bridge Publishing - R
Broadman & Holman
Christopher Publishing Hs
Concordia - R
Creation House - R
Eerdmans Publishing
HarperSanFrancisco - R
Harvest House - R
Huntington House - R
InterVarsity Press
Kregel - R
Life Enrichment
Living Flame Press
Morning Star Press - R
Nelson, Thomas - R
New Hope - R
New Leaf Press - R
Open Court - R
Our Sunday Visitor
Presbyterian/Reformed - R
Prescott Press - R
PROBE Ministries - R
Proclaim Publishing - R
Revell, Fleming H.
Review & Herald
Servant Publications - R
Son-Rise
Starburst Publishers
TEACH Services - R
Trinity Foundation - R
Trinity Press Intl. - R
Triumph Books - R
Tyler Press - R
Tyndale House - R
VESTA
Victor Books
Victory House - R
Welch Publishing - R
Women's Miss. Union - R
Zondervan - R
Zondervan/Academic

CURRENT/SOCIAL ISSUES

Alba House - R
AMG Publishers - R
Baker Book House - R
Barclay Press - R
Brentwood - R
Bridge Publishing - R
Bristol House - R
Center for Learning
Chalice Press
Chosen Books
Christian Publications - R
Christopher Publishing Hs
Collier/Macmillan
Companion Press - R
Concordia - R
Cornell Univ Press - R
Creation House - R
Crossway
DaBaR Services - R
Eerdmans Publishing
Fairway Press - R
Forward Movement - R
Franciscan Press - R
Friendship Press
HarperSanFrancisco - R
Harvest House - R
Haworth Press - R
Herald Press - R
Horizon House - R
Huntington House - R
InterVarsity Press
Judson Press - R
Kindred Press
Kregel - R
Life Cycle Books - R
Lifetime Books
Liguori Publications
Loyola Univ Press - R
LuraMedia
Moody Press
Morehouse Publishing - R
Nazarene Publishing House
Nelson, Thomas - R
New Hope - R
New Leaf Press - R
New Society Publishers - R
Pilgrim Press
Presbyterian/Reformed - R
Prescott Press - R
Proclaim Publishing - R
Questar - R
Resurrection Press - R
Review & Herald
Servant Publications - R
Shaw Publishers, Harold - R
Son-Rise
Starburst Publishers
Star Song - R
Still Waters Revival - R
Trinity Foundation - R
Trinity Press Intl. - R
Triumph Books - R
Tyler Press - R
Tyndale House - R
University Press/America - R
Upper Room Books
VESTA
Victor Books
Victory House - R
Welch Publishing - R
Westminster Press
Women's Miss. Union - R
Zondervan - R

CURRICULUM

Accent
Augsburg Fortress
Center for Learning
Christian Ed. Publishers
Christopher Publishing Hs
Church Growth Institute
Companion Press - R
Concordia - R
CSS Publishing
Didaskon Publishing - R
Educational Ministries
Franciscan Press - R
Friends United Press - R
Group Publishing
Hensley, Virgil W. - R
Master Books - R
Morehouse Publishing - R
New Society Publishers - R
Novalis
Scripture Press

Trinity Foundation - R
United Church Press
University Press/America - R
Welch Publishing - R
Wellness

DEVOTIONAL BOOKS

Alba House - R
Augsburg Fortress - R
Baker Book House - R
Barbour & Co. - R
Barclay Press - R
Bible Discovery
Brentwood - R
Bridge Publishing - R
Broadman & Holman
Brownlow Publishing
Center for Learning
Chosen Books
Christian Classics - R
Christian Publications - R
Christopher Publishing Hs
Companion Press - R
Concordia - R
Contemporary Drama Service
Creation House - R
CREDO
Crossway
CSS Publishing
DaBaR Services - R
Eerdmans Publishing
Emerald Books - R
Fairway Press - R
Forward Movement - R
Friends United Press - R
Good Book
Gibson, C.R. - R
Gilgal
Group Publishing
HarperSanFrancisco - R
Harrison House - R
Harvest House - R
Herald Press - R
Honor Books
Kindred Press
Kregel - R
Life Enrichment
Liguori Publications
Living Flame Press
Loyola Univ Press - R
Morehouse Publishing - R
Morning Star Press - R
Nazarene Publishing House
Nelson, Thomas - R
New Leaf Press - R
Novalis
OMF Books
Our Sunday Visitor
Pacific Press
Paraclete Press - R
Praxis Inst. Press - R
Proclaim Publishing - R
Questar - R
Resurrection Press - R
Revell, Fleming H.
Review & Herald
Servant Publications - R
Sheed & Ward - R
Sheer Joy! Press
Son-Rise
Standard - R (for kids)
Starburst Publishers
Star Song - R
TEACH Services - R
Trinity Press Intl. - R
Tyler Press - R
Tyndale House - R
United Church Publishing
United Methodist
Upper Room Books
VESTA
Victory House - R
Warner Press
Welch Publishing - R
Westminster Press
World Bible - R
Zondervan - R

DISCIPLESHIP

Accent
Aglow
AMG Publishers - R
Baker Book House - R
Barclay Press - R
Brentwood - R
Bridge Publishing - R
Bristol House - R
Broadman & Holman
Chalice Press
Chosen Books
Christian Classics - R
Christian Liter. Crusade - R
Christian Publications - R
Christopher Publishing Hs
Church Growth Institute
Companion Press - R
Concordia - R
Creation House - R
Crossway
DaBaR Services - R
Discipleship Resources
Eerdmans Publishing
Fairway Press - R
Forward Movement - R
Friends United Press - R
HarperSanFrancisco - R
Harvest House - R
Hendrickson Publishers - R
Hensley, Virgil W. - R
Herald Press - R
Horizon House - R
InterVarsity Press
Judson Press - R
Kregel - R
Liguori Publications
Living Flame Press
LuraMedia
Morehouse Publishing - R
Nazarene Publishing House
Neibauer Press - R
Nelson, Thomas - R
New Hope - R
New Leaf Press - R
Paraclete Press - R
Pillar Books- R
Presbyterian/Reformed - R
Proclaim Publishing - R
Questar - R
Revell, Fleming H.
Review & Herald
Roper Press - R
Scarecrow Press
Servant Publications - R
Shaw Publishers, Harold - R
Sheed & Ward - R
Southern Baptist Press - R
TEACH Services - R
Tyler Press - R
Tyndale House - R
United Church Press

United Methodist
VESTA
Victor Books
Victory House - R
Welch Publishing - R
Westminster Press
Zondervan - R

DIVORCE

AMG Publishers - R
Ave Maria Press
Baker Book House - R
Bantam Books
Brentwood - R
Bridge Publishing - R
Broadman & Holman
Chalice Press
Christopher Publishing Hs
Collier/Macmillan
Companion Press - R
Concordia - R
Creation House - R
Eerdmans Publishing
Forward Movement - R
Franciscan Press - R
Gilgal
HarperSanFrancisco - R
Harvest House - R
Haworth Press - R
Hensley, Virgil W. - R
InterVarsity Press
Lifetime Books
Liguori Publications
Living Flame Press
LuraMedia
Morehouse Publishing - R
Nazarene Publishing House
Nelson, Thomas - R
New Leaf Press - R
Presbyterian/Reformed - R
Proclaim Publishing - R
Questar - R
Resurrection Press - R
Review & Herald
Servant Publications - R
Sheer Joy! Press
Southern Baptist Press - R
Starburst Publishers
TEACH Services - R
Tyndale House - R
United Methodist
VESTA
Victor Books
Victory House - R
Welch Publishing - R
Zondervan - R

DOCTRINAL

AMG Publishers - R
Ave Maria Press
Baker Book House - R
Brentwood - R
Broadman & Holman
Christian Classics - R
Christopher Publishing Hs
Church Growth Institute
Collier/Macmillan
Concordia - R
Creation House - R
CREDO
Crossway
Discipleship Resources
Eerdmans Publishing
Fairway Press - R
Franciscan Press - R
Franciscan Univ Press - R
Friends United Press - R
HarperSanFrancisco - R
Harrison House - R
InterVarsity Press
Kregel - R
Liguori Publications
Liturgical Press
Living Flame Press
Loyola Univ Press - R
Nazarene Publishing House
Nelson, Thomas - R
New Leaf Press - R
Novalis
Omega Publications
OMF Books
Pillar Books - R
Praxis Inst. Press - R
Presbyterian/Reformed - R
Proclaim Publishing - R
Promise Publishers
Questar - R
Review & Herald
Scarecrow Press
Sheed & Ward - R
Southern Baptist Press - R
Star Song - R
Still Waters Revival - R
TEACH Services - R
Trinity Foundation - R
Tyler Press - R
Tyndale House - R
VESTA
Welch Publishing - R
Westminster Press
World Bible - R
Zondervan - R

DRAMA

A.D. Players
Baker Book House - R
Brentwood - R
Chalice Press
Concordia - R
Contemporary Drama Service
CSS Publishing
Fairway Press - R
Group Publishing
Lillenas Publishing
Loyola Univ Press - R
Meriwether Publishing - R
Proclaim Publishing - R
Resource Publications
Sheer Joy! Press
Shining Star
Southern Baptist Press
TEACH Services - R
United Methodist
University Press/America - R
Welch Publishing - R

ECONOMICS

Baker Book House - R
Brentwood - R
Broadman & Holman
Christopher Publishing Hs
Collier/Macmillan
Concordia - R
Dimension Books - R
Eerdmans Publishing
Focus on the Family - R
Franciscan Press - R
HarperSanFrancisco - R
Haworth Press - R
Herald Press - R
Huntington House - R
InterVarsity Press
Lifetime Books

Moody Press
Nelson, Thomas - R
New Leaf Press - R
New Society Publishers - R
Pilgrim Press
Proclaim Publishing - R
Review & Herald
Starburst Publishers
TEACH Services - R
Trinity Foundation - R
Trinity Press Intl. - R
Tyler Press - R
University Press/America - R
Welch Publishing - R
WRS Publishing - R
Zondervan - R

ENVIRONMENTAL ISSUES

Baker Book House - R
Bantam Books
Broadman & Holman
Chalice Press
Chosen Books
Christopher Publishing Hs
Concordia - R
Eerdmans Publishing
Forward Movement - R
Franciscan Press - R
Friendship Press
HarperSanFrancisco - R
Hensley, Virgil W. - R
Herald Press - R
Liguori Publications
Morehouse Publishing - R
New Society Publishers - R
Oxford University
Pilgrim Press
Prescott Press - R
Proclaim Publishing - R
Questar - R
Resurrection Press - R
Shining Star
Southern Baptist Press - R
Starburst Publishers
Trinity Foundation - R
Triumph Books - R
Tyler Press - R
WRS Publishing - R
Zondervan - R

ETHICS

Augsburg Fortress - R
Baker Book House - R
Bantam Books
Brentwood - R
Broadman & Holman
Chalice Press
Christian Classics - R
Christian Publications - R
Christopher Publishing Hs
Collier/Macmillan
Companion Press - R
Concordia - R
Cornell Univ Press - R
Creation House - R
Crossway
Eerdmans Publishing
Forward Movement - R
Franciscan Press - R
Friendship Press
HarperSanFrancisco - R
Harvest House - R
Haworth Press - R
Herald Press - R
InterVarsity Press
Kregel - R
Life Cycle Books - R
Liguori Publications
Loyola Univ Press - R
Morehouse Publishing - R
Nelson, Thomas - R
New Leaf Press - R
New Society Publishers - R
Omega Publications
Open Court - R
Our Sunday Visitor
Oxford University
Pilgrim Press
Presbyterian/Reformed - R
PROBE Ministries - R
Proclaim Publishing - R
Questar - R
Review & Herald
Sheed & Ward - R
Star Song - R
Still Waters Revival - R
TEACH Services - R
Trinity Foundation - R
Trinity Press Intl. - R
Triumph Books - R
Tyler Press - R
United Methodist
University Press/America - R
VESTA
Victor Books
Welch Publishing - R
Westminster Press
Yale - R
Zondervan - R
Zondervan/Academic

*ETHNIC BOOKS

Aglow
Augsburg Fortress - R
August House
Baker Book House - R (black)
Chalice Press
College Press - R
Concordia - R
DaBaR Services - R
Discipleship Resources
Eerdmans Publishing
Forward Movement - R
Franciscan Univ. Press - R
Guernica Editions - R
Herald Press - R
Judson Press - R
Kregal Publications - R
Liguori Publications
Living Sacrifice - R
National Baptist - R
Pacific Press (some)
Pelican Publishing - R
Pilgrim Press
Proclaim Publishing - R
Star Song - R
Triumph Books - R
United Church Press
United Methodist
VESTA Publications
Women's Miss. Union - R
World Bible - R
WRS Publishing - R

EVANGELISM

Accent
Aglow
Baker Book House - R
Bethel Publishing - R
Brentwood - R
Bridge Publishing - R

Bristol House - R
Broadman & Holman
Chalice Press
Chosen Books
Christian Liter. Crusade - R
Christian Publications - R
Christopher Publishing Hs
Church Growth Institute
Collier/Macmillan
Companion Press - R
Concordia - R
Creation House - R
Crossway
Discipleship Resources
Eerdmans Publishing
Fairway Press - R
Forward Movement - R
Franciscan Press - R
Friends United Press - R
HarperSanFrancisco - R
Harrison House - R
Harvest House - R
Hendrickson Publishers - R
Hensley, Virgil W. - R
Herald Press - R
Horizon House - R
InterVarsity Press
Judson Press - R
Kindred Press
Kregel - R
Langmarc Publishing
Liguori Publications
Morehouse Publishing - R
Morning Star Press - R
Nazarene Publishing House
Neibauer Press - R
Nelson, Thomas - R
New Hope - R
New Leaf Press - R
Omega Publications
Pillar Books - R
Presbyterian/Reformed - R
Proclaim Publishing - R
Promise Publishing
Questar - R
Resurrection Press - R
Review & Herald
Roper Press - R
Sheer Joy! Press
Son-Rise
Southern Baptist Press - R
Star Song - R
Still Waters Revival - R
TEACH Services - R
Trinity Foundation - R
Tyler Press - R
Tyndale House - R
United Church Press
United Methodist
VESTA
Victory House - R
Warner Press
Welch Publishing - R
Westminster Press
Women's Miss. Union - R
Zondervan - R
Zondervan/Academic

EXPOSÉS

Brentwood - R
Huntington House - R
Nelson, Thomas - R
New Leaf Press - R
Open Court - R
Prescott Press - R
Questar - R
Southern Baptist Press - R
Trinity Foundation - R
Tyler Press - R
Victor Books
Welch Publishing - R
Zondervan - R

FAMILY LIFE

ACTA Publications
Aglow
Alba House - R
AMG Publishers - R
Augsburg Fortress - R
Ave Maria Press
Baker Book House - R
Bantam Books
Bethel Publishing - R
Bosco Multimedia, Don
Brentwood - R
Broadman & Holman
Brownlow Publishing
Chalice Press
Christian Classics - R
Christian Publications - R
Christopher Publishing Hs
Church Growth Institute
College Press - R
Collier/Macmillan
Companion Press - R
Concordia - R
Crossway
Discipleship Resources
Eerdmans Publishing
Emerald Books - R
Fairway Press - R
Focus on the Family - R
Friends United Press - R
Gibson, C.R. - R
HarperSanFrancisco - R
Harrison House - R
Harvest House - R
Haworth Press - R
Hensley, Virgil W. - R
Herald Press - R
Honor Books
Huntington House - R
InterVarsity Press
Kregel - R
Langmarc Publishing
Life Cycle Books - R
Liguori Publications
Living Flame Press
LuraMedia
Morehouse Publishing - R
Nazarene Publishing House
Nelson, Thomas - R
New Hope - R
New Leaf Press - R
Novalis
Pelican Publishing - R
Pillar Books - R
Presbyterian/Reformed - R
Prescott Press - R
PROBE Ministries - R (values)
Proclaim Publishing - R
Promise Publishing
Questar - R
Rainbow Books (FL)
Rainbow's End
Resurrection Press - R
Revell, Fleming H.
Review & Herald
Roper Press - R
Servant Publications - R
Shaw Publishers, Harold - R

Shining Star
Son-Rise
Southern Baptist Press - R
Standard - R (activities)
Starburst Publishers
Star Song - R
Still Waters Revival - R
TEACH Services - R
Triumph Books - R
Tyler Press - R
Tyndale House - R
United Methodist
Upper Room Books
VESTA
Victor Books - R
Warner Press
Welch Publishing - R
Wellness
Westminster Press
WRS Publishing - R
Zondervan - R

FICTION: ADULT

Baker Book House - R
Barbour - R
Bethel Publishing - R
Bridge Publishing - R
Christian Classics - R
Christian Publications - R
Christopher Publishing Hs
Companion Press - R
Creation House - R
Crossway
Didaskon Publishing - R
Emerald Books - R
Friendship Press
Friends United Press - R
Harvest House - R
Heartsong Presents
Hensley, Virgil W. - R
Herald Press - R
Horizon House - R
Huntington House - R
InterVarsity Press
LifeJourney Books
Lifetime Books
Moody Press
Nazarene Publishing House
Nelson, Thomas - R
New Leaf Press - R
Pacific Press (true)
Proclaim Publishing - R
Questar - R
Regency Press
Revell, Fleming H.
Roper Press - R
Servant Publications - R
Sheer Joy! Press
Starburst Publishers
Star Song - R
VESTA
Victor Books
Victory House - R
Zondervan - R

FICTION: ADVENTURE

Bantam Books
Bethel Publishing
Brentwood - R
Broadman & Holman
Christopher Publishing Hs
Companion Press - R
Concordia - R
Crossway
Didaskon Publishing - R
Eerdmans Publishing
Emerald Books - R
Harvest House - R
Hensley, Virgil W. - R
Huntington House - R
InterVarsity Press
LifeJourney Books
Moody Press
Morehouse Publishing - R
Morrow and Co., William (juv) - R
Nelson, Thomas - R
New Leaf Press - R
Omega Publications
Prescott Press - R
Proclaim Publishing - R
Questar - R
Regency Press
Roper Press - R
Southern Baptist Press - R
Starburst Publishers
Victory House - R
Zondervan - R

FICTION: ALLEGORY

Bridge Publishing - R
Christopher Publishing Hs
Creation House - R
Crossway
Eerdmans Publishing
InterVarsity Press
Moody Press
Morehouse Publishing - R
New Leaf Press - R
Proclaim Publishing - R
Questar - R
Star Song - R
Victory House - R

FICTION: BIBLICAL

Bethel Publishing - R
Brentwood - R
Bridge Publishing - R
Christopher Publishing Hs
College Press - R
Companion Press - R
Concordia - R
Creation House - R
CSS Publishing
Eerdmans Publishing
Fairway Press - R
Friends United Press - R
Harvest House - R
Herald Press - R
InterVarsity Press
Lifetime Books
Living Flame Press
Morehouse Publishing - R
Morris, Joshua
Nazarene Publishing House
New Leaf Press - R
Proclaim Publishing - R
Questar - R
Regency Press
Roper Press - R
Sheer Joy! Press
Shining Star (juvenile)
Southern Baptist Press - R
Tyndale House - R
United Church Press
Victory House - R
Zondervan - R

FICTION: CONTEMPORARY

Baker Book House - R
Bantam Books
Brentwood - R
Broadman & Holman
Christopher Publishing Hs
Companion Press - R
Concordia - R
Creation House - R
Crossway
Eerdmans Publishing
Gibson, C.R. - R
HarperSanFrancisco - R
Hensley, Virgil W. - R
Huntington House - R
InterVarsity Press
LifeJourney - R
Living Flame Press
Moody Press
Morehouse Publishing - R
Morris, Joshua
National Baptist - R
Nelson, Thomas - R
New Leaf Press - R
Proclaim Publishing - R
Questar - R
Regency Press
Southern Baptist Press - R
Starburst Publishers
Star Song - R
Victory House - R
Zondervan - R

FICTION: FANTASY

Christopher Publishing Hs
Companion Press - R
Crossway
Didaskon Publishing - R
Eerdmans Publishing
Huntington House - R
InterVarsity Press
New Leaf Press - R
Proclaim Publishing - R
Questar - R
Starburst Publishers
Victory House - R
Zondervan - R

FICTION: FRONTIER

Bantam Books
Bethel Publishing - R
Brentwood - R
Broadman & Holman
Christopher Publishing Hs
Crossway
Eerdmans Publishing
Harvest House - R
Hensley, Virgil W. - R - R
Nazarene Publishing House
Nelson, Thomas - R
New Leaf Press - R
Proclaim Publishing - R
Questar - R
Regency Press
Roper Press - R
Servant Publications - R
Southern Baptist Press - R
Starburst Publishers
Victory House - R
Welch Publishing - R
Zondervan - R

FICTION: FRONTIER/ ROMANCE

Bantam Books
Bethel Publishing - R
Brentwood - R
Eerdmans Publishing
Harvest House - R
Heartsong Presents
Hensley, Virgil W. - R
Huntington House - R
Moody Press
Nelson, Thomas - R
New Leaf Press - R
Pacific Press (true)
Proclaim Publishing - R
Questar - R
Regency Press
Revell, Fleming H.
Roper Press - R
Servant Publications - R
Southern Baptist Press - R
Starburst Publishers
Victory House - R
Welch Publishing - R
Zondervan - R

FICTION: HISTORICAL

Bantam Books
Bethel Publishing - R
Brentwood - R
Broadman & Holman
Christian Publications - R
Christopher Publishing Hs
Companion Press - R
Crossway
Didaskon Publishing - R
Eerdmans Publishing
Friends United Press - R
HarperSanFrancisco - R
Harvest House - R
Hensley, Virgil W. - R
Herald Press - R
Horizon House - R
InterVarsity Press
LifeJourney Books
Misty Hill Press
Moody Press
Morehouse Publishing - R
Morrow and Co., William
Nazarene Publishing House
Nelson, Thomas - R
New Leaf Press - R
Proclaim Publishing - R
Questar - R
Regency Press
Roper Press - R
Servant Publications - R
Son-Rise
Southern Baptist Press - R
Starburst Publishers
Star Song - R
Victor Books
Victory House - R
Zondervan - R

FICTION: HISTORICAL/ ROMANCE

Bantam Books
Bethel Publishing - R
Brentwood - R
Christian Publications - R
Creation House - R

Eerdmans Publishing
Emerald Books - R
Harvest House - R
Heartsong Presents
Hensley, Virgil W. - R
Horizon House - R
LifeJourney - R
Moody Press
Nazarene Publishing House
Nelson, Thomas - R
New Leaf Press - R
Proclaim Publishing - R
Questar - R
Regency Press
Revell, Fleming H.
Roper Press - R
Servant Publications - R
Southern Baptist Press - R
Starburst Publishers
Victor Books
Victory House - R
Zondervan - R

FICTION: HUMOR

Bethel Publishing - R
Bridge Publishing - R
Broadman & Holman
Christopher Publishing Hs
Companion Press - R
Crossway
Emerald Books - R
Fairway Press - R
InterVarsity Press
LifeJourney - R
Morehouse Publishing - R
Morris, Joshua
Nelson, Thomas - R
New Leaf Press - R
Prescott Press - R
Proclaim Publishing - R
Questar - R
Sheer Joy! Press
Star Song - R
Victory House - R

FICTION: JUVENILE

(Ages 8-12)
AMG Publishers - R
Baker Book House - R
Bay Publications, Mel - R
Bethel Publishing - R
Bob Jones - R
Broadman & Holman
Christian Publications - R
Concordia - R
Crossway
Didaskon Publishing - R
Eerdmans Publishing
Emerald Books - R
Fairway Press - R
Friendship Press
Friends United Press - R
Gold/N/Honey
Harvest House - R
Herald Press - R
Horizon House - R
Misty Hill Press
Morehouse Publishing - R
Morris, Joshua
Nelson, Thomas - R
Pacific Press (true)
Prescott Press - R
Proclaim Publishing - R
Questar - R
Review & Herald
Roper Press - R
Sheer Joy! Press
Shining Star
Tyler Press - R
United Church Press
Upper Room Books
Victor Books
Victory House - R
Zondervan - R

FICTION: LITERARY

Baker Book House - R
Christopher Publishing Hs
Crossway
Gibson, C.R. - R
Guernica - R
Herald Press - R
InterVarsity Press
Morris, Joshua
Morrow and Co., William
New Leaf Press - R
Proclaim Publishing - R
Questar - R
Star Song - R
VESTA
Victor Books
Victory House - R

FICTION: MYSTERY

Baker Book House - R
Bantam Books
Bethel Publishing - R
Broadman & Holman
Christopher Publishing Hs
Companion Press - R
Concordia - R
Crossway
Didaskon Publishing - R
Harvest House - R
Hensley, Virgil W. - R
InterVarsity Press
LifeJourney - R
Moody Press
Morehouse Publishing - R
Morrow and Co., William
Nelson, Thomas - R
New Leaf Press - R
Prescott Press - R
Proclaim Publishing - R
Questar - R
Regency Press
Roper Press - R
Servant Publications - R
Victor Books
Victory House - R
Zondervan - R

FICTION:MYSTERY/ ROMANCE

Bantam Books
Brentwood - R
Heartsong Presents
Hensley, Virgil W. - R
Herald Press - R
Huntington House - R
LifeJourney - R
Moody Press
Nelson, Thomas - R

New Leaf Press - R
Proclaim Publishing - R
Questar - R
Regency Press
Revell, Fleming H.
Roper Press - R
Servant Publications - R
Southern Baptist Press - R
Victor Books
Victory House - R

FICTION: PLAYS

Bay Publications, Mel - R
Brentwood - R
CSS Publishing
Fairway Press - R
Lillenas
Meriwether Publishing - R
National Baptist - R
Pacific Theatre Press - R
Proclaim Publishing - R
Resource Publications
Sheer Joy! Press (dramatic readings/puppet plays)
Shining Star (juvenile)
Southern Baptist Press - R
Victory House - R

FICTION:ROMANCE

Christian Publications - R
Companion Press - R
Harvest House - R
Heartsong Presents
LifeJourney - R
Morrow and Co., William
Nazarene Publishing House
Nelson, Thomas - R
New Leaf Press - R
Proclaim Publishing - R
Regency Press
Sheer Joy! Press
Victory House - R
Zondervan - R

FICTION: SCIENCE FICTION

Christopher Publishing Hs
Companion Press - R
Crossway
Didaskon Publishing - R
Harvest House - R
Huntington House - R
InterVarsity Press
Moody Press
Morrow and Co., William
Nelson, Thomas - R
New Leaf Press - R
Prescott Press - R
Proclaim Publishing - R
Victory House - R

FICTION: SHORT-STORY COLLECTION

AMG Publishers - R
Christopher Publishing Hs
Concordia - R
Emerald Books - R
Friends United Press - R
Gibson, C.R. - R
Herald Press - R
Morehouse Publishing - R
National Baptist - R
Nazarene Publishing House
Proclaim Publishing - R
Resource Publications
Victory House - R

FICTION: TEEN/YOUNG ADULT

AMG Publishers - R
Bay Publications, Mel - R
Bob Jones - R
Bosco Multimedia, Don
Christian Publications - R
Companion Press - R
Eerdmans Publishing
Emerald Books - R
Fairway Press - R
Focus on the Family - R
Friendship Press
Hensley, Virgil W. - R
Herald Press - R
Horizon House - R
Huntington House - R
LifeJourney - R
Lifetime Books
Living Flame Press
Nelson, Thomas - R
Pacific Press (true)
Proclaim Publishing - R
Review & Herald
Sheer Joy! Press
Victor Books
Victory House - R
Zondervan - R

GAMES/CRAFTS

Bay Publications, Mel - R
Brown-ROA (religious)
Concordia - R
Contemporary Drama Service
CSS Publishing
Educational Ministries
Group Publishing
Meriwether Publishing - R
Morris, Joshua (kids)
Proclaim Publishing - R
Rainbow Books (CA)
St. Paul Books - R
Shining Star
Standard - R
United Methodist
Zondervan - R

GIFT BOOKS

Baker Book House - R
Berrie, Russ
Brownlow Publishing
Calligraphy Collection
Christopher Publishing Hs
Companion Press - R
Contemporary Drama Service
Current Inc.
Focus on the Family - R
Franciscan Press - R
Gibson, C.R. - R
HarperSanFrancisco - R
Herald Press - R
Honor Books
Living Flame Press
Mailaways
Manhattan Greeting Card Co
Morehouse Publishing - R.
Morning Star Press - R
Nelson, Thomas - R
New Leaf Press - R
Proclaim Publishing - R
Questar - R
Resurrection Press - R

Revell, Fleming H.
Roserich Designs
Starburst Publishers
Star Song - R
Sunrise Publications
Triumph Books - R
Upper Room Books
Victor Books
Victory House - R
Welch Publishing - R
Westminster Press
Zondervan - R

GROUP STUDY BOOKS

Aglow
Alban Institute
AMG Publishers - R
Baker Book House - R
Brentwood - R
Center for Learning
Chalice Press
Christopher Publishing Hs
Church Growth Institute
Companion Press - R
Concordia - R
DaBaR Services - R
Didaskon Publishing - R
Discipleship Resources
Fairway Press - R
Group Publishing
HarperSanFrancisco - R
Hensley, Virgil W. - R
Herald Press - R
Judson Press - R
Kregel - R
Langmarc Publishing
Liguori Publications
LuraMedia
Morehouse Publishing - R
Morning Star Press - R
Nazarene Publishing House
Nelson, Thomas - R
New Hope - R
New Leaf Press - R
Our Sunday Visitor
Presbyterian/Reformed - R
Proclaim Publishing - R
Questar - R
Review & Herald
St. Anthony Messenger - R
Sheed & Ward - R
Southern Baptist Press - R
Star Song - R
TEACH Services - R
VESTA
Victor Books
Victory House - R
Welch Publishing - R
Women's Miss. Union - R
World Bible - R
Zondervan - R

HEALING

Aglow
Baker Book House - R
Bantam Books
Brentwood - R
Bridge Publishing - R
Chosen Books
Christian Classics - R
Christopher Publishing Hs
Companion Press - R
Concordia - R
Creation House - R
DaBaR Services - R
Eerdmans Publishing
Fairway Press - R
Gilgal
Good Book
HarperSanFrancisco - R
Harrison House - R
Haworth Press - R
Hendrickson Publishers - R
InterVarsity Press
Life Enrichment
Liguori Publications
Living Flame Press
Loyola Univ Press - R
LuraMedia
Morehouse Publishing - R
Morning Star Press - R
Nazarene Publishing House
Nelson, Thomas - R
New Leaf Press - R
Our Sunday Visitor
Pillar Books - R
Prescott Press - R
Proclaim Publishing - R
Questar - R
Rainbow's End
Resurrection Press - R
Review & Herald
Servant Publications - R
Son-Rise
Southern Baptist Press - R
Starburst Publishers
TEACH Services - R
Triumph Books - R
Tyler Press - R
VESTA
Victor Books
Victory House - R
Welch Publishing - R
WRS Publishing - R

HEALTH

Bantam Books
Bob Jones - R
Brentwood - R
Broadman & Holman
Brownlow Publishing
Christopher Publishing Hs
Concordia - R
Eerdmans Publishing
Fairway Press - R
Focus on the Family - R
Good Book
HarperSanFrancisco - R
Herald Press - R
InterVarsity Press
Life Cycle Books - R
Lifetime Books
Loyola Univ Press - R
LuraMedia
Nelson, Thomas - R
New Leaf Press - R
Omega Publications
Prescott Press - R
Proclaim Publishing - R
Promise Publishing
Review & Herald
Son-Rise
Southern Baptist Press - R
Starburst Publishers
TEACH Services - R
Tyler Press - R
VESTA
Victor Books
Victory House - R
Welch Publishing - R
Wellness
WRS Publishing - R

Zondervan - R

HISTORICAL

Augsburg Fortress - R
Baker Book House - R
Bantam Books
Blue Dolphin - R
Bob Jones - R
Brentwood - R
Chalice Press
Catholic Univ of America - R
Christian Classics - R
Christian Publications - R
Christopher Publishing Hs
Cistercian Publications - R
College Press - R
Concordia - R
Cornell Univ Press - R
Custom Communications
Didaskon Publishing - R
Dimension Books - R
Eerdmans Publishing
Franciscan Press - R
Friends United Press - R
Good Book
HarperSanFrancisco - R
Harrison House - R
Hendrickson Publishers - R
Herald Press - R (Mennonite)
InterVarsity Press
Loyola Univ Press - R
Morehouse Publishing - R
Morning Star Press - R
Morrow and Co., William
Nelson, Thomas - R
New Leaf Press - R
Omega Publications
Our Sunday Visitor
Oxford University
Pillar Books - R
Prescott Press - R
Proclaim Publishing - R
Regnery Gateway - R
Review & Herald
St. Bede's Publications - R
Scarecrow Press
Son-Rise
Southern Baptist Press - R
Star Song - R
Still Waters Revival - R
TEACH Services - R
Trinity Foundation - R
Trinity Press Intl. - R
Tyler Press - R
United Church Press
Univer of NC Press
University Press/America - R
VESTA
Victory House - R
Welch Publishing - R
World Bible - R
Zondervan - R
Zondervan/Academic

HOW-TO/SELF-HELP

Accent
ACTA Publications
Aglow
Alba House - R
Augsburg Fortress - R
Ave Maria Press - R
Baker Book House - R
Bantam Books
Blue Dolphin - R
Brentwood - R
Bridge Publishing - R
Broadman & Holman
Brown-ROA
Chosen Books
Christian Media
Christopher Publishing Hs
Church & Synagogue Lib
Collier/Macmillan
Companion Press - R
Concordia - R
DaBaR Services - R
Emerald Books - R
Fairway Press - R
Focus on the Family - R
Gibson, C.R. - R
Gilgal
HarperSanFrancisco - R
Harrison House - R
Harvest House - R
Herald Press - R
Honor Books
InterVarsity Press
Lifetime Books
Liguori Publications
Living Flame Press
Loyola Univ Press - R
Meriwether Publishing - R
(how-to only)
Moody Press
Morehouse Publishing - R
Morning Star Press - R
Morrow and Co., William
Nazarene Publishing House
Nelson, Thomas - R
New Hope - R
New Leaf Press - R
Omega Publications
OMF Books
Pilgrim Press
Prescott Press - R
Proclaim Publishing - R
Rainbow Books (FL)
Rainbow's End
Resurrection Press - R
Revell, Fleming H.
Review & Herald
St. Paul Books - R
Servant Publications - R
Shaw Publishers, Harold - R
Son-Rise
Southern Baptist Press - R
Standard - R
Starburst Publishers
Star Song - R
Still Waters Revival - R
TEACH Services - R
Triumph Books - R
Tyler Press - R
Tyndale House - R
Victor Books
Victory House - R
Welch Publishing - R
Westminster Press
Women's Miss.
Union - R
World Bible - R
Zondervan - R

HUMOR

Aglow
August House
Baker Book House - R
Bethel Publishing - R
Bob Jones - R
Brentwood - R
Broadman & Holman
Christian Publications - R
Christopher Publishing Hs

Companion Press - R
Concordia - R
CSS Publishing
Dimension Books - R
Emerald Books - R
Fairway Press - R
Focus on the Family - R
Friends United Press - R
Gibson, C.R. - R
HarperSanFrancisco - R
Harvest House - R
InterVarsity Press
Liguori Publications
Living Flame Press
LuraMedia
Meriwether Publishing - R
Morehouse Publishing - R
Nazarene Publishing House
Nelson, Thomas - R
New Leaf Press - R
Prescott Press - R
Proclaim Publishing - R
Questar - R
Review & Herald
Servant Publications - R
Shaw Publishers, Harold - R
Son-Rise
Southern Baptist Press - R
Starburst Publishers
Star Song - R
Tyler Press - R
Victor Books
Welch Publishing - R
Zondervan - R

INSPIRATIONAL

Aglow
Baker Book House - R
Bantam Books
Bethel Publishing - R
Blue Dolphin - R
Brentwood - R
Bridge Publishing - R
Broadman & Holman
Christian Classics - R
Christian Publications - R
Christopher Publishing Hs
Companion Press - R
Concordia - R
Crossway
DaBaR Services - R
Eerdmans Publishing
Fairway Press - R
Forward Movement - R
Franciscan Press - R
Friends United Press - R
Gibson, C.R. - R
Gilgal
Good Book
HarperSanFrancisco - R
Harvest House - R
Herald Press - R
Honor Books
ICS Publications - R
Langmarc Publishing
Lifetime Books
Liguori Publications
Living Flame Press
Loyola Univ Press - R
LuraMedia
Morehouse Publishing - R
Morning Star Press - R
Nazarene Publishing House
Nelson, Thomas - R
New Leaf Press - R
Our Sunday Visitor
Pacific Press
Paraclete Press - R
Pelican Publishing - R
Proclaim Publishing - R
Questar - R
Rainbow's End
Resurrection Press - R
Review & Herald
St. Paul Books - R
Servant Publications - R
Sheed & Ward - R
Sheer Joy! Press
Shining Star
Son-Rise
Southern Baptist Press - R
Starburst Publishers
Star Song - R
TEACH Services - R
Triumph Books - R
Tyler Press - R
Tyndale House - R
United Church Press
United Methodist
VESTA
Victor Books
Victory House - R
Welch Publishing - R
Wellness
Westminster Press
World Bible - R
Zondervan - R

LITURGICAL STUDIES

Alba House - R
American Catholic Press - R
Brentwood - R
Center for Learning
Chalice Press
Christian Classics - R
Christopher Publishing Hs
Concordia - R
Cornell Univ Press - R
CSS Publishing
Discipleship Resources
Eerdmans Publishing
Fairway Press - R
Forward Movement - R
Franciscan Press - R
HarperSanFrancisco - R
Liguori Publications
Living Flame Press
Morehouse Publishing - R
Morning Star Press - R
Novalis
Our Sunday Visitor
Oxford University
Pastoral Press
Paulist Press
Pillar Books - R
Presbyterian/Reformed - R
Proclaim Publishing - R
Resource Publications
St. Bede's Publications - R
Scarecrow Press
Sheed & Ward - R
Southern Baptist Press - R
Star Song - R
University Press/America - R
VESTA
Welch Publishing - R
Westminster Press

MARRIAGE

ACTA Publications
Aglow
Alba House - R

AMG Publishers - R
Augsburg Fortress - R
Ave Maria Press
Baker Book House - R
Bantam Books
Brentwood - R
Broadman & Holman
Center for Learning
Chalice Press
Christian Classics - R
Christian Publications - R
Christopher Publishing Hs
College Press - R
Collier/Macmillan
Companion Press - R
Concordia - R
Crossway
CSS Publishing
DaBaR Services - R
Eerdmans Publishing
Fairway Press - R
Focus on the Family - R
Forward Movement - R
Franciscan Press - R
Gibson, C.R. - R
HarperSanFrancisco - R
Harrison House - R
Harvest House - R
Haworth Press - R
Hendrickson Publishers - R
Hensley, Virgil W. - R
Herald Press - R
Honor Books
InterVarsity Press
Kregel - R
LifeJourney - R
Liguori Publications
Living Flame Press
Loyola Univ Press - R
LuraMedia
Moody Press
Morehouse Publishing - R
Nazarene Publishing House
Nelson, Thomas - R
New Leaf Press - R
Novalis
Our Sunday Visitor
Pacific Press
Pillar Books - R
Presbyterian/Reformed - R
Proclaim Publishing - R
Questar - R
Rainbow Books (FL)
Resurrection Press - R
Revell, Fleming H.
Review & Herald
St. Paul Books - R
Servant Publications - R
Shaw Publishers, Harold - R
Sheed & Ward - R
Sheer Joy! Press
Southern Baptist Press - R
Starburst Publishers
Star Song - R
Still Waters Revival - R
TEACH Services - R
Tyler Press - R
Tyndale House - R
United Methodist
Upper Room Books
VESTA
Victor Books
Victory House - R
Welch Publishing - R
Westminster Press
Zondervan - R

*MEN'S BOOKS

Baker Book House - R
Blue Dolphin - R
Chosen Books
Christopher Publishing Hs
Concordia - R
Discipleship Resources
Focus on the Family - R
Forward Movement - R
Hensley, Virgil W. - R
Herald Press - R
InterVarsity Press
Moody Press
Morehouse Publishing - R
Nazarene Publishing House
Nelson, Thomas - R
New Leaf Press - R
Pacific Press
Pilgrim Press
Proclaim Publishing - R
Questar - R
Resurrection Press - R
Roper Press - R
Son-Rise
Starburst Publishers
Star Song - R
TEACH Services - R
Triumph Books - R
Tyler Press - R
United Church Press
Victory House - R

MIRACLES

Baker Book House - R
Brentwood - R
Bridge Publishing - R
Broadman & Holman
Center for Learning
Chosen Books
Christian Classics - R
Christopher Publishing Hs
Fairway Press - R
Franciscan Press - R
Friends United Press - R
HarperSanFrancisco - R
Harrison House
Liguori Publications
Living Flame Press
LuraMedia
Morning Star Press - R
Nelson, Thomas - R
New Leaf Press - R
Our Sunday Visitor
Pillar Books - R
Proclaim Publishing - R
Questar - R
Review & Herald - R
Servant Publications - R
Southern Baptist Press - R
TEACH Services - R
Tyler Press - R
VESTA
Victory House - R
Welch Publishing - R

MISSIONARY

Bob Jones - R
Brentwood - R
Center for Learning
Chosen Books
Christian Liter. Crusade - R
Christian Publications - R
Christopher Publishing Hs
Concordia - R
Crossway
Didaskon Publishing - R

Eerdmans Publishing
Fairway Press - R
Forward Movement - R
Franciscan Press - R
Friendship Press
Friends United Press - R
HarperSanFrancisco - R
Hendrickson Publishers - R
Herald Press - R
Horizon House - R
InterVarsity Press
Liguori Publications
Nazarene Publishing House
Nelson, Thomas - R
New Hope - R
New Leaf Press - R
OMF Books
Pillar Books - R
Prescott Press - R
Proclaim Publishing - R
Questar - R
Review & Herald
Southern Baptist Press - R
TEACH Services - R
Tyler Press - R
VESTA
Welch Publishing - R
Westminster Press
Women's Miss. Union - R
Zondervan/Academic

MONEY MANAGEMENT

Alban Institute
Baker Book House - R
Barbour & Co. - R
Brentwood - R
Broadman & Holman
Christopher Publishing Hs
Collier/Macmillan
Concordia - R
Discipleship Resources
Fairway Press - R
Focus on the Family - R
HarperSanFrancisco - R
Harvest House - R
Haworth Press - R
Hensley, Virgil W. - R
Herald Press - R
Honor Books
InterVarsity Press
Moody Press
Nazarene Publishing House
Nelson, Thomas - R
New Leaf Press - R
Omega Publications
Pillar Books - R
Prescott Press - R
Proclaim Publishing - R
Promise Publishing
Questar - R
Review & Herald
Servant Publications - R
Shaw Publishers, Harold - R
Southern Baptist Press - R
Starburst Publishers
TEACH Services - R
Tyler Press - R
Tyndale House - R
Victor Books
Victory House - R
Welch Publishing - R
Zondervan - R

MUSIC-RELATED BOOKS

American Catholic Press - R
Bay Publications, Mel - R
Christopher Publishing Hs
Companion Press - R
Concordia - R
Contemporary Drama Service
Cornell Univ Press - R
Eerdmans Publishing
HarperSanFrancisco - R
Huntington House - R
Lillenas Publishing
Morehouse Publishing - R
Nelson, Thomas - R
Pastoral Press
Pillar Books - R
Prescott Press - R
Proclaim Publishing - R
Star Song - R
TEACH Services - R
Welch Publishing - R

PARENTING

ACTA Publications
Aglow
Augsburg Fortress - R
Ave Maria Press
Baker Book House - R
Bantam Books
Bethel Publishing - R
Brentwood - R
Broadman & Holman
Brownlow Publishing
Center for Learning
Chalice Press
Chosen Books
Christian Publications - R
Christopher Publishing Hs
College Press - R
Collier/Macmillan
Companion Press - R
Concordia - R
CSS Publishing
DaBaR Services - R
Discipleship Resources
Eerdmans Publishing
Fairway Press - R
Focus on the Family - R
HarperSanFrancisco - R
Harrison House - R
Harvest House - R
Haworth Press - R
Hensley, Virgil W. - R
Herald Press - R
Honor Books
Horizon House - R
Huntington House - R
InterVarsity Press
Kregel - R
Lifetime Books
Liguori Publications
Living Flame Press
Loyola Univ Press - R
LuraMedia
Moody Press
Morehouse Publishing - R
Nazarene Publishing House
Nelson, Thomas - R
New Leaf Press - R
Omega Publications
Our Sunday Visitor
Pacific Press
Pilgrim Press
Pillar Books - R
Presbyterian/Reformed - R
Prescott Press - R
Proclaim Publishing - R
Questar - R

Rainbow Books (FL)
Resurrection Press - R
Revell, Fleming H.
Review & Herald
St. Paul Books - R
Servant Publications - R
Shaw Publishers, Harold - R
Sheed & Ward - R
Shining Star
Starburst Publishers
Still Waters Revival - R
Tabor Publishing
TEACH Services - R
Tyler Press - R
Tyndale House - R
United Church Press
United Methodist
Upper Room Books
VESTA
Victor Books
Victory House - R
Welch Publishing - R
Westminster Press
Zondervan - R

PASTORS' HELPS

Accent
Alban Institute
AMG Publishers - R
Augsburg Fortress - R
Baker Book House - R
Brentwood - R
Bristol House - R
Broadman & Holman
Brown-ROA
Chalice Press
Christian Publications - R
Christopher Publishing Hs
Church Growth Institute
Companion Press - R
Concordia - R
Crossway
CSS Publishing
Didaskon Publishing - R
Discipleship Resources
Eerdmans Publishing
Fairway Press - R
Franciscan Press - R
Friends United Press - R
Group Publishing
HarperSanFrancisco - R
Harrison House - R
Haworth Press - R
Hendrickson Publishers - R
Herald Press - R
Inter Varsity
Judson Press - R
Kregel - R
Langmarc Publishing
Liguori Publications
Meriwether Publishing - R
Morehouse Publishing - R
Nazarene Publishing House
Neibauer Press - R
Nelson, Thomas - R
New Leaf Press - R
Our Sunday Visitor
Pastor's Choice Press
Pillar Books - R
Presbyterian/Reformed - R
Proclaim Publishing - R
Questar - R
Resurrection Press - R
Review & Herald
Southern Baptist Press - R
TEACH Services - R
Tyndale House - R
United Church Press
United Methodist
Victor Books
Victory House - R
Welch Publishing - R
Wellness
Westminster Press
World Bible - R
Zondervan - R

PERSONAL EXPERIENCE

Brentwood - R
Chosen Books
Christopher Publishing Hs
Companion Press - R
Concordia - R
DaBaR Services - R
Eerdmans Publishing
Fairway Press - R
Friends United Press - R
Gilgal
HarperSanFrancisco - R
Harvest House - R
Herald Press - R
Kindred Press
Living Flame Press
Loyola Univ Press - R
LuraMedia
Nelson, Thomas - R
New Leaf Press - R
Omega Publications
Pacific Press
Prescott Press - R
Proclaim Publishing - R
Rainbow's End
Review & Herald
Son-Rise
Southern Baptist Press - R
TEACH Services - R
Tyler Press - R
Tyndale House - R
Upper Room Books
VESTA
Victor Books
Victory House - R
Welch Publishing - R
WRS Publishing - R
Zondervan - R

PHILOSOPHY

Alba House - R
Brentwood - R
Catholic Univ of America - R
Christian Classics - R
Christopher Publishing Hs
Concordia - R
Cornell Univ Press - R
Crossway
Eerdmans Publishing
Fairway Press - R
Franciscan Press - R
Friends United Press - R
HarperSanFrancisco - R
InterVarsity Press
Loyola Univ Press - R
New Leaf Press - R
Open Court - R
Oxford University
Pilgrim Press
Proclaim Publishing - R
St. Bede's Publications - R
Star Song - R
Still Waters Revival - R
Tabor Publishing
Trinity Foundation - R

Trinity Press Intl. - R
Triumph Books - R
University Press/America - R
VESTA
Wadsworth Publishing
Welch Publishing - R
World Bible - R
WRS Publishing - R
Yale - R
Zondervan - R
Zondervan/Academic

POETRY

Brentwood - R
Christopher Publishing Hs
Companion Press - R
Fairway Press - R
Gibson, C.R. - R
HarperSanFrancisco - R
Poets Cove Press
Proclaim Publishing - R
Rainbow's End
Southern Baptist Press - R
TEACH Services - R
Upper Room Books
VESTA
Welch Publishing - R
Wesleyan University Press
Westminster Press

POLITICAL THEORY

Brentwood - R
Catholic Univ of America - R
Christian Media
Christopher Publishing Hs
Concordia - R
Crossway
Franciscan Press - R
Friendship Press
Friends United Press - R
HarperSanFrancisco - R
Huntington House - R
Lifetime Books
Loyola Univ Press - R
New Leaf Press - R
New Society Publishers - R
Open Court - R
Pilgrim Press
PROBE Ministries - R
Proclaim Publishing - R
Questar - R
Regnery Gateway - R - R
Servant Publications - R
Star Song - R
Still Waters Revival - R
Trinity Foundation - R
Tyler Press - R
University Press/America - R
Univer of NC Press
VESTA
Welch Publishing - R
WRS Publishing - R

PRAYER

Aglow
Alba House - R
Augsburg Fortress - R
Ave Maria Press
Baker Book House - R
Bantam Books
Barclay Press - R
Bethel Publishing - R
Brentwood - R
Bridge Publishing - R
Bristol House - R
Broadman & Holman
Brown-ROA
Center for Learning
Chalice Press
Chosen Books
Christian Classics - R
Christian Publications - R
Christopher Publishing Hs
Companion Press - R
Concordia - R
Creation House - R
Crossway
CSS Publishing
DaBaR Services - R
Eerdmans Publishing
Emerald Books - R
Fairway Press - R
Forward Movement - R
Franciscan Press - R
Franciscan Univ Press - R
Friends United Press - R
Good Book
HarperSanFrancisco - R
Harrison House - R
Harvest House - R
Hensley, Virgil W. - R
Herald Press - R
ICS Publications - R
InterVarsity Press
Kregel - R
Life Enrichment
Liguori Publications
Living Flame Press
Loyola Univ Press - R
LuraMedia
Morehouse Publishing - R
Morning Star Press - R
Morris, Joshua (kids)
Nazarene Publishing House
Nelson, Thomas - R
New Hope - R
New Leaf Press - R
Novalis
Our Sunday Visitor
Pacific Press
Paraclete Press - R
Pastoral Press
Paulist Press
Pillar Books - R
Praxis Inst. Press - R
Presbyterian/Reformed - R
Proclaim Publishing - R
Questar - R
Resurrection Press - R
Revell, Fleming H.
Review & Herald
St. Anthony Messenger - R
St. Paul Books - R
Shaw Publishers, Harold - R
Sheed & Ward - R
Southern Baptist Press - R
Starburst Publishers
Star Song - R
Still Waters Revival - R
TEACH Services - R
Trinity Press Intl. - R
Tyler Press - R
Tyndale House - R
United Church Press
VESTA
Victor Books
Victory House - R
Warner Press
Welch Publishing - R
Westminster Press
Women's Miss. Union - R
Zondervan - R

PROPHECY

AMG Publishers - R
Brentwood - R
Bridge Publishing - R
Chosen Books
Christian Classics - R
Christian Media
Christopher Publishing Hs
Companion Press - R
Creation House - R
Eerdmans Publishing
Fairway Press - R
Friends United Press - R
HarperSanFrancisco - R
Harvest House - R
Huntington House - R
Kregel - R
Morning Star Press - R
Nelson, Thomas - R
New Leaf Press - R
Pillar Books - R
Proclaim Publishing - R
Questar - R
Southern Baptist Press - R
Starburst Publishers
Still Waters Revival - R
TEACH Services - R
Trinity Press Intl. - R
Tyler Press - R
VESTA
Victory House - R
Welch Publishing - R
World Bible - R
Zondervan - R

PSYCHOLOGY

Alba House - R
Augsburg Fortress - R
Baker Book House - R
Bantam Books
Brentwood - R
Broadman & Holman
Christopher Publishing Hs
Collier/Macmillan
Concordia - R
Eerdmans Publishing
Fairway Press - R
Focus on the Family - R
Franciscan Press - R
Good Book
HarperSanFrancisco - R
Harvest House - R
Haworth Press - R
Herald Press - R
InterVarsity Press
Lifetime Books
Living Flame Press
Loyola Univ Press - R
LuraMedia
Morning Star Press - R
Nelson, Thomas - R
New Leaf Press - R
Open Court - R
Oxford University
Paulist Press
Proclaim Publishing - R
Religious Education Press
Resurrection Press - R
Review & Herald
Servant Publications - R
Southern Baptist Press - R
Starburst Publishers
Tabor Publishing
TEACH Services - R
Trinity Foundation - R
Trinity Press Intl. - R
Triumph Books - R
Tyler Press - R
Tyndale House - R
University Press/America - R
VESTA
Victor Books
Victory House - R
Welch Publishing - R
World Bible - R
Yale - R
Zondervan - R
Zondervan/Academic

REFERENCE BOOKS

AMG Publishers - R
Baker Book House - R
Brentwood - R
Broadman & Holman
Christopher Publishing Hs
Companion Press - R
Concordia - R
CREDO
CSS Publishing
Eerdmans Publishing
Fairway Press - R
HarperSanFrancisco - R
Harvest House - R
Hendrickson Publishers - R
InterVarsity Press
Kregel - R
Morehouse Publishing - R
Nelson, Thomas - R
OMF Books
Our Sunday Visitor
Oxford University
Pillar Books - R
Prescott Press - R
Review & Herald
St. Bede's Publications - R
Scarecrow Press
Southern Baptist Press - R
Star Song - R
Still Waters Revival - R
TEACH Services - R
Trinity Foundation - R
Trinity Press Intl. - R
Triumph Books - R
Tyndale House - R
University Press/America - R
VESTA
Victor Books
Victory House - R
Welch Publishing - R
Westminster Press
World Bible - R
Zondervan - R
Zondervan/Academic

RELIGION

Alba House - R
AMG Publishers - R (world)
Augsburg Fortress - R
Baker Book House - R
Bantam Books
Brentwood - R
Catholic Univ of America - R
Center for Learning
Chalice Press
Christian Classics - R
Christopher Publishing Hs
Concordia - R
Cornell Univ Press - R
Crossway
CSS Publishing
Dimension Books - R
Eerdmans Publishing
Fairway Press - R

Forward Movement - R
Franciscan Press - R
Friendship Press
Friends United Press - R
Good Book
HarperSanFrancisco - R
Hendrickson Publishers - R
Herald Press - R
InterVarsity Press
Kregel - R
Liguori Publications
Living Flame Press
Loyola Univ Press - R
Thomas More Press
Morehouse Publishing - R
Morning Star Press - R
Morris, Joshua
Morrow and Co, William
Nazarene Publishing House
Nelson, Thomas - R
New Leaf Press - R
Open Court - R
Our Sunday Visitor
Oxford University
Pilgrim Press
Praxis Inst. Press - R
Proclaim Publishing - R
Promise Publishing
Questar - R
Religious Education Press
Resurrection Press - R
Review & Herald
St. Bede's Publications - R
St. Paul Books - R
Sheed & Ward - R
Sheer Joy! Press
Southern Baptist Press - R
Star Song - R
Still Waters Revival - R
Tabor Publishing
TEACH Services - R
Trinity Press Intl. - R
Triumph Books - R
Tyndale House - R
United Church Press
United Church Publishing
University Press/America - R
University of NC Press
VESTA
Victory House - R
Wadsworth Publishing
Welch Publishing - R
Westminster Press
World Bible - R
Yale - R
Zondervan - R
Zondervan/Academic

RETIREMENT

Baker Book House - R
Broadman & Holman
Christopher Publishing Hs
College Press - R
Concordia - R
Fairway Press - R
Forward Movement - R
HarperSanFrancisco - R
Hensley, Virgil W. - R
Nazarene Publishing House
Nelson, Thomas - R
New Leaf Press - R
Proclaim Publishing - R
Questar - R
Review & Herald
Southern Baptist Press - R
Starburst Publishers
VESTA
Welch Publishing - R
Westminster Press
Zondervan - R

SCIENCE

Bob Jones - R
Christopher Publishing Hs
Cornell Univ Press - R
Crossway
Didaskon Publishing - R
HarperSanFrancisco - R
Huntington House - R
InterVarsity Press
Master Books - R
New Leaf Press - R
Open Court - R
Oxford University
Pilgrim Press
Proclaim Publishing - R
Review & Herald
Trinity Foundation - R
Tyler Press - R
Welch Publishing - R
World Bible - R

SENIOR ADULT CONCERNS

Baker Book House - R
Broadman & Holman Publishers
Chalice Press
Christian Classics - R
Christian Publications - R
Christopher Publishing Hs
Concordia - R
Discipleship Resources
Eerdmans Publishing
Fairway Press - R
Friends United Press - R
HarperSanFrancisco - R
Haworth Press - R
Herald Press - R
Horizon House - R
Judson Press - R
Langmarc Publishing
Living Flame Press
Loyola Univ Press - R
LuraMedia
Morehouse Publishing - R
Nazarene Publishing House
Nelson, Thomas - R
New Leaf Press - R
Prescott Press - R
Proclaim Publishing - R
Questar - R
Review & Herald
Shaw Publishers, Harold - R
Southern Baptist Press - R
Star Song - R
Welch Publishing - R
Westminster Press
Women's Miss. Union - R
Zondervan - R

SERMONS

AMG Publishers - R
Baker Book House - R
Brentwood - R
Christian Classics - R
Christopher Publishing Hs
Companion Press - R
Concordia - R
CSS Publishing
Eerdmans Publishing
Fairway Press - R

Franciscan Press - R
HarperSanFrancisco - R
Herald Press - R
Kregel - R
Liturgical Press
Meriwether Publishing - R
Morning Star Press - R
Nazarene Publishing House
Nelson, Thomas - R
New Leaf Press - R
Pastor's Choice Press
Pillar Books - R
Proclaim Publishing - R
Review & Herald
Southern Baptist Press - R
Still Waters Revival - R
TEACH Services - R
Trinity Press Intl. - R
Tyler Press - R
Tyndale House - R
United Church Press
VESTA
Welch Publishing - R

SINGLES ISSUES

Baker Book House - R
Brentwood - R
Broadman & Holman
Chalice Press
Christian Classics - R
Christian Publications - R
Christopher Publishing Hs
Collier/Macmillan Books
Concordia - R
DaBaR Services - E
Eerdmans Publishing
Focus on the Family - R
HarperSanFrancisco - R
Harvest House - R
Haworth Press - R
Hensley, Virgil W. - R
Herald Press - R
Horizon House - R
InterVarsity Press
Langmarc Publishing
Living Flame Press
LuraMedia
Moody Press
Morehouse Publishing - R
Nazarene Publishing House
Nelson, Thomas - R
New Leaf Press - R
Pillar Books - R
Proclaim Publishing - R
Questar - R
Revell, Fleming H.
Review & Herald
Shaw Publishers, Harold - R
Tyndale House - R
United Methodist
VESTA
Victor Books
Welch Publishing - R
WRS Publishing - R
Zondervan - R

SOCIAL JUSTICE ISSUES

ACTA Publications
Alban Institute
Baker Book House - R
Barclay Press - R
Brentwood - R
Center for Learning
Chalice Press
Chosen Books
Christian Classics - R
Christian Publications - R
Christopher Publishing Hs
Collier/Macmillan
Concordia - R
Crossway
Discipleship Resources
Eerdmans Publishing
Forward Movement - R
Franciscan Press - R
Friendship Press
HarperSanFrancisco - R
Hendrickson Publishers - R
Herald Press - R
Huntington House - R
InterVarsity Press
Life Cycle Books - R
Lifetime Books
Loyola Univ Press - R
LuraMedia
Morehouse Publishing - R
Nelson, Thomas - R
New Leaf Press - R
New Society Publishers - R
Oxford University
Paulist Press
Pilgrim Press
Proclaim Publishing - R
Questar - R
Regnery Gateway - R
Resurrection Press - R
Review & Herald
Shaw Publishers, Harold - R
Sheed & Ward - R
Star Song - R
Still Waters Revival - R
Trinity Press Intl. - R
Tyler Press - R
United Church Publishing
United Methodist
VESTA
Welch Publishing - R
Westminster Press
WRS Publishing - R
Zondervan - R
Zondervan/Academic

SOCIOLOGY

Alba House - R
Baker Book House - R
Brentwood - R
Christian Publications - R
Christopher Publishing Hs
Crossway
Franciscan Press - R
HarperSanFrancisco - R
Haworth Press - R
Herald Press - R
InterVarsity Press
Lifetime Books
Loyola Univ Press - R
New Leaf Press - R
New Society Publishers - R
Oxford University
Prescott Press - R
Proclaim Publishing - R
Review & Herald
Still Waters Revival - R
Triumph Books - R
Tyler Press - R
Univer of NC Press
Welch Publishing - R
WRS Publishing - R
Zondervan - R
Zondervan/Academic

SPIRITUALITY

Aglow
Alban Institute
Ave Maria Press
Baker Book House - R
Bantam Books
Barclay Press - R
Brentwood - R
Bridge Publishing - R
Broadman & Holman
Center for Learning
Chalice Press
Chosen Books
Christian Classics - R
Christian Publications - R
Christopher Publishing Hs
Collier/Macmillan
Companion Press - R
DaBaR Services - R
Dimension Books - R
Discipleship Resources
Eerdmans Publishing
Fairway Press - R
Forward Movement - R
Franciscan Press - R
Friends United Press - R
Good Book
HarperSanFrancisco - R
Hendrickson Publishers - R
Herald Press - R
InterVarsity Press
Judson Press - R
Kregel - R
Liguori Publications
Living Flame Press
Loyola Univ Press - R
LuraMedia
Thomas More Press
Morehouse Publishing - R
Morning Star Press - R
Nazarene Publishing House
Nelson, Thomas - R
New Leaf Press - R
New Society Publishers - R
Novalis
Omega Publishers
Our Sunday Visitor
Oxford University
Pacific Press
Paraclete Press - R
Pastoral Press
Pillar Books - R
Praxis Inst. Press - R
Presbyterian/Reformed - R
Proclaim Publishing - R
Questar - R
Resurrection Press - R
Revell, Fleming H.
Review & Herald
St. Anthony Messenger - R
St. Bede's Publications - R
St. Paul Books - R
Servant Publications - R
Shaw Publishers, Harold - R
Sheed & Ward - R
Southern Baptist Press - R
TEACH Services - R
Trinity Press Intl. - R
Triumph Books - R
Tyler Press - R
Tyndale House - R
United Church Press
United Methodist
VESTA
Victor Books
Victory House - R
Welch Publishing - R
Westminster Press
World Bible - R
Zondervan - R
Zondervan/Academic

SPORTS

Christopher Publishing Hs
Prescott Press - R
Proclaim Publishing - R
Starburst Publishers
Star Song - R
WRS Publishing - R
Zondervan - R

THEOLOGICAL

Alba House - R
AMG Publishers - R
Augsburg Fortress - R
Baker Book House - R
Brentwood - R
Bridge Publishing - R
Broadman & Holman
Chalice Press
Catholic Univ of America - R
Center for Learning - R
Christian Classics - R
Christopher Publishing Hs
Cistercian Publications - R
Collier/Macmillan
Companion Press - R
Concordia - R
Creation House - R
CREDO
Crossway
Dimension Books - R
Discipleship Resources
Eerdmans Publishing
Fairway Press - R
Forward Movement - R
Franciscan Press - R
Franciscan Univ Press - R
Friends United Press - R
HarperSanFrancisco - R
Harvest House - R
Hendrickson Publishers - R
Herald Press - R
InterVarsity Press
Kregel - R
Life Enrichment
Liturgical Press
Loyola Univ Press - R
Morehouse Publishing - R
Morning Star Press - R
Nazarene Publishing House
Nelson, Thomas - R
New Leaf Press - R
Novalis
Omega Publications
OMF Books
Open Court - R
Our Sunday Visitor
Oxford University
Pastoral Press
Paulist Press
Pilgrim Press
Pillar Books - R
Praxis Inst. Press - R
Presbyterian/Reformed - R
Proclaim Publishing - R
Religious Education Press
Resurrection Press - R
Review & Herald
St. Anthony Messenger - R
Servant Publications - R
Sheed & Ward - R

Southern Baptist Press - R
Star Song - R
Still Waters Revival - R
TEACH Services - R
Trinity Foundation - R
Trinity Press Intl. - R
Triumph Books - R
Tyler Press - R
Tyndale House - R
United Church Press
United Church Publishing
United Methodist
University Press/America - R
Upper Room Books
VESTA
Victory House - R
Welch Publishing - R
Westminster Press
World Bible - R
Zondervan - R
Zondervan/Academic

TRAVEL

Bob Jones - R
Brentwood - R
Bridge Publishing - R
Christopher Publishing Hs
Pelican Publishing - R
Prescott Press - R
Proclaim Publishing - R
Rainbow Books (FL)

WOMEN'S ISSUES

Aglow
Alban Institute
AMG Publishers - R
Augsburg Fortress - R
Baker Book House - R
Bantam Books
Blue Dolphin - R
Bridge Publishing - R
Broadman & Holman
Chalice Press
Chosen Books
Christian Publications - R
Christopher Publishing Hs
Collier/Macmillan
College Press - R
Concordia - R
Cornell Univ Press - R
Crossway
DaBaR Services - R
Didaskon Publishing - R
Eerdmans Publishing
Emerald Books - R
Fairway Press - R
Focus on the Family - R
Forward Movement - R
Franciscan Press - R
HarperSanFrancisco - R
Harvest House - R
Haworth Press - R
Hendrickson Publishers - R
Hensley, Virgil W. - R
Herald Press - R
Honor Books
Horizon House - R
InterVarsity Press
Judson Press - R
Kregel - R
Life Cycle Books - R
Lifetime Books
Liguori Publications
LuraMedia
Moody Press
Morehouse Publishing - R
Morning Star Press - R
Nazarene Publishing House
Nelson, Thomas - R
New Hope - R
New Leaf Press - R
New Society Publishers - R
Pacific Press
Pastoral Press
Paulist Press
Pelican Publishing - R
Pilgrim Press
Pillar Books - R
Prescott Press - R
Proclaim Publishing - R
Questar - R
Resurrection Press - R
Review & Herald
Roper Press - R
St. Bede's Publications - R
St. Paul Books - R
Servant Publications - R
Shaw Publishers, Harold - R
Sheed & Ward - R
Son-Rise
Southern Baptist Press - R
Starburst Publishers
Star Song - R
Still Waters Revival - R
TEACH Services - R
Trinity Press Intl. - R
Triumph Books - R
Tyler Press - R
United Church Press
United Church Publishing
United Methodist
Upper Room Books
VESTA
Victor Books
Victory House - R
Welch Publishing - R
Westminster Press
Women's Miss. Union - R
Zondervan - R
Zondervan/Academic

WORLD ISSUES

Baker Book House - R
Bridge Publishing - R
Center for Learning
Christian Publications - R
Christopher Publishing Hs
Companion Press - R
Franciscan Press - R
HarperSanFrancisco - R
Herald Press - R
Guernica - R
InterVarsity Press
Loyola Univ Press - R
Nelson, Thomas - R
New Leaf Press - R
New Society Publishers - R
Orbis Books
Pilgrim Press
Pillar Books - R
Prescott Press - R
PROBE Ministries - R
Proclaim Publishing - R
Questar - R
Regnery Gateway - R
Still Waters Revival - R
Trinity Foundation - R
Trinity Press Intl. - R
Triumph Books - R
Tyler Press - R
VESTA
Victory House - R
Welch Publishing - R

Zondervan - R

WORSHIP RESOURCES

AMG Publishers - R
Baker Book House - R
Bridge Publishing - R
Broadman & Holman
Center for Learning
Chalice Press
Christian Classics - R
Christopher Publishing Hs
Collier/Macmillan
Companion Press - R
Concordia - R
CSS Publishing
Didaskon Publishing - R
Discipleship Resources
Educational Ministries
Eerdmans Publishing
Emerald Books - R
Fairway Press - R
Franciscan Press - R
Group Publishing
HarperSanFrancisco - R
Judson Press - R
Kindred Press
Kregel - R
Liguori Publications
Liturgical Press
Loyola Univ Press - R
Meriwether Publishing - R
Morehouse Publishing - R
Nazarene Publishing House
Nelson, Thomas - R
Our Sunday Visitor
Pastoral Press
Pillar Books - R
Proclaim Publishing - R
St. Anthony Messenger - R
Sheed & Ward - R
Star Song - R
TEACH Services - R
Tyndale House - R
United Church Press
United Church Publishing
Upper Room Books
VESTA
Victory House - R
Welch Publishing - R
Westminster Press
Zondervan - R

YOUTH BOOKS (Nonfiction)

Note: Listing denotes books for 8-12 year olds, junior highs or senior highs. If all three, it will say "all".

Augsburg Fortress - R (8-12)
Baker Book House - R (all)
Bible Discovery (all)
Bob Jones - R (all)
Bosco Multimedia, Don
Bridge Publishers
Broadman & Holman (all)
Center for Learning (all)
Christian Liter. Crusade - R (Jr High)
Christian Publications - R (all)
Concordia - R (all)
Contemporary Drama Service
CREDO (all)
Eerdmans Publishing (8-12)
Emerald Books - R (all)
Fairway Press - R (all)
Forward Movement - R (all)
Friends United Press - R (8-12/Jr High)
Group Publishing (all)
Harvest House - R (8-12 & Sr High)
Herald Press - R (Sr High)
Honor Books
Horizon House - R (Jr/Sr. High)
Langmarc Publishing (Jr/Sr High)
Liguori Publications (all)
Morehouse Publishing - R (8-12/Jr high)
Morris, Joshua (all)
Nelson, Thomas - R (all)
New Hope - R
Novalis (all)
OMF Books (all)
Our Sunday Visitor (all)
Proclaim Publishing - R (all)
Questar - R (all)
Resurrection Press - R
Review & Herald (all)
St. Paul Books - R (all)
Son-Rise (all)
So. Baptist Press - R (all)
Still Waters Revival - R (all)
United Church Press (all)
Upper Room Books
Victor Books (Jr/Sr High)
Victory House - R
Welch Publishing - R
Women's Miss. Union - R
Zondervan - R (all)

YOUTH PROGRAMS

Baker Book House - R
Bridge Publishing - R
Center for Learning - R
Church Growth Institute
Concordia - R
Contemporary Drama
Discipleship Resources
Educational Ministries
Fairway Press - R
Group Publishing
Hensley, Virgil W. - R
Judson Press - R
Langmarc Publishing
Liguori Publications
Meriwether Publishing - R
Morehouse Publishing - R
Morris, Joshua
Nazarene Publishing House
Nelson, Thomas - R
Proclaim Publishing - R
Resurrection Press - R
Sheer Joy! Press
Welch Publishing - R

ALPHABETICAL LISTINGS OF BOOK PUBLISHERS

(*) An asterisk before a listing indicates no or unconfirmed information update.

(#) A number symbol before a listing indicates it was updated from their guidelines or other sources.

(+) A plus sign before a listing indicates it's a new listing.

ABINGDON PRESS - See The United Methodist Publishing House.

ACCENT BIBLE CURRICULUM, Box 15337, Denver CO 80215. (303)988-5300. Mary B. Nelson, mng. ed. Buys all rights as work for hire of assigned projects. Writers must be Baptist or baptistic. Submit query letter explaining qualifications to write curriculum; experience; published works. No freelance submissions.
Special Needs: Writers for Kindergarten & Adult.

ACCENT PUBLICATIONS, Imprint of David C. Cook Publishing, Box 15337, Denver CO 80215. (303)988-5300. Mary B. Nelson, mng. ed. Publishes 9-12 titles/yr. Receives 700-1,000 submissions annually. 75% of books from first-time authors. Accepts mss through agents (reluctantly). Royalty on retail; no advance. Publication within 9-12 mos. Accepts simultaneous submissions. Reports in 8-12 wks. Guidelines; catalog for 9x12 SAE/4 stamps.
Nonfiction: Query letter/one-pg synopsis/1st 3 chapters; no phone query.
Tips: "We publish Church Resource books which include Bible study series, or books which can be used to enhance the teaching/education ministry of the local church. No trade books, fiction or children's books."

ACTA PUBLICATIONS, 4848 N. Clark St., Chicago IL 60640. (312)271-1030. Fax: (312)271-1030. Catholic. Gregory F. Augustine Pierce, co-pub. Publishes 10 titles/yr. Receives 100 submissions annually. 95% of books from first-time authors. Accepts mss through agents. Prefers 125 pgs or 50,000 wds. Royalty 7.5-10% on wholesale; no advance. Average first printing 2,000. Publication within 1 yr. No simultaneous submissions. Reports in 6 wks. Guidelines; catalog for 9x12 SAE/2 stamps.
Nonfiction: Query or proposal/1 chapter; no phone query.
Tips: "Most open to books that are useful to a large number of average Christians. Read our catalog first."

+A.D. PLAYERS, 2710 W. Alabama, Houston TX 77098. (713)526-2721. Christian. Martha Doolittle, literary mngr. Professional theater company that produces plays. Produces 10 full plays and several shorter ones/season. Receives 50-100 submissions annually. Accepts plays through agents. Payment and advance negotiable/contract.

Production in 1 year or less. Considers simultaneous submissions. Reports in 6-12 mos. Guidelines; free script catalog.
Special Needs: Children's shows with 4-6 actors only.
Plays: Query. Any genre; also biographical or on social issues.
Tips: "We have a staged reading series especially for the development of plays by new authors."

AGLOW, Box 1548, Lynnwood WA 98046-1548. (206)775-7282x163. Fax: (206)778-9615. Women's Aglow Fellowship Intl. Karen E. Anderson, ed. Publishes 3-4 titles/yr. Receives 400 submissions annually. 65% of books from first-time authors. Accepts mss through agents. Prefers 40,000-50,000 wds or 175-225 pgs. Royalty to 10% on retail; advance $1,000-2,500. Average first printing 10,000. Publication within 12-18 mos. Accepts simultaneous submissions. Reports in 8 wks. Guidelines; catalog for 9x12 SAE/3 stamps.
Nonfiction: Query letter; phone query ok. "Most open to women's, family issues, always from the perspective of spiritual healing for brokenness."
Ethnic Books: Prints Bible studies and brochures in Spanish.
Tips: "Prepare a very thorough proposal that includes extensive research on target audience and market niche for your book. Market research with proposal is increasingly important to us. It shows an author `gets it'."

#ALBA HOUSE, 2187 Victory Blvd., Staten Island NY 10314. (718)761-0047. Fax: (718)761-0057. Catholic/Society of St. Paul. Aloysius Milella, ed; Edmund C. Lane, mng. ed. Publishes 30 titles/yr. Receives 1,000 submissions annually. 50% of books from first-time authors. Accepts mss through agents. Reprints books. Royalty 10% on retail; no advance. Publication within 9 mos. Accepts simultaneous submissions. Reports in 1 month. Guidelines; catalog for SASE.
Nonfiction: Query.

#THE ALBAN INSTITUTE, INC., 4125 Nebraska Ave. NW, Washington DC 20016. (202)244-7320. Episcopal Church. Celia A. Hahn, ed-in-chief. Publishes 10 titles/yr. Receives 100 submissions annually. No mss through agents. Prefers 100 pgs. Royalty 7-10% on net; advance $100. Publication within 1 yr. Reports in 3-4 mos. Guidelines; catalog for 9x12 SAE/3 stamps.
Nonfiction: Proposal only first. Books for clergy and laity.
Tips: "Books on congregational issues: problems and opportunities in congregational life; the clergy role and career; the ministry of the laity in church and world." Intelligent/liberal audience.

AMERICAN CATHOLIC PRESS, 16160 S. Seton Dr., South Holland IL 60473. (708)331-5485. Catholic worship resources. Father Michael Gilligan, ed. dir. Publishes 4 titles/yr. Reprints books. Pays $25-$100 for outright purchases only. Publication within 8 mos. Accepts simultaneous submissions. Reports in 2 mos.
Nonfiction: Query first.
Tips: "We publish only materials on the Roman Catholic liturgy. Especially interested in new music for church services."

#AMG PUBLISHERS, 6815 Shallowford Rd., Box 22000, Chattanooga TN 37422. (615)894-6060. Fax: (615)894-6863. Evangelical/AMG Intl. Dale Anderson, dir. Publishes 10 religious titles/yr. Receives 30 submissions annually. 20% of books from first-time authors. Accepts ms through agents. Reprints books. Prefers 150-250 pgs. Royalty 8% on retail (negotiable); no advance. Average first printing 2,500. Publication within 6 mos. Accepts simultaneous submissions. Reports in 8-12 wks. No guidelines; free catalog.
Nonfiction: Proposal/sample chapters.
Fiction: Query first. Juvenile/teen-yg adult.
Tips: "Must be a needed subject. Our focus is on pastoral helps."

#AUGSBURG FORTRESS, 426 S. 5th St., Box 1209, Minneapolis MN 55440. (612)330-3433. Evangelical Lutheran Church in America. Paul Nockleby, ed. dir.; Ron Klug, sr acq ed. Publishes 50 titles/yr. Receives 3,000 submissions annually. 20% of books from first-time authors. Accepts mss through agents. Reprints books. Prefers 128 pgs. Royalty 10% on retail; advance $1,000. Average first printing 4,000. Publication within 2 yrs. Accepts simultaneous submissions. Reports in 6 wks. Free guidelines/catalog.
Nonfiction: Query first. "Looking for devotional books and books for 8-12 yr olds."
Ethnic Books: African-American, Hispanic, Asian-American; contextual theology.

+AUGUST HOUSE PUBLISHERS, INC., P.O. Box 3223, Little Rock AR 72203. (501)372-5450. Fax: (501)372-5579. Liz Parkhurst, ed-in-chief. Publishes 8-10 titles/yr. Receives 200-300 submissions annually. 20% of books from first-time authors. Accepts mss through agents. Subsidy publishes 7% of books. Prefers less than 450 pgs. Pays royalty. Occasionally pays advance. Publication within 12-18 mos. Accepts simultaneous submissions. Reports in 120 days. Guidelines; catalog $2.
Nonfiction: Query or proposal/sample chapters; no phone queries.
Ethnic Books: African-American; Mexican-American; other multicultural titles.
Tips: "Our focus is on books pertaining to American folklore and storytelling; how to use story in your professional life."

AVE MARIA PRESS, Notre Dame IN 46556. (219)287-2831. Fax: (219)239-2904. Catholic. Frank J. Cunningham, dir. of publishing. Publishes 12-15 titles/yr. Receives 250 submissions annually. 50% of books from first-time authors. Accepts mss through agents. Royalty on retail; occasional advance. Average first printing 12,000. Publication within 8 mos. Accepts simultaneous submissions. Reports as soon as necessary. Guidelines; catalog for 9x12 SAE/5 stamps.
Nonfiction: Proposal/3 chapters or complete ms; no phone query.

BAKER BOOK HOUSE, Box 6287, Grand Rapids MI 49507. (616)676-9185. Fax: (616)676-9573. Evangelical. Allan Fisher, dir. of publications; submit to Jane Dekker, asst. Publishes 130 titles/yr. Receives 1,500-2,000 submissions annually. 5-10% of books from first-time authors. Accepts mss through agents. Reprints books. Prefers 200-350 pgs. Royalty 14-17.5% on net; sometimes pays advance. Average first

printing 5,000. Publication within 12 mos. Accepts simultaneous submissions. Reports in 2-4 wks. Guidelines; catalog for 9x12 SAE/3 stamps.
Nonfiction: Proposal/2-3 chapters; phone query ok, but mail preferred.
Fiction: Proposal/2-3 chapters. "We are specifically interested in mysteries and contemporary women's fiction. Trying to avoid romances, fantasy and historical fiction. Nothing preachy or didactic."
Ethnic Books: Would be interested in publishing specifically for the African-American market.
Tips: "Please prepare a complete, well-organized proposal. Request our guidelines for guidance."

#BANTAM BOOKS, 1540 Broadway, New York NY 10036. (216)354-6500. General trade publisher with a religious/inspirational list. Maria Mack & Michelle Rapkin, eds. Accepts mss only through agents. Prefers at least 80,000-100,000 wds. Royalty 4-15%; advance. Publication within 1 yr. Accepts simultaneous submissions. Reports in 2 mos. No guidelines/catalog.
Nonfiction: Proposal/1-2 chapters. "Want all types of religious/ inspirational books." No humor, no triumph over tragedy unless subject is well-known or a celebrity.
Fiction: Proposal/2-3 chapters. "Books must cross over into the trade market."
Tips: "We want books that appeal to a large, general audience and fresh ideas. Be sure to investigate the competition and include an author bio. The author's relevant experience and authority is very important to us."

BARBOUR & CO., INC., 1810 Barbour Dr., P.O. Box 719, Uhrichsville OH 44683. (614)922-6045. Fax: (614)922-5948. Stephen Reginald, V.P. editorial. Publishes 40 titles/yr. Receives 200 submissions annually. 15% of books from first-time authors. Accepts mss through agents. Reprints books. Prefers 50,000 wds. Royalty 5-10% on wholesale; outright purchases $500-2,500; advance $500. Average first printing 10,000. Publication within 6-8 mos. Accepts simultaneous submissions. Reports in 1-3 mos. Guidelines; catalog for 9x12 SAE/4 stamps.
Nonfiction: Proposal/3 chapters; phone query ok.
Tips: "Present a neat, well-organized proposal with return postage."

BARCLAY PRESS, 600 E. Third St., Newberg OR 97132-3106. (503)538-7345. Fax: (503)538-7033. Friends/Quaker. Dan McCracken, general manager. Publishes 2 titles/yr. Receives 15 submissions annually. 50% of books from first-time authors. Accepts mss through agents. Reprints books. Prefers 100-200 pgs. Royalty 10%; no advance. Average first printing 1,500. Publication within 18 mos. Accepts simultaneous submissions. Reports in 2 wks-2 mos. No guidelines; free catalog.
Nonfiction: Proposal/2 chapters. "Looking for books on spirituality and current social issues."

***MEL BAY PUBLICATIONS, INC.**, #4 Industrial Dr., Pacific MO 63069. (314)257-3970. William Bay, V.P.; submit to L. Dean Bye, gen mgr. Publishes 25 inspirational/religious titles/yr. Accepts mss through agents. Reprints books. Royalty 10% on retail; no advance. Publication within 6-9 mos. Reports in 1-6 wks. Free

guidelines/catalog.
Nonfiction: Proposal/chapters (photocopy only).
Fiction: Complete ms or proposal. Children's picture books, juvenile, plays.
Tips: Specializes in music books. "In case of musical submissions, we appreciate a cassette recording."

BEACON HILL PRESS OF KANSAS CITY - see **NAZARENE PUBLISHING HOUSE**

BETHANY HOUSE PUBLISHERS, 11300 Hampshire Ave. S, Minneapolis MN 55438. Steve Laube, acq. ed. Accepting no freelance material until further notice.

BETHEL PUBLISHING, 1819 S. Main, Elkhart IN 46516. (219)293-8585. Fax: (219)522-5670. Missionary Church. Rev. Richard Oltz, pres.; submit to Senior Editor. Publishes 5+ titles/yr. Receives 1400+ submissions annually. 85% of books from first-time authors. Accepts mss through agents. Reprints books. Prefers 30,000-40,000 wds. Royalty 5-10% on wholesale; no advance. Average first printing 10,000. Publication within 12 mos. Accepts simultaneous submissions. Reports in 1-2 mos. Guidelines; catalog for 9x12 SAE/3 stamps.
Nonfiction: Query or complete ms; no phone query.
Fiction: Query or complete ms. Adult/teen/juvenile.

+BIBLE DISCOVERY, Chariot Family Publishing, 20 Lincoln Ave., Elgin IL 60120. (708)741-0800. Fax: (708)741-0499. David C. Cook Publishing Co. Jeannie Harmon, ed. To acquaint children of all ages (1-14 yrs) with the truths of God's Word. Publishes 35-45 titles/yr. Receives 150-200 submissions annually. Few from first-time authors. Might accept mss through agents. Would consider reprinting books. Royalty or outright purchase; advance. Average first printing 15,000. Publication within 6-12 mos. Accepts simultaneous submissions. Reports in 3-5 mos.
Nonfiction: Summary of idea and sample; complete ms for books for very young children; no phone query. "Most open to accurate, quality Bible stories and devotional material that effectively bridges Scripture to a child's life. We look for unique ideas that are clear, concise, and age-appropriate."
Special Needs: Bible portions/devotional material; new ways to utilize Scripture for 8-14 year olds. Bible storybooks; product ideas for using Scripture text; devotional; Bible portions for 0-3 and 3-8 year olds.
Note: They are accepting no submissions until August 1994.

+BLUE DOLPHIN PUBLISHING, INC., P.O. Box 1920, Nevada City CA 95959. (916)265-6925. Fax: (916)265-0787. Paul M. Clemens, pres. Imprint: Pelican Pond. Publishes 6-10 titles/yr. Receives 2,400 submissions annually. 90% of books from first-time authors. Accepts mss though agents. Reprints books. Prefers about 60,000 wds or 200 pgs. Royalty 10-15% on wholesale; no advance. Average first printing 5,000. Publication within 2-6 mos. Accepts simultaneous submissions. Reports in 1-2 mos. Guidelines; catalog for 9x12 SAE/3 stamps.
Nonfiction: Complete ms; no phone query. "We will accept most categories, depending on preferences at the time and presentation of the work."

Special Needs: Books on early Christianity, personal mysticism, relationships, self-help/inspirational, men's and women's issues.
Tips: "Re-write the manuscript seven times before submission."

BOB JONES UNIVERSITY PRESS, Light Line and Pennant Books Imprints (for children & youth only), Greenville SC 29614. (803)242-5100x4315. George Collins, ed-in-chief; Gloria Rapp, acq. ed. for Light Line & Pennant books. Goal is to publish books for children that excel in both literary and moral content. Publishes 6-10 titles/yr. Receives 400 submissions annually. 30% of books from first-time authors. Accepts mss through agents. Reprints books. Prefers 3,000-60,000 wds (depends on age group). Outright purchases of $1,000-1,500; no advance. Average first printing 5,000. Publication within 12-18 months. Accepts simultaneous submissions. Reports in 2 mos. Guidelines; catalog for 9x12 SAE/2 stamps.
Nonfiction: Query or proposal/5 chapters; no phone query. "Looking for juvenile biography and history books."
Fiction: Proposal/5 chapters or complete ms. "Looking for humor; problem realism; historical fiction."
Tips: "Most open to realistic or historical fiction for upper elementary through teens; biography with a good moral tone."

#DON BOSCO MULTIMEDIA, 475 North Ave., Box T, New Rochelle NY 10802. (914)576-0122. Fax: (914)654-0443. Catholic. James T. Morgan, ed. Publishes 30 titles/yr. Receives 50 submissions annually. 15% of books from first-time authors. No mss through agents. Royalty 5-10% on retail; $100 advance. Subsidy publishes 10% (for nonprofit and religious societies). Prefers 150 pgs. Average first printing 2,500. Publication within 10 mos. Reports in 5 wks. Guidelines; free catalog.
Nonfiction: Query or proposal/2 chapters. For youth and adults.

BRENTWOOD CHRISTIAN PRESS, 4000 Beallwood Ave., Columbus GA 31904. (706)576-5787. Mainline. Jerry L. Luquire, exec. ed. Publishes 267 titles/yr. Receives 2,000 submissions annually. Accepts mss through agents. Reprints books. Subsidy publishes 95%. Prefers 120 pgs. Average first printing 500. Publication within 2 mos. Accepts simultaneous submissions. Reports in 2 days. Guidelines; no catalog.
Nonfiction: Complete ms. "Collection of sermons on family topics; poetry; relation of Bible to current day."
Fiction: Complete ms. "Stories that show how faith helps overcome small, day-to-day problems. Prefer under 200 pgs."
Tips: "Keep it short; support facts with reference."

BRIDGE PUBLISHING, INC., 2500 Hamilton Blvd., South Plainfield NJ 07080. (908)754-0745. Fax: (908)754-0617. Catherine J. Barrier, ed. Publishes 35 titles/yr. Receives 400 submissions annually. 70% of books from first-time authors. Accepts mss through agents. Subsidy publishes 10%. Reprints books. Prefers 200-300 pgs. Royalty 6-25% of wholesale; sometimes pays advance. Average first printing 10,000. Publication within 4 mos. Accepts simultaneous submissions. Reports in 6-18 wks. Guidelines; free catalog.

Nonfiction: Proposal/3 chapters or complete ms; phone query ok. "Most open to evangelism, spiritual growth and Christian classics."
Fiction: Proposal/3 chapters or complete ms. For all ages.
Tips: "Call us. We are always ready to give specific advice depending on the circumstances."

BRISTOL HOUSE, LTD., 3131 E. 67th St., Anderson IN 46013. (317)644-0856. Fax: (317)622-1045. Sara Anderson, sr. ed.; submit to James S. Robb, ed. Imprint: Bristol Books. Publishes 6 titles/yr. Receives 35-55 submissions annually. 33-50% of books from first-time authors. Accepts mss through agents. Reprints books. Some subsidy. Prefers 160-240 pgs. Royalty 14% of net; no advance. Average first printing 3,000. Publication within 6-9 mos. No simultaneous submissions. Reports in 3 mos. No guidelines; catalog for 9x12 SAE/2 stamps.
Nonfiction: Proposal/2 chapters; phone query ok (606)273-7142. "Looking for books on renewal."

BROADMAN & HOLMAN PUBLISHERS, 127 9th Ave. N, Nashville TN 37234. (615)251-2401. Southern Baptist. Vicki Crumpton, acq./dev. ed. Publishes 65 titles/yr. Receives 1,500+ submissions annually. 20-30% of books from first-time authors. Accepts mss through agents. Length varies. Variable royalty (on wholesale) and advance. Average first printing 3,000-5,000. Publication within 9-12 mos. Accepts simultaneous submissions. Reports in 6-8 wks. Guidelines; catalog for 9x12 SAE/3 stamps.
Nonfiction: Proposal/2 chapters (see guidelines for format); no phone query. "Looking for men's books and practical theology."
Fiction: Proposal (complete synopsis)/2 chapters. Only publishes juvenile fiction in a series.
Tips: "Follow guidelines when submitting. Be informed about the market in general and specifically related to the book you want to write."

#BROWN PUBLISHING-ROA MEDIA, 2460 Kerper Blvd., Dubuque IA 52001. (319)588-1451. Fax: (319)589-4705. Catholic. Mary Jo Graham, sr. ed. Publishes 50-100 titles/yr. Receives 100-300 submissions annually. Accepts mss through agents. Variable royalty or outright purchase; rarely pays advance. Average first printing 1,000-3,000. Publication within 1 yr. Accepts simultaneous submissions. Reports in 2 mos. No guidelines; free catalog.
Nonfiction: Complete ms. "Looking primarily for school and parish textbooks and easy-to-use help books."

THE CATHOLIC UNIVERSITY OF AMERICA PRESS, 620 Michigan Ave. NE, Washington DC 20064. (202)319-5052. Fax: (202)319-5802. Catholic. Dr. David J. McGonagle, dir. Publishes 4-5 titles/yr. No mss through agents. Reprints books. Prefers 250 pgs. Royalty 10% on wholesale; no advance. Average first printing varies. Publication within 1 yr. Considers simultaneous submissions. Reports in 3 mos. Guidelines; free catalog.
Nonfiction: Query first; phone query ok. "Looking for history, literature, philosophy,

political theory and theology."
Tips: "We publish only works of original scholarship of interest to practicing scholars and academic libraries; works that are aimed at college and university classrooms. We do not publish for the popular religious audience."

+THE CENTER FOR LEARNING, 21590 Center Ridge Rd., Rocky River OH 44116. (216)331-1404. Fax: (216)331-5414. Catholic/Sisters of the Humility of Mary. Amy Richards, edit. dir. Publishes 15 titles/yr. Receives 100 submissions annually. 20% of books from first-time authors. No mss through agents. Royalty 8-10% on net; advance $250-$1,000. Average first printing 500-1,000. Publication within 6 mos. Accepts simultaneous submissions. Reports in 2 mos. Free guidelines/catalog.
Nonfiction: Proposal/as many chapters as available or complete ms. "Most open to values-based curriculum guides or models. Most of our curriculum materials are written by full-time teachers."
Tips: "Our mission is to improve education by writing and publishing values-based curriculum materials that enable teachers to foster student responsibility for learning."

CHALICE PRESS, Box 179, St. Louis MO 63166. (314)231-8500. Fax: (314)231-8524. Christian Church (Disciples of Christ). Dr. David P. Polk, ed. Books for a thinking, caring church. Publishes 12 titles/yr. Receives 200 submissions annually. 25% of books from first-time authors. No mss through agents. Rarely reprints books. Prefers 150 pgs. Royalty 14-17% on wholesale; no advance. Average first printing 2,500. Publication within 9 mos. Accepts simultaneous submissions. Reports in 3 mos. Guidelines; catalog for 9x12 SAE/2 stamps.
Nonfiction: Proposal/2 chapters; no phone query. "Looking for informed treatments of current social issues; preaching; stewardship."
Tips & Ethnic Books: "We want to publish a greater number of female and ethnic minority writers."

CHARIOT BOOKS (juvenile books), Imprint of Chariot Family Publishing, David C. Cook Publishing Co., 20 Lincoln Ave., Elgin IL 60120. (708)741-9558. Julie Smith, mng. ed. "For at least a year, Chariot Books (children's imprint), will not be accepting unsolicited manuscripts. We're overwhelmed with mss, and have cut back on editorial staff."
Tips: They will look at manuscripts recommended by current authors, or those submitted through The Writer's Edge Manuscript Service (see listing in Editorial Services).

CHARIOT FAMILY PUBLISHING - A division of David C. Cook Publishing Company. See Chariot Books (children), LifeJourney Books (adults), and Bible Discovery.

CHOSEN BOOKS, Division of Baker Book House, 2956 Valera Ct., Vienna VA 22181. Phone/Fax: (703)242-2080. Charismatic. Jane Campbell, ed. Publishes 6-8 titles/yr. Receives 500 submissions annually. 10% of books from first-time authors. Accepts mss through agents. Prefers 60,000 wds or 200 pgs. Royalty 14% on wholesale; advance. Average first printing 5,000. Publication within 12 mos. Accepts simultaneous

submissions. Reports in 2-3 mos. Guidelines; no catalog.
Nonfiction: Proposal/2-3 chapters; no phone query. "Looking for books on missions/evangelism."
Tips: "Narratives must have a strong theme and reader benefits."

CHRISTIAN CLASSICS, INC., Box 30, 73 W. Main St., Westminster MD 21158. (410)848-3065. Fax: (410)857-2805. Catholic. John J. McHale, ed. Publishes 10 titles/yr. Receives 100+ submissions annually. 25% of books from first-time authors. Accepts mss through agents. Reprints books. Royalty 12.5% on net; advance $750. First printing 1,000-2,000. Publication within 4 months. No simultaneous submissions. Reports in 2-5 wks. Guidelines; free catalog.
Nonfiction: Query/proposal/2-3 chapters; phone query ok.
Fiction: Query only. "Would have to be religious in nature and of high interest; related to prominent religious figures or teaching by nature."
Special Needs: "Something on religious renewal of youth; treatises on resolution of diversities in faith; studies of Catholicism in the 1990's."
Tips: "Most open to something of solid intellectual nature or inspirational; something that will help direct sound religious development. We are geared mainly to the adult scholarly market."

#CHRISTIAN ED. PUBLISHERS, Box 261129, San Diego CA 92196. (619)578-4700. Evangelical. Carol Rogers, mng. ed. Publishes 28 titles/yr. 25% of books from first-time authors. No mss through agents. Outright purchases for .02-.03 per wd; no advance. Publication within 9 mos. Reports in 90 days. Guidelines; catalog for 9x12 SAE/2 stamps.
Nonfiction: Query first. Bible studies, curriculum and take-home papers.
Fiction: Query first. Juvenile fiction for take-home papers. "Each story is divided into 4-5 sections of about 300 wds ea."
Tips: "All writing done on assignment. Send letter with age level you want to write for, with your qualifications."

CHRISTIAN LITERATURE CRUSADE, Box 1449, Fort Washington PA 19034. (215)542-1242. Fax: (215)542-7580. Ken Brown, pub. mngr. Publishes 6 titles/yr. Receives 50-100 submissions annually. 100% of books from first-time authors. Accepts mss through agents. Reprints books. Prefers 200-250 pgs. Royalty 5-10% on retail; rarely pays $500 advance. Average first printing 2,000-3,000. Publication within 18 mos. Accepts simultaneous submissions. Reports in 2-3 wks. Guidelines; catalog for 9x12 SAE.
Nonfiction: Proposal/3 chapters; no phone query. "Looking for adult and senior high mission biographies; books on deeper Christian life."
Tips: "Send only a proposal and 3 chapters. You are less likely to get a favorable notice if you send the complete manuscript unasked."

CHRISTIAN MEDIA, Box 448, Jacksonville OR 97530. (503)899-8888. James Lloyd, ed./pub. New publisher. Query.
Tips: "Interested in media-oriented materials with a specific focus on Christian music,

video, film, broadcasting or drama. Includes manuals, instructional or otherwise. Also books of prophetic interpretation, end times, escatology, interpolations of political events, etc."

#CHRISTIAN PUBLICATIONS, 3825 Hartzdale Dr., Camp Hill PA 17011. (717)761-7044. Fax: (717)761-7273. Christian and Missionary Alliance. Jonathan Graf, ed. dir. Publishes 24 titles/yr. Receives 700 submissions annually. 5-10% of books from first-time authors. Accepts mss through agents. Subsidy publishes 2%. Reprints books. Prefers 160-200 pgs. Royalty 5-10% on retail; outright purchases $100-2,000; advance $500. Average first printing 5,000. Publication within 12-16 mos. Accepts simultaneous submissions. Reports in 2-3 mos. Guidelines; catalog for 9x12 SAE/3 stamps.
Nonfiction: Proposal/3 chapters; no phone query. "Looking for books on contemporary Christian living that have a solid biblical base."
Fiction: Proposal/3 chapters. Adult, teen, children. "Something that could be a series. No 'end times' or science fiction please!"
Tips: "Most open to a well-written, contemporary-sounding book that moves the reader toward a deeper relationship with Jesus Christ."

THE CHRISTOPHER PUBLISHING HOUSE, 24 Rockland St., Hanover MA 02339. (617)826-7474. Fax: (617)826-5556. Nancy A. Lucas, mng. ed. Publishes 8-12 titles/yr. Receives over 1,000-1,200 submissions annually. 90% of books from first-time authors. Accepts mss through agents. Subsidy publishes 10-15%. Prefers at least 64 ms pgs. Royalty 10-30% of net; no advance. Average first printing 2,000. Publication within 12-15 mos. Accepts simultaneous submissions. Reports in 4-6 wks. Guidelines; catalog for #10 SAE/2 stamps.
Nonfiction: Complete ms.
Fiction: Complete ms. Adult.

***CHURCH AND SYNAGOGUE LIBRARY ASSN., INC.**, Box 19357, Portland OR 97280. (503)244-6919. Lorraine E. Burson, ed. Publishes 2-3 titles/yr. Usually recruits books from membership. Receives 2-3 submissions annually. 80% of books from first-time authors. No mss through agents. Prefers 35-40 pgs. Pays in copies. Average first printing 1,000. Publication within 12 mos. Reports in 2 wks. Guidelines/catalog for #10 SAE/1 stamp.
Nonfiction: Query first. "How-to helps for the congregational librarian."

CHURCH GROWTH INSTITUTE, Box 4404, Lynchburg VA 24502. (804)525-0022. Fax: (804)525-0608. Conservative/evangelical. Cindy G. Spear, ed; submit to Marvin Osborn, dir. of resource development. Publishes 8 titles/yr. 30% of books from first-time authors. No mss through agents. Prefers 208 pgs (printed). Royalty on retail or outright purchase. Average first printing 5,000. Publication within 6 mos. Accepts simultaneous submissions. Reports in 90 days. Guidelines; no catalog.
Nonfiction: Proposal/1 chapter; no phone query.
Tips: "Book must be able to fit in an entire resource packet as part of a theme related to church growth or ministry. Our products are educational tools for pastors or churches. Books are lay-oriented, while related packets are leadership oriented."

#CISTERCIAN PUBLICATIONS INC., Wallwood Hall, WMU Station, Kalamazoo MI 49008. (616)387-8920. Fax: (616)387-8921. Catholic/Order of Cistercians of the Strict Observance. Dr. E. Rozanne Elder. ed. dir. Publishes 8-10 titles/yr. Receives 25-50 submissions annually. No mss through agents. Reprints books. Prefers 204-286 pgs. No payment. Average first printing 1,500. Publication within 18-48 mos. Reports in 3 mos. Free guidelines/catalog.
Nonfiction: Proposal/2 chapters; no phone query. Christian living, historical and theology.
Tips: "Christian monastic studies only."

COLLEGE PRESS PUBLISHING CO., INC., 223 W. Third St., Box 1132, Joplin MO 64802. (417)623-6280 or (800)289-3300. Fax: (417)623-8250. Christian Church/Church of Christ. John M. Hunter, ed. Imprint: Forerunner Books. Publishes 36 titles/yr. Receives 300+ submissions annually. 16% of books from first-time authors. Accepts mss through agents. Reprints books. Prefers 200-300 pgs/40,000-60,000 wds. Royalty 10% on net; no advance. Average first printing 2,000-3,000. Publication within 6-12 mos. Accepts simultaneous submissions. Reports in 2-3 wks. Guidelines; catalog for 9x12 SAE/9 stamps.
Nonfiction: Proposal/2-3 chapters only; no phone query. "Looking for apologetics and Christian reactions to politics in 21st century; Christian holiness."
Fiction: None for now; maybe next year.
Ethnic Books: Reprints their own books in Spanish.
Tips: "Most open to exegetically documented works in Bible study."

***COLLIER-MACMILLAN PUBLISHING CO.,** 866 Third Ave., New York NY 10022. (212)702-9865. Trade book publisher with a religious line. Stephen Wilburn, dir., religious books. Publishes 8-12 titles/yr. Prefers 50,000 wds & up. Royalty & advance.
Nonfiction: Proposal/3-5 chapters.

#COMPANION PRESS, 167 Walnut Bottom Rd., Shippenburg PA 17257. (717)532-3040. Fax: (717)532-9291. Inter-denominational. Imprint: Destiny Image Books. Keith Carroll, pub. Publishes 38 titles/yr. Receives 300 submissions annually. 80% of books from first-time authors. Accepts mss through agents. Reprints books. Subsidy publishes 80%. Prefers 60,000 wds. Royalty 4-8% on retail; for subsidy, purchase books at 70% of retail price; no advance. Average first printing 5,000. Publication within 3 mos. Accepts simultaneous submissions. Reports in 4 wks. Free guidelines & catalog.
Nonfiction & Fiction: Query or complete ms.

CONCORDIA PUBLISHING HOUSE, 3558 S. Jefferson Ave., St. Louis MO 63118-3968. (314)268-1000. Fax: (314)268-1329. Lutheran Church/Missouri Synod. Rev. David V. Koch, chief ed; Rev. Mervin Marquardt, mng. ed; Ruth Geisler, family/children's editor; and Rev. Bruce Cameron, academic/theological editor. Publishes 75 titles/yr. Receives 1,200+ submissions annually. 25% of books from first-time authors. Accepts mss through agents. Rarely reprints books. Royalty 6-10% on retail; some outright purchases; seldom pays advances. Publication within 10-12 mos.

Accepts simultaneous submissions. Reports in 8 wks. Free guidelines/catalog.
Nonfiction: Proposal/2 chapters; no phone query.
Fiction: Proposal/2 chapters. For children or teens only; also picture books. Fiction guidelines available on request. Christian fiction only.
Ethnic Books: Publishes books for Hispanic, Chinese, African-American, Hmong, and Vietnamese.
Tips: "Most open to family, inspirational/devotional, or children's books."

CONTEMPORARY DRAMA SERVICE - See Meriwether Publishing, Ltd.

DAVID C. COOK PUBLISHING CO. - See Chariot Books & LifeJourney Books.

#CORNELL UNIVERSITY PRESS, Box 250, 124 Roberts Pl., Ithaca NY 14851. (607)257-7000. Fax: (607)257-3552. Nondenominational. Bernard Kendler & Roger Hayden, eds. Publishes 6-8 titles/yr. Receives 20 submissions annually. 50% of books from first-time authors. Accepts mss through agents. Reprints books. Prefers 100,000 wds. Royalty 5-10%; rarely pays advance. Average first printing 1,250. Publication within 1 yr. May consider simultaneous submission. Reports in 3 mos. Free guidelines/catalog.
Nonfiction: Query first. "Looking for historical (esp. medieval & early modern) and philosophical books."

#COVENANT PUBLISHERS, Box 26361, Philadelphia PA 19141. (215)638-4324. Mainline Protestant. Dr. Matthew Sadiku, exec. ed. Publishes 2 titles/yr. Receives 4 submissions annually. 50% of books from first-time authors. Prefers 250 pgs. Royalty 10% on wholesale; no advance. Publication within 6 mos. Reports in 2 wks. Catalog for SASE.
Nonfiction: Complete ms. "Looking for Christian living topics."

CREATION HOUSE, 190 N. Westmonte Dr., Altamonte Springs FL 32714. (407)862-7565. Fax: (407)869-6051. Strang Communications Co. Debbie Cole, mng ed; submit to Barb Dycus. Imprint: Christian Life Books. Publishes 18 titles/yr. Receives 500 submissions annually. Less than 5% of books from first-time authors. Accepts mss through agents. Reprints books. Prefers 40,000 wds. Royalty on wholesale; pays advance. Average first printing 15,000. Publication within 6-9 mos. Accepts simultaneous submissions. Reports in 8 wks. Guidelines; catalog for 9x12 SAE/3 stamps.
Nonfiction: Proposal/3 chapters; no phone query. "Need books of special interest to charismatics and pentecostals; also practical Christian living."
Fiction: Proposal/3 chapters. "Strong Christian message is most important." Also reprints public-domain books.
Tips: "Send something that meets a strong felt need in our audience."

***CREATIVELY YOURS**, 2906 W. 64th Pl., Tulsa OK 74132. Publishes individual scripts and books of plays, poems, and related material; general religious. Jill Morris, pub. Send complete ms. Reports in 2 mos or less. Pays $25 for plays; $5 for poems

(4-20 lines/action), and $10 for choral readings. Buys all rts. Guidelines; free brochure.
Tips: "Try the material on children—if they don't like it, don't send it to us. Use humor whenever possible. The plays we publish can be used with puppets or children, so don't overload on characters, props or setting—keep it simple."
Note: Since this publisher wants individual plays or poems, it is listed in the topical section for periodicals.

#CREDO PUBLISHING CORP., Box 3175, Langley BC V3A 4R5 Canada. (604)533-8355. Evangelical. Jocelyn Cameron, acq. ed. Publishes 3-6 titles/yr. Subsidy publishes 60%. Prefers 112-350 pgs. Royalty 7-10%; advance. Accepts simultaneous submissions. Reports in 90 days. Guidelines.
Nonfiction: Proposal/sample chapters.
Special Needs: Material for children and youth.

+CROSSWAY BOOKS, 1300 Crescent St., Wheaton IL 60187. (708)682-4300. Fax: (708)682-4785. A Division of Good News Publishers. Leonard G. Goss, editorial dir. Publishes 50-60 titles/yr. Receives 4,500 submissions annually. 25% of books from first-time authors. Accepts mss through agents. Rarely reprints books. Royalty 15-20+% on net; advance. Publication within 7-9 mos. Accepts simultaneous submissions. Reports in 4-8 wks. Guidelines; catalog for 9x12 SAE.
Nonfiction: Query/proposal/2-3 chapters; no phone query.
Fiction: Query/proposal/most of finished book. Also takes western or intrigue novels.
Tips: "Most open to books that are consistent with what the Bible teaches and stand within the stream of historic Christian truth; books that give a clear sense that the author is a genuine Christian seeking to live a consistent Christian life."

#C.S.S. PUBLISHING CO., 517 S. Main St., Lima OH 45802. (419)227-1818. Fax: (419)228-9184. Protestant. Fred Steiner, ed. dir. Publishes 52 titles/yr. Receives 300 submissions annually. 90% of books from first-time authors. No mss through agents. Subsidy publishes 20% through Fairway Press. Prefers 100-125 pgs. Outright purchases for $25-300. Average first printing 2,000. Publication within 9-12 mos. Accepts simultaneous submissions. Reports in 3 mos. Guidelines/needs list; catalog for 9x12 SAE/2 stamps.
Nonfiction: Complete ms; phone query ok. "Need lectionary-related subjects; Thanksgiving, Christmas and Easter coloring books; sermons for special occasions/holidays."
Fiction: Complete ms. Plays only.

***CUSTOM COMMUNICATIONS SERVICES, INC./SHEPHERD PRESS/CUSTOMBOOK**, 77 Main St., Tappan NJ 10983. (914)365-0414. Norman Shaifer, pres. Publishes 50-75 titles/yr. 50% of books from first-time authors. No mss through agents. Royalty on wholesale; some outright purchases for specific assignments. Publication within 6 mos. Reports in 1 month. Guidelines; no catalog.
Nonfiction: Query/proposal/chapters. "Histories of individual congregations, denominations, or districts."
Tips: "Find stories of larger congregations (750 or more households) who have played

a role in the historic growth and development of the community or region."

+DABAR SERVICES, P.O. Box 35377, Detroit MI 48235. (313)861-2806. Fax: (313)864-9444. Diane Reeder, content ed. Publishes 1-2 titles/yr. Receives 3 submissions annually. 100% of books from first-time authors. No mss through agents. Open to subsidy publishing, especially of established speakers. Would reprint books. Royalty 10-15% on retail; no advance. Average first printing 3,000. Publication time undetermined. Accepts simultaneous submissions. Reports in 3 mos. No guidelines/catalog.
Nonfiction: Query first. "We look for books that speak to the specific needs of African-American women while not necessarily excluding the needs of other women."
Ethnic Books: "Black women are our target audience."
Tips: "Explore and exhaust all other avenues. We're small and new. But if a book is burning within and no other doors have opened, contact us. The book needs to have a strong, scriptural base."

***DIDASKON PUBLISHING**, 3601 - 42nd St., Lubbock TX 79413. (806)799-8655. David Unfred, pres. Publishes 3-5 titles/yr. Receives 50+ submissions annually. 90% of books from first-time authors. No mss through agents. Some subsidy publishing. Prefers less than 500 pgs. Escalating royalty on retail or wholesale; no advance. Average first printing 5,000. Publication within 18 months. Accepts simultaneous submissions. Reports in 3 months. No guidelines or catalog.
Nonfiction: Complete ms.
Fiction: Complete ms. "Apologetic orientation."
Tips: "Christian education/apologetics focusing on non-fiction archaeology, history, science for youth, and fiction."

DIMENSION BOOKS, INC., Box 811, Denville NJ 07834. (201)627-4334. Catholic. Thomas P. Coffey, ed. Publishes 7 titles/yr. Receives hundreds of submissions annually. 20% of books from first-time authors. Accepts mss through agents. Reprints books. Prefers 200 pgs. Royalty on retail; pays advance. Average first printing 10,000. Publication within 6 mos. Accepts simultaneous submissions. Reports in 2-5 wks. No guidelines; catalog for #10 SAE/1 stamp.
Nonfiction: Query; no phone query.

DISCIPLESHIP RESOURCES, Box 840, Nashville TN 37202. (615)340-7068. Fax: (615)340-7006. United Methodist. Craig Gallaway, ed. dir. Publishes 15-20 titles/yr. Receives 200-250 submissions annually. 40% of books from first-time authors. Accepts mss through agents. Prefers 80-150 pgs. Royalty 10% on net; outright purchases $250-$1,500; rare advances $250. Average first printing 4,000. Publication within 6 mos. Reports in 1-3 mos. Free guidelines/catalog.
Nonfiction: Query; proposal/2 chapters; no phone query.
Special Needs: Shepherding programs (discipling); youth ministry programs; family ministry programs.
Ethnic Books: Produces titles related to ministries for African-American, Hispanic, Korean, Native-American, and other ethnic groups.

Tips: "Most open to books to support ministries/programs related to Christian discipleship that are also focused on congregational life and leadership."

***DISCOVERY PUBLISHING HOUSE**, Box 3566, Grand Rapids MI 49501. Radio Bible Class. Robert DeVries, pub.; submit to Carol Holquist, assoc. pub. Guidelines. Not included in topical listings.

#EDUCATIONAL MINISTRIES, INC., 165 Plaza Dr., Prescott AZ 86303-5549. (602)771-8601. Fax: (602)771-8621. Christian education publisher/Mainline Protestant. Robert Davidson, ed.; Suzanne Rood Cox, project ed. Publishes 10 titles/yr. Prefers 40-100 pgs. Royalty 10% on retail; some outright purchases $500. Reports in 3 mos. Guidelines; catalog for 9x12 SAE/4 stamps.
Nonfiction: Complete ms. Christian education resource books.

WM B. EERDMANS PUBLISHING CO., 255 Jefferson Ave. SE, Grand Rapids MI 49503. (616)459-4591. Fax: (616)459-6540. Protestant/Academic/Theological. Jon Pott, ed-in-chief; Amy Eerdmans, children's bk. ed.; Nueva Creacion, Spanish imprint. Publishes 90 titles/yr. Receives 1,000 submissions annually. Accepts mss through agents. Occasionally subsidy publishes and reprints books. Royalty 7.5-10% on retail; occasional advance, $1,000. Average first printing 5,000. Publication within 2 yrs. Accepts simultaneous submissions. Reports in 4 wks. Guidelines; free catalog.
Nonfiction: Proposal/2 chapters. "Looking for women's issues, spirituality, men's issues, and aging."
Fiction: Complete ms. Adult/juvenile/picture books. Rarely buys fiction.
Ethnic Books: Spanish Imprint.
Tips: "Most open to material with general appeal, but well researched. Cutting edge material that bridges the gap between evangelical and mainline world."

+EMERALD BOOKS, P.O. Box 635, Lynnwood WA 98046. (206)771-1153. Fax: (206)775-2383. Non-denominational. Warren Walsh, owner/ed. Publishes 4-6 titles/yr. Receives 20-30 submissions annually. Accepts mss through agents. Subsidy publishes 5% of books. Prefers 150-200 pgs. Royalty 15% on net; seldom pays an advance. Average first printing 7,500. Publication within 6 mos. Accepts simultaneous submissions. Reports in 30-60 days. Guidelines; free catalog.
Nonfiction: Proposal/2 chapters. "Looking for solid Christian living books and solid books for youth."
Fiction: Proposal/2-4 chapters. For all ages.

***EVERGREEN PUBLICATIONS INC.**, Box 220, Davison MI 48423. Dr. Robert Busha, pub.; Mary Beckwith Busha, assoc. pub. Not publishing for now.

FAIRWAY PRESS, Subsidy Division for C.S.S. Publishing Company. 517 S. Main St., Box 4503, Lima OH 45802. (419)227-1818. Fax: (419)228-9184. A subsidy publisher. Niki C. Dunham, gen mgr. Publishes 60-75 titles/yr. Receives 365 submissions annually. 98% of books from first-time authors. Accepts mss through agents. Reprints books. **100% SUBSIDY**. Royalty; no advance. Average first printing 2,000. Publication

within 8-9 mos. Accepts simultaneous submissions. Reports in up to 1 month. Free guidelines/catalog for 9x12 SAE.
Nonfiction: Complete ms. "Looking for mss with a Christian theme, and seasonal material."
Fiction: Complete ms. For adults, teens, or children.

FOCUS ON THE FAMILY PUBLISHERS, 8605 Explorer Dr., Colorado Springs CO 80920-1051. (719)531-3400. Fax: (719)531-3484. Gwen Weising, mng. ed. Publishes 15 titles/yr. Receives 1,200 submissions annually. 1% from first-time authors. Accepts mss through agents. Reprints books. Prefers 225 pgs. Royalty on net; advance. Average first printing 25,000. Publication within 18 mos. Considers simultaneous submissions. Reports in 8 wks. Guidelines; catalog for 9x12 SASE.
Nonfiction: Query only.
Fiction: Query only. "Lines are full."
Tips: "Most open to helpful, practical books that meet a felt need. We're looking for a unique angle on family issues."

FORWARD MOVEMENT PUBLICATIONS, 412 Sycamore St., Cincinnati OH 45202. (513)721-6659. Fax: (513)421-0315. Episcopal. Charles H. Long, ed. Publishes 25 books/yr. No mss through agents. Reprints books. Prefers 98-128 published pgs. One-time honorarium; no advance. Average first printing 6,000. Accepts simultaneous submissions. Reports in 1-3 mos. Guidelines; catalog for #10 SAE/3 stamps.
Nonfiction: Complete ms; no phone query. "We really aren't looking for books although we publish about 8 a year. We need short works for pamphlets and booklets."
Ethnic books: Hispanic.

#FRANCISCAN PRESS, 1800 College Ave., Quincy IL 62301-2670. (217)228-5670. Fax: (217)228-5672. Catholic/Franciscan. Imprints: Franciscan Herald Press and Franciscan Press. Est. 1991. Dr. Terrence J. Riddell, dir. Publishes 5-10 titles/yr. Receives 50-100 submissions annually. 10% of books from first-time authors. No mss through agents. Reprints books. Royalty 5-10% on wholesale; outright purchases negotiated; no advance. Average first printing 2,500. Publication within 12-18+ mos. Accepts simultaneous submissions. Reports in up to 6 mos. No guidelines; free catalog.
Nonfiction: Query first. "Looking for moral theology; Franciscan history; works on life and writings of SS, Francis, Clare, Bonaventure."
Tips: "Please observe our somewhat specific subject area limitations."

FRANCISCAN UNIVERSITY PRESS, Franciscan Way, Steubenville OH 43952. (614)283-6357. Fax: (614)283-6442. Catholic. Dawn C. Harris, ed. Publishes 10 titles/yr. Receives 30 submissions annually. 5% of books from first-time authors. No mss through agents. Reprints books. Prefers 250 pgs. Royalty 5-15% on retail; no advance. Average first printing 2,000-5,000. Publication within 1 yr. Accepts simultaneous submissions. Reports in several mos. Guidelines; free catalog.
Nonfiction: Proposal/1 chapter; author vita; table of contents; no phone query. "Looking for Catholic apologetics and biblical studies."

Ethnic books: "Spanish translations of our best-selling devotional works."
Tips: "Most of our books are solicited from university professors and associates."

FRIENDSHIP PRESS, 475 Riverside Dr., Room 860, New York NY 10115. (212)870-2496. Fax: (212)870-2550. National Council of Churches of Christ. Margaret Larom, ed.; submit to Audrey A. Miller, dir. Publishes 12-20 titles/yr. Receives 35 submissions annually. 50% of books from first-time authors. Accepts mss through agents. Prefers 40-130 pgs. Royalty; some outright purchases; advance. Average first printing 10,000. Publication within 9-12 mos. Occasionally considers simultaneous submissions. Reports in 1-3 mos. Guidelines; catalog for 9x12 SAE.
Nonfiction: Complete ms; no phone query. "Looking for books on life in a multicultural society; the churches and the United Nations."
Fiction: Complete ms. For all ages.
Special Needs: Global perspective, mission education and political and religious issues, peace and justice education, cultural understanding and appreciation, spiritual reflection and development related to mission and social action.
Tips: "Most open to a book that fits a theme stated in our guidelines (one global/one topical), or one with a secured market. Church people primary audience."

FRIENDS UNITED PRESS, 101 Quaker Hill Dr., Richmond IN 47374. (317)962-7573. Fax: (317)966-1293. Friends United Meeting (Quaker). Ardith Talbot, ed. Publishes 14 titles/yr (6 new/8 reprints). Receives 75 submissions annually. 85% of books from first-time authors. Accepts mss through agents. Reprints books. Subsidy publishes 2%. Prefers 250-275 pgs. Royalty 7.5% on wholesale (after printing costs are recouped); no advance. Average first printing 1,500. Publication within 14 mos. Reports in 6 mos. Free guidelines/catalog.
Nonfiction: Complete ms/phone query ok. "Looking for books on spirituality; Quaker biography and autobiography."
Fiction: Complete ms. For all ages.
Tips: "We are restricted to Quaker authors, history, doctrine, etc."

***C.R. GIBSON CO.**, 32 Knight St., Norwalk CT 06856. (203)847-4543. Julie Mitchell, asst. ed. Publishes 10 titles/yr. Receives 500 submissions annually. 10% of books from first-time authors. Accepts mss through agents. Reprints books. Subsidy publishes 20%. Prefers 40-60 pgs. Royalty or outright purchase; advance. Average first printing 10,000. Publication within 1 yr. Accepts simultaneous submissions. Reports in 2 mos. No guidelines/ catalog.
Nonfiction: Proposal/1 chapter. Specializes in gift books.
Fiction: Proposal/1 chapter. Adult and children's picture books.

GILGAL PUBLICATIONS, Box 3386 or 3399, Sunriver OR 97707. (503)593-8639. Fax: (503)593-5604. Judy Osgood, exec. ed. Publishes 1 title/yr. Receives 100 submissions annually. No mss through agents. Pays $10 for each short article accepted for the anthologies, plus royalties. Pays on acceptance. Reports in 3-13 wks (only if SASE is included). Guidelines when available for new book projects.
Nonfiction: Complete ms (after reading guidelines). "Our books are all anthologies on

coping with stress and resolving grief. Not interested in other book mss."

GOLD'N'HONEY BOOKS, Imprint of Questar Publishers for children's books, Box 1720, Sisters OR 97759. (503)549-1144. Brenda Saltzer, ed. Publishes 10-20 titles/yr. See **Questar Publishers**.

+GOOD BOOK PUBLISHING COMPANY, P.O. Box 276, Corte Madera CA 94976-0276. (415)924-8902. Fax: (808)874-4876. Christian/Protestant Bible Fellowship. Researches and publishes books on the biblical/Christian roots of Alcoholics Anonymous. Publishes 3 titles/yr. Receives 5 submissions annually. 20% of books from first-time authors. Accepts mss through agents. Prefers 300 pgs. Royalty on wholesale or outright purchase; no advance. Publication within 3 mos. Accepts simultaneous submission. Reports in 6 mos. No guidelines; free catalog.
Nonfiction: Query letter only; no phone query. Books on the spiritual roots of A.A.

GOSPEL LIGHT PUBLICATIONS - See **REGAL BOOKS**.

#GROUP PUBLISHING, INC., Box 481, Loveland CO 80539. (303)669-3836. Fax: (303)669-3269. Imprint: Group Books. Stephen Parolini, ed. Publishes 75 titles/yr. Receives 150 submissions annually. 3% of books from first-time authors. Reluctantly accepts mss through agents. Prefers 96-120 pgs. Royalty 10% on net; some outright purchases; advance $1,000. Average first printing 7,000. Publication within 18 mos. Accepts simultaneous submissions. Reports in 4-6 wks. Guidelines; free catalog.
Nonfiction: Query or proposal/1 chapter; no phone query. "Practical resources for youth workers, parents and teenagers. Resources for children's ministry." Nothing else.
Tips: "Most open to programming/curriculum materials. Send SASE for curriculum trial assignment."

#GUERNICA EDITIONS, Box 633, Stn. NDG, Montreal, QB H4A 3R1 Canada. (514)987-7411. Fax: (514)982-9793. Antonio D'Alfonso, ed. Publishes 2 titles/yr. Receives 500 submissions annually. 5% of books from first-time authors. Accepts mss through agents. Reprints books. Subsidy publishes 50%. Prefers 128 pgs. Royalty 3-10% on retail; outright purchases $200-5,000; no advance. Average first printing 1,000. Publication within 18 mos. Reports in 3 mos. No guidelines; for catalog send money order for stamps (if from US).
Nonfiction: Query first. "Looking for books on world issues."
Fiction: Query first. "Looking for literary fiction that is an analysis of world situations."
Ethnic Books: Concentration on Italian culture. "We are involved in translations and ethnic issues."

#HARPER SAN FRANCISCO, 1160 Battery St., San Francisco CA 94111-1213. (415)477-4400. Fax: (415)477-4444. Religious division of a general trade publisher (HarperCollins). Tom Grady, pub; John Shopp, sr. ed., religious reference/religious trade. Publishes 180 titles/yr. Receives 10,000 submissions annually. 5% of books from first-time authors. Accepts mss through agents. Reprints books. Prefers 160-256

ms pgs. Royalty 10-15% on cloth, 7.5% on paperback, on retail; advance. Average first printing 7,500-10,000. Publication within 18 mos. Accepts simultaneous submissions. Reports in 6-8 wks. Free guidelines/catalog.
Nonfiction: Query or proposal/3 chapters.

#HARRISON HOUSE PUBLISHERS, Box 35035, Tulsa OK 74153. (918)582-2126. Evangelical/charismatic. Submit to Editorial Asst. Publishes 36 titles/yr. Receives 1,500 submissions annually. 1% of books from first-time authors. No books through agents. Reprints books. Prefers 128-160 pgs. Royalty on wholesale, no advance. Average first printing 10,000. Publication within 18 mos. Accepts simultaneous submissions. Reports in 6 wks. Guidelines; no catalog.
Nonfiction: Query only; no phone query. "Looking for Charismatic teaching books from active ministers. Historical books should be on revivalists."
Tips: "Books should teach the power of the name of Jesus, the authority of the believer, and a revelation of God's grace for mankind."

HARVEST HOUSE PUBLISHERS, 1075 Arrowsmith, Eugene OR 97402. (503)343-0123. Evangelical. Eileen L. Mason, ed-in-chief; submit to Manuscript Coordinator. Books that help the hurts of people. Publishes 70-80 titles/yr. Receives 3,500 submissions annually. 10% of books from first-time authors. Accepts mss through agents. Reprints books. Prefers 180-250 pgs. Royalty 14-18% on wholesale; advance. Average first printing 10,000. Publication within 1 yr. Accepts simultaneous submissions. Reports in 2-8 wks. Guidelines; catalog for 9x12 SAE/2 stamps.
Nonfiction: Prefers query.
Fiction: Prefers query. Children's picture books & adult novels. "We have discontinued our Rhapsody Romance (contemporary romance) line."

+THE HAWORTH PASTORAL PRESS, An imprint of The Haworth Press, 10 Alice St., Binghamton NY 13904. (607)722-5857. Fax: (607)722-8465. Dr. William Clements, sr. ed. Publishes 5-10 titles/yr. Receives 25-50 submissions annually. 25% of books from first-time authors. Prefers no mss through agents. Reprints books. Prefers up to 250 pgs. Royalty 7.5-12% on wholesale; no advance. Average first printing 1,500. Publication within 18 mos. Prefers no simultaneous submissions. Reports in 2 mos. Free guidelines/catalog.
Nonfiction: Proposal/2 chapters; no phone query. "Looking for books on psychology/social work, etc., with a pastoral perspective."

+HEARTSONG PRESENTS, Imprint of Barbour and Company, Inc., P.O. Box 719, 1810 Barbour Dr., Uhrichsville OH 44683. (614)922-6045. Fax: (614)922-5948. Karen Carroll, ed. Publishes 48 titles/yr. Receives 100-200 submissions annually. 20% of books from first-time authors. Accepts mss through agents. Prefers 45,000-50,000 wds. Royalty 5-10% on wholesale; outright purchases; $500 advance. Average first printing 20,000. Publication within 6-8 months. Accepts simultaneous submissions. Reports in 3-5 wks. Guidelines; no catalog.
Fiction: Proposal/3 chapters or complete ms. All types of inspirational romances.

***HELMERS & HOWARD PUBLISHERS**, Box 7407, Colorado Springs CO 80933. No guidelines.

HENDRICKSON PUBLISHERS, INC., 137 Summit St./Box 3473, Peabody MA 01961. (800)358-3111. Fax: (508)531-8146. Patrick Alexander, sr. academic ed; submit to Dr. Philip H. Anderson. Publishes 14-18 titles/yr. Receives 150-200 submissions annually. 20% of books from first-time authors. No mss through agents. Reprints books. Prefers 200-500 pgs. Royalty 14% on wholesale; no advance. Average first printing 1,500-2,000. Publication within 12-14 mos. Accepts simultaneous submissions. Reports in 2-3 mos. Guidelines; free catalog.
Nonfiction: Proposal; no phone query. "Looking for biblical studies and reference works."
Tips: "A well-organized, thought provoking, clear and accurate proposal has the best chance of being read."

VIRGIL W. HENSLEY, INC., 6116 E. 32nd St., Tulsa OK 74135. (918)644-8520. Fax: (918)664-8562. Terri Kalfas, ed. Publishes 5-10 titles/yr. Receives 700 submissions annually. 50% of books from first-time authors. Accepts mss through agents. Reprints books. Prefers 65,000 wds for fiction; Bible studies vary. Royalty 5% on retail; no advance. Average first printing 5,000. Publication within 12-18 mos. Accepts simultaneous submissions. Reports in 8-10 wks. Guidelines; catalog for 9x12 SAE/4 stamps.
Nonfiction: Proposal/3 consecutive chapters (preferably 1st 3); no phone query. "If it's good we'll consider it even if it doesn't fit the categories we've indicated."
Fiction: Proposal/3 consecutive chapters. For teens and adults. "Christianity must be an integral part of the story, not tacked on. A real page-turner."

HERALD PRESS, 616 Walnut Ave., Scottdale PA 15683. (412)887-8500. Fax: (412)887-3111. Canadian address: Herald Press Canada, 490 Dutton Dr., Waterloo ON N2L 6H7 Canada. Mennonite Church. David Garber, book ed. Publishes 30 titles/yr. Receives 1,100 submissions annually. 30% of books from first-time authors. Reluctantly accepts mss through agents. Rarely reprints books. Prefers 160-200 pgs. Royalty 10-12% on retail; no advance. Average first printing 3,500. Publication within 10 mos. Dislikes simultaneous submissions. Reports in 2 mos. Free guidelines; catalog $.60.
Nonfiction: Query first; phone query ok.
Fiction: Query first. Juvenile/teen/adult. "Currently overstocked."
Special Needs: Bible study books; peace and social concerns, conflict resolution.
Ethnic Books: Native American (California focus); Amish and Mennonite.
Tips: "Most open to quality writing compatible with Mennonite beliefs."

HIGLEY PUBLISHING CORPORATION, Box 5398, Jacksonville FL 32247. (904)396-1918. Wesley C. Reagan, ed. Publishes 1 title/yr. No mss through agents. Outright purchase of $900-3,600. Average first printing 70,000. Not in topical listings. Guidelines; no catalog.
Tips: "Our purpose is to publish an annual undenominational resource for adult

teachers, based on International Sunday school outlines."

HOLMAN BIBLE PUBLISHERS - See **BROADMAN & HOLMAN PUBLISHERS.**

#HONOR BOOKS, Box 55388, Tulsa OK 74155. (918)585-5033. Evangelical. Submit to Acquisitions. Publishes 12 titles/yr. 0% of books from first-time authors. Accepts mss through agents. Prefers 192 pgs. Royalty on wholesale; no advance. Publication within 2 yrs. Accepts simultaneous submissions. Reports in 6 wks. Guidelines; no catalog.
Nonfiction: Query or proposal/2 chapters. "Looking for motivational books for the Christian professional who balances a relationship with God with responsibilities to family, church and work; business-related books; books on personal excellence."
Tips: "Also need holiday-focused gift books and books to strengthen families."

HORIZON HOUSE PUBLISHERS, Subsidiary of Christian Publications, 3825 Hartzdale Dr., Camp Hill PA 17011. (717)761-7044. Jonathan Graf, ed. dir. See listing for Christian Publications for details.

#HUNTINGTON HOUSE PUBLISHERS, Box 53788, Lafayette LA 70505-3788. (318)237-7049. Mark Anthony, ed-in-chief. Publishes 25-30 titles/yr. Receives 1,500 submissions annually. 25% of books from first-time authors. Accepts mss through agents. Reprints books. Prefers 60,000-95,000 wds. Royalty to 10% on retail; negotiable advance. Average first printing 5,000-10,000. Publication within 1 yr. Accepts simultaneous submissions. Reports in 4 mos. Free guidelines/catalog.
Nonfiction: Query/proposal. "We need current social and political issues, biographies, self-help, inspirational, and children's books."
Tips: "Our goal is to keep readers abreast of critical current events."

#ICS PUBLICATIONS, 2131 Lincoln Rd NE, Washington DC 20002. (202)832-8489. Catholic/Institute of Carmelite Studies. Steven Payne OCD, ed. Publishes 8 titles/yr. Receives 20-30 submissions annually. 10% of books from first-time authors. Reprints books. Prefers 200 pgs. Royalty 2-6% on retail; some outright purchases; advance $500. Average first printing 3,000-7,000. Publication within 12-24 mos. Accepts simultaneous submissions. Reports in 8 wks. Guidelines; catalog for 7x10 SAE/2 stamps.
Nonfiction: Query first; phone query ok. "Most open to translation of Carmelite classics; popular introductions to Carmelite themes which shows a solid grasp of the tradition."
Special Needs: Popular commentaries on Carmelite authors—John of the Cross, Teresa of Avila, Therese of Lisieux, etc.

INTERVARSITY PRESS, Box 1400, Downers Grove IL 60515. (708)964-5700. Fax: (708)964-1251. Andrew T. LePeau, ed. dir. Publishes 70 titles/yr. Receives 1,200 submissions annually. 10% of books from first-time authors. Accepts mss through agents. Prefers 120-200 pgs. Royalty 5-15% on retail; negotiable advance. Average first printing 6,000. Publication within 1 yr. Accepts simultaneous submissions. Reports in 8-12 wks. Guidelines; catalog for 9x12 SAE/5 stamps.

Nonfiction: All unsolicited mss (from people they have had no previous contact with) are referred to The Writer's Edge (see their listing under Editorial Services); no phone queries.
Fiction: See Nonfiction above. Adult. "Fiction need not be explicitly Christian or religious, but should arise out of a Christian perspective."
Tips: "We publish books of substance that aim to change people's lives rather than to entertain or confirm their beliefs."

+JEWS FOR JESUS BOOKS, 60 Haight St., San Francisco CA 94102. (415)864-2600. Fax: (415)552-8325. Steven Lawson, Director of Publications. They are not generally open to submissions, but they did say: "We would like to hear from Jewish believers who are writers. We do have a need from time to time for editing and freelance ghost writing. And on a rare occasion have published a book by someone who is not on our staff. But we would like to establish a relationship with such a person, rather than seeing a manuscript without any previous contact."

JOY PUBLISHING, Box 827, San Juan Capistrano CA 92675. (714)493-8161. Woody Young, pub. Publishes 15 titles/yr. Receives 200 submissions annually. 80% of books from first-time authors. No mss through agents. Subsidy publishes 10% of books. Reprints books. No royalty or advance. Average first printing 2,500. Publication within 6 mos. No simultaneous submissions. Reports in 90 days. Not in topical listings. No guidelines or catalog.
Nonfiction: Proposal/3 chapters; no phone query.
Tips: "We are only interested in writers who have or are planning to have a ministry where this book is an important part. We assist writers/speakers who feel so strongly about their work they will self-publish it if they have to."

JUDSON PRESS, Box 851, Valley Forge PA 19482. (215)768-2118. American Baptist Churches U.S.A. Harold Rast, pub; submit to Kristy Arnesen Pullen, assoc. pub. Publishes 18-20 titles/yr. Receives 500+ submissions annually. 50% of books from first-time authors. Accepts mss through agents. Reprints books. Prefers 128-160 pgs. Royalty 10% on retail; advance $250. Average first printing 2,000. Publication within 6-12 mos. Accepts simultaneous submissions. Reports in 3-6 mos. Free guidelines/catalog.
Nonfiction: Proposal/1 chapter; phone query ok (but not preferred). "Looking for practical how-to for local church leaders and pastors."
Ethnic Books: African-American.
Tips: "Develop a proposal before you write the whole ms."

+KINDRED PRESS, 4-169 Riverton Ave., Winnepeg MB R2L 2E5 Canada. (204)669-6575. Fax: (204)654-1865. Mennonite Brethren. Marilyn Hudson, dir. Publishes 3-4 titles/yr. Receives 20-25 submissions annually. 10% of books from first-time authors. No mss through agents. Prefers 200-250 pgs. Royalty 10-15%; no advance. Publication within 10 mos. Accepts simultaneous submissions. Reports in 3 mos. Free guidelines/catalog.
Nonfiction: Proposal/3 chapters; no phone query.

Fiction: Proposal/2 chapters. Children/teen/adult. "Teen books are always in demand, but for now we are restricting ourselves to Mennonite authors."
Tips: "Send an inspiring query that will sell me your book." Guidelines are being revised.

KREGEL PUBLICATIONS, P.O. Box 2607, Grand Rapids MI 49501. (616)451-4775. Fax: (616)451-9330. Dennis R. Hillman, sr. ed. Publishes 50-60 titles/yr. Receives 150 submissions annually. 5% of books from first-time authors. Accepts mss through agents. Reprints books. Prefers 160-192 pgs (open). Royalty 10-14% on wholesale; Some outright purchases; negotiable advance. Average first printing 5,000. Publication within 6 mos. Accepts simultaneous submissions. Reports in 1-2 mos. Guidelines; free catalog.
Nonfiction: Query only; no phone query. "Looking for ministry-related materials, Bible and biblical/theological studies, and contemporary issues."
Ethnic Books: Spanish Division: Editorial Portaroz.

+LANGMARC PUBLISHING, P.O. Box 33817, San Antonio TX 78265. (210)822-2521. Fax: (210)822-5014. Lutheran. Renee Hermanson, ed. Focuses on spiritual growth of readers. Publishes 5 titles/yr. Receives 50-60 submissions annually. 50% of books from first-time authors. No mss through agents. Prefers 150-300 pgs. Royalty 8-10% on retail; no advance. Average first printing 1,500. Publication within 9-12 mos. No simultaneous submissions. Reports in 1 mo. Brochure for #10 SAE/1 stamp.
Nonfiction: Query or proposal/3 chapters; phone query ok. "Most open to inspirational, congregational helps, or materials for teens."

***LIFE BOOKS**, Subsidy Division of Barbour & Co., Inc., Box 1219, Westwood NJ 07675. (201)664-2463. Ellen Caughey, ed. Publishes 5 titles/yr. No books through agents. 100% subsidy. Author pays for books, royalty if reprinted; no advance. Publication within 2 mos. Accepts simultaneous submissions. Reports in 1-3 wks. No guidelines/catalog.
Nonfiction & Fiction: Proposal/3 chapters.

#LIFE CYCLE BOOKS, Box 420, Lewiston NY 14092. (416) 690-5860. Fax: (416)690-5860. Paul Broughton, gen. mgr. Publishes 1-3 inspirational/religious titles/yr. Receives 50 submissions annually. 50% of books from first-time authors. Accepts mss through agents. Reprints books. Royalty 8% on wholesale; outright purchase of brochure material, $250; advance $100-300. Subsidy publishes 10%. Publication within 10 mos. Reports in 6 wks. Guidelines; free catalog.
Nonfiction: Query or complete ms. "Our emphasis is on pro-life and pro-family titles."
Tips: "We are most involved in publishing leaflets of about 1,500 wds, and welcome submissions of mss of this length."

***LIFE ENRICHMENT PUBLISHERS**, Daring Publishing Group, Inc., 2221-9th St SW, Canton OH 44706. (216)454-7519. Patrice Bartow, ed. Publishes 3 titles/yr. Receives 100 submissions annually. 80% of books from first-time authors. Accepts mss through agents. Reprints books. Subsidy publishes 10%. Prefers 200+ pgs. Royalty 6-12% on

wholesale; advance $100. Average first printing 2,000. Publication within 1 yr. Accepts simultaneous submissions. Reports in 1-6 mos. No guidelines; free catalog.
Nonfiction: Query first. "Most open to unique, well-done projects."
Tips: "Go to the library and study the industry and know what to realistically expect if your book gets published."

***LIFEJOURNEY BOOKS** (adult books) Imprint of Chariot Family Publishing, David C. Cook Publishing Co., 850 N. Grove Ave., Elgin IL 60120. (708)741-0800x229. Submit to Editor. Publishes 12 titles/yr. Receives 500 submissions annually. 50% of books from first-time authors. Accepts mss through agents. Reprints books. Royalty on net, negotiable advance. Average first printing 15,000. Publication within 12 mos. Accepts simultaneous submissions. Reports in 3 mos. Guidelines; catalog for 9x12 SAE/5 stamps.
Nonfiction: Query first. Books on Christian living or marriage.
Fiction: Proposal/2-3 chapters.
Tips: "Since this line is still in early development, we are looking for good writers who want an opportunity to grow with the line—especially fiction writers."

#LIFETIME BOOKS, Fell Publishers, Inc., 2131 Hollywood Blvd., Hollywood FL 33020. (305)925-4252. George Sheldon, ed. General publisher that publishes 4 religious titles/yr. Receives 50 submissions annually. 50% of books from first-time authors. Accepts mss through agents. Prefers 224 pgs. Royalty 6-15% on wholesale; variable advance. Average first printing 10,000. Publication within 1 yr. Accepts simultaneous submissions. Reports in 3 mos. Guidelines; catalog for 9x12 SAE/5 stamps.
Nonfiction: Query first. "Most open to business and self-help titles."
Fiction: Query first. Adult, teen, biblical.

#LIGUORI PUBLICATIONS, 1 Liguori Dr., Liguori MO 63057-9999. (314)464-2500. Catholic/Redemptionists. Rev. Paul Coury, ed-in-chief; Audrey Vest, mng. ed. Publishes 35 titles/yr. Receives 200 submissions annually. 20% of books from first-time authors. Accepts mss through agents. Prefers 20-200 pgs. Royalty 10% on retail; outright purchase of 20-page pamphlets for $400-450; advance $1,000. Average first printing 5,000 on books, 10,000 on pamphlets. Publication within 12 mos. Accepts simultaneous submissions. Reports in 6-8 wks. Free guidelines/catalog.
Nonfiction: Proposal/2 chapters (complete ms for pamphlets). "Looking for pastoral, practical material targeted to parishes and individuals with specific needs."
Ethnic Books: Publishes books in Spanish.
Tips: "Manuscripts accepted by us must have a strong, practical application."

#LILLENAS PUBLISHING CO., (Drama Division of Beacon Hill Press), Program Builder Series and Other Drama Resources, Box 419527, Kansas City MO 64141. (816)931-1900. Church of the Nazarene. Paul M. Miller, ed. Publishes 15 drama resource books and 5 program builders/yr. Royalties for drama resources; outright purchase of program builder material. Accepts simultaneous submissions. Reports in 8-12 wks. Guidelines; catalog.
Nonfiction: Query or complete ms. Accepts readings, plays, puppet scripts, program

and service features.

LION PUBLISHING CORP., 20 Lincoln Ave., Elgin IL 60120. (708)741-4256. David C. Cook Publishing Co. Robert Bittner, ed. "No longer able to consider unsolicited manuscripts or proposals."

#THE LITURGICAL PRESS, Collegeville MN 56321. (612)363-2213. Fax: (612)363-3299. St. John's Abbey (a Benedictine group). Mark Twomey, mng. ed. Publishes 25 titles/yr. Prefers 100-600 pgs. Royalty 10% of net; some outright purchases; no advance. Reports in 2 mos. Guidelines; free catalog.
Nonfiction: Query/proposal. Adult only.
Tips: Sermon helps, homily hints.

***LIVING FLAME PRESS**, 325 Rabro Dr., Hauppauge NY 11788. (516)348-5251. Catholic/ecumenical. Nancy Benvenga & Emily Teutshman, eds. Publishes 10 titles/yr. Receives 50 submissions annually. 25% of books from first-time authors. No mss through agents. Royalty 5% on retail (negotiable). Publication within 24 mos. Reports in 1 week on query. Guidelines; free catalog.
Nonfiction: Proposal/chapters. Needs theology and liturgy.
Fiction: Proposal/chapters. No "biblical" novels based on outdated or literal understandings of Scripture.
Tips: "Most open to a well-researched, well-written book on timely pastoral issues."

+LIVING SACRIFICE BOOK CO., A Division of Voice of the Martyrs, Inc., 200 E Frank Phillips Blvd., P.O. Box 443, Bartlesville OK 74005. (918)337-8015. Fax: (918)337-9185. Tom White, C.E.O. Publishes 2 titles/yr. Accepts mss through agents. Reprints books. Prefers 200 pgs. Terms negotiable. Average first printing 5,000. Publication within 8 mos. Accepts simultaneous submissions. Reports in 1 month. No guidelines; free catalog.
Nonfiction: Complete mss; phone query ok. "Books related to the subject of the persecuted church in Communist/Moslem countries."
Ethnic Books: Publishes some titles in Spanish.
Tips: "Most open to biographies or autobiographies on Christians who are persecuted for their faith, or informational books relating to Islam or Communism."

#LOYOLA UNIVERSITY PRESS, 3441 N. Ashland Ave., Chicago IL 60657. (312)281-1818. Fax: (312)281-0555. Catholic. Rev. Joseph F. Downey, S.J., ed. dir. Publishes 12-15 titles/yr, Campion Books Imprint, Values & Ethics Series (Dr. Rugh McGugan, ed). Receives 150 submissions annually. 60% of books from first-time authors. No mss through agents. Reprints books. Prefers 60,000-80,000 wds or 180-230 pgs. Royalty 10% on net; no advance. Average first printing 1,500-2,000. Publication within 1 yr. Accepts simultaneous submissions. Reports in 2 mos. Free guidelines/catalog.
Nonfiction: Query or proposal/chapters. "Most open to professionally written mss, more or less in the Catholic tradition (but not conservative), written out of solid field training and experience."
Tips: "Review our catalog, sample our published books from last five years, and find a

match there to your book in treatment and viewpoint."

+LURA MEDIA, INC., 7060 Miramar Rd., Ste. 104, San Diego CA 92121. (619)578-1948. Fax: (619)578-7560. Ecumenical. Lura Jane Geiger, ed-in-chief. Specializes in books on personal growth with spiritual and feminine dimensions. Publishes 6 titles/yr. Receives 500 submissions annually. 80% of books from first-time authors. Accepts mss through agents. Prefers 125-225 pgs. Royalty 10-12% on wholesale; seldom offers advance, $500. Average first printing 3,000. Publication within 20-24 mos. Accepts simultaneous submissions. Responds immediately; decision within 2 mos. Guidelines: catalog for 6x9 SAE/2 stamps.
Nonfiction: Book proposal/1 chapter; no phone query. "Looking for books on spirituality, women's issues, and personal experience."
Tips: "Most open to books on renewal for body, mind and spirit that are relational, creative, and well integrated."

MASTER BOOKS, Box 26060, Colorado Springs CO 80936-6060. (719)591-0800. Fax: (719)591-1446. Creation Life Publisher, Inc. Ron Hillestad, general manager. Publishes 55 titles/yr. Receives 300 submissions annually. 5% of books from first-time authors. Accepts mss through agents. Subsidy publishes 5%. Reprints books. Royalty 7-12% of wholesale; some advances. Average first printing 5,000. Publication within 6 mos. Accepts simultaneous submissions. Reports in 7-10 days. No guidelines; free catalog.
Nonfiction: Proposal/3 chapters or complete ms; no phone query. "Looking for biblical creationism; biblical science; creation/evolution debate material."

MERIWETHER PUBLISHING LTD., 885 Elkton Dr., Colorado Springs CO 80907. (719)594-4422. Fax: (719)594-9916. General trade publisher that does some religious titles. Ted Zapel, ed. Publishes 3-4 titles/yr; 35 plays/yr. Receives 700 submissions annually (mostly plays). 80% of books from first-time authors. Accepts mss through agents. Reprints books. Prefers 200 pgs. Royalty 10% on retail for books; plays are a 10% royalty to a (varying) fixed amount. Average first printing 5,000. Publication within 12-18 mos. Accepts simultaneous submissions. Reports in 4-6 wks. Guidelines; catalog for 9x12 SAE/3 stamps.
Nonfiction: Proposal/1 chapter. "Looking for creative worship books, i.e., drama, using the arts in worship, how-to books with ideas for Christian education.
Fiction: Children's picture books (prefers an author who can also illustrate) or plays only, including religious plays. Send complete ms.
Tips: "No religious titles with fundamentalist themes or approaches; we prefer mainstream religion titles. Most open to drama-related books."

***MISTY HILL PRESS**, 5024 Turner Rd., Sebastopol CA 95472. (707)823-7437. Small press that does some religious titles. Sally C. Karste, ed. Publishes 1 title/yr. Negotiable royalty. Reports in 1 week. Guidelines; catalog for 9x12 SAE/2 stamps.
Fiction: Query first. Historical fiction for children.

MOODY PRESS, 820 N. LaSalle Blvd., Chicago IL 60610. (312)329-2101. Fax:

(312)329-4157. Imprint: Northfield Publishing. Submit to Moody Press Editor. To provide books that evangelize, edify the believer, and educate concerning the Christian life. Publishes 60-80 titles/yr. Receives 1,200-1,500 submissions annually. 5% of books from first-time authors. Accepts mss through agents. Occasionally reprints books. Royalty on retail; variable advance. Average first printing 5,000-10,000. Publication within 12-18 mos. Accepts simultaneous submissions. Reports in 6-8 wks. Guidelines; catalog for 9x12 SAE/5 stamps.
Nonfiction: Proposal/1-2 chapters; no phone query.
Fiction: Proposal/1-3 chapters. Adult.
Tips: "Become well-informed (investigate thoroughly) the need in the book marketplace before attempting to write a book—and then target that need."

#THOMAS MORE PRESS, 205 W. Monroe, 6th Floor, Chicago IL 60606. (312)609-8880. Fax: (312)609-8891. Catholic/Thomas More Assn. Joel Wells, ed. Publishes 6-10 titles/yr. Prefers 40,000 wds. Royalty 7.5% on retail; advance. Reports in 2 wks. Guidelines; free catalog.
Nonfiction: Complete ms or proposal/chapters. Religion and spirituality.
Tips: "Looking for books on theology, commentary, reflection, spirituality and reference."

MOREHOUSE PUBLISHING CO., 871 Ethan Allen Hwy., Ste. 204, Ridgefield CT 06877. (203)431-3927. Fax: (203)431-3964. Episcopal/ecumenical. Deborah Grahame-Smith, sr. ed. Publishes 15-20 titles/yr. Receives 500-600 submissions annually. 60% of books from first-time authors. Accepts mss through agents. Reprints books. Prefers 100-200 pgs. Royalty 6-12% on retail; advance $250-500. Average first printing 2,500. Publication within 6-9 mos. Accepts simultaneous submissions. Reports in 6-8 wks. Guidelines; catalog for 9x12 SAE/4 stamps.
Nonfiction: Proposal/3 chapters; no phone query. "Looking for environmental issues, family life, parenting, how-to/self-help, group-study books, current social issues, and retirement."
Fiction: Proposal/2-3 chapters. For children.
Tips: "Most open to a book for which there is a specific need; one that has been `field tested' by congregations (study guides and programs); one to which the writer brings a special expertise or sensibility."

***MORNING STAR PRESS**, Box 1095, Grand Central Station, New York NY 10163. (212)661-4304. Morning Star Chapel. Rev. Kathleen Shedaker, pub. Publishes 2 titles/yr. Receives 3 submissions annually. 50% of books from first-time authors. No books through agents. Reprints books. Prefers 120 pgs. Royalty 10% on retail; no advance. Publication within 6 mos. Accepts simultaneous submissions. Reports in 3-6 wks. No guidelines/catalog.
Nonfiction: Query first. "Only religious/inspirational books."
Tips: "We encourage members of all denominations to live a more Christian life."

+JOSHUA MORRIS PUBLISHING, 206 Danbury Rd., Wilton CT 06897. (203)834-9878. Fax: (203)762-5655. Anglican/evangelical. Sally Lloyd Jones, editorial dir. A

Christian children's book packager. Publishes 60 titles/yr. Receives 40 submissions annually. 5% of books from first-time authors. Accepts mss through agents. Makes outright purchases. Average first printing 25,000-50,000. Publication within 1 yr. Usually reports in 3-4 mos. No guidelines or catalog.
Nonfiction: Query; no phone query. "We usually assign story ideas to writers, but we are open to hearing ideas."
Fiction: Query. "Looking for rhyme/poetry for young children; Bible stories in rhyme."
Special Needs: "Factual-based, fun writing for children—about 7 years old—that makes study of Bible-related subjects fun."
Tips: "On books for young children, we prefer 1-2 lines of text per 2-page spread."

#WILLIAM MORROW AND CO., 1350 Avenue of the Americas, New York NY 10019. (212)261-6500. Fax: (212)261-6595. General trade publisher that does a few religious titles. Debbie Mercer-Sullivan, mng. ed. Publishes 5 religious titles/yr. Receives 10,000 submissions annually. 30% of books from first-time authors. Prefers 50,000-100,000 wds. Standard royalty on retail; advance. Publication within 1-2 yrs. Accepts simultaneous submissions. Reports in 3 mos. No guidelines/catalog.
Nonfiction & Fiction: Query only through agent.

MOTT MEDIA, INC., PUBLISHERS, 1000 E. Huron St., Milford MI 48381. (313)685-8773. Fax: (313)685-8776. Imprint of Baker Book House. Sharon J. Peterson, ed. Accepting no freelance submissions for now.

MULTNOMAH BOOKS - See **Questar Publishers.**

+NATIONAL BAPTIST PUBLISHING BOARD, 6717 Centennial Blvd., Nashville TN 37209. (615)350-8000. Fax: (615)350-9018. National Missionary Baptist Convention of America. Rev. Kenneth H. Dupree, dir. of publications. To provide quality Christian education resources to be used by African-American churches. Receives 200 submissions annually. 30% of books from first-time authors. Accepts mss through agents. Reprints books. Prefers 130 pgs. Outright purchases; advance. Average first printing 20,000. Publication within 1 yr.
Nonfiction: Complete ms; phone query ok.
Fiction: Complete ms. "We need biblical-based fiction for children."
Ethnic Books: African-American publisher.
Tips: "Most open to religious books that can be used for Christian education."

NAVPRESS/PINON PRESS, Box 35001, Colorado Springs CO 80935. (719)548-9222. Debby Weaver, sub. ed. "We are no longer accepting <u>any</u> unsolicited submissions, proposals, queries, etc."

NAZARENE PUBLISHING HOUSE/BEACON HILL PRESS OF KANSAS CITY, 6401 The Paseo, Kansas City MO 64131. (816)333-7000. Fax: (816)333-1748. Church of the Nazarene. Bonnie Perry, ed. coordinator. Publishes 50-60 titles/yr. Receives 350-400 submissions annually. 40% of books from first-time authors. No mss through agents. Prefers 125-150 pgs. Royalty 12-16% on net; no advance. Average first

printing 4,000. Publication within 8-12 mos. Accepts simultaneous submissions. Reports in 2-3 mos. Free guidelines/catalog.
Nonfiction: Proposal/3 chapters; no phone query.
Fiction: Complete ms. For adults.
Tips: "Most open to practical, lay-oriented books on personal growth and applied Christianity. Inspirational and devotional books also considered."

#NEIBAUER PRESS, 20 Industrial Dr., Warminster PA 18974. (215)322-6200. Fax: (215)322-2495. Evangelical/Protestant clergy and church leaders. Nathan Neibauer, ed. Publishes 8 titles/yr. Receives 100 submissions annually. 5% of books from first-time authors. No mss through agents. Reprints books. Prefers 200 pgs. Royalty on wholesale; some outright purchases. Some subsidy. Publication within 6 mos. Accepts simultaneous submissions. Reports in 2 wks. No guidelines; catalog for 9x12 SAE.
Nonfiction: Query first.
Tips: "Need religious books on stewardship, church enrollment, and bulletin fillers. Also tracts and pamphlets."

THOMAS NELSON PUBLISHERS, P.O. Box 141000, 506 Nelson Pl., Nashville TN 37214. (615)889-9000. Evangelical. Darryl Winburne, mng. ed. Publishes 300+ titles/yr. Receives over 2,000 submissions annually. 15% of books from first-time authors. Accepts mss through agents. Reprints books. Subsidy publishes 10% of books. Prefers 250 pgs. Variable royalty and advance. Average first printing 7,500. Publication within 18 mos. Accepts simultaneous submissions. Reports in 10 wks. Guidelines; catalog for 9x12 SAE.
Nonfiction: Proposal/3 chapters. "Looking for books on seniors and aging; biblical reference; career planning; biblical counseling; singles; and theology."
Fiction: Proposal/3 chapters. "Must have some benefit for the reader."

NEW HOPE PUBLISHERS, Box 12065, Birmingham AL 35202. (205)991-8120. Woman's Missionary Union; Auxiliary to Southern Baptist Convention. Cindy McClain, ed. Publishes 10 titles/yr. Receives 40-50 submissions annually. 85% of books from first-time authors. Accepts mss through agents. Reprints books. Prefers 150-250 pgs. Royalty or outright purchases; no advance. Average first printing 5,000-10,000. Publication within 12-18 mos. Accepts simultaneous submissions. Reports in 6 mos. Guidelines; free catalog for 9x12 SAE.
Nonfiction: Proposal/3 chapters or complete ms; no phone query. "All of our materials must have a missions focus (local or global) in some way."
Tips: "Most open to books which lead to spiritual growth toward a missions lifestyle or that lead to involvement in missions or support of missions."

NEW LEAF PRESS, Box 311, Green Forest AR 72638. (501)438-5288. Fax: (501)438-5120. Pentecostal/charismatic. Jim Flector, ed. Publishes 25 titles/yr. Receives 1,000-1,500 submissions annually. 10% of books from first-time authors. Accepts mss through agents. Reprints books. Subsidy publishes 5%. Prefers 150-250 pgs. Royalty on wholesale; advance. Average first printing 7,500-10,000. Publication within 6 mos. Accepts simultaneous submissions. Reports in 30-60 days. Guidelines:

catalog for 9x12 SAE/4 stamps.
Nonfiction: Query; no phone query. "Looking for humor and gift books."
Fiction: Query. Adult fiction; any genre.
Tips: "Tell us why this book is marketable and why it will be a blessing and fulfill the needs of others."

NEW SOCIETY PUBLISHERS, 4527 Springfield Ave., Philadelphia PA 19143. (215)382-6543. (Canadian address: Box 189, Gabriola Island, BC, V0R 1X0 Canada) Barbara Hirshkowitz, ed. mgr. Publishes 1-2 titles/yr. Receives dozens of submissions annually. 90% of books from first-time authors. Accepts mss through agents. Reprints books. Prefers up to 220 pgs. Royalty 10-15% on wholesale; advance to $3,000 (if needed). Average first printing 3,000. Publication within 6 mos. Accepts simultaneous submissions. Guidelines; free catalog.
Nonfiction: Query only; no phone query. "Looking for nonviolent traditions in religions other than Christianity or Judaism (we have those). Also economics or environmental issues."
Tips: "We publish books about fundamental social change through nonviolent action. We emphasize success stories and tool books."

#NOVALIS, 223 Main St., Ottawa ON K1S 1C4 Canada. (612)236-1393. Fax: (613)236-1393. University of St. Paul. Michael O'Hearn, acq. ed. Publishes 18 titles/yr. Prefers 200 pgs. Royalty & outright purchases; no advance. Accepts simultaneous submissions. Reports in 12 wks. No guidelines/catalog.
Nonfiction: Query or proposal/chapters.
Special Needs: Sacramental preparation, materials on the revised rite of Christian funerals.

***OMEGA PUBLICATIONS**, 6425 Crater Lake Hwy, Central Point OR 97501. (503)826-1030. Jim Andrews, pres. Publishes 2 titles/yr. Reports in 2 wks. Prefers 150-200 pgs.
Nonfiction & Fiction: Query first.

***OMF BOOKS**, 1058 Avenue Rd., Toronto ON M5N 2C6 Canada. (416)483-0427. Overseas Missionary Fellowship. Edyth Banks, public. mngr. Publishes 6-12 titles/yr. Subsidy publishes 20%. Prefers up to 200 pgs. Royalty about 7.5%; advance. Reports in 10 wks. No guidelines.
Nonfiction: Query. "Must relate to mission work or Christian living in East Asia." Most books written by OMF members.

#OPEN COURT PUBLISHING CO., 332 S. Michigan Ave., Ste. 2000, Chicago IL 60604. David Ramsey Steele, ed. dir. Publishes 4 religious titles/yr. Receives 500 submissions annually. 20% of books from first-time authors. Accepts mss through agents. Reprints books. Prefers 350-400 pgs. Royalty 5-12% of wholesale; advance $1,000. Average first printing 500 (cloth), 1,500 (paperback). Publication within 1 yr. Accepts simultaneous submissions. Reports in 3-6 mos. Free guidelines/catalog.
Nonfiction: Query or proposal/2 chapters. "We're looking for works of high intellectual

quality for a scholarly or general readership on comparative religion, philosophy of religion, and religious issues. We have special interest in religions of other cultures, notably oriental."

#ORBIS BOOKS, Maryknoll NY 10545. (914)941-7590. Fax: (914)945-0670. Catholic Foreign Mission Society. Robert Ellsberg, ed. Publishes 50 titles/yr. Prefers 250-350 pgs. Royalty 10-15% on net; advance $1,000. Reports in 2 mos. Guidelines; catalog.
Nonfiction: Proposal/2 chapters. "Global justice and peace; religious development in Asia, Africa, and Latin America; Christianity and world religions."

#OUR SUNDAY VISITOR, INC., 200 Noll Plaza, Huntington IN 46750. (219)356-8400. Catholic. Jacquelyn M. Murphy, ed. Publishes 25-30 titles/yr. Receives 100+ submissions annually. 10% of books from first-time authors. Accepts mss through agents. Prefers 30,000-50,000 wds. Royalty 8-12% on net; advance $1,000. Average first printing 5,000. Publication within 1 yr. Accepts simultaneous submissions. Reports in 3 mos. Free guidelines/catalog.
Nonfiction: Proposal/2 chapters; no phone query. "Catholic viewpoint."
Tips: "Most open to solid devotional books (not first-person), well-researched church histories or lives of the saints, or self-help for those over 55."

+OXFORD UNIVERSITY PRESS, 200 Madison Ave., New York NY 10016. (212)725-9272. (212)679-7300. Fax: (212)725-9272. Academic press. Cynthia Read, sr. ed. Publishes 40 titles/yr. Receives hundreds of submissions annually. 10% of books from first-time authors. Accepts mss through agents. Prefers 240 pgs. Royalty. Average first printing 1,200. Publication within 9 mos. Accepts simultaneous submissions. Reports in 3 mos. No guidelines; free catalog.
Nonfiction: Proposal/2 chapters; no phone query.

PACIFIC PRESS PUBLISHING ASSN., Box 7000, Boise ID 83707. (208)465-2500. Fax: (208)465-2531. Seventh-day Adventist. Russell Holt, ed; Marvin Moore, acq. ed. Publishes 30 titles/yr. Receives several hundred submissions annually. 15-20% of books from first-time authors. No mss through agents. Prefers 33,000-85,000 wds or 128-256 pgs. Royalty 12-16% on wholesale; advance $500. Average first printing 5,000. Publication within 6-12 mos. Accepts simultaneous submissions. Reports in 8 wks. Guidelines/catalog for 9x12 SAE/3 stamps.
Nonfiction: Query or proposal/1-2 chapters; complete ms ok; phone queries ok. "Looking for inspirational, devotional, family life, and Christian living books."
Fiction: Query, proposal/2 chapters, or complete ms. "Stories must be based on events that actually happened but written in good fiction style."
Ethnic Books: Occasionally publishes for ethnic market.
Tips: "Most open to inspirational/devotional book that focuses on a specific type of person and his/her needs—singles, parents of various age children, people struggling with specific issues/addictions, etc."

***PACIFIC THEATRE PRESS,** 5375 University Blvd., Vancouver BC V6T 1K3 Canada. (604)222-8226. Ron Reed, artistic dir. Publishes 10 plays/yr. Reprints plays. Prefers

full-length or one-act plays and sketches. Royalty 15% on retail for plays, flat fee for sketches; advances only on commissioned work. Accepts simultaneous submissions. No guidelines.
Plays: Query/summary & sample scene or complete script/summary pg.
Special Needs: "Producible plays by Christians, but not necessarily religious, for college or community theater; strong or unusual sketches for church/street/youth/revue settings.

+PARACLETE PRESS, P.O. Box 1568, Orleans MA 02653. (508)255-4685. Fax: (508)255-5705. Ecumenical. David Manuel, editor; submit to Pam Jordan. Publishes 3-4 titles/yr. Receives 30 submissions annually. 85% of books from first-time authors. Accepts mss through agents. Reprints books. Prefers less than 300 pgs (typeset). Royalty on wholesale; no advance. Average first printing 3,000 or 10,000. Publication within 14 mos. No simultaneous submissions. No guidelines; free catalog.
Nonfiction: Proposal; no phone query. "Looking for books on deeper spirituality that appeals to all denominations."

#THE PASTORAL PRESS, 225 Sheridan St. NW, Washington DC 20011. (202)723-1254. Fax: (202)723-2262. Catholic/National Assn. of Pastoral Musicians. Lawrence Johnson, dir. Publishes 16 titles/yr. Receives 12 submissions annually. 60% of books from first-time authors. Accepts mss through agents. Prefers 250 pgs. Royalty 10% on net; no advance. Publication within 10 mos. Accepts simultaneous submissions. Reports in 2 mos. No guidelines; free catalog.
Nonfiction: Complete ms.
Tips: "Most open to theology and planning of Roman Catholic liturgies."

PASTOR'S CHOICE PRESS, 4000 Beallwood Ave., Columbus GA 31904. (706)576-5787. Subsidiary of Brentwood Publishers Group. Jerry Luquire, ed. dir. New Imprint. **Subsidy publishes 100%.** Focus is on sermon notes, outlines, illustrations, plus news that pastors would find interesting. Publishes 300-500 copies. Cost of about $3-4/book. Publication in 45 days. Same day response.

#PAULIST PRESS, 997 Macarthur Blvd., Mahwah NJ 07430. (201)825-7300. Fax: (201)825-8345. Catholic/ecumenical. Rev. Kevin A. Lynch, ed; Donald Brophy, mng. ed. Publishes 80-100 titles/yr. Receives 500 submissions annually. 5-8% of books from first-time authors. Accepts mss through agents. Prefers 150-250 pgs. Royalty 10% on retail; advance $500. Average first printing 3,500. Publication within 10 mos. Reports in 4-6 wks. Guidelines; free catalog.
Nonfiction: Proposal/2 chapters. "Looking for theology (Catholic and ecumenical Christian), popular spirituality, liturgy, and religious education texts."
Tips: "Most open to progressive, world-affirming, theologically sophisticated, growth-oriented, well-written books. Have strong convictions but don't be pious. Stay well-read. Pay attention to contemporary social needs."

PELICAN PUBLISHING CO., INC., 1101 Monroe St., Box 189, Gretna LA 70053. (504)368-1175. Mostly Southern Baptist. Nina Kooij, ed. Publishes 1 religious title/yr.

Receives 1,200 submissions annually. No books from first-time authors. Accepts books through agents. Reprints books. Prefers 75,000 wds/300 pgs. Royalty 10%; some advances. Average first printing 6,000. Publication within 9-18 mos. No simultaneous submissions. Reports in 1 mo. Guidelines; catalog for 9x12 SAE/8 stamps.
Nonfiction: Proposal/2 chapters; no phone query.
Ethnic Books: Fiction for blacks, Hispanics, Native Americans, Asian-Americans, etc. Ethnic history for above groups.
Tips: "We're only publishing one inspirational book a year in this category. The one we will pick will be an author who already has a strong, established lecture circuit."

PILGRIM PRESS, 700 Prospect Ave. E., Cleveland OH 44115. (216)736-3700. Fax: (216)736-3703. United Church of Christ. Richard E. Brown, ed. Publishes 20-25 titles/yr. Receives 250-275 submissions annually. 0% of books from first-time authors. Accepts mss through agents. Prefers 50,000 wds/125-275 book pgs. Royalty 8% on net; negotiable advance. Average first printing 3,000. Publication within 9-12 mos. Accepts simultaneous submissions. Reports in 8-10 wks. Free guidelines/catalog.
Nonfiction: Query; no phone query. "Looking for books on ethics and social issues for academic, trade, and religious audiences."
Ethnic Books: African-American theology; womanist theology.

#PILLAR BOOKS AND PUBLISHING CO., INC., 5840 S. Memorial Dr., Ste. 111, Tulsa OK 74145. (918)665-3240. Fax: (918)663-7690. Elizabeth Sherman, ed. Publishes 5 titles/yr. Receives 50 submissions annually. No mss through agents. **100% subsidy**. Reprints books. Prefers 150-200 pgs. Royalty 10-15% on wholesale; no advance. Average first printing 15,000. Publication within 2-3 mos. Accepts simultaneous submissions. Reports in 4 wks. Free guidelines & catalog.
Nonfiction: Complete ms or query; phone query ok. "Looking for Bible teaching materials, commentaries on scripture or areas of study, scholarly studies on topical subjects."
Tips: "Most open to powerful biblically-based ideas comprised of sound doctrine, ideas that will edify, exhort, admonish, and build up the body of Christ."

POETS COVE PRESS, 4000 Beallwood Ave., Columbus GA 31904. (404/706)576-5787. Subsidiary of Brentwood Publishers Group. Jerry Luquire, exec. ed. Publishes 125 titles/yr. **SUBSIDY PUBLISHES 100%.** Specializes in self publishing books of religious or inspirational poetry, in small press runs of under 500 copies. Publication in 45 days. Same day response.
Tips: "Type one poem per page; include short bio and photo with first submission.

***PRAXIS INSTITUTE PRESS,** 275 High Rd., Newbury MA 01951. (508)462-0563. Non-denominational. Robin Amis, dir. Publishes 3 titles/yr. No mss through agents. Reprints books. Prefers 100-300 pgs. Does mostly translations. Royalty 10% on wholesale; no advance. Average first printing 3,000. Publication within 12-16 mos. Accepts simultaneous submissions. Reports slowly. No guidelines; free catalog.
Nonfiction: Query only; phone query ok. "Most open to translations within the tradition of spirituality; or original works by living authors only if based on actual experience."

PRESBYTERIAN AND REFORMED PUBLISHING CO., Box 817, Phillipsburg NJ 08865. (908)454-0505. Fax: (908)859-2390. Not a denominational house. Thom E. Notaro, ed. Publishes 6-8 titles/yr. Receives 130 submissions annually. 20% of books from first-time authors. Accepts mss through agents. Reprints books. Royalty 10-14% on wholesale. Publication within 9-12 mos. Accepts simultaneous submissions. Reports in 4-8 wks. Free guidelines/catalog.
Nonfiction: Proposal/3 chapters.
Tips: "Clear, engaging, and insightful applications of reformed theology to life. Offer us fully developed proposals and polished sample chapters."

PRESCOTT PRESS PUBLISHERS, Box 53777, Lafayette LA 70505. (318)237-0109. Fax: (318)237-7060. David England, ed-in-chief. Publishes 10-15 titles/yr. Receives 300 submissions annually. 80% of books from first-time authors. Accepts mss through agents. Reprints books. Prefers 30,000-100,000 words or 224 pgs. Royalty 10-20% on wholesale; no advance. Average first printing 1,500-3,000. Publication within 6-8 mos. Accepts simultaneous submissions. Reports in 4-8 wks. Guidelines: free catalog.
Nonfiction & Fiction: Proposal/5 chapters and cover letter.
Tips: "Tell us about the author and why this book needs to be published."

#PROBE MINISTRIES INTERNATIONAL, 1900 Firman Dr., Ste. 100, Richardson TX 75081-6796. (214)480-0240. Fax: (214)644-9664. Conservative/evangelical. Louis D. Whitworth, sr. ed. Publishes 2-3 titles/yr. Receives 10 submissions annually. Few from first-time authors. No mss through agents. Occasionally reprints books. Prefers 120-250 pgs. Pays $1,000 on acceptance, plus a percentage of sales. Average first printing 2,000+. Publication within 9-10 mos. Accepts simultaneous submissions. Reports in 2 mos. No guidelines; free copy.
Nonfiction: Query only; phone query ok. "Christian approaches to all the academic disciplines; national issues: political, social, medical; education; family values."
Tips: "Most open to a popular level book on issues, apologetics, etc., with sound theology and a Christian world view written by a well-educated person of credible reputation and scholarship."

PROCLAIM PUBLISHING, 1117 Marquette Ave., Ste. 2303, Minneapolis MN 55403. (612)376-0570. Fax: (612)673-0866. Jo Reaves, pub. Publishes 24 titles/yr. Receives 200 submissions annually. 80% of books from first-time authors. Accepts mss through agents. **SUBSIDY PUBLISHES 100%.** Prefers 100-250 pgs (any length ok). Average first printing 2,500. Publication within 2-3 mos. Accepts simultaneous submissions. Reports in 2-4 wks. Guidelines; no catalog.
Nonfiction: Query only; no phone query. Any topic.
Fiction: Query only. Juvenile, teen, adult. Any genre.
Ethnic Books: Interested in publishing some.
Tips: "We are now able to offer a total marketing program, as well as warehousing and order fulfillment services with an 800 number. Our services are affordable."

***PROMETHEUS BOOKS, INC.**, 700 E. Amhearst St., Buffalo NY 14215. (716)837-2475. Scholarly publisher that does a few religious titles. Steven L. Mitchell, ed-in-

chief. Publishes 40 titles/yr. (all types). Royalty 5-10% on wholesale; advance negotiable. Not in topical listings.
Nonfiction: Proposal/first few chapters.

***PROMISE PUBLISHING**, Box 41179, Pasadena CA 91114. (714)997-8450. Dan Wooding, VP/exec. ed. Publishes 15 titles/yr. Receives 30 submissions annually. No books from first-time authors. Accepts mss through agents. **100% SUBSIDY** (author buys back 5,000 copies). Royalty 10% on net; no advance. Publication within 3 mos. Accepts simultaneous submissions. Reports in 2-4 wks. No guidelines/catalog.
Nonfiction: Query or proposal/chapters. "We do evangelical books that can be used by a ministry or the author in their work."

QUESTAR PUBLISHERS, Box 1720, Sisters OR 97759. (503)549-1144. Fax: (503)549-2044. Brenda Saltzer, editorial asst. Multnomah Books is their imprint for youth and adult books; Gold 'N' Honey is imprint for children's books. Publishes 35-40 titles/yr. Receives 1,800-2,000 submissions annually. 1% of books from first-time authors. Prefers not to work with agents. Reprints few books. Length depends on book. Negotiable royalty and advance. Average first printing 10,000-15,000. Publication within 6-12 mos. Accepts simultaneous submissions. Reports in 2 mos. Guidelines; catalog for 9x12 SAE/3 stamps.
Nonfiction: Proposal/2-3 chapters; no phone query.
Fiction: Proposal/2-3 chapters. "Looking for clean, moral, uplifting fiction—not necessarily religious."
Tips: "We evaluate specifically on a book-by-book basis. Most books are shaped by our editors based on input from our marketing and sales departments. We use about 1% or less of our unsolicited mss."

***RAINBOW BOOKS**, Box 261129, San Diego CA 92196. (619)578-4700. Carol Rogers, ed. dir. Publishes 12 titles/yr. Receives 200 submissions annually. 50% of books from first-time authors. No mss through agents. Prefers 64 pgs. Outright purchases $500. Publication within 12-24 mos. Accepts simultaneous submissions. Reports in 3-5 mos. Guidelines; catalog for 9x12 SAE/2 stamps.
Nonfiction: Proposal/2-3 chapters or complete ms; phone query ok. "Looking for 64-pg. activity books for teachers to use in teaching the Bible to children."
Tips: "Most open to book of creative activities that encourage Bible learning for Christian educators to use with children age 2 through grade 6."

+RAINBOW BOOKS, P.O. Box 430, Highland City FL 33846-0430. Phone/Fax: (813)648-4420. Protestant. Betsy A. Lampe, ed. dir. Publishes 10-15 titles/yr. Receives 600 submissions annually. 70% of books from first-time authors. Accepts mss through agents. Royalty 6-8% on retail; advance. Publication within 8 mos. Accepts simultaneous submissions. Reports in 2 mos. Guidelines; copy for 6x9 SAE/3 stamps.
Nonfiction: Query only. "No religious titles with a doomsday thrust." Features home study books.

RAINBOW'S END COMPANY, 354 Golden Grove Rd., Baden PA 15005. (412)266-

4997. Judith Blanarik, sr. ed.; submit to Wayne P. Brumagin. Publishes 5-10 titles/yr. Receives 50+ submissions annually. 80% of books from first-time authors. No mss through agents. Cooperative publishing (author pays half) of 95%. Prefers 150-250 pgs. After initial investment (@ $3,500), author gets all profits from first printing. Average first printing 1,000. Publication within 10-15 mos. Accepts simultaneous submissions. Reports in 4-6 wks. Guidelines; no catalog; book samples $3 ea.
Nonfiction: Complete ms; no phone query. "All books must make a difference in lives—that difference being Jesus Christ."
Special Needs: Books on recovery from addictions.
Tips: "We are offering Christian writers a reputable way of getting their work into print through a reasonably-priced publishing program. Standards are high. Don't be too wordy. Make sure Scripture quotes are accurate. Stay within specified length."

REGAL BOOKS, 2300 Knoll Dr., Ventura CA 93003. (800)235-3415. Kyle Duncan, ed. dir.; Jean Daly, curriculum. Publishes 12 titles/yr. Receives 1,000 submissions annually. No books from first-time authors. No mss through agents. Reprints books. Prefers 200-300 pgs. Royalty 15% on wholesale (10% on curriculum books); advance $1,500-5,000. Average first printing 10,000-20,000. Publication within 9-12 mos. Reports in 90 days. No guidelines/catalog.
Nonfiction: NOT ACCEPTING MSS OR QUERIES AT THIS TIME. All unsolicited mss will be returned unopened.

+REGENCY PRESS, P.O. Box 2306, Bandera TX 78003. (210)796-7215. Gayle Buck, ed. New publisher. No mss through agents. Prefers 70,000-74,000 wds. Royalty 7-10% on retail; no advance. Publication within 18 mos. Accepts simultaneous submissions. Reports ASAP. Guidelines; no catalog.
Fiction: Proposal/3 chapters or complete ms. "Romantic adventure preferred, either contemporary or historical, with believable characters. Must include Christian, Bible-based teaching without preaching—character's lives show growth in Christian principles."
Tips: "Make it professional; no haphazard, lazy format. Biblical and historical references must be accurate."

#THE REGINA PRESS, 145 Sherwood Ave., Farmingdale NY 11735. (516)694-8600. Fax: (516)694-2205. Catholic/Christian. George Malhame, juvenile ed. Publishes 5 titles/yr. Royalty on wholesale; some outright purchases; some advances. No guidelines; sometimes sends free catalog.
Fiction: Query/proposal. Children's picture books for ages 3-8.

#REGNERY GATEWAY, INC., 1130 17th St. NW, Ste. 600, Washington DC 20036. (202)457-0978. Fax: (202)457-0774. Trade publisher that does scholarly Catholic books and evangelical Protestant books. Alfred S. Regnery, ed. Publishes 2-3 religious titles/yr. Receives 20 submissions annually, 70% of books from first-time authors. Accepts mss through agents. Subsidy publishes 2%. Reprints books. Prefers 200-300 pgs. Royalty 10% on retail; usually no advance. Average first printing 5,000. Publication within 9 mos. Accepts simultaneous submissions. Reports in 2-3 mos.

Guidelines; free catalog.
Nonfiction: Proposal/3 chapters or complete ms.
Tips: "Religious books should relate to politics, history, current affairs, biography, and public policy."

#RELIGIOUS EDUCATION PRESS, 5316 Meadow Brook Rd., Birmingham AL 35242. (205)991-1000. Fax: (205)991-9669. Nancy J. Vickers, mng. ed. Publishes 5-6 titles/yr. Receives 280 submissions annually. 40% of books from first-time authors. Accepts mss through agents. Prefers 250-300 pgs. Royalty 10% on retail; no advance. Average first printing 2,000. Publication within 9 mos. Reports in 2 mos. Guidelines; free catalog.
Nonfiction: Query first. "Serious, scholarly books of special interest to professional religious educators and pastoral ministers."
Tips: "Personally examine 2-4 of our books first to see if your book fits representative specifications."

***REMNANT PUBLICATIONS**, 272 Union City Rd., Coldwater MI 49036. (517)278-4011/2665. Seventh-day Adventist. Bill Smith, dir. Publishes 11 titles/yr. This is a new company only reprinting books at this time. Not in topical listings.

***RENEWAL PRESS, INC.**, 1117 Hellmers Ln., Ocean Springs MS 39564. (601)875-4128. Southern Baptist. Grant Shipp, pres. Publishes 1 title/yr. Receives 1 submission annually. 100% of books from first-time authors. No mss through agents. Prefers 175 pgs. Average first printing 2,000. Publication within 3 mos. Reports in 2 wks. Free guidelines/brochure.
Nonfiction: Query first. "Information and procedures concerning church renewal, and small groups."

#RESOURCE PUBLICATIONS, INC., Ste. 290, 160 E. Virginia St., San Jose CA 95112. (408)286-8505. Kenneth E. Guentert, ed. dir. Publishes 15 titles/yr. Receives 250 submissions annually. 60% of books from first-time authors. Accepts mss through agents. Prefers 150 pgs. Royalty 8% on wholesale: no advance. Average first printing 3,000. Publication within 1 yr. Accepts simultaneous submissions. Reports in 3 mos. Guidelines; catalog for 9x12 SAE/2 stamps.
Nonfiction: Proposal/chapters. "Practical resources related to worship." No inspirational works.
Fiction: Proposal. "We publish only short (3-10 minute) dramatic sketches and stories suitable for use in worship or religious education."

RESURRECTION PRESS LTD, Box 248, Williston Park NY 11596. (516)742-5686. Fax: (516)746-6872. Catholic. Emilie Cerar, sr. ed. Publishes 8-10 titles/yr. Receives 80-100 submissions annually. 50% of books from first-time authors. Accepts mss through agents. Reprints books. Prefers 60-200 pgs. Royalty 7-10% on wholesale; advance $200. Average first printing 3,000. Publication within 6-12 mos. Accepts simultaneous submissions. Reports in 2-3 mos. Free guidelines & catalog.
Nonfiction: Query only; no phone query. "Most open to pastoral resources and

spirituality for the active Christian."

FLEMING H. REVELL CO., Box 6287, Grand Rapids MI 49516. (616)676-9185. Fax: (616)676-9573. Evangelical. William J. Petersen, ed. dir. Publishes 60 titles/yr. Receives 1,000 submissions annually. 5% of books from first-time authors. Accepts mss through agents. Prefers 192 pgs. Royalty 14% on wholesale; advance $2,000. Average first printing 5,000. Publication within 14 mos. Accepts simultaneous submissions. Reports in 30 days. Guidelines; catalog for SASE.
Nonfiction: Query only.
Fiction: Query only. Adult.

#REVIEW AND HERALD PUBLISHING ASSN., 55 W. Oak Ridge Dr., Hagerstown MD 21740-7390. (301)791-7000. Seventh-day Adventist. Penny E. Wheeler, acq. ed. Publishes 35 titles/yr. Receives 300-400 submissions annually. 15% of books from first-time authors. No mss through agents. Prefers 128 pgs. Royalty 12-14% retail; advance $500. Average first printing 5,000-7,500. Publication within 18 mos. Accepts simultaneous submissions. Reports in 4 mos. Guidelines; catalog for 10x13 SAE.
Nonfiction: Query or proposal/2-3 chapters. "Accepting fewer but better-written mss."
Fiction: Proposal/3 chapters. Juvenile or teen/yg. adult.
Tips: "Not accepting music, puzzles, or games, and very few children's mss."

ROPER PRESS, 4737 A Gretna, Dallas TX 75207. (214)630-4808. Fax: (214)630-4822. Evangelical. Billy O. Hoskins, pres. Publishes 4-5 titles/yr. Receives 50-100 submissions annually. 90% of books from first-time authors. Accepts mss through agents. Reprints books. Royalty on wholesale; no advance. Average first printing 5,000. Publication within 9-18 mos. Accepts simultaneous submissions. Reports in 1-2 mos. Guidelines; catalog for 9x12 SAE/2 stamps.
Nonfiction: Proposal/3 chapters; no phone queries. "Most interested in Bible study and Bible stories."
Fiction: Proposal/3 chapters. Adult and juvenile. "Christian principles must be integral to the story, not a tacked-on afterthought."
Tips: "Finish the title before submission; have an independent reader evaluate it; provide complete background on author."

ST. ANTHONY MESSENGER PRESS, 1615 Republic St., Cincinnati OH 45210. (513)241-5615. Fax: (513)241-1197/0399. Catholic. Lisa Biedenbach, mng. ed. Publishes 12-15 titles/yr. Receives 250 submissions annually. 10% of books from first-time authors. No mss through agents. Reprints books. Prefers 100-250 pgs. Royalty 10-12% on net; advance $600. Average first printing 5,000. Publication within 12-18 mos. Reports in 4-6 wks. Guidelines: catalog for 9x12 SAE/2 stamps.
Nonfiction: Query only. "Looking for books that discuss Catholic identity—what it means to be Catholic; that support Catholic Christian life; that can be used as resources for pastoral ministry and faith sharing groups; for RCIA."
Tips: "Ms must be written in popular style with anecdotes, examples from real life experience."

#ST. BEDE'S PUBLICATIONS, Box 545, Petersham MA 01366. (508)724-3407. Fax: (508)724-3574. Catholic. Sr. Scholastica Crilly, OSB, ed. Publishes 8-12 titles/yr. Receives 100 submissions annually. 30-40% of books from first-time authors. Accepts mss through agents. Reprints books. Prefers 100-150 pgs. Royalty 5-10% on retail or wholesale; no advance. Average first printing 1,500. Publication within 2 yrs. Accepts simultaneous submissions. Reports in 2 mos. Guidelines; catalog for 9x13 SAE/2 stamps.
Nonfiction: Query first; no phone query. "Looking for titles in monastic spirituality."
Tips: "Just state what you've got simply without gimmicks or attention-getting ploys that usually turn off editors before they've even read your proposal. If your work is worthy of publication, it will stand on its own."

***ST. HILDA'S PRESS**, c/o Longstreet Press, 2150 Newmarket Parkway, Ste. 102, Marietta GA 30067. (404)980-1488. Episcopal Press of the western NC diocese. Gail Godwin, ed. Publishes artistic and spiritual books, tracts, and music. Not included in topical listings.

ST. PAUL BOOKS AND MEDIA, 50 St. Paul's Ave., Boston MA 02130. (617) 522-8911. Fax: (617)541-9805. Catholic/Christian. Sr. Mary Mark Wickenhiser, ed. dir. Publishes 20-25 titles/yr. Receives 400-500 submissions annually. 40% of books from first-time authors. Reluctantly accepts ms through agents. Some reprints. Royalty 6-12% on retail; negotiable outright purchases; occasional advance. Average first printing 3,000-5,000. Publication within 18-24 mos. Reports in 6-8 weeks. Guidelines; catalog for 9x12 SAE/4 stamps.
Nonfiction: Proposal/3 chapters; no phone query. "Looking for self-help and religious instruction works; parenting books."
Tips: "Need books on coping with contemporary problems, such as alcoholism, as long as approach is consonant with Catholic teaching and practice. Books on family life from a Catholic perspective." Use inclusive language when possible. Put footnotes on separate sheets.

SCARECROW PRESS INC., 52 Liberty St., Box 4167, Metuchen NJ 08840. (908)548-8600. Division of Grolier that does a few religious titles. Norman Horrocks, V.P., Editorial. Publishes 5 religious titles/yr. Receives 600-700 submissions annually. 70% of books from first-time authors. Accepts mss through agents. Prefers 250+ pgs. Royalty 10-15% on retail; no advance. Average first printing 1,000. Publication within 12-18 mos (6-12 mos if camera ready). Accepts simultaneous submissions. Reports in 1 month. Free guidelines/catalog.
Nonfiction: Query first. "Only looking for reference material of interest to libraries."

SCRIPTURE PRESS - See Victor Books.

#SERVANT PUBLICATIONS/VINE BOOKS, Box 8617, Ann Arbor MI 48107. (313)761-8505. Fax: (313)761-1577. Elizabeth Feia, sr. ed. Vine Books for Evangelical Christians. Publishes 40 titles/yr. 5% of books from first-time authors. Accepts mss through agents. Reprints books. Prefers 70,000-100,000 wds. Royalty 10% on retail;

advance. Publication within 1 yr. Accepts simultaneous submissions. Reports in 2 mos. No guidelines; catalog for 9x12 SAE/5 stamps.
Nonfiction: Nonfiction only from agents or published authors; all other returned unopened.
Fiction: Query or proposal/1 chapter. Historical. "We would like our fiction to support Christian values."

#HAROLD SHAW PUBLISHERS, Box 567, Wheaton IL 60189. (708)665-6700. Fax: (708)665-6793. Ramona Tucker, dir. of ed. services; Carol Pleuddemann, Bible study ed. Publishes 32 titles/yr. Receives 4,000 submissions annually. 10% of books from first-time authors. Accepts mss through agents. Reprints books. Prefers 160-240 pgs. Royalty 5-10% on retail; outright purchases $1,000-2,500; advance. Average first printing 5,000. Publication within 12-15 mos. Reports in 1 mo. Guidelines; catalog for 9x12 SAE/5 stamps.
Nonfiction: Proposal/3 chapters; no phone query. "Looking for books on family issues; men's and women's issues."
Tips: "Most open to practical books on family living or spiritual life."

#SHEED & WARD, Box 419492, Kansas City MO 64141. (816)531-0538. Fax: (816)931-5082. Catholic/ecumenical. Robert Heyer, ed-in-chief. Publishes 30 titles/yr. Receives 200 submissions annually. 10% of books from first-time authors. No mss through agents. Subsidy publishes 2%. Reprints books. Prefers 100-200 pgs. Royalty 6% on retail; work-for-hire; no advance. Average first printing 2,000. Publication within 4-7 mos. Reports in 3 mos. Guidelines; catalog for 7x11 SAE/2 stamps.
Nonfiction: Complete ms. "Looking for euthanasia, health care, spirituality, leadership, sacraments, small group or priestless parish facilitating books."
Tips: "Be in touch with needs of progressive/changing parishes."

#SHEER JOY! PRESS/PROMOTIONS, Rt 1 Box 110E, Pink Hill NC 28572. (919)568-6101. Fax: (919)568-4171. Protestant. James R. Adams, pres.; submit to Patricia Adams, ed. Publishes 1-2 titles/yr. Receives 5-10 submissions annually. No mss through agents. Subsidy publishes 85%. Prefers 20,000-30,000 wds (200 pgs). Royalty on retail; no advance. Average first printing 1,000. Publication within 6 mos. Accepts simultaneous submissions. Reports in 3-4 wks. No guidelines/ catalog.
Nonfiction: Complete ms. "Need Bible-based dramatic readings."
Fiction: Complete ms. "Need Bible-based puppet skits."
Tips: "Be very illustrative and forceful in writing Christian drama."

#SHINING STAR PUBLICATIONS, Box 299, Carthage IL 62321. (800)435-7234; (217)357-3981. Fax: (217)357-3987. Good Apple, Inc. Becky Daniel, ed. Publishes 20 titles/yr. Receives 1,000 submissions annually. 50% of books from first-time authors. Accepts mss through agents. Prefers 64-144 pgs. Outright purchases $640-1,440 ($10.50/page for ideas). Average first printing 3,000. Publication within 1 yr. Accepts simultaneous submissions. Reports in 6 wks. Guidelines; free catalog.
Nonfiction: Proposal/2 chapters or complete ms. "We do reproducible workbooks to teach scriptures and Christian values."

Fiction: Book proposal or complete ms. "Biblical fiction; retell story using only Scripture facts."
Tips: "Teachers appreciate things that can be presented in a short time. We have new 3-Minute & 5-Minute Bible stories series. Most open to crafts, bulletin board ideas. etc."

+SON-RISE PUBLICATIONS, 143 Greenfield Rd., New Wilmington PA 16142. (800)358-0777. Fax: (412)946-8700. Florence W. Biros, acq. ed. Publishes 5-6 titles/yr. Receives 20 submissions annually. 50% of books from first-time authors. Accepts mss through agents. Subsidy publishes 50%. Prefers 25,000-40,000 wds or 90-196 pgs. Royalty 7.5-10% on retail; no advance. Average first printing 3,000. Publication within 8-9 mos. No simultaneous submissions. Reports ASAP. No guidelines or catalog.
Nonfiction: Query; no phone query. "Most open to Christian teaching and testimony combined."
Fiction: Query. "Looking for an historical novel series."

SOUTHERN BAPTIST PRESS, 4000 Beallwood Ave., Columbus GA 31904. (706) 576-5787. Jerry L. Luquire, exec. ed. Publishes 42 books/yr. Receives 600 submissions annually. Accepts mss through agents. Reprints books. Subsidy publishes 95%. Prefers 120 pgs. Average first printing 500. Publication within 2 mos. Accepts simultaneous submissions. Reports in 1 week. Guidelines; no catalog.
Nonfiction: Complete ms. "Collections of sermons on family topics; poetry; relation of Bible to current day."
Fiction: Complete ms. "Stories that show how faith helps overcome small, day-to-day problems. Prefers under 200 wds."
Tips: "Keep it short; support facts with reference."

STANDARD PUBLISHING, 8121 Hamilton Ave., Cincinnati OH 45231. (513)931-4050. Theresa Hayes, acq. ed. An evangelical Christian publisher of curriculum, classroom resources, and children's books. Publishes 40-80 titles/yr. Receives 1,600-1,700 submissions annually. 33% of books from first-time authors. Accepts mss through agents. Reprints books. Variable royalty or outright purchase; pays advance. Average first printing 7,500-15,000. Publication within 12-18 mos. Accepts simultaneous submissions. Reports in 1-6 mos. Guidelines; seasonal catalog for 9x12 SAE/4 stamps; full trade catalog $2.
Nonfiction: Query or proposal/one chapter; no phone query. "Looking for tips for teachers, training material, bulletin board helps, classroom activity books."
Fiction: Complete ms. Children's picture books.
Tips: "Most open to picture books or teacher resource books."

STARBURST PUBLISHERS, Box 4123, Lancaster PA 17604. (717)293-0939. Ellen Hake, ed. dir. Publishes 8-10 titles/yr. Receives 300-400 submissions annually. 50% of books from first-time authors. Accepts mss through agents. Prefers 200 pgs minimum. Royalty 6-16% on wholesale. Average first printing 5,000. Publication within 12 mos. Accepts simultaneous submissions. Reports in 1 month. Guidelines; catalog for 9x12

SAE/4 stamps.
Nonfiction: Query or proposal/3 chapters; no phone query.
Fiction: Query or proposal/3 chapters. Adult. "Looking for good fiction by published authors."
Tips: "60% of our line goes into the Christian marketplace; 40% into the secular."

STAR SONG PUBLISHING GROUP, 2325 Crestmoor, Nashville TN 37215. (615)269-0196. Fax: (615)385-2708. Matthew A. Price, VP. Serving those who serve the church. Publishes 20-25 titles/yr. Receives 500-600 submissions annually. 5% of books from first-time authors. Accepts mss through agents. Reprints books. Prefers 75,000-125,000 words or 224 pgs. Royalty 12-18% on wholesale; advance $1,500. Average first printing 5,000. Publication within 6 mos. Accepts simultaneous submissions. Reports in 4-6 weeks. Free guidelines/catalog.
Nonfiction: Query; no phone query. "Looking for reference books."
Fiction: Query. For all ages. Contemporary.
Ethnic Books: African-American.
Tips: "Send a cover letter, summary, brief marketing proposal, and vita."

#STILL WATERS REVIVAL BOOKS, 4710 - 37A Ave., Edmonton, AB T6L 3T5 Canada. (403)450-3730. Reformed Church. Reg Barrow, pres. Publishes 15 titles/yr. Receives few submissions. Very few books from first-time authors. Accepts mss through agents. Reprints books. Prefers 128-160 pgs. Negotiated royalty or outright purchase. Accepts simultaneous submissions. No guidelines; catalog for 9x12 SAE/2 stamps.
Nonfiction: Proposal/2 chapters. "Reformed and Reconstructionistic books of scholarly value, for the use of educated laymen." No non-Reformed or pre-millennial.
Tips: "Most open to books based on the system of doctrine found in the Westminster confession of faith, as it applies to our contemporary setting."

#TABOR PUBLISHING, 25115 Avenue Stanford, Ste. 130, Valencia CA 91355. Catholic/mainline Christian. Cullen W. Shippe, pres.; Carol Prochaska, mng. ed. Publishes 15-20 titles/yr. Receives 150 submissions annually. 75% of books from first-time authors. Accepts mss through agents. Prefers up to 75,000 wds. Royalty 4-12% on wholesale; some outright purchases for $500-2,000; advance $1,000. Publication within 18 mos. Reports in 1 mo.
Nonfiction: Query only. All unsolicited mss returned unopened. Textbooks.

+TEACH SERVICES, INC., Rt 1 Box 182, Brushton NY 12916. (518)358-3028. Fax: (518)358-3028. Timothy Hullquist, pres. Publishes 50 titles/yr. Receives 10-15 submissions annually. 20% of books from first-time authors. No mss through agents. Subsidy publishes 20% of books. Reprints books. Royalty 10% on retail; no advance. Average first printing 5,000. Publication within 3 mos. No simultaneous submissions. Reports in 10 days. No guidelines; free catalog.
Nonfiction: Query only; phone query ok. "Looking for books on health and prophecy."
Tips: "Most open to Bible-related studies."

THE TRINITY FOUNDATION, Box 700, Jefferson MD 21755. (301)371-7155. John W. Robbins, pres. Advocates a systematic presentation of the whole doctrine of God. Publishes 4+ titles/yr. Receives 20+ submissions annually. Accepts mss through agents. Reprints books. Subsidy publishes 10%. Prefers 200 pgs. Outright purchase; free books; no advance. Average first printing 3,000. Publication within 6 mos. Accepts simultaneous submissions. Reports in 3 mos. No guidelines; catalog for #10 SAE/1 stamp.
Nonfiction: Proposal/3 chapters; phone query ok.
Special Needs: Contra Catholicism.

#TRINITY PRESS INTERNATIONAL, Box 851, Valley Forge PA 19482. (215)768-2120. Fax: (215)768-2056. Dr. Harold W. Rast, dir./ed. Publishes 20-25 titles/yr. Receives 150-200 submissions annually. 3% of books from first-time authors. Accepts mss through agents. Reprints books. Royalty 7.5-10% on retail; advance $500 and up. Subsidy publishes 10%. Publication within 8 mos. Reports in 8 wks. Guidelines; free catalog.
Nonfiction: Complete ms or proposal/1 chapter. "Religious material only in the area of Bible studies, theology, ethics, etc." No dissertations or essays.
Tips: "Give small amount of information for first submission."

+TRIUMPH BOOKS, 333 Glen Head Rd., Old Brookville NY 11545. (516)759-7402. Fax: (516)759-8619. Ecumenical (Mainline). Patricia A. Kossmann, exec. ed. Publishes 16-20 titles/yr. Receives 75 submissions annually. 25% of books from first-time authors. Accepts mss through agents. Reprints books. Prefers at least 40,000 wds. Royalty 6-15% on retail; variable advance. Average first printing 5,000. Publication within 7 mos. Considers simultaneous submissions. Reports in 3-4 wks. Free guidelines/catalog.
Nonfiction: Proposal/1-2 chapters; no phone query. "Looking for challenging, intellectually and spiritually stimulating (books that engage both head and heart) for serious readers. No pop stuff! Subjects must speak to the cultural, social, moral, and other issues that affect one's life and values."
Fiction: None at this time.
Ethnic Books: Parent company, Liguori Publications, publishes books in Spanish.
Tips: "Know what's already out there in the same general subject area and articulate what makes your book different, better, etc. Sell us on why we should publish it."

+TYLER PRESS, 1221 W.S.W. Loop 323, Tyler TX 75701. (903)581-2255. Fax: (903)581-7841. Non-denominational. Jennie Urrego, mng. ed. Our goal is to restore Christ as the center of the American character. Publishes 6 titles/yr. Receives 40 submissions annually. 70% of books from first-time authors. Reluctantly accepts mss through agents. Reprints books. Prefers 204 pgs and up. Works on a joint publishing venture with the author; no advance. Average first printing 1,500-2,000. Publication within 2 mos. Considers simultaneous submissions. Reports in 3-4 wks. No guidelines/catalog.
Nonfiction: Query. "We enthusiastically promote self-help/how-to, historical, creation science, current social & political issues, biographies, autobiographies, marriage &

family, and women's issues."
Fiction: Complete ms. For children only.

#TYNDALE HOUSE PUBLISHERS, 351 Executive Dr., Box 80, Wheaton IL 60189. (708)668-8300. Fax: (708)668-6885. Ronald Beers, V.P editorial; submit to Marilyn Dellorto. Publishes 100 titles/yr. Receives 3,000 submissions annually. 5-10% of books from first-time authors. Accepts mss through agents. Reprints books. Royalty; outright purchase of some children's books up to $1,000; advance up to $5,000. Subsidy publishes 30%. Average first printing 5,000-10,000. Publication within 12-18 mos. Accepts simultaneous submissions. Reports in up to 3 mos. Guidelines (separate guidelines for children's books - request specifically); catalog for 9x12 SAE/9 stamps.
Nonfiction: Query.
Fiction: Query. Also children's books, especially for ages 6-12.

UNITED CHURCH PRESS, 700 Prospect Ave. E., Cleveland OH 44115. (216)736-3704. Fax: (216)736-3703. United Church of Christ/Board for Homeland Missions. Kim M. Sadler, ed. Receives 60+ submissions annually. 50% of books from first-time authors. Accepts mss through agents. Royalty 8-12% on net; work for hire, one-time fee; advance negotiable. Average first printing 3,000. Publication within 9-12 mos. Rarely considers simultaneous submissions. Reports in 8-12 wks. Free guidelines/catalog.
Nonfiction: Proposal/2 or more chapters or complete ms.; no phone query.
Fiction: Proposal/2 or more chapters or complete ms. Biblical, for children or teens.
Special Needs: Children's sermons, worship resources, youth materials, religious materials for racial/ethnic persons.
Ethnic Books: African-American, Native-American, Asian-American, Pacific Islanders, and Hispanic.
Tips: "Most open to well-written mss that are United Church of Christ specific and/or religious topics that cross denominations. Use inclusive language and follow the Chicago Manual of Style."

#THE UNITED CHURCH PUBLISHING HOUSE, 85 St. Clair Ave. E., Toronto ON M4T 1M8, Canada. (416)925-5931. Fax (416)925-9692. The United Church of Canada. Peter Gordon White, ed-in-chief. Publishes 15 titles/yr. Receives 30-40 submissions annually. 15% of books from first-time authors. Accepts mss through agents. Prefers 200 pgs. Royalty 8-12% on retail; some advances. Average first printing 2,000. Publication within 8 mos. Accepts simultaneous submissions. Reports in 4 wks. No guidelines; free catalog.
Nonfiction: Query; no phone query. "Must be of interest to Canadians and address some aspect of Canadian living."

THE UNITED METHODIST PUBLISHING HOUSE, Box 801, Nashville TN 37202. (615)749-6000. Fax: (615)749-6512. United Methodist. Imprints: Abingdon Press and Dimensions for Living. Michael E. Lawrence, mng. ed. Resources for mainline Christians & mainline churches. Publishes 100 titles/yr. Receives 2,500 submissions annually. Less than 5% of books from first-time authors. Accepts mss through agents.

Reprints books. Prefers 32-300 pgs. Royalty on retail & advance (rare) always negotiated. Average first printing 4,000-5,000. Publication within 10 mos. Accepts simultaneous submissions. Reports in 6-8 wks. No guidelines; catalog for 9x12 SAE/10 stamps.
Nonfiction: Proposal/2 chapters; no phone query. "Most open to a book that offers a unique perspective on issues or concerns before clergy and thoughtful lay people."
Special Needs: United Methodism, Wesleyan studies, family life, & parenting.
Ethnic Books: African-American, Native-American, and Asian-American.
Tips: "Most open to a well-argued position by a recognized voice. Have a proven track record in sales of previously published titles."

#UNIVERSITY OF NORTH CAROLINA PRESS, Box 2288, Chapel Hill NC 27515-2288. (919)966-3561. Academic publisher that does a few books of religious studies. Kate Douglas Torrey, dir. Publishes 65 titles/yr. 70% of books from first-time authors. Accepts mss through agents. Prefers 75,000-125,000 wds. Royalty varies; occasional advance. Publication within 1 yr. Reports in 5 mos. Guidelines; free catalog.
Nonfiction: Proposal/chapters. Religious studies.

#UNIVERSITY PRESS OF AMERICA, 4720 Boston Way, Lanham MD 20706. (301)459-3366. Fax: (301)459-2118. Academic press; imprint Madison Books. James E. Lyons, pub.; Jonathan Sisk, ed. Publishes 50 religious titles/yr. Receives 100 submissions annually. Accepts mss through agents. Reprints books. Prefers 100-400 pgs. Royalty 5-15% on net; occasional advance. Some subsidy. Publication within 6-8 mos. Accepts simultaneous submissions. Reports in 6 wks. Guidelines/catalog for SASE.
Nonfiction: Send outline or request proposal questionnaire. Religion. "Scholarly texts with appeal to college level."

***UPPER ROOM BOOKS**, 1908 Grand Ave., Box 189, Nashville TN 37202. (615)340-7332. United Methodist. Dr. Lynne Deming, sr. ed. Publishes 20-25 titles/yr. Receives 100 submissions annually. 10% of books from first-time authors. Accepts mss through agents. Reprints books. Royalty on retail; advance. Accepts simultaneous submissions. Reports in 6-8 wks. Guidelines; catalog for 9x12 SAE/3 stamps.
Nonfiction: Proposal/3 chapters or complete ms.
Tips: "Need books that are well written with a high literary value; books that focus on spirituality, spiritual formation, and related themes."

#VESTA PUBLICATIONS, LTD., Box 1641, Cornwall ON K6H 5V6 Canada. (613)932-2135. Fax: (613)932-7735. General trade publisher that does a few religious titles. Ajay Gill, pres. Publishes 4 titles/yr. Receives 350 submissions annually. 80% of books from first-time authors. No mss through agents. Subsidy publishes 5%. Prefers 75,000 wds & up. Royalty 10% on wholesale; no advance. Publication within 2 mos. Considers simultaneous submissions if noted. Reports in 1 mo. Free catalog.
Nonfiction & Fiction: Query; phone query ok.
Ethnic Books: Ethnic fiction.

VICTOR BOOKS, 1825 College Ave., Wheaton IL 60187. (708)668-6000. Scripture Press Publications, Inc. David Horton, sr. acq. ed.; Liz Duckworth, mng. ed. for Children's Products and SonPower Youth Resources. Publishes over 100 titles/yr. Receives 5,000 submissions annually. 10% of books from first-time authors. Accepts mss through agents. Reprints books (name authors only). Prefers 200-250 pgs or 80-100,000 wds. Royalty 10-15% on retail; some outright purchases; advance $2,000-3,000. Average first printing 7,500-10,000. Publication within 8-12 mos. Accepts simultaneous submissions. Reports in 60-90 days. Guidelines; catalog for 2 stamps.
Nonfiction: Proposal/2-3 chapters; no phone query. "Most open to fresh, marketable concepts; well-thought-out, and well-written books."
Fiction: Proposal/5 chapters. Adult/teen/juvenile/picture books.
Tips: "Develop your writing skill; develop a platform; know the industry."

VICTORY HOUSE, INC., Box 700238, Tulsa OK 74170. (918)747-5009. Fax: (918)747-1970. Lloyd B. Hildebrand, mng. ed. Publishes 5-7 titles/yr. Receives 600 submissions annually. 10% of books from first-time authors. Accepts mss through agents. Subsidy publishes 5-10%. Reprints books. Prefers 250 pgs. Royalty; rarely pays advance. Average first printing 5,000. Publication within 10-12 mos. Accepts simultaneous submissions. Reports in 3 mos. Guidelines; catalog for #10 SAE/1 stamp.
Nonfiction: Complete ms; sometime accepts phone query. "Looking for books on prayer, Christian living, and contemporary issues."
Fiction: Complete ms. For all ages.
Tips: "Most open to a well-written book with substance and a fresh approach. Keep the writing simple and direct. Show, don't tell. Avoid preachiness. Illustrate teaching with personal examples. Don't overwrite."

WADSWORTH PUBLISHING COMPANY, 10 Davis Dr., Belmont CA 94002. (415)595-2350. Fax: (415)637-7544. Secular publisher that does some religious books. Tammy Goldfeld, ed. Publishes 3-4 higher education religious textbooks/yr. Receives 30 submissions annually. 50% of books from first-time authors. No mss through agents. Royalty 10-13% on wholesale; rarely offers advance. Average first printing 5,000. Publication within 9 mos. Accepts simultaneous submissions. Reports in 2-4 mos. Guidelines/catalog available only to college professors.
Nonfiction: Query only; no phone query. "Looking for textbooks on religion, Judaism, and non-Christian religions. Open only to mainstream undergraduate college texts by a professor with teaching experience."

WARNER PRESS, Box 2499, Anderson IN 46018-2499. (317)644-7721. Church of God. David C. Schultz, ed-in-chief; Dan Harman, book ed. Publishes 10-15 titles/yr. Receives 200 submissions annually. 5% of books by first-time authors. Accepts mss through agents. Prefers 120 pgs. Royalty 15% on wholesale; seldom makes advances. Average first printing 5,000. Publication within 8 mos. Reports in 2 wks. No guidelines; free catalog.
Nonfiction: Query only; no phone query.

#WELLNESS PUBLICATIONS, Box 2397, Holland MI 49423. (616)335-5553. Darrell Franken, pres. Specializes in health and faith books. Publishes 1 title/yr. Receives 25 submissions annually. All books from first-time authors. Accepts mss through agents. Prefers 250 pgs. Royalty 10% on retail; no advance. Average first printing 2,000. Publication within 3 mos. Reports in 3 mos. No guidelines; free catalog.
Nonfiction: Complete ms.
Tips: "Most open to self-help books, especially dealing with marriage and family life."

***WESLEYAN UNIVERSITY PRESS**, 110 Mt. Vernon St., Middletown CT 06457. Peter J. Potter, ed. Royalty.
Nonfiction: Complete ms. Books of poetry, 64-80 pgs.

#WESTMINSTER/JOHN KNOX PRESS, 100 Witherspoon St., Louisville KY 40202-1396. (502)569-5043. Fax: (502)569-5018. Presbyterian Church (U.S.A.). Davis Perkins, ed dir; Walter Sutton & Alexa Smith, professional & general books; Cynthia Thompson & Jeffries Hamilton, academic books; Harold Twiss, general books. Publishes 80-100 titles/yr. Prefers 200 pgs. Royalty 7-10%; negotiable advance. Reports in 2-3 mos. Guidelines; free catalog.
Nonfiction: Proposal/chapters. Emphasizes ethics and theology.

+WOMAN'S MISSIONARY UNION, P.O. Box 830010, Birmingham AL 35283-0010. (205)991-8100. Fax: (205)991-4990. Southern Baptist. Cindy McClain, editorial group manager. Publishes 40 titles/yr (many are work for hire). Receives 40-50 submissions annually. 85% of books from first-time authors. Accepts mss through agents. Reprints books. Prefers 150-250 pgs. Royalty on retail or outright purchase; no advance. Average first printing 5,000-10,000. Publication within 12-18 mos. Accepts simultaneous submissions. Reports in 6 mos. Guidelines; copy for 9x12 SAE.
Nonfiction: Proposal/3 chapters or complete ms. "All that we produce must have a missions/ministry emphasis."
Ethnic Books: Publishes books for Hispanic market.
Tips: "Most open to how-to for missions involvement or books that address involvement in missions or lead persons into involvement."

+WORLD BIBLE PUBLISHERS, INC., 1500 Riverside Dr., P.O. Box 370, Iowa Falls IA 50126. (515)648-4271. Fax: (515)648-4801. Dan Penwell, Dir. of New Product Development. Seeks to make the Bible more understandable to the masses. Publishes 6-10 titles/yr. 25% of books from first-time authors. Accepts mss through agents. Does some subsidy publishing. Reprints books. Prefers 200-300 pgs. Royalty 10-15% on wholesale; some outright purchases; some advances. Average first printing 5,000-7,500. Publication within 6 mos. Accepts simultaneous submissions. Reports in 2-4 wks. No guidelines; catalog for 9x12 SAE/$2.90 postage.
Nonfiction: Query or book proposal; phone query ok. "Most open to popular-style reference book or popular-style Bible study book."
Ethnic Books: African-American & Spanish.
Tips: "Have a well-defined statement of purpose.; a well-developed outline of the book with a good summary of each chapter; and actual formatted page layouts of what

author perceives the book should look like."

W.R.S. PUBLISHING, Box 21207, Waco TX 76702. (817)776-6461. Fax: (817)776-6321. W.R. Spence, pres. Publishes 6 titles/yr. Receives 200 submissions annually. 60% of books from first-time authors. Accepts mss through agents. Reprints books. Prefers 75,000 wds. Royalty 15% on wholesale; advance $3,000. Publication within 1 yr. Considers simultaneous submissions. Reports in 30 days. Guidelines; catalog for 9x12 SAE.
Nonfiction: Query letter only; no phone query. "Looking for biographical and inspirational books—ordinary people with extraordinary accomplishments. Impossible dream stories."
Ethnic Books: For African-Americans.
Tips: "Most open to promotable author or subject."

YALE UNIVERSITY PRESS, 92A Yale Station, New Haven CT 06520. (203)432-0900. Charles Grench, exec. ed. Publishes 10 religious titles/yr. Receives 175 submissions annually. 15% of books from first-time authors. Accepts mss through agents. Reprints books. Prefers up to 100,000 wds or 400 pgs. Royalty to 15% on retail; advances as needed. Average first printing 1,500. Publication within 1 yr. Reports in 2-13 wks. No guidelines; free catalog.
Nonfiction: Query first. "Excellent and saleable scholarly books."

#ZONDERVAN PUBLISHING HOUSE, General Trade Books, 5300 Patterson Ave. S E, Grand Rapids MI 49530. (616)698-6900. Division of HarperCollins Publishers. Submit to Manuscript Review ed. Publishes 130 trade titles/yr. Receives 3,000 submissions annually. 20% of books from first-time authors. Accepts mss through agents. Reprints books. Royalty 12-14% on net; variable advance. Average first printing 5,000. Publication within 14 mos. Accepts simultaneous submissions. Reports in 3 mos. Guidelines; no catalog. For a recording about submissions, call (616)698-3447.
Nonfiction: Proposal/1 chapter (follow guidelines); no phone query. "Looking for books for men and seniors."
Fiction: Query or proposal/2 chapters. "Looking for series for adults and juveniles."
Tips: "Send something unique, distinctive in content. Proposal must show strong understanding of competition and audience."

#ZONDERVAN PUBLISHING HOUSE, Academic and Professional Books, 5300 Patterson Ave. SE, Grand Rapids MI 49530. (616)698-6900. Division of HarperCollins Publishers. Rachel Berrens, ed. Publishes 40-45 academic titles/yr. Accepts mss through agents. Seldom reprints books or dissertations. Royalty 14% on net; usually pays advance. Publication within 3 months. Free guidelines/catalog.
Nonfiction: Query or proposal/1-2 chapters. Academic books only.
Tips: "Includes books on preaching, counseling, discipleship, worship, and church renewal for pastors, professionals, and lay leaders in ministry." Wesleyan perspective.

BOOK PUBLISHERS NOT INCLUDED

Following is a list of book publishers who did not return a questionnaire, have gone out of business, or asked to be deleted for various reasons. Their inclusion on this list indicates a lack of interest in freelance submissions. The following codes indicate the reason for each: OB - Out of business, ABD - Asked to be deleted, NF - No freelance,NQ - Did not return questionnaire, or BA - Bad address.Abbey Press (ABD)

Affirmation Books (OB)
Anglican Book Centre, The (NQ)
Arbuta House (NQ)
Arnold Publications (NF)
A.S. Barnes (BA)
Back To the Bible Books (OB)
Banner of Truth Trust (NF)
Bible Temple Publishing (NF)
Brethren Press (NF)
Brownlow Publishing Co. (NQ)
Canec Publishing House (NQ)
Canyonview Press (NF)
Christian Schools Intl (NF)
Doubleday (ABD)
Falcon Press (NQ)
Gazelle Publications (NF for now)
Michael Glazier Inc (BA)
Gospel Publishing House (ABD)
Great Ocean Publishers (NQ)
Guideposts Books (ABD)
Harpers Ferry Press (BA)
Here's Life Publishers (OB)
Holman Bible Publishers
(now Broadman & Holman)
Hope Publishing House (NQ)
Ideals Publishing Corp (NQ)
Krieger Publishing (NF)
LifeCare Books (ABD)
Lion Publishing (NF)
Loizeaux Brothers (NF)
Magnificat Press (OB)
Majestic Books (ABD)
Ministry Pub Co (OB)
Morse Press (BA)
Mott Media (NF for now)
Mustard Seed Books (NF)
Nelson-Hall Publishers (ABD)
Parthenon Press (NQ)
Pastoral Fisherman (BA)
Pathway Press (NQ)
Peregrine Press (NF for now)
Pine Mt Press (BA)
Pointe Publishers (NQ)
Polaris Press (NF)
Provident Press (OB)
Randall House Publications (NF)
Regular Baptist Press (NQ)
Richelieu Court Pub (BA)
Russell House (BA)
Rutledge Hill Press (ABD)
William H. Sadlier (NF)
Scroll Publishing (NF for now)
Silver Burdett Ginn Inc. (ABD)
Skipjack Press (NF)
Sparrow Press (NF)
Sherwood Sugden (NQ)
Star Books (NF for now)
Sweetwater Publications (NF for now)
Today's Christian Woman Books (NF)
Twenty-Third Publications (NF)
Union Gospel Press (NF)
Welch Publishing Co (OB)
Westport Publishers (ABD)
Whitaker House (NF for now)
Windflower Communications (OB)
Windy Willow Press (OB)
Wolgemuth & Hyatt (OB)
Word Inc. (NF)

TOP 26 BOOK PUBLISHERS IN ORDER OF MOST BOOKS PUBLISHED PER YEAR

1. Thomas Nelson 300+
2. HarperSanFrancisco 180
3. Baker Book House 130
4. Zondervan 130
5. Victor Books 100+
6. Tyndale House 100
7. United Methodist Pub Hs 100
8. Wm B Eerdmans 90
9. Paulist Press 80-100
10. Westminster/John Knox 80-100
11. Concordia 75
12. GROUP Publishing 75
13. Harvest House 70-80
14. InterVarsity Press 70-80
15. Broadman & Holman 65
16. University of NC
17. Moody Press 60-80
18. Joshua Morris 60
19. Fleming H. Revell 60
20. Master Books 55
21. CSS Publishing 52
22. Brown/ROA 50-100
23. Custom Communications 50-75
24. Crossway 50-60
25. Kregel Publications 50-60
26. Nazarene Publishing House 50-60

ALL PUBLISHERS IN ORDER OF MOST BOOKS PUBLISHED PER YEAR

Thomas Nelson 300+
HarperSanFrancisco 180
Baker Book House 130
Zondervan 130
Victor Books 100+
Tyndale House 100
United Methodist 100
Wm B Eerdmans 90
Paulist Press 80-100
Westminster/John Knox 80-100
Concordia 75
GROUP Publishing 75
Harvest House 70-80
InterVarsity Press 70
Broadman & Holman 65
University of NC 65
Moody Press 60-80
Joshua Morris 60
Fleming H. Revell 60
Master Books 55
CSS Publishing 52
Brown/ROA 50-100
Custom Communications 50-75
Crossway 50-60
Kregel 50-60
Nazarene Pub House 50-60
Augsburg Fortress 50
Chariot Books 50
Orbis Books 50
TEACH Services 50
University Press of America 50
Heartsong Presents 48
Standard 40-80
Zondervan Academic 40-45
Barbour & Co 40
Bridge Publishing 40
Oxford University 40
Servant Publications 40
Woman's Missionary Union 40
College Press 36
Harrison House 36
Bible Discovery 35-45
Questar 35-40
Bridge Publishing 35
Liguori Publications 35
Meriwether (plays) 35
Review & Herald 35
Harold Shaw 32
Alba House 30
Don Bosco Multimedia 30
Herald Press 30
Pacific Press 30

Sheed & Ward 30
Christian Ed Publishers 28
Huntington House 25-30
Our Sunday Visitor 25-30
Mel Bay Publications 25
Forward Movement 25
Liturgical Press 25
New Leaf Press 25
Christian Publications 24
Pilgrim Press 20-25
St Paul Books 20-25
Star Song 20-25
Trinity Press Intl. 20-25
Upper Room Books 20-25
Shining Star 20
Judson Press 18-20
Creation House 18
Novalis 18
Triumph books 16-20
Pastoral Press 16
Discipleship Resources 15-20
Morehouse Publishing 15-20
New Leaf Press 15-20
Rainbow Books (FL) 15-20
Tabor Publishing 15-20
Lillenas 15+
Center for Learning 15
Focus on the Family 15
Joy Publishing 15
New Hope 15
Resource Publications 15
Still Waters 15
United Church Publishing Hs 15
Hendrickson Publishers 14-18
Friends United Press 14
Friendship Press 12-20
Ave Maria Press 12-15
Loyola University Press 12-15
St. Anthony Messenger Press 12-15
United Church Press 12-15
Chalice Press 12
Honor Books 12
LifeJourney Books 12
Pastoral Press 12
Rainbow Books (CA) 12
Regal Books 12
Remnant Publications 11
Gold 'N Honey 10-20
Prescott Press 10-15
Rainbow Books (FL) 10-15
Warner Press 10-15
ACTA Publications 10
Alban Institute 10
AMG Publishers 10
Christian Classics 10
Educational Ministries 10
Franciscan Univ Press 10
C.R. Gibson 10
Living Flame 10
New Hope 10
Pacific Theatre (plays) 10
Yale University Press 10
Accent Publications 9-12
Christopher Pub Hs 8-12
Collier-MacMillan 8-12
St. Bede's Publications 8-12
August House 8-10
Cistercian Publications 8-10
Resurrection Press 8-10
Starburst Publishers 8-10
Church Growth Institute 8
ICS Publications 8
Neibauer Press 8
Dimension Books 7
OMF Books 6-12
Blue Dolphin 6-10
Bob Jones University Press 6-10
Thomas More Press 6-10
World Bible 6-10
Chosen Books 6-8
Cornell University Press 6-8
Presbyterian/Reformed 6-8
Bristol House 6
Christian Literature Crusade 6
Lura Media 6
WRS Publishing 6
Franciscan Press 5-10
Haworth Press 5-10
Hensley, Virgil W. 5-10

Rainbow's End 5-10
Victory House 5-7
Religious Education Press 5-6
Son-Rise 5-6
Bethel Publishing 5+
Langmarc Publishing 5
Regina Press 5
Scarecrow Press 5
Emerald Books 4-6
Catholic Univ of America 4-5
Roper Press 4-5
Trinity Foundation 4+
American Catholic Press 4
Covenant Publishers 4
Lifetime Books 4
Open Court 4
VESTA Publications 4
CREDO Publishing 3-6
Didaskon Publishing 3-5
Aglow 3-4
Kindred Press 3-4
Meriwether Publishing 3-4
Paraclete Press 3-4
Wadsworth Publishing 3-4
Good Book 3
Life Enrichment 3
Praxis Institute 3
Church/Synagogue Library 2-3
Probe Ministries 2-3
Regnery Gateway 2-3
Barclay Press 2
Covenant Publishers 2
Guernica Editions 2
Krieger Publishing 2
Living Sacrifice 2
Morning Star Press 2
Omega Publications 2
Life Cycle Books 1-3
DaBaR Services 1-2
New Society Publishers 1-2
Gilgal Publications 1
Higley Publishing 1
Pelican Publishing 1
Renewal Press 1
Wellness Publications 1

SUBSIDY PUBLISHERS:

Brentwood 267
Poet's Cove 125
Fairway Press 60-75
Southern Baptist Press 42
Companion Press 38
Proclaim Publishing 24
Promise Publishing 15
Life Books 5
Pillar Books 5
Sheer Joy! Press 1-2

MARKET ANALYSIS

BOOK PUBLISHERS WITH THE MOST BOOKS ON THE BEST SELLER LIST FOR THE LAST YEAR

Note: This tally is based on actual sales in Christian bookstores for January-December 1993. Numbers behind the names indicate the number of titles each publisher had on the best-seller list during the year. The number in parentheses following that number indicates their place on the list last year (if different).

Adult Books

1. Word Inc. 22 (#2)
2. Bethany House 19 (#1)
3. Thomas Nelson 12
4. Zondervan 7
5. Harvest House 6 (#9)
6. Moody Press 5 (#10)
7. Questar/Multnomah 5 (#6)

8. Crossway 4 (#7)
9. Tyndale House 4 (#12)
10. Baker/Revell 3 (#13/17)
11. Macmillan 3 (#15)
12. NavPress 3 (#11)
13. Augsburg Fortress 1 (#20)
14. Harrison House 1 (#21)
15. Living Truth 1
16. Regal Books 1 (#22)
17. Rutledge Hill 1
18. Servant 1 (#18)
19. Sparrow 1
20. Walker 1

Children's Books

1. Thomas Nelson 10 (#2)
2. Questar/Gold 'N Honey 6 (#3)
3. Bethany House 5 (#1)
4. Crossway Books 5 (#5)
5. Word, Inc. 5 (#8)
6. Chariot Books 4
7. Zondervan 4
8. Tyndale House 2 (#11)
9. Baker Books 1 (#4)
10. Barbour Books 1 (#9)
11. HarperCollins 1
12. Moody Press 1 (#15)
13. Regina Press 1
14. Victor Books 1 (#16)
15. World Bible 1 (#12)

Comments:

* Unfortunately, of the publishers listed above with best-selling books: Word, Bethany House, NavPress, Rutledge Hill, and Walker are not open to unsolicited manuscripts.
* Of the best-selling books represented by the above list: most of Moody's had to do with money management or investing; Bethany's books appear to be exclusively fiction (children's and adults); Crossway's are all Peretti books except one; NavPress' were women's books; Questar's and Chariot's children's books were all children's Bibles or Bible-related books. Some of the best sellers were public-domain classics reprinted by more than one publisher.

BOOK TOPICS MOST POPULAR WITH PUBLISHERS

Note: The numbers following the topics indicate how many publishers said they were interested in seeing a book on that topic.

1. Christian Living 98
2. Bible Studies 93
3. Family Life 87
4. Prayer 87
5. Women's Issues 86
6. Theological 80
7. Devotional Books 79
8. Spirituality 79
9. Marriage 78
10. Parenting 78
11. Christian Education 77
12. Religion 76
13. How-To/Self-Help 74
14. Current/Social Issues 72
15. Evangelism 72
16. Inspirational 70
17. Discipleship 67
18. Church Renewal 64
19. Counseling Aids 64
20. Biography 62
21. Pastor's Helps 60
22. Historical 59
23. Church Life 58
24. Ethics 58
25. Doctrinal 53
26. Social Justice Issues 53

27. Psychology 51
28. Healing 50
29. Worship Resources 48
30. Divorce 47
31. Group Study Books 47
32. Youth Books (nonfiction) 47
33. Apologetics 46
34. Cults/Occult 43
35. Reference Books 43
36. Children's Picture Books 42
37. Humor 42
38. Fiction: Adult 41
39. Autobiography 40
40. Singles Issues 40
41. Missionary 39
42. Money Management 39
43. Liturgical Studies 38
44. Fiction: Historical 37
45. Fiction: Juvenile 36
46. Gift Books 36
47. Health 36
48. Personal Experience 36
49. Philosophy 36
50. Senior Adult Concerns 35
51. Christian Home Schooling 32
52. Fiction: Adventure 32
53. Fiction: Biblical 32
54. Prophecy 32
55. Sermons 32
56. Economics 31
57. Fiction: Contemporary 31
58. World Issues 31
59. Environmental Issues 30
60. Ethnic 30
61. Miracles 30
62. Political 30
63. Archaeology 29
64. Controversial Issues 29
65. Men's Books 29
66. Fiction: Historical/Romance 27
67. Fiction: Mystery 27
68. Fiction: Teen/Young Adult 26
69. Sociology 26
70. Curriculum 23
71. Fiction: Frontier/Romance 23
72. Youth Programs 23
73. Fiction: Frontier 22
74. Celebrity Profiles 21
75. Retirement 21
76. Drama 20
77. Fiction: Humor 20
78. Music-Related Books 20
79. Fiction: Mystery/Romance 19
80. Science 18
81. Christian School Books 16
82. Cookbooks 16
83. Fiction: Literary 16
84. Games/Crafts 16
85. Poetry 16
86. Fiction: Plays 15
87. Fiction: Romance 14
88. Fiction: Science Fiction 14
89. Fiction: Allegory 13
90. Fiction: Fantasy 13
91. Short Story Collections 13
92. Exposés 12
93. Travel 8
94. Sports 7

Comments:

* If you are a fiction writer, you are more likely to sell adult fiction (41 possible publishers—2 fewer than last year), than you are juvenile fiction (36 publishers—two more than last year) or teen fiction (26 publishers—three fewer than last year). The most popular genres with publishers are historical fiction (37), adventure and biblical (32 each), contemporary (31), and historical/romance (27). This remains the same as last year. Interest in both adult and teen fiction dropped this year, along with interest in fantasy and mystery romance. Interest increased in humorous, frontier/romance, frontier, historical, and literary fiction.

* If you are a poet, there are only 16 book publishers who publish poetry books (up two from last year), so you will probably have to self-publish (look for subsidy

publishers in this book), or sell to periodicals. Go to the topical listings in this book to find periodical markets.

* Compared to last year, the top 20 topics are virtually the same, with a slight difference in order. Bible Studies, Women's Issues, Theological, Spirituality, Christian Education, How-to/Self-Help, and Biography showed slight gains in interest this year. Family Life, Devotional Books, Parenting, Religion, and Current/Social Issues showed a slight decrease in interest.
* In a general comparison to last year, the following topics showed a significant increase or decrease in interest among the publishers. The numbers indicate how many places they moved up or down.

Decreased in interest:
Games/Crafts 14
World Issues 10
Fiction: Teen/Young Adult 9
Health 9
Drama 8
Fiction: Adult 7
Cookbooks 6
Fiction: Fantasy 6
Fiction: Mystery/Romance 6
Political 6
Controversial Issues 5
Gift Books 5

Increased in interest:
Economics 11
Christian School Books 8
Cults/Occult 8
Fiction: Humorous 7
Children's Picture Books 6
Fiction: Frontier/Romance 6
Science 6
Curriculum 5
Fiction: Frontier 5
Fiction: Historical 5
Fiction: Literary 5
Missionary 5
Sermons 5
Youth Programs 5

Comments:

* The following topics showed a decrease in interest for the second year in a row: Fiction: Teen/Young Adult, Gift Books, Drama, and Fiction: Fantasy.
* The following topics were down last year, but up this year: Fiction: Frontier/Romance, Fiction: Historical, and Cults/Occult.

* The following topics showed an increase in interest for the second year in a row: Economics, Science, and Missionary.

* The following topics were up last year, but down this year: Sermons, Games/Crafts, World Issues, Political, Controversial Issues, and Health.

SUMMARY OF INFORMATION ON CHRISTIAN BOOK PUBLISHERS FOUND IN THE ALPHABETICAL LISTINGS

Note: The following numbers are based on the maximum total estimate for each company. For example, if a company gave a range of 5-10, the averages were based on the higher number, 10.

TOTAL MANUSCRIPTS RECEIVED:

One-hundred-fifty-five publishers indicated they received a combined total of about 97,000 manuscripts during the year. That is an average of 625 manuscripts per editor, per year (that's a 10-11% drop from last year). The actual number of manuscripts received ranged from one to 10,000.

NUMBER OF BOOKS PUBLISHED:

One-hundred-eighty-eight publishers reported that they will publish a combined total of nearly 5,350 titles during the coming year. That is an average of 28.4 books per publisher (a decrease of 5% from last year). The actual number per publisher ranges from one to 267 (for a subsidy publisher). If each publisher actually publishes his maximum estimate of books for the year, only 5.5% of the manuscripts submitted will be published (that's an increase of .02% over last year).

AVERAGE FIRST PRINT RUN:

Based on 133 book publishers who indicated their average first print run, the average first printing of a book for a new author is about 5,550 books. That's an increase of about 3% over last year. Actual print runs ranged from 500 to 25,000 copies.

ROYALTIES:

Of the 167 publishers who reported that they paid royalties, 61 (36.5%) pay on the retail price; 78 (46.7%) pay on the wholesale price or net; and 28 (16.8%) didn't tell which. (Those percentages are virtually unchanged from last year.) The average royalty based on the retail price of the book was 8% to 11%. (Actual royalties varied from 2% to 15%.) The average royalty based on net varied from 10% to 13%. (Actual royalties varied from 4-30%.) The recommended royalty based on wholesale is 18%, but few Christian publishers are paying that much.

ADVANCES:

One-hundred-sixty-two publishers responded to the question about whether or not they paid advances. Of those, 55% pay advances (down from 59% last year) and 45% do not. Of those who pay advances, only 23% (37 publishers) gave a specific amount. The average advance for those 37 was $834-1153. The actual range was from $100 to $5,000. Of course, a number of these publishers pay more than that for established authors or potentially best-selling books. It is not unusual for a first author to get no advance or a small one. Once you have one or more books published, feel free to ask for an advance, and raise the amount for each book. Don't be afraid to ask for an advance, even on a first book, if you need the money to support you while you finish the manuscript.

REPORTING TIME:

Waiting for a response from an editor is often the hardest part of the writing business. Of the 175 editors who indicated how long you should have to wait for a response from them, the average time was 8-10 weeks. However, since the times they actually gave ranged from one to 26 weeks, be sure to check the listing for the publisher you are interested in. Give them a week or two grace period, then feel free to write a polite letter asking about the current status of your manuscript. Give them another month to respond, and if you don't hear anything, you can call as a last resort.

TOPICAL LISTINGS OF PERIODICALS

As soon as you have an article or story idea, look up that topic in the following topical listings (see Table of Contents for a full list of topics). Study the appropriate periodicals in the primary/alphabetical listings (as well as their writers' guidelines and sample copies), and select those that are most likely targets for the piece you are writing.

Note that most ideas can be written for more than one periodical if you slant them to the needs of different audiences; for example, money management for teens, or families, or senior citizens. Have a target periodical and audience in mind before you start writing. Each topic is divided by age-group/audience, so you can pick appropriate markets for your particular slant.

If the magazine prefers or requires a query letter, be sure to write that letter first and then follow any guidelines or suggestions they make if they give you a go-ahead.

R - TAKES REPRINTS

(*) - Indicates new topic this year.

BIBLE STUDIES

ADULT/GENERAL
ADVOCATE - R
America
Annals of St. Anne
Assoc Ref Presbyterian - R
Baptist Beacon - R
Baptist Informer
Bible Advocate - R
Bible Today
Canadian Catholic Review
Catholic Digest - R
Catholic Twin Circle - R
Charisma & Christian Life
Christian Century
Christian Standard - R
Church Herald
Church Herald/Holiness Banner - R
Compass
Conquest
Connecting Point - R
Creation Social Science - R
Emphasis/Faith & Living - R
Evangelical Baptist
Evangelical Friend
Family, The - R
Friends Journal - R
God's Revivalist - R
God's Special People - R
Hallelujah - R
Inspirer, The - R
John Milton - R
Life Advocate - R
Living Church
Lutheran, The
Lutheran Digest - R
Lutheran Layman
Lutheran Witness
Maranatha - R
Mennonite, The - R
Mennonite Brethren Herald - R
MESSAGE
MESSAGE of the Open Bible - R
Messenger, The (NC) - R
Messenger of St. Anthony - R
Ministry Today - R
Morning Glory - R
North American Voice
Other Side, The
Our Family - R
Our Sunday Visitor
Pentecostal Evangel
Pentecostal Homelife - R
Plowman, The
Presbyterian Outlook
Presbyterian Record - R
Presbyterian Survey - R
St. Willibrord Journal
Signs of the Times - R
Tree of Life
Wesleyan Advocate - R
Witness, The
Writer's Forum - R

CHILDREN
Crusader - R
Focus/Clubhouse/Clubhouse Jr
Touch - R

CHRISTIAN EDUCATION/LIBRARY
CE Connection - R
Christian School
Church Educator - R
GROUP
Leader - R
Lutheran Education
Shining Star
Youth Leader - R

MISSIONS
Childlife
Maryknoll
New World Outlook
Urban Mission - R

PASTORS/LEADERS
Christian Ministry
Congregational Journal
Cross Currents
Five Stones, The - R
Group's Jr High
Journal/Christian Healing - R
Liturgy
Lutheran Forum - R
Paraclete - R
Preacher's Magazine - R
Priest, The
PROCLAIM - R
Pulpit/Bible Study Helps - R
Quarterly Review
Review for Religious
Single Ad. Ministries Jour.
Word & World

TEEN/YOUNG ADULT
Certainty
Conqueror - R
event
High School I.D. - R
Kiln, The - R
Magazine/Youth! - R
Pathway I.D. - R
Student, The - R
Student Leadership - R
Teenage Christian - R
Young Adult Today
Young Salvationist - R

WOMEN
Anna's Journal - R
Church Woman
Co-Laborer - R
Contempo
Daughters of Sarah
Horizons - R
Lutheran Woman Today
Response
Royal Service
Salt and Light
Sisters Today - R
Woman's Touch - R

BOOK EXCERPTS

ADULT/GENERAL
Advent Christian Witness
African-American Heritage - R
All About Issues - R
Assoc Reformed Presbyterian - R
AXIOS - R
Better Tomorrow
Bible Advocate - R
Canadian Catholic Review
Charisma & Christian Life
Christian Century
Christian Edge - R
Christian Research - R
Christian Reader - R
Christian Single - R
Christianity Today - R
Church Herald/Holiness Banner - R
Columbia - R
Covenant Companion
Door, The
Emphasis/Faith & Living - R
Evangelical Friend
Expression
God's Revivalist - R
Gospel Tidings - R
Hallelujah - R
Home Life
Home Times - R
Indian Life - R
InterVarsity
John Milton - R
Journal/Christian Nursing - R
Kansas City Christian - R
Living - R
Maranatha - R
MESSAGE of the Open Bible - R
Ministry Today - R
Moody
Morning Glory - R
New Covenant - R
New Heart, A - R
New Thought Journal - R
Pentecostal Evangel
Presbyterian Outlook
Presbyterian Record - R
Religious Broadcasting - R
SCP Journal - R
Signs of the Times - R
Sunday Digest - R
Today's Better Life
Vista - R
Witness, The

CHILDREN
High Adventure - R

CHRISTIAN EDUCATION/LIBRARY
CE Connection - R
Changing Lives - R
Christian School
GROUP
Memos - R

MISSIONS
Aeropagus - R
Intl. Journal/Frontier - R
Maryknoll
World Vision - R

PASTORS/LEADERS
Bible-Science - R
Diaconalogue - R
Five Stones, The - R
Ivy Jungle Report - R
Journal/Christian Healing - R
Ministries Today
Networks - R
Single Ad. Ministries Jour.
Worldwide Challenge - R
Youthworker - R

TEEN/YOUNG ADULTS
Breakaway - R
Freeway - R
High School I.D. - R
Kiln, The - R
Straight - R
Young Salvationist - R

WOMEN
Co-Laborer - R
Conscience - R
Daughters of Sarah
Horizons - R
Link & Visitor - R
Parent Care - R
Today's Christian Woman
Women Alive! - R

WRITERS
Writers Connection - R
Writing Right - R

BOOK REVIEWS

ADULT/GENERAL
AGAIN - R
All About Issues - R
Anglican Journal - R
Assoc Ref Presbyterian - R
AXIOS - R
Burning Light - R
Canadian Catholic Review
Catholic Family Media Guide - R
Catholic Twin Circle - R
Charisma & Christian Life
Christian Century
Christian Courier (Canada) - R
Christian Edge - R

Christian Renewal - R
Christian Research - R
Christianity Today - R
ChristianWeek
Church Advocate, The - R
Compass
Congregational Journal
Connecting Point - R
Cornerstone - R
Creation Social Science - R
Cresset
Discovery - R
Evangelical Baptist
Expression
Friends Journal - R
Good News Journal
His Garden
Home Life
Home Times - R
Impact Magazine - R
Indian Life - R
Interim - R
Joyful Noise
Mennonite, The - R
John Milton - R
Minnesota Chronicle, The - R
National Catholic Reporter
National Christian Reporter
New Thought Journal - R
Parenting Treasures - R
Pentecostal Testimony - R
Perspectives on Science
Presbyterian Outlook
Presbyterian Record - R
Presbyterian Survey - R
Psychology for Living - R
Ratio
Religious Broadcasting - R
Religious Education
St. Anthony Messenger
SCP Journal - R
Servant
Shantyman, the - R
Spiritual Life
Spokane/Inland NW Christian
Thirteen Poetry
Touchstone
Tree of Life
United Methodist Reporter

CHILDREN

Skipping Stones

CHRISTIAN EDUCATION/LIBRARY

CE Counselor - R
Christian Librarian - R
Christian School Librarian's World - R
Memos - R
Vision - R
Youth & CE Leadership - R
Youth Leader - R

MISSIONS

Areopagus - R
Intl. Journal/Frontier - R
Missiology
New World Outlook
World Christian - R

MUSIC

Hymn, The
Worship Today - R

PASTORS/LEADERS

Advance - R
Bethany Choice - R
Christian Management - R
Christian Sentinel - R
Clergy Journal
Congregational Journal
Five Stones, The - R
Journal/Christian Healing - R
Ministries Today
Networks - R
Paraclete - R
Preacher's Magazine - R
Quarterly Review
Resource - R
Review for Religious
Search
Single Ad. Ministries Jour.
Word & World

TEEN/YOUNG ADULT

Insight - R
Magazine/Youth! - R
Student Leadership - R
Teenage Christian - R
You! - R
Young Salvationist - R

WOMEN

Co-Laborer - R
Conscience - R
Esprit - R
Parent Care - R
Wesleyan Woman
Woman's Touch - R

WRITERS

Canadian Writer's Jour - R
Christian Vision - R
Cross & Quill - R
Gotta Write
Writers Anchor - R
Writers Connection
Writer's Guidelines
Writer's Infor Network
Writer's Nook News
Writing Right - R

CELEBRITY PIECES

ADULT/GENERAL

All About Issues - R
American Tract Society - R
AXIOS - R
Beacon Christian News - R
Bookstore Journal - R
Canada Lutheran - R
Canadian Catholic Review
Catholic Digest - R
Catholic Family Media Guide - R
Catholic Sentinel - R
Catholic Twin Circle - R
Charisma & Christian Life
Christian Reader - R
Christian Single - R
Christianity Today - R
Columbia - R
Companion
Critic, The
Door, The
Emphasis/Faith & Living - R
Expression
Family, The - R
Good News, Etc - R
Guideposts
Herald of Holiness - R
Home Life
Home Times - R
John Milton - R
Kansas City Christian - R
Indian Life - R
Living - R
Lutheran Layman
Maranatha - R
Mature Years - R
MESSAGE
Messenger, The (NC) - R
Minnesota Chronicle, The - R
Ministry Today - R
National Christian Reporter
New Thought Journal - R
Our Sunday Visitor
Parents of Teenagers

Pentecostal Evangel
Pentecostal Testimony - R
Presbyterian Record - R
Pursuit - R
St. Anthony Messenger
Signs of the Times - R
Sports Spectrum
Standard - R
Sunday Digest - R
United Methodist Reporter
Vibrant Life - R
Writer's Forum - R

CHILDREN
Church Outreach - R
Counselor
Crusader - R
Faith 'n Stuff
GUIDE - R
My Friend
Pockets - R

CHRISTIAN EDUCATION/LIBRARY
Changing Lives - R
Teachers in Focus

MISSIONS
IMPACT
Worldwide Challenge - R

TEEN/YOUNG ADULT
Breakaway - R
Brio
Edge, The - R
Event
HiCall - R (Chr. athletes)
High School I.D. - R
Insight - R
Insight/Out - R
Magazine/Youth! - R
Spirit
Straight - R
Teenage Christian - R
You! - R
Young Salvationist - R

WOMEN
Today's Christian Woman

WRITERS
Christian Communicator - R
Exchange - R
Gotta Write
Writer's Infor Network

CHRISTIAN BUSINESS

ADULT/GENERAL
Annals of St. Anne
AXIOS - R
Beacon Christian News - R
Bookstore Journal - R
Canada Lutheran - R
Catholic Digest - R
Catholic Twin Circle - R
Charisma & Christian Life
Christian Century
Christian Courier (Canada)
Christian Reader - R
Christian Retailing
Christian Single - R
Christianity Today - R
Decision
Discovery - R
Emphasis/Faith & Living - R
Evangelical Visitor - R
Expression
Faith Today
God's Revivalist - R
Guideposts
Herald of Holiness - R
Home Times - R
InterVarsity
Kansas City Christian
Maranatha - R
Mature Years - R
Mennonite, The - R
MESSAGE
Messenger, The (NC) - R
Messenger of St. Anthony - R
Ministry Today - R
Minnesota Chronicle, The - R
Nat/Intl Religion Report
New Covenant - R
PCA Messenger - R
Pentecostal Evangel
Pentecostal Homelife - R
Presbyterian Record - R
Religious Broadcasting - R
Social Justice Review
Tree of Life
Writer's Forum - R

MISSIONS
Childlife
World Vision - R
Worldwide Challenge - R

PASTORS/LEADERS
Advance - R
Christian Management - R
Clergy Journal
Faith & Renewal - R
Today's Parish
Your Church - R

TEEN/YOUNG ADULT
Teenage Christian - R

WOMEN
Lutheran Woman Today
Salt and Light
Woman's Touch - R

CHRISTIAN EDUCATION

ADULT/GENERAL
America
Anglican Journal - R
Annals of St. Anne
Assoc Ref Presbyterian - R
AXIOS - R
Baptist Informer
B.C. Catholic - R
Canada Lutheran - R
Canadian Catholic Review
Catholic Accent
Catholic Digest - R
Catholic Parent
Catholic Twin Circle - R
Charisma & Christian Life
Christian Century
Christian C.L. RECORD - R
Christian Courier (Canada) - R
Christian Edge - R
Christian Home & School
Christian Parenting Today - R
Christian Reader - R
Christianity Today - R
Church Herald/Holiness Banner - R
Columbia - R
Compass
Covenant Companion
Creation Social Science - R
Decision
Discovery - R
Emphasis/Faith & Living - R
Evangelical Baptist
Evangelical Beacon
Evangelical Friend
Evangelical Visitor - R
Faith Today
God's Revivalist - R
Good News, Etc - R

Herald of Holiness - R
John Milton - R
Joyful Noise
Kansas City Christian - R
Liguorian
Living Church
Lookout - R
Lutheran Digest - R
Maranatha - R
Mature Years - R
Mennonite, The - R
Mennonite Brethren Herald - R
MESSAGE
Messenger, The (Canada) - R
Messenger, The (NC) - R
Messenger of St. Anthony - R
Ministry Today - R
Minnesota Chronicle, The - R
National Christian Reporter
New Covenant - R
North American Voice
NW Christian Journal - R
Our Family - R
Our Sunday Visitor
Parenting Treasures - R
Parents of Teenagers
PCA Messenger - R
Pentecostal Evangel
Pentecostal Homelife - R
Pentecostal Testimony - R
Plowman, The
Presbyterian Outlook
Presbyterian Record - R
Religious Education
SCP Journal - R
Social Justice Review
Table Talk - R
Tree of Life
United Church Observer - R
United Methodist Reporter
Vista - R
Witness, The
Writer's Forum - R

CHRISTIAN EDUCATION/LIBRARY
(See Alphabetical listings)

MISSIONS
Compassion Update - R
Maryknoll
World Vision - R

PASTORS/LEADERS
Advance - R
Bible-Science - R
Christian Management - R
Church Administration
Church Business - R
Discipleship Training
Faith & Renewal - R
Five Stones, The - R
Groups's Jr High
Ministries Today
Networks - R
Pastoral Life - R - R
Preacher's Magazine - R
Pulpit/Bible Study Helps - R
Quarterly Review
Resource - R
Review for Religious
Search
Today's Parish
Word & World
Youthworker - R

TEEN/YOUNG ADULT
Conqueror - R
You! - R
Young Salvationist - R

WOMEN
Esprit - R
Lutheran Woman Today
Response
Salt and Light
Woman's Touch - R

CHRISTIAN LIVING

ADULT/GENERAL
ADVOCATE - R
Alive! - R
alive now! - R
All About Issues - R
America
American Tract Society - R
Annals of St. Anne
Arkansas Catholic
Assoc Ref Presbyterian - R
At Ease - R
AXIOS - R
Baptist Beacon - R
B.C. Catholic - R
Better Tomorrow
Bible Advocate - R
Canada Lutheran - R
Canadian Catholic Review
Catholic Digest - R
Catholic New York
Catholic Parent
Catholic Sentinel - R
Catholic Twin Circle - R
Charisma & Christian Life
Christian Courier - R
Christian Courier (Canada) - R
Christian Edge - R
Christian Home & School
Christian Living - R
Christian Parenting Today - R
Christian Reader - R
Christian Renewal - R
Christian Single - R
Christian Standard - R
Christianity Today - R
Church Herald
Church Herald/Holiness Banner - R
Church of God Evangel
Columbia - R
Commonweal
Companion
Companions - R
Connecting Point - R
Conquest
Cornerstone - R
Covenant Companion
Decision
Discipleship Journal - R
Emphasis/Faith & Living - R
Evangel - R
Evangelical Baptist
Evangelical Beacon - R
Evangelical Friend
Evangelical Visitor - R
Family, The - R
Family Digest, The - R
Fellowship Today - R
Focus on the Family - R
Foursquare World ADVANCE - R
Gem, The - R
God's Revivalist - R
God's Special People - R
Good News - R
Good News, Etc - R
Gospel Tidings - R
Guideposts
Hallelujah - R
Herald of Holiness - R
Home Times - R
Impact Magazine - R
Indian Life - R
Inspirer, The - R
Interim - R
InterVarsity
John Milton - R
Journal/Christian Nursing - R
Kansas City Christian - R
Lifeglow - R

Light and Life
Liguorian
Live - R
Living - R
Living Church
Lookout - R
Lutheran, The
Lutheran Digest - R
Lutheran Layman
Maranatha - R
Marian Helpers Bulletin - R
Mature Years - R
Mennonite, The - R
Mennonite Brethren Herald - R
MESSAGE
MESSAGE of the Open Bible - R
Messenger, The (Canada) - R
Messenger, The (NC) - R
Messenger of St. Anthony - R
Messenger of the Sacred Heart
Ministry Today - R
Moody
Morning Glory - R
National Christian Reporter
New Covenant - R
New Oxford Review
North American Voice
Other Side, The
Our Family - R
Our Sunday Visitor
Parenting Treasures - R
Parents of Teenagers
PCA Messenger - R
Pentecostal Evangel
Pentecostal Homelife - R
Pentecostal Messenger - R
Pentecostal Testimony - R
Positive Approach - R
Power for Living - R
Presbyterian Record - R
Presbyterian Survey - R
PROGRESS - R
Psychology for Living - R
Purpose - R
St. Anthony Messenger
SCP Journal - R
Seek - R
Servant
Sharing - R
Signs of the Times - R
Social Justice Review
Standard - R
Sunday Digest - R
Table Talk - R
Today's Better Life
Tree of Life
United Church Observer - R
United Methodist Reporter
U.S. Catholic
Vision (MO) - R
Vista - R
Vital Christianity - R
War Cry
Wesleyan Advocate
Witness, The
Writer's Forum - R

CHILDREN
GUIDE - R
High Adventure - R
Junior Trails - R
Partners - R
Primary Pal
Touch - R
Wonder Time

CHRISTIAN EDUCATION/LIBRARY
Brigade Leader - R
Changing Lives - R
Church Educator - R
Lutheran Education
Perspective - R
Shining Star
Youth Leader - R

MISSIONS
American Horizon - R
Maryknoll
Worldwide Challenge - R

PASTORS/LEADERS
Advance - R
Diaconalogue - R
Discipleship Training
Eucharistic Minister - R
Faith & Renewal - R
Five Stones, The - R
Journal/Christian Healing - R
Media Update
Ministries Today
Pastoral Life - R
Preacher's Illus. Service - R
Preacher's Magazine - R
Pulpit/Bible Study Helps - R
Review for Religious
Word & World

TEEN/YOUNG ADULT
Certainty
Challenge (IL)
Conqueror - R
Edge, The - R
event
Freeway - R
HiCall - R
High School I.D. - R
Insight - R
Insight/Out - R
Kiln, The - R
Magazine/Youth! - R
Student Leadership - R
Teenage Christian - R
Teen Life - R
Teen Power - R
Teen Quest - R
Venture - R
YOU! - R
Young Adult Today
Young & Alive - R
Young Salvationist - R
Youth World - R

WOMEN
Co-Laborer - R
Daughters of Sarah
Esprit - R
Helping Hand - R
Horizons - R
Link & Visitor - R
Lutheran Woman Today
Salt and Light
Sisters Today - R
Today's Christian Woman
Virtue - R
Woman's Touch - R
Women Alive! - R

CHURCH MANAGEMENT

ADULT/GENERAL
Acts 29
AXIOS - R
Canada Lutheran - R
Canadian Catholic Review
Christian Century
Christian Edge - R
Church of God Evangel
Covenant Companion
Emphasis/Faith & Living - R
Good News, Etc - R
John Milton - R
Joyful Noise
Kansas City Christian - R
Living Church
Lutheran Digest - R
MESSAGE of the Open Bible - R
Ministry Today - R

Nat/Intl Religion Report
NW Christian Journal - R
Our Sunday Visitor
Presbyterian Outlook
United Methodist Reporter
Wesleyan Advocate

CHRISTIAN EDUCATION/LIBRARY

CE Connection - R
Leader - R
Leader/Church School Today

PASTORS/LEADERS

Advance - R
Christian Management - R
Church Growth Network- R
Group's Jr High
Leadership Journal - R
Pastoral Life - R
Preacher's Magazine - R
Priest, The
Pulpit/Bible Study Helps - R
Resource - R
Word & World
Worship Leader
Your Church - R
Youthworker - R

CHURCH OUTREACH

ADULT/GENERAL

Acts 29
Advent Christian Witness
ADVOCATE - R
Alive! - R
America
Assoc Ref Presbyterian - R
At Ease - R
AXIOS - R
Baptist Beacon - R
Baptist Informer
Bible Advocate - R
Canada Lutheran - R
Canadian Catholic Review
Catholic Sentinel - R
Catholic Twin Circle - R
Charisma & Christian Life
Christian Edge - R
Christian Reader - R
Christianity Today - R
Church Herald
Church Herald/Holiness Banner - R
Columbia - R
Companion
Companions - R
Cornerstone - R
Covenant Companion
Decision
Emphasis/Faith & Living - R
Episcopal Life - R
Evangel - R
Evangelical Beacon - R
Evangelical Friend
Evangelical Visitor - R
Expression
Faith Today
Family, The - R
Fellowship Today - R
God's Revivalist - R
Good News - R
Good News, Etc - R
Inspirer, The - R
Interchange
John Milton - R
Kansas City Christian - R
Light and Life
Living Church
Lookout - R
Lutheran, The
Lutheran Digest - R
Lutheran Layman
Maranatha - R
Mature Years - R
Mennonite, The - R
Mennonite Brethren Herald - R
Mennonite Reporter
MESSAGE
MESSAGE of the Open Bible - R
Messenger, The (Canada) - R
Messenger, The (NC) - R
Messenger of St. Anthony - R
Ministry Today - R
Moody
National Christian Reporter
Nat/Intl Religion Report
New Covenant - R
New Oxford Review
North American Voice
NW Christian Journal - R
Other Side, The
Our Family - R
Our Sunday Visitor
Pentecostal Evangel
Pentecostal Messenger - R
Pentecostal Testimony - R
Positive Approach - R
Presbyterian Outlook
Presbyterian Record - R
Presbyterian Survey - R
Purpose - R
Religious Broadcasting - R
Religious Education
St. Joseph Messenger - R
SCP Journal - R
Seek - R
Sharing - R
Social Justice Review
Sunday Digest - R
Tree of Life
United Church Observer - R
United Methodist Reporter
Vista - R
Wesleyan Advocate

CHILDREN

High Adventure - R

CHRISTIAN EDUCATION/LIBRARY

CE Connection - R
CE Counselor - R
Changing Lives - R
Church Educator - R
Church Recreation - R
Insight - R
Leader - R
Lutheran Education
Perspective - R
Youth & CE Leadership - R
Youth Leader - R

MISSIONS

American Horizon - R
Catholic Near East
Childlife
Compassion Update - R
IMPACT
Intl. Journal/Frontier - R
Maryknoll
Urban Mission - R
Worldwide Challenge - R

PASTORS/LEADERS

Advance - R
Bible-Science - R
Church Administration
Church Growth Network - R
Faith & Renewal - R
Five Stones, The - R
Group's Jr High
Growing Churches
Leadership Journal - R
Ministries Today
Pastoral Life - R
Preacher's Magazine - R
Priest, The
Pulpit/Bible Study Helps - R
Resource - R

Review for Religious
Search
Single Ad. Ministries Jour.
Today's Parish
Word & World

TEEN/YOUNG ADULT
Freeway - R
HiCall - R
Insight - R
Insight/Out - R
Magazine/Youth! - R
Teen Power - R
YOU! - R
Young Adult Today

WOMEN
Esprit - R
Horizons - R
Lutheran Woman Today
Sisters Today - R
Wesleyan Woman
Woman's Touch - R

CONTROVERSIAL ISSUES

ADULT/GENERAL
ADVOCATE - R
AFA Journal - R
All About Issues - R
American Tract Society - R
Answers in Action
At Ease - R
AXIOS - R
Beacon Christian News - R
Bible Advocate - R
Canada Lutheran - R
Canadian Catholic Review
Charisma & Christian Life
Christian Century
Christian Courier (Canada) - R
Christian Single - R
Christian Research - R
Christian Social Action
Christianity Today - R
Columbia - R
Commonweal
Compass
Cornerstone - R
Covenant Companion
Creation Social Science - R
Cresset
Critic, The
Door, The
Episcopal Life - R
Evangelical Friend
Expression
Faith Today
Family, The - R
God's Special People - R
Good News, Etc - R
Hallelujah - R
Home Life
Home Times - R
John Milton - R
Journal/Christian Camping - R
Journal/Christian Nursing - R
Joyful Noise
Kansas City Christian - R
Life Advocate - R
Light and Life
Living Church
Lookout - R
Lutheran, The
Lutheran Witness
Maranatha - R
Mature Years - R
Mennonite Brethren Herald - R
Messenger, The (NC) - R
Messenger of St. Anthony - R
Minnesota Chronicle, The - R
Moody
National Catholic Reporter
National Christian Reporter
Nat/Intl Religion Report
New Oxford Review
New Thought Journal - R
Other Side, The
Our Family - R
Parents of Teenagers
Pentecostal Evangel
Pentecostal Testimony - R
Presbyterian Outlook
Presbyterian Record - R
Presbyterian Survey - R
Religious Education
Religious Broadcasting - R
St. Anthony Messenger
SCP Journal - R
Seek - R
Social Justice Review
Table Talk - R
United Methodist Reporter
Vista - R
War Cry
Wesleyan Advocate
Witness, The
Writer's Forum - R

CHILDREN
Faith 'n Stuff

CHRISTIAN EDUCATION/LIBRARY
CE Connection - R
CE Counselor - R
Youth Leader - R

MISSIONS
American Horizon - R
Maryknoll
Worldwide Challenge - R

PASTORS/LEADERS
Bethany Choice - R
Christian Sentinel - R
Congregational Journal
Cross Currents
Diaconalogue - R
Faith & Renewal - R
Group's Jr High
Lutheran Forum - R
Media Update
Ministries Today
Networks - R
Pastoral Life - R
Preacher's Magazine - R
Resource - R
Search
Single Ad. Ministries Jour.
Word & World
Youthworker - R

TEEN/YOUNG ADULT
Brio
Conqueror - R
Freeway - R
HiCall - R
Insight/Out - R
Issues & Answers - R
Kiln, The - R
Magazine/Youth! - R
Straight - R
Student Leadership - R
Teenage Christian - R
You! - R
Young Adult Today
Young Salvationist - R

WOMEN
Conscience - R
Daughters of Sarah
Esprit - R
Horizons - R

CULTS/OCCULT

ADULT/GENERAL

Acts 29
America
American Tract Society - R
AXIOS - R
Baptist Beacon - R
Bible Advocate - R
Canada Lutheran - R
Catholic Digest - R
Catholic Twin Circle - R
Charisma & Christian Life
Christian Research - R
Christianity Today - R
Church Herald/Holiness Banner - R
COMMENTS - R
Companions - R
Conquest
Cornerstone - R
Creation Social Science - R
Evangelical Friend
Good News, Etc - R
John Milton - R (sects)
Journal/Christian Nursing - R
Journal/Church & State
Kansas City Christian - R
Light and Life
Lutheran Digest - R
Maranatha - R
MESSAGE of the Open Bible - R
Messenger, The (NC) - R
Minnesota Chronicle, The - R
Moody
Nat/Intl Religion Report
New Heart, A - R
New Oxford Review
New Thought Journal - R
Our Sunday Visitor
Pentecostal Evangel
Pentecostal Messenger - R
Pentecostal Testimony - R
Power for Living - R
Psychology for Living - R
SCP Journal - R
Vista - R
VISION - R

CHILDREN

Crusader - R

CHRISTIAN EDUCATION/LIBRARY

Team - R
Youth Leader - R

MISSIONS

American Horizon - R
Areopagus - R
IMPACT
World Christian - R

PASTORS/LEADERS

Christian Sentinel - R
Discipleship Training
Faith & Renewal - R
Journal/Christian Healing - R
Preacher's Magazine - R
Word & World

TEEN/YOUNG ADULT

Brio
Certainty
Challenge (IL)
Freeway - R
HiCall - R
High School I.D. - R
Insight - R
Insight/Out - R
Issues & Answers - R
Kiln, The - R
Magazine/Youth! - R
Pathway I.D. - R
Straight - R
Student, The - R
Teenage Christian - R
Teen Power - R
Teen Quest - R
YOU! - R
Young Adult Today
Young Salvationist - R
Youth Update

WOMEN

Woman's Touch - R

CURRENT/ SOCIAL ISSUES

ADULT/GENERAL

ADVOCATE - R
AFA Journal - R
AGAIN - R
Alive! - R
alive now! - R
All About Issues - R
America
American Tract Society - R
Anglican Journal - R
Arlington Catholic Herald
Assoc Ref Presbyterian - R
AXIOS - R
Baptist Informer
B.C. Catholic - R
Beacon Christian News - R
Bible Advocate - R
Bookstore Journal - R
Canada Lutheran - R
Canadian Catholic Review
Catholic Courier
Catholic New York
Catholic Parent
Catholic Sentinel - R
Catholic Twin Circle - R
Charisma & Christian Life
Christian Century
Christian Courier - R
Christian Courier (Canada) - R
Christian Crusade
Christian Home & School
Christian Living - R
Christian Reader - R
Christian Renewal - R
Christian Research - R
Christian Single - R
Christian Social Action
Christian Standard - R
Christianity Today - R
Church & State - R
Church Herald
Church Herald/Holiness Banner - R
Columbia - R
Commonweal
Companions - R
Compass
Conquest
Cornerstone - R
Covenant Companion
Creation Social Science - R
Cresset
Critic, The
Discipleship Journal - R
Door, The
Emphasis/Faith & Living - R
Episcopal Life - R
Evangelical Baptist
Evangelical Friend
Evangelical Visitor - R
Faith Today
Family, The - R
Fellowship Today - R
Friends Journal - R
God's Special People - R
Good News - R
Good News, Etc - R
Good News Journal
Gospel Tidings - R

Hallelujah - R
Herald of Holiness - R
Home Times - R
Impact Magazine - R
Interim - R
InterVarsity
John Milton - R
Journal/Christian Nursing - R
Journal/Church & State
Kansas City Christian - R
Liberty - R
Life Advocate - R
Light and Life
Liguorian
Live - R
Lookout - R
Lutheran, The
Lutheran Journal - R
Lutheran Layman
Maranatha - R
Marion Helpers Bulletin
Mature Living
Mennonite, The - R
Mennonite Brethren Herald - R
Mennonite Reporter
MESSAGE
MESSAGE of the Open Bible - R
Messenger, The (NC) - R
Messenger of St. Anthony - R
Ministry Today - R
Minnesota Chronicle, The - R
Montana Catholic
Moody
National Christian Reporter
National/Intl Religion Report
New Covenant - R
New Heart, A - R
New Oxford Review
New Thought Journal - R
North American Voice
NW Christian Journal - R
Other Side, The
Our Family - R
Our Sunday Visitor
Pentecostal Evangel
Pentecostal Homelife - R
Pentecostal Messenger - R
Pentecostal Testimony - R
Plowman, The
Power for Living - R
Presbyterian Outlook
Presbyterian Record - R
Presbyterian Survey - R
Psychology for Living - R
Purpose - R
Quiet Revolution - R
Religious Broadcasting - R
Religious Education
Review for Religious
St. Anthony Messenger - R
St. Joseph Messenger - R
Salt
SCP Journal - R
Seek - R
Servant
Signs of the Times - R
Social Justice Review
Standard - R
Star of Zion
Touchstone
Tree of Life
United Methodist Reporter
Vista - R
Vital Christianity - R
War Cry
Wesleyan Advocate
Witness, The
World
Writer's Forum - R

CHILDREN

Crusader - R
God's World Today
GUIDE - R
High Adventure - R
Skipping Stones

CHRISTIAN EDUCATION/LIBRARY

Brigade Leader - R
CE Connection - R
CE Counselor - R
Memos - R
Team - R
Today's Catholic Teacher - R
Vision - R
Youth Leader - R

MISSIONS

American Horizon - R
Areopagus - R
Childlife - R
Compassion Update - R
IMPACT
P.I.M.E. World - R
Urban Mission - R
World Christian - R
World Vision - R
Worldwide Challenge - R

PASTORS/LEADERS

Advance - R
Bible-Science - R
Christian Sentinel - R
Church Growth Network - R
Diaconalogue - R
Discipleship Training
Faith & Renewal - R
Five Stones, The - R
Ivy Jungle Report - R
Liturgy
Lutheran Forum - R
Media Update
Ministries Today
Pastoral Life - R
Preacher's Magazine - R
Resource - R
Search
Single Ad. Ministries Jour.
Word & World
Youthworker - R

TEEN/YOUNG ADULT

Brio
Certainty
Conqueror - R
event
Freeway - R
HiCall - R
High School I.D. - R
Insight - R
Insight/Out - R
Issues & Answers - R
Kiln, The - R
Magazine/Youth! - R
Pathway I.D. -R
Pioneer - R
Straight - R
Student, The - R
Student Leadership - R
Teenage Christian - R
Teen Power - R
Teen Quest - R
Venture - R
With - R
YOU! - R
Young Adult Today
Young Salvationist - R
Youth Update

WOMEN

Co-Laborer - R
Conscience - R
Contempo
Daughters of Sarah
Esprit - R
Horizons - R
Jour/Women's Ministries
Link & Visitor - R
Lutheran Woman Today
Response
Royal Service

Salt and Light
Sisters Today - R
Today's Christian Woman
Virtue - R
Wesleyan Woman
Woman's Touch - R

DEVOTIONALS/ MEDITATIONS

ADULT/GENERAL
Acts 29
alive now! - R
Annals of St. Anne
Assoc Ref Presbyterian - R
At Ease - R
Baptist Beacon - R
Baptist Informer
Bible Advocate - R
Broken Streets
Burning Light - R
Canadian Catholic Review
Catholic Digest - R
Catholic Twin Circle - R
Charisma & Christian Life
Christian Century
Christian Living - R
Christian Reader - R
Christian Renewal - R
Christianity Today - R
Companion
Companions - R
Conquest
Cornerstone - R
Covenant Companion
Creation Social Science - R
Emphasis/Faith & Living - R
Evangel - R
Evangelical Baptist
Evangelical Friend
Family Digest, The - R
Fellowship Today - R
Foursquare World ADVANCE - R
Friends Journal - R
God's Revivalist - R
Gospel Tidings - R
Inspirer, The - R
John Milton - R
Kansas City Christian - R
Lifeglow - R
Light and Life
Liguorian
Living Church
Lookout - R
Lutheran Journal - R
Lutheran Witness
Maranatha - R
Mennonite Brethren Herald - R
MESSAGE
MESSAGE of the Open Bible - R
Messenger, The (Canada) - R
Messenger, The (NC) - R
Messenger of St. Anthony - R
Messenger of the Sacred Heart
Morning Glory - R
New Covenant - R
New Heart, A - R
North American Voice
Our Sunday Visitor
Pentecostal Evangel
Pentecostal Homelife - R
Pentecostal Messenger - R
Prayer Line, The - R
Presbyterian Record - R
Presbyterian Survey - R
Prism
Queen of All Hearts
Seek - R
Sharing - R
Standard - R
Starlight
Today's Single - R
War Cry

CHILDREN
Focus/Clubhouse/Clubhouse Jr
GUIDE - R
High Adventure - R
Keys for Kids - R
Power & Light - R
Primary Pal

CHRISTIAN EDUCATION/LIBRARY
Church Recreation - R
Church Worship
KEY - R
Lutheran Education
Today's Catholic Teacher - R

DAILY DEVOTIONAL
(See alphabetical list)

MISSIONS
Areopagus - R

PASTORS/LEADERS
Christian Ministry
Diaconalogue - R
Five Stones, The - R
Journal/Christian Healing - R
Preacher's Magazine - R
Priest, The
Pulpit/Bible Study Helps - R
Review for Religious

TEEN/YOUNG ADULT
Breakaway - R
Brio
Certainty
Challenge (IL)
Conqueror - R
High School I.D. - R
Insight - R
Insight/Out - R
Magazine/Youth! - R
Straight - R
Take Five - R
Teenage Christian - R
YOU! - R
Young Adult Today
Young Salvationist - R

WOMEN
Co-Laborer - R
Daughters of Sarah
Esprit - R
Helping Hand - R
Horizons - R
Jour/Women's Ministries
Lutheran Woman Today
Parent Care - R
Response
Salt and Light
Woman's Touch - R
Women Alive! - R

WRITERS
Cross & Quill - R

DISCIPLESHIP

ADULT/GENERAL
Acts 29
American Tract Society - R
At Ease - R
Baptist Beacon - R
Bible Advocate - R
Canada Lutheran - R
Canadian Catholic Review
Catholic Digest - R
Catholic Sentinel - R
Christian Century
Christian Living - R
Christian Parenting Today - R
Christianity Today - R
Church Herald/Holiness Banner - R
Companion
Cornerstone - R
Covenant Companion
Decision
Discipleship Journal - R
Emphasis/Faith & Living - R

Evangel - R
Gospel Tidings - R
Hallelujah - R
Herald of Holiness - R
Indian Life - R
John Milton - R
Kansas City Christian - R
Light and Life
Liguorian
Living Church
Lookout - R
Lutheran Digest - R
Maranatha - R
Mature Years - R
Mennonite, The - R
Mennonite Brethren Herald - R
Messenger, The (Canada) - R
Ministry Today - R
Moody
National Christian Reporter
New Covenant - R
New Oxford Review
Our Family - R
Parents of Teenagers
Pentecostal Evangel
Pentecostal Homelife - R
Pentecostal Messenger - R
Pentecostal Testimony - R
Power for Living - R
Prism
Purpose - R
Religious Education
St. Joseph Messenger - R
Seek - R
Standard - R
Sunday Digest - R
United Methodist Reporter
Vision (MO) - R
Vista - R
Vital Christianity - R
Wesleyan Advocate - R
Witness, The

CHILDREN
High Adventure - R

CHRISTIAN EDUCATION/LIBRARY
CE Connection - R
CE Counselor - R
Changing Lives - R
Christian School
Church Educator - R
Leader - R
Team - R
Youth & CE Leadership - R
Youth Leader - R

MISSIONS
American Horizon - R
Urban Mission - R
Worldwide Challenge - R

MUSIC
Worship Today - R

PASTORS/LEADERS
Advance - R
Church Growth Network - R
Group's Jr High
Ivy Jungle Report - R
Journal/Christian Healing - R
Ministries Today
Preacher's Magazine - R
PROCLAIM - R
Pulpit/Bible Study Helps - R
Quarterly Review
Resource - R
Review for Religious
Word & World
Youthworker - R

TEEN/YOUNG ADULT
Conqueror - R
Edge, The - R
Freeway - R
High School I.D. - R
Insight - R
Kiln, The - R
Magazine/Youth! - R
Straight - R
Student Leadership - R
Teenage Christian - R
Teen Power - R
Young Salvationist - R

WOMEN
Co-Laborer - R
Esprit - R
Helping Hand - R
Link & Visitor - R
Today's Christian Woman
Virtue - R
Women Alive! - R

DIVORCE

ADULT/GENERAL
America
At Ease - R
Bible Advocate - R
Canada Lutheran - R
Catholic Digest - R
Catholic Twin Circle - R
Charisma & Christian Life
Christian Home & School
Christian Living - R
Christian Parenting Today - R
Christian Single - R
Church Herald/Holiness Banner - R
Family, The - R
Focus on the Family - R
Friends Journal - R
Good News, Etc - R
Hallelujah - R
Home Life
Home Times - R
Impact Magazine - R
John Milton - R
Jour/Religion in Psychotherapy
Jour/Religious Gerontology
Kansas City Christian - R
Liguorian
Living - R
Lookout - R
Lutheran Digest - R
Maranatha - R
Mature Years - R
Mennonite, The - R
MESSAGE
MESSAGE of the Open Bible - R
Messenger, The (NC) - R
Minnesota Chronicle, The - R
Moody
National Christian Reporter
New Covenant - R
New Heart, A - R
Our Family - R
Parents of Teenagers
PCA Messenger - R
Pentecostal Evangel
Pentecostal Messenger - R
Power for Living - R
Presbyterian Record - R
Presbyterian Survey - R
Psychology for Living - R
Seek - R
Signs of the Times - R
Smart Dads
Standard - R
Table Talk - R
Today's Single - R
United Methodist Reporter
U.S. Catholic
VISION - R
Vista - R
Vital Christianity - R
CHILDREN GUIDE - R

CHRISTIAN EDUCATION/LIBRARY
Lutheran Education

MISSIONS
Worldwide Challenge - R

PASTORS/LEADERS
Chicago Studies
Faith & Renewal - R
Ministries Today
Pastoral Life - R
Preacher's Magazine - R
PROCLAIM - R
Pulpit/Bible Study Helps - R
Single Ad. Ministries Jour.
Word & World

TEEN/YOUNG ADULT
Insight - R
Insight/Out - R
Magazine/Youth! - R
With - R
YOU! - R
Young Adult Today
Youth Update

WOMEN
Daughters of Sarah
Esprit - R
Helping Hand - R
Lutheran Woman Today
Salt and Light
Today's Christian Woman
Virtue - R
Woman's Touch - R

DOCTRINAL

ADULT/GENERAL
ADVOCATE - R
America
Anglican Journal - R
Assoc Ref Presbyterian - R
At Ease - R
Baptist Beacon - R
Baptist Informer
B.C. Catholic - R
Bible Advocate - R
Canadian Catholic Review
Catholic Digest - R
Christian Century
Christian Reader - R
Christian Renewal - R
Christian Research - R
Christianity Today - R
Church Herald/Holiness Banner - R
Church of God Evangel
Companions - R
Compass
Cornerstone - R
Cresset
Critic, The
Emphasis/Faith & Living - R
Evangelical Baptist
Evangelical Friend
Evangelical Visitor - R
God's Revivalist - R
Good News - R
Hallelujah - R
Interim - R
John Milton - R
Kansas City Christian - R
Liguorian
Living Church
Lutheran Layman
Lutheran Witness
Maranatha - R
Mennonite Brethren Herald - R
Messenger, The (NC) - R
Messenger of St. Anthony - R
Ministry Today - R
New Thought Journal - R
North American Voice
Our Family - R
Our Sunday Visitor
Pentecostal Evangel
Pentecostal Testimony - R
Presbyterian Outlook
Presbyterian Record - R
Presbyterian Survey - R
Queen of All Hearts
St. Willibrord Journal
SCP Journal - R
Sharing - R
Signs of the Times - R
Social Justice Review
Tree of Life

CHRISTIAN EDUCATION/LIBRARY
CE Counselor - R
Lutheran Education
Youth Leader - R

MISSION
Urban Mission - R
Worldwide Challenge - R

PASTORS/LEADERS
Advance - R
Bible-Science - R
Chicago Studies
Congregational Journal
Discipleship Training
Homiletic & Pastoral Review
Lutheran Forum - R
Paraclete - R
Preacher's Magazine - R
Priest, The
PROCLAIM - R
Pulpit/Bible Study Helps - R
Review for Religious
Word & World

TEEN/YOUNG ADULT
event
High School I.D. - R
Magazine/Youth! - R
YOU! - R
Young Adult Today
Youth Update

WOMEN
Lutheran Woman Today
Sisters Today - R
Woman's Touch - R

ECONOMICS

ADULT/GENERAL
All About Issues - R
America
AXIOS - R
Bookstore Journal - R
Canadian Catholic Review
Catholic Sentinel - R
Catholic Twin Circle - R
Christian Century
Christian C.L. RECORD - R
Christian Courier (Canada) - R
Christian Parenting Today - R
Christian Retailing
Christian Social Action
Christianity Today - R
Compass
Creation Social Science - R
Cresset
Discovery - R
Evangelical Friend
Expression
Faith Today
Good News, Etc - R
Home Times - R
John Milton - R
Kansas City Christian - R
Mennonite, The - R
Minnesota Chronicle, The - R
Moody

National Christian Reporter
Other Side, The
Our Sunday Visitor
Parents of Teenagers
PCA Messenger - R
Pentecostal Messenger - R
Prism
Quiet Revolution - R
SCP Journal - R
Social Justice Review
Sunday Digest - R
Today's Better Life
United Methodist Reporter
Vista - R
Witness, The
Writer's Forum - R

MISSIONS
IMPACT
Urban Mission - R

PASTORS/LEADERS
Cross Currents
Five Stones, The - R
Pastoral Life - R
Preacher's Magazine - R
Today's Parish
Word & World
Your Church - R

TEEN/YOUNG ADULT
Issues & Answers - R
Young Adult Today
Youth Update

WOMEN
Horizons - R
Salt and Light
Virtue - R
Woman's Touch - R

WRITERS
Writer's Nook News

ENVIRONMENTAL ISSUES

ADULT/GENERAL
All About Issues - R
Anglican Journal - R
AXIOS - R
Beacon Christian News - R
Canada Lutheran - R
Canadian Catholic Review
Charisma & Christian Life
Catholic Exponent
Catholic Sentinel - R
Christian Century
Christian Courier (Canada) - R
Christian Living - R
Christian Social Action
Christianity Today - R
Church Herald
Commonweal
Companion
Compass
Creation Social Science - R
Cresset
Emphasis/Faith & Living - R
Evangelical Baptist
Evangelical Friend
Herald of Holiness - R
Home Times - R
John Milton - R
Journal/Christian Camping - R
Kansas City Christian - R
Liguorian
Living - R
Living Church
Lookout - R
Lutheran, The
Lutheran Digest - R
Mature Years - R
Mennonite, The - R
Mennonite Brethren Herald - R
Messenger, The (NC) - R
Messenger of St. Anthony - R
Ministry Today - R
Minnesota Chronicle, The - R
Moody
National Christian Reporter
NW Christian Journal - R
Other Side, The
Our Family - R
Our Sunday Visitor
Plowman, The
Prairie Messenger
Presbyterian Outlook
Presbyterian Record - R
Presbyterian Survey - R
Prism
Purpose - R
St. Anthony Messenger
SCP Journal - R
Signs of the Times - R
Social Justice Review
United Church Observer - R
United Methodist Reporter
War Cry
Witness, The

CHILDREN
Crusader - R
Faith 'n Stuff
GUIDE - R
High Adventure - R
My Friend
On the Line - R
Pockets - R
Primary Days
Skipping Stones
Touch - R

CHRISTIAN EDUCATION/LIBRARY
Christian School
Lutheran Education
Today's Catholic Teacher - R

MISSIONS
IMPACT
Maryknoll
P.I.M.E. World - R
World Vision - R

PASTORS/LEADERS
Bible-Science - R
Church Business - R
Congregational Journal
Five Stones, The - R
Preacher's Magazine - R
Search
Word & World

TEEN/YOUNG ADULT
Freeway - R
HiCall - R
Insight/Out - R
Issues & Answers - R
Kiln, The - R
Magazine/Youth! - R
Straight - R
Student Leadership - R
Teenage Christian - R
Teen Power - R
Teen Quest - R
YOU! - R
With - R
Young Adult Today
Youth Update

WOMEN
Daughters of Sarah
Esprit - R
Horizons - R

ESSAYS

ADULT/GENERAL

African-American Heritage - R
alive now! - R
All About Issues - R
Assoc Ref Presbyterian - R
AXIOS - R
Burning Light - R
Catholic Answer
Catholic Sentinel - R
Catholic Twin Circle
Christian Living - R
Christian Reader - R
Christian Research - R
Christianity Today - R
Christmas - R
Church & State - R
Church Herald/Holiness Banner - R
Columbia - R
Compass
Cornerstone - R
Creation Social Science - R
Cresset
Critic, The
Emphasis/Faith & Living - R
Evangelical Friend
Evangelical Visitor - R
Explorer
Home Times - R
Inspirer, The - R
John Milton - R
Kansas City Christian - R
Lookout - R
Messenger of St. Anthony - R
Ministry Today - R
Montana Catholic
National Catholic Reporter
New Oxford Review
New Thought Journal - R
Plenty Good Room
Poetry Forum
Power for Living - R
Presbyterian Outlook
Presbyterian Survey - R
Prism
Ratio
Religious Education
SCP Journal - R
Sharing - R
Social Justice Review
Touchstone
Tree of Life
Vista - R

CHILDREN

Nature Friend - R

MISSIONS

Areopagus - R
Catholic Near East
World Vision - R

PASTORS/LEADERS

Homiletic & Pastoral Review
Leadership Journal - R
Quarterly Review
Word & World
Youthworker - R

TEEN/YOUNG ADULT

Insight - R
Student Leadership - R
Young Adult Today
Youth Focus - R

WOMEN

Link & Visitor - R
Lutheran Woman Today

WRITERS

Canadian Writer's Jour - R
Writer's Infor Network
Writer's Nook News

ETHICS

ADULT/GENERAL

All About Issues - R
At Ease - R
AXIOS - R
Beacon Christian News - R
Bible Advocate - R
Canadian Catholic Review
Catholic Digest - R
Catholic Exponent
Christian Century
Christian Courier (Canada) - R
Christian Parenting Today - R
Christian Single - R
Christian Social Action
Christianity Today - R
Church Herald/Holiness Banner - R
Columbia - R
Commonweal
Compass
Cornerstone - R
Creation Social Science - R
Emphasis/Faith & Living - R
Faith Today
Good News, Etc - R
Herald of Holiness - R
Home Times - R
Impact Magazine - R
John Milton - R
Journal/Christian Nursing - R
Journal/Church & State
Kansas City Christian - R
Life Advocate - R
Living Church
Lookout - R
Maranatha - R
Mature Years - R
Ministry Today - R
Minnesota Chronicle, The - R
Moody
National Christian Reporter
Nat/Intl Religion Report
New Covenant - R
New Oxford Review
New Thought Journal - R
NW Christian Journal - R
Our Family - R
Our Sunday Visitor
Parents of Teenagers
PCA Messenger - R
Pentecostal Evangel
Pentecostal Testimony - R
Power for Living - R
Presbyterian Outlook
Presbyterian Record - R
Prism
Religious Broadcasting - R
Religious Education
Seek - R
Social Justice Review
Today's Better Life
United Church Observer - R
United Methodist Reporter
Vista - R
Witness, The

CHILDREN

High Adventure - R
Wonder Time

CHRISTIAN EDUCATION/LIBRARY

CE Connection - R
Journal/Adventist Educ. - R

MISSIONS

Areopagus - R
Urban Mission - R
World Vision - R
Worldwide Challenge - R

PASTORS/LEADERS

Bethany Choice - R
Cross Currents
Ivy Jungle Report - R
Journal/Christian Healing - R

Preacher's Magazine - R
Priest, The
PROCLAIM - R
Resource - R
Review for Religious
Word & World
Youthworker - R

TEEN/YOUNG ADULT
Conqueror - R
Kiln, The - R
Student Leadership - R
Teenage Christian - R
With - R

WOMEN
Conscience - R
Esprit - R
Link & Visitor - R
Salt and Light
Virtue - R

WRITERS
Canadian Writer's Jour - R

*ETHNIC MARKETS

ADULT/GENERAL
African-American Heritage - R
Baptist Informer
Christian Living - R
Class
Common Boundary
El Orador
Hallelujah! - R
Impact Magazine
Indian Life - R
Joyful Noise
Message of the Open Bible - R
Plenty Good Room
Plowman, The
Purpose - R
Star of Zion

CHILDREN
On the Line - R
Preschool Playhouse
Primary Street
Skipping Stones
Story Friends - R

CHRISTIAN EDUCATION/LIBRARY
Student Leadership Journal - R

MISSIONS
Urban Mission

TEEN/YOUNG ADULT
Take Five (photos)
Young Adult Today
Youth Focus - R

EVANGELISTIC

ADULT/GENERAL
Acts 29
Advent Christian Witness
ADVOCATE - R
American Tract Society - R
Anglican Journal - R
At Ease - R
Baptist Beacon - R
Baptist Informer
Better Tomorrow
Bible Advocate - R
Canadian Catholic Review
Catholic Accent
Catholic Digest - R
Charisma & Christian Life
Christian Chronicle
Christian Courier - R
Christian Reader - R
Christian Research - R
Christian Single - R
Church Herald/Holiness Banner - R
Church of God Evangel
Companions - R
Conquest
Cornerstone - R
Decision
Discipleship Journal - R
Emphasis/Faith & Living - R
Evangelical Baptist
Evangelical Visitor - R
God's Revivalist - R
God's Special People - R
Good News, Etc - R
Hallelujah - R
Indian Life - R
Inspirer, The - R
InterVarsity
John Milton - R
Journal/Christian Nursing - R
Journal/Church & State
Kansas City Christian - R
Light and Life
Liguorian
Live - R
Living Church
Lutheran, The
Lutheran Digest - R
Lutheran Layman
Lutheran Witness
Maranatha - R
MESSAGE of the Open Bible - R
Messenger, The (NC) - R
Ministry Today - R
Morning Glory - R
Nat/Intl Religion Report
New Covenant - R
New Heart, A - R
New Oxford Review
NW Christian Journal - R (news)
Parenting Treasures - R
Pentecostal Evangel
Pentecostal Messenger - R
Pentecostal Testimony - R
Power for Living - R
Presbyterian Record - R
Presbyterian Survey - R
Pursuit - R
Railroad Evangelist - R
Religious Broadcasting - R
Religious Education
Seek - R
Servant
Shantyman, The - R
Sharing - R
Standard - R
Star of Zion
Sunday Digest - R
Together - R
Tree of Life
Vision (MO) - R
Vista - R
Vital Christianity - R
War Cry
Wesleyan Advocate
Writer's Forum - R

CHILDREN
Counselor
High Adventure - R

CHRISTIAN EDUCATION/LIBRARY
CE Connection - R
Evangelizing Today's Child
Lutheran Education
Youth & CE Leadership - R
Youth Leader - R

MISSIONS
American Horizon - R
IMPACT
Urban Mission - R

World Christian - R
World Vision - R
Worldwide Challenge - R

PASTORS/LEADERS

Advance - R
Bible-Science - R
Christian Sentinel - R
Church Administration
Church Growth Network - R
Evangelism - R
Faith & Renewal - R
Networks - R
Pastoral Life - R
Preacher's Magazine - R
Priest, The
PROCLAIM - R
Pulpit/Bible Study Helps - R
Resource - R
Search
Youthworker - R

TEEN/YOUNG ADULT

Certainty
event
Freeway - R
HiCall - R
High School I.D. - R
Pathway I.D. - R
Teenage Christian - R
Teen Power - R
Venture - R
YOU! - R
Young Adult Today

WOMEN

Co-Laborer - R
Helping Hand - R
Joyful Woman - R
Salt and Light
Today's Christian Woman
Woman's Touch - R

FAMILY LIFE

ADULT/GENERAL

Acts 29
Advent Christian Witness
ADVOCATE - R
AFA Journal - R
Alive! - R (grandparenting)
All About Issues - R
America
American Tract Society - R
Annals of St. Anne
Arlington Catholic Herald
Assoc Ref Presbyterian - R
At Ease - R
AXIOS - R
Baptist Beacon - R
Baptist Informer
B.C. Catholic - R
Better Tomorrow
Bible Advocate - R
Canada Lutheran - R
Canadian Catholic Review
Catholic Digest - R
Catholic Exponent
Catholic Parent
Catholic Sentinel - R
Catholic Twin Circle - R
Charisma & Christian Life
Christian C.L. RECORD - R
Christian Courier - R
Christian Courier (Canada) - R
Christian Edge - R
Christian Home & School
Christian Living - R
Christian Parenting Today - R
Christian Reader - R
Christian Renewal - R
Church Herald/Holiness Banner - R
Columbia - R
Companion
Companions - R
Connecting Point - R
Conquest
Cornerstone - R
Covenant Companion
Emphasis/Faith & Living - R
Evangel - R
Evangelical Baptist
Evangelical Beacon - R
Evangelical Friend
Evangelical Visitor - R
Expression
Family, The - R
Family Digest, The - R
Fellowship Today - R
Focus on the Family - R
Foursquare World ADVANCE - R
Friends Journal - R
Gem, The - R
God's Revivalist - R
God's Special People - R
Good News, Etc - R
Good News Journal
Gospel Tidings - R
Hallelujah - R
Herald of Holiness - R
Home Life
Home Times - R
Impact Magazine - R
Indian Life - R
Interim - R
John Milton - R
Journal/Christian Nursing - R
Jour/Religion in Psychotherapy
Jour/Religious Gerontology
Kansas City Christian - R
LA Catholic Agitator
Light and Life
Liguorian
Live - R
Living - R
Living Church
Lookout - R
Lutheran, The
Lutheran Digest - R
Lutheran Layman
Lutheran Witness
Maranatha - R
Mature Years - R
Mennonite, The - R
Mennonite Brethren Herald - R
MESSAGE
MESSAGE of the Open Bible - R
Messenger (KY)
Messenger, The (Canada) - R
Messenger, The (NC) - R
Messenger of St. Anthony - R
Ministry Today - R
Minnesota Chronicle, The - R
Moody
Morning Glory - R
National Christian Reporter
New Oxford Review
Our Family - R
Our Sunday Visitor
Parenting Treasures - R
Parents of Teenagers
PCA Messenger - R
Pentecostal Evangel
Pentecostal Homelife - R
Pentecostal Messenger - R
Pentecostal Testimony - R
Positive Approach - R
Power for Living - R
Presbyterian Record - R
Presbyterian Survey - R
PROGRESS - R
Psychology for Living - R
Purpose - R
Pursuit - R
Railroad Evangelist - R
Religious Education
St. Anthony Messenger
Seek - R
Servant
Signs of the Times - R

Smart Dads
Social Justice Review
Standard - R
Sunday Digest - R
Table Talk - R
Today's Better Life
Together - R
United Church Observer - R
United Methodist Reporter
U.S. Catholic
VISION - R
Vision (MO) - R
Vista - R
Vital Christianity - R
Voice, The - R
War Cry
Wesleyan Advocate
Writer's Forum - R

CHILDREN
BREAD for God's Children - R
Faith 'n Stuff
GUIDE - R
High Adventure - R
Junior Trails - R
Skipping Stones
Touch - R
Wonder Time
Young Crusader - R

CHRISTIAN EDUCATION/LIBRARY
Brigade Leader - R
CE Connection - R
CE Counselor - R
Children's Ministry
Church Educator - R
Church Recreation - R
GROUP
Leader - R
Lutheran Education
Shining Star
Youth Leader - R

MISSIONS
American Horizon - R
Childlife - R
IMPACT
World Christian - R
Worldwide Challenge - R

MUSIC
Tradition - R

PASTORS/LEADERS
Advance - R
Bethany Choice - R
Bible-Science - R
Chicago Studies
Diaconalogue - R
Faith & Renewal - R
Journal/Christian Healing - R
Leadership Journal - R
Media Update
Networks - R
Pastoral Life - R
Preacher's Illus. Service - R
PROCLAIM - R
Pulpit/Bible Study Helps - R
Today's Parish
Word & World
Youthworker - R

TEEN/YOUNG ADULT
Breakaway - R
Certainty
Challenge (IL)
Conqueror - R
event
Freeway - R
Insight - R
Insight/Out - R
Kiln, The - R
Magazine/Youth! - R
Pioneer - R
Teenage Christian - R
Teen Quest - R
YOU! - R
With - R
Young Adult Today
Youth Update

WOMEN
Co-Laborer - R
Contempo
Esprit - R
Helping Hand - R
Joyful Woman - R
Link & Visitor - R
Lutheran Woman Today
Royal Service
Today's Christian Woman
Virtue - R
Woman's Touch - R
Women Alive! - R

WRITERS
Housewife-Writers Forum - R

FILLERS: ANECDOTES

ADULT/GENERAL
Acts 29
African-American Heritage - R
Alive! - R
All About Issues - R
AXIOS - R
Catholic Digest - R
Christian Courier - R
Christian Parenting Today - R
Christian Retailing
Church Herald/Holiness Banner - R
Companion
Companions - R
Conquest
Decision
Evangel - R
Explorer
Family, The - R
Family Digest, The - R
Foursquare World ADVANCE - R
Guideposts
Home Times - R
Impact Magazine - R
Inspirer, The - R
John Milton - R
Kansas City Christian - R
Life Advocate - R
Liguorian
Live - R
Living - R
Lutheran Digest - R
Lutheran Journal - R
Maranatha - R
Mature Living
Morning Glory - R
NW Christian Journal - R
Our Family - R
Parenting Treasures - R
Parents of Teenagers
Power for Living - R
Presbyterian Record - R
Presbyterian Survey - R
Railroad Evangelist - R
Standard - R
Sunday Digest - R

CHILDREN
High Adventure - R

CHRISTIAN EDUCATION/LIBRARY
Christian School
Christian Librarian - R
Lutheran Education
Religion Teacher's Journal
Vision - R

MUSIC
Church Pianist, etc.
Tradition

PASTORS/LEADERS
Art+ Repro Resource
Eucharistic Minister - R
Ivy Jungle Report - R
Journal/Christian Healing - R

TEEN/YOUNG ADULT
Campus Life - R
Certainty
Challenge (IL)
HiCall - R
Insight - R
Insight/Out - R
Kiln, The - R
Teenage Christian - R
YOU! - R
Young Salvationist - R

WOMEN
Anna's Journal
Co-Laborer - R
Esprit - R
Today's Christian Woman

WRITERS
Byline
Cross & Quill - R
Canadian Writer's Jour - R
Housewife-Writers Forum - R
Writers Anchor - R
Writer's Digest - R
Writer's Exchange - R
Writer's Nook News
Writer's Resource - R

FILLERS: CARTOONS

ADULT/GENERAL
Alive! - R
alive now! - R
At Ease - R
AXIOS - R
Bookstore Journal - R
Catholic Twin Circle - R
Christian Century
Christian Edge - R
Christian Reader - R
Christian Retailing
ChristianWeek
Companion
Connecting Point - R
Cornerstone - R
Door, The
Evangel - R
Family, The - R
Family Digest, The - R
Foursquare World ADVANCE - R
Herald of Holiness - R
Home Life
Home Times - R
Impact Magazine - R
Inspirer, The - R
INTEREST - R
Journal/Christian Camping - R
Kansas City Christian - R
Life Advocate - R
Live - R
Living - R
Lutheran, The
Lutheran Digest - R
Lutheran Journal - R
Lutheran Witness
Maranatha - R
Mature Living
Mature Years - R
Mennonite, The - R
NW Christian Journal - R
Our Family - R
Parenting Treasures - R
PCA Messenger - R
Pentecostal Testimony - R
Power for Living - R
Prayer Line, The - R
Presbyterian Record - R
Presbyterian Survey - R
Prism
Pursuit - R
Railroad Evangelist - R
Shantyman, The - R
Standard - R
Starlight
Star of Zion
Table Talk - R
Together - R
Touchstone
United Church Observer - R
Vista - R
Vital Christianity - R
World

CHILDREN
CLUBHOUSE - R
Counselor
Crusader - R
GUIDE - R
High Adventure - R
Junior Trails - R
On the Line - R
Power & Light - R
R-A-D-A-R - R
Touch - R

CHRISTIAN EDUCATION/LIBRARY
Baptist Leader
CE Counselor - R
Christian Librarian - R
Church Recreation - R
Journal/Adventist Educ. - R
Leader/Church School Today
Teachers in Focus
Teacher's Interaction
Team - R
Today's Catholic Teacher - R

MUSIC
Church Pianist, etc.
Creator
Glory Songs
Senior Musician - R

PASTORS/LEADERS
Art+ Repro Resource
Celebration
Christian Ministry
Eucharistic Minister - R
Ivy Jungle Report - R
Preacher's Magazine - R
Preaching
Reformed Worship
Resource - R
Your Church - R

TEEN/YOUNG ADULT
Breakaway - R
Brio
Challenge (TN) - R
Edge, The - R
Freeway - R
HiCall - R
Insight - R
Insight/Out - R
Kiln, The - R
Magazine/Youth! - R
Teenage Christian - R
Teen Power - R
Teen Quest - R
With - R
YOU! - R
Young Salvationist - R

WOMEN
Daughters of Sarah
Esprit - R
Women Alive! - R

WRITERS
Byline
Canadian Writer's Jour - R
Christian Communicator - R

Cross & Quill - R
Gotta Write
Home Office - R
Housewife-Writers Forum - R
Writers Anchor - R
Writer's Exchange - R
Writer's Guidelines
Writer's Nook News

FILLERS:FACTS

ADULT/GENERAL

African-American Heritage - R
Alive! - R
All About Issues - R
AXIOS - R
Bible Advocate - R
Catholic Digest - R
Christian Courier - R
Church Herald/Holiness Banner - R
Conquest
Creation Social Science - R
God's Revivalist - R
Hallelujah - R
Home Times - R
Inspirer, The - R
Life Advocate - R
Lutheran Digest - R
Maranatha - R
Mature Living
Mature Years - R
Morning Glory - R
Parenting Treasures - R
PCA Messenger - R
Presbyterian Record - R
Vista - R

CHILDREN

Counselor
Faith 'n Stuff
GUIDE - R
High Adventure - R
My Friend
Pockets - R
Young Crusader - R

CHRISTIAN EDUCATION/LIBRARY

Leader/Church School Today
Lutheran Education
Today's Catholic Teacher - R
Vision - R
Youth Leader - R

PASTORS/LEADERS

Christian Ministry
Ivy Jungle Report - R
Journal/Christian Healing - R
Preacher's Magazine - R
Single Ad. Ministries Jour.

TEEN/YOUNG ADULT

Breakaway - R
Brio
Campus Life - R
Certainty
Challenge (IL)
Insight - R
Insight/Out - R
Student Leadership - R
Teenage Christian - R
YOU! - R
Young Salvationist - R

WOMEN

Co-Laborer - R

WRITERS

Cross & Quill - R
Housewife-Writers Forum - R
Writers Anchor - R
Writers Connection
Writer's Exchange - R
Writer's Guidelines
Writer's Resource - R

FILLERS:GAMES

ADULT/GENERAL

Alive! - R
Catholic Digest - R
Christian Edge - R
Connecting Point - R
Family, The - R
Inspirer, The - R
INTEREST - R
Living - R
Maranatha - R
Standard - R
Table Talk - R

CHILDREN

CLUBHOUSE - R
Counselor
Crusader - R
Faith 'n Stuff
Focus/Clubhouse/Clubhouse Jr
GUIDE - R
High Adventure - R
In the Line - R
Listen
Pockets - R
Power & Light - R
Primary Pal
Wonder Time
Young Crusader - R

CHRISTIAN EDUCATION/LIBRARY

Church Educator - R (Bible)
Church Recreation - R
Leader/Church School Today
Perspective - R
Religion Teacher's Journal
Today's Catholic Teacher - R

TEEN/YOUNG ADULT

Certainty
Challenge (IL)
Challenge (TN) - R
Conqueror - R
Student Leadership - R
Teenage Christian - R
Young Salvationist - R

FILLERS:IDEAS

ADULT/GENERAL

Alive! - R
Catholic Digest - R
Christian Drama - R
Christian Edge - R
Christian Retailing
Conquest
Family, The - R
God's Revivalist - R
Home Times - R
Inspirer, The - R
John Milton - R
Kansas City Christian - R
Maranatha - R
Presbyterian Record - R
St. Joseph Messenger - R
Seek - R
Sunday Digest - R
Table Talk - R

CHILDREN

High Adventure - R
Listen
Pockets - R
Young Crusader - R

CHRISTIAN EDUCATION/LIBRARY

Church Worship
Leader - R
Leader/Church School Today

Lutheran Education
Parish Teacher - R
Religion Teacher's Journal
Team - R

MUSIC
Glory Songs
Senior Musician - R

PASTORS/LEADERS
Ivy Jungle Report - R
Journal/Christian Healing - R
Preacher's Illus. Service - R
Preacher's Magazine - R
Single Ad. Ministries Jour.

TEEN/YOUNG ADULT
Brio
Campus Life - R
Certainty
Insight/Out - R
Magazine/Youth! - R
Teenage Christian - R
YOU! - R

WOMEN
Anna's Journal
Co-Laborer - R
Parent Care - R
Writers Anchor - R

WRITERS
Canadian Writer's Jour - R
Exchange - R
Housewife-Writers Forum - R
Writers Connection (tips)
Writer's Exchange - R
Writing Right - R

FILLERS:JOKES

ADULT/GENERAL
Alive! - R
Catholic Digest - R
Family, The - R
Home Times - R
Impact Magazine - R
Lutheran, The
Lutheran Digest - R
Lutheran Journal - R
Maranatha - R
Mature Years - R
NW Christian Journal - R
Our Family - R
Seek - R

CHILDREN
Counselor
High Adventure - R
My Friend
On the Line - R
Pockets - R
Power & Light - R
R-A-D-A-R - R

CHRISTIAN EDUCATION/LIBRARY
Baptist Leader
Lutheran Education

MUSIC
Tradition

PASTORS/LEADERS
Art+ Repro Resource
Ivy Jungle Report - R
Journal/Christian Healing - R
Preacher's Illus. Service - R
Preacher's Magazine - R

TEEN/YOUNG ADULT
Kiln, The - R
YOU! - R

WRITERS
Writer's Exchange - R

FILLERS: NEWSBREAKS

ADULT/GENERAL
Anglican Journal - R
Arkansas Catholic
B.C.Catholic - R
Canada Lutheran - R
Catholic Family Media - R
Catholic Telegraph
Christian Courier - R
Christian Renewal - R
Common Boundary
Conquest
Hallelujah - R
Home Times - R
Indian Life - R
INTEREST - R
Interchange
Interim - R
John Milton - R
Kansas City Christian - R
Life Advocate - R
Maranatha - R
Mennonite Weekly Review
Morning Glory - R
Religious Broadcasting - R

CHILDREN
Faith 'n Stuff
GUIDE - R

CHRISTIAN EDUCATION/LIBRARY
Christian Librarian - R
Vision - R
Youth Leader - R

MUSIC
Worship Today - R

PASTORS/LEADERS
Christian Ministry, The
Church Business - R
Ivy Jungle Report - R
Journal/Christian Healing - R
Preacher's Illus. Service - R
Single Ad. Ministries Jour.

TEEN/YOUNG ADULT
Certainty
Challenge (IL)
Insight - R
Magazine/Youth! - R
Teenage Christian - R

WOMEN
Conscience - R

WRITERS
Gotta Write
Writers Connection
Writer's Exchange - R
Writer's Guidelines
Writer's Resource - R
Writing Right - R

FILLERS: PARTY IDEAS

CHILDREN
Focus/Clubhouse/Clubhouse Jr
My Friend

CHRISTIAN EDUCATION/LIBRARY
Church Recreation - R
Perspective - R
Team - R

MUSIC
Glory Songs
Senior Musician - R

PASTORS/LEADERS
Ivy Jungle Report - R

TEEN/YOUNG ADULT
Conqueror - R
Insight - R
Insight/Out - R
Student Leadership - R

FILLERS: PROSE

ADULT/GENERAL
Bible Advocate - R
Broken Streets - R
Church Herald/Holiness Banner - R
Companions - R
Conquest
Creation Social Science - R
Decision
Discovery - R
Explorer
Family, The - R
God's Revivalist - R
Hallelujah - R
Inspirer, The - R
Liguorian
Live - R
Mennonite, The - R
Presbyterian Record - R
Presbyterian Survey - R
Starlight
Table Talk - R
Wesleyan Advocate

PASTORS/LEADERS
Preacher's Illus. Service - R

TEEN/YOUNG ADULT
Brio
Certainty
Challenge (IL)
Conqueror - R
Freeway - R
Insight/Out - R
Magazine/Youth! - R
Teen Power - R
Venture - R

WOMEN
Anna's Journal - R
Co-Laborer - R
Esprit - R

WRITERS
Chip Off Writer's Block - R
Writers Anchor - R
Writer's Exchange - R

FILLERS:QUIZZES

ADULT/GENERAL
Alive! - R
Catholic Digest - R
Catholic Twin Circle - R
Creation Social Science - R
Door, The
Impact Magazine - R
John Milton - R
Living - R
Maranatha - R
Mature Living
Mature Years - R
MESSAGE
Power for Living - R
St. Willibrord Journal
Standard - R
Sunday Digest - R
Together - R

CHILDREN
Counselor
Faith 'n Stuff
Focus/Clubhouse/Clubhouse Jr
GUIDE - R
High Adventure - R
On the Line - R
Partners - R
Power & Light - R
Story Mates - R
Young Crusader - R

CHRISTIAN EDUCATION/LIBRARY
Church Recreation - R
Leader - R

MUSIC
Glory Songs
Senior Musician - R

PASTORS/LEADERS
Ivy Jungle Report - R

TEEN/YOUNG ADULT
Breakaway - R
Brio
Conqueror - R
Freeway - R
HiCall - R
Insight/Out - R
Magazine/Youth! - R
Student Leadership - R
Teenage Christian - R
Teen Power - R
Young Salvationist - R

WRITERS
Gotta Write
Writers Anchor - R

*FILLERS: PRAYERS

ADULT/GENERAL
alive now!
All About Issues - R
Bible Advocate - R
Companion
Congregational Journal
Explorer
Family Digest, The - R
Liguorian
Morning Glory - R
Starlight

CHRISTIAN EDUCATION/LIBRARY
Baptist Leader
Religion Teacher's Journal

TEEN/YOUNG ADULT
Freeway - R
Young Salvationist - R

WOMEN
Anna's Journal - R
Co-Laborer - R
Esprit - R

WRITERS
Cross & Quill - R

FILLERS:QUOTES

ADULT/GENERAL
Acts 29
Bible Advocate - R
Christian Edge - R
Church Herald & Holiness Banner - R
Companion
Creation Social Science - R

Guideposts
Hallelujah - R
Home Times - R
INTEREST - R
John Milton - R
Kansas City Christian - R
Life Advocate - R
Maranatha - R
Morning Glory - R
Railroad Evangelist - R
Seek - R
Together - R

CHRISTIAN EDUCATION/LIBRARY
Youth Leader - R

PASTORS/LEADERS
Ivy Jungle Report - R
Journal/Christian Healing - R
Single Adult Min Journal

TEENS/YOUNG ADULTS
Kiln, The - R

WOMEN
Co-Laborer - R
Esprit - R

WRITERS
Christian Communicator - R
Cross & Quill - R
Exchange - R
Writers Anchor - R
Writer's Exchange - R

FILLERS: SHORT HUMOR

ADULT/GENERAL
Alive! - R
All About Issues - R
Annals of St. Anne
Catholic Digest - R
Christian Parenting Today - R
Christian Reader - R
Companion
Conquest
Cornerstone - R
Door, The
Friends Journal - R
God's Revivalist - R
Guideposts
Home Times - R
Impact Magazine - R
Inspirer, The - R
John Milton - R
Kansas City Christian - R
Life Advocate - R
Liguorian
Live - R
Living - R
Lutheran, The
Lutheran Digest - R
Lutheran Journal - R
Lutheran Witness
Maranatha - R
Mature Living
Mature Years - R
Morning Glory - R
NW Christian Journal - R
Our Family - R
Parenting Treasures - R
PCA Messenger - R
Pentecostal Testimony - R
Prayer Line, The - R
Presbyterian Record - R
Presbyterian Survey - R
St. Willibrord Journal
Seek - R
Starlight
Star of Zion
Vista - R

CHILDREN
Focus/Clubhouse/Clubhouse Jr
GUIDE - R
Junior Trails - R
R-A-D-A-R - R
Touch - R
Young Crusader - R

CHRISTIAN EDUCATION/LIBRARY
Christian Librarian - R
Leader - R
Lutheran Education
Teachers in Focus
Team - R

MUSIC
Creator
Glory Songs
Senior Musician - R

PASTORS/LEADERS
Ivy Jungle Report - R
Journal/Christian Healing - R
Eucharistic Minister - R
Preacher's Illus. Service - R
Preacher's Magazine - R
Resource - R

TEEN/YOUNG ADULT
Brio
Certainty
Freeway - R
HiCall - R
Insight - R
Insight/Out - R
Kiln, The - R
Magazine/Youth! - R
Straight - R
Teenage Christian - R
Teen Power - R
Venture - R
YOU! - R
Young Salvationist - R

WOMEN
Co-Laborer - R
Daughters of Sarah
Today's Christian Woman

WRITERS
Byline
Canadian Writer's Jour - R
Cross & Quill - R
Writers Anchor - R
Writer's Digest - R
Writer's Exchange - R

FILLERS: WORD PUZZLES

ADULT/GENERAL
Alive! - R
Christian Edge - R
Christian Reader - R
Companion
Connecting Point - R
Conquest
Friends Journal - R
Impact Magazine - R
Inspirer, The - R
INTEREST - R
Living - R
Maranatha - R
Mature Living
Mature Years - R
Power for Living - R
Standard - R
Today's Single
Together - R

CHILDREN
CLUBHOUSE - R
Counselor
Crusader - R
Faith 'n Stuff

Focus/Clubhouse/Clubhouse Jr
GUIDE - R
High Adventure - R
Junior Trails - R
On the Line - R
Our Little Friend
Partners - R
Pockets - R
Power & Light - R
Primary Days
Primary Pal
Story Mates - R
Touch - R
Wonder Time
Young Crusader - R

CHRISTIAN EDUCATION/LIBRARY
Church Educator - R (Bible)
Church Recreation - R
Leader - R
Parish Teacher - R
Today's Catholic Teacher - R

MUSIC
Young Musicians

TEEN/YOUNG ADULT
Certainty
Challenge (IL)
Challenge (TN) - R
Conqueror - R
Freeway - R
Teenage Christian - R
Teen Power - R
Young Salvationist - R

WOMEN
Esprit - R

WRITERS
Gotta Write
Writers Anchor - R

FOOD/RECIPES

ADULT/GENERAL
AXIOS - R
Better Tomorrow
Christian C.L. RECORD - R
Christian Parenting Today - R
Christian Reader - R
Christian Single - R
Home Life
Ideals - R
Lutheran Digest - R
MESSAGE
Pentecostal Homelife - R
PROGRESS - R
Table Talk - R
Today's Better Life

CHILDREN
CLUBHOUSE - R
On the Line - R

CHRISTIAN EDUCATION/LIBRARY
Church Recreation - R
Shining Star

WOMEN
Helping Hand - R
Joyful Woman - R
Woman's Touch - R
Women Alive ! - R

HEALING

ADULT/GENERAL
Acts 29
ADVOCATE - R
At Ease - R
Catholic Digest - R
Catholic Twin Circle - R
Charisma & Christian Life
Church Herald/Holiness Banner - R
Common Boundary
Connecting Point - R
God's Revivalist - R
Good News, Etc - R
Guideposts
Hallelujah - R
John Milton - R
Journal/Christian Nursing - R
Kansas City Christian - R
Liguorian
Live - R
Living - R
Living Church
Lutheran Digest - R
Maranatha - R
Mennonite, The - R
MESSAGE of the Open Bible - R
Messenger, The (NC) - R
National Christian Reporter
New Covenant - R
New Oxford Review
Our Family - R
Pentecostal Evangel
Pentecostal Homelife - R
Pentecostal Messenger - R
Pentecostal Testimony - R
Presbyterian Record - R
Presbyterian Survey - R
Purpose - R
Railroad Evangelist - R
SCP Journal - R
Sharing - R
Sunday Digest - R
Today's Better Life
Total Health
United Methodist Reporter
VISION - R
Vision (MO) - R

CHRISTIAN EDUCATION/LIBRARY
Youth Leader - R

MISSIONS
American Horizon - R
Areopagus - R

PASTORS/LEADERS
Diaconalogue - R
Eucharistic Minister - R
Faith & Renewal - R
Journal/Christian Healing - R
Ministries Today
Networks - R
Paraclete - R
Priest, The
Word & World

TEEN/YOUNG ADULT
Conqueror - R
Pathway I.D. - R
Sharing the VICTORY - R
YOU! - R
Young Adult Today

WOMEN
Esprit - R
Helping Hand - R
Lutheran Woman Today
Response
Virtue - R
Woman's Touch - R

HEALTH

ADULT/GENERAL
Alive! - R
Anglican Journal - R
B.C. Catholic - R
Better Tomorrow
Canada Lutheran - R
Catholic Digest - R
Catholic Exponent
Catholic Sentinel - R

Catholic Twin Circle - R
Charisma & Christian Life
Christian Courier - R
Christian Courier (Canada) - R
Christian Edge - R
Christian Living - R
Christian Parenting Today - R
Christian Single - R
Christian Social Action
Church Herald/Holiness Banner - R
Companion
Conquest
Creation Social Science - R
Discovery - R
Evangelical Friend
Guideposts
Home Life
Home Times - R
Interim - R
John Milton - R
Journal/Christian Camping - R
Journal/Christian Nursing - R
Kansas City Christian - R
Lifeglow - R
Liguorian
Living - R
Lookout - R
Lutheran Digest - R
Lutheran Witness
Mature Years - R
Mennonite, The - R
MESSAGE
MESSAGE of the Open Bible - R
Messenger, The (NC) - R
Montana Catholic
National Christian Reporter
New Heart, A - R
NW Christian Journal - R
Pentecostal Evangel
Pentecostal Homelife - R
Poetry Forum
SCP Journal - R
Sharing - R
Star of Zion
Table Talk - R
Today's Better Life
Today's Single - R
Total Health
United Methodist Reporter
Vibrant Life - R

CHILDREN

CLUBHOUSE - R
GUIDE - R
Touch - R

CHRISTIAN EDUCATION/LIBRARY

CE Connection - R
Church Recreation - R

MISSIONS

Areopagus - R
Childlife - R
Compassion Update - R

PASTORS/LEADERS

Bible-Science - R
Chicago Studies
Journal/Christian Healing - R
Word & World

TEEN/YOUNG ADULT

Conqueror - R
Insight - R
Insight/Out - R
Magazine/Youth! - R
Pioneer - R
Straight - R
Teenage Christian - R
YOU! - R
Young Adult Today
Young & Alive - R

WOMEN

Esprit - R
Helping Hand - R
Joyful Woman - R
Lutheran Woman Today
Parent Care - R
Response
Virtue - R
Woman's Touch - R

HISTORICAL

ADULT/GENERAL

African-American Heritage - R
AGAIN - R
All About Issues - R
America
Annals of St. Anne
At Ease - R
AXIOS - R
Baptist History & Heritage
Bible Advocate - R
Canadian Catholic Review
Catholic Answer
Catholic Digest - R
Catholic Heritage
Catholic Sentinel - R
Catholic Twin Circle - R
Charisma & Christian Life
Christian C.L. RECORD - R
Christian Courier (Canada) - R
Christian Edge - R
Christian History - R
Christian Renewal - R
Christianity Today - R
Church & State - R
Church Herald
Class
Compass
Conquest
Creation Social Science - R
Evangelical Friend
Friends Journal - R
Herald of Holiness - R
(Wesleyan)
Home Times - R
Ideals - R
Indian Life - R
InterVarsity
John Milton - R
Journal/Christian Nursing - R
Journal/Church & State
Lifeglow - R
Living Church
Lutheran Digest - R
Lutheran Journal - R
Lutheran Layman
Lutheran Witness
MESSAGE
Messenger, The (NC) - R
Methodist History
Minnesota Chronicle, The - R
Morning Glory - R
Mountain Laurel - R
National Christian Reporter
Our Sunday Visitor
Pentecostal Evangel
Pentecostal Testimony - R
Presbyterian Outlook
Presbyterian Record - R
Presbyterian Survey - R
Purpose - R
Religious Broadcasting - R
Religious Education
SCP Journal - R
Sharing - R
Social Justice Review
Sunday Digest - R
United Methodist Reporter

CHILDREN

Faith 'n Stuff
High Adventure - R
Junior Trails - R

My Friend
Partners - R

CHRISTIAN EDUCATION/LIBRARY
Changing Lives - R
Lutheran Education
Today's Catholic Teacher - R

MISSIONS
American Horizon - R
Areopagus - R
Catholic Near East
IMPACT
Urban Mission - R
World Vision - R
Worldwide Challenge - R

MUSIC
Church Pianist, etc.
Tradition - R

PASTORS/LEADERS
Bible-Science - R
Congregational Journal
Five Stones, The - R
Journal/Christian Healing - R
Lutheran Forum - R
Paraclete - R
Preacher's Magazine - R
Today's Parish - R
Word & World

TEEN/YOUNG ADULT
Certainty
Challenge (IL)
Issues & Answers - R
Kiln, The - R
Magazine/Youth! - R
Pioneer - R
Student Leadership - R
Young Adult Today
Young & Alive - R
Youth Focus - R

WOMEN
Esprit - R
Link & Visitor - R
Virtue - R

HOLIDAY THEMES

ADULT/GENERAL
Advent Christian Witness
ADVOCATE - R
Alive! - R
alive now! - R
All About Issues - R
American Tract Society - R
Annals of St. Anne
Assoc Ref Presbyterian - R
At Ease - R
AXIOS - R
Baptist Beacon - R
Bible Advocate - R
Canada Lutheran - R
Canadian Catholic Review
Catholic Accent
Catholic Digest - R
Catholic New York
Catholic Parent
Catholic Sentinel - R
Catholic Twin Circle - R
Charisma & Christian Life
Christian C.L. RECORD - R
Christian Courier - R
Christian Edge - R
Christian Home & School
Christian Living - R
Christian Parenting Today - R
Christian Reader - R
Christian Standard - R
Christianity Today - R
Christmas - R
Church Herald/Holiness Banner - R
Church of God Evangel
Connecting Point - R
Conquest
Cornerstone - R
Covenant Companion
Decision
Discovery - R
Emphasis/Faith & Living - R
Evangel - R
Evangelical Friend
Evangelical Visitor - R
Explorer
Expression
Family Digest, The - R
Fellowship Today - R
Friends Journal - R
Gem, The - R
God's Revivalist - R
Good News, Etc - R
Gospel Tidings - R
Herald of Holiness - R
Home Life
Home Times - R
Ideals - R
Inspirer, The - R
John Milton - R
Lifeglow - R
Liguorian
Live - R
Living - R
Lookout - R
Lutheran Digest - R
Lutheran Witness
Maranatha - R
Mature Years - R
Mennonite, The - R
Mennonite Brethren Herald - R
MESSAGE of the Open Bible - R
Messenger (KY)
Messenger, The (Canada) - R
Messenger, The (NC) - R
Messenger of St. Anthony - R
Minnesota Chronicle, The - R
Ministry Today - R
Morning Glory - R
National Christian Reporter
Our Sunday Visitor
Parenting Treasures - R
PCA Messenger - R
Pentecostal Evangel
Pentecostal Homelife - R
Pentecostal Messenger - R
Pentecostal Testimony - R
Plenty Good Room
Power for Living - R
Presbyterian Outlook
Presbyterian Record - R
Presbyterian Survey - R
PROGRESS - R
Psychology for Living - R
Purpose - R
Religious Broadcasting - R
St. Anthony Messenger
St. Joseph Messenger - R
Seek - R
Sharing - R
Standard - R
Star of Zion
Sunday Digest - R
Today's Single - R
United Church Observer - R
United Methodist Reporter
Vista - R
Vital Christianity - R
Voice, The - R
War Cry
Wesleyan Advocate

CHILDREN
Counselor
Faith 'n Stuff
Focus/Clubhouse/Clubhouse Jr
GUIDE - R
High Adventure - R
Junior Trails - R
My Friend
On the Line - R

Pockets - R
Power & Light - R
Primary Pal
R-A-D-A-R - R
Touch - R
Wonder Time
Young Crusader - R

CHRISTIAN EDUCATION/LIBRARY
Baptist Leader
CE Connection - R
Changing Lives - R
Church Educator - R
Church Recreation - R
Cornerstone Connections - R
GROUP
KEY - R
Leader - R
Leader/Church School Today
Parish Teacher - R
Perspective - R
Religion Teacher's Journal (religious)
Vision - R

MISSIONS
Catholic Near East
Door of Hope
Worldwide Challenge - R

MUSIC
Church Pianist
Music Leader

PASTORS/LEADERS
Advance - R
Celebration
Preacher's Magazine - R
Proclaim
Pulpit/Bible Study Helps - R
Youth Leader - R

TEEN/YOUNG ADULT
Breakaway - R
Conqueror - R
Cornerstone - R
Freeway - R
HiCall - R
High School I.D.
Insight - R
Kiln - R
Mag/Christian Youth - R
Straight - R
Teenage Christian - R
Teen Power - R
With - R
Young & Alive - R
Young Salvationist - R

WOMEN
Co-Laborer - R
Helping Hand - R
Just Between Us
Link & Visitor - R
Probe
Today's Christian Woman
Virtue - R

HOME SCHOOLING

ADULT/GENERAL
Anglican Journal - R
AXIOS - R
Charisma & Christian Life
Christian C.L. RECORD - R
Christian Parenting Today - R
Creation Social Science - R
Expression
Friends Journal - R
Good News, Etc - R
Gospel Tidings - R
Home Times - R
Journal/Christian Camping - R
Kansas City Christian - R
Lookout - R
Lutheran Life - R
MESSAGE of the Open Bible - R
Messenger, The (NC) - R
Minnesota Chronicle, The - R
Moody
NW Christian Journal - R
Parents of Teenagers
PCA Messenger - R
Pentecostal Homelife - R
Pentecostal Messenger - R
Pentecostal Testimony - R
Positive Approach - R
Psychology for Living - R
Religious Education
Social Justice Review
Table Talk - R
Tree of Life
Vista - R
Wesleyan Advocate
Writer's Forum - R

CHILDREN
BREAD for God's Children - R
GUIDE - R

CHRISTIAN EDUCATION/LIBRARY
CE Connection - R
Christian Educators Jour - R
Christian School
Lutheran Education
Shining Star

PASTORS/LEADERS
Bible-Science - R
Pulpit/Bible Study Helps - R

TEEN/YOUNG ADULT
Conqueror - R
You! - R

WOMEN
Esprit - R
Helping Hand - R
Joyful Woman - R
Virtue - R

HOW-TO ACTIVITIES (JUV.)

ADULT/GENERAL
Christian Drama - R
John Milton - R
Living - R
Lutheran Life - R
MESSAGE - R
Ministry Today - R
Pentecostal Evangel

CHILDREN
Bible Time 4's & 5's
BREAD for God's Children - R
Counselor
God's World Today
High Adventure - R
Junior Trails - R
Listen
My Friend
Nature Friend - R
On the Line - R
Partners - R
Primary Days
Primary Pal
R-A-D-A-R - R
Touch - R
Wonder Time

CHRISTIAN EDUCATION/LIBRARY
Church Recreation - R
Evangelizing Today's Child
Junior Teacher - R
Leader - R
Memos - R
Perspective - R

Shining Star

PASTORS/LEADERS
Bible-Science - R
Group's Jr High
Networks - R

TEEN/YOUNG ADULT
Breakaway - R
Freeway - R
Insight - R
Insight/Out - R
Teenage Christian - R
Teen Power - R
Magazine/Youth! - R
You! - R
Young Salvationist - R

WOMEN
Joyful Woman - R

HOW-TO/ SELF-HELP

ADULT/GENERAL
Advent Christian Witness
African-American Heritage - R
Alive! - R
At Ease - R
Baptist Informer
Better Tomorrow
Bible Advocate - R
Canada Lutheran - R
Catholic Digest - R
Catholic Twin Circle - R
Charisma & Christian Life
Christian Edge - R
Christian Home & School
Christian Living - R
Christian Reader - R
Christian Retailing
Christian Standard - R
Church Herald
Columbia - R
Companion
Connecting Point - R
Conquest
Cornerstone - R
Emphasis/Faith & Living - R
Evangel - R
Family, The - R
Family Digest, The - R
Gospel Tidings - R
Guideposts
Home Life
Home Times - R
Indian Life - R
John Milton - R
Journal/Christian Camping - R
Liguorian
Living - R
Lookout - R
Lutheran Digest - R
Lutheran Journal - R
Lutheran Layman
Mature Living
Mature Years - R
Mennonite, The - R
MESSAGE
Messenger, The (NC) - R
Ministry Today - R
NW Christian Journal - R
Our Sunday Visitor
Pentecostal Evangel
Pentecostal Homelife - R
Power for Living - R
Psychology for Living - R
Quiet Revolution - R
Sharing - R
Standard - R
Sunday Digest - R
Today's Better Life
Today's Single - R
Vista - R
Vital Christianity - R

CHILDREN
High Adventure - R
My Friend

CHRISTIAN EDUCATION/LIBRARY
Brigade Leader - R
CE Connection - R
CE Counselor - R
Children's Ministry
Christian School
Church & Synagogue Libraries - R
GROUP
Journal/Adventist Educ. - R
Level D Teacher - R
Librarian's World - R
Lollipops

MISSIONS
IMPACT

MUSIC
Church Music Report
Music Leader

PASTORS/LEADERS
Church Administration
Church Business - R
Faith & Renewal - R
Group's Jr High
Ivy Jungle Report - R
Journal/Christian Healing - R
Leadership Journal - R
Networks - R
Priest, The
Youthworker - R

TEEN/YOUNG ADULT
Breakaway - R
Certainty
Challenge (IL)
Challenge (TN) - R
event
Insight - R
Insight/Out - R
Magazine/Youth! - R
Pioneer - R
Straight - R
Student Leadership - R
Teenage Christian - R
You ! - R
Youth Update

WOMEN
Co-Laborer - R
Esprit - R
Helping Hand - R
Joyful Woman - R
Just Between Us
Link & Visitor - R
Lutheran Woman Today
Parent Care - R
Probe
Salt and Light
Today's Christian Woman
Virtue - R
Woman's Touch - R

WRITERS
Byline
Canadian Writer's Jour - R
Chips Off Writer's Block - R
Christian Communicator - R
Christian Vision - R
Cross & Quill - R
Exchange - R
Home Office - R
Writers Anchor - R
Writers Connection - R
Writer's Exchange - R
Writer's Guidelines
Writer's Infor Network

HUMOR

ADULT/GENERAL
ADVOCATE - R
African-American Heritage - R
Alive! - R
alive now! - R
All About Issues - R
At Ease - R
AXIOS - R
Beacon Christian News - R
Better Tomorrow
Canada Lutheran - R
Catholic Digest - R
Catholic Parent
Catholic Twin Circle - R
Christian C.L. RECORD - R
Christian Drama - R
Christian Edge - R
Christian Living - R
Christian Parenting Today - R
Christian Reader - R
Christian Single - R
Church Herald
Church of God Evangel
Companion
Connecting Point - R
Cornerstone - R
Covenant Companion
Critic, The
Door, The (satire)
Emphasis/Faith & Living - R
Evangelical Visitor - R
Family, The - R
Family Digest, The - R
Focus on the Family - R
Friends Journal - R
Home Life
Home Times - R
Impact Magazine - R
Inspirer, The - R
John Milton - R
Journal/Christian Nursing - R
Light and Life
Live - R
Living Church
Lookout - R
Lutheran, The
Lutheran Digest - R
Lutheran Journal - R
Lutheran Layman
Lutheran Witness
Maranatha - R
Mature Living
Mature Years - R
Mennonite, The - R
MESSAGE
MESSAGE of the Open Bible - R
Messenger, The (NC) - R
Ministry Today - R
Minnesota Chronicle, The - R
Morning Glory - R
Mountain Laurel - R
National Christian Reporter
NW Christian Journal - R
Our Family - R
Parents of Teenagers
PCA Messenger - R
Pentecostal Homelife - R
Pentecostal Testimony - R
Power for Living - R
Presbyterian Outlook
Presbyterian Record - R
Presbyterian Survey - R
Pursuit - R
Salt
Standard - R
Starlight
Table Talk - R
Today's Single - R
United Methodist Reporter
U.S. Catholic
Vista - R
Voice, The - R

CHILDREN
Crusader - R
Faith 'n Stuff
Focus/Clubhouse/Clubhouse Jr
GUIDE - R
High Adventure - R
My Friend
On the Line - R
Power & Light - R
R-A-D-A-R - R
Touch - R
Wonder Time
Young Crusader - R

CHRISTIAN EDUCATION/LIBRARY
Brigade Leader - R
Christian School
Shining Star
Teachers in Focus
Team - R

MISSIONS
Areopagus - R
World Christian - R
Worldwide Challenge - R

MUSIC
Church Pianist, etc.

PASTORS/LEADERS
Five Stones, The - R
Journal/Christian Healing - R
Leadership Journal - R
Networks - R
Preacher's Illus. Service - R
Preacher's Magazine - R
Priest, The
Resource - R
Today's Parish

TEEN/YOUNG ADULT
Breakaway - R
Brio
Certainty
Challenge (IL)
Conqueror - R
event
Freeway - R
HiCall - R
High School I.D. - R
Insight - R
Insight/Out - R
Kiln, The - R
Magazine/Youth! - R
Pioneer - R
Straight - R
Student, The - R
Teenage Christian - R
Teen Power - R
Teen Quest - R
Venture - R
With - R
YOU! - R
Young Adult Today
Young Salvationist - R
Youth Focus - R

WOMEN
Co-Laborer - R
Esprit - R
Helping Hand - R
Horizons - R
Lutheran Woman Today
Today's Christian Woman
Virtue - R
Woman's Touch - R

WRITERS
Byline
Canadian Writer's Jour - R
Exchange - R
Housewife-Writers Forum - R
Writers Anchor - R
Writer's Exchange - R
Writer's Guidelines

INSPIRATIONAL

ADULT/GENERAL

Acts 29
ADVOCATE - R
African-American Heritage - R
Annals of St. Anne
Assoc Ref Presbyterian - R
At Ease - R
Baptist Beacon - R
Better Tomorrow
Bible Advocate - R
Broken Streets
Canada Lutheran - R
Catholic Accent
Catholic Answer
Catholic Digest - R
Catholic Parent
Catholic Sentinel - R
Catholic Twin Circle - R
Charisma & Christian Life
Christian Century
Christian Edge - R
Christian Reader - R
Christian Single - R
Church Herald
Church Herald/Holiness Banner - R
Columbia - R
Companion
Companions - R
Connecting Point - R
Conquest
Cornerstone - R
Covenant Companion
Discipleship Journal - R
Emphasis/Faith & Living - R
Evangel - R
Evangelical Beacon - R
Evangelical Friend
Evangelical Visitor - R
Explorer
Family, The - R
Family Digest, The - R
Fellowship Today - R
Foursquare World ADVANCE - R
Friends Journal - R
Gem, The - R
God's Revivalist - R
God's Special People - R
Good News - R
Gospel Tidings - R
Guideposts
Herald of Holiness - R
His Garden
Home Times - R
Ideals - R
Indian Life - R
Inspirer, The - R
John Milton - R
Lifeglow - R
Light and Life
Liguorian
Live - R
Living - R
Living Church
Lookout - R
Lutheran, The
Lutheran Digest - R
Lutheran Journal - R
Lutheran Layman
Lutheran Witness
Maranatha - R
Marian Helpers Bulletin - R
Mature Living
Mature Years - R
Mennonite Brethren Herald - R
MESSAGE
MESSAGE of the Open Bible - R
Messenger, The (Canada) - R
Messenger, The (NC) - R
Messenger of St. Anthony - R
Messenger of the Sacred Heart
Ministry Today - R
Morning Glory - R
New Covenant - R
New Heart, A - R
New Thought Journal - R
Oblates
Our Sunday Visitor
Parenting Treasures - R
PCA Messenger - R
Pentecostal Evangel
Pentecostal Homelife - R
Pentecostal Messenger - R
Pentecostal Testimony - R
Plenty Good Room
Positive Approach - R
Power for Living - R
Prayer Line, The - R
Presbyterian Outlook
Presbyterian Record - R
Presbyterian Survey - R
Pursuit - R
Queen of all Hearts
St. Anthony Messenger
St. Joseph Messenger - R
Seek - R
Shantyman, The - R
Sharing - R
Standard - R
Sunday Digest - R
Table Talk - R
Teaching Home, The
Today's Better Life
Today's Single - R
Total Health
VISION - R
Vision (MO) - R
Vista - R
Voice, The - R
War Cry
Wesleyan Advocate
Worldwide Challenge - R
Writer's Forum - R

CHILDREN

GUIDE - R
High Adventure - R
Partners - R
Touch - R
Wonder Time

CHRISTIAN EDUCATION/LIBRARY

Brigade Leader - R
CE Connection - R
Changing Lives - R
Christian School
Junior Teacher - R
Librarian's World - R
Lutheran Education
Perspective - R
Vision - R
Youth Leader - R

MISSIONS

American Horizon - R
Areopagus - R

MUSIC

Senior Musician - R

PASTORS/LEADERS

Christian Ministry
Eucharistic Minister - R
Five Stones, The - R
Group's Jr High
Journal/Christian Healing - R
Networks - R
Preacher's Magazine - R
Priest, The
PROCLAIM - R
Pulpit/Bible Study Helps - R
Review for Religious

TEEN/YOUNG ADULT

Breakaway - R
Certainty
Challenge (IL)
Conqueror - R
Freeway - R
High School I.D. - R

Insight - R
Insight/Out - R
Kiln, The - R
Magazine/Youth! - R
Straight - R
Teenage Christian - R
Teen Power - R
Teen Quest - R
With - R
Young Adult Today
Young & Alive - R
Young Salvationist - R

WOMEN
Co-Laborer - R
Esprit - R
Helping Hand - R
Horizons - R
Lutheran Woman Today
Salt and Light
Sisters Today - R
Today's Christian Woman
Woman's Touch - R

WRITERS
Byline
Canadian Writer's Jour - R
Writer's Guidelines
Writer's Infor Network

INTERVIEWS/ PROFILES

ADULT/GENERAL
Acts 29
ADVOCATE - R
African-American Heritage - R
AGAIN - R
Alive! - R
Anglican Journal - R
Arkansas Catholic
Arlington Catholic Herald
Assoc Ref Presbyterian - R
At Ease - R
AXIOS - R
Better Tomorrow
Bookstore Journal - R
Burning Light - R
Canadian Catholic Review
Catholic Digest - R
Catholic Family Media Guide - R
Catholic New York
Catholic Parent
Catholic Sentinel - R
Catholic Twin Circle - R
Charisma & Christian Life
Christian Century
Christian C.L. RECORD - R
Christian Courier - R
Christian Courier (Canada) - R
Christian Edge - R
Christian Parenting Today - R
Christian Reader - R
Christian Renewal - R
Christian Research - R
Christianity Today - R
Church & State - R
Church Herald/Holiness Banner - R
Class
Columbia - R
Companion
Cornerstone - R (music)
Creation Social Science - R
Critic, The
Door, The
Emphasis/Faith & Living - R
Episcopal Life - R
Evangelical Friend
Expression
Faith Today
Family, The - R
Family Digest, The - R
Friends Journal - R
God's Special People - R
Good News, Etc - R
Good News Journal
Guideposts
Herald of Holiness - R
Home Life
Home Times - R
Impact Magazine - R
Indian Life - R
Interim - R
InterVarsity
John Milton - R
Journal/Christian Camping - R
Journal/Christian Nursing - R
Joyful Noise
Kansas City Christian - R
Life Advocate - R
Lifeglow - R
Liguorian
Living - R
Living Church
Lookout - R
Lutheran, The
Lutheran Layman
Lutheran Witness
Maranatha - R
Mature Living
Mature Years - R
Mennonite, The - R
Mennonite Brethren Herald - R
Mennonite Reporter
MESSAGE
Messenger (KY)
Messenger, The (NC) - R
Minnesota Chronicle, The - R
National Christian Reporter
New Covenant - R
New Heart, A - R
News Network Intl.
New Thought Journal - R
Other Side, The
Our Sunday Visitor
Parents of Teenagers
Pentecostal Evangel
Pentecostal Testimony - R
Plenty Good Room
Positive Approach - R
Power for Living - R
Presbyterian Outlook
Presbyterian Record - R
Presbyterian Survey - R
Prism
Pursuit - R
Quiet Revolution - R
Religious Broadcasting - R
St. Anthony Messenger
Salt
SCP Journal - R
Servant
Shantyman, The - R
Sharing - R
Signs of the Times - R
Standard - R
Star of Zion
Sunday Digest - R
Today's Better Life
Touchstone
United Church Observer - R
United Methodist Reporter
Vista - R
Witness, The

CHILDREN
Crusader - R
Focus/Clubhouse/Clubhouse Jr
My Friend

CHRISTIAN EDUCATION/LIBRARY
CE Counselor - R
Changing Lives - R
Christian Educators Jour - R
Christian School
GUIDE - R
Lutheran Education
Perspective - R
Teachers in Focus

Vision - R
Youth & CE Leadership - R
Youth Leader - R

MISSIONS
American Horizon - R
Childlife - R
Compassion Update - R
IMPACT
P.I.M.E. World - R
Urban Mission - R
World Christian - R
World Vision - R
Worldwide Challenge - R

MUSIC
Church Music World
Worship Today - R

PASTORS/LEADERS
Bible-Science - R
Christian Sentinel - R
Diaconalogue - R
Faith & Renewal - R
Five Stones, The - R
Ivy Jungle Report - R
Journal/Christian Healing - R
Leadership Journal - R
Ministries Today
Networks - R
Preacher's Magazine - R
PROCLAIM - R
Resource - R
Search
Single Ad. Ministries Jour.
Worship Leader
Youthworker - R

TEEN/YOUNG ADULT
Breakaway - R
event
Freeway - R
HiCall - R
High School I.D. - R
Insight - R
Insight/Out - R
Issues & Answers - R
Magazine/Youth! - R
Pathway I.D. - R
Sharing the VICTORY - R
Spirit
Straight - R
Teenage Christian - R
Teen Power - R
Teen Quest - R
Venture - R
YOU! - R
Young Adult Today
Young & Alive - R
Young Salvationist - R
Youth Focus - R

WOMEN
Church Woman
Contempo
Daughters of Sarah
Esprit - R
Horizons - R
Jour/Women's Ministries
Joyful Woman - R
Link & Visitor - R
Lutheran Woman Today
Probe
Royal Service
Salt and Light
Sisters Today - R
Today's Christian Woman
Virtue - R

WRITERS
Canadian Writer's Jour - R
Christian Communicator, The - R
Christian Vision - R
Cross & Quill - R
Writers Connection - R
Writer's Info
Writer's Infor Network

LEADERSHIP

ADULT/GENERAL
Acts 29
At Ease - R
ADVOCATE - R
Baptist Beacon - R
Bible Advocate - R
Canada Lutheran - R
Canadian Catholic Review
Catholic Digest - R
Christian Century
Christian Edge - R
Christianity Today - R
Church Herald/Holiness Banner - R
Columbia - R
Companion
Covenant Companion
Discipleship Journal - R
Emphasis/Faith & Living - R
Evangelical Baptist
Faith Today
Good News, Etc - R
John Milton - R
Journal/Christian Nursing - R
Liguorian
Living Church
Lutheran Digest - R
Mennonite, The - R
Mennonite Brethren Herald - R
MESSAGE of the Open Bible - R
Ministry Today - R
Nat/Intl Religion Report
NW Christian Journal - R
Our Family - R
Our Sunday Visitor
Pentecostal Evangel
Pentecostal Homelife - R
Pentecostal Messenger - R
Presbyterian Outlook
Religious Education
Sunday Digest - R
United Methodist Reporter
Vista - R

CHILDREN
High Adventure - R

CHRISTIAN EDUCATION/LIBRARY
Baptist Leader
Brigade Leader - R
CE Connection - R
CE Counselor - R
Changing Lives - R
Church Educator - R
Church Worship
GROUP
Leader - R
Leader/Church School Today
Memos - R
Perspective - R
Team - R
Vision - R
Youth & CE Leadership - R
Youth Leader - R

MISSIONS
American Horizon - R
Urban Mission - R
World Vision - R
Worldwide Challenge - R

PASTORS/LEADERS
Advance - R
Christian Management - R
Christian Ministry
Church Business - R
Church Growth Network - R
Group's Jr High
Ivy Jungle Report - R
Journal/Christian Healing - R

Leadership Journal - R
Ministries Today
Preacher's Magazine - R
Priest, The
Pulpit/Bible Study Helps - R
Resource - R
Word & World
Worship Leader
Youthworker - R

TEEN/YOUNG ADULT
Kiln, The - R
Student Leadership - R
Teenage Christian - R

WOMEN
Esprit - R
Link & Visitor - R
Virtue - R
Women Alive ! - R
Writers Anchor - R

LITURGICAL

ADULT/GENERAL
Acts 29
AGAIN - R
alive now! - R
Canada Lutheran - R
Canadian Catholic Review
Catholic Digest - R
Church Herald/Holiness Banner - R
Commonweal
Companion
Covenant Companion
Cresset
Episcopal Life - R
Family Digest, The - R
John Milton - R
Liguorian
Living Church
Messenger (KY)
North American Voice
Our Family - R
Our Sunday Visitor
Presbyterian Outlook
Presbyterian Record - R
Queen of All Hearts
Social Justice Review
Tree of Life
United Church Observer - R
United Methodist Reporter
U.S. Catholic

CHRISTIAN EDUCATION/LIBRARY
Church Worship
Lutheran Education
Parish Teacher - R
Religion Teacher's Journal
Today's Catholic Teacher - R

MISSIONS
Areopagus - R
Catholic Near East

MUSIC
Church Pianist, etc.
Creator
Hymn, The

PASTORS/LEADERS
Celebration
Chicago Studies
Christian Ministry
Church Administration
Congregational Journal
Eucharistic Minister - R
Five Stones, The - R
Journal/Christian Healing - R
Liturgy
Lutheran Forum - R
Pastoral Life - R - R
Preaching
Preacher's Illus. Service - R
Preacher's Magazine - R
Priest, The
PROCLAIM - R
Quarterly Review
Reformed Worship
Review for Religious
Today's Parish
Word & World

TEENS/YOUNG ADULTS
You! - R

WOMEN
Daughters of Sarah
Esprit - R
Horizons - R
Lutheran Woman Today
Sisters Today - R

MARRIAGE

ADULT/GENERAL
Advent Christian Witness
ADVOCATE - R
Alive! - R
All About Issues - R
America
American Tract Society - R
Assoc Ref Presbyterian - R
At Ease - R
AXIOS - R
Better Tomorrow
Bible Advocate - R
Canada Lutheran - R
Canadian Catholic Review
Catholic Digest - R
Catholic Parent
Catholic Sentinel - R
Catholic Twin Circle - R
Charisma & Christian Life
Christian C.L. RECORD - R
Christian Century
Christian Courier (Canada) - R
Christian Edge - R
Christian Home & School
Christian Living - R
Christian Parenting Today - R
Christian Reader - R
Church Herald/Holiness Banner - R
Columbia - R
Companion
Companions - R
Conquest
Covenant Companion
Creation Social Science - R
Decision
Emphasis/Faith & Living - R
Evangel - R
Evangelical Beacon - R
Evangelical Friend
Evangelical Visitor - R
Expression
Family, The - R
Family Digest, The - R
Fellowship Today - R
Focus on the Family - R
Friends Journal - R
Good News, Etc - R
Gospel Tidings - R
Guideposts
Hallelujah - R
Home Life
Home Times - R
Impact Magazine - R
Indian Life - R
John Milton - R
Journal/Christian Nursing - R
Jour/Religion in Psychotherapy
Jour/Religious Gerontology
Joyful Noise
Kansas City Christian - R
Lifeglow - R
Light and Life

Liguorian
Live - R
Living - R
Lookout - R
Lutheran, The
Lutheran Digest - R
Lutheran Witness
Mature Years - R
Mennonite, The - R
Mennonite Brethren Herald - R
MESSAGE
MESSAGE of the Open Bible - R
Messenger, The (Canada) - R
Messenger, The (NC) - R
Messenger of St. Anthony - R
Ministry Today - R
Minnesota Chronicle, The - R
Montana Catholic
Moody
National Christian Reporter
New Covenant - R
New Oxford Review
North American Voice
NW Christian Journal - R
Our Family - R
Our Sunday Visitor
Parenting Treasures - R
Parents of Teenagers
PCA Messenger - R
Pentecostal Evangel
Pentecostal Homelife - R
Pentecostal Messenger - R
Pentecostal Testimony - R
Power for Living - R
Presbyterian Record - R
Presbyterian Survey - R
Psychology for Living - R
Purpose - R
Pursuit - R
St. Anthony Messenger
Seek - R
Signs of the Times - R
Social Justice Review
Standard - R
Sunday Digest - R
Table Talk - R
Today's Better Life
Tree of Life
United Methodist Reporter
U.S. Catholic
VISION - R
Vision (MO) - R
Vista - R
Vital Christianity - R
Voice, The - R
Wesleyan Advocate
Writer's Forum - R

CHRISTIAN EDUCATION/LIBRARY
Brigade Leader - R
CE Connection - R
CE Counselor - R
Leader - R
Lutheran Education

MISSIONS
Worldwide Challenge - R

PASTORS/LEADERS
Bethany Choice - R
Chicago Studies
Christian Ministry
Congregational Journal
Faith & Renewal - R
Journal/Christian Healing - R
Ministries Today
Networks - R
Pastoral Life - R
Preacher's Illus. Service - R
PROCLAIM - R
Pulpit/Bible Study Helps - R
Search
Today's Parish
Word & World

TEEN/YOUNG ADULT
Insight - R
Student, The - R
YOU! - R
Young Adult Today
Young & Alive - R

WOMEN
Anna's Journal - R
Co-Laborer - R
Daughters of Sarah
Esprit - R
Helping Hand - R
Joyful Woman - R
Link & Visitor - R
Lutheran Woman Today
Today's Christian Woman
Virtue - R
Woman's Touch - R
Women Alive! - R

WRITERS
Housewife-Writer's Forum - R

*MEN'S ISSUES

ADULT/GENERAL
All About Issues - R
Annals of St. Anne
At Ease - R
AXIOS - R
Canada Lutheran - R
Catholic Parent
Catholic Sentinel - R
Christian Edge - R
Christian Single - R
Christian Social Action
Christianity Today - R
Companion
Critic, The
Emphasis/Faith & Living - R
Expression
Family, The - R
Good News, Etc - R
Gospel Tidings - R
Herald of Holiness - R
Indian Life - R
Joyful Noise
Kansas City Christian - R
Liguorian
Mature Years - R
Mennonite, The - R
Mennonite Brethren Herald - R
MESSAGE of the Open Bible - R
Ministry Today - R
Moody
NW Christian Journal - R
Our Family - R
Pentecostal Evangel
Pentecostal Messenger - R
Pentecostal Testimony - R
Power for Living - R
Smart Dads
Sunday Digest - R
Today's Better Life
Vibrant Life - R (health)
Vista - R
Witness, The

CHRISTIAN EDUCATION/LIBRARY
Brigade Leader - R

MISSIONS
American Horizon - R
New World Outlook
Worldwide Challenge - R

PASTORS/LEADERS
Bethany Choice - R
Ministries Today
Preacher's Magazine - R
Resource - R
Word & World

MIRACLES

ADULT/GENERAL

Acts 29
ADVOCATE - R
America
Annals of St. Anne
At Ease - R
Canadian Catholic Review
Catholic Digest - R
Catholic Twin Circle - R
Charisma & Christian Life
Church Herald/Holiness Banner - R
Companion
Connecting Point - R
Evangel - R
Explorer
Friends Journal - R
God's Revivalist - R
Good News, Etc - R
Guideposts
Hallelujah - R
Impact Magazine - R
Inspirer, The - R
Liguorian
Live - R
Lutheran Digest - R
Maranatha - R
Mennonite, The - R
MESSAGE of the Open Bible - R
Messenger, The (NC) - R
New Oxford Review
New Thought Journal - R
Pentecostal Evangel
Pentecostal Homelife - R
Pentecostal Messenger - R
Power for Living - R
Queen of All Hearts
Sharing - R
Standard - R
Sunday Digest - R
Table Talk - R
Tree of Life
VISION - R
Vision (MO) - R
Vista - R
Writer's Forum - R

CHILDREN

GUIDE - R

CHRISTIAN EDUCATION/LIBRARY

Changing Lives - R

MISSIONS

American Horizon - R
Areopagus - R

PASTORS/LEADERS

Faith & Renewal - R
Journal/Christian Healing - R
Ministries Today
Networks - R
Preacher's Magazine - R
Word & World

TEEN/YOUNG ADULT

Conqueror - R
HiCall - R
Insight - R
Insight/Out - R
Pathway I.D. - R
YOU! - R
Young Adult Today

WOMEN

Esprit - R
Lutheran Woman Today
Woman's Touch - R

MISSIONS

ADULT/GENERAL

Acts 29
ADVOCATE - R
Alive! - R
Annals of St. Anne
Anglican Journal - R
Assoc Ref Presbyterian - R
At Ease - R
Baptist Informer
B.C. Catholic - R
Canada Lutheran - R
Canadian Catholic Review
Catholic Digest - R
Catholic Sentinel - R
Catholic Twin Circle - R
Charisma & Christian Life
Christian Century
Christian Reader - R
Christian Renewal - R
Christianity Today - R
Church Herald/Holiness Banner - R
Columbia - R
Companion
Companions - R
Connecting Point - R
Conquest
Cornerstone - R
Decision
Episcopal Life - R
Evangelical Baptist
Evangelical Friend
Explorer
God's Revivalist - R
Good News, Etc - R
Gospel Tidings - R
Hallelujah - R
Indian Life - R
Inspirer, The - R
InterVarsity
John Milton - R
Journal/Christian Nursing - R
Live - R
Living Church
Lookout - R
Lutheran, The
Lutheran Witness
Maranatha - R
Mennonite, The - R
Mennonite Reporter
MESSAGE of the Open Bible - R
Messenger, The (NC) - R
Messenger of St. Anthony - R
Moody
National Christian Reporter
Nat/Intl Religion Report
New Heart, A - R (medical)
New Oxford Review
News Network Intl.
North American Voice
Other Side, The
Our Family - R
Our Sunday Visitor
Pentecostal Evangel
Pentecostal Homelife - R
Pentecostal Messenger - R
Power for Living - R
Presbyterian Outlook
Presbyterian Record - R
Presbyterian Survey - R
Psychology for Living - R
Purpose - R
Railroad Evangelist - R
Religious Broadcasting - R
Seek - R
Servant
Social Justice Review
Standard - R
Star of Zion
Sunday Digest - R
Tree of Life
United Methodist Reporter
Vision (MO) - R
Vista - R

CHILDREN

Partners - R
Primary Pal

CHRISTIAN EDUCATION/LIBRARY
Brigade Leader - R
Changing Lives - R
Church Educator - R
Church Recreation - R
Evangelizing Today's Child
Youth Leader - R

MISSIONS
(see alphabetical listings)

PASTORS/LEADERS
Bible-Science - R
Christian Ministry
Church Administration
Discipleship Training
Evangelism - R
Five Stones, The - R
Journal/Christian Healing - R
Ministries Today
Networks - R
Paraclete - R
Preacher's Magazine - R
PROCLAIM - R
Pulpit/Bible Study Helps - R
Resource - R
Search
Word & World
Youthworker - R

TEEN/YOUNG ADULT
Certainty
Challenge (IL)
Conqueror - R
Edge, The - R
Freeway - R
Insight - R
Insight/Out - R
Kiln, The - R
Magazine/Youth! - R
Pathway I.D. - R
Priest, The
Student, The - R
Teen Power - R
Teen Quest - R
YOU! - R
Young Adult Today
Young Salvationist - R

WOMEN
Co-Laborer - R
Contempo
Esprit - R
Link & Visitor - R
Lutheran Woman Today
Response
Royal Service
Virtue - R
Wesleyan Woman
Woman's Touch - R

MONEY MANAGEMENT

ADULT/GENERAL
Anglican Journal - R
At Ease - R
AXIOS - R
Better Tomorrow
Catholic Digest - R
Catholic Parent
Catholic Twin Circle - R
Charisma & Christian Life
Christian C.L. RECORD - R
Christian Edge - R
Christian Parenting Today - R
Christian Single - R
Church Herald/Holiness Banner - R
Connecting Point - R
Discovery - R
Emphasis/Faith & Living - R
Evangelical Baptist
Evangelical Friend
Evangelical Visitor - R
Expression
Focus on the Family - R
Good News, Etc - R
Good News Journal
Gospel Tidings - R
Guideposts
Herald of Holiness - R
Home Life
Home Times - R
Indian Life - R
John Milton - R
Journal/Christian Camping - R
Lookout - R
Lutheran Digest - R
Mennonite, The - R
MESSAGE
MESSAGE of the Open Bible - R
Messenger, The (NC) - R
Ministry Today - R
Parents of Teenagers
PCA Messenger - R
Pentecostal Evangel
Pentecostal Homelife - R
Pentecostal Messenger - R
Pentecostal Testimony - R
Power for Living - R
Purpose - R
Religious Broadcasting - R
Servant
Signs of the Times - R
Social Justice Review
Sunday Digest - R
Today's Better Life
United Methodist Reporter
Vista - R

CHILDREN
Crusader - R

CHRISTIAN EDUCATION/LIBRARY
Brigade Leader - R
CE Connection - R
Christian School

MISSIONS
World Christian - R

PASTORS/LEADERS
Advance - R
Christian Ministry
Church Business - R
Clergy Journal
Journal/Christian Healing - R
Leadership Journal - R
Ministries Today
Networks - R
Pastoral Life - R
Pastor's Tax & Money
Preacher's Magazine - R
Today's Parish
Your Church - R
Youthworker - R

TEEN/YOUNG ADULT
Kiln, The - R
Student, The - R
Teenage Christian - R
With - R
Young Adult Today

WOMEN
Esprit - R
Helping Hand - R
Joyful Woman - R
Lutheran Woman Today
Salt and Light
Today's Christian Woman
Virtue - R
Woman's Touch - R
Women Alive! - R

WRITERS
Writers Anchor - R

*MUSIC REVIEWS

ADULT/GENERAL
Canadian Catholic Review
Christian Edge - R
Cornerstone - R
Expression
Home Life
Home Times - R
Impact Magazine - R
Presbyterian Record - R

MUSIC
Hymn, The
Worship Today - R

TEEN/YOUNG ADULT
Insight - R
Young Salvationist - R

NATURE

ADULT/GENERAL
Alive! - R
AXIOS - R
Canadian Catholic Review
Catholic Digest - R
Christian Living - R
Companion
Companions - R
Creation Social Science - R
Explorer
John Milton - R
Lifeglow - R
Lutheran Digest - R
Mature Years - R
Pentecostal Evangel
Purpose - R
Seek - R
Sunday Digest - R

CHILDREN
Crusader - R
GUIDE - R
High Adventure - R
Junior Trails - R
My Friend
Nature Friend
On the Line
Skipping Stones

CHRISTIAN EDUCATION/LIBRARY
Church Recreation - R

PASTORS/LEADERS
Journal/Christian Healing - R
Word & World

TEEN/YOUNG ADULT
Insight - R
Magazine/Youth! - R
Teenage Christian - R
Venture - R
Young & Alive - R

WOMEN
Esprit - R

*NEWSPAPERS

Anglican Journal - R
Arkansas Catholic
Arlington Catholic Herald
B.C. Catholic - R
Beacon Christian News
Catholic Accent
Catholic Courier
Catholic Exponent
Catholic New York
Catholic Sentinel
Catholic Telegraph
Catholic Twin Circle - R
Christian Chronicle
Christian Courier (WI) - R
Christian Courier (Canada) - R
Christian Crusade
Christian Edge - R
ChristianWeek
Discovery - R
Episcopal Life - R
Expression Christian Newspaper
Good News, Etc. - R
Good News Journal
Home Times - R
Interchange
The Interim - R
Issues & Answers - R
Kansas City Christian - R
Maranatha - R
Mennonite Reporter
Mennonite Weekly Review
Messenger (KY)
Minnesota Chronicle - R
Montana Catholic
National Catholic Reporter
Northwest Christian Journal
Our Sunday Visitor
Probe
Pulpit/Bible Study Helps - R
Spokane/Inland NW Christian
Today's Single
United Methodist Reporter
World

OPINION PIECES

ADULT/GENERAL
Acts 29
African-American Heritage - R
All About Issues - R
Arlington Catholic Herald
Assoc Ref Presbyterian - R
At Ease - R
AXIOS - R
B.C. Catholic - R
Better Tomorrow
Bible Advocate - R
Canadian Catholic Review
Catholic New York
Catholic Sentinel - R
Charisma & Christian Life
Christian Chronicle
Christian Renewal - R
Christian Research - R
Christianity Today - R
Commonweal
Compass
Cornerstone - R
Creation Social Science - R
Door, The
Episcopal Life - R
Evangelical Baptist
Evangelical Friend
Expression
Family, The - R
Fellowship Today - R
Good News, Etc - R
Home Times - R
Interim - R
John Milton - R
Journal/Christian Nursing - R
Kansas City Christian - R
Life Advocate - R
Light and Life (600 wds)
Living Church
Lookout - R
Lutheran, The
Maranatha - R
Mennonite Brethren Herald - R
Mennonite Reporter
Mennonite Weekly Review
MESSAGE of the Open Bible - R
Messenger (KY)
Minnesota Chronicle, The - R
National Christian Reporter
New Oxford Review
News Network Intl.
New Thought Journal - R
Pentecostal Messenger - R
Presbyterian Record - R
Presbyterian Survey - R

Prism
Purpose - R
Quiet Revolution - R
Religious Broadcasting - R
Salt
Servant
Social Justice Review
Tree of Life
United Methodist Reporter
U.S. Catholic
Vista - R

CHRISTIAN EDUCATION/LIBRARY
CE Connection - R
Lutheran Education

MISSIONS
American Horizon - R
Areopagus - R
World Vision - R

PASTORS/LEADERS
Journal/Christian Healing - R
Leadership Journal - R
Ministries Today
Preacher's Magazine - R
Priest, The
Single Ad. Ministries Jour.
Word & World

TEEN/YOUNG ADULT
Insight - R
Insight/Out - R
Magazine/Youth! - R
You! - R
Young Adult Today
Youth Focus - R

WOMEN
Conscience - R
Joyful Woman - R
Lutheran Woman Today
Virtue - R

WRITERS
Canadian Writer's Jour - R
Christian Vision - R
Exchange - R
Writers Anchor - R

PARENTING

ADULT/GENERAL
Advent Christian Witness
ADVOCATE - R
American Tract Society - R
Annals of St. Anne
AXIOS - R
Baptist Beacon - R
Bible Advocate - R
Canada Lutheran - R
Catholic Digest - R
Catholic Parent
Catholic Sentinel - R
Charisma & Christian Life
Christian Courier (Canada) - R
Christian Edge - R
Christian Home & School
Christian Living - R
Christian Parenting Today - R
Christian Reader - R
Christian Single - R
Church Herald/Holiness Banner - R
Columbia - R
Companion
Companions - R
Covenant Companion
Creation Social Science - R
Emphasis/Faith & Living - R
Evangel - R
Evangelical Beacon - R
Evangelical Friend
Evangelical Visitor - R
Expression
Family, The - R
Family Digest, The - R
Fellowship Today - R
Focus on the Family - R
Foursquare World ADVANCE - R
Friends Journal - R
Good News, Etc - R
Gospel Tidings - R
Herald of Holiness - R
Home Life
Home Times - R
Impact Magazine - R
Indian Life - R
John Milton - R
Kansas City Christian - R
Light and Life
Liguorian
Living - R
Lookout - R
Lutheran, The
Lutheran Digest - R
Mature Years - R
Mennonite, The - R
MESSAGE
MESSAGE of the Open Bible - R
Messenger, The (Canada) - R
Messenger, The (NC) - R
Messenger of St. Anthony - R
Ministry Today - R
Moody
National Christian Reporter
New Covenant - R
New Oxford Review
NW Christian Living - R
Our Family - R
Our Sunday Visitor
Parenting Treasures - R
Parents of Teenagers
PCA Messenger - R
Pentecostal Evangel
Pentecostal Homelife - R
Pentecostal Messenger - R
Pentecostal Testimony - R
Positive Approach - R
Power for Living - R
Presbyterian Survey - R
Psychology for Living - R
Purpose - R
Pursuit - R
Religious Education
St.Anthony Messenger
St. Joseph Messenger - R
Seek - R
Smart Dads
Social Justice Review
Standard - R
Sunday Digest - R
Table Talk - R
Today's Better Life
Today's Single - R
Tree of Life
United Church Observer - R
United Methodist Reporter
Vision (MO) - R
Vista - R
Vital Christianity - R
Wesleyan Advocate
Writer's Forum - R

CHRISTIAN EDUCATION/LIBRARY
Brigade Leader - R
CE Connection - R
Christian School
Church Educator - R
GROUP
Leader - R
Lutheran Education
Shining Star

MISSIONS
Worldwide Challenge - R

PASTORS/LEADERS
Bethany Choice - R
Bible-Science - R
Christian Ministry
Diaconalogue - R
Discipleship Training

Faith & Renewal - R
Group's Jr High
Journal/Christian Healing - R
Media Update
Networks - R
Preacher's Illus. Service - R
Pulpit/Bible Study Helps - R
Single Ad. Ministries Jour.
Youthworker - R

WOMEN

Co-Laborer - R
Esprit - R
Helping Hand - R
Joyful Woman - R
Lutheran Woman Today
Today's Christian Woman
Virtue - R
Women Alive! - R

WRITERS

Housewife-Writer's Forum - R

PERSONAL EXPERIENCE

ADULT/GENERAL

Acts 29
Advent Christian Witness
African-American Heritage - R
AGAIN - R
alive now! - R
All About Issues - R
Annals of St. Anne
Assoc Ref Presbyterian - R
At Ease - R
B.C. Catholic - R
Better Tomorrow
Bible Advocate - R
Canada Lutheran - R
Canadian Catholic Review
Catholic Digest - R
Catholic New York
Catholic Sentinel - R
Catholic Twin Circle - R
Charisma & Christian Life
Christian Courier (Canada) - R
Christian Edge - R
Christian Parenting Today - R
Christian Reader - R
Christian Renewal - R
Christian Research - R
Church Herald
Church Herald/Holiness Banner - R
Commonweal
Companion
Companions - R
Compass
Conquest
Cornerstone - R
Covenant Companion
Decision
Door, The
Evangel - R
Evangelical Baptist
Evangelical Friend
Evangelical Visitor - R
Explorer
Family, The - R
Family Digest, The - R
Fellowship Today - R
Focus on the Family - R
Friends Journal - R
Gem, The - R
God's Revivalist - R
God's Special People - R
Good News - R
Good News, Etc - R
Good News Journal
Guideposts
Hallelujah - R
Herald of Holiness - R
His Garden
Home Times - R
Ideals - R
Impact Magazine - R
Indian Life - R
Inspirer, The - R
Interim - R
InterVarsity
John Milton - R
Journal/Christian Nursing - R
Life Advocate - R
Light and Life
Liguorian
Living - R
Living Church
Lookout - R
Lutheran, The
Lutheran Digest - R
Lutheran Journal - R
Lutheran Layman
Maranatha - R
Marian Helpers Bulletin - R
Mature Years - R
Mennonite, The - R
Mennonite Brethren Herald - R
Mennonite Reporter
MESSAGE of the Open Bible - R
Messenger, The (NC) - R
Minnesota Chronicle, The - R
Moody
Morning Glory - R
New Covenant - R
New Thought Journal - R
Other Side, The
Our Family - R
Parenting Treasures - R
Parents of Teenagers
Pentecostal Evangel
Pentecostal Homelife - R
Pentecostal Messenger - R
Pentecostal Testimony - R
Plenty Good Room
Power for Living - R
Presbyterian Record - R
Presbyterian Survey - R
PROGRESS - R
Psychology for Living - R
Purpose - R
Pursuit - R
Railroad Evangelist - R
Religious Broadcasting - R
SCP Journal - R
Seek - R
Servant
Shantyman, The - R
Sharing - R
Standard - R
Star of Zion
Sunday Digest - R
Table Talk - R
Today's Single - R
Tree of Life
Touchstone
United Church Observer - R
VISION - R
Vision (MO) - R
Vista - R
Vital Christianity - R
Voice, The - R
Wesleyan Advocate

CHILDREN

Counselor
GUIDE - R
Touch - R
Venture
Young Crusader - R

CHRISTIAN EDUCATION/LIBRARY

CE Connection - R
CE Counselor - R
Changing Lives - R
Journal/Adventist Educ. - R
KEY - R
Lutheran Education
Perspective - R

Religion Teacher's Journal
Youth & CE Leadership - R

MISSIONS
American Horizon - R
Areopagus - R
Heartbeat - R
P.I.M.E. World - R
World Christian - R
Worldwide Challenge - R

MUSIC
Music Leader

PASTORS/LEADERS
Church Business - R
Congregational Journal
Diaconalogue - R
Discipleship Training
Eucharistic Minister - R
Faith & Renewal - R
Five Stones, The - R
Journal/Christian Healing - R
Leadership Journal - R
Ministries Today
Networks - R
Preacher's Illus. Service - R
Preacher's Magazine - R
Today's Parish
Youthworker - R

TEEN/YOUNG ADULT
Breakaway - R
Campus Life - R
Certainty
Challenge (IL)
Conqueror - R
event
Freeway - R
HiCall - R
Insight - R
Insight/Out - R
Spirit
Straight - R
Student, The - R
Teen Life - R
Teen Power - R
Teen Quest - R
With - R (1st person teen)
You! - R
Young Adult Today
Young Salvationist - R
Youth Focus - R
Youth World - R

WOMEN
Contempo
Esprit - R
Helping Hand - R
Jour/Women's Ministries
Joyful Woman - R
Just Between Us
Link & Visitor - R
Lutheran Woman Today
Probe
Response
Royal Service
Salt and Light
Today's Christian Woman
Virtue - R
Woman's Touch - R
Women Alive ! - R

WRITERS
Byline
Chips Off Writer's Block - R
Christian Vision - R
Exchange - R
Home Office - R
Housewife-Writer's Forum - R
Writer's Infor Network
Writer's Nook News

PHOTOGRAPHS

Note: `Reprint' indicators (R) have been deleted from this section, and 'B' for black & white glossy prints or 'C' for color transparencies inserted.

ADULT/GENERAL
ABS RECORD
Advent Christian Witness - B
ADVOCATE - B & C
African-American Heritage - B
Alive! - B
alive now! - B
All About Issues - B & C
American Tract Society
Anglican Journal - B & C
Annals of St. Anne
Arlington Catholic Herald - B & C
Assoc Ref Presbyterian - B
At Ease - B & C
Better Tomorrow - C
Bible Today - B
Bookstore Journal - B & C
Calvinist Contact - B & C
Canada Lutheran
Catholic Courier - B
Catholic Digest - B & C
Catholic Exponent - B
Catholic Family Media Guide
Catholic Heritage
Catholic New York - B
Catholic Sentinel - B
Catholic Telegraph - B
Catholic Twin Circle
Charisma/Christian Life - C
Christian Century - B
Christian Chronicle - B
Christian Courier - B
Christian Crusade - B
Christian Drama - B
Christian History - B & C
Christian Home & School - B & C
Christian Living - B
Christian Parenting Today - B/C
Christian Reader - B & C
Christian Research - B & C
Christian Retailing - B & C
Christian Single - B
Christian Social Action - B
Christian Standard - B & C
Christianity Today - B & C
Church & State
Church Herald - B & C
Church of God Evangel - C
Class
Columbia - C/prints
Companion - B
Connecting Point - B
Conquest - B
Cornerstone - B & C
Covenant Companion - B & C
Discipleship Journal - C
Episcopal Life - B
Evangel - B
Evangelical Beacon - B & C
Evangelical Friend - B
Evangelical Visitor - B
Expression - B
Faith Today - B
Family, The - B & C
Fellowship Today - B
Focus on the Family - C
Foursquare World ADVANCE - B/C
Good News, Etc - B & C
Gospel Tidings - B
Guideposts - B & C
Hallelujah - B
Herald of Holiness - B & C
Home Life - C
Home Times - B
Ideals - C (No 35mm)
Impact Magazine - C
Indian Life - C
Inspirer, The - B
Interchange - B
INTEREST - B & C
Interim

InterVarsity - B
Journal/Christian Camping - B/C
Journal/Christian Nursing - B/C
Joyful Noise
Liberty - B & C
Lifeglow - B & C
Light and Life - B & C
Liguorian
Live - B & C
Living - B & C
Living Church - B
Lookout - B & C
Lutheran, The - B
Lutheran Journal - C
Lutheran Witness - B & C
Maranatha - B
Marian Helpers Bulletin - B & C
Mature Living
Mature Years - C
Mennonite, The - B
Mennonite Brethren Herald - B
Mennonite Reporter - B & C
Mennonite Weekly Review - B
MESSAGE - B & C
MESSAGE of the Open Bible - C
Messenger (KY) - B
Messenger, The (Canada) - B
Messenger, The (NC) - B
Messenger of St. Anthony - B/C
Montana Catholic - B & C
Nat. Christian Reporter - B & C/prints
News Network Intl.
New Thought Journal - B (cover)
Other Side, The - B & C
Our Family - B & C
Our Sunday Visitor - B & C
Parents of Teenager - B
PCA Messenger - B
Pentecostal Evangel - B & C
Pentecostal Messenger - C
Pentecostal Testimony - B & C
Plenty Good Room - B
Plowman, The - B
Power for Living - B
Prayer Line - B
Prairie Messenger - B
Presbyterian Outlook
Presbyterian Record - B & C
Presbyterian Survey - B & C
Prism
Purpose - B
Pursuit - B
Quiet Revolution - B
St. Anthony Messenger - B & C
Salt - B
SCP Journal - B & C
Seek - B
Signs of the Times - C
Spiritual Life - B
Sports Spectrum - C
Standard - B
Starlight - B (drawings)
Star of Zion - B & C
Sunday Digest - B & C
Thema - B
Today's Better Life - C
Today's Single - B
Together - B & C
Twin Cities Christian - B
United Church Observer - B & C
United Methodist Reporter - B & C/prints
VISION - B & C
Vista - B & C
War Cry - C
Wesleyan Advocate - C
Witness, The

CHILDREN

Counselor - B & C
Faith 'n Stuff - B & C
Focus/Clubhouse/Clubhouse Jr - C
God's World Today - C
Junior Trails - C
Listen - C
Nature Friend - B & C
My Friend
On the Line - B
Pockets - C
Power & Light - B & C
Primary Days - B & C
R-A-D-A-R - C
Story Friends - B
Together Time - C
Touch - B
Wonder Time - B & C

CHRISTIAN EDUCATION/LIBRARY

Baptist Leader - B
Brigade Leader - B
CE Counselor - B & C
Children's Ministry - B
Christian Librarian - B
Christian School - C
Church Recreation - C
Evang. Today's Child - B & C
GROUP - B
Journal/Adventist Education - B
Junior Teacher - B & C
KEY - B
Leader/Church School Today - B
Level C Teacher - B
Lollipops
Parish Teacher - B
Perspective - B & C
Preschool Playhouse - B & C
Primary Street - B & C
Religion Teacher's Journal - B & C
Teachers in Focus - C
Teachers Interaction - B
Team - B & C
Today's Catholic Teacher - B & C
Youth & CE Leadership - B & C

DAILY DEVOTIONALS

Daily Dev for Deaf - C
Light From the Word - C
Pathways to God - B & C
Secret Place - B & C
Upper Room - C

MISSIONS

American Horizon - R
Areopagus - B & C
Catholic Near East - C
P.I.M.E. World - C
Childlife
Impact - B & C
Maryknoll - B & C
New World Outlook - B & C
Wherever - B (with ms)
World Christian - B & C
World Vision - C
Worldwide Challenge - C

MUSIC

Church Musician - B
Creator - B
Music Leader - B & C

PASTORS/LEADERS

Advance - B & C
Celebration - B & C
Christian Ministry - B
Christian Sentinel - B & C
Discipleship Training - B
Group's Jr High - B
Growing Churches - B & C
Leadership Journal
Liturgy - B
Lutheran Forum - R - B
Media Update - B
Networks - B
Pastoral Life - B
Preacher's Magazine - B & C
Preaching - B & C
Resource - B & C
Today's Parish - B & C
Your Church - B & C

TEEN/YOUNG ADULT
Breakaway - C
Brio - C
Campus Life - C
Certainty - B
Challenge (IL) -B
Challenge (TN) - B & C
Conqueror, The - B & C
Freeway - B
HiCall - B & C
High School I.D.
Insight - B & C
Lighted Pathway - B & C
Magazine/Youth! - B & C
Pioneer - B
Sharing the VICTORY - C
Spirit - B & C
Straight - B & C
Student, The - B
Student Leadership - B & C
Take Five - B & C
Teenage Christian - C
Teen Power - B
Teen Quest - B & C
Teens Today - B
Venture - B
With - B
YOU! - B & C
Young Adult Today - B
Young & Alive - B (prefer) & C
Young Salvationist - C
Youth Focus (with article)

WOMEN
Anna's Journal - B
Conscience - B
Daughters of Sarah - B
Esprit (few)
Helping Hand - B
Horizons - B
Jour/Women's Ministries - B
Joyful Woman - B & C
Just Between Us
Link & Visitor - B
Lutheran Woman Today - B
Probe - B & C
Response - B & C
Sisters Today - B & C
Today's Christian Woman - C
Virtue - B & C
Woman's Touch - C
Women Alive! - B

WRITERS
Gotta Write - B
Home Office - B
Housewife-Writers Forum - B

POETRY

ADULT/GENERAL
ADVOCATE - R
African-American Heritage - R
alive now! - R
All About Issues - R
America
At Ease - R
AXIOS - R
Baptist Beacon - R
Bible Advocate - R
Broken Streets - R
Burning Light - R
Christian Century
Christian Courier (Canada) - R
Christian Drama - R
Christian Living - R
Christian Reader - R
Christian Single - R
Christmas - R
Church Herald/Holiness Banner - R
Class
Commonweal
Companion
Companions - R
Connecting Point - R
Cornerstone - R
Covenant Companion
Creation Social Science - R
Cresset
Decision
Door, The
Evangel - R
Explorer
Friends Journal - R
God's Revivalist - R
God's Special People - R
Guideposts
Hallelujah - R
Herald of Holiness - R
His Garden
Home Life
Home Times - R
Ideals - R
Impact Magazine - R
Inspirer, The - R
INTEREST - R
John Milton - R
Journal/Christian Camping - R
Journal/Christian Nursing - R
Liberty (little) - R
Life Advocate - R
Light and Life
Lighthouse Fiction Collection
Liguorian
Live - R
Living Church
Lutheran Digest - R
Lutheran Journal - R
Manna
Mature Living
Mature Years - R
Mennonite, The - R
Mennonite Brethren Herald - R
Messenger, The (Canada) - R
Messenger of St. Anthony - R
Miraculous Medal
Morning Glory - R
National Christian Reporter
New Thought Journal - R
North American Voice
Oblates
Other Side, The
Our Family - R
Parenting Treasures - R
PCA Messenger - R
Pegasus Review
Pentecostal Evangel
Pentecostal Messenger - R
Pentecostal Testimony - R
Plowman, The
Poetry Forum
Power for Living - R
Prayer Line - R
Presbyterian Record - R
Presbyterian Survey - R
Purpose - R
Queen of all Hearts
Railroad Evangelist - R
Ratio
St. Anthony Messenger
St. Joseph Messenger - R
Shantyman, The - R
Sharing - R
Standard - R
Starlight
Star of Zion
Sunday Digest - R
Thema - R
Thirteen Poetry
Time of Singing - R
Today's Single - R
Touchstone
United Methodist Reporter
Vision (MO) - R
Vital Christianity - R
Voice, The - R
Wesleyan Advocate
Witness, The

CHILDREN
CLUBHOUSE - R
Creatively Yours

Faith 'n Stuff
Focus/Clubhouse/Clubhouse Jr
Junior Trails - R
Listen
Mission
Nature Friend - R
On the Line - R
Our Little Friend - R
Partners - R
Pockets - R
Primary Treasure - R
R-A-D-A-R - R
Story Friends - R
Story Mates - R
Together Time
Touch - R
Wonder Time
Young Crusader - R

CHRISTIAN EDUCATION/LIBRARY
Baptist Leader
Christian Educators Jour - R
Christian School
Church Educator - R
Church Worship
Level C Teacher - R
Lollipops
Teacher Interaction - R
Vision - R

DAILY DEVOTIONALS
Living Words - R
Secret Place

MISSIONS
Areopagus - R
Maryknoll
New World Outlook

MUSIC
Choir Herald, etc.
Church Musician
Church Pianist, etc.
Glory Songs
Hymn, The (hymns only)
Music Leader
Senior Musician - R
Tradition

PASTORS/LEADERS
Art+ Repro Resource
Congregational Journal
Cross Currents
Diaconalogue - R
Journal/Christian Healing - R
Liturgy
Lutheran Forum - R
Networks - R
Preacher's Illus. Service - R
Review for Religious
Today's Parish

TEEN/YOUNG ADULT
Campus Life - R
event
Freeway - R
HiCall - R
Insight - R
Insight/Out - R
Magazine/Youth! - R
Sharing the Victory - R
Straight - R
Student Leadership - R
Take Five - R
Teenage Christian - R
Teen Life - R
Teen Power - R (by teens)
Teen Quest - R (by teens)
With - R
Young Salvationist - R
Youth Focus - R
Youth World - R

WOMEN
Anna's Journal - R
Co-Laborer - R
Conscience - R
Daughters of Sarah
Esprit - R
Helping Hand - R
Horizons - R
Jour/Women's Ministries
Link & Visitor - R
Lutheran Woman Today
Parent Care - R
Probe
Salt and Light
Sisters Today - R
Virtue - R
Woman's Touch - R
Women Alive! - R

WRITERS
Byline
Canadian Writer's Jour - R
Christian Communicator - R
Christian Vision - R
Cross & Quill - R
Gotta Write
Housewife-Writers Forum - R
Writers Anchor - R
Writer's Digest - R
Writer's Exchange - R
Writer's Guidelines - R

POLITICAL

ADULT/GENERAL
AFA Journal - R
All About Issues - R
Anglican Journal - R
AXIOS - R
Bible Advocate - R
Canadian Catholic Review
Catholic Courier
Catholic Sentinel - R
Charisma & Christian Life
Christian C.L. RECORD - R
Christian Courier - R
Christian Courier (Canada) - R
Christian Crusade
Christian Renewal - R
Christian Single - R
Christian Social Action
Christianity Today - R
Commonweal
Compass
Cornerstone - R
Critic, The
ESA Advocate
Evangelical Friend
Expression
Faith Today
Friends Journal - R
Good News, Etc - R
Home Times - R
Interim - R
John Milton - R
Journal/Church & State
Kansas City Christian - R
Life Advocate - R
Lookout - R
Messenger, The (NC) - R
Minnesota Chronicle, The - R
National Christian Reporter
Nat/Intl Religion Report
Other Side, The
Perspectives on Science
Presbyterian Outlook
Presbyterian Survey - R
Religious Education
SCP Journal - R
Social Justice Review
United Methodist Reporter
Witness, The
World

CHRISTIAN EDUCATION/LIBRARY
Today's Catholic Teacher - R

MISSIONS
Areopagus - R

PASTORS/LEADERS
Christian Ministry
Faith & Renewal - R
Lutheran Forum - R
Networks - R
Preacher's Illus. Service - R
Preacher's Magazine - R
Word & World

TEEN/YOUNG ADULT
Issues & Answers - R
Magazine/Youth! - R
With - R
Young Adult Today

WOMEN
Conscience - R
Horizons - R

PRAYER

ADULT/GENERAL
Acts 29
Advent Christian Witness
ADVOCATE - R
alive now! - R
All About Issues - R
Annals of St. Anne
At Ease - R
Baptist Beacon - R
Baptist Informer
Better Tomorrow
Bible Advocate - R
Broken Streets
Canadian Catholic Review
Catholic Digest - R
Catholic Parent
Catholic Sentinel - R
Charisma & Christian Life
Christian Reader - R
Christianity Today - R
Church Herald/Holiness Banner - R
Christian Living - R
Companion
Companions - R
Compass
Connecting Point - R
Conquest
Cornerstone - R
Discipleship Journal - R
Emphasis/Faith & Living - R
Episcopal life - R
Evangel - R
Evangelical Beacon - R
Evangelical Friend
Evangelical Visitor - R
Explorer
Family Digest, The - R
Fellowship Today - R
Focus on the Family - R
Foursquare World ADVANCE - R
Friends Journal - R
God's Revivalist - R
Good News, Etc - R
Gospel Tidings - R
Guideposts
Hallelujah - R
Herald of Holiness - R
Home Times - R
Indian Life - R
John Milton - R
Journal/Christian Nursing - R
Kansas City Christian - R
Light and Life
Liguorian
Live - R
Living Church
Lookout - R
Lutheran, The
Lutheran Digest - R
Lutheran Layman
Lutheran Witness
Marian Helpers Bulletin - R
Mature Years - R
Mennonite, The - R
Mennonite Brethren Herald - R
MESSAGE
MESSAGE of the Open Bible - R
Messenger, The (NC) - R
Messenger of St. Anthony - R
Messenger of the Sacred Heart
Ministry Today - R
Moody
Morning Glory - R
National Christian Reporter
New Covenant - R
New Oxford Review
North American Voice
Other Side, The
Our Family - R
Our Sunday Visitor
Pentecostal Evangel
Pentecostal Homelife - R
Pentecostal Messenger - R
Plowman, The
Power for Living - R
Prayer Line - R
Presbyterian Record - R
Presbyterian Survey - R
Purpose - R
Queen of All Hearts
Railroad Evangelist - R
St. Anthony Messenger
Salt
Seek - R
Sharing - R
Social Justice Review
Spiritual Life
Standard - R
Sunday Digest - R
Table Talk - R
Today's Better Life
United Methodist Reporter
U.S. Catholic
Vision (MO) - R
Vista - R
Vital Christianity - R
Wesleyan Advocate
Writer's Forum - R

CHILDREN
Counselor
High Adventure - R
Primary Pal
Touch - R
Wonder Time

CHRISTIAN EDUCATION/LIBRARY
Brigade Leader - R
CE Connection - R
Changing Lives - R
Church Educator - R
Church Worship
Evangelizing Today's Child - R
Leader - R
Lutheran Education
Pastoral Life - R
Religion Teacher's Journal
Youth Leader - R

MISSIONS
American Horizon - R
Areopagus - R
Childlife - R
Worldwide Challenge - R

PASTORS/LEADERS
Advance - R
Chicago Studies
Christian Ministry
Church Growth Network - R
Congregational Journal
Five Stones, The - R
Journal/Christian Healing - R
Ministries Today
Networks - R

Paraclete - R
Pastoral Life - R
Preacher's Illus. Service - R
Preacher's Magazine - R
Priest, The
PROCLAIM - R
Pulpit/Bible Study Helps - R
Resource - R
Review for Religious
Search
Today's Parish
Word & World

TEEN/YOUNG ADULT
Certainty
Challenge (IL)
Conqueror - R
Freeway - R
High School I.D. - R
Insight - R
Insight/Out - R
Magazine/Youth! - R
Pathway I.D. - R
Straight - R
Student, The - R
Student Leadership - R
Teenage Christian - R
Teen Power - R
YOU! - R
Vision - R
With - R
Young Adult Today
Young Salvationist - R
Youth Update

WOMEN
Co-Laborer - R
Contempo
Daughters of Sarah
Esprit - R
Helping Hand - R
Horizons - R
Lutheran Woman Today
Response
Royal Service
Salt and Light
Sisters Today - R
Today's Christian Woman
Virtue - R
Women Alive! - R

PROPHECY

ADULT/GENERAL
Acts 29
ADVOCATE - R
Baptist Beacon - R
Bible Advocate - R
Charisma & Christian Life
Church Herald/Holiness Banner - R
Conquest
Evangelical Friend
God's Revivalist - R
Good News, Etc - R
Hallelujah - R
Home Times - R
John Milton - R
Kansas City Christian - R
MESSAGE of the Open Bible - R
Messenger, The (NC) - R
Our Family - R
Pentecostal Messenger - R
Pentecostal Testimony - R
SCP Journal - R
Signs of the Times - R
Writer's Forum - R

CHRISTIAN EDUCATION/LIBRARY
Youth Leader - R

PASTORS/LEADERS
Faith & Renewal - R
Journal/Christian Healing - R
Ministries Today
Paraclete - R
Preacher's Magazine - R
PROCLAIM - R
Pulpit/Bible Study Helps - R
Word & World

TEEN/YOUNG ADULT
Certainty
Challenge (IL)
Insight/Out - R
Issues & Answers - R
Pathway I.D. - R
Young Adult Today

WOMEN
Daughters of Sarah
Esprit - R
Woman's Touch - R

PSYCHOLOGY

ADULT/GENERAL
AXIOS - R
Catholic Digest - R
Catholic Sentinel - R
Catholic Twin Circle - R
Christian Reader - R
Christian Single - R
Common Boundary
Companion
Cornerstone - R
Creation Social Science - R
Cresset
Evangelical Friend
Good News, Etc - R
Home Times - R
John Milton - R
Journal/Christian Nursing - R
Jour/Religion in Psychotherapy
Jour/Religious Gerontology
Lutheran Journal - R
Lutheran Layman
MESSAGE
MESSAGE of the Open Bible - R
New Covenant - R
New Thought Journal - R
Parenting Treasures
Perspectives on Science
Psychology for Living - R
Ratio
Religious Education
St. Anthony Messenger
SCP Journal - R
Social Justice Review
Today's Better Life
Vista - R
Writer's Forum - R

CHRISTIAN EDUCATION/LIBRARY
Church Educator - R
Lutheran Education

PASTORS/LEADERS
Advance - R
Bible-Science - R
Congregational Journal
Eucharistic Minister - R
Faith & Renewal - R
Group's Jr High
Journal/Christian Healing - R
Pastoral Life - R
Preacher's Magazine - R
Priest, The
Review for Religious
Single Ad. Ministries Jour.
Word & World

WOMEN
Daughters of Sarah
Esprit - R
Woman's Touch - R

*RELATIONSHIPS

ADULT/GENERAL
ADVOCATE - R
At Ease - R
AXIOS - R
Better Tomorrow
Bible Advocate - R
Canada Lutheran - R
Catholic Digest - R
Catholic Sentinel - R
Christian Edge - R
Christian Living - R
Christian Parenting Today - R
Christian Single - R
Columbia - R
Companion
Cornerstone
Discipleship Journal - R
Evangel - R
Explorer
Family, The - R
Good News, Etc - R
Herald of Holiness - R
Indian Life - R
Journal/Christian Nursing - R
Kansas City Christian - R
Liguorian
Lutheran Digest - R
Mature Years - R
Mennonite, The - R
Mennonite Brethren Herald - R
Ministry Today - R
Moody
NW Christian Journal - R
Parenting Treasures - R
Parents of Teenagers
Pentecostal Evangel
Pentecostal Messenger - R
Pentecostal Testimony - R
Power for Living - R
Pursuit - R
Sunday Digest - R
Today's Better Life
Vista - R

CHILDREN
GUIDE - R

CHRISTIAN EDUCATION/LIBRARY
Brigade Leader - R

MISSIONS
American Horizon - R
Worldwide Challenge - R

PASTORS/LEADERS
Ministries Today
Preacher's Magazine - R
Resource - R
Youthworker - R
Word & World

TEEN/YOUNG ADULT
Challenge (TN) - R
Edge, The - R
Freeway - R
HiCall - R
Insight - R
Straight - R
Student Leadership - R
Teen Power - R
With - R

WOMEN
Anna's Journal - R
Co-Laborer - R
Helping Hand - R
Today's Christian Woman
Virtue - R

RELIGIOUS FREEDOM

ADULT/GENERAL
AFA Journal - R
AGAIN - R
America
AXIOS - R
Bible Advocate - R
Catholic Digest - R
Catholic Twin Circle - R
Charisma & Christian Life
Christian C.L. RECORD - R
Christian Century
Christian Courier - R
Christian Courier (Canada) - R
Christian Social Action
Christianity Today - R
Church & State - R
Church Herald/Holiness Banner - R
Columbia - R
Connecting Point - R
Cornerstone - R
Creation Social Science - R
Cresset
Episcopal Life - R
Evangelical Friend
Faith Today
God's Revivalist - R
Good News, Etc - R
Hallelujah - R
Herald of Holiness - R
Home Times - R
Inspirer, The - R
John Milton - R
Journal/Church & State
Kansas City Christian - R
Liberty - R
Lookout - R
Mature Years - R
MESSAGE
Messenger, The (NC) - R
Messenger of St. Anthony - R
MESSAGE of the Open Bible - R
Minnesota Chronicle, The - R
Moody
Morning Glory - R
Nat/Intl Religion Report
News Network Intl.
New Thought Journal - R
NW Christian Journal - R
Our Family - R
Our Sunday Visitor
Pentecostal Evangel
Pentecostal Messenger - R
Pentecostal Testimony - R
Presbyterian Outlook
Presbyterian Survey - R
Prism
Purpose - R
Religious Education
SCP Journal - R
Social Justice Review
United Church Observer - R
Vista - R

CHRISTIAN EDUCATION/LIBRARY
CE Connection - R
Church Worship
Youth Leader - R

MISSIONS
Areopagus - R
Maryknoll
Worldwide Challenge - R

PASTORS/LEADERS
Bible-Science - R
Congregational Journal
Cross Currents
Discipleship Training
Faith & Renewal - R
Journal/Christian Healing - R
Ministries Today
Networks - R
Pastoral Life - R
Preacher's Magazine - R

Pulpit/Bible Study Helps - R
Search
Word & World

TEEN/YOUNG ADULT
Conqueror - R
Issues & Answers - R
Kiln, The - R
Young Adult Today

WOMEN
Daughters of Sarah
Esprit - R
Response
Woman's Touch - R

SALVATION TESTIMONIES

ADULT/GENERAL
Acts 29
AGAIN - R
American Tract Society - R
At Ease - R
Bible Advocate - R
Broken Streets
Charisma & Christian Life
Christian Reader - R
Christian Research - R
Church Herald/Holiness Banner - R
Companions - R
Connecting Point - R
Conquest
Decision
Emphasis/Faith & Living - R
Evangel - R
Evangelical Friend
Explorer
God's Revivalist - R
God's Special People - R
Good News - R
Good News, Etc - R
Good News Journal
Hallelujah - R
Herald of Holiness - R
Home Times - R
Indian Life - R
Inspirer, The - R
Light and Life
Liguorian
Maranatha - R
Mennonite Brethren Herald - R
MESSAGE
MESSAGE of the Open Bible - R
Messenger, The (NC) - R
Ministry Today - R
Moody
Morning Glory - R
New Covenant - R
New Heart, A - R
New Oxford Review
Pentecostal Evangel
Pentecostal Messenger - R
Pentecostal Testimony - R
Power for Living - R
PROGRESS - R
Railroad Evangelist - R
SCP Journal - R
Shantyman, The - R
Sharing - R
Standard - R
Starlight
Sunday Digest - R
Together - R
Tree of Life
VISION - R
Vista - R
Vital Christianity - R
Voice, The - R
Wesleyan Advocate
Writer's Forum - R

CHILDREN
Counselor
Power & Light - R
Primary Days

CHRISTIAN EDUCATION/LIBRARY
Evangelizing Today's Child
Youth Leader - R

MISSIONS
American Horizon - R
Childlife - R
Worldwide Challenge - R

PASTORS/LEADERS
Journal/Christian Healing - R
Networks - R
Preacher's Magazine - R

TEEN/YOUNG ADULT
Certainty
Challenge (IL)
Conqueror - R
Freeway - R
Insight - R
Pathway I.D. - R
Teen Power - R
Young Adult Today

WOMEN
Esprit - R
Joyful Woman - R
Salt and Light
Sisters Today - R
Woman's Touch - R

SCIENCE

ADULT/GENERAL
AXIOS - R
Canadian Catholic Review
Catholic Digest - R
Catholic Twin Circle - R
Christian C.L. RECORD - R
Christian Courier (Canada) - R
Christian Reader - R
Companions - R
Compass
Friends Journal - R
Home Times - R
John Milton - R
Kansas City Christian - R
Lutheran Journal - R
National Christian Reporter
Nat/Intl Religion Report
Perspectives on Science
Religious Education
SCP Journal - R
United Methodist Reporter

CHILDREN
My Friend
Nature Friend - R
Primary Days
Primary Pal

CHRISTIAN EDUCATION/LIBRARY
Journal/Adventist Educ. - R
Today's Catholic Teacher - R

PASTORS/LEADERS
Bible-Science - R
Cross Currents
Journal/Christian Healing - R
Word & World

TEEN/YOUNG ADULT
Certainty
Challenge (IL)
HiCall - R
Issues & Answers - R
Young Adult Today

WOMEN
Esprit - R

SENIOR ADULT ISSUES

ADULT/GENERAL
Acts 29
Alive! - R
Anglican Journal - R
AXIOS - R
B.C. Catholic - R
Better Tomorrow
Bible Advocate
Canada Lutheran - R
Catholic Digest - R
Catholic Exponent
Catholic Sentinel - R
Charisma & Christian Life
Christian Century
Christian Courier (Canada) - R
Christian Home & School
Christian Living - R
Christian Reader - R
Church Herald/Holiness Banner - R
Columbia - R
Companion
Companions - R
Conquest
Covenant Companion
Creation Social Science - R
Decision
Discovery - R
Emphasis/Faith & Living - R
Evangel - R
Evangelical Baptist
Evangelical Friend
Expression
Family, The - R
Foursquare World ADVANCE - R
Good News, Etc - R
Herald of Holiness - R
Home Times - R
John Milton - R
Kansas City Christian - R
Light and Life
Liguorian
Lookout - R
Lutheran, The
Lutheran Digest - R
Mature Years - R
Mennonite, The - R
Mennonite Brethren Herald - R
MESSAGE
MESSAGE of the Open Bible - R
Messenger, The (NC) - R
Minnesota Chronicle, The - R
Montana Catholic
Moody
National Christian Reporter
New Thought Journal - R
NW Christian Journal - R
Our Family - R
Our Sunday Visitor
PCA Messenger - R
Pentecostal Evangel
Pentecostal Messenger - R
Presbyterian Record - R
Presbyterian Survey - R
Purpose - R
Standard - R
Star of Zion
Sunday Digest - R
United Methodist Reporter
Vista - R
Wesleyan Advocate
Witness, The

CHRISTIAN EDUCATION/LIBRARY
CE Connection - R
Church Educator - R
Church Recreation - R
Leader - R
Leader/Church School Today

MISSIONS
Worldwide Challenge - R

MUSIC
Senior Musician - R

PASTORS/LEADERS
Diaconalogue - R
Journal/Christian Healing - R
Preacher's Magazine - R
Search
Single Ad. Ministries Jour.
Word & World

WOMEN
Co-Laborer - R
Esprit - R
Link & Visitor - R
Parent Care - R

SERMONS

ADULT/GENERAL
Baptist Beacon - R
Bible Advocate - R
Church Herald/Holiness Banner - R
God's Revivalist - R
Hallelujah - R
John Milton - R
Joyful Noise
Maranatha - R
Messenger, The (NC) - R
Morning Glory - R
Pentecostal Evangel
Presbyterian Survey - R
Tree of Life
Writer's Forum - R

CHRISTIAN EDUCATION/LIBRARY
Church Worship
Youth Leader - R

PASTORS/LEADERS
Christian Ministry
Clergy Journal
Congregational Journal
In Season
Journal/Christian Healing - R
Liturgy
Lutheran Forum - R
Paraclete - R
Preacher's Illus. Service - R
Preacher's Magazine - R
Preaching
PROCLAIM - R
Pulpit/Bible Study Helps - R
Today's Parish

SHORT STORY: ADULT

African-American Heritage - R
Alive! - R
alive now! - R
Annals of St. Anne
Assoc Ref Presbyterian - R
Baptist Informer
Burning Light - R
Byline
Canadian Writer's Jour - R
Chips Off Writer's Block - R
Christian Century
Christian Courier (Canada) - R
Christian Educators Journal - R
Christian Living - R
Christian Reader - R
Christian Renewal - R
Christian School
Christmas - R
Church Herald
Church Musician
Companion
Connecting Point - R
Conquest

Cornerstone - R
Critic, The
Daughters of Sarah
Door, The (satire)
Emphasis/Faith & Living - R
Esprit - R
Evangel - R
Evangelical Visitor - R
Explorer
Family, The - R
God's Revivalist - R
Helping Hand - R
His Garden
Home Life
Home Office - R
Home Times - R
Horizons - R
Housewife-Writer's Forum - R
Ideals
Impact Magazine - R
Indian Life - R
Inspirer, The - R
John Milton - R
Journal/Christian Healing - R
Junebugs Knocking
Lighthouse Fiction Collection
Liguorian
Live - R
Lookout - R
Lutheran Journal - R
Lutheran Witness
Lutheran Woman Today
Maranatha - R
Mature Living
Mature Years - R
Mennonite Brethren Herald - R
Messenger, The (NC) - R
Messenger of the Sacred Heart
Ministry Today - R
Miraculous Medal
Moody
Mountain Laurel - R
North American Voice
Other Side, The
Pegasus Review
Pentecostal Homelife - R
Poetry Forum
Presbyterian Record - R
Probe
Purpose - R
Queen of all Hearts
Ratio
St. Anthony Messenger
St. Joseph Messenger - R
Seek - R
Standard - R
Starlight
Star of Zion
Sunday Digest - R
Today's Christian Woman
Today's Single - R
Touchstone
U.S. Catholic
Virtue - R
Vision - R
Vista - R (seniors)
Vital Christianity - R
Wherever
Women Alive! - R
Writers Anchor - R
Writer's Guidelines
Writing Right - R

SHORTSTORY: ADVENTURE

CHILDREN

CLUBHOUSE - R
Connecting Point - R
Counselor
Crusader - R
Discoveries - R
Faith 'n Stuff
Focus/Clubhouse/Clubhouse Jr
GUIDE - R
John Milton - R
Junior Trails - R
Lighthouse Fiction Collection
Lollipops (young)
My Friend
Power & Light - R
R-A-D-A-R - R
Shantyman, The - R
Starlight
Touch - R
Young Crusader - R

TEEN/YOUNG ADULT

Breakaway - R
Certainty
Challenge (IL)
HiCall - R
Insight - R
Insight/Out - R
Lighthouse Fiction Collection
John Milton - R
Magazine/Youth! - R
Teenage Christian - R
Student, The - R
Teen Life - R
Teen Quest - R
Teens Today - R
Venture - R
Young Adult Today
Young Salvationist - R
Youth World - R

ADULT

African-American Heritage - R
Alive! - R
Byline
Chip Off Writer's Block - R
Christian Courier (Canada) - R
Emphasis/Faith & Living - R
John Milton - R
Junebugs Knocking
Lighthouse Fiction Collection
Live - R
Miraculous Medal
Pentecostal Testimony - R
Standard - R
StarLight
Thema - R
Vision (MO) - R
Writer's Guidelines

SHORT STORY: ALLEGORY

CHILDREN

CLUBHOUSE - R
John Milton - R
Pockets - R
Starlight

TEENS

Conqueror - R
I.D.
Magazine/Youth! - R
John Milton - R
Student Leadership - R
Teen Life - R
Youth World - R

ADULT

Burning Light - R
Chip Off Writer's Block - R
Discipleship Journal - R
Esprit - R
Home Times - R
John Milton - R
Life Advocate - R
Mennonite Brethren Herald - R
Pentecostal Homelife - R
Ratio
Starlight
Thema - R
Vision (MO) - R

Writer's Guidelines

SHORT STORY:BIBLICAL

CHILDREN
Church Educator - R
Discoveries - R
Focus/Clubhouse/Clubhouse Jr
Gospel Tidings - R
Messenger, The (NC) - R
Pockets - R
Power & Light - R
Preacher's Illus. Service - R
R-A-D-A-R - R
Shining Star
StarLight

TEEN/YOUNG ADULT
Certainty
Conqueror - R
Gospel Tidings - R
High School I.D.
Magazine/Youth! - R
Maranatha - R
Messenger, The (NC) - R
Preacher's Illus. Service - R
Student, The - R
Teenage Christian - R
Young Adult Today
Young Salvationist - R

ADULT
Annals of St. Anne
Assoc Ref Presbyterian - R
Christian Courier (Canada) - R
Christian Reader - R
Church Herald/Holiness Banner - R
Church Worship
Connecting Point - R
Dreams & Visions
Esprit - R
Emphasis/Faith & Living - R
Explorer
Five Stones, The - R
Helping Hand - R
Horizons - R
Impact Magazine - R
Inspirer, The - R
Junebugs Knocking
Live - R
Lutheran Woman Today
Maranatha - R
Mature Years - R
Messenger, The (NC) - R
Ministry Today - R
Miraculous Medal
Pentecostal Homelife - R
Pentecostal Testimony - R
Preacher's Illus. Service - R
Presbyterian Record - R
Purpose - R
Ratio
Sharing - R
StarLight

SHORT STORY: CONTEMPORARY

CHILDREN
BREAD for God's Children - R
Canada Lutheran - R
Focus/Clubhouse/Clubhouse Jr
GUIDE - R
Junior Trails - R
Lighthouse Fiction Collection
Listen
My Friend
Power & Light - R
Shantyman, The - R
Story Friends - R

TEEN/YOUNG ADULT
Campus Life - R
Certainty
Challenge (IL)
Freeway - R
High School I.D. - R
Insight - R
Insight/Out - R
Lighthouse Fiction Collection
Spirit
StarLight
Straight - R
Teenage Christian - R
Teen Power - R
Teen Quest - R
Teens Today - R
Tradition - R
Venture - R

ADULT
Byline
Chip Off Writer's Block - R
Christian Living - R
Christian Reader - R
Companion
Connecting Point - R
Cornerstone - R
Critic, The
Dreams & Visions
Esprit - R
Evangel - R
Explorer
Family, The - R
Home Life
Home Times - R
Housewife-Writers Forum - R
Inspirer, The - R
Junebugs Knocking
Lighthouse Fiction Collection
Liguorian
Lookout - R
Lutheran Journal - R
Maranatha - R
Miraculous Medal
Moody
Other Side, The
Pentecostal Testimony - R
St. Anthony Messenger
St. Joseph Messenger - R
Standard - R
StarLight
Thema - R
Tradition - R
U.S. Catholic
Virtue - R
Vital Christianity - R
Writer's Guidelines

SHORT STORY: FANTASY

CHILDREN
Faith 'n Stuff
Focus/Clubhouse/Clubhouse Jr
John Milton - R
Lollipops (young)
Touch - R
Venture

TEEN/YOUNG ADULT
John Milton - R
Magazine/Youth! - R
Spirit
With - R
Young Adult Today
Young Salvationist - R

ADULT
Byline
Chip Off Writer's Block - R
Christian Courier (Canada) - R
Connecting Point - R
Dreams & Visions
Esprit - R
Home Times - R
Housewife-Writers Forum - R

John Milton - R
Junebugs Knocking
Presbyterian Record - R
Ratio
Thema - R
Writer's Guidelines

SHORT STORY: FRONTIER

CHILDREN
CLUBHOUSE - R
Faith 'n Stuff
Focus/Clubhouse/Clubhouse Jr
High Adventure - R
John Milton - R
Junior Trails - R
Lighthouse Fiction Collection

TEEN/YOUNG ADULT
Challenge (IL)
John Milton - R
Lighthouse Fiction collection

ADULT
Byline
Chip Off Writer's Block - R
Connecting Point - R
Explorer
John Milton - R
Junebugs Knocking
Lighthouse Fiction Collection
Miraculous Medal
Thema - R
Writer's Guidelines

SHORT STORY: FRONTIER/ ROMANCE

Byline
Challenge (IL)
Chip Off Writer's Block - R
CLUBHOUSE - R
Connecting Point - R
Helping Hand - R
Lighthouse Fiction Collection
Miraculous Medal
Writer's Guidelines

SHORT STORY: HISTORICAL

CHILDREN
CLUBHOUSE - R
Counselor
Faith 'n Stuff
Focus/Clubhouse/Clubhouse Jr
High Adventure - R
Indian Life - R
John Milton - R
Junior Trails - R
Lighthouse Fiction Collection
Messenger, The (NC) - R
My Friend
R-A-D-A-R - R
Shantyman, The - R

TEEN/YOUNG ADULT
Certainty
Challenge (IL)
Indian Life - R
John Milton - R
Lighthouse Fiction Collection
Messenger, The (NC) - R
Tradition - R
Young Adult Today
Youth - R

ADULT
African-American Heritage - R
Alive! - R
Burning Light - R
Byline
Chip Off Writer's Block - R
Christian Courier (Canada) - R
Connecting Point - R
Conquest
Esprit - R
Explorer
Home Times - R
Horizons - R
Housewife-Writers Forum - R
Indian Life - R
John Milton - R
Junebugs Knocking
Lighthouse Fiction Collection
Live - R
Maranatha - r
Messenger, The (NC) - R
Miraculous Medal
Mountain Laurel - R
North American Voice
Presbyterian Record - R
Purpose - R
Ratio
Seek - R
Thema - R
Tradition - R
Writer's Guidelines

SHORT STORY: HISTORICAL/ ROMANCE

Byline
Chip Off Writer's Block - R
CLUBHOUSE - R
Connecting Point - R
Home Times - R
Lighthouse Fiction Collection
Miraculous Medal
Writer's Guidelines

SHORT STORY: HUMOROUS

CHILDREN
CLUBHOUSE - R
Crusader - R
Faith 'n Stuff
Focus/Clubhouse/Clubhouse Jr
GUIDE - R
High Adventure - R
John Milton - R
Lighthouse Fiction Collection
Messenger, The (NC) - R
My Friend
On the Line - R
Preacher's Illus. Service - R
R-A-D-A-R - R
Touch - R
Wonder Time

TEEN/YOUNG ADULT
Breakaway - R
Brio - R
Campus Life - R
Certainty
Challenge (IL)
Freeway - R
HiCall - R
High School I.D. - R
Insight - R
Insight/Out - R
John Milton - R
Lighthouse Fiction Collection
Magazine/Youth! - R
Messenger, The (NC) - R
Preacher's Illus. Service - R
Straight - R
Student, The - R

Student Leadership - R
Teenage Christian - R
Teen Power - R
Teen Quest - R
Teens Today - R
Tradition - R
Venture - R
With - R
Young Adult Today
Young Salvationist - R

ADULT
African-American Heritage - R
Alive! - R
Byline
Canada Lutheran - R
Chip Off Writer's Block - R
Christian Courier (Canada) - R
Christian Reader - R
Christian Single - R
Companion
Connecting Point - R
Conquest
Door, The
Dreams & Visions
Esprit - R
Family, The - R
Five Stones, The - R
Helping Hand - R
Home Life
Home Times - R
Horizons - R
Housewife-Writers Forum - R
Impact - R
Inspirer, The - R
John Milton - R
Junebugs Knocking
Life Advocate - R
Lighthouse Fiction Collection
Live - R
Lookout - R
Lutheran Journal - R
Maranatha - R
Mature Years - R
Messenger, The (NC) - R
Miraculous Medal
Other Side, The
Pentecostal Homelife - R
Pentecostal Testimony - R
Preacher's Illus. Service - R
Presbyterian Record - R
Seek - R
Standard - R
Thema - R
Tradition - R
Virtue - R
Vista - R (seniors)
Writer's Guidelines

SHORT STORY: JUVENILE

Assoc Ref Presbyterian - R
Bible Time 4's & 5's
BREAD for God's Children - R
Children's Church - R (6-8)
Christian Home & School
Christmas - R
Counselor
Crusader - R
Discoveries - R
Evangelizing Today's Child
Faith 'n Stuff
Focus/Clubhouse/Clubhouse Jr
Gospel Tidings - R
GUIDE - R
High Adventure - R
John Milton - R (8-12)
Junior Trails - R
Lighthouse Fiction Collection
Listen (4-6)
Lollipops
Lutheran Woman Today (some)
Messenger, The (NC) - R
My Friend
On the Line - R
Partners - R
Pentecostal Testimony - R
Pockets - R
Power & Light - R
Presbyterian Record - R
Primary Days
Primary Pal
R-A-D-A-R - R
Shantyman, The - R
Skipping Stones
StarLight
Story Friends - R
Today's Catholic Teacher - R
Touch - R
Venture - R
Venture (MN)
Wonder Time
Young Crusader - R
Young Musicians

SHORT STORY: LITERARY

CHILDREN
John Milton - R

TEEN/YOUNG ADULT
Certainty
John Milton - R

ADULT
Burning Light - R
Byline
Chip Off Writer's Block - R
Christian Courier (Canada) - R
Christian Living - R
Christian Reader - R
Compass
Conquest
Cornerstone - R
Critic, The
Dreams & Visions
Esprit - R
Explorer
Home Times - R
John Milton - R
Junebugs Knocking
Live - R
Lutheran Journal - R
Mennonite Brethren Herald-R
Miraculous Medal
Other Side, The
Ratio
Thema - R
Writer's Guidelines

SHORT STORY:MYSTERY

CHILDREN
BREAD for God's Children - R
Faith 'n Stuff
Focus/Clubhouse/Clubhouse Jr
GUIDE - R
Lighthouse Fiction Collection
John Milton - R
Junior Trails - R
On the Line - R
R-A-D-A-R - R
Touch - R

TEEN/YOUNG ADULT
Certainty
Challenge (IL)
Lighthouse Fiction Collection
John Milton - R
Venture - R
Young Adult Today

ADULT
African-American Heritage - R
Assoc Ref Presbyterian - R

Burning Light - R
Byline
Chip Off Writer's Block - R
Christian Courier (Canada) - R
Connecting Point - R
Housewife-Writers Forum - R
John Milton - R
Lighthouse Fiction Collection
Liguorian
Miraculous Medal
Thema - R
Writer's Guidelines

SHORT STORY: MYSTERY/ ROMANCE

Byline
Chip Off Writer's Block - R
Christian Single - R
Connecting Point - R
Lighthouse Fiction Collection
Miraculous Medal
Standard - R
Writer's Guidelines

SHORT STORY: PARABLES

CHILDREN
Annals of St. Anne
CLUBHOUSE - R
High Adventure - R
Indian Life - R
My Friend
Pockets - R
Preacher's Illus. Service - R
R-A-D-A-R - R
Shining Star
Touch - R

TEEN/YOUNG ADULT
Annals of St. Anne
Indian Life - R
Insight - R
Insight/Out - R
Preacher's Illus. Service - R
Student, The - R
Student Leadership - R
Teenage Christian - R
With - R
Young Adult Today

ADULT
alive now! - R
America
Annals of St. Anne
Burning Light - R
Catholic Twin Circle - R
Christian Courier (Canada) - R
Christian Reader - R
Church Worship
Companion
Discovery - R
Door, The
Emphasis/Faith & Living - R
Esprit - R
Five Stones, The - R
God's Revivalist - R
Helping Hand - R
Horizons - R
Impact Magazine - R
Indian Life - R
Inspirer, The - R
LA Catholic
Live - R
Lutheran
Maranatha - R
MESSAGE
Ministry Today - R
Pentecostal Testimony - R
Preacher's Illus. Service - R
Presbyterian Record - R
Psychology for Living - R
Purpose - R
Ratio
Response
StarLight
Tree of Life
Woman's Touch - R

SHORT STORY: PLAYS

A.D. Players (book section)
Burning Light - R
Certainty
Children's Story Scripts
Christian Drama - R
Church Worship
Creatively Yours
Esprit - R
Five Stones, The - R
Focus/Clubhouse/Clubhouse Jr
Horizons - R
Music Leader
My Friend
Plowman, The
Ratio
Shining Star
Student, The - R
Thema - R (short)
Touch - R

SHORT STORY: ROMANCE

TEEN/YOUNG ADULT
Brio
Lighthouse Fiction Collection
Teen Quest - R
Teens Today - R
Young Salvationist - R

ADULT
African-American Heritage - R
Alive! - R
Byline
Chip Off Writer's Block - R
Connecting Point - R
Housewife-Writers Forum - R
Lighthouse Fiction Collection
Miraculous Medal
Ratio
Virtue - R
Writer's Guidelines

SHORT STORY: SCIENCE FICTION

CHILDREN
Focus/Clubhouse/Clubhouse Jr
John Milton - R

TEEN/YOUNG ADULT
Breakaway - R
John Milton - R
Teen Quest - R
Young Adult Today
Young Salvationist - R

ADULT
Burning Light - R
Byline
Chip Off Writer's Block - R
Christian Courier (Canada) - R
Connecting Point - R
Housewife-Writers Forum - R
Impact Magazine - R
John Milton - R
Junebugs Knocking
Ratio
Thema - R
Writer's Guidelines

SHORT STORY: SKITS

CHILDREN
Christian Drama - R
Church Recreation - R
On the Line - R
Shining Star
Touch - R

TEEN
Christian Drama - R
Church Recreation - R
Student Leadership - R

ADULT
Christian Drama - R
Church Recreation - R
Church Worship
Esprit - R
Five Stones, The - R

SHORT STORY: TEEN/YOUNG ADULT

BREAD for God's Children - R
Breakaway - R
Brio
Campus Life - R
Canada Lutheran - R
Certainty
Challenge (IL)
Conqueror - R
Evangel- R
Event
Freeway - R
Gospel Tidings - R
HiCall - R
High Adventure - R
Insight - R
Insight/Out - R
John Milton - R
Lighthouse Fiction Collection
Magazine/Youth! - R
Messenger, The (NC) - R
Pentecostal Testimony - R
Presbyterian Record - R
Spirit
Straight - R
Student
Student Leadership
Teenage Christian - R
Teen Life - R
Teen Power - R
Teens Today - R
Touch - R
Venture - R
With - R
Young Adult Today
Young Crusader - R
Young Salvationist - R
Youth World - R

SINGLES ISSUES

ADULT/GENERAL
Acts 29
All About Issues - R
American Tract Society - R
At Ease - R
Catholic Digest - R
Charisma & Christian Life
Christian Courier (Canada) - R
Christian Living - R
Christian Parenting Today - R
Christian Reader - R
Christian Single - R
Christian Social Action
Church Herald/Holiness Banner - R
Columbia - R
Companion
Covenant Companion
Discipleship Journal - R
Emphasis/Faith & Living - R
Evangelical Friend
Expression
Family, The - R
Foursquare World ADVANCE - R
Herald of Holiness - R
Home Times - R
John Milton - R
Kansas City Christian - R
Light and Life
Liguorian
Live - R
Living - R
Lookout - R
Lutheran, The
Lutheran Digest - R
Mature Years - R
Mennonite, The - R
Mennonite Brethren Herald - R
MESSAGE
Messenger, The (Canada) - R
Messenger, The (NC) - R
Messenger of St. Anthony - R
Ministry Today - R
Minnesota Chronicle, The - R
Moody
National Christian Reporter
NW Christian Journal - R
PCA Messenger - R
Pentecostal Evangel
Pentecostal Messenger - R
Pentecostal Testimony - R
Power for Living - R
Presbyterian Record - R
Presbyterian Survey - R
Purpose - R
St. Anthony Messenger
Signs of the Times - R
Standard - R
Table Talk - R
United Methodist Reporter
Vista - R
Wesleyan Advocate
Writer's Forum - R

CHRISTIAN EDUCATION/LIBRARY
CE Connection - R
CE Counselor - R
Leader - R

MISSIONS
Worldwide Challenge - R

PASTORS/LEADERS
Church Administration
Church Growth Network - R
Faith & Renewal - R
Journal/Christian Healing - R
Ministries Today
Pastoral Life - R
Preacher's Magazine - R
Pulpit/Bible Study Helps - R
Resource - R
Search
Single Ad. Ministries Jour.
Word & World

TEEN/YOUNG ADULT
Conqueror - R
YOU! - R
Young Adult Today

WOMEN
Co-Laborer - R
Esprit - R
Joyful Woman - R
Salt and Light
Today's Christian Woman
Virtue - R
Women Alive! - R

SOCIOLOGY

ADULT/GENERAL
Anglican Journal - R
Catholic Digest - R
Christian Courier (Canada) - R
Christian Century
Compass
Cornerstone - R
Creation Social Science - R
Critic, The
Evangelical Friend
Faith Today
Herald of Holiness - R
Home Times - R
John Milton - R
Journal/Church & State
Lutheran Journal - R
Moody
New Oxford Review
New Thought Journal - R
Other Side, The
Quiet Revolution - R
Religious Broadcasting - R
SCP Journal - R
Seek - R
Social Justice Review
Star of Zion
Vista - R
Witness, The

CHRISTIAN EDUCATION/LIBRARY
CE Connection - R
Church Educator - R

MISSIONS
Areopagus - R
Urban Mission - R

PASTORS/LEADERS
Bible-Science - R
Congregational Journal
Eucharistic Minister - R
Faith & Renewal - R
Five Stones, The - R
Group's Jr High
Journal/Christian Healing - R
Pastoral Life - R
Preacher's Magazine - R
Single Ad. Ministries Jour.
Word & World

TEEN/YOUNG ADULT
Student Leadership - R
Young Adult Today

WOMEN
Daughters of Sarah
Esprit - R

SPIRITUALITY

ADULT/GENERAL
Acts 29
ADVOCATE - R
alive now! - R
American Tract Society - R
Annals of St. Anne
At Ease - R
Baptist Beacon - R
Bible Advocate - R
Bible Today
Canada Lutheran - R
Canadian Catholic Review
Catholic Digest - R
Catholic Exponent
Catholic Sentinel - R
Christian Century
Christian Chronicle
Christian Home & School
Christian Living - R
Christian Reader - R
Christian Single - R
Christianity Today - R
Church Herald/Holiness Banner - R
Columbia - R
Common Boundary
Commonweal
Companion
Companions - R
Compass
Conquest
Covenant Companion
Cresset
Discipleship Journal - R
Door, The
Emphasis/Faith & Living - R
Evangelical Beacon - R
Episcopal Life - R
Evangelical Friend
Faith Today
Family, The - R
Family Digest, The - R
Fellowship Today - R
Friends Journal - R
God's Revivalist - R
Good News, Etc - R
Guideposts
Hallelujah - R
Herald of Holiness - R
John Milton - R
Journal/Christian Nursing - R
Liguorian
Living - R
Living Church
Lookout - R
Lutheran, The
Lutheran Digest - R
Maranatha - R
Mature Years - R
Mennonite, The - R
Mennonite Brethren Herald - R
MESSAGE
Messenger, The (Canada) - R
Messenger, The (NC) - R
Messenger of St. Anthony - R
Ministry Today - R
Morning Glory - R
National Christian Reporter
New Covenant - R
New Oxford Review
New Thought Journal - R
North American Voice
Other Side, The
Our Family - R
Our Sunday Visitor
Parenting Treasures - R
Pentecostal Evangel
Pentecostal Homelife - R
Pentecostal Messenger - R
Presbyterian Outlook
Presbyterian Record - R
Presbyterian Survey - R
Purpose - R
Queen of All Hearts
Religious Education
St. Anthony Messenger
St. Willibrord Journal
SCP Journal - R
Sharing - R
Signs of the Times - R
Social Justice Review
Spiritual Life
Standard - R
Starlight
Sunday Digest - R
United Church Observer - R
United Methodist Reporter
Vision (MO) - R
Vista - R
Wesleyan Advocate
Witness, The

CHILDREN
Wonder Time

CHRISTIAN EDUCATION/LIBRARY
CE Connection - R

Christian School
Church Educator - R
Church Worship
Lutheran Education
Religion Teacher's Journal
Youth & CE Leadership - R
Youth Leader - R

MISSIONS
Areopagus - R
Worldwide Challenge - R

PASTORS/LEADERS
Chicago Studies
Congregational Journal
Christian Ministry
Diaconalogue - R
Eucharistic Minister - R
Five Stones, The - R
Homiletic & Pastoral Review
Journal/Christian Healing - R
Ministries Today
Paraclete - R
Pastoral Life - R
Preacher's Illus. Service - R
Preacher's Magazine - R
Priest, The
PROCLAIM - R
Pulpit/Bible Study Helps - R
Review for Religious
Search
Today's Parish
Word & World
Youthworker - R

TEEN/YOUNG ADULT
Certainty
Conqueror - R
Insight - R
Kiln, The - R
Magazine/Youth! - R
Student, The - R
Student Leadership - R
Teenage Christian - R
YOU! - R
Young Adult Today
Young Salvationist - R
Youth Update

WOMEN
Daughters of Sarah
Esprit - R
Horizons - R
Lutheran Woman Today
Response
Sisters Today - R
Today's Christian Woman
Virtue - R

SPORTS

ADULT/GENERAL
American Tract Society - R
AXIOS - R
Christian Courier - R
Christian Courier (Canada) -R
Christian Reader - R
Christian Single - R
Columbia - R
Connecting Point - R
(Special Olympics)
Expression
Good News, Etc - R
Home Times - R
Indian Life - R
John Milton - R (for blind)
Kansas City Christian - R
Lifeglow - R
Live - R
Lutheran Layman
Lutheran Witness
Messenger, The (NC) - R
Minnesota Chronicle, The - R
National Christian Reporter
NW Christian Journal - R
PCA Messenger - R
Power for Living - R
Sports Spectrum
United Methodist Reporter

CHILDREN
Counselor
Crusader - R
Faith 'n Stuff
Focus/Clubhouse/Clubhouse Jr
GUIDE - R
High Adventure - R
My Friend
On the Line - R
Primary Days

CHRISTIAN EDUCATION/LIBRARY
Christian School
Church Recreation

MISSIONS
Worldwide Challenge - R

PASTORS/LEADERS
Preacher's Illus. Service - R

TEEN/YOUNG ADULT
Breakaway - R
Certainty
Challenge (IL)
Challenge (TN) - R
Edge, The - R
event
Freeway - R
HiCall - R
Insight - R
Insight/Out - R
Issues & Answers - R
Magazine/Youth! - R
Pioneer - R
Sharing the VICTORY - R
Straight - R
Teenage Christian - R
Teen Power - R
Teen Quest - R
With - R
YOU! - R
Young Adult Today
Young & Alive - R
Young Salvationist - R

WOMEN
Esprit - R

THEOLOGICAL

ADULT/GENERAL
Acts 29
ADVOCATE - R
AGAIN - R
America
Anglican Journal - R
Annals of St. Anne
Assoc Ref Presbyterian - R
At Ease - R
Baptist Beacon - R
Baptist Informer
B.C. Catholic - R
Bible Advocate - R
Canadian Catholic Review
Catholic Digest - R
Catholic Twin Circle - R
Charisma & Christian Life
Christian Century
Christian Reader - R
Christian Renewal - R
Christian Research - R
Christian Social Action
Christianity Today - R
Church Herald
Church Herald/Holiness Banner - R
Columbia - R
Commonweal
Companion

Companions - R
Compass
Cornerstone - R
Covenant Companion
Cresset
Critic, The
Emphasis/Faith & Living - R
Episcopal Life - R
Evangelical Baptist
Evangelical Friend
Evangelical Visitor - R
Friends Journal - R
God's Revivalist - R
God's Special People - R
Good News - R
Hallelujah - R
Inspirer, The - R
Interim - R
John Milton - R
Journal/Church & State
Jour/Religion in Psychotherapy
Jour/Religious Gerontology
Living Church
Lutheran, The
Lutheran Digest - R
Lutheran Layman
Maranatha - R
Mature Years - R
Mennonite Brethren Herald - R
MESSAGE
MESSAGE of the Open Bible - R
Messenger, The (NC) - R
Messenger of St. Anthony - R
Ministry Today - R
Montana Catholic
Moody (applied)
National Christian Reporter
New Oxford Review
New Thought Journal - R
North American Voice
Other Side, The
Our Family - R
Our Sunday Visitor
Pentecostal Evangel
Plowman, The
Presbyterian Outlook
Presbyterian Record - R
Presbyterian Survey - R
Ratio
Religious Education
St.Willibrord Journal
SCP Journal - R
Social Justice Review
Spiritual Life
United Church Observer - R
United Methodist Reporter
Voice, The - R
Witness, The
Writer's Forum - R

CHRISTIAN EDUCATION/LIBRARY

CE Connection - R
Church Educator - R
Church Worship
Journal/Adventist Educ. - R
Lutheran Education
Youth Leader - R

MISSIONS

Areopagus - R
Maryknoll
Urban Mission - R
Worldwide Challenge - R

PASTORS/LEADERS

Bible-Science - R
Chicago Studies
Christian Sentinel - R
Church Growth Network - R
Congregational Journal
Cross Currents
Eucharistic Minister - R
Five Stones, The - R
Homiletic & Pastoral Review
Journal/Christian Healing - R
Liturgy
Lutheran Forum - R
Ministries Today
Networks - R
Paraclete - R
Pastoral Life - R
Preacher's Illus. Service - R
Preacher's Magazine - R
Priest, The
PROCLAIM - R
Pulpit/Bible Study Helps - R
Quarterly Review
Review for Religious
Search
Today's Parish
Word & World
Youthworker - R

TEEN/YOUNG ADULT

Certainty
Student, The - R
Young Adult Today

WOMEN

Conscience - R
Daughters of Sarah
Esprit - R
Horizons - R
Jour/Women's Ministries
Lutheran Woman Today
Sisters Today - R
Woman's Touch - R

THINK PIECES

ADULT/GENERAL

ADVOCATE - R
American Tract Society - R
Annals of St. Anne
AXIOS - R
Burning Light - R
Canada Lutheran - R
Canadian Catholic Review
Catholic Digest - R
Catholic Twin Circle - R
Christian Century
Christian C.L. RECORD - R
Christian Courier (Canada) - R
Christian Edge - R
Christian Parenting Today - R
Christian Research - R
Christian Retailing
Christianity Today - R
Church Herald
Commonweal
Companion
Compass
Conquest
Covenant Companion
Cresset
Door, The
Episcopal Life - R
Evangelical Friend
Evangelical Visitor - R
Explorer
Family, The - R
Friends Journal - R
Good News, Etc - R
Herald of Holiness - R
Home Times - R
Inspirer, The - R
John Milton - R
Kansas City Christian - R
Living Church
Lookout - R
Lutheran, The
Lutheran Digest - R
Lutheran Journal - R
Maranatha - R
Mature Years - R
MESSAGE of the Open Bible - R
Messenger, The (NC) - R
Minnesota Chronicle, The - R

National Christian Reporter
New Oxford Review
News Network Intl.
New Thought Journal - R
NW Christian Journal - R
PCA Messenger - R
Pentecostal Homelife - R
Pentecostal Messenger - R
Presbyterian Record - R
Presbyterian Survey - R
Purpose - R
Ratio
Religious Broadcasting - R
Religious Education
Seek - R
Starlight
United Methodist Reporter
U.S. Catholic
Vista - R
Voice, The - R
Wesleyan Advocate
Writer's Forum - R

CHRISTIAN EDUCATION/ LIBRARY

CE Connection - R
Changing Lives - R
Lutheran Education

MISSIONS

Areopagus - R
Catholic Near East

MUSIC

Tradition - R

PASTORS/LEADERS

Congregational Journal
Eucharistic Minister - R
Faith & Renewal - R
Journal/Christian Healing - R
Leadership Journal - R
Ministries Today
Networks - R
Priest, The
Word & World

TEEN/YOUNG ADULT

Certainty
Conqueror - R
event
Freeway - R
Insight - R
Insight/Out - R
Kiln, The - R
Magazine/Youth! - R
Teenage Christian - R
Teen Quest - R
Vision - R
YOU! - R
Young Adult Today

WOMEN

Anna's Journal - R
Daughters of Sarah
Esprit - R
Horizons - R
Joyful Woman - R
Link & Visitor - R
Lutheran Woman Today
Virtue - R
Woman's Touch - R

WRITERS

Exchange - R
Writers Anchor - R

TRAVEL

ADULT/GENERAL

African-American Heritage - R
Alive! - R
Better Tomorrow
Catholic Digest - R
Catholic Twin Circle - R
Christian Courier (Canada) - R
Christian Single - R
Class
Columbia - R
Companion
Explorer
Family Digest, The - R
Home Times - R
John Milton - R
Joyful Noise
Lifeglow - R
Living - R
Lookout - R
Lutheran Layman
Mature Living
Mature Years - R
Pentecostal Homelife - R
Seek - R
Star of Zion
United Methodist Reporter

CHRISTIAN EDUCATION/LIBRARY

Church Recreation - R

MISSIONS

Areopagus - R
Childlife - R

PASTORS/LEADERS

Preacher's Illus. Service - R

TEEN/YOUNG ADULT

Conqueror - R
Teenage Christian - R
Young Adult Today
Young & Alive - R
Youth Focus - R

TRUE STORIES

ADULT/GENERAL

Acts 29
ADVOCATE - R
AGAIN - R
Annals of St. Anne
At Ease - R
Baptist Beacon - R
Better Tomorrow
Bible Advocate - R
Canada Lutheran - R
Catholic Digest - R
Catholic Twin Circle - R
Charisma & Christian Life
Christian Edge - R
Christian Living - R
Christian Parenting Today - R
Christian Reader - R
Church Herald/Holiness Banner - R
Companion
Conquest
Emphasis/Faith & Living - R
Evangel - R
Evangelical Friend
Evangelical Visitor - R
Family, The - R
Friends Journal - R
Gem, The - R
God's Revivalist - R
God's Special People - R
Good News, Etc - R
Good News Journal
Guideposts
Hallelujah - R
Herald of Holiness - R
Home Times - R
Impact Magazine - R
Indian Life - R
Inspirer, The - R
InterVarsity
John Milton - R
Journal/Christian Nursing - R
Kansas City Christian - R
Life Advocate - R

Lifeglow - R
Light and Life
Liguorian
Live - R
Living - R
Lookout - R
Lutheran, The
Lutheran Digest - R
Lutheran Journal - R
Lutheran Layman
Lutheran Witness
Maranatha - R
Mennonite, The - R
MESSAGE
MESSAGE of the Open Bible - R
Messenger, The (NC) - R
Ministry Today - R
Minnesota Chronicle, The - R
Moody
Morning Glory - R
Nat/Intl Religion Report
New Heart, A - R
New Thought Journal - R
Our Family - R
Parenting Treasures - R
Pentecostal Evangel
Pentecostal Homelife - R
Pentecostal Messenger - R
Power for Living - R
Presbyterian Record - R
Purpose - R
Quiet Revolution - R
Railroad Evangelist - R
SCP Journal - R
Seek - R
Sharing - R
Signs of the Times - R
Standard - R
Starlight
Sunday Digest - R
Table Talk - R
Together - R
Vision (MO) - R
Vista - R
Wesleyan Advocate

CHILDREN
Bible Time 4's & 5's
Counselor
Crusader - R
Focus/Clubhouse/Clubhouse Jr
GUIDE - R
High Adventure - R
Junior Trails - R
Listen
Mission
Nature Friend - R
Our Little Friend - R
Partners - R
Pockets - R
Primary Days
Primary Treasure - R
Touch - R
Young Crusader - R (family)

CHRISTIAN EDUCATION/LIBRARY
CE Connection - R
Changing Lives - R
Church Media Library - R
Lutheran Education
Perspective - R
Teacher Interaction - R
Youth Leader - R

MISSIONS
American Horizon - R
Areopagus - R
Childlife
Heartbeat - R
Urban Mission - R
World Christian - R
Worldwide Challenge - R

PASTORS/LEADERS
Eucharistic Minister - R
Five Stones, The - R
Networks - R
Preacher's Illus. Service - R
Preacher's Magazine - R

TEEN/YOUNG ADULT
Certainty
Challenge (IL)
Conqueror - R
event
Freeway - R
HiCall - R
Insight - R
Insight/Out - R
Kiln, The - R
Magazine/Youth! - R
Pioneer - R
Straight - R
Teenage Christian - R
Teen Life - R
Teen Power - R
With - R
Young Adult Today
Young & Alive - R
Young Salvationist - R
Youth World - R

WOMEN
Esprit - R
Joyful Woman - R
Link & Visitor - R
Lutheran Woman Today
Today's Christian Woman
Virtue - R
Woman's Touch - R

WRITERS
Writers Anchor - R
Writer's Nook News

WITNESSING

ADULT/GENERAL
Acts 29
ADVOCATE - R
American Tract Society - R
Annals of St. Anne
At Ease - R
Baptist Beacon - R
Bible Advocate - R
Canada Lutheran - R
Canadian Catholic Review
Catholic Digest - R
Charisma & Christian Life
Christian Reader - R
Christian Research - R
Christian Social Action - R
Church Herald/Holiness Banner - R
Companion
Companions - R
Conquest
Cornerstone - R
Decision
Discipleship Journal - R
Emphasis/Faith & Living - R
Evangel - R
Evangelical Friend
Evangelical Visitor - R
Friends Journal - R
God's Revivalist - R
Good News, Etc - R
Hallelujah - R
Herald of Holiness - R
Indian Life - R
Inspirer, The - R
InterVarsity
John Milton - R
Journal/Christian Nursing - R
Light and Life
Live - R
Lutheran Layman
Lutheran Witness
Maranatha - R
MESSAGE of the Open Bible - R
Messenger, The (NC) - R
Ministry Today - R

Moody
Morning Glory - R
New Covenant - R
New Heart, A - R
New Oxford Review
Our Family - R
Pentecostal Evangel
Pentecostal Messenger - R
Power for Living - R
Presbyterian Survey - R
Purpose - R
Railroad Evangelist - R
SCP Journal - R
Seek - R
Standard - R
Starlight
Sunday Digest - R
Tree of Life
Vision - R
Vista - R
Wesleyan Advocate

CHILDREN
Counselor
GUIDE - R
Primary Days
Touch - R

CHRISTIAN EDUCATION/LIBRARY
Brigade Leader - R
CE Connection - R
Changing Lives - R
Church Media Library - R
Evangelizing Today's Child
Insight
Journal/Adventist Educ. - R
Lutheran Education
Youth & CE Leadership - R
Youth Leader - R

MISSIONS
American Horizon - R
IMPACT
Mission Frontier - R
Urban Mission - R
World Christian - R
Worldwide Challenge - R

PASTORS/LEADERS
Advance - R
Bible-Science - R
Church Administration
Discipleship Training
Eucharistic Minister - R
Evangelism - R
Faith & Renewal - R
Journal/Christian Healing - R
Ministries Today
Networks - R
Paraclete - R
Pastoral Life - R
Preacher's Magazine - R
PROCLAIM - R
Pulpit/Bible Study Helps - R

TEEN/YOUNG ADULT
Certainty
Challenge (IL)
Conqueror - R
event
Freeway - R
Insight - R
Magazine/Youth! - R
Student, The - R
Teenage Christian - R
Teen Power - R
Teen Quest - R
YOU! - R
Young Adult Today
Young Salvationist - R

WOMEN
Co-Laborer - R
Esprit - R
Joyful Woman - R
Lutheran Woman Today
Salt and Light
Sisters Today - R
Today's Christian Woman
Wesleyan Woman
Woman's Touch - R

WOMEN'S ISSUES

ADULT/GENERAL
Advent Christian Witness
All About Issues - R
Anglican Journal - R
Annals of St. Anne
At Ease - R
Better Tomorrow
Canada Lutheran - R
Canadian Catholic Review
Catholic Digest - R
Catholic Exponent
Catholic Parent
Catholic Twin Circle - R
Charisma & Christian Life
Christian Century
Christian C.L. RECORD - R
Christian Courier (Canada) - R
Christian Edge - R
Christian Reader - R
Christian Single - R
Christian Social Action - R
Columbia - R
Companion
Compass
Cornerstone - R
Covenant Companion
Creation Social Science - R
Critic, The
Emphasis/Faith & Living - R
Episcopal Life - R
Evangelical Friend
Expression
Family, The - R
Foursquare World ADVANCE - R
Friends Journal - R
Good News, Etc - R
Gospel Tidings - R
Hallelujah - R
Herald of Holiness - R
Home Life
Home Times - R
Interim - R
John Milton - R
Journal/Christian Nursing - R
Joyful Noise
Kansas City Christian - R
Liguorian
Live - R
Living - R
Lookout - R
Lutheran, The
Mature Years - R
Mennonite, The - R
Mennonite Brethren Herald - R
MESSAGE
MESSAGE of the Open Bible - R
Messenger, The (NC) - R
Ministry Today - R
Minnesota Chronicle, The - R
Moody
National Christian Reporter
NW Christian Journal - R
Other Side, The
Our Sunday Visitor
Pentecostal Evangel
Pentecostal Messenger - R
Power for Living - R
Prairie Messenger (church)
Presbyterian Outlook
Presbyterian Survey - R
Prism
Purpose - R
St. Joseph Messenger - R
Salt
Signs of the Times - R

Standard - R
Sunday Digest - R
Today's Better Life
United Church Observer - R
United Methodist Reporter
Vista - R
Witness, The

MISSIONS
American Horizon - R
Maryknoll
New World Outlook
Urban Mission - R
World Vision - R
Worldwide Challenge - R

PASTORS/LEADERS
Bethany Choice - R
Christian Ministry
Diaconalogue - R
Faith & Renewal - R
Journal/Christian Healing - R
Ministries Today (little)
Single Ad. Ministries Jour.
Youthworker - R
Word & World

TEEN/YOUNG ADULT
Brio
Vision - R
Young Adult Today

WOMEN
(See alphabetical listing)

WRITERS
Housewife-Writer's Forum - R

WORLD ISSUES

ADULT/GENERAL
ADVOCATE - R
Alive!
All About Issues - R
America
Annals of St. Anne
At Ease - R
AXIOS - R
Baptist Informer
Bible Advocate - R
Canada Lutheran - R
Canadian Catholic Review
Catholic Sentinel - R
Catholic Twin Circle - R
Charisma & Christian Life
Christian Century
Christian Courier (Canada) - R
Christian Crusade
Christian Living - R
Christian Research - R
Christian Single - R
Christian Social Action
Church Herald/Holiness Banner - R
Columbia - R
Companion
Compass
Cornerstone - R
Creation Social Science - R
Critic, The
Emphasis/Faith & Living - R
Evangelical Friend
Evangelical Visitor - R
Expression
Faith Today
Family, The - R
Friends Journal - R
Gotta Write
Hallelujah - R
Home Times - R
Interchange
InterVarsity
John Milton - R
Journal/Church & State
Kansas City Christian - R
Liberty - R
Lookout - R
Lutheran, The
Lutheran Layman
Mennonite, The - R
Mennonite Brethren Herald - R
MESSAGE
MESSAGE of the Open Bible - R
Messenger (KY)
Messenger, The (NC) - R
Messenger of St. Anthony - R
Ministry Today - R
Minnesota Chronicle, The - R
Moody
Morning Glory - R
National Christian Reporter
Nat/Intl Religion Report
News Network Intl.
New Thought Journal - R
NW Christian Journal - R
Other Side, The
Our Sunday Visitor
PCA Messenger - R
Pentecostal Evangel
Pentecostal Messenger - R
Power for Living - R
Presbyterian Outlook
Presbyterian Record - R
Presbyterian Survey - R
Prism
Quiet Revolution - R
Religious Broadcasting - R
St. Anthony Messenger
SCP Journal - R
United Church Observer - R
United Methodist Reporter
Vision (MO) - R
Witness, The

CHILDREN
Counselor
Faith 'n Stuff
God's World Today

MISSIONS
Areopagus - R
Catholic Near East
Childlife - R
Compassion Update - R
IMPACT
Maryknoll
New World Outlook
P.I.M.E. World - R
Urban Mission - R
World Christian - R
World Vision - R
Worldwide Challenge - R

PASTORS/LEADERS
Christian Ministry
Liturgy
Networks - R
Preacher's Illus. Service - R
Preacher's Magazine - R
Word & World
Youthworker - R

TEEN/YOUNG ADULT
Conqueror - R
Insight - R
Insight/Out - R
Issues & Answers - R
Magazine/Youth! - R
Student, The - R
Student Leadership - R
Teenage Christian - R
Young Adult Today
Young Salvationist - R

WOMEN
Contempo
Esprit - R
Helping Hand - R
Horizons - R
Link & Visitor - R
Lutheran Woman Today
Response

Royal Service
Sisters Today - R
Woman's Touch - R

WORSHIP

ADULT/GENERAL

Acts 29
ADVOCATE - R
alive now! - R
Annals of St. Anne
At Ease - R
Baptist Beacon - R
Baptist Informer
Bible Advocate - R
Canada Lutheran - R
Canadian Catholic Review
Catholic Digest - R
Catholic Sentinel - R
Charisma & Christian Life
Christian Reader - R
Church Herald/Holiness Banner - R
Companion
Companions - R
Conquest
Covenant Companion
Decision
Discipleship Journal - R
Emphasis/Faith & Living - R
Evangelical Beacon - R
Evangelical Friend
Evangelical Visitor - R
Family Digest, The - R
Fellowship Today - R
Friends Journal - R
God's Revivalist - R
Good News - R
Good News, Etc - R
Herald of Holiness - R
Inspirer, The - R
John Milton - R
Joyful Noise
Light and Life
Liguorian
Living Church
Lookout - R
Lutheran, The
Maranatha - R
Mature Years - R
Mennonite, The - R
Mennonite Brethren Herald - R
Mennonite Reporter
MESSAGE
MESSAGE of the Open Bible - R
Messenger, The (Canada) - R
Messenger, The (NC) - R
Ministry Today - R
Moody
Morning Glory - R
North American Voice
NW Christian Journal - R
Our Family - R
Our Sunday Visitor
Pentecostal Evangel
Pentecostal Homelife - R
Pentecostal Messenger - R
Plenty Good Room
Presbyterian Outlook
Presbyterian Record - R
Presbyterian Survey - R
Religious Broadcasting - R
St. Willibrord Journal
Seek - R
Sunday Digest - R
Tree of Life
United Church Observer - R
United Methodist Reporter
Vista - R
Vital Christianity - R
Wesleyan Advocate

CHILDREN

Wonder Time

CHRISTIAN EDUCATION/LIBRARY

CE Connection - R
Changing Lives - R
Christian Ed Journal - R
Church Educator - R
Church Media Library - R
Church Worship
Journal/Adventist Educ. - R
Leader - R
Lutheran Education
Youth & CE Leadership - R
Youth Leader - R

MISSIONS

American Horizon - R
Areopagus - R
Catholic Near East
IMPACT
Worldwide Challenge - R

MUSIC

Church Pianist, etc.
Creator
Glory Songs
Hymn, The
Worship Today - R

PASTORS/LEADERS

Advance - R
Chicago Studies
Christian Ministry
Church Growth Network - R
Clergy Journal
Faith & Renewal - R
Five Stones, The - R
Journal/Christian Healing - R
Leadership Journal - R
Liturgy
Lutheran Forum - R
Ministries Today
Networks - R
Paraclete - R
Pastoral Life - R
Preacher's Illus. Service - R
Preacher's Magazine - R
Priest, The
PROCLAIM - R
Pulpit/Bible Study Helps - R
Reformed Worship
Review for Religious
Search
Today's Parish
Word & World
Worship Leader
Youthworker - R

TEEN/YOUNG ADULT

Certainty
Conqueror - R
Freeway - R
Insight - R
Pathway I.D. - R
Teenage Christian - R
Teen Power - R
Student Leadership - R
Young Adult Today
Young Salvationist - R
Youth Update

WOMEN

Esprit - R
Horizons - R
Lutheran Woman Today
Sisters Today - R
Today's Christian Woman
Virtue - R
Women Alive ! - R

YOUTH ISSUES

ADULT/GENERAL

Acts 29
American Tract Society - R
Annals of St. Anne
AXIOS - R

Canada Lutheran - R
Canadian Catholic Review
Catholic Digest - R
Catholic Exponent
Catholic Parent
Catholic Sentinel - R
Christian Courier (Canada) - R
Christian Edge - R
Christian Parenting Today - R
Christian Social Action
Church Herald/Holiness Banner - R
Columbia - R
Companion
Companions - R
Covenant Companion
Creation Social Science - R
Decision
Emphasis/Faith & Living - R
Evangelical Friend
Expression
Faith Today
Family, The - R
Foursquare World ADVANCE - R
Good News, Etc - R
Gospel Tidings - R
Herald of Holiness - R
Home Times - R
John Milton - R
Kansas City Christian - R
Light and Life
Living - R
Lutheran, The
Lutheran Digest - R
Maranatha - R
Mennonite, The - R
Mennonite Brethren Herald - R
MESSAGE
Messenger, The (Canada) - R
Messenger, The (NC) - R
Messenger of St. Anthony - R
Ministry Today - R
National Christian Reporter
New Oxford Review
NW Christian Journal - R
Our Family - R
PCA Messenger - R
Pentecostal Evangel
Pentecostal Messenger - R
Pentecostal Testimony - R
Presbyterian Outlook
Presbyterian Record - R
Presbyterian Survey - R
Religious Broadcasting - R
Religious Education
Social Justice Review
United Church Observer - R
United Methodist Reporter
Witness, The

CHILDREN
BREAD for God's Children - R
Crusader - R
Focus/Clubhouse/Clubhouse Jr
GUIDE - R
High Adventure - R
Power & Light - R
R-A-D-A-R - R
Touch - R
Young Crusader - R

CHRISTIAN EDUCATION/LIBRARY
CE Connection - R
CE Counselor - R
Changing Lives - R
Church Educator - R
Church Recreation - R
GROUP
Journal/Adventist Educ. - R
KEY - R
Leader - R
Leader/Church School Today
Lutheran Education
Parish Teacher - R
Perspective - R
Religion Teacher's Journal
Team - R
Youth & CE Leadership - R
Youth Leader - R

MISSIONS
American Horizon - R
New World Outlook
Worldwide Challenge - R

PASTORS/LEADERS
Bethany Choice - R
Christian Ministry
Church Growth Network - R
Congregational Journal
Faith & Renewal - R
Five Stones, The - R
Group's Jr High
Ivy Jungle Report - R
Journal/Christian Healing
Leadership Journal - R
Ministries Today
Pastoral Life - R
Preacher's Magazine - R
Pulpit/Bible Study Helps - R
Search
Word & World
Youthworker - R

TEEN/YOUNG ADULT
(See alphabetical listing)

ALPHABETICAL LISTINGS OF PERIODICALS

Following are the listings of periodicals. They are arranged alphabetically by type of periodical (see Table of Contents for a list of types). Nonpaying markets are indicated in bold letters within those listings, e.g. **NO PAYMENT**.

If a listing is preceded by an asterisk (*), it indicates that publisher did not send updated information. If it is preceded by a number symbol (#) it was updated from available sources or by phone. If it is preceded by a (+) it is a new listing. It is important that freelance writers request writers' guidelines and a recent sample copy before submitting to any of these publications, but especially to those with these symbols.

If you do not find the publication you are looking for, check the supplementary listings at the back of the book for those periodicals that have ceased publication, changed names, or are not open to freelance submissions.

For a detailed explanation of how to understand and get the most out of these listings, see the "How to Use This Book" section at the front of the book. Unfamiliar terms are explained in the Glossary at the back of the book.

(*) An asterisk before a listing indicates no or unconfirmed information update.

(#) A number symbol before a listing means it was updated from their current writers' guidelines or other sources.

(+) A plus sign means it is a new listing.

ADULT/GENERAL MARKETS

ACTS 29, P.O. Box 4237,Evergreen CO 80439-3745. (303)674-9744. Fax: (303) 674-9709. Episcopal Renewal Ministries. Tom Beckwith, ed. To report, support, and encourage parish renewal within the Anglican community and as a forum for apostolic teaching. Bimonthly mag; circ. 55,000. Free subscription. 50% freelance. Complete ms/cover letter; no phone query. **NO PAYMENT**, for all rts. Articles (24/yr) 500-1,400 wds; book & music reviews, 800 wds. Free copy.
Fillers: Anecdotes, quotes; 25-75 wds.
Columns/Departments: Personal Testimonies, 500 wds; Teaching Articles (doctrine/policy), 1,200-1,400 wds; Reports (Episcopal Parish Renewal), 800 wds; Parish Articles, 1,200 wds.
Tips: "Manuscripts from Episcopal lay people and clergy are welcome."

#ADVENT CHRISTIAN WITNESS, Box 23152, Charlotte NC 28212. (704)545-6161. Fax: (704)573-0712. Advent Christian General Conference. Robert J. Mayer, ed. Denominational. Monthly mag; 20 pgs; circ 4,000. Subscription $11. 10% freelance. Complete ms. Pays $15-25, on publication, for one-time rts. Articles 750-1,200 wds (4/yr). Reports in 8 wks. Seasonal 6 mos ahead. Accepts simultaneous submissions. Guidelines; copy $2.

ADVOCATE, (International Pentecostal Holiness ADVOCATE), Box 12609, Oklahoma City OK 73157. (405)787-7110. Fax: (405)789-3957. International Pentecostal Holiness Church. Shirley Spencer, exec. ed. Denominational; conservative in viewpoint; full-gospel. Monthly mag; 20 pgs; circ 3,000. Subscription $9.75. 10% freelance. Complete ms/no cover letter; no phone query. Pays $15-30, on acceptance, for 1st, reprint, or simultaneous rts. Articles 500-1,200 wds. Reports in 3 wks. Seasonal 3 mos ahead. Accepts simultaneous submissions & reprints. Guidelines; free copy.
Poetry: Buys 6/yr. Free verse, traditional; to 15 lines. Pays $15. Submit max. 3 poems.

#AFA JOURNAL, Box 2440, 107 Parkgate Dr., Tupelo MS 38801. (601)844-5036. American Family Assn. Don Wildmon, exec. ed; Randall Murphree, articles ed. Urges people to become involved, as change agents, with social/moral issues, such as pornography, TV programming, abortion, and First Amendment rights. Monthly (11X) journal; 24 pgs; circ 400,000. 5% freelance. Query; phone query ok. **NO PAYMENT**. Not copyrighted. Articles (2-3/yr) 1,000 wds. Accepts simultaneous query & reprints. Reports in 2 mos. No guidelines; free copy.
Tips: "Most open to articles on social and moral issues with impact on the family."

+AFRICAN-AMERICAN HERITAGE, 8443 S. Crenshaw Blvd., Ste. 103, Inglewood CA 90305. (213)752-3706. General publication that includes inspirational and religious articles. Dennis DeLoach, ed. To cultivate self-esteem, pride and appreciation for ethnic heritage. Quarterly mag; circ. 25,000. 30% freelance. Query. Pays $25-300; on publication; for 1st, one-time, or simultaneous rts. Articles 200-2,000 wds (6/yr); fiction 200-2,000 wds (6/yr). Reports in 1-2 mos. Seasonal 6 mos ahead. Accepts simultaneous submissions & reprints. Kill fee 25%. Guidleines; copy for 9x12 SAE/4 stamps.
Special Needs: February is Black History Month.
Poetry: Buys 60/yr. Avant-garde, free verse, haiku, light verse, traditional; 4-36 lines. Pays $1-25. Submit max. 5 poems.
Fillers: Buys 12/yr. Anecdotes, facts; 10-200 wds. pays $25-100.

#AGAIN MAGAZINE, Box 76, Ben Lomond CA 95005. (408)336-5118. Fax: (408)336-8882. Orthodox/Conciliar Press. Weldon Hardenbrook, ed. A call to the people of God to return to their roots of historical orthodoxy once AGAIN. Quarterly mag; 32 pgs; circ 4,500. Subscription $12. 1% freelance. Query. **PAYS IN COPIES**. Accepts simultaneous submissions & reprints. Articles 1,500-2,000 wds; fiction 1,500-2,500 wds; book reviews 500-700 wds. Reports in 4 mos. Seasonal 2 mos ahead. Serials 2 parts. Guidelines; copy $2.50/9x12 SAE/5 stamps.

#ALIVE! A MAGAZINE FOR CHRISTIAN SENIOR ADULTS, Box 46464, Cincinnati OH 45246-0464. (513)825-3681. Christian Seniors Fellowship. J. David & June Lang, eds. Focuses on activities and opportunities for active, Christian senior adults, age 55 & older. Bimonthly mag; 12-16 pgs; circ 6,000. 60% freelance. Complete ms/cover letter optional; no phone query. Pays .03-.05/wd ($18-75), on publication, for 1st rts. Articles (25/yr), 600-1,200 wds; fiction (12/yr), 600-1,500 wds. Reports in 1-2 mos. Seasonal 6 mos ahead. Accepts simultaneous submissions & reprints. Guidelines; copy for 9x12 SAE/2 stamps.
Fillers: Buys 15/yr. Anecdotes, facts, jokes & short humor; 50-500 wds; $2-15.
Columns/Departments: Buys 50/yr. Heart Medicine (humor, grandparent/grandchild anecdotes), to 100 wds; $2.50-5; Games 'n Stuff (word puzzles/games), $2-25.
Tips: "No queries, no dot matrix. Prefer not to get a bundle of mss. We don't have time to do critiques."

#ALIVE NOW!, 1908 Grand Ave., Box 189, Nashville TN 37202-0189. (615)340-7218. Fax:(615)340-7006. United Methodist/The Upper Room. George Graham, ed. Short writings in attractive graphic setting for reflection and meditation. Bimonthly mag; 64 pgs; circ 65,000. 90% freelance. Complete ms/cover letter. Pays $15-20, on acceptance, for all, one-time or reprint rts. Articles 250 wds; fiction 250-750 wds. Reports in 2-3 wks. Seasonal 6-8 mos ahead. Guidelines/theme list; free copy.
Poetry: Free verse, traditional; to 25 lines.
Fillers: Cartoons, prayers.

ALL ABOUT ISSUES, Box 1350, Stafford VA 22554. (703)659-4171. Fax: (703)659-2586. American Life League. Steve Dunham, mng. ed. A pro-life educational group. Bimonthly mag; circ. 100,000. Subscription $12.95. 80% freelance. Query; phone query only if necessary. Pays $50/pg ($25/pg for reprints); on publication; for one-time rts. Articles 200-2,000 wds (50/yr); book reviews 250-500 wds, $25-50. Reports in 2-6 wks. Seasonal 6 mos ahead. Accepts simultaneous query & reprints. Kill fee. Guidelines/theme list; copy for 9x12 SAE/4 stamps.
Poetry: Buys up to 6/yr. Pays $25.
Fillers: Buys 6/yr. Anecdotes, facts, prayers, short humor; 25-100 wds. Pays $15-25.
Columns/Departments: Commentary, 500 wds. Pays $25.
Tips: "Looking for articles on pro-life action by individuals and churches. We often print human interest articles about people society wouldn't protect—children of rape or incest, or who were predicted to be deformed."
** This periodical was #46 on the 1993 Top 50 Plus Christian Publishers list.

#AMERICA, 106 W. 56th St., New York NY 10019. (212)581-4640. Catholic. George Hunt, S.J., ed. A national journal of opinion. Weekly mag; 24-32 pgs; circ 36,000. 100% freelance. Query or complete ms/cover letter. Pays $75-250, on acceptance, for 1st rts. Articles 1,500-2,000 wds. Reports in 1 mo. Seasonal 3 mos ahead. Guidelines; copy $1.50/SASE.
Poetry: Patrick Samway, S.J. Light verse, serious poetry, unrhymed; 15-30 lines. Pays $7.50-25, on publication. Submit max. 3 poems.

***THE AMERICAN BAPTIST**, Box 851, Valley Forge PA 19482. American Baptist Church. Philip E. Jenks, ed. Denominational. Little freelance. Not in topical listings.
Tips: "Interested in denominational-oriented news and issues stories."

#AMERICAN BIBLE SOCIETY RECORD, 1865 Broadway, New York NY 10023. (212)408-1480. Fax: (212)408-1456. Clifford P. Macdonald, ed. Report of stewardship for ABS members. Monthly mag; 32 pgs; circ. 275,000. 2% freelance. Query; phone query ok. Negotiable payment, on acceptance, for all rts. Not copyrighted. Articles 500-600 wds (1/yr). Accepts simultaneous query & reprints. Not in topical listings. No guidelines; free copy.
Tips: "Only articles concerning the Bible or the work and mission of the ABS."

***AMERICAN TRACT SOCIETY**, Box 462008, Garland TX 75046. (214)276-9408. Perry Brown, tract ed. Majority of tracts written to win unbeliever. Bimonthly tracts; 25 million produced annually. 10% freelance. Query or complete ms/cover letter; phone query ok. Pays $100-150, on publication, for simultaneous rts. Tracts 800-1,200 wds (3-6/yr). Reports in 4-6 wks. Seasonal 8-9 mos ahead. Accepts reprints. Guidelines; free samples.
Special Needs: Youth issues.
Tips: "Choose a subject that is very relevant and evident to potential readers."

#ANGLICAN JOURNAL, 600 Jarvis St., Toronto ON M4Y 2J6 Canada. (416)924-9192. Anglican Church of Canada. Carolyn Purden, ed; submit to Vianney Carriere, news ed. Informs Canadian Anglicans about the church at home and overseas. Newspaper (10x/yr); 24 pgs; circ. 272,000. 25% freelance. Query; phone query ok. Pays $50-500 (Canadian), on publication, for 1st rts. Articles 200-800 wds. Reports in 2 wks. Seasonal 2 mos ahead. Accepts reprints. Guidelines.

THE ANNALS OF SAINT ANNE DE BEAUPRE, Box 1000, St. Anne de Beaupre, QB G0A 3C0 Canada. (418)827-4538. Fax: (418)827-4530. Redemptorist Fathers. Father Roch Achard, C.Ss.R., ed. Promotes Catholic family values. Monthly (11X) mag; 32 pgs; circ 50,000. Subscription $8 U.S. 80% freelance. Complete ms/cover letter; phone query ok. Pays .03-.04/wd, on acceptance, for 1st NA Serial rts. Articles 500-1,500 wds (30/yr); fiction 500-1,500 wds (15/yr). Reports in 2 wks. Seasonal 3 mos ahead. Free guidelines/copy.
Poetry: Overstocked for now.
Tips: "Write something educational, inspirational, objective and uplifting. No articles without a spiritual thrust. Good, solid stories, no heavy or long quotes or citations, or borrowing from other authors."

***ANSWERS IN ACTION JOURNAL**, Box 2067, Costa Mesa CA 92628. (714)646-9042. Answers in Action. Gretchen Passantino, ed. Education and analysis of current religious scene. Monthly; circ. 2,000. Query. Articles; book reviews.

THE APOCALYPSE CHRONICLES, Box 448, Jacksonville OR 97530. (503)899-8888. James Lloyd, ed/pub. Deals with the apocalypse exclusively. Quarterly. Query. Payment negotiable. Articles. No guidelines; copy for #10 SAE/2 stamps.

+ARKANSAS CATHOLIC, P.O. Box 7417, Little Rock AR 72217. (501)664-0340. Catholic. Pete Hoelscher, ed. Regional newspaper for the local Diocese. Published 40X/yr; 16 pgs; circ. 7,000. 5% freelance. Query/clips only. Pays $2.50/column inch, on publication, for 1st rts.
Articles 500-1,300 wds. Reports in 3 wks. Accepts simultaneous submissions. Guidelines; copy for 9x12 SAE/2 stamps.
Columns/Departments: Viewpoint (issues-related opinion pieces); Scripture Speaks Today (Bible commentary); 500 wds.
Tips: "Most open to news of the Diocese or pieces that inspire readers to consider what it means to be Catholic today."

+ARLINGTON CATHOLIC HERALD, 200 N. Glebe Rd., Ste. 614, Arlington VA 22203. (703)841-2590. Catholic. Michael Flach, ed. Regional newspaper for the local Diocese. Weekly newspaper; 24 pgs; circ. 45,000. 20-25% freelance. Complete ms/cover letter. Pays $50-200, on publication, for one-time rts. Articles 500-2,000 wds. Reports in 2 mos. Guidelines; free copy.
Columns/Departments: Sports; School News; Local Entertainments; 500 wds.
Tips: "All submissions must be Catholic-related. Avoid controversial issues within the Church."

#THE ASSOCIATE REFORMED PRESBYTERIAN, 1 Cleveland St., Greenville SC 29601-3696. (803)232-8297. Fax: (803)271-3729. Associate Reformed Presbyterian Church. Ben Johnston, ed. Denominational. Monthly mag; 40 pgs; circ 6,300. Subscription $15. 10% freelance. Query or complete ms/cover letter. Pays $20-50; on

acceptance; for 1st, one-time or reprint rts. Not copyrighted. Articles (10-15/yr) 800-850 wds; fiction & children's stories 400-2,000 wds. Reports in 1 month. Seasonal 4 mos ahead. Accepts simultaneous query & reprints. Guidelines; copy $1.50.
Columns/Departments: Higher Education, Witness & Outreach, World Missions; 200-500 wds.
Annual Contest: Children's stories. Send SASE for contest rules in January. April 1 deadline.
Tips: "Most open to feature articles."

AT EASE, 1445 Boonville Ave., Springfield MO 65802. (417)862-2781. Fax: (417)863-7276. Assemblies of God. Lemuel D. McElyea, ed; articles to Janet Walker, mng. ed. For military personnel. Bimonthly mag; 4 pgs; circ 28,000. 90% freelance. Complete ms/cover letter; phone query ok. Pays .03/wd, on publication, for 1st or one-time rts. Articles 400-800 wds (20/yr). Reports in 3-4 wks. Seasonal 6 mos ahead. Accepts simultaneous submissions & reprints. Guidelines/copy for #10 SAE/1 stamp.
Poetry: Buys 4/yr. Avant-garde, free verse, light verse, traditional; $10.
Fillers: Buys 5/yr. Cartoons; $20-40.
Tips: "Strong human interest; talk about real life. Make subject inspiring and uplifting. We want to win souls."

AXIOS, P.O. Box 279, Belmopan, Belize, Central America. Orthodox Christian. Fr. Daniel John Gorham, ed. Review of public affairs, religion, literature and the arts, and is especially interested in the Orthodox Catholic Church and its world view. Bimonthly newsletter; 32 pgs; circ 15,672. Subscription $25. 90% freelance. Complete ms/cover letter; no phone query. Pays .04/wd & up ($25-500), on publication, for 1st rts. Articles, any length (29/yr); book reviews 2,000 wds. Reports in 4-8 wks. Seasonal 4 mos ahead. Accepts simultaneous submissions & reprints. Kill fee 25%. Copy $4.20/9x12 SAE/$1.20 currency.
Poetry: Buys 6/yr. Traditional; any length. Pays $5-25. Submit max. 3 poems.
Fillers: Buys 25/yr. Anecdotes, cartoons, facts.
Columns/Departments: Buys 80 religious book and film reviews/yr. Query.
Tips: "Most open to articles. Be sure you have an idea of who and what an orthodox Christian is."

+THE BAPTIST BEACON, RR 1, Waterford ON N0E 1Y0 Canada. (519)443-8525. Baptist. Sterling Clark, ed. For adults, emphasizing biblical doctrine, evangelism, prophesy, and inspirational articles. Monthly mag; 20 pgs; circ. 300. Subscription $12. 15% freelance. Complete ms/cover letter; phone query ok. **NO PAYMENT** for one-time use. Articles any length. Seasonal 3 mos ahead. Accepts reprints. Free copy.
Poetry: Accepts 24+/yr. Traditional; any length. Submit any number.
Tips: "Most open to devotional, inspirational and biblical teaching."

+BAPTIST HISTORY AND HERITAGE, 901 Commerce St., Ste. 400, Nashville TN 37203. (615)244-0344. Southern Baptist. Dr. Charles W. DeWeese, ed. A scholarly journal focusing on Baptist history. Quarterly journal; 64 pgs; circ. 2,000. 15-20% freelance. Query. Pays $192 (for assigned only), for all rts. Articles to 4,000 wds. Reports in 2 mos. Guidelines; no copy.
Tips: "Most open to lesser known aspects of Baptist history based on primary sources."

+THE BAPTIST INFORMER, 603 S. Wilmington St., Raleigh NC 27601. (919)821-7466. Fax: (919)836-0061. General Baptist. Archie D. Logan, ed. Regional African-American publication. Monthly tabloid; 16 pgs; circ. 10,000. 10% freelance. Query or complete ms/cover letter. **PAYS IN COPIES**, for one-time rts. Articles & fiction. Reports in 3 mos. Accepts simultaneous submissions. No guidelines; free copy.

+THE B.C. CATHOLIC, 150 Robson St., Vancouver BC V6B 2A7 Canada. (604) 683-0281. Fax: (604)683-8117. Catholic. Rev. Vincent Hawkswell, ed. News, education, and inspiration for Canadian Catholics. Weekly (47X) newspaper; 16 pgs; circ. 20,000. Query. Pays variable rate, on publication, for 1st rts. Articles 400-500 wds. Reports in 4 wks. Accepts simultaneous submissions & reprints. No guidelines or copy.
Tips: "We prefer to use Catholic writers."

+THE BEACON, P.O. Box 381985, Miami FL 33138. (305)787-1307. Submit to the Editor. Bimonthly newsletter. 20% freelance. Free subscription. Not in topical listings.

+THE BEACON CHRISTIAN NEWS, 1733 Sheepshead Bay Rd., Brooklyn NY 11235. (718)769-4400. Fax: (718)769-5048. Karen L. Santiago, ed. For evangelical Christians in Metro New York; hard and soft (feature) news about what God is doing with and through His people. Monthly newspaper; circ. 35,000. Subscription $19.95. Est. 1992. 50% freelance. Query; phone query ok. Pays $25, on publication, for one-time rts. Articles 200-300 wds (120/yr). Reports in 1 wk. Seasonal 3 mos ahead. Accepts reprints. Free guidelines/theme list/copy.
Special Needs: Hard news about Christians in Metro New York.
Tips: "I am eagerly looking for news journalists who will be responsible for covering Christian news in specific boroughs of Metro New York. Please call."

+A BETTER TOMORROW, 5301 Wisconsin Ave. NW #620, Washington DC 20015. (202)364-8000. Fax: (202)364-8910. Nondenominational. Cathy Constant, asst. ed. For Christian seniors who want to make the most of their later years (most 55-75). Quarterly mag; 110 pgs; circ. 100,000. Subscription $19.80. Est. 1992. 25% freelance. Query. Pays .10/wd, on acceptance, for 1st rts. Articles 1,200-1,700 wds. Reports in 8-10 wks. Seasonal 8 mos ahead. Guidelines; no copy.
Columns/Departments: Buys 16-20/yr. My Story (personal experience), 1,500 wds; Opinion (idea on faith); Profiles (Christian senior making a difference—tips/ideas only).
Tips: "Read back issues."

BIBLE ADVOCATE, Box 33677, Denver CO 80233. (303)452-7973. Fax: (303)452-0657. Church of God (Seventh Day). Roy Marrs, ed; Sherri Langton, asst. ed. Mostly older adult readers; general reading. Monthly (11X) mag; 24 pgs; circ 12,000. Free subscription. 25% freelance. Complete ms/cover letter; no phone query. Pays $10/printed pg, to $25; on publication; for one-time use. Articles 1,000-2,500 wds (20-30/yr). Reports in 4-6 wks. Seasonal 3-6 mos ahead. Accepts simultaneous submissions & reprints. Kill fee to $25. Guidelines; copy for 9x12 SAE/3 stamps.
Poetry: Uses 10-20/yr. Free verse, light verse, traditional; 5-25 lines. **PAYS IN COPIES**. Submit max. 5 poems.
Fillers: Buys 5/yr. Facts, prayers, prose, quotes; 10-250 wds. Pays $5-10.
Columns/Departments: Uses 6/yr. Viewpoint (social or religious issues), to 700 wds. **PAYS IN COPIES.**
Tips: "Viewpoint column & poetry most open. Keep your writing fresh. Have something different to say that is biblically sound and insightful, and stick to your focus."

#BIBLE REVIEW, 3000 Connecticut Ave. NW, #300, Washington DC 20008. (202)387-8888. Fax: (202)483-3423. Biblical Archaeological Society. Hershel Shanks, ed. Bimonthly mag; 80 pgs; circ 40,000. 5% freelance. Query only. Pays to $300, on publication, for one-time rts. Accepts reprints. Articles 700-1,500, to 5,000. Reports in 1 yr. Not in topical listings. No guidelines or copy.
Tips: "Looking for interesting, historical, critical analysis of the Bible."

THE BIBLE TODAY, Saint John's Abbey, Collegeville MN 56321-7500. (612)363-2213. Fax: (800)445-5899. Catholic. Mss to: Rev. Leslie J. Hoppe, O.F.M., ed., 5401 S. Cornell Ave., Chicago IL 60615. Explains the meaning and context of particular biblical passages and books and encourages a regular, prayerful reading of the Bible. Bimonthly mag; 64 pgs; circ 8,500. Subscription $20. 20% freelance. Complete ms/cover letter; phone query ok. **PAYS 5 COPIES & SUBSCRIPTION.** Articles to 2,000 wds (15/yr). Reports in 4-9 wks. Seasonal 6 mos ahead. Free guidelines/copy.
Tips: "Most open to general articles on the Bible or biblical themes, biblical archaeology, biblical spirituality."

BOOKSTORE JOURNAL, Box 200, Colorado Springs CO 80901. (719)576-7880. Fax: (719)576-0795. Christian Booksellers Assn. Todd Hafer, ed. To provide Christian bookstore owners with professional retail skills, product information, and industry news. Monthly trade journal; 175 pgs; circ 10,000. Subscription $45. 50% freelance. Query/clips. Pays .11-.14/wd, on publication, for all or 1st rts. Articles 800-3,500 wds (12/yr). Reports in 6 wks. Seasonal 5 mos ahead. Accepts simultaneous submissions & reprints. Kill fee 90%. Guidelines; copy $5/9x12 SAE/3 stamps.
Fillers: Buys 12/yr. Cartoons; $100.
Tips: "Know the Christian retail industry. Do your homework and get facts straight, quotes accurate, etc."

BROKEN STREETS, 57 Morningside Dr. E., Bristol CT 06010. (203)582-2943. Ron Grossman, ed. For Christian writers of poetry, especially new writers. Quarterly journal; 40-50 pgs; circ 500. 100% freelance. Complete ms/cover letter; no phone query. **PAYS IN COPIES**, for one-time rts. Articles 100-500 wds (5-10/yr). Reports in 1 wk. Accepts reprints. Guidelines; copy $2.50.
Poetry: Accepts 200/yr. All types; no length limit. Submit max. 5 poems.
Fillers: Accepts 50/yr. Prose, devotionals, prayers, journal entries; 5-15 lines.
Tips: "Buy a sample, write a good cover letter, and pray for guidance."

+BURNING LIGHT: A Journal of Christian Literature, 98 Constitution Way, Franklin NJ 07416. (201)209-0365. Carl Simmons, ed/pub. Quarterly journal; circ. 200. Subscription $12. Est. 1993. 75 % freelance. Complete ms/cover letter; phone query ok. **PAYS IN COPIES/SUBSCRIPTION**, for all rts (negotiable). Articles 1,000-3,000 wds (3-4/yr); fiction 1,000-3,000 wds, longer if serialized (15/yr). Reports in 2-3 wks. No seasonal. Reluctantly accepts simultaneous submissions & reprints. Guidelines; copy $3.50.
Poetry: Buys 30-40/yr. Avant-garde, free verse, haiku, traditional; 1-500 lines.
Columns/Departments: Buys about 10/yr. Reviews (Christian/literary), 150-500 wds.
Tips: "Be adventurous; don't be slick; be honest. Don't be a Christian writer; be a Christian who writes. If it's rough, we'll work with you."

CANADA LUTHERAN, 1512 St. James St., Winnipeg MB R3H 0L2 Canada. (204)786-6707, Fax: (204)783-7548. Evangelical Lutheran Church of Canada. Kenn Ward, ed. Denominational. Monthly (11X) mag; 40 pgs; circ. 25,500. Subscription $17 U.S./yr. 45% freelance. Complete ms/cover letter; no phone query. Pays $40-120 (Canadian), on publication. Articles 600-2,000 wds (15/yr); fiction 800-1,500 wds (4/yr). Reports in 1 wk. Seasonal 10 mos ahead. Accepts simultaneous submissions & reprints. Guidelines.
Tips: "Canadians/Lutherans receive priority, but not the only consideration. Want material that is clear, concise and fresh. Articles that talk about real life experiences of faith receive our best reader response."

THE CANADIAN CATHOLIC REVIEW, St. Thomas More College, 1437 College Dr., Saskatoon, SK S7N 0W6 Canada. (306)966-8959. Fax: (306)966-8904. Catholic. Donald Ward, mng. ed. For intelligent (but not scholarly) Catholics who take their faith seriously. Monthly (11X) mag; 40 pgs; circ 1,100. Subscription $26.75/yr. 30% freelance. Query; phone query ok. Pays $50-300, on publication, for 1st N.A. serial rts. Articles 1,000-6,000 wds (10/yr); book & music reviews 500 wds/$25. Reports in 2-4 wks. Seasonal 6 mos ahead. No guidelines; copy $3/9x12 SAE/$1 Canadian postage.
Columns/Departments: Buys 10/yr. Scripture; Liturgy; American Notes; The Church in Quebec; all 1,000 wds/$50.
Tips: "Most open to columns and general articles. Be lucid, articulate, faithful and brief."

#CATHEDRAL AGE, Mount St. Alban, Massachusetts & Wisconsin Aves, Washington DC 20016. (202)537-6247. Fax: (202)364-6600. National Cathedral (Episcopal). Kelly Ferguson, ed. About what's happening in and to cathedrals and their programs. Quarterly mag; 32 pgs; circ 35,000. Good percentage freelance written. Query only. Pays $125, on publication, for all rts. Articles 1,000-2,000 wds; meditations & book reviews 500 wds. Reports immediately. Not in topical listings. Guidelines; copy $3.75.
Tips: Works on themes, but no theme list available.

+THE CATHOLIC ACCENT, P.O. Box 850, Greensburg PA 15601. (412)834-4010. Catholic. Alice Laurich, ed. Local news and inspiration for the Diocese of Greenburg PA (western & southwestern PA). Weekly newspaper; 20 pgs; circ. 48,000. Complete ms/cover letter. Variable payment, for one-time rts. Articles 300-500 wds. Reports in 1-2 mos. No guidelines; copy $.35.
Tips: "Most open to inspirational articles."

#THE CATHOLIC ANSWER, 207 Adams St., Newark NJ 07105. (219)356-8400. Our Sunday Visitor/Catholic. Father Peter Stravinskas, mng. ed. Answers to questions of belief for orthodox Catholics. Bimonthly mag; 64 pgs; circ 60,000. 50% freelance. Query/clips. Pays $100, on publication, for 1st rts. Articles 1,200-2,200 wds (80/yr). Seasonal 6 mos ahead. Guidelines; free copy (from 200 Noll Plaza, Huntington IN 46750).

+CATHOLIC COURIER, 1150 Buffalo Rd., Rochester NY 14624. (716)328-4340. Catholic. Karen Franz, ed. Independent newspaper for the Diocese of Rochester NY. Weekly newspaper; 20 pgs; circ. 48,000. 5% freelance. Complete ms/cover letter. Pays $30-100, on publication, for one-time rts. Articles 1,200 wds. Reports in 1-2 mos. Accepts simultaneous submissions.
Columns/Departments: Et Cetera; Leisure; Opinion; Sports; Youth; 750 wds.

CATHOLIC DIGEST, Box 64090, St. Paul MN 55164-0090. (612)962-6749. Fax: (612)962-6755. Catholic. Richard Reece, ed. Primarily for Catholic families with teens or grown children; most reprinted from other publications. Monthly mag; 128 pgs; circ 550,000. 10% freelance. Complete ms (for original material)/cover letter, tear sheets for reprints; no phone query. Pays to $100-400, on acceptance, for one-time or reprint rts. Articles 1,500-2,500 wds (75-100/yr). Reports in 4 wks. Seasonal 4-5 mos ahead. Accepts reprints. Guidelines; copy for 7x10 SAE/4 stamps.
Fillers: Buys 250/yr. Anecdotes, facts, games, ideas, jokes, quizzes, short humor; 1 line to 150 wds. Pays $4-50.
Columns/Departments: Buys 50-100/yr. Open Door (personal stories of conversion to Catholicism); 300-500 wds; $20-50. See guidelines for full list.
Tips: "We use a broad selection of articles."
** This periodical was #5 on the 1993 Top 50 Plus Christian Publishers list.

+THE CATHOLIC EXPONENT, P.O. Box 6787, Youngstown OH 44501-6787. (216)744-5251. Catholic. Denny Finneran, ed. Family-oriented paper for Catholics in northern OH Diocese. Biweekly newspaper; 24 pgs; circ. 37,000. 20% freelance. Query. Pays variable rates, on publication, for one-time rts. Articles to 500 wds. Accepts simultaneous submissions. No guidelines; free copy.
Tips: "Our emphasis is on moral/ethical issues."

+CATHOLIC FAMILY MEDIA GUIDE, P.O. Box 369, Durand IL 61024. (815)248-4407. Fax: (815)248-2330. Catholic. Owen C. Phelps, ed. Provides families with concise information about their current media choices—including books, movies, videos, and TV shows. Monthly (10X) mag; 32 pgs; circ. 3,000. Est. 1992. Limited freelance. Complete ms/brief biographical cover letter; query for seasonal material. Pays $50 (for profiles) or .05/wd for reviews; within 30 days of publication; for 1st rts. Articles to 1,000 wds.; book reviews 250-750 wds. Reports in 6-8 wks. Seasonal 6 mos ahead. Accepts reprints (if published regionally). Guidelines; copy for 9x12 SAE/7 stamps.
Special Needs: Profiles of Catholic sports and entertainment figures. Photo required.

+CATHOLIC HERITAGE, 200 Noll Plaza, Huntington IN 46750. (219)356-8400. Fax: (219)356-8472. Catholic. Robert Lockwood, ed. For those interested in Catholic history. Bimonthly mag. 15% freelance. Query; no phone query. Pays $100, on acceptance, for 1st rts. Articles 1,000-1,500 wds. Reports in 4-8 wks. No reprints. No guidelines; copy available.

+CATHOLIC NEW YORK, 1011 1st Ave, 17th Fl., New York NY 10126. (212)688-2399. Catholic. Anne Buckley, ed-in-chief. To inform New York Catholics. Weekly newspaper; 44 pgs; circ. 130,000. 10% freelance. Query or complete ms/cover letter. Pays $15-100, on publication, for one-time rts. Articles 500-800 wds. Reports in 1 mo. No guidelines; copy $1.
Columns/Departments: Comment; Catholic New Yorkers (profiles of unique individuals); 325 wds.
Tips: "Most open to articles that show how to integrate Catholic faith into work, hobbies or special interests."

+CATHOLIC PARENT, 200 Noll Plaza, Huntington IN 46750. (219)356-8400. Catholic. Woodeene Koenig-Bricker, ed. Practical advice for Catholic parents, with a specifically Catholic slant. Bimonthly mag; 48 pgs; circ. 18,500. Subscription $18. Est. 1993. 90%

freelance. Complete ms/cover letter; no phone query. Pays variable rates, on acceptance, for 1st rts. Articles 800-1,000 wds (70/yr). Reports in 6-8 wks. Seasonal 6-8 mos ahead. No reprints. Kill fee. Guidelines; copy $3/10x13 SAE/5 stamps.
Tips:"Be practical, be useful. Have a Catholic tie-in and slant. Most open to articles."

+CATHOLIC SENTINEL, P.O. Box 18030, Portland OR 97218-0030. (503)281-1191. Fax: (503)282-3486. Catholic. Robert Pfohman, ed. For Catholics in the Archdiocese of western and eastern Oregon. Weekly newspaper; 20 pgs; circ 16,500. Subscription $22. 25% freelance. Query; phone query ok. Pays $25-150, on publication, for 1st rts. Articles 600-1,200 wds. Reports in 1-6 wks. Seasonal 1 month ahead. Accepts simultaneous submissions and reprints (if not in nearby publication). Kill fee 100%.
Columns/Departments: Buys about 100/yr. Send complete ms. Pays in copies up to $20.
Tips: "We are especially interested in stories about Oregon Catholics living their faith. We focus on local issues and personalities."

+CATHOLIC TELEGRAPH, 100 E. 8th St., Cincinnati OH 45202. (513)421-3131. Catholic. Tricia Hempel, gen. mng. Diocese newspaper for Cincinnati area. Weekly newspaper; 16 pgs; circ. 40,000. 10% freelance. Send resume & writing samples for assignment. Pays varying rates, on publication, for all rts. Articles. Reports in 2-3 wks. Kill fee. Guidelines sent/acceptance; free copy.
Fillers: Newsbreaks (local).

#CATHOLIC TWIN CIRCLE, 15760 Ventura Blvd., Ste. 1201, Encino CA 91436-3002. Catholic. Loretta G. Seyer, ed. Features writing for Catholics and/or Christian families of all ages. Weekly newspaper; 20 pgs; circ 30,000. 45% freelance. Complete ms/cover letter. Pays .10/wd; on publication; for all, 1st, one-time or reprint rts (.03-.05/wd). Articles 1,200-2,000 wds; book reviews 750 wds. Reports in 2 mos. Seasonal 3 mos ahead. Serials 3 parts. Guidelines; copy for 9x12 SAE/2 stamps or $2.
Fillers: Cartoons, quizzes.
Columns/Departments: Opinions/editorials on topics of interest to Catholic families; 600-800 wds.

+CELEBRATION, 207 Hillsboro, Silver Spring MD 20902. (301)681-4927. Interdenominational. Bill Freburger, ed. To help Christian clergy prepare for Sunday celebrations (baptism, marriage, funerals, etc.) Monthly mag; 48 pgs; circ. 9,000. Some freelance. Query. Pays .10/wd, on acceptance, for 1st rts. Articles any length. Reports in 2 wks. No guidelines; free copy.
Fillers: Cartoons.

#CHARISMA & CHRISTIAN LIFE, 600 Rinehart Rd., Lake Mary FL 32746. (407)644-8720. Fax: (407)333-9753. Strang Communications. Stephen Strang, ed: articles to John Archer; news to Nancy Justice. Primarily for the pentecostal and charismatic Christian community. Monthly mag; 100 pgs; circ 200,000. Subscription $19.97. 75% freelance. Query or complete ms. Pays $75-400, on publication, for 1st rts. Articles 1,500-2,500 wds; fiction only for annual contest. Reports in 1 mo. Seasonal 8 mos ahead. Kill fee. Guidelines; copy for 9x12 SAE.
Contest: Sponsors annual fiction contest.
Tips: "Tell us in the cover letter why you are qualified to write the story. Ask yourself if the story would be of special interest to a charismatic/pentecostal Christian audience."

#CHRISTIAN CENTURY, 407 S. Dearborn St., Chicago IL 60605. (312)427-5380. James M. Wall, ed. For ecumenically-minded, progressive church people, both clergy and lay. Weekly journal; 46 pgs; circ 35,000. 90% freelance. Complete ms/cover letter. Pays $75-125, on publication, for all rts. Articles (60/yr) 1,500-3,000 wds; fiction (1/yr); book reviews 500 wds. Kill fee. Reports in 1 mo. Seasonal 3 mos ahead. Guidelines; copy $1.75/9x12 SAE/3 stamps.
Poetry: Dean Peerman. Buys 70/yr. Free verse; to 20 lines; $20.
Fillers: Cartoons.

+CHRISTIAN CHRONICLE, P.O. Box 11000, Oklahoma City OK 73136. (405)425-5070. Church of Christ. Glover Shipp, mng. ed. Denominational; international; focus on evangelism. Monthly (10X) newspaper; 32 pgs; circ. 112,000. 5% freelance. Complete ms/cover letter. Pays varying rates, on acceptance, for one-time rts. Articles to 1,000 wds. Reports in 2-3 wks. No guidelines; free copy.
Tips: "We prefer to get submissions from members of the Church of Christ."

#THE CHRISTIAN CIVIC LEAGUE OF MAINE RECORD, Box 5459, Augusta ME 04332. (207)622-7634. Jasper S. Wyman, ed. Focuses on church, public service, and political action. Monthly newsletter; 12 pgs; circ 4,600. 10% freelance. Query. **NO PAYMENT** for one-time rts. Articles (10-12/yr). Reports in 4-8 wks. Seasonal 2 mos ahead. Accepts simultaneous query & reprints. Free copy.

THE CHRISTIAN COURIER, 1933 W. Wisconsin Ave., Milwaukee WI 53233. (414)344-7300. Fax: (414)344-7375. ProBuColls Assn. John M. Fisco, Jr., pub. To propagate the gospel of Jesus Christ in the Midwest. Monthly newspaper; circ 10,000. 10% freelance. Query. **PAYS IN COPIES**, for one-time rts. Not copyrighted. Articles 300-1,500 wds (6/yr). Reports in 2-4 wks. Seasonal 2 mos ahead. Accepts reprints. Guidelines; free copy.
Fillers: Anecdotes, facts, newsbreaks; 10-100 wds.

#CHRISTIAN COURIER, 4-261 Martindale Rd., St. Catherines, ON L2W 1A1 Canada. (U.S. address: Box 110, Lewiston NY 14092). (416)682-8311. Independent (Protestant Reformed). Bert Witvoet, ed; Bob Vander Vennen, book review ed. To present Canadian and international news, both religious and secular, from a Reformed Christian perspective. Weekly newspaper; 20 pgs; circ 6,000. 15% freelance. Complete ms/cover letter; phone query ok. Pays .05-.10/wd, on publication, for one-time rts. Articles 700-1,000 wds (20/yr); fiction 1,000-2,000 wds (10/yr); book reviews 100-500 wds. Reports in 1 mo. Seasonal 1 yr ahead. Accepts simultaneous submissions & reprints. Guidelines; copy for 9x12 SAE/IRC.
Poetry: Buys 20/yr. Avant-garde, free verse, traditional; 10-30 lines; $15-30. Submit max. 5 poems.

+CHRISTIAN CRUSADE NEWSPAPER, P.O. Box 279, Neosho MO 64850. (918)438-4234. Fax: (417)451-4319. Interdenominational. Billy James Hargis, pub. A Christian, pro-American approach to current social and political issues. Monthly newspaper; 24 pgs; circ. 25,000. 50% freelance. Query. Pays varying rates, on publication, for all rts. Articles. Reports in 2 mos. No guidelines; free copy.

CHRISTIAN DRAMA MAGAZINE, 1824 Celestia Blvd., Walla Walla WA 99362-3619. (509)529-0089. Judy Tash, ed. For Christian dramatists; promoting the gospel through drama. Quarterly mag; 28 pgs; circ 300. Subscription $5.50. Estab. 1990. 40%

freelance. Complete ms/cover letter; phone query ok. Pays $25; on publication; for 1st, one-time, reprint & simultaneous rts. Articles 300-1,000 wds (6/yr); plays/skits 50-1,500 wds (6/yr); play reviews 50-200 wds/$25. Reports in 4-12 wks. Seasonal 6 mos ahead. Accepts simultaneous submissions and reprints. Guidelines; copy for 8x10 SAE/3 stamps.
Special Needs: Drama, drama directing, scriptwriting, acting, set design, special effects, puppetry, mime, sound design, play scripts, lighting, costumes, performance reviews, script reviews, news about Christian drama groups, publishers who buy scripts, Christian dance.
Poetry: Accepts 4-6/yr. Poetry appropriate for dramatic readings. Pays $25.
Fillers: Ideas (about Christian drama), news; to 100 wds; $5-10.
Columns/Departments: Questions & Answers (drama production); 50-200 wds; $10-25.

+THE CHRISTIAN EDGE, 6501 Bronson Ln., Bakersfield CA 93009. (805)837-1378. Fax: (805)397-2661. Evangelical. Don Chase, pub/ed. Activity & resources guide; not an issues driven publication. Monthly newspaper; circ. 1,500. Subscription $15. 30% freelance. Complete ms/cover letter; no phone query. **PAYS IN COPIES**, for reprint rts. Articles 150-350 wds (20-30/yr); book & music reviews 350 wds. Reports in 2 wks. Seasonal 2 mos ahead. Accepts simultaneous submissions & reprints. No guidelines; copy $1 + $1.25 postage (no SAE).
Fillers: Cartoons, games, ideas, quotes, word puzzles; 50-150 wds.

#CHRISTIAN HISTORY, 465 Gundersen Dr.,Carol Stream IL 60188. (708)260-6200. Fax: (708)260-0114. Christianity Today, Inc. Kevin Miller, ed. To teach Christian history to contemporary readers. Theme oriented. Quarterly mag; 50 pgs; circ 60,000. Subscription $16. 75% freelance. Query. Pays .10/wd, on publication, for 1st rts. Articles 1,000-2,500 wds. Reports in 1 mo. Accepts reprints. Guidelines/theme list; copy $4.40.
Columns/Departments: Buys 4/yr. Christian History Sampler; History Behind the News; Faith Behind the Famous; 1,500 wds.
Tips: "Let us know your particular areas of specialization and any books or papers you have written in the area of Christian history."

#CHRISTIAN HOME & SCHOOL, 3350 East Paris Ave. SE, Box 8709, Grand Rapids MI 49512. (616)957-1070. Fax: (616)957-5022. Christian Schools Intl. Dr. Gordon L. Bordewyk, ed; submit to Roger Schmurr, sr. ed. Focuses on parenting and Christian education; for parents who send their children to Christian schools. Bimonthly mag; 32 pgs; circ 52,000. Subscription $11.95. 50% freelance. Complete ms/cover letter; no phone query. Pays $75-150, on publication, for 1st rts. Articles 1,200-2,000 wds (40/yr); fiction 1,200-2,000 wds. Reports in 1 mo. Seasonal 4 mos ahead. Accepts simultaneous query. Guidelines/theme list; copy for 9x12 SAE/4 stamps.
Tips: Most open to features.

CHRISTIAN LIVING, 616 Walnut Ave., Scottdale PA 15683. (412)887-8500. Mennonite. David Graybill, ed. Denominational with emphasis on community, family and spirituality. Monthly (8X) mag; 28 pgs; circ 6,100. 50% freelance. Complete ms/no cover letter or phone query. Pays .05/wd, on acceptance, for one-time rts. Articles 700-1,200 wds (50/yr); fiction 700-1,200 wds (2/yr). Reports in 2-4 wks. Seasonal 5 mos ahead. Accepts simultaneous submissions & reprints. Guidelines; copy for 9x12 SAE/3 stamps.

Poetry: Buys 10-15/yr. Free verse, haiku, light verse; 3-24 lines; $10-25. Submit max. 6 poems.
Ethnic: Targets all ethnic groups involved in the Mennonite religion.
Tips: "We want well-written, non-formulaic fiction."
** This periodical was #41 on the 1993 Top 50 Plus Christian Publishers list.

CHRISTIAN MEDIA, Box 448, Jacksonville OR 97530. (503)899-8888. James Lloyd, ed/pub. For emerging Christian songwriters, artists, and others professionals involved in music, video, film and broadcasting. Bimonthly newsletter; 8 pgs. Query. Payment negotiable. Articles. No guidelines; copy for 9x12 SAE/2 stamps.

#THE CHRISTIAN OBSERVER, 9400 Fairview Ave., Ste. 200, Manassas VA 22110. (703)335-2844. Fax: (703)368-4817. The Christian Observer, Inc.; Presbyterian Reformed. Edwin Elliott, ed. To encourage and edify God's people and families. Mag. published 2X/month; circ. 7,200. Subscription $27. Not in topical listings.

CHRISTIAN PARENTING TODAY, Box 850, Sisters OR 97759-0850. (503)549-8261. Fax: (503)549-0153. David Kopp, ed. Practical advice for parents, from a Christian perspective, that runs the whole gamut of needs: social, educational, spiritual, medical, etc. Bimonthly mag; 80 pgs; circ 250,000. Subscription $16.97. 70% freelance. Query; no phone query. Articles 850-1,500 wds (15-20/yr). Pays .15-.25/wd, on acceptance for assigned (on publication for unsolicited), for 1st rts. Reports in 6-8 wks. Seasonal 6 mos ahead. Accepts reprints. Kill fee. Guidelines; copy for 9x12 SAE/5 stamps.
Fillers: Buys 60-100/yr. Anecdotes, short humor, parenting tips; 25-100 wds; $25-40.
Columns/Departments: Buys 15/yr. Parent News, to 500 wds; Life in Our House (humorous anecdotes), 25-100 wds/$25; Parent Exchange (practical tips) 25-100 wds/$40; My Story 800-1,500 wds (query).
Tips: "Use the presence of people in your writing. Quotes from authorities and examples from real life make a strong article. No preaching."
** This periodical was #4 on the 1993 Top 50 Plus Christian Publishers list.

#THE CHRISTIAN READER, 465 Gundersen Dr., Carol Stream IL 60188. (708)260-6200. Fax: (708)260-0114. Christianity Today, Inc. Bonne Steffen, ed. A Christian "Readers Digest" that uses both reprints & original material. Bimonthly mag; 110 pgs; circ 200,000. Subscription $14.95. 80% freelance. Complete ms.; phone query ok. Pays $45-100 (.10/wd); on acceptance; for 1st, one-time, or reprint rts. Articles (120/yr) & fiction (2/yr); 500-1,500 wds. Reports in 1-6 mos. Seasonal 9 mos ahead. Accepts reprints. Kill fee $50. Guidelines; copy for 6x9 SAE/2 stamps.
Poetry: Buys 3/yr. Free verse, light verse, traditional; 25-75 lines; $40-65. Submit max. 6 poems.
Fillers: Buys 36/yr. Cartoons, short humor (see Lite Fare), word puzzles; 30-50 wds; $25.
Columns/Departments: Mary Ann Jeffreys. Buys 200/yr. Lite Fare (adult church humor), 25-150 wds; Kids of the Kingdom (kids say & do funny things), 25-150 wds; Rolling Down the Aisle (wedding humor), 25-250 wds; Ordinary Heroes. Pays $25.
Tips: "Keep articles short; we edit everything. First-person non-fiction stories are a top priority editorially for final selection."

CHRISTIAN RENEWAL, Box 770, Lewiston NY 14092. (416)562-5719. Fax: (416)562-7828. Reformed (Conservative). John Van Dyk, mng. ed. Church-related and world news for members of the Reformed community of churches in North America. Biweekly tabloid; 20 pgs; circ. 4,500. Subscription $27/yr. 25% freelance. Complete ms. Pays $10-50, on publication, for one-time and reprint rts. Articles 500-2,000 wds; fiction (6/yr). Reports in 4 wks. Seasonal 2 mos ahead. Accepts simultaneous submissions & reprints.

#CHRISTIAN RESEARCH JOURNAL, Box 500, San Juan Capistrano CA 92693-0500. (714)855-4428. Fax: (714)855-4428. Christian Research Institute. Elliot Miller, ed-in-chief. For those who have been affected by cults and the occult. Quarterly journal; 48 pgs; circ 24,000. Subscription $16. 80% freelance. Query or complete ms. Pays .10/wd, on publication, for 1st or reprint rts. Articles 500-6,000 wds; book reviews 500-2,500 wds. Reports in 12 wks. Accepts simultaneous submissions and reprints. Kill fee 50%. Guidelines; copy $4.
Special Needs: Fully-documented critiques; apologetics.
Tips: "Send sample of previous writing on topics relevant to our focus, with brief resume showing qualifications to write in this field. Most open to features, book reviews, opinion pieces, and witnessing tips."

#CHRISTIAN RETAILING, 600 Rinehart Rd., Lake Mary FL 32746. (407)333-0600. Strang Communications, Inc. Brian Peterson, ed. Business/trade publication directed toward Christian retail/bookstore owners, managers and clerks. Monthly trade journal/tabloid; 72 pgs; circ 9,500. 60% freelance. Complete ms. Pays .10-.12/wd; on publication; for all rts. Articles to 700-2,300 wds (36/yr). Reports in 6-8 wks. Seasonal 5 mos ahead. Kill fee. Accepts reprints. Guidelines; copy $3.
Fillers: Buys 5/yr. Anecdotes, cartoons, ideas; 50-300 wds. Pays $20-50.
Tips: " Most open to features. Think about interesting subjects for Christian retailers."

CHRISTIAN SINGLE, 127 9th Ave. N, Nashville TN 37234. (615)251-2228. Fax: (615)251-5058. Southern Baptist. Leigh Neely, mng. ed. For Christian single persons, 25-45. Monthly mag; 52 pgs; circ 65,000. Subscription $13.30. 40% freelance. Query/clips; no phone query. Pays .055/wd; on acceptance; for all, 1st, one-time or reprint rts. Articles (60/yr) & fiction (4-5/yr), 600 wds & up. Reports in 4-8 wks. Seasonal 6 mos ahead. Accepts reprints. Guidelines; copy for 9x12 SAE/4 stamps.
Special Needs: "Advice and words of encouragement for those who are suddenly single. Single adults who successfully faced challenge and change in their lives."
Poetry: Buys 8-10/yr. Traditional. Variable payment. Submit max. 3 poems.
Tips: "We want articles that feature single adults as happy fulfilled persons, pleased with their lives and looking to God for their comfort."

CHRISTIAN SOCIAL ACTION, 100 Maryland Ave. NE, Washington DC 20002. (202)488-5621. Fax: (202)488-5621. United Methodist. Lee Ranck, ed. Information and analysis of critical social issues from the perspective of Christian faith. Monthly (11X) mag; 48 pgs; circ 3,000. Subscription $13.50. 15% freelance. Complete ms/cover letter. Pays $125, on publication, for all rts. Articles 2,000 wds (10-12/yr). Reports in 4-5 wks (longer for accepted material). Sometimes accepts reprints. Guidelines; copy for 6x9 SAE.
Tips: "We look for experts on an issue who can write, instead of writers who can research an issue; know the issue well. Our audience is Christian social activists."

#CHRISTIAN STANDARD, 8121 Hamilton Ave., Cincinnati OH 45231. (513)931-4050. Fax: (513)931-0904. Standard Publishing/Christian Churches/Churches of Christ. Sam E. Stone, ed. Devoted to the restoration of New Testament Christianity, its doctrines, its ordinances, and its fruits. Weekly mag; 16-24 pgs; circ 62,000. Subscription $17. 60% freelance. Complete ms/cover letter. Pays $10-80, on publication, for 1st or one-time rts. Articles 400-1,600 wds (200/yr). Reports in 2 mos. Seasonal 8-12 mos ahead. Accepts reprints. Guidelines; copy $1.

CHRISTIANITY TODAY, 465 Gundersen Dr., Carol Stream IL 60188. (708)260-6200. Fax: (708)260-0114. David Neff, mng. ed; submit to Articles Editor. For evangelical Christian thought leaders who seek to integrate their faith commitment with responsible action. Magazine published 15X/yr; 90 pgs; circ 200,000. Subscription $24.95. 50% freelance. Query/clips; no phone query. Pays .10/wd, on publication, for 1st rts. Articles 2,000-5,000 wds (60/yr); book reviews 500-750 wds, pays $75. Reports in 2-4 wks. Seasonal 6 mos ahead. Accepts reprints. Kill fee. Guidelines; copy for 9x12 SAE/3 stamps.
Columns/Departments: Buys 15/yr. Church in Action (profile of unusual person/ministry), 1,500 wds (query); Speaking Out (op/ed), 650 wds (complete ms); $75-150.

+**CHRISTIANWEEK**, The Fellowship for Print Witness, Inc., Box 725, Winnipeg MB R3C 2K3 Canada. (204)943-1147. Fax: (204)947-5632. Doug Koop, mng. ed. News and opinion written from an evangelical perspective, and produced to give readers a window on Christian faith and life in Canada. Biweekly newspaper; 16-20 pgs; circ. 11,000. Subscription $23 in Canada, $35 outside. 5% freelance. Query; phone query ok. Pays $50-100, after publication, for one-time rts. Articles 500-1,000 wds (10-15/yr). Reports immediately on queries, 3-4 wks on mss. Accepts simultaneous submissions. Not copyrighted. Guidelines; copy for $1. Not in topical listings.
Fillers: Cartoons, pays $15-25.
Tips: "Most open to a news or feature query with a Canadian setting. A genuine news story in some part of the country we haven't covered recently would have a good chance."

#**CHRISTMAS,** The Annual of Christmas Literature and Art, Box 1209, Minneapolis MN 55440. (612)330-3442. Augsburg Fortress. Kristine Oberg, ed. Birth of Christ central to celebration of Christmas. Annual book; 64 pgs; circ 40,000. 70-100% freelance. Complete ms/cover letter; no phone query. Pays $300-450, on acceptance, for negotiable rts. Articles (3-4/yr) 2,000-3,000 wds; fiction (3-4/yr)1,500-5,000 wds. Reports in 1-3 mos. Works 18 mos ahead. Accepts reprints. Guidelines; copy $12.95 + postage (call 800-328-4648).
Poetry: Buys 2-3/yr. Free verse, light verse, traditional; to 30 lines; $75-150. Submit max. 3 poems. Nothing on Santa Claus.
Tips: "Short stories related to Christmas only."
** This periodical was #47 on the 1993 Top 50 Plus Christian Publishers list.

CHURCH & STATE, 8120 Fenton St., Silver Springs MD 20910. (301)589-3707. Americans United for Separation of Church and State. Joseph L. Conn, mng. ed. Emphasizes religious liberty and church/state relations matters. Monthly mag; 24-32 pgs; circ 33,000. 10% freelance. Query. Pays negotiable fee, on acceptance, for all rts. Articles 600-3,000 wds, prefers 800-1,600 (11/yr). Reports in 1 month. Accepts simultaneous query & reprints. Guidelines; copy for 9x12 SAE/3 stamps.
Tips: "We are not a religious magazine. You need to see our magazine before you try to write for it."

#THE CHURCH ADVOCATE, Box 926, 700 E. Melrose Ave., Findlay OH 45839. (419)424-1961. Fax: (419)424-3433. Churches of God General Conference. Linda M. Draper, ed. Denominational. Monthly mag; circ 6,660. Subscription $10. Little freelance. Query or complete ms. Pays $10/printed pg, on publication. Articles 1,000-2,500 wds. Accepts reprints. Free guidelines/copy.

THE CHURCH HERALD, 4500 - 60th St. SE, Grand Rapids MI 49512-9642. (616)698-7071. Fax: (616)698-6606. Reformed Church in America. Jeffrey Japinga, ed. We are seeking to relate the Christian faith to the problems and issues our denominational audience faces everyday. Monthly mag; circ 40,000. Subscription $15. 5% freelance. Query only (complete ms for fiction). Pays $50-200 ($40-120 for fiction); on acceptance; for 1st, one-time, all, simultaneous & reprint rts. Articles 400-1,500 wds (30/yr); fiction 400-1,500 wds (5/yr). Reports in 1-2 mos. Seasonal 6 mos ahead. Accepts simultaneous query & reprints. Kill fee 50%. Guidelines; copy $2/9x12 SAE.
Tips: "Most open to feature articles."

#CHURCH HERALD AND HOLINESS BANNER, 7415 Metcalf, Box 4060, Overland Park KS 66204. (913)432-0331. Fax: (913)722-0351. Church of God (Holiness)/Herald and Banner Press. Ray Crooks, ed. Denominational; conservative/ evangelical people. Biweekly mag; 20 pgs; circ 2,500. Subscription $10. 50% freelance. Complete ms/cover letter; no phone query. **NO PAYMENT**, for one-time rts. Not copyrighted. Articles 200-800 wds (25+/yr); fiction 500-1,000 wds. Reports in 2 mos. Seasonal 6 mos ahead. Accepts simultaneous submissions & reprints. Guidelines; no copy.
Poetry: Buys few. Traditional; 8-24 lines.
Fillers: Anecdotes, facts, prose, quotes; 150-400 wds.
Tips: "Most open to devotional articles. Must be concise, well-written, and get one main point across; 200-400 wds."

CHURCH OF GOD EVANGEL, Box 2250, Cleveland TN 37320-2250. (615)476-4512. Fax: (615)478-7521. Church of God (Cleveland, TN). Homer G. Rhea, ed-in-chief. Denominational. Monthly mag; 36 pgs; circ 45,000. Subscription $10. 40% freelance. Complete ms/no cover letter; no phone query. Pays .03/wd, on acceptance, for 1st or one-time rts. Articles 300-1,200 wds (30/yr). Reports in 2 wks. Seasonal 6 mos ahead. Accepts simultaneous submissions. Guidelines; copy for 9x12 SAE/4 stamps.
Tips: "Always willing to buy thoughtful, well-written pieces that speak to people where they live. Always need good humor."

+CLASS, 900 Broadway, New York NY 10003. (212)677-3055. General publication that accepts religious articles. Constance M. Weaver, exec. ed. Geared toward Caribbean, Latin, and African-American readers, 18-49 years old. Monthly mag; circ. 250,000. 25% freelance. Query/clips. Pays up to .10/wd, 45 days after publication, for 1st and reprint rts. Articles 500-1,300 wds. Reports in 6 wks. Seasonal 3 mos ahead. Guidelines; copy for 9x12 SAE/4 stamps.
Poetry: Buys 10-20/yr. Pays up to $10. Submit max. 5 poems.

COLUMBIA, P.O. 1670, New Haven CT 06510. (203)772-2130. Fax: (203)777-0114. Knights of Columbus (Catholic). Richard McMunn, ed. Geared to a general Catholic family audience. Monthly mag; 92 pgs; circ 1.5 million. Subscription $6; foreign add $2. 50-60% freelance. Query or complete ms/cover letter; no phone query. Pays to $250-500, on acceptance, for 1st rts. Articles 750-2,000 wds (15-20/yr). Reports in 2-3 wks. Seasonal 4 mos ahead. Accepts reprints. Kill fee 20%. Free guidelines/copy.

Tips: "Keep eye out for K of C activity in local area and send a query letter about it."

COMMENTS FROM THE FRIENDS, Box 840, Stoughton MA 02072. No calls. David A. Reed, ed. For ex-Jehovah's Witnesses, their relatives, Christians reaching out to them, and dissident Witnesses. Quarterly mag; circ 1,500. 5% freelance. Complete ms. Pays $2-20, on publication, for one-time rts. Articles 50 wds & up (4/yr); book reviews 500 wds. Reports in 4 wks. Seasonal 4 mos ahead. Accepts simultaneous submissions & reprints. Guidelines; copy $1.
Tips: "Acquaint us with why you are qualified to write about J.W.'s. Write well-documented, concise articles relevant to J.W.'s today. We automatically reject all material not specifically about Jehovah's Witnesses."

+COMMON BOUNDARY, 4304 East-West Hwy, Bethesda MD 20814. (301)652-9495. Ecumenical. Mark Judge, ed. asst. Explores relationship between psychotherapy and spirituality. Bimonthly mag; 64 pgs; circ. 26,000. 50% freelance. Query. Pays varying rates, on publication, for 1st rts. Articles 3,000-4,000 wds. Reports in 3-6 mos. Accepts simultaneous submissions. Kill fee 1/3. Guidelines; copy $5.
Fillers: Newsbreaks, 200-600 wds.

COMMONWEAL, 15 Dutch St., New York NY 10038. (212)732-0800. Catholic. Submit to The Editor. A review of public affairs, religion, literature, and the arts. Biweekly mag; 32 pgs; circ 18,000. Subscription $39. 15% freelance. Query; phone query ok. Pays .03/wd, on acceptance, for all rts. Articles 1,000-3,000 wds (20/yr). Reports in 3-4 wks. Kill fee. Copy for 9x12 SASE.
Poetry: Buys 35/yr. Free verse; to 75 lines; .50/line.
Columns/Departments: Upfronts (brief, newsy, facts, & info behind the headlines), 750-1,000 wds.
Tips: "Most open to meaningful articles on social, political, religious, and cultural topics."

COMPANION MAGAZINE (formerly **THE COMPANION OF ST. FRANCIS AND ST. ANTHONY**), Box 535, Station F., Toronto, ON M5R 2S6 Canada. (416)463-5442, Fax: (416)463-4392. Catholic/Franciscan. Mrs. B. McCrimmon, mng. ed. An adult, Catholic, inspirational, devotional family magazine. Monthly mag; 31 pgs; circ 4,200. 15% freelance. Complete ms, with cover letter. Pays .06/wd (Canadian funds), on publication, for 1st rts. Articles 500-1,500 wds (35/yr); fiction 500-1,000 wds (7/yr). Reports in 6 wks. Seasonal 3 mos ahead. Occasionally accepts reprints. Guidelines; copy for 7x10 SAE with IRCs.
Special Needs: Articles on St. Francis, Franciscan spirituality, and social justice.
Poetry: Free verse, light verse, traditional. Pays .60/line (Canadian).
Fillers: Anecdotes, cartoons, prayers, quotes, short humor, word puzzles.
Tips: Most open to human interest.

COMPANIONS, Box 1212, Harrisonburg VA 22801-1212. (703)434-0768. Conservative Mennonite. Roger L. Berry, ed. Consistent with Mennonite doctrine: believer baptism, nonresistance, and nonconformity. Weekly take-home paper; circ 8,000. Subscription $9.50. 70% freelance. Complete ms; no cover letter or phone query. Pays .015-.02/wd, on acceptance, for 1st, one-time or reprint rts. Articles 100-900 wds (200/yr). Reports in 4-6 wks. Seasonal 5 mos ahead. Accepts reprints. Guidelines; copy for 9x12 SAE/2 stamps.
Poetry: Buys 40/yr. Traditional, 4-20 lines; $.15-.20/line. Submit max. 3 poems.

Fillers: Buys 10-15/yr. Anecdotes/prose; 25-150 wds.
Columns/Departments: Buys 12/yr. Science and Scripture (creationist/biblicist), and Archaeology and Scripture (archaeology that support biblical truths); both to 800 wds.
Tips: "Study guidelines and get a feel for our very distinctive approach to Christian living. Most open to articles; everything must have a strong spiritual emphasis."
** This periodical was #32 on the 1993 Top 50 Plus Christian Publishers list.

COMPASS: A Jesuit Journal, 10 St. Mary St. #300, Toronto ON M4Y 1P9 Canada. (416)921-0653. Fax: (416)921-1864, Catholic. Robert Chodos, ed. Ethical and ecumenical discussion of social and religious topics; for educated, but non-specialized readership. Bimonthly mag; 48 pgs; circ 4,000. Subscription $19. 80% freelance. Query/clips; no phone query. Pays $100-500 (Canadian), on publication, for 1st rts. Articles 750-2,000 wds (60/yr); fiction 1,000-2,500 wds (pays $100-250); book reviews 2,000 wds/$300. Reports in 4-8 wks. Seasonal 4 mos ahead. Kill fee 50%. Guidelines/theme list; copy $2/9x12 SAE/$1.35 postage (Canadian).
Fillers: Accepts 60/yr. Short, pithy quotes from other writers; 10-150 wds. Pays 1-yr subscription.
Columns/Departments: Buys 24/yr. Testament (contemporary application of scripture); Colloquy (theology & daily life); Saint (fresh perspective on a saint); all 750 wds. Pays $100-150. Query.
Tips: "We are interested primarily in analytical and reflective articles. Write for themes."

#CONNECTING POINT, Box 685, Cocoa FL 32923. (407)632-0130. Linda G. Howard, ed. For and by the mentally challenged (retarded) community; primarily deals with spiritual and self-advocacy issues. Monthly mag; circ 1,000. Estab. 1989. 75% freelance. Complete ms. **NO PAYMENT** for 1st rts. Articles (24/yr) & fiction (12/yr), 250-750 wds; book reviews 150 wds. Reports in 3-6 wks. Seasonal 3 mos ahead. Accepts simultaneous submissions & reprints. Guidelines; copy for 9x12 SAE/6 stamps.
Special Needs: Record reviews, self-advocacy, integration/normalization, justice system.
Poetry: Uses 4/yr. Any type; 4-66 lines. Submit max. 10 poems.
Fillers: Uses 12/yr. Cartoons, games, word puzzles; 50-250 wds.
Columns/Departments: Uses 24/yr. Devotion Page, 1,000 wds; Bible Study, 500 wds. Query.
Tips: "All ms need to be in primary vocabulary."

#CONQUEST, 1300 N Meacham Rd., Schaumburg IL 60173. (708)843-1600. Regular Baptist. Joan E. Alexander, ed. Take-home paper for adults; conservative, fundamental. Weekly take-home paper. New writers query. Pays .03-.05/wd, on acceptance, for all or 1st rts. Articles & fiction 500-1,500 wds (some multi-part fiction). Reports in 2-8 wks. Seasonal 1 yr ahead. Guidelines; copy for #10 SAE/2 stamps.
Fillers: Anecdotes, facts, ideas, newsbreaks, prose, short humor, word puzzles.
Tips: Not everything that is Christian is suitable for readers in fundamental Baptist churches. Most open to fiction and nonfiction."

CORNERSTONE, 939 W. Wilson, Chicago IL 60640. (312)989-2080. Fax: (312)989-2076. Evangelical Covenant Church. Dawn Herrin, ed. (articles); Jennifer Ingerson, submissions ed. For young adults, 18-35; covers contemporary issues in light of evangelical Christianity. Quarterly (3-4x) mag; 64 pgs; circ 50,000. Up to 20%

freelance. Complete ms/cover letter; no phone query. Pays .08-.10/wd, on publication, for one-time rts. Articles to 2,700 wds (3-4/yr); fiction 250-2,500 wds (3-4/yr); book & music reviews 500-1,000 wds. Reports in 4-6 mos. Seasonal 6 mos ahead. Accepts simultaneous submissions & reprints. Guidelines; copy $2 or 9x12 SAE/5 stamps.
Special Needs: Homosexual issues; homeless/the poor.
Poetry: Tammy Boyd. Buys 15-25/yr. Any type & length; $10-25. Submit max. 5 poems.
Fillers: Buys 1-4/yr. Cartoons, short humor; 500-1,000 wds.
Tips: "Issues pertinent to contemporary society seen with a biblical world view. No pornography, cheap shots about non-Christians, or unrealistic/sugar-sweet articles. Looking for high-quality fiction and book or music reviews."

#THE COVENANT COMPANION, 5101 N. Francisco Ave., Chicago IL 60625. (312)784-3000. Fax: (312)784-4366. Evangelical Covenant Church. Rev. James R. Hawkinson, ed. Denominational. Monthly mag; 44 pgs; circ 22,500. Subscription $26. 10-15% freelance. Complete ms/cover letter. Pays $15-50; on publication; for all, 1st or one-time rts. Articles 500-2,000 wds (20-25/yr); book reviews 500-1,000 wds/$15-25. Reports in 2-3 mos. Seasonal 4 mos ahead. Accepts simultaneous submissions & reprints. Guidelines; copy $2.25/9x12 SAE/5 stamps.
Poetry: Buys 10-15/yr. Free verse; $10-15. Submit max. 10 poems.
Tips: "Study guidelines and send general articles of universal interest and pertinence. Also open to church year/holiday material."

#CREATION SOCIAL SCIENCE AND HUMANITIES QUARTERLY, 1429 N. Holyoke, Wichita KS 67208. (316)683-3610. Creation Social Science and Humanities Society. Dr. Paul D. Ackerman, ed; Ellen Myers, book review ed. For Christians interested in technical and in-depth articles regarding biblical creation, scientific creationism and its impact on the social sciences and humanities. Quarterly mag; 32 pgs; circ 600. 50% freelance. Query or complete ms/cover letter; phone query ok. **PAYS IN COPIES** for all rts. Articles 1,000-3,000 wds (20-25/yr); book reviews 1,000-2,000 wds. Reports in 3 mos. Seasonal 6 mos ahead. Accepts reprints. Guidelines; free copy.
Poetry: Uses 8/yr. Free verse, haiku, traditional; 4-24 lines. Submit max. 2 poems.
Fillers: Accepts 8/yr. Facts, prose, quizzes, quotes; 50-200 wds.
Tips: "All articles must relate to biblical creation and/or evolution. We prefer 2,000-3,000 words."

***CRESSET,** A Review of Arts, Literature & Public Affairs, Box VAL, Valparaiso IN 46383. Valparaiso University/Lutheran. G. Eifrig, ed. For college educated, professors, pastors, lay people; serious review essays on religious-cultural affairs. Monthly mag; circ 4,000. Complete ms. Pays $25 honorarium, on publication, for all rts. Articles to 5,000 wds (9-12/yr); book reviews 300 wds. Free copy.
Poetry: Rene Steinke, ed. Buys 36/yr. Avant-garde, free verse, traditional; $10.

+THE CRITIC, 205 W. Monroe St., 6th Floor, Chicago IL 60606. (312)609-8880. Fax: (312)609-8891. Catholic. John Sprague, ed. Focuses primarily on American Catholic culture. Quarterly journal; 130 pgs; circ. 2,000. Subscription $20. 80% freelance. Query (complete ms for fiction); no phone query. Pays, on acceptance, for one-time rts. No reprints. Articles (8/yr); fiction (8/yr). No guidelines; copy $6.
Special Needs: Literary profiles/interviews; ecumenical issues.
Poetry: Buys 15/yr. Submit max. 3 poems.

DECISION, 1300 Harmon Pl., Minneapolis MN 55440. (612)338-0500. Fax: (612)335-1299. Billy Graham Evangelistic Assn. Roger C. Palms, ed. Evangelism/Christian nurture. Monthly (11X) mag; 42 pgs; circ 1,700,000. Subscription $7. 25% freelance. Query; no phone query. Pays $10-200, on publication, for all, 1st or reprint rts. Articles 1,600-1,800 wds (90/yr). Reports 1-2 wks. Seasonal 10-12 mos ahead. Kill fee. Guidelines/theme list; copy for 10x13 SAE/3 stamp.
Special Needs: Vignettes - Concise narratives relating incidents from life written with a spiritual application; 400-1,000 wds.
Poetry: Buys 40/yr. Free verse, light verse, traditional; 4-20 lines; $.50/pub. wd. Submit max. 7 poems.
Fillers: Buys 30-40/yr. Anecdotes, prose; 400-1,000 wds; $50-75.
Columns/Departments: Buys 11/yr. Where Are They Now? (people who have become Christian through Billy Graham ministries); 600-900 wds; $70.
Tips: "Most open to first-person testimonies of people from all walks of life that clearly show how an individual committed life to Jesus Christ."

DISCIPLESHIP JOURNAL, Box 35004, Colorado Springs CO 80935. (719)548-9222. Fax: (719)598-7128. The Navigators. Deena Davis, mng ed. For motivated, maturing Christians desiring to grow spiritually and to help others grow; biblical and practical. Bimonthly mag; 80 pgs; circ 90,000. Subscription $18.97. 95% freelance. Query; no phone query. Pays .17/wd, on acceptance, for 1st or reprint rts. Articles 500-3,000 wds (50/yr); fiction published rarely. Reports in 4-6 wks. Seasonal 6 mos ahead. Accepts simultaneous submissions. Kill fee. Guidelines/theme list; copy for 9x12 SAE/7 stamps.
Columns/Departments: Buys 6/yr. On the Home Front (Q & A regarding family issues); 950 wds. Pays $175.
Tips: "Most open to non-theme articles."
** This periodical was #36 on the 1993 Top 50 Plus Christian Publishers list.

+DISCOVERY, P.O. Box 607702, Orlando FL 32860-7702. (407)682-9494. Fax: (407)682-7005. Radio Station WTLN FM/AM. Janice Willis, ed. For Christian community in Central Florida. Bimonthly newspaper; circ. 20,000. Subscription $3. Query. **NO PAYMENT**. Not copyrighted. Articles & book reviews. Seasonal 3 mos ahead. Accepts reprints.
Columns/Departments: Christian Walk (general interest), 500 wds; Family Life (babies-seniors), 500 wds.
Tips: "We've never used fiction but would be open to parables."

THE DOOR, Box 530, Yreka CA 96097. (916)842-2701. Fax: (916)842-7729. Youth Specialties. Bob Darden, ed. Satire of evangelical church plus issue-oriented interviews. Bimonthly mag; 36 pgs; circ 10,000. Subscription $24. 50% freelance. Query; no phone query. Pays $50-300, on publication, for 1st rts. Not copyrighted. Articles (20-30/yr) & fiction (25/yr), 750-2,500 wds. Reports in 6-12 wks. Seasonal 6 mos ahead. Kill fee $40-50. Guidelines/theme list; copy for 9x12 SAE/5 stamps.
Poetry: Mike Yaconelli. Buys 2-3/yr. Avant-garde, free verse. Pays $40-100. Submit max. 6 poems.
Fillers: Buys 10/yr. Cartoons, quizzes, short humor, mock ads; 100-250 wds; $50-100.
Tips: "We look for biting satire/humor—National Lampoon not Reader's Digest. You must understand our satirical slant. Read more than one issue to understand our 'wavelength'."

DREAMS & VISIONS, RR 1, Washago, ON L0K 2B0 Canada. Skysong Press. Steve Stanton, ed. Quality fiction for Christian readers. Triannual journal; 52 pgs; circ 200. Subscription $12 U.S. 100% freelance. Complete ms. **NO PAYMENT** ($100 for Best of Year as chosen by subscribers), for 1st rts and one non-exclusive reprint. Fiction 2,000-6,000 wds (uses 28/yr). Reports in 8 wks. Accepts simultaneous submissions. Guidelines; copy $3.95.
Tips: "Be concise, powerful and unique."

***EL ORADOR**, 10101 Slater Ave., Ste. 111, Fountain Valley CA 92708. (714)965-9369. Carlos A. Alvarado, ed. To evangelize. Monthly mag; circ. 20,000. Not in topical listings.

EMPHASIS ON FAITH AND LIVING, Box 9127, Fort Wayne IN 46899. (219)747-2027. Fax: (219)747-5331. Missionary Church. Robert Ransom, mng. ed. Denominational; for adults 40 and older. Bimonthly mag; 16 pgs; circ 13,000. Subscription free. 10% freelance. Complete ms/ cover letter; no phone query. Pays .03-.04/wd; on publication; for 1st, one-time, reprint or simultaneous rts. Not copyrighted. Articles 200-800 wds (3/yr); fiction 200-1,600 wds (1-2/yr). Reports in 4-8 wks. Seasonal 4 mos ahead. Accepts simultaneous submissions & reprints. Guidelines; copy for 9x12 SAE/2 stamps.
Tips: "Our publication provides church news, missions information, and spiritual reading for members and friends of the Missionary Church denomination. We seek material that is compatible with our Wesleyan-Arminian church doctrine."

#EPISCOPAL LIFE, 815 2nd Ave., New York NY 10017. (212)922-5398. Episcopal Church. Jerrold F. Hames, ed; Edward P. Stannard, news ed. Denominational. Monthly newspaper; 32 pgs; circ 170,000. Estab. 1990. 40-50% freelance. Query/clips or complete ms/cover letter; phone query on breaking news only. Pays $50-300, on publication, for 1st, one-time or simultaneous rts. Articles 250-1,200 wds (12/yr); assigned book reviews 400 wds ($35). Reports in 2 mos. Seasonal 4 mos ahead. Accepts simultaneous submissions & reprints. Kill fee 50%. No guidelines; free copy.
Columns/Departments: Nan Cobbey. Buys 36/yr. Commentary on political/religious topics, 300-600 wds. Pays $35-75. Query or complete ms.
Tips: "All articles must have Episcopal Church slant or specifics. We need topical/issues, not devotional stuff. Most open to feature stories about Episcopalians—clergy, lay, churches, involvement in local efforts, movements, ministries."

EVANGEL, Box 535002, Indianapolis IN 46253. (317)244-3660. Fax: (317)244-1247. Free Methodist. Carolyn Smith, ed. For young adults and over 50's. Weekly take-home paper; 8 pgs; circ 25,000. Subscription $6.50. 95% freelance. Complete ms/cover letter; no phone query. Pays .04/wd; on publication; for one-time rts. Articles to 1,200 wds; fiction 1,000-1,200 wds. Reports in 4-6 wks. Seasonal 6 mos ahead. Accepts simultaneous submissions & reprints. Guidelines; copy for #10 SAE/1 stamp.
Poetry: Buys 15/yr. Free verse, haiku, light verse, traditional; 3-16 lines; $10. Submit max. 6 poems.
Fillers: Buys 20/yr. Anecdotes, cartoons; 200-400 wds; $7.50-10.
Tips: "Most open to first-person stories."

#THE EVANGELICAL BAPTIST, 679 Southgate Dr., Guelph ON N1G 4S2 Canada. (519)821-9829. The Fellowship of Evangelical Baptist Churches of Canada. Tom Scura, ed. Denominational; conservative Christian. Monthly (11X) mag; 32 pgs; circ.

5,000. 50% freelance. Prefers query. Negotiable payment, for 1st rts. Articles 700-1,200 wds. Reports in 8 wks. Seasonal 2 mos ahead. Accepts simultaneous submissions. Guidelines; copy for 9x12 SAE/Canadian postage.

THE EVANGELICAL BEACON, 901 E. 78th St., Minneapolis MN 55420. (612)854-1300. Fax: (612)853-8488. Evangelical Free Church of America. Susan Brill, asst. ed. Denominational; informational, inspirational, and evangelistic. Monthly (8x) mag; 40 pgs; circ 35,000. Subscription $12. 30% freelance. Complete ms/no cover letter; no phone query. Pays .07/wd (reprints .03/wd), on publication, for one-time or reprint rts. Articles 600-2,000 wds (20/yr). Reports in 6 wks. Seasonal 4 mos ahead. Accepts simultaneous submissions & reprints. Kill fee. Guidelines/theme list; copy for 9x12 SAE/4 stamps.
Tips: "Indicate which issue/theme article relates to; articles are all theme related. We prefer to publish members of the denomination."

#EVANGELICAL FRIEND, Box 232, Newberg OR 97132. (503)538-7345. Evangelical Friends Intl. Paul Anderson, ed. Denominational organ. Bimonthly mag; 27 pgs; circ 10,500. 5% freelance. Query. **NO PAYMENT.** Not copyrighted. Articles 500-1,800 wds (6/yr). Reports in 4 wks. Seasonal 4 mos ahead. Accepts simultaneous submissions. Guidelines; copy for 9x12 SASE.

#EVANGELICAL VISITOR, Box 166, Nappanee IN 46550-0166. (219)773-3164. Fax: (219)773-5934. Brethren in Christ. Glen Pierce, ed. Denominational. Monthly mag; circ 5,500. Subscription $12. 10% freelance. Complete ms. Pays $15-39, on publication, for reprint rts. Articles 750-1,200 wds (3-5 pgs); fiction or true stories 900 wds. Reports in 10 wks. Seasonal 3-4 mos ahead. Accepts simultaneous submissions. Guidelines; copy $1.

EXPLORER MAGAZINE, Box 210, Notre Dame IN 46556. (219)277-3465. Ray Flory, ed. Short, inspirational material. Semiannual mag; circ 200+. Subscription $6. 95% freelance. Complete ms/cover letter; phone query ok. Pays small cash prizes (winners determined by readers), for one-time rts. Not copyrighted. Articles 100-300 wds (10/yr); fiction to 300-800 wds (10/yr). Reports in 1-2 wks. Seasonal 6 mos ahead. Accepts simultaneous submissions. Guidelines; copy $3/#10 SAE/3 stamps.
Poetry: Uses 100/yr. Free verse, traditional; to 16 lines. Submit max. 5 poems.
Fillers: Uses 6/yr. Anecdotes, prose, prayers; 100-300 wds.
Tips: "Send one poem/pg and camera-ready, if possible."

+EXPRESSION CHRISTIAN NEWSPAPER, P.O. Box 44148, Pittsburgh PA 15205. (412)921-1300. Fax: (412)921-1537. Barbara Wilson, dir. of operations; Cathy Hinkling, articles ed. Geared toward bringing unity among the churches in the Pittsburgh and west PA area. Monthly newspaper; circ. 15,000. Free subscription/donations accepted. 25-35% freelance. Complete ms/cover letter; no phone query. Pays $25, on publication. Articles 300-500 or 750-1,000 wds; no payment for book or music reviews. Seasonal 2 mos ahead. Accepts simultaneous submissions. Guidelines; copy for 9x12 SAE/3 stamps.
Columns/Departments: Editorial and news summary.
Tips: "Send local/state stories, for example: Interview with local guy, Mel Blount (ex-Steeler), who has a half-way house for boys. Most open to editorials; PA stories of interest."

FAITH TODAY, Box 8800, Sta. B, Willowdale, ON M2K 2R6 Canada. (905)479-5885. Fax: (905)479-4742. Evangelical Fellowship of Canada. Audrey Dorsch, mng. ed. Canadian news and current issues from an evangelical perspective. Bimonthly mag; 4 pgs; circ 18,000. Subscription $17.99. 75% freelance. Query; no phone query. Pays $65-800, on publication, for 1st rts. Articles (90/yr) 400-2,000 wds. Reports in 6-8 wks. Kill fee 30-50%. Guidelines/theme list; copy for 9x12 SAE/$1.35 Canadian postage.
Columns/Departments: Buys 6/yr. Guest Column (current social/political/religious issues of concern to Canadian church); 900 wds; $75-85.
Tips: "Most open to independent features. Interview lots of pertinent source people from all sides of the issue. We do not use generic Christian-living, spiritual development material. Understand the difference between journalism and other types of writing."

THE FAMILY, 50 St. Paul's Ave., Boston MA 02130. (617)522-8911. Fax: (617)541-9805. Catholic. Submit to Acquisitions Editor. Stresses the special place of the family within society as an irreplaceable center of life, love and faith. Monthly (11X) mag; 40 pgs; circ 7,000. Subscription $12. 50% freelance. Complete ms/cover letter; NO phone calls. Pays .07-.10/wd, on publication (on acceptance for less than 100 wds), for 1st or reprint rts. Articles 800-1,600 wds (20/yr) & fiction (12/yr) 1,500-2,000 wds. Reports in 3-6 wks. Seasonal 6 mos ahead. Accepts reprints. Kill fee 25%. Guidelines; copy $1.75/10x13 SAE/2 stamps.
Special Needs: Material related to Year of the Family. Life vignettes.
Fillers: Buys 20/yr. Anecdotes, cartoons, ideas, jokes, prose, short humor; 25-100 wds; $10-25.
Columns/Departments: Buys 12/yr. Family Spirituality (examples of), 1,000 wds; Views (on current issues), 800 wds. Pays .06-.10/wd.
Tips: "Most open to fiction: Stories portraying family life, either dealing with crisis issues with a faith perspective or humorous. No preaching. Also helpful articles for families."

THE FAMILY DIGEST (formerly **PARISH FAMILY DIGEST**), P.O. Box 40137, Fort Wayne IN 46804. Our Sunday Visitor/Catholic. Corine B. Erlandson, ed. Geared to young Catholic families. Bimonthly digest; 48 pgs; circ 150,000. 95% freelance. Complete ms/with or without cover letter; no phone query. Pays .05/wd, on acceptance, for 1st rts. Articles 700-1,200 wds (60/yr). Reports in 4-8 wks. Seasonal 7 mos ahead. Accepts reprints. Guidelines; copy for 6x9 SAE/2 stamps.
Fillers: Buys 30/yr. Anecdotes, cartoons, prayers; 25-150 wds. Pays $5-10.
Tips: "Reading and getting to know the publication (and guidelines) is the best way to break in."
** This periodical was #37 on the 1993 Top 50 Plus Christian Publishers list.

#FELLOWSHIP TODAY, Fellowship Press, 4909 E. Buckeye Rd., Madison WI 53716. (608)221-1528. Fax: (608)221-4934. Fellowship of Christian Assemblies. James E. Mattson, ed. Inspirational and teaching, informational. Monthly mag; circ 4,500. Subscription $14. 15% freelance. Complete ms. Pays $7-20, on publication, for 1st or reprint rts. Articles 500-1,800 wds (12/yr). Reports in 8 wks. Seasonal 3-4 mos ahead. Accepts simultaneous submissions. Guidelines; copy for 9x12 SAE/3 stamps.

FOCUS ON THE FAMILY MAGAZINE, 8605 Explorer Dr., Colorado Springs CO 80920. (719)531-3400. Fax: (719)531-3499. Focus on the Family. Mike Yorkey, ed. To help families utilize Christian principles in the problems and situations of everyday

living. Monthly mag; 16 pgs; circ 2 million. Free subscription. 20% freelance. Complete ms/cover letter; no phone query. Pays $50-500, on acceptance, for 1st rts. Articles 400-1,500 wds (0-1/yr). Reports in 2 wks. Seasonal 6 mos ahead. Accepts simultaneous submissions & reprints. Kill fee 1/3. Guidelines; copy for 9x12 SAE/5 stamps.
Tips: "We are always on the lookout for interesting, first-person accounts and helpful how-tos for our `Family News' pages."
** This periodical was #11 on the 1993 Top 50 Plus Christian Publishers list.

FOURSQUARE WORLD ADVANCE, 1910 W. Sunset Blvd., Ste. 200, Los Angeles CA 90026-3282. (213)484-2400. Fax: (213)484-8401. International Church of the Foursquare Gospel. Ronald D. Williams, ed. Denominational. Bimonthly magazine; 24 pgs; circ 95,000. Free subscription. 10% freelance. Query; no phone query. Pays $75; on publication; for 1st or one-time rts. Not copyrighted. Articles 1,200-1,400 wds (3/yr). Reports in 2-4 wks. Seasonal 6 mos ahead. Accepts simultaneous submissions & reprints. Free guidelines/copy.
Fillers: Buys 1-2/yr. Anecdotes, cartoons; 250-300 wds; $50.

#FRIENDS JOURNAL, 1501 Cherry St., Philadelphia PA 19102-1497. (215)241-7277. Quaker. Vinton Deming, ed. Denominational. Monthly mag; 48 pgs; circ 9,500. 98% freelance. Query or complete ms/cover letter. **PAYS 4 COPIES**, for 1st & reprint rts. Articles 500-2,500 wds; book reviews 500 wds. Reports in 6 mos. Seasonal 3 mos ahead. Accepts simultaneous submissions. Guidelines; free copy.
Poetry: Free verse, haiku, traditional; to 25 lines. Submit max. 3 poems. Only on Quaker themes: meditation, peace concerns.
Fillers: Quaker-related humor and crossword puzzles.

THE GEM, 700 E. Melrose Ave., Box 926, Findlay OH 45839. (419)424-1961. Fax: (419)424-3433. Churches of God, General Conference. Kathy Rodabaugh, ed. Weekly take-home paper for youth and adults; circ 8,000. Subscription $7. 98% freelance. Complete ms; no cover letter or phone query. Pays $7.50-15, on publication, for reprint rts. Not copyrighted. Articles 200-1,700 wds (125/yr). Reports in several months. Seasonal 4 mos ahead. Accepts simultaneous submissions & reprints. Guidelines/copy for #10 SAE/1 stamp.
Tips: "We are accepting more material that is 400 wds or less as fillers. Holiday material always welcome, although often we don't use it the first year we have it."

#GOD'S REVIVALIST , 1810 Young St., Cincinnati OH 45210. (513)721-7944x296. Ron E. Shew, ed. Salvation theme; Wesleyan persuasion. Monthly mag; 24 pgs; circ 21,000. 80% freelance. Complete ms/cover letter (query for fiction). **NO PAYMENT** for one-time rts. Articles 600-1,400 wds (3/yr); fiction 200-700 wds (few). Reports in 2 mos. Seasonal 3 mos ahead. Accepts simultaneous submissions & reprints. Guidelines; copy $.50.
Poetry: Accepts 5/yr. Free verse, light verse, traditional; 8-20 lines. Submit max. 10 poems.
Fillers: Accepts 5/yr. Facts, ideas, prose, short humor; 50-90 wds.

#GOD'S SPECIAL PEOPLE, Box 729, Ocean Shores WA 98569. (206)289-2540. Independent Baptist. Dan Lindsey, ed. Conservative Christian; concerning disabilities. Quarterly mag; 36 pgs; circ 400. 100% freelance. Complete ms. **NO PAYMENT.** Articles (30/yr) to 1,000 wds (prefers shorter). Reports in 1-2 mos. Accepts

simultaneous submissions & reprints. Guidelines; copy $2.
Poetry: Uses 2-3/yr.
Tips: "Articles must be definitely Christian and concern those who are disabled or have disabled children."

#GOOD NEWS, Box 150, Wilmore KY 40390. (606)858-4661. Fax: (606)858-4972. United Methodist. James V. Heidinger II, ed. Focus is church renewal—a return to scriptural Christianity. Bimonthly mag; circ 18,000. Subscription $14.95. 20% freelance. Query only. Pays .05-.07/wd; on acceptance; for 1st, simultaneous or reprint rts. Articles 1,500-1,800 wds (25/yr). Reports in 3 mos. Seasonal 6 mos ahead. Kill fee. Guidelines; copy $2.75.

+GOOD NEWS, ETC., P.O. Box 2660, Vista CA 92085. (619)724-3075. Fax: (619)724-8311. Good News Publishers, Inc. of California. Rick Monroe, ed/pub. Feature stories and local news of interest to Christians in San Diego County. Monthly newspaper; circ. 44,000. Subscription $15. 5% freelance. Query/clips or complete ms/cover letter. Pays $20, on publication, for 1st rts. Articles 400-700 wds (20/yr). Reports in 2 wks. Seasonal 2 mos ahead. Accepts simultaneous submissions and reprints. No guidelines; copy for 9x12 SAE/4 stamps.
Special Needs: Short, local articles in newspaper style.
Tips: "Most open to material for youth and family sections."

#GOOD NEWS JOURNAL, Box 1882, 10900 E Hwy WW, Columbia MO 65205. (314)875-8755. Fax: (314)874-4964. Teresa Shields Parker, ed. Christian newspaper for mid-Missouri area. Quarterly newspaper; 16 pgs; circ 50,000. Subscription $10. 50% freelance. Complete ms/cover letter. **NO PAYMENT.** Articles 900-1,000 wds. Reports in 2 mos. Accepts simultaneous submissions. No guidelines; copy for 9x12 SAE/3 stamps.
Tips: Issues are topical. "Interested in testimonies and personal experience stories that illustrate Christian growth or Christian principles."

GOSPEL TIDINGS, 5800 S. 14th St., Omaha NE 68107. (402)731-4780. Fax: (402)731-1173. Fellowship of Evangelical Bible Churches. Robert L. Frey, ed. To inform, educate, and edify members of affiliate churches. Bimonthly mag; 16-20 pgs; circ 2,200. Subscription $8. 2% freelance. Complete ms/cover letter; no phone query. **NO PAYMENT** to $35. Articles 400-2,500 wds (3/yr); fiction (1-2/yr) 500-1,000 wds. Reports in 4 wks. Seasonal 2 mos ahead. Accepts simultaneous submissions & reprints. Copy for 9x12 SAE/2 stamps.
Poetry: Light verse, traditional.

GUIDEPOSTS, 16 E 34th St., New York NY 10016. (212)251-8100. Interfaith. Fulton Oursler, Jr., ed-in-chief; submit to The Editors. Personal faith stories showing how faith in God helps each person cope with life in some particular way. Monthly mag; 48 pgs; circ 3.9 million. 30% freelance. Complete ms; no cover letter; phone query ok. Pays $200-400 (sometimes more for repeat sales), on acceptance, for all rts. Articles 750-1,500 wds (50/yr). Reports in 2-4 wks. Seasonal 6 mos ahead. Kill fee 25%. Free guidelines/copy.
Poetry: Colleen Hughes. Buys 2-3/yr. Free verse, light verse, traditional; 2-20 lines; $10-25.
Fillers: Colleen Hughes. Buys 10-12/yr. Anecdotes; quotes, short humor; 10-200 wds; $15-200. "This is new for us."

Columns/Departments: Colleen Hughes. Buys 30-40/yr. His Mysterious Ways, 250 wds; This Thing Called Prayer, 250 wds; The Quiet People, 300 wds ("This is our most open area. Write in 3rd person."); $50-200.
Tips: "Be able to tell a good story, with drama, suspense, description & dialogue. The point of the story should be some practical spiritual help the reader receives from what the author learned through his experience." First person only.

+HALLELUJAH!, P.O. Box 223, Stn. A, Vancouver BC V6C 2M3 Canada. (604)498-3895. Bible Holiness Movement. Wesley H. Wakefield, ed. For evangelism and promotion of holiness revivals; readership mostly ethnic, non-white minorities. Bimonthly mag; 40 pgs; circ 6,000. Subscription $10. 2% freelance. Query or complete ms; no phone query. Pays $15-50, on acceptance, for any rts. Articles 300-2,500 wds (6/yr). Reports in 3-6 wks. Accepts simultaneous submissions & reprints. Guidelines; copy for 6x9 SAE/.86 Canadian postage.
Special Need: Holiness emphasis.
Ethnic: Distributes to Nigeria, Canada, and U.S.
Poetry: Buys 6 poems/yr. Traditional, any length. Variable pay rate. Submit max. 2 poems.
Fillers: Buys a few/yr. Facts, newsbreaks, prose, quotes; 10-50 wds. Pays 0-$5.
Tips: "Avoid Americanisms. No Calvinistic articles or premillenialism."

HERALD OF HOLINESS, 6401 The Paseo, Kansas City MO 64131. (816)333-7000x2302. (816)333-1748. Church of the Nazarene. Dr. Wesley D. Tracy, ed. Denominational. Monthly mag; 64 pgs; circ 81,000. Subscription $10. 20% freelance. Complete ms/cover letter; no phone query. Pays .05/wd (.04/wd for reprints), on acceptance, for one-time rts. Not copyrighted. Articles 350-1,500 wds. Reports in 6-8 wks. Seasonal 6 mos ahead. Accepts reprints. Kill fee 50%. Guidelines/theme list; no copy.
Poetry: Buys 30/yr. Free verse & traditional. Pays .75/line. Submit max. 3 poems.
Fillers: Buys 30 cartoons/yr. Pay negotiable.
Tips: "Need personality pieces about Nazarenes who are making a difference in their world (need not be celebrities); plus personal experiences of God at work in a person's life."
** This periodical was #16 on the Top 50 Plus Christian Publishers list.

+HIS GARDEN, 216 N. Vine St., Kewanee IL 61443. Christian. Margi Washburn, ed. A forum for new and unpublished Christian writers. Triannual mag. Est. 1992. 90% freelance. Query (for nonfiction) or complete ms. Pays $5, on acceptance, for all rts. Articles to 2,500 wds (3-4/yr); fiction 250-2,500 wds (6-10/yr). Reports in 3-9 wks. Seasonal 6 mos ahead. Accepts reprints. Guidelines; copy $3.50.
Poetry: Buys 15-25/yr. Free verse, haiku, light verse, traditional. Submit max. 5 poems.

HOME LIFE, 127 9th Ave. N., Nashville TN 37234. (615)251-2272. Southern Baptist. Charlie Warren, ed. Christian family leisure reading. Monthly mag; 66 pgs; circ 600,000. Subscription $12.60. 50% freelance. Query; no phone query. Pays $20-275; on acceptance; for all or 1st rts. Articles 200-1,500 wds (60/yr); fiction 1,200-1,500 wds (12/yr); book & music reviews, $50-75. Reports in 3-12 wks. Seasonal 8 mos ahead. Accepts simultaneous submissions. Guidelines; copy $1/9x12 SAE/7 stamps.
Special Needs: Humor about family life. Fiction on family relationships.
Poetry: Buys 20/yr. Free verse, light verse, traditional; 4-24 lines; $13-24. Submit max.

3 poems.
Fillers: Cartoons. Pays $38-50.
Columns/Departments: Buys 36/yr. Coupletime or Familytime (an event or activity that strengthens a family or marriage), 350-500 wds. Pays $75.
Tips: "Our new Familytime column is a good way to break in (description in guidelines). Also open to fiction."
** This periodical was #17 on the 1993 Top 50 Plus Christian Publishers list.

#HOME TIMES, Box 16096, West Palm Beach FL 33416. (407)439-3509. Dennis Lombard, ed. Conservative, pro-Christian, pro-Jewish community newspaper. Monthly newspaper; 24 pgs; circ 8,000. 90% freelance. Complete ms/cover letter; no phone query. Pays $5-25, on publication, for one-time rts. Articles to 900 wds (20/yr); fiction 500-1,200 wds (5/yr); book reviews 500 wds/$5. Reports in 1 wk. Seasonal 1 mo ahead. Accepts simultaneous submissions & reprints. Guidelines; copy for $1/9x12 SAE/3 stamps.
Special Needs: Op-eds and new columnists.
Poetry: Buys 3/yr. Light verse, traditional; any length; $5-10. Submit max. 3 poems.
Fillers: Uses 10/yr. Various; any length; $0.
Columns/Departments: Buys 25/yr. Numerous; open to ideas, to 700 wds. Pays $5-15.
Tips: "Very open to new writers, but study guidelines and sample first; we are different."

+HOMEWORK, The Home Business Newsletter with a Christian Perspective, 20 Whitcomb Dr., P.O. Box 394, Simsbury CT 06070. (203)651-5503. Christian. Posy Lough, ed. For people who work at home, or plan to. Bimonthly newsletter; 8 pgs. Subscription $20. Open to freelance. Complete ms. Short articles relating to home business. No additional information. Not included in topical listings.

#IDEALS, Ideals Publishing, 565 Marriott Dr., Box 140300, Nashville TN 37214. (615)885-8270. Tim Hamling, ed. Seasonal, inspirational, nostalgic magazine for mature men and women of traditional values. Mag published 8 times/yr; 80 pgs; circ 180,000+. 95% freelance. Query (for fiction) or complete ms (copies only, doesn't return). Pays .10/wd, on publication, for one-time rts. Articles (20/yr) 500-800 wds; fiction (10/yr). Reports in 3 mos. Seasonal 8 mos ahead. Accepts simultaneous submissions & reprints. Kill fee. Guidelines/theme list; copy $3.
Poetry: Buys 250/yr. Light verse & traditional; 12-50 lines; $10. Submit max. 15 poems.
Tips: "Most open to optimistic poetry oriented around a season or theme."

IMPACT MAGAZINE, 12 B East Coast Rd., 1542 Singapore. 65-345-0444. Fax: 65-345-3045. Evangelical Fellowship of Singapore. Andrew Goh, ed. To help young working adults apply Christian principles to contemporary issues. Bimonthly mag; circ. 6,000. Subscription $22. 10-15% freelance. Complete ms/cover letter; phone query ok. **NO PAYMENT** up to $20/pg, for all rts. Articles (12/yr) and short stories (6/yr), 1,000-2,000 wds. Seasonal 2 mos ahead. Accepts reprints. No guidelines; copy for $3 and $1.70 postage (surface mail).
Poetry: Accepts 2-3 poems/yr. Free verse, 20-40 lines. Submit max. 3 poems.
Fillers: Accepts 6/yr. Anecdotes, cartoons, jokes, quizzes, short humor, and word puzzles.
Columns/Departments: Closing Thoughts (current social issues), 600-800 wds;

Testimony (personal experience), 1,500-2,000 wds; Parenting (Asian context), 1,000-1,500 wds.
Tips: "We're most open to fillers."

INDIAN LIFE, Box 3765, Sta. B, Winnipeg, MB R2W 3R6 Canada. U.S. address: Box 32, Pembina ND 58271. (204)661-9333. Fax: (204)661-3982. Intertribal Christian Communications. Ed Hughes, ed. Speaking to the social, cultural, and spiritual needs of the North American Indians. Bimonthly mag; circ 34,000. Subscription $7. 10% freelance. Complete ms/cover letter; phone query ok. **NO PAYMENT**, for one-time rts. Articles 500-1,400 wds (10/yr); fiction, 500-1,500 wds; book reviews, 500 wds. Reports in 1-2 wks. Seasonal 6 mos ahead. Accepts simultaneous submissions & reprints. Guidelines/copy $2/IRC.
Special Needs: News items of positive achievements by native groups or individuals.
Fillers: Accepts 6/yr. News items; 100-400 wds.
Tips: "Know the Indian people well and write from their perspective. No talking down. Native authors preferred."

#THE INSPIRER, 737 Kimsey Ln. #620, Henderson KY 42420-4917. (502)826-5720. Billy Edwards, ed. To encourage other believers in their Christian life. (Especially open to writers who are physically disabled.) Quarterly newsletter; 8 pgs; circ 2,000. 50% freelance. Complete ms. Articles 500 wds. **PAYS IN COPIES**. Not copyrighted. Reports in 2 wks. Seasonal 2 mos ahead. Accepts simultaneous submissions & reprints. No guidelines; copy for #10 SASE/1 stamp.
Special Needs: Issues of interest to the physically disabled.
Poetry: Accepts 10/yr. Free verse. Submit max. 5 poems.
Fillers: Accepts 10/yr. Various; 25-100 wds.
Columns/Departments: Accepts 10/yr. Food for Thought (Christian living); The Lighter Side; Prayer Works Wonders; all 300 wds.

+INTERCHANGE, 412 Sycamore St., Cincinnati OH 45202. (513)421-0311. Episcopal. Michael Barwell, ed. Regional paper for the Episcopal and Anglican Church in southern Ohio. Newspaper published 8X/yr; 28 pgs; circ. 12,800. 10% freelance. Query/clips. Pays $35-50, on publication, for all rts. Articles 500-2,000 wds. Reports in 2 mos. Accepts simultaneous submissions. No guidelines; copy for 9x12 SASE.

#INTEREST MAGAZINE, Box 190, Wheaton IL 60189. (708)653-6573. Fax: (708)653-6595. Christian (Plymouth) Brethren. William W. Conrad, ed. Denominational. Monthly (11X) mag; circ. 15,000. Subscription $14. Query; no phone query. Pays $30-75, on publication. Articles 600-1,200 wds (3/yr). Seasonal 3 mos ahead. Accepts reprints. Free guidelines/copy.
Poetry: Free verse, light verse, traditional; $30.
Fillers: Buys 10/yr. Various; $35.
Tips: "Most open to articles on people in the Christian Brethren movement or related organizations.

***THE INTERIM**, 53 Dundas St. E., Toronto ON M5B 1C6 Canada. (416)368-0250. Catholic. Alphonse de Valk, ed. Abortion, euthanasia, pornography, feminism, and religion for a pro-life perspective. Monthly newspaper; circ. 25,000. 50% freelance. Complete ms; phone query ok. Pays $50-150 (Canadian), on publication. Articles 500-1,500 wds. Reports in 4 wks. Seasonal 2 mos ahead. Accepts reprints.

***INTERNATIONAL REPORT**, Box 16044, Colorado Springs CO 80935. (719)632-0755. Karen White, ed. To publish news and truth of interest to Christians. Quarterly; circ. 9,500. Query. Not in topical listings.

#INTERVARSITY, Box 7895, Madison WI 53707-7895. (608)274-9001. Fax: (608) 274-7882. InterVarsity Christian Fellowship. Neal Kunde, ed. To inform donors and other interested readers of InterVarsity's work on campus. Quarterly mag; circ 50,000. Subscription for donation. 5% freelance. Prefers query. Pays $250, on publication, for 1st rts. Articles 750 wds (21/yr). Seasonal 6 mos ahead. Guidelines; free copy.
Columns/Departments: Buys 4/yr. Campus Datelines (news about life on college campuses); 100 wds; $50.
Tips: "Most open to nonfiction features. Call the editor and ask specific questions."

***JOHN MILTON MAGAZINE**, 475 Riverside Dr., Rm. 455, New York NY 10115. (212)870-3335. John Milton Society for the Blind/nonsectarian. Pam Toplisky, ed. For visually impaired church members, some blind. Monthly mag; bimonthly record (talking book); circ 16,400. 0.1% freelance. Complete ms/cover letter; phone query ok. **NO PAYMENT**, for one-time or simultaneous rts. Articles 200-2,500 (5-6/yr); fiction 200-3,000 (1-2/yr); book reviews 200-500 wds. Reports in 8-10 wks. Seasonal 6 mos ahead. Accepts reprints. Free copy.
Special Needs: Archaeology; children's stories.
Poetry: Accepts 20-25/yr. Free verse, haiku, light verse, traditional; to 40 lines. Submit max. 5 poems.
Fillers: Accepts 4-5/yr. Various; 100-200 wds.
Tips: "Well-researched articles on any subject; concise writing."

JOURNAL OF CHRISTIAN NURSING, Box 1650, Downers Grove IL 60515. (708) 964-5700. Fax: (708)964-5700. Nurses Christian Fellowship of InterVarsity Christian Fellowship. Melodee Yohe, mng. ed. Personal, professional, practical articles that help nurses integrate Christian faith with nursing profession. Quarterly journal; 12 pgs; circ 10,000. Subscription $17.95. 30% freelance. Complete ms/cover letter; no phone query. Pays $25-80; on publication; for all, 1st, one-time or reprint rts. Articles 6-12 pgs (20/yr). Reports in 1-4 wks. Seasonal 12 mos ahead. Rarely accepts reprints. Kill fee rarely. Guidelines/theme list; copy for $4/9x12 SAE/6 stamps.
Special Needs: Faith & nursing; nursing issues; transcultural nursing experiences; vignettes that exemplify Christian nursing; ethical dilemmas/case studies. All topics must relate to nursing.
Poetry: Buys 1-3/yr. Light verse, traditional (by, about, or of interest to nurses); any length; $25. Submit max. 4 poems.
Department: Buys 4/yr. The Last Word (opinion related to nursing), 750-900 wds; $25-50.
Tips: "Learn our style from our publication. Only submit articles appropriate for our audience. Most open to first person (nurses) experiences—interviewed and written by a freelancer."

+JOURNAL OF CHURCH & STATE, P.O. Box 97308, Baylor University, Waco TX 76798. (817)755-1510. Fax: (817)755-3740. Interdenominational. Derek Davis, mng. ed. Provides a forum for the critical examination of the interaction of religion and government worldwide. Quarterly jour; 200+ pgs; circ. 1,700. Subscription $20. 100% freelance. Complete ms/cover letter; no phone query. **NO PAYMENT**, for all rights. Articles 30 pgs/footnotes. Reports in 3-4 mos. Guidelines; copy $8.
Special Needs: Church-state issues.

***THE JOURNAL OF RELIGION IN PSYCHOTHERAPY,** 1325 N. College Ave., Claremont CA 91711. (714)626-3521. Dr. William M. Clements, ed. Academic/applied audience. Quarterly journal. Complete ms. **No Payment.** Articles to 6,000 wds (20/yr). Reports in 12 wks. Guidelines; free copy.

***THE JOURNAL OF RELIGIOUS GERONTOLOGY,** 1325 N. College Ave., Claremont CA 91711. (714)626-3521. Dr. William M. Clements, ed. Academic/applied audience. Quarterly journal. Complete ms. **No Payment.** Articles to 6,000 wds (20/yr). Reports in 12 wks. Guidelines; free copy.

+JOYFUL NOISE, 310 N. Tulane Dr., Archer FL 32618. (904)486-3232. Nondenominational. William W. Maxwell, ed. Deals with African-American life and religious culture. Bimonthly mag. Est. 1993. Complete ms/cover letter or query/clips. Pays $50-250, on acceptance, for 1st rts. Articles 700-3,000 wds. Guidelines; no copy.

***JUNEBUGS KNOCKING,** Rt.4 Box 274, West Frankfort IL 62896. D. Ivan Rodden IV, pub. A Christian literary magazine. Journal published 3x/yr; circ 100. Estab. 1991. 100% freelance. Complete ms. Pays $5, on publication, for one-time rts. Not copyrighted. Fiction only 1,000-10,000 wds (20-30/yr). Reports in 4-8 wks. Seasonal 8 mos ahead. Guidelines; copy $3.
Tips: "We are very new and looking for well-written fiction based on truth and honest human experience."

+KANSAS CITY CHRISTIAN NEWSPAPER, P.O. Box 1114, Lee's Summit MO 64063. (816)524-4522. Fax: (816)525-3444. Non-denominational. Dwight Widaman, pub; Alecia Chai, ed. To promote Christian business, ministries, and organizations; provide thought-provoking commentary for edification of the body of Christ. Monthly newspaper; circ. 35,000. Subscription $14. 50% freelance. Complete ms/cover letter; short phone query ok. **PAYS IN COPIES** or limited amount for well-researched pcs, for one-time or reprint rts. Not copyrighted. Articles to 1,200 wds (100/yr). Reports in 6 wks. Seasonal 6 mos ahead. Accepts reprints. Guidelines; copy for 9x12 SAE/$1 postage.
Fillers: Accepts 12/yr. Anecdotes, cartoons, ideas, newsbreaks, quotes, short humor; to 500 wds.
Tips: "We look for up-to-date information. Willing to work with new writers who want to learn."

#LIBERTY, Religious Liberty Dept., 12501 Old Columbia Pike, Silver Springs MD 20904. (310)680-6691. Fax: (310)680-6695. Seventh-day Adventist. Roland R. Hegstad, ed. Deals with religious liberty issues for government officials, civic leaders, and laymen. Bimonthly mag; 32 pgs; circ 250,000. 90% freelance. Query. Pays .06-.08/wd, on acceptance, for 1st or reprint rts. Articles & essays 2,000-3,000 wds. Reports in 4 wks. Guidelines; copy $1.

***LIFE ADVOCATE**, Box 13656, Portland OR 97213. (503)257-7023. Advocates for Life Ministry. Paul deParrie, ed. Pro-life, pro-family, activist. Monthly mag; circ. 5,500. 100% freelance. Query or complete ms/cover letter; phone query ok. **NO PAYMENT** for 1st rts. Articles 100-700 wds; fiction 150-400 wds (few). Reports in 2-4 wks. Seasonal 3 mos ahead. Accepts simultaneous submissions & reprints.
Special Needs: Satire; news pieces; current rescue news.
Poetry: Accepts 1/yr.

Fillers: Accepts many. Various types.
Columns/Departments: Uses 48/yr. Commentary (editorials on life issues), 700 wds; FYI (educational, how-to, pro-life work), 700 wds.
Send good self-photo.

#LIFEGLOW, Box 6097, Lincoln NE 68506. (402)488-0981. Christian Record Services. Richard Kaiser, ed. For sight-impaired adults over 25; interdenominational Christian audience. Quarterly mag; 65-70 pgs (lg. print); circ 28,000. 90% freelance. Query; phone query ok. Pays .03-.05/wd, on acceptance, for one-time rts. Articles & true stories 800-1,400 wds. Reports in 2-3 mos. Seasonal 1 yr ahead. Accepts simultaneous query & reprints. Guidelines; copy for 9x12 SAE/6 stamps.
Columns/Departments: Healthwatch (current, health-related topics).
Tips: "I will read any ms which has first been queried and is written in an interesting manner on the topics I've indicated in the topical listing section."

LIGHT AND LIFE, Box 535002, Indianapolis IN 46253. (317)244-3660. Fax: (317)244-1247. Free Methodist Church of North America. Robert B. Haslam, ed. Christian growth, ministry to saved and unsaved, denominational news. Monthly mag; 32 pgs; circ 33,000. Subscription $15. 40% freelance. Complete ms/cover letter; no phone query. Pays .04/wd; on publication; for 1st, one-time, or simultaneous rts. Articles 500-1,200 wds (35/yr). Reports in 6 wks. Seasonal 6 mos ahead. Accepts simultaneous submissions. Kill fee 50%. Guidelines; copy $1.50.
Poetry: Buys 15/yr. Free verse, traditional; 4-12 lines; $10. Send max. 5 poems.
Tips: "Most open to feature articles. Write solid, biblically-based material that is relevant to Christian living."

LIGHTHOUSE FICTION COLLECTION, Box 1377, Auburn WA 98071-1377. Tim Clinton, ed/pub. Timeless fiction for the whole family. Bimonthly booklet; circ 300+. Subscription $7.95. 100% freelance. Complete ms/cover letter; no phone query. Pays to $4-50, on publication, for 1st rts. Fiction for all ages 250-5,000 wds (60+/yr). Reports in 10 wks or more. Seasonal any time. Guidelines; copy $3.
Poetry: Buys 20/yr. Free verse, haiku, light verse, traditional; 4-80 lines; pays $.50-$5. Submit max. 5 poems.
Tips: "Read and follow guidelines. Basic need is for good stories and poems—well-written, interesting, etc."

LIGUORIAN, One Liguori Dr., Liguori MO 63057. (314)464-2500. Catholic. Susan M. Schuster, mng. ed.; Allan Weinert, CSSR, ed-in-chief. To help readers lead a fuller Christian life through the sharing of experiences, scriptural knowledge, and a better understanding of the church. Monthly mag; 72 pgs; circ 360,000. Subscription $15. 40% freelance. Query or complete ms/cover letter; phone query ok. Pays .10-.12/wd, on acceptance, for all rts. Articles to 2,000 wds (45/yr); fiction to 2,000 wds (6/yr). Reports in 2-8 wks. Seasonal 6 mos ahead. Kill fee 50%. Guidelines; copy for 6x9 SAE/3 stamps.
Poetry: Buys 10/yr. Traditional; 8-24 lines. Submit max. 4 poems. Pays $25-35.
Fillers: Anecdotes, prose, prayers, short humor. Pays .10/wd.
Columns/Departments: Buys 6/yr. Five-Minute Meditation, to 750 wds. Complete ms.
Tips: "Polish your own ms. Need marriage and parenting articles, articles that touch a reader's life in a personal way. If writing a personal experience piece, beware of limited subjectivity."

LIVE, 1445 Boonville Ave., Springfield MO 65802. (417)862-2781. Fax: (417)862-6059. Assemblies of God. Submit to The Editor. For adults in Sunday school. Weekly take-home paper; 8 pgs; circ 150,000. Subscription $5.80. 100% freelance. Complete ms (a copy only). Pays .03/wd (.02/wd for reprints and simultaneous), on acceptance, for 1st, one-time or reprint rts. Articles 800-2,000 wds; fiction 800-2,000 wds (100/yr). Reports in 12 wks. Seasonal 1 yr ahead. Accepts simultaneous submissions & reprints. Guidelines/copy for #10 SAE/1 stamp.
Special Needs: Holiday stories—Christmas, July 4th, Easter, Thanksgiving, Mothers/Fathers Day.
Poetry: Buys 50+/yr. Free verse, haiku, light verse, traditional; to 20 lines; $5. Submit max. 4 poems.
Fillers: Anecdotes, cartoons, prose, short humor; 200-800 wds. Pay .02-.03/wd.
Columns/Departments: Reflections (pithy sayings/anecdotes), 50-100 wds. **NO PAYMENT.**
Tips: "Send scanable copy. Do not send original/only copy. Send SASpostcard for reply. Be patient, staff is limited. Proofread your ms. Be concise."
** This periodical was #26 on the 1993 Top 50 Plus Christian Publishers list.

***LIVING**, Rt. 2 Box 656, Grottoes VA 24441. (703)249-3177. Eugene K. Souder, mng. ed. A positive, practical, and uplifting publication for the whole family; mass distribution. Quarterly tabloid; circ. 100,000. Estab. 1991. 60% freelance. Complete ms; no cover letter or phone query. Pays $25-100, on publication, for all rts. Articles 500-1,200 wds (25/yr). Reports in 4 wks. Seasonal 4-6 mos ahead. Accepts simultaneous submissions & reprints. Guidelines; copy for 9x12 SAE/4 stamps.
Fillers: Buys 15/yr. Various; 30-100 wds; $10-25.
Columns/Departments: Open to new family-related columns.
Tips: "Most open to first-person stories on family relationships—spouse and parent-child. Strong on anecdotes, short on moralism. Touch family needs in a practical way with a Christian slant, without being overly religious."

THE LIVING CHURCH, P.O. Box 92936, Milwaukee WI 53202-0936. (414)276-5420. Fax: (414)276-7483. Episcopal. David Kalvelage, ed. For members of the denomination, many theologically conservative. Weekly mag; 16-20 pgs; circ 9,000. Subscription $39.50. 75% freelance. Complete ms/cover letter; phone query ok. **NO PAYMENT.** Articles to 1,200 wds (150/yr). Reports in 2 wks. Seasonal 2 mos ahead. Free copy.
Poetry: John Schuessler, poetry ed. Accepts 25/yr. Free verse, light verse, traditional; 3-15 lines. Submit max. 3 poems.
Columns/Departments: Buys 50/yr. Viewpoint (opinion), 500-1,000 wds. Complete ms.
Tips: "Most open to features of interest to Episcopalians."

#THE LOOKOUT, 8121 Hamilton Ave., Cincinnati OH 45231-9981. (513)931-4050. Fax: (513)931-0904. Standard Publishing. Simon J. Dahlman, ed. For adults in Sunday school who are interested in learning more about applying the gospel to their lives. Weekly take-home paper; 16 pgs; circ 118,000. Subscription $19. 50-60% freelance. Query or complete ms/cover letter; no phone query. Pays .04-.08/wd; on acceptance; for 1st, one-time, simultaneous rts. Articles 500-2,000 wds (160/yr); fiction 1,000-2,000 wds (40/yr). Reports in 4 mos. Seasonal 6 mos ahead. Accepts simultaneous submissions & reprints. Kill fee 33%. Guidelines/theme list; copy for 9x12 SAE/2 stamps.

Columns/Departments: Buys 45/yr. Outlook (personal opinion), 500-900 wds; Growing in Groups (small group tips), 50-250; $25-50.
Tips: "Show evidence of solid research. In feature articles on hot issues, present accurate information and measured judgements and let the reader decide. Most open to Outlook column."
** This periodical was #2 on the 1993 Top 50 Plus Christian Publishers list.

#THE LUTHERAN, 8765 W. Higgins Rd., Chicago IL 60631-4183. (312)380-2540. Fax: (312)380-2751. Evangelical Lutheran Church in America. Edgar R. Trexler, ed.; David L. Miller, articles ed. Addresses broad constituency of the church. Monthly mag; 68 pgs; circ 960,000. 25-50% freelance. Complete ms. Pays $400-1,000 (assigned), $50-400 (unsolicited); on acceptance, for 1st rts. Articles 300-2,000 wds (40/yr). Reports in 3-6 wks. Seasonal 4 mos ahead. Kill fee 50%. Guidelines/theme list; free copy.
Fillers: Roger Kahle. Buys 50/yr. Cartoons, jokes, short humor.
Columns/Departments: Roger Kahle. Lite Side (church and religious humor) and Reader's Viewpoint, 25-100 wds; $10.
Tips: "Most open to feature articles."
** This periodical was #14 on the 1993 Top 50 Plus Christian Publishers list.

THE LUTHERAN DIGEST, Box 4250, Hopkins MN 55343. (612)933-2820. Lutheran. David L. Tank, ed. Blend of secular and light theological material used to win non-believers to the Lutheran faith. Quarterly mag; circ 150,000. Subscription $20/2 yrs (min.). 30% freelance. Complete ms/cover letter; no phone query. Pays $15-25, on acceptance, for 1st, one-time or reprint rts. Articles to 1,000 wds (25-30/yr). Reports in 4-6 wks. Seasonal 6-9 mos ahead. Accepts reprints. Guidelines; copy $1.75/6x9 SAE/3 stamps.
Poetry: Accepts 45-50/yr. Light verse, traditional; 4-30 lines. **NO PAYMENT**. Submit max. 3 poems.
Fillers: Anecdotes, cartoons, facts, jokes, short humor. **NO PAYMENT**.
Tips: "We would like more short articles, 1 page or less. We also look for good-quality nature articles."

#THE LUTHERAN JOURNAL, 7317 Cahill Rd., Edina MN 55439-2081. (612)941-6830. Lutheran. Rev. Armin U. Deye, ed. Family magazine for church members, middle age & older. Quarterly mag; 32 pgs; circ 136,000. 60% freelance. Complete ms/cover letter or query. Pays .01-.03/wd (.01-.015/wd for fiction); on publication; for all, 1st, or one-time rts. Articles (25/yr) to 2,000 wds (prefers 1,500), fiction (2/yr) to 2,000 wds. Reports in 3-4 mos. Seasonal 6 mos ahead. Accepts simultaneous submissions & reprints (occasionally). No guidelines; copy for 9x12 SAE/2 stamps.
Poetry: Buys 6/yr. Free verse, traditional; to 20 lines. Submit max. 3 poems.

#THE LUTHERAN LAYMAN, 2185 Hampton Ave., St. Louis MO 63139-2983. (314)647-4900x18 or (800)944-3450. Lutheran Laymen's League/Lutheran Church-Missouri Synod. Gerald Perschbacher, ed. Lutheran news for lay adults. Monthly tabloid; 16 pgs; circ 80,000. 10% freelance. Query. Pays negotiable fees (about $110/tabloid pg), on acceptance, for all rts. Not copyrighted. Articles 600-1,500 wds (10+/yr). Reports in 2 wks. Seasonal 3 mos ahead. Guidelines; free copy.
Columns/Departments: Buys 5/yr. Celebrities or Personalities (L.L.L. related, when possible—members, supporters); 600-1,500 wds.
Tips: "No opinion pieces or heavy doctrine. Be in Lutheran Church-Missouri Synod and know about Intl. L.L.L."

#LUTHERAN WITNESS, 1333 S. Kirkwood Rd., St. Louis MO 63122-7295. (314)965-9917. Lutheran Church-Missouri Synod. David L. Strand, mng. ed. Denominational. Monthly mag; 26 pgs; circ 350,000. 75% freelance. Complete ms/cover letter. Pays $100-300, on acceptance, for 1st rts. Articles 500-1,500 wds (25+/yr); fiction 500-1,500 wds. Reports in 6-8 wks. Seasonal 6 mos ahead. Accepts simultaneous submissions (non-competitive). Kill fee 50%. Guidelines; free copy.
Fillers: Accepts 60+/yr. Cartoons ($50), short humor **(NO PAYMENT)**.

+MANNA, 2966 W Westcove Dr., West Valley City UT 84119-5940. Christian. Roger A. Ball, ed. Features short, unrhymed poetry by beginning and intermediate writers. Biannual mag; 40 pgs; circ. 250. 100% freelance. Complete ms. **NO PAYMENT** but gives cash prizes of $3-7 for best poems in each issue; for 1st rts. Reports in 1 mo. Guidelines; copy $3.50.
Poetry: Free verse. Submit max. 5 poems.

+MARANATHA, P.O. Box 936, Newark NJ 07101. (201)589-3166. Fax: (201) 589-6212. Assemblies of God. Waldir DeOliveira, ed. General publication in Portuguese/English. Bimonthly newspaper; circ. 5,000. Free subscription. 100% freelance. Complete ms/cover letter; no phone query. **NO PAYMENT.** Not copyrighted. Articles 1 page (20/yr); fiction (5/yr). Accepts reprints. Guidelines/theme list; free copy.
Fillers: Accepts 25/yr. Anecdotes, cartoons, facts, games, ideas, jokes, newsbreaks, quizzes, quotes, short humor, and word puzzles.
Columns/Departments: This World, Happening This Way, Conflict, Evangelism; all 1/4 pg.
Tips: "Our publication is 90% in Portuguese language. All the material (English) suitable will be translated into Portuguese."

***MARIAN HELPERS BULLETIN**, Eden Hill, Stockbridge MA 01263. (413)298-3691. Catholic. Vincent Flynn, ed. Quarterly mag; circ 500,000. 20% freelance. Query/pub. clips or complete ms/cover letter. Pays .10/wd, on acceptance, for all, 1st, or reprint rts. Articles 500-900 wds; book reviews. Reports in 3 wks. Seasonal 6 mos ahead. Accepts reprints. Kill fee 30%. Free guidelines/copy.
Tips: "Also needs articles on mercy in action or devotion to Blessed Virgin Mary."

#MATURE LIVING, 127 9th Ave. N., Nashville TN 37234. (615)251-2274. Southern Baptist. Al Shackleford, ed. Christian leisure-reading for senior adults (60+) characterized by human interest and Christian warmth. Monthly mag; circ 350,000. 75% freelance. Complete ms. Pays .055/wd, on acceptance, for all or one-time rts. Articles (100/yr) & fiction (12/yr), 900-1,475. Reports in 1-3 mos. Seasonal 12-18 mos ahead. Serials. Guidelines; copy for 9x12 SAE/4 stamps.
Poetry: Buys 50/yr. Light verse, traditional; senior adult themes; any length; $5-24. Submit max. 5 poems.
Fillers: Buys 180/yr. Anecdotes, facts, short humor; to 50 wds; $5.
Tips: "Most open to human-interest stories. All articles and fiction must relate to senior adults."

MATURE YEARS, Box 801, Nashville TN 37202. (615)749-6292. Fax: (615)749-6512. United Methodist. Marvin W. Cropsey, ed. Inspiration, information, and leisure reading for persons of retirement age. Quarterly mag; 112 pgs; circ 77,000. Subscription $12. 40% freelance. Complete ms/cover letter; no phone query. Pays .04/wd; on acceptance; for one-time rts. Articles 400-2,000 wds (40/yr); fiction 1,500-1,800 wds

(4/yr). Reports in 3-8 wks. Seasonal 14 mos ahead. Accepts reprints. Guidelines; copy $2.50.
Special Needs: Articles on crafts & pets. Fiction on older adult situation.
Poetry: Buys 8/yr. Free verse, haiku, light verse, traditional; to 16 lines; .50-$1/line. Submit max. 6 poems.
Fillers: Buys 12/yr. Cartoons, facts, jokes, quizzes, short humor, word puzzles (religious only); $2-5.
Columns/Departments: Buys 16/yr. Health Hints, 1,000-1,800 wds; Modern Revelations (inspirational), 900-1,500 wds; Fragments of Life (true life inspirational), 400-800 wds.
** This periodical was #40 on the 1993 Top 50 Plus Christian Publishers list.

+THE MENNONITE, Box 347, Newton KS 67114. (316)283-5100. Fax: (316)283-0454. General conference Mennonite Church. Gordon Houser, ed. Practical articles on aspects of Christian living. Semimonthly magazine; 24 pgs; circ. 9,000. Subscription $22. 10% freelance. Complete ms/cover letter; phone query ok. Pays .05/wd, on publication, for one-time rts. Articles 600-1,000 wds (25/yr); book reviews, 300 wds ($10). Reports in 1-2 wks. Seasonal 3-4 mos ahead. Accepts simultaneous submissions and reprints. Guidelines; copy for $1 and 9x12 SAE/3 stamps.
Special Needs: Christmas-related articles that are different.
Poetry: Buys 5/yr. Avant-garde, free verse. Pays $10-30. Submit max. 5 poems.
Fillers: Buys 5/yr. Cartoons and prose, 50-200 wds. Pays $15-30.
Tips: "Send practical article with anecdotes, sidebars, graphs, photos, lists of e.g., advantages/disadvantages, ways to..., etc. Most open to book reviews of interest to Mennonites."

MENNONITE BRETHREN HERALD, 3-169 Riverton Ave., Winnipeg, MB R2L 2E5 Canada. (204)669-6575. Fax: (204)654-1865. Mennonite Brethren Conference of Canada. Ron Geddert, ed. Denominational; for spiritual nurture and awareness of our conference and the world around us. Biweekly mag; 32 pgs; circ 14,800. Subscription $44. 25% freelance. Complete ms/cover letter; no phone query. Pays .06/wd, on publication, for one-time & reprint rts. Articles 750-2,000 wds (20/yr); fiction to 750-1,500 wds (6/yr). Reports in 26 wks. Seasonal 3 mos ahead. Accepts simultaneous submissions & reprints. Guidelines; copy $1/9x12 SAE/.86 Canadian postage.
Poetry: Buys 10/yr. Avant-garde, free verse, traditional; any length; pays to $10.

+MENNONITE REPORTER, 3-312 Marsland Dr., Waterloo ON N2J 3Z1 Canada. Mennonite. Ron Rempel, ed. Denominational. Biweekly newspaper; 20 pgs; circ. 11,000. 15% freelance. Query. Pays .10/wd, on publication, for 1st rts. Articles 500-1,500 wds. Reports in 3-4 wks. Accepts simultaneous submissions. Guidelines; free copy.
Tips: "Most of our readers are Canadians; give us a Canadian perspective."

+MENNONITE WEEKLY REVIEW, Box 568, Newton KS 67114-0568. (316)283-3670. Mennonite. Robert Schrag, ed. Features religious and Mennonite news. Weekly newspaper; 12-16 pgs; circ. 11,000. 5% freelance. Complete ms/cover letter. Pays .05/wd, on publication, for one-time rts. Articles 400-500 wds. Reports in 1 mo. Accepts simultaneous submissions. No guidelines; copy $1/SAE/2 stamps.

#MESSAGE, Review and Herald Pub. Assn., 55 W. Oak Ridge Dr., Hagerstown MD 21740. (301)791-7000 x 2614, 2565. Fax: (301)791-7012. Seventh-day Adventist.

Stephen P. Ruff, ed. Blacks and other minorities who have an interest in current issues and are seeking a better lifestyle. Bimonthly mag; 32 pgs; circ 50,000. Subscription $11.95. 90% freelance. Complete ms/cover letter. Pays $80-150, on acceptance, for 1st rts. Articles (150/yr) 800-1,200 wds; parables; fiction for children, 400 wds. Reports in 1-2 mos. Seasonal 6 mos ahead. Accepts simultaneous submissions. Some kill fees. Guidelines/theme list; free copy.
Fillers: Quizzes/$25.
Tips: "Most open to feature articles on topics of current interest (drugs, sex, teen pregnancy, etc.); personality profiles on well-known Black Christian personalities."

MESSAGE OF THE OPEN BIBLE, 2020 Bell Ave., Des Moines IA 50315. (515)288-6761. Fax: (515)288-2510. Open Bible Standard Churches. Delores Winegar, ed. To inspire, inform, and educate the Open Bible family. Monthly (10x) mag; 20 pgs; circ 4,000. Subscription $6. 10% freelance. Complete ms/cover letter; phone query ok. **NO PAYMENT**. Not copyrighted. Articles 500-1,500 wds (10-15/yr). Reports in 2 wks. Seasonal 3 mos ahead. Accepts simultaneous submissions & reprints. Guidelines/theme list; copy for 9x12 SAE/3 stamps.
Special Needs: 1994 - Year of Ethnic Ministries.
Tips: "A well-written, 700-750 wd 1st-person testimony or article would catch my attention. Would like to occasionally see a humorous article (used to drive home a point)."

+MESSENGER, Box 18068, Covington KY 41018-0068. Catholic. Jean Bach, news ed. Diocese paper of Covington KY. Weekly newspaper; 24 pgs; circ. 16,000. 40% freelance. Query/clips. Pays $1.25/column inch, on publication, for 1st rts. Articles 500-800 wds. Reports in 1 wk. Seasonal 1 mo ahead. Accepts simultaneous submissions. Guidelines; free copy.

+THE MESSENGER, Box 1268, Steinbach MB R0A 2A0 Canada. (204)326-6401. Fax: (204)326-1613. Evangelical Mennonite Conference. Menno Hamm, ed. Denominational; informational and devotional. Biweekly mag; circ. 3,700. Subscription $6. 4% freelance. Query; no phone query. Pays $5-25, on publication, for one-time rts. Not copyrighted. Articles 300-1,600 wds (5/yr). Reports in 3-6 wks. Seasonal 2 mos ahead. Accepts simultaneous submissions & reprints. No guidelines; copy for 9x12 SAE/ $1.10 Canadian postage.
Poetry: Buys 5/yr. Light verse, traditional; pays $5-10. Submit max. 2 poems.

#THE MESSENGER, Box 1568, Dunn NC 28335-1568. (919)892-4161. Fax: (919)892-6876. Pentecostal Free Will Baptist. Rev. Don Sauls, ed. Denominational. Monthly (10X) mag; 16 pgs; circ 3,000. 15% freelance. Complete ms. Pays $2.50-10, on publication, for simultaneous rts. Not copyrighted. Articles 2-6 pgs (12/yr); fiction to 5.5 pgs (1-2/yr). Reports in 4 wks. Seasonal 6 mos ahead. Accepts reprints. Guidelines; copy .65.
Tips: "Accepting material only from members of local congregations."

#MESSENGER OF THE SACRED HEART, 661 Greenwood Ave., Toronto, ON M4J 4B3 Canada. (416)466-1195. Catholic/Apostleship of Prayer. Rev. F.J. Power, S.J., ed. Help for daily living on a spiritual level. Monthly (11X) mag; 32 pgs; circ 18,000. 40% freelance. Complete ms/cover letter; no phone query. Pays .04/wd, on publication, for 1st rts. Articles 800-1,500 wds (30/yr); fiction 800-1,500 wds (12/yr). Reports in 1 mo. Seasonal 5 mos ahead. Guidelines; copy $1.
Tips: "Most open to inspirational stories and articles."

***THE MESSENGER OF ST. ANTHONY**, (Padua, Italy), U.S. address: 1105 W. 8th St., Yankton SD 57078. Catholic. Rev. Ronald Mrozinski, U.S. ed. Published in 6 languages/international. Monthly mag; circ 200,000. 35% freelance. Complete ms. Pays $50-100, on publication, for one-time rts. Articles 700-1,800 wds (3/ yr). Reports in 3-5 wks. Seasonal 9 mos ahead. Accepts reprints. Copy for 9x12 SAE/3 stamps.
Poetry: Buys 1/yr. Free verse, traditional. Submit max. 3 poems.
Tips: "Send material for review."

#METHODIST HISTORY, Box 127, Madison NJ 07940. (201)822-2787. Fax: (201)408-3909. United Methodist. Charles Yrigoyen Jr., ed. History of the United Methodism and Methodist/Wesleyan churches. Quarterly journal; 64 pgs; circ 1,200. 100% freelance. Complete ms/with cover letter; phone query ok. **PAYS IN COPIES** for 1st rts. Historical articles (20/yr) to 5,000 wds. Reports in 3 mos. Guidelines; no copy.

MINISTRY TODAY, Box 9127, Fort Wayne IN 46899. (219)747-2027. Fax: (219)747-5331. Missionary Church. Robert Ransom, mng. ed. Denominational; for young adults, 20-45 years old. Bimonthly tabloid; 4 pgs; circ. 5,000. Est. 1992. 15% freelance. Complete ms/cover letter; no phone query. Pays .03-.04/wd; on publication; for 1st, one-time, reprint or simultaneous rts. Not copyrighted. Articles 200-800 wds (3-4/yr); fiction 200-1,600 wds (1-2/yr). Reports in 4-8 wks. Seasonal 4 mos ahead. Accepts simultaneous submissions & reprints. Guidelines; copy for 9x12 SAE/2 stamps.
Tips: "Limited due to being only 4 tabloid pages with six issues/yr. Family and parenting material is most selected category."

#THE MINNESOTA CHRONICLE (formerly **TWIN CITIES CHRISTIAN NEWSPAPER**), 1619 Portland Ave. S., Minneapolis MN 55404. (612)339-9579. Doug Trouten, ed. Local news and features of interest to the Christian community. Biweekly newspaper; 36 pgs; circ 7,500. Subscription $19.95. 10% freelance. Query; phone query ok. Pays .05/wd, after publication, for one-time rts. Articles 500-1,000 wds (50/yr); book reviews 500 wds. Reports in 3 mos. Seasonal 2 mos ahead. Accepts simultaneous query & reprints. Guidelines; copy $2.
Tips: "Not interested in anything without a Minnesota 'hook'. Inspiration section has room for two general personality features each issue; tell us about people and ministries we're not aware of."

#THE MIRACULOUS MEDAL, 475 E. Chelten Ave., Philadelphia PA 19144-5785. (215)848-1010. Fax: (215)848-1014. Catholic. Rev. John W. Gouldrick, ed. For Catholic adult readers. Quarterly mag; 30 pgs; circ 340,000. 40% freelance. Query or complete ms. Pays .02/wd & up, on acceptance, for 1st rts. Articles (10/yr); fiction 1,600-2,000 wds (6/yr). Reports in 3-6 mos. Seasonal 1 yr ahead. Accepts simultaneous submissions. Guidelines; copy for 6x9 SAE/2 stamps.
Poetry: Buys 10/yr. Traditional; to 20 lines; .50/line. Send any number. "Must have religious theme, preferably about the Blessed Virgin Mary."

+MONTANA CATHOLIC, P.O. Box 1729, Helena MT 59624-1729. (406)442-5820. Catholic. Gerald M. Korson, ed. Diocese paper for Helena, MT. Newspaper published 16X/yr; 20-24 pgs; circ. 8,300. 2% freelance. Query/clips or complete ms/cover letter. Pays varying rates, on publication, for one-time rts. Articles 400-1,000 wds. Reports in 1 mo. Accepts simultaneous submissions.
Poetry: To fit themes.

MOODY MAGAZINE, 820 N. LaSalle Blvd., Chicago IL 60089. (312)329-2164. Fax: (312)329-2149. Moody Bible Institute. Andrew Scheer, mng. ed. To encourage and equip evangelical Christians to think and live biblically. Monthly (11X) mag; 76 pgs; circ 142,000. Subscription $19.95. 75% freelance. Query only; no phone query. Pays $180-500 ($210-375 for fiction), or .15/wd (.20 for assigned);on acceptance, for 1st rts. Articles 1,200-2,500 wds (80/yr); fiction 1,400-2,500 wds (3-4/yr). Reports in 8-10 wks. Seasonal 9 mos ahead. Kill fee 50%. Guidelines; copy for 9x12 SASE/3 stamps.
Columns/Departments: Buys 22/yr. Just For Parents (practical), 1,500 wds; First Person (salvation testimonies - may be "as-told-to"), 800 wds; $150-225.
Tips: "Send a sharp, well-written query that includes a paragraph or two of your article. Include a working title, approx. length, slant, and intended take-away. We're looking for crisp narratives with well-developed scenes and anecdotes, not just generalizations and summaries." No articles on recovery or AIDS.
** This periodical was #19 on the 1993 Top 50 Plus Christian Publishers list.

MORNING GLORY, 314 Spruce St., Fergus Falls MN 56537. Lutheran. Rev. Arnold E. Windahl, ed. Godly living in light of the return of Christ. Quarterly mag; 12 pgs; circ 800. 100% freelance. Query or complete ms/cover letter: no phone query. **NO PAYMENT.** Accepts reprints. Articles to 300 wds. Reports in 4-6 wks. Seasonal 6 mos ahead. Accepts simultaneous submissions & reprints. Guidelines; copy for 9x12 SAE/3 stamps.
Poetry: Accepts 10/yr. Free verse, traditional; to 20 lines. Submit max. 2 poems.
Fillers: Accepts 40/yr. Anecdotes, facts, newsbreaks, prayers, quotes, short humor; to 50 wds.
Tips: "No liberal theology or photography."

***THE MOUNTAIN LAUREL**, Box 562, Wytheville VA 24382. (203)228-7282. A secular family publication that stresses old-fashioned high moral values and integrity. Susan Thigpen, ed. Quarterly tabloid; circ. 4,000. Variable freelance. Complete ms. **PAYS IN COPIES**, for one-time rts. Articles 750 wds (150/yr) & fiction to 1,000 wds. Reports in 1 month. Seasonal 3 mos ahead. Accepts simultaneous submissions & reprints. Copy for 9x12 SAE/3 stamps.
Tips: "We (only) publish stories about the Blue Ridge Mountains in every category—religious history would be one part of that."

+NATIONAL CATHOLIC REPORTER, 115 E. Armour Blvd., Kansas City MO 64141. (816)531-0538. Catholic. Thomas Fox, ed. Independent. Weekly (44X) newspaper; 44-48 pgs; circ. 48,000. Query/clips. Pays varying rates, on publication. Articles any length. Reports in 2 mos. Accepts simultaneous submissions.
Columns/Departments: Query with ideas for columns.

***NATIONAL CHRISTIAN REPORTER,** Box 660275, Dallas TX 75266. (214)630-6495. United Methodist. Diane Balay, assoc. ed. Weekly newspaper; circ 15,000. 5% freelance. Complete ms/cover letter; phone query ok. Pays .04/wd, on publication, for 1st rts. Articles 250-700 wds (12-15/yr). Reports in 3 wks. Seasonal 6 mos ahead. Accepts simultaneous submissions. Free guidelines/copy.
Poetry: Any type; 4-36 lines; $2.
Columns/Departments: Features, 500-700 wds; Arts & Entertainment (popular culture), 500-700 wds.
Tips: See United Methodist Reporter.

***NETWORK**, Box 320627, Birmingham AL 35232. (205)328-7112. Interdenominational. Dolores Milazzo Hicks, ed/pub. To encourage and nurture dialog, understanding, and unity in Jewish and Christian communities. Monthly tabloid; circ. 15,000. 50% freelance. Negotiable payment. Not copyrighted. Accepts simultaneous submissions. Articles and news.

#NEW COVENANT, 200 Noll Plaza, Huntington IN 46750. (313)668-4896. Fax: (313)668-6104. Catholic/Our Sunday Visitor. Jim Manney, ed. Serves readers involved in Catholic charismatic renewal. Monthly mag; 36 pgs; circ 42,000. 85% freelance. Query/clips or complete ms/cover letter; phone query ok. Pays .10/wd ($100-400); on acceptance; for 1st or one-time rts. Articles 750-3,000 wds (40/yr). Reports in 1 mo. Seasonal 5 mos ahead. Kill fee 50%. Accepts simultaneous submissions & reprints. Guidelines; copy for 9x12 SAE/5 stamps.
Tips: "Most open to testimonies. Speak from experience, not teaching. Be familiar with New Covenant's style so you can speak to our audience."
** This periodical was #28 on the 1993 Top 50 Plus Christian Publishers list.

#A NEW HEART, Box 4004, San Clemente CA 92674-4004. (714)496-7655. Interdenominational. Aubrey Beauchamp, ed. Evangelism among healthcare givers and their patients. Quarterly mag; 16 pgs; circ 5,000. 25-30% freelance. Complete ms or query/clips. **NO PAYMENT** for one-time rts. Not copyrighted. Articles (4-6/yr) 400-500 wds. Reports 3 mos before publication. Seasonal 3 mos ahead. Accepts simultaneous submissions & reprints. Guidelines/theme list; free copy.
Tips: "Most open to true stories, short, medically related, including caregivers."

+NEW OXFORD REVIEW, 1069 Kains Ave., Berkeley CA 94706. (510)526-5374. Catholic. Dale Vree, ed. Orthodox Catholic, but open to compatible evangelical views; highly educated audience. Monthly mag; circ. 14,000. Subscription $19. 50% freelance. Query or complete ms; phone query ok. **PAYS IN COPIES**, for all rts. Articles 750-3,750 wds (15/yr). Reports in 3-6 wks. Seasonal 4 mos ahead. No guidelines: copy for $3.50.
Tips: "Manuscripts must have intellectual depth."

NEWS NETWORK INTERNATIONAL NEWS SERVICE, Box 28001, Santa Ana CA 92799. (714)775-4900. Fax: (714)775-7315. CNNI Intl. Submit to exec. ed. A religious freedom news and information agency; provides wholesale news to retail news outlets. Monthly news service. Subscription $75. 65% freelance. Query; phone query ok. Call for quote on payment. Pays on publication, for 1st rts. Articles 600-1,800 wds. Reports in 2-3 wks. Seasonal 1 month ahead. Kill fee 50%. No guidelines; free copy.
Special Needs: Human rights issues.
Columns/Departments: Buys 24/yr. World Perspectives (world affairs and religious liberty issues); 750 wds.
Tips: "Most open to news (spot news/analysis) and features. Focus very specifically on issues/news along the topic of religious freedom. Not interested in reflective, how-to reports. We work with straight, hard news. We welcome internationally-based correspondents with access to developing trends and issues facing the church."

NEW THOUGHT JOURNAL, Box 700754, Tulsa OK 74170. Fax: (918)492-6237. Edward Wincentsen, ed. An inspirational magazine to stimulate thought. Bimonthly journal; circ. 600. Subscription $15. 75% freelance. Query or complete ms/cover letter; no phone query. **PAYS IN COPIES**, for 1st rts. Articles 1-3 pgs. Reports in 3 wks.

Accepts simultaneous submissions & reprints. Guidelines/theme list; copy $2.
Poetry: Avant-garde, free verse, haiku. Overstocked on poetry.
Columns/Departments: Open to column ideas and proposals.
Tips: "The best writers for us are the ones who already have a sincere interest in spirituality, truth, open-mindedness, philosophy and thought. Most all areas open for good writing."

#THE NORTH AMERICAN VOICE OF FATIMA, 1023 Swan Rd., Youngstown NY 14174. (716)754-7489. Catholic. Rev. Stephen McGee, C.R.S.P., ed. To foster Christian ideals with emphasis on Mary, Mother of God, and Mother of the Church. Bimonthly mag; 20 pgs; circ 3,000. 40% freelance. Query or complete ms. Pays .02/wd, on publication, for 1st rts. Not copyrighted. Articles & fiction 700 wds. Reports in 6 wks. Seasonal 6 mos ahead. Accepts simultaneous submissions. Free copy.

NORTHWEST CHRISTIAN JOURNAL, Box 59014, Renton WA 98058. (206)255-3552. Fax: (206)228-8749. Non-denominational/ evangelical. Tami Tedrow, ed. News with an evangelical perspective for NW Christians; local features & news stories. Monthly newspaper; circ. 27,000. Subscription $15. 10-20% freelance. Complete ms/cover letter; no phone query. Pays $5-35, on publication, for 1st, one-time & reprint rts. Articles 250-1,200 wds (24/yr). Reports in 6 wks. Seasonal 4 mos ahead. Accepts simultaneous submissions & reprints. Guidelines; copy $1.50.
Fillers: Buys 2-3/yr. Anecdotes, cartoons, jokes, short humor; 50-200 wds. Pays $5.
Tips: "This is a news publication, which means we look for stories that are timely and reflect what's happening in the Northwest. No devotional material; we have a news focus/news style and don't want the kind of articles a magazine would publish. Most open to news/interviews assigned by the editor."

OBLATES, 15 S. 59th St., Belleville IL 62223. (618)233-2238. Catholic. Priscilla Kurz, mss ed. To inspire, comfort, uplift, and motivate an older Catholic/Christian audience. Bimonthly mag; 20 pgs; circ 500,000. 25% freelance. Complete ms; no phone query. Pays $80, on acceptance, for 1st rts. Articles 500 wds (12/yr). Reports in 8 wks. Seasonal 6 mos ahead. Guidelines; copy for 7x10 SAE/2 stamps.
Poetry: Buys 12/yr. Traditional; 8-20 lines; pays $30.
Tips: "Need good, inspirational articles with a strong spiritual theme firmly grounded to a particular incident."

#THE OTHER SIDE, 300 W. Apsley, Philadelphia PA 19144-4285. (215)849-2178. Fax: (215)849-3755. Doug Davidson, mng. ed; Jennifer Wilkins, fiction ed. Peace, justice, and faith from a Christian perspective. Bimonthly mag; 64 pgs; circ 9,500. Subscription $29.50. 80% freelance. Complete ms/cover letter. Pays $25-300; on acceptance; for 1st or all rts. Articles (100/yr) 500-6,000 wds & fiction (6/yr, $25-250) 300-4,000 wds. Reports in 1-3 mos. Seasonal 6 mos ahead. Guidelines; copy $4.50.
Poetry: Rod Jellema, ed. Buys 15/yr. Traditional; 3-50 lines; $15. Submit max. 3 poems.

OUR FAMILY, Box 249, Battleford, SK S0M 0E0 Canada. (306)937-7771. Fax: (306)937-7644. Catholic. Nestor Gregoire, ed. All aspects of family life in the light of Christian faith. Monthly mag; 40 pgs; circ 10,000. Subscription $15.98. 50% freelance. Complete ms/no cover letter. Pays .07-.12/wd, on acceptance, for 1st rts. Articles 500-2,000 wds (75/yr). Reports in 4 wks. Seasonal 4 mos ahead. Accepts simultaneous submissions & reprints. Guidelines; copy $2.50.

Poetry: Buys 44/yr. Free verse, haiku, light verse, traditional; 2-25 lines; $1/line.
Fillers: Buys 40/yr. Anecdotes, cartoons, jokes, short humor; to 150 wds.
Tips: "Your SASE must have Canadian postage. We aim at the average reader. Our goal is to strengthen, encourage families as they strive to live their faith today. Articles need an experiential point of view with practical guidelines."
** This periodical was #42 on the 1993 Top 50 Plus Christian Publishers list.

OUR SUNDAY VISITOR, 200 Noll Plaza, Huntington IN 46750. (219)356-8400. Fax: (219)356-8472. Catholic. David Scott, ed. Vital news, spirituality for today's Catholic. Weekly newspaper; 24 pgs; circ 125,000. Subscription $36. 90% freelance. Query/pub. clips; no phone query. Pays $200, on acceptance, for 1st rts. Articles 1,200 wds (300/yr). Reports in 4-8 wks. Seasonal 3 mos ahead. Kill fee. Guidelines; no copy.
Columns/Departments: Buys 50/yr. Viewpoint (editorial/op-ed), 750 wds. Pays $100.
Tips: "Need familiarity with Catholic Church issues and with Catholic press—newspapers and magazines."
** This periodical was #43 on the 1993 Top 50 Plus Christian Publishers list.

PARENTING TREASURES, 400 West Blvd. South, Elkhart IN 46514. (219)522-1491. Fax: (219)522-0114. Lutheran-Missouri Synod. Deb Graf, administrative ed.; Toni Blackwood, articles ed. Encouraging parents of newborns through college age to apply Christian faith to parenting actions and attitudes. Quarterly mag; 24 pgs; circ 400. Subscription $8. 100% freelance. Complete ms/cover letter; no phone query. **PAYS 4 COPIES**, for one-time rts. Articles 500-1,500 wds (40-50/yr); book reviews 500 wds. Reports in 6-8 wks. Seasonal 6 mos ahead. Accepts simultaneous submissions & reprints. Guidelines/theme list; copy for 9x12 SAE/4 stamps or $1.
Special Needs: Discipline, self-esteem, sibling rivalry; see theme list.
Poetry: Uses 8/yr. Free verse, haiku, light verse, traditional; 4-20 lines. Submit max. 4 poems.
Fillers: Accepts 16/yr. Anecdotes, cartoons, facts, short humor; 50-500 wds.
Columns/Departments: Deb Graf. Uses 8/yr. A Time to Laugh (funny things kids say or do), 50-150 wds.
Tips: "As long as an article fits topic, there is a good chance we'll publish it (if well written). Avoid use of Christian jargon and judgmental attitudes. We address both the joys and frustrations of parenting."

PARENTS OF TEENAGERS, Box 850, Sisters OR 97759-0850. (503)549-8261. Fax: (503)549-0153. Good Family Magazines/D.C. Cook. Gloria Chisholm, ed. For youth workers and parents of teenagers. Bimonthly mag; 40 pgs; circ. 50,000. 75% freelance. Query/clips preferred or complete ms; no phone query. Pays .10-.15/wd, on acceptance, for 1st rts. Articles 1,000-1,800 wds (24/yr). Reports in 6-8 wks. Seasonal 6 mos ahead. Accepts simultaneous query & reprints. Kill fee. Guidelines/theme list; copy for 9x12 SAE/4 stamps.
Fillers: Buys 6/yr. Anecdotes, to 150 wds.
Columns/Departments: Buys 24/yr. Personal Help for Parents (practical tips), 300-500 wds, $25-40; Prize Kids (about positive teen examples) 250 wds, $25; Product Review, 200 wds, $25; Devotions, 500-800 wds, $75.
Tips: "Writer must be in touch with both parents and teenagers' needs and hurts and be able to write in a non-preachy, compassionate tone. Most open to 'Personal Help for Parents'."
** This periodical was #13 on the 1993 Top 50 Plus Christian Publishers list.

+THE PEGASUS REVIEW, P.O. Box 134, Flanders NJ 07836-0314. Art Bounds, ed. Theme oriented poetry/prose. Bimonthly journal; 10-12 pgs; circ. 100. 100% freelance. Complete ms/cover letter. **PAYS IN COPIES** for one-time rts. Fiction to 650 wds. Reports in 2 mos. Accepts simultaneous submissions. Guidelines/theme list; copy $2.
Poetry: Theme oriented, to 24 lines.

PENTECOSTAL EVANGEL, 1445 Boonville, Springfield MO 65802. (417)862-2781x4100. Fax: (417)862-0416. Assemblies of God. Richard Champion, ed. Denominational; pentecostal. Weekly mag; 32 pgs; circ 280,000. Subscription $14.95. 33% freelance. Complete ms/cover letter; no phone query. Pays .06/wd (1/2 for reprints), on acceptance, for 1st or reprint rts. Articles 400-1,200 wds (150/yr). Reports in 6-8 wks. Seasonal 4 mos ahead. Accepts reprints. Kill fee. Free guidelines/theme list/copy.
Tips: "A writer needs to know the doctrines and traditions of the Assemblies of God, tie into those, and have something significant to say. We need short, nonpreachy articles directed to the unconverted."

#PENTECOSTAL HOMELIFE, 8855 Dunn Rd., Hazelwood MO 63042-2299. (314)837-7300. United Pentecostal Church. Mark Christian, ed. To help couples and parents in everyday living. Monthly (7X) mag; circ 6,000. 90% freelance. Complete ms; no phone query. Pays $15-30, on publication, for reprint rts. Articles 400-800 wds or 1,000-1,500 wds (48/yr); fiction 1,000-1,500 wds. Reports in 1-2 mos. Seasonal 1 yr ahead. Accepts simultaneous submissions & reprints. Guidelines/theme list; copy for 9x12 SAE/2 stamps.
Tips: Prefers use of King James Version of the Bible.

THE PENTECOSTAL MESSENGER, Box 850, Joplin MO 64802. (417)624-7050. Fax: (417)624-7102. Pentecostal Church of God. Peggy Allen, mng. ed. Denominational. Monthly (11X) mag; 32 pgs; circ 8,000. Subscription $11. 25% freelance. Complete ms. Pays .015/wd; on publication; for one-time, simultaneous or reprint rts. Articles 900-2,400 wds (35/yr). Reports in 4 wks. Seasonal 4 mos ahead. Accepts simultaneous submissions & reprints. Guidelines; copy for 9x12 SAE/$1.05 postage.
Poetry: Buys a few/yr. Any type. Pays .25/line. Submit max. 5 poems.
Columns/Departments: Buys 2-3/yr. Ladies column (Diana Gee, ed), 900 wds; youth column (Eddie Vansell, ed), 900 wds.
Tips: "Submit articles that build faith in God and in His Word, that provide encouragement in dealing with the problems of life, that present instruction for growing the Kingdom of God through the church."

+THE PENTECOSTAL TESTIMONY. 6745 Century Ave., Mississauga ON L5N 6P7 Canada. (905)542-7400. Fax: (905)542-7313. The Pentecostal Assemblies of Canada. Rick Hiebert, ed. Focus is inspirational and Christian living; pentecostal slant. Monthly mag; circ. 27,000. Subscription $24. 30-40% freelance. Query/clips. Pays $20-100, on publication, for 1st or reprint rts. Articles 300-2,000 wds (30-40/yr); fiction 700-1,500 wds (12/yr); book reviews 200-300 wds, $20. Reports in 3-6 wks. Seasonal 4 mos ahead. Accepts reprints. No guidelines yet; copy $2/9x12 SAE/$1 Canadian postage.
Poetry: Buys 6/yr. Avant-garde, free verse; 8-20 lines. Pays $20-40. Submit max. 2 poems.
Fillers: Buys 12/yr. Cartoons, short humor; 100-300 wds. Pays $20-30.
Tips: "It helps if you're Pentecostal or at least informed and sympathetic to pentecostal issues. Most open to fiction and fillers."

#PERSPECTIVES ON SCIENCE AND CHRISTIAN FAITH, Box 668, Ipswich MA 01938. (508)356-5656. Fax: (508)356-4375. American Scientific Affiliation. Dr. J.W. Haas, Jr., ed. Scholarly articles and essays dealing with the interaction between the sciences and Christian faith. Quarterly journal; 72 pgs; circ 3,500. Subscription $25. Little freelance. Complete ms (3 copies). **PAYS 2 COPIES** for 1st or all rts. Articles to 9 pgs; book reviews 2-4 pgs. Reports within 1 month. Seasonal 3 mos ahead. Accepts serials. Guidelines; copy for 9x12 SAE/$1.05 postage.

+PLENTY GOOD ROOM, 1800 N. Hermitage Ave., Chicago IL 60622-1101. (312)486-8970. Catholic. J. Glen Murray, ed. Focuses on African-American worship within the church. Bimonthly mag; 12 pgs. Est. 1993. Query. Pays $25/pg, for all rts. Articles. Reports in 3 mos. Guidelines; free copy.

+THE PLOWMAN, 510 Athol St., Whitby ON L1N 5S4 Canada. (416)668-7803. Christian. Tony Scavetta, ed. Poetry (and prose) of social commentary. Quarterly tabloid; 56 pgs; circ. 1,500. 100% freelance. Query/clips or complete ms/cover letter. **NO PAYMENT**, but writers eligible for cash prizes. Buys all or one-time rts. Articles & fiction. Reports in 1 mo. Accepts simultaneous submissions. Guidelines; free copy.
Special Needs: Drama, plays & novellas.
Poetry: Submit max. 5 poems.
Tips: "We buy material from our subscribers first."

+POETRY FORUM SHORT STORIES, 5713 Larchmont Dr., Erie PA 16509. (819)866-2543. Fax: (819)866-2543. Interdenominational. Gunvor Skogsholm, ed. Poetry and prose that takes an honest look at the human condition. Quarterly journal; 24 pgs; circ. 500. 90% freelance. Complete ms/cover letter. **NO PAYMENT** for one-time rts. Articles 100-800 wds; fiction 800-3,000 wds. Reports in 1-3 mos. Accepts simultaneous submissions. Guidelines; copy $3.
Poetry: Inspirational; any type.

A POSITIVE APPROACH, A National Magazine for the Physically Challenged, Box 910, Millville NJ 08332. (609)451-4777. Fax: (609)451-6678. Pat Swart, ed. For the physically and mentally disabled and churches serving their needs. Quarterly mag; 64 pgs; circ 200,000. Subscription $15. 100% freelance. Query or complete ms/cover letter; phone query ok. **PAYS 10 COPIES**; for one-time or simultaneous rts. Articles 500-1,000 wds (120/yr). Reports in 2 wks. Seasonal 4 mos ahead. Accepts simultaneous submissions & reprints. Guidelines; copy $1.50 or a 9x12 SAE/8 stamps.
Tips: "We stress person first/disability last. We encourage people with newly incurred disabilities. Articles must pertain to a person with a disability or a church working with the problems of the disabled."

POWER FOR LIVING, Box 632, Glen Ellyn IL 60138. (708)668-6000. Fax: (708)668-3806. Don Crawford, ed. To help readers apply biblical truths; to demonstrate God's work in people's lives. Weekly take-home paper; 8 pgs; circ 250,000. Subscription $9.45. 67% freelance. complete ms/no cover letter; phone query ok. Pays .07-.10/wd (reprints .05-.07/wd), on acceptance, for one-time or reprint rts. Articles 300-1,500 wds (120/yr). Reports in 2-10 wks. Seasonal 1 yr ahead. Accepts reprints. Guidelines/copy for #10 SAE/1 stamp.
Poetry: Buys 10/yr. Free verse, light verse, traditional; 2-80 lines. Pays $25-50. Submit max. 6 poems.
Fillers: Buys 12/yr. Anecdotes, cartoons, quizzes, word puzzles; 75-250 wds; $25-50.

Tips: "Most open to vignettes, 450-1,000 wds; personal experiences, 400-1,500 wds. Writing must clearly demonstrate the Lord's work in individuals' lives. Signed releases required."

PRAIRIE MESSENGER, Box 190, Muenster, SK S0K 2Y0 Canada. (306)682-1770. Fax: (306)682-5285. Catholic. Submit to The Editor. Focuses on justice/family/native/women's/church (in the broad sense) issues. Weekly (46X) tabloid; circ 9,200. Subscription $21.50. 10% freelance. Complete ms/cover letter; no phone query. Pays to $40 ($2/column inch for news items), on publication, for 1st rts. Not copyrighted. Articles to 800 wds (40/yr). Reports in 4 wks. Seasonal 3 mos ahead. Guidelines; copy for .55/9x12 SAE/.84 Canadian/$1.05 U.S.
Special Needs: Ecumenism; social justice; native concerns.
Tips: "Comment/feature section is most open. Send topic of concern or interest to Prairie readership. It's difficult to break into our publication."

#THE PRAYER LINE, Box 55146, Seattle WA 98155-0146. (206)363-3586. Prayer By Mail Society. Dr. Jonathan E. Nisbet, ed. To proclaim the gospel and encourage believers in their prayer life. Quarterly newsletter; 4 pgs; circ 3,800. Subscription free. 50% freelance. Query. Pays variable amount, on publication, for 1st or one-time rts. Not copyrighted. Articles 1,500-2,000 wds (5-6/yr). Reports in 25 wks. Accepts reprints (in ms form). Guidelines; copy for #10 SAE/2 stamps.
Poetry: "We use very small poems as fillers."
Fillers: Cartoons, short humor.
Tips: "Would like articles on teaching how to pray. Tell us what you expect to be paid."

THE PRESBYTERIAN OUTLOOK, Box 85623, Richmond VA 23285-5623. (804)359-8442. Fax: (804)353-6369. Presbyterian Church (USA)/Independent. Robert H. Bullock Jr., ed. For ministers, members, and staff of the denomination. Weekly (43X) mag; 16 pgs; circ 11,500. Subscription $24.95. 5% freelance. Query; phone query ok. **NO PAYMENT**. Not copyrighted. Articles to 1,000 wds; book reviews 300 wds. Reports in 1-2 wks. Seasonal 2 mos ahead. Free guidelines/copy.
Columns/Departments: Forum (current issues before the church); 400 wds.
Tips: "Correspond with editor regarding current needs. Most material is commissioned; anything submitted should be of interest to Presbyterians."

PRESBYTERIAN RECORD, 50 Wynford Dr., North York, ON M3C 1J7 Canada. (416)444-1111 x307. Fax: (416)441-2825. Presbyterian Church in Canada. Rev. John Congram, ed. Denominational. Monthly (11X) mag; 52 pgs; circ 60,300. 50% freelance. Query or complete ms/cover letter; no phone query. Pays $25-75; on publication; for 1st, one-time, or simultaneous rts. Articles (50/yr) & fiction (2/yr-query), 1,500 wds; book & music reviews, 500 wds/no pay. Reports in 4-6 wks. Seasonal 6 mos ahead. Accepts simultaneous submissions & reprints. Guidelines; copy for 9x12 SAE/$1 Canadian postage or IRCs (no U.S. postage).
Poetry: Tom Dickey. Buys 5/yr. Free verse, haiku, traditional; any length; $25-50. Send any number.
Fillers: Buys 6/yr. Anecdotes, cartoons, facts, ideas, prose, short humor; to 200 wds; $15-25.
Columns/Departments: Buys 12/yr. Full Count (controversial issues), 750 wds; $35-50.

PRESBYTERIAN SURVEY, 100 Witherspoon St., Louisville KY 40202. (502) 569-5637. Presbyterian Church (USA). Catherine Cottingham, mng. ed. Denominational; not as conservative or evangelical as some. Monthly (10X) mag; 44 pgs; circ 105,000. Subscription $11. 70% freelance. Query or complete ms/cover letter; phone query ok. Pays to $50-200, on acceptance, for 1st or (some) reprint rts. Articles 800-1,800 wds/1,200-1,500 preferred (50/yr). Reports in 2-5 wks. Seasonal 4 mos ahead. Kill fee. Guidelines; free copy.
Poetry: Buys 8-10/yr. Free verse, light verse, traditional (if religious); 4-100 lines, prefers 25-30; $50. Submit max. 2 poems.
Fillers: Buys 5-6/yr. Anecdotes, cartoons, prose, short humor; to 100 wds; $10-50.
Tips: "Most open to feature articles or news articles about Presbyterian people and programs (600-800 wds, $50-75). Do not often use inspirational or testimony-type articles."
** This periodical was #21 on the 1993 Top 50 Plus Christian Publishers list.
Note: This magazine will cease publication July 1, 1994.

#PRISM (formerly **ESA ADVOCATE**), 10 Lancaster Ave., Wynnewood PA 19096. (215)645-9390. Fax: (215)649-3834. Evangelicals for Social Action. David R. Gushee, mng. ed. For Christians who are interested in the social and political dimensions of the gospel. Monthly newsletter; circ. 2,100. Subscription $25. 10-25% freelance. Query; phone query ok. Pays to $25 for one-time rts. Articles 600-2,300 wds (2-3/yr). Reports in 1-2 wks. Seasonal 2-3 mos ahead. Accepts simultaneous query & reprints. Free guidelines/copy.
Fillers: Buys 5-7/yr. Cartoons; $20.
Columns/Departments: Buys 2-3/yr. Perspective (analysis of public policy issue), 2,300 wds; Global Intercessors (Christian community outside U.S.), 1,400 wds; Here I Stand (editorial), 600 wds. Pays $25.
Tips: "Contact us and present your idea. Most open to editorials for Here I Stand—speak concisely, with passion, make your case."

#PROGRESS, Box 9609, Kansas City MO 64134. (816)763-7800. Stonecroft Ministries. Susan Collard, mng. ed. For women and their families who are involved in some aspect of Stonecroft Ministries. Bimonthly mag; 64 pgs; circ 30,000. 10% freelance. Query or complete ms/cover letter; no phone query. **PAYS IN COPIES**, for 1st rts. Not copyrighted. Feature articles 300-600 wds, personal testimonies 1,500-2,000 wds (20/yr). Reports in 1 mo. Seasonal 5 mos ahead. Accepts reprints. Guidelines; copy for 6x9 SASE.
Columns/Departments: Buys 12/yr. Ministry in the Marketplace (meeting spiritual needs of Christians in the work force); Coping Series (how God helped through crisis or stress); 1,000-1,500 wds.
Tips: "We do not include controversial or doctrinal issues about which Christian disagree. Material should be Christ-centered and biblically based."

#PSYCHOLOGY FOR LIVING, Narramore Christian Foundation, Box 5000, Rosemead CA 91770. (818)288-7000. Fax: (818)288-5333. Ruth E. Narramore, ed. A faith ministry devoted to preventing and solving human problems. Bimonthly mag; 20 pgs; circ 14,000. 40% freelance. Complete ms or query. **NO PAYMENT.** Accepts reprints. Articles 1,000-1,500 wds. Reports in 3 mos. Seasonal 6 mos ahead. Guidelines; free copy.

#PURPOSE, 616 Walnut Ave., Scottdale PA 15683. (412)887-8500. Fax: (412)887-3111. Mennonite Church. James E. Horsch, ed. Denominational. Weekly mag; 8 pgs; circ 17,100. Subscription $13.25. 95% freelance. Complete ms/cover letter; no phone query. Pays .03-.05/wd, on acceptance, for one-time rts. Articles & fiction 300-900 wds (175-200/yr). Reports in 2-4 mos. Seasonal 6 mos ahead. Accepts simultaneous submissions & reprints. Kill fee. Guidelines; copy for 6x9 SAE/2 stamps.
Poetry: Buys 150/yr. Free verse, light verse, traditional; 3-12 lines; $5-15.
Ethnic: Targets all ethnic groups involved in the Mennonite religion.
Tips: "Write in first person. All areas open."
** This periodical was #6 on the 1993 Top 50 Plus Christian Publishers list.

PURSUIT, 901 E. 78th St., Minneapolis MN 55420. (612)853-1750. Submit to Manuscript Ed. An evangelistic mag. written for the unchurched. Quarterly mag; 32 pgs; circ. 35,000. Subscription $8. 100% freelance. Complete ms/no cover letter; no phone query. Pays .07/wd (.03/wd for reprints), on publication, for one-time, reprint or simultaneous rts. Articles 800-2,000 wds (8/yr). Reports in 6 wks. Seasonal 6 months ahead. Accepts simultaneous submissions & reprints. Kill fee. Guidelines; copy $1/9x12 SAE.
Special Needs: Cartoons & humor articles related to themes.
Tips: "Articles should be written to the nonChristian. Write from a Christian worldview, but without religious language."

QUEEN OF ALL HEARTS, 26 S. Saxon Ave., Bay Shore NY 11706. (516)665-0726. Fax: (516)665-4349. Catholic. Submit to Editor. Focus is Mary, the Mother of Jesus. Bimonthly mag; 48 pgs; circ 4,500. Subscription $15. 100% freelance. Complete ms/cover letter; phone query ok. Pays $40-60, on publication, for one-time rts. Not copyrighted. Articles 750-2,500 wds (25/yr); fiction 1,500-2,500 wds (6/yr). Reports in 3-4 wks. Seasonal 6 mos ahead. Guidelines; copy for $3.
Special Needs: "Articles on Shrines of Our Lady and Saints devoted to Our Lady."
Poetry: Buys 10/yr. Free verse. **PAYS IN SUBSCRIPTION & COPIES**. Submit max. 2 poems.

#THE QUIET REVOLUTION, 1655 St. Charles St., Jackson MS 39209. (601)353-1635. Voice of Calvary Ministries. Cornelius J. Jones, ed. Interracial ministry to the poor; conservative/evangelical. Quarterly mag; 7 pgs; circ 3,000. 10% freelance. Query or complete ms/cover letter. **NO PAYMENT** for one-time rts. Articles 3-4 pgs. Reports in 1 mo. Accepts reprints. No guidelines; free copy.
Tips: "Most open to articles about ministering to the poor."

***RATIO: Essays in Christian Thought**, 126 W. Whiting Ave. #3, Fullerton CA 92632. (714)441-3454. Jeff Bearce, ed. For an academic/ intellectual audience anchored in the humanities; deals with theology, biblical studies, psychology, science, etc. Semiannual journal; circ. 100. Estab. 1992. 15-20% freelance. Query. **NO PAYMENT.** Not copyrighted. Articles, fiction & book reviews.

RELIGIOUS BROADCASTING, National Religious Broadcasters, 7839 Ashton Ave., Manassas VA 22110. (703)330-7000. Fax: (703)330-7100. Elizabeth Guetschow, features ed. Topics relate to Christian radio, television and satellite; promoting access excellence in religious broadcasting. Monthly mag; 56 pgs; circ 10,000. Subscription $24. 90% freelance. Complete ms/cover letter; phone query ok. **PAYS IN COPIES** for one-time rts. Articles 1,200-2,500 wds (55-60/yr); book reviews 300 wds. Reports in 4

wks. Seasonal 5 mos ahead. Accepts simultaneous submissions & reprints. Guidelines/theme list; free copy.
Special Needs: Electronic media; education. All articles must relate in some way to broadcasting.
Columns/Departments: Sarah E. Smith. Uses 100/yr. Trade Talk or Media Focus (news items/events in religious broadcasting), 300 wds; Socially Speaking (social issues), 1,000 wds.
Tips: "Our features dept. depends on freelance contributions. Must show clear tie to religious broadcasting—strong, well-written, and well-researched pieces."

RELIGIOUS EDUCATION, 15600 Mulholland Dr., Los Angeles CA 90077. (310)476-9777x326. Fax: (310)471-1278. Religious Education Assn. Hanan A. Alexander, ed-in-chief. A forum for interreligious dialogue for people concerned with issues surrounding religious education. Quarterly journal; circ. 3,000. Subscription/membership $40. 95% freelance. Complete ms/cover letter; no phone query. **PAYS 3 COPIES**, for all rts. Articles to 6,500 wds; book reviews, 250 wds. Reports in 2-3 wks. Guidelines; copy $2.
Special Needs: Religious, theological, values, moral education, spiritual formation or development, character development.
Columns/Departments: Insights from Scholarship; Insights from Practice; Forum (diverse points of view on topics of interest); and Critique (reviews of books, media and curricula).

ST. ANTHONY MESSENGER, 1615 Republic St., Cincinnati OH 45210. (513)241-5615. Fax: (513)241-0399. Catholic. Norman Perry, O.F.M., ed. National Catholic family magazine. Monthly mag; 59 pgs; circ 325,000. 50% freelance. Prefers query; complete ms/cover letter ok; phone query ok. Pays .14/wd, on acceptance, for 1st and (rarely) one-time rts. Articles to 3,000 wds (30-40/yr); fiction to 3,000 wds (12/yr); book reviews 500 wds/$25. Reports in 6-8 wks. Seasonal 6 mos ahead. Free guidelines/copy.
Poetry: Catherine Walsh. Buys 50/yr. All types; 3-25 lines; $2/line ($10 min.) Submit max. 5 poems.
Tips: "Any article accepted will employ a Catholic perspective and vocabulary and be in accord with Catholic teaching."

#ST. JOSEPH'S MESSENGER AND ADVOCATE OF THE BLIND, Box 288, Jersey City NJ 07303-0288. (201)798-4141. Catholic. Sister Ursula Maphet, CSJP, ed. For older Catholics interested in supporting ministry to the aged, young blind, and needy. Quarterly mag; 16 pgs; circ 20,000. 30% freelance. Complete ms; no phone query. Pays $5-25, on acceptance, for 1st rts. Articles 300-1,500 wds (24/yr); fiction (30/yr), 600-1,600 wds. Reports in 1 mo. Seasonal 3 mos ahead. Accepts simultaneous submissions & reprints. Guidelines; copy for 9x12 SAE/2 stamps.
Poetry: Buys 25/yr. Light verse, traditional; 10-30 lines; $5-20, on publication. Submit max. 10 poems.
Fillers: Buys 20/yr. Ideas, 50-100 wds; $5-10.
Tips: "Most open to fiction."

#ST. WILLIBRORD JOURNAL, Box 271751, Houston TX 77277-1751. Christ Catholic Church. Charles E. Harrison, ed. Strictly Catholic; concentrating on the unchurched. Quarterly journal; 40 pgs; circ 500. 5% freelance. Complete ms/cover letter. **NO PAYMENT** for one-time rts. Not copyrighted. Articles to 1,000 wds. Reports in 2 mos. Seasonal 6 mos ahead. No guidelines; copy $2.

Columns/Departments: Question Box; Q & A column on doctrinal and biblical questions.
Tips: "We will read anything if it is sincere and orthodox. Most open to what's happening in the Christian church: doctrinal changes, attitude adjustments, moral attitudes."

+SALT, 205 W. Monroe St., Chicago IL 60606. (312)236-7782. Christian. Mary Lynn Hendrickson, mng. ed. Focus is on social justice and prayer. Monthly (10X) mag; 32 pgs; circ. 11,000. 50% freelance. Query/clips or complete ms/cover letter. Pays $200-400, on acceptance, for 1st rts. Articles 1,000-3,500 wds. Reports in 1-2 mos. Kill fee. Guidelines; free copy.

SCP JOURNAL/SCP NEWSLETTER, (Spiritual Counterfeits Project), 2606 Dwight Way, Berkeley CA 94704. (510)540-0300. Fax: (510)540-1107. Tal Brooke, ed. Christian apologetics for the college educated. Quarterly; 55 pgs; circ 18,000. Subscription $25. 20-60% freelance. Query/clips; phone query encouraged. Pays $20-35/type-set pg, on publication, for negotiable rts. Articles 2,500-3,500 wds (5/yr); book reviews 1,500 wds. Reports in 1-3 mos. Accepts simultaneous query & reprints. Guidelines; copy $5.
Tips: "Talk to us first."

#SEEK, 8121 Hamilton Ave., Cincinnati OH 45231. (513)931-4050x365. Standard Publishing. Eileen H. Wilmoth, ed. For young & middle-age adults. Weekly take-home paper; 8 pgs; circ 45,000. 98% freelance. Complete ms/cover letter; no phone query. Pays .05/wd; on acceptance; for 1st rts, .025/wd for reprint rts. Articles 400-1,200 wds (150-200/yr); fiction 400-1,200 wds. Reports in 2-3 mos. Seasonal 1 yr ahead. Accepts reprints. Guidelines; copy for 6x9 SAE/2 stamps.
Fillers: Buys 50/yr. Ideas, jokes, short humor; $15.
** This periodical was #48 on the 1993 Top 50 Plus Christian Publishers list.

#SERVANT MAGAZINE, Box 4000, Three Hills AB T0M 2A0 Canada. (403)443-5511. Fax: (403)443-5540. Prairie Bible Institute. Phil Callaway, mng. ed. General Christian readership. Bimonthly mag; circ 17,500. Estab. 1989. Subscription free. 10% freelance. Query. Pays $20-50, on publication, for all rts. Articles 600-1,500 wds (2/yr); book reviews 150 wds/no pay. Seasonal 6 mos ahead. Accepts simultaneous submissions. Reports in 8 wks. Guidelines; copy $3.

THE SHANTYMAN, 6981 Millcreek Dr., Unit 17, Mississauga, Ontario L5N 6B8 Canada. (905)821-1175. Fax: (905)821-8400. Shantymen's Christian Assn. Submit to The Editor. Distributed by their missionaries in remote areas of Canada and northern U.S. as an evangelism tool. Bimonthly mag; 16 pgs; circ 15,000. Subscription $6. 80-90% freelance. Complete ms only/cover letter; no phone query. Pays $20-50 ($20-25 for fiction), on publication, for one-time or simultaneous rts. Articles 800-2,000 wds (24/yr); fiction 500-800 (3/yr); book reviews, 500 wds, pays in copies. Reports in 3-4 wks. Seasonal 6 mos ahead. Accepts simultaneous submissions & reprints. Guidelines; copy for #10 SAE/2 IRC's.
Special Needs: Testimonies and poetry in French. Children's fiction for 8-14 yr. olds.
Poetry: Accepts 6/yr. Free verse, light verse, traditional; any length. No payment. Submit max. 2 poems.
Fillers: Accepts 3-4 cartoons/yr. No payment.
Tips: "Write in a clear, concise, down-to-earth manner; avoid preachiness and the

temptation to moralize. Let your story speak for itself. Keep scripture references to a minimum. Most open to salvation testimonies. We prefer stories of less than 1,200 wds."

#SHARING, A Journal of Christian Healing, Box 1974, Snoqualmie WA 98065. (206)391-9510x512. Fax: (206)391-9512. Order of St. Luke the Physician. Rusty Rae, ed. For Christian interested in spiritual and physical healing. Monthly (10X) journal; 32 pgs; circ 10,000. 100% freelance. Complete ms/cover letter; phone query ok. **NO PAYMENT.** Not copyrighted. Articles 300-2,000 wds (100-150/yr); fiction 300-2,000 wds (few). Reports in 6 wks. Seasonal 2 mos ahead. Accepts simultaneous submissions & reprints. Guidelines; free copy.
Poetry: Accepts 20-30/yr. Any type or length.
Tips: "Most open to stories of personal healing."

SIGNS OF THE TIMES, Box 7000, Boise ID 83707. (208)465-2577. Seventh-day Adventist. Greg Brothers, ed. Biblical principles relevant to all of life; for general public. Monthly mag; 32 pgs; circ 270,000. 60% freelance. Complete ms/no cover letter or phone query. Pays $150-450; on acceptance; for 1st or reprint rts. Articles 750-2,500 wds (20/yr). Reports in 1-5 wks. Seasonal 8-9 mos ahead. Accepts reprints. Kill fee 50%. Free guidelines/copy.
Tips: "Looking for personality profiles."
** This periodical was #22 on the 1993 Top 50 Plus Christian Publishers list.

#SMART DADS (formerly **DADS ONLY)**, Box 270616, San Diego CA 92198. (619)487-7099. Paul Lewis, ed. Bimonthly fathering/parenting newsletter; circ 15,000. Little freelance. Pays $25, on publication, for 1st rts & some reprints. Articles 350-900 wds. Reports in 4 wks. Seasonal 4 mos ahead. Copy for 9x12 SASE.

SOCIAL JUSTICE REVIEW, 3835 Westminster Pl., St. Louis MO 63108. (314)371-1653. Catholic. Rev. John H. Miller, C.S.C., ed. For those interested in the social teaching of the Catholic Church. Bimonthly journal; 32 pgs; circ 1,250. 80% freelance. Complete ms/cover letter. Pays .02/wd, on publication, for 1st rts. Not copyrighted. Articles 800-3,000 wds (25/yr); book reviews 750 wds. Reports in 2 wks. Seasonal 3 mos ahead. Accepts simultaneous submissions & reprints. Guidelines; copy for 9x12 SAE/3 stamps.
Tips: "Fidelity to papal teaching & clarity & simplicity of style; thoughtful & thought-provoking writing."

#SPIRITUAL LIFE, 2131 Lincoln Rd. NE, Washington DC 20002-1199. (800)832-8489. Fax: (202)832-8967. Catholic. Steven Payne O.C.D., ed.; Br. Edward O'Donnell, O.C.D., book review ed. The contemporary experience of God (with special attention to the Carmelite tradition). Quarterly journal; 64 pgs; circ 12,000. 80-90% freelance. Complete ms/cover letter; no phone query. Pays $50 min. ($10/ms pg), on acceptance, for 1st rts. Articles 3,000-5,000 wds (20/yr); book reviews 3-5 pgs, $15. Reports in 6-8 wks. Seasonal 6 mos ahead. Accepts simultaneous submissions (if indicated). Guidelines; copy $1/7x10 SAE/4 stamps.
Tips: "No stories of personal healing, conversion, miracles, etc."

+SPOKANE & THE INLAND NORTHWEST CHRISTIAN NEWS, 222 W. Mission #118, Spokane WA 99201. (509)328-0820. Fax: (509)325-2025. Zeda Leonard, ed. To inform, motivate, and encourage evangelical Christians in the region. Monthly newspaper; circ. 42,000. Subscription $12.95. Accepts freelance. Query. Articles; book reviews. Not in topical listings.

SPORTS SPECTRUM, Box 3566, Grand Rapids MI 49501. (616)954-1276. Fax: (616)957-5741. Radio Bible Class. Dave Branon, mng. ed. An evangelistic tool that sports fans can use to witness to non-Christian friends. Monthly mag; 32 pgs; circ 52,000. Subscription $18.97. 40% freelance. Query/clips. Pays .15/wd, on acceptance, for 1st rts; no phone query. Articles 500-2,000 wds (25/yr). Reports in 3 wks. Kill fee. Guidelines; free copy.
Columns/Departments: Buys 10/yr. Leaderboard (Christian athletes serving others), 500 wds. Pays $20-40.
Tips: "Show an ability to interview professional athletes and create a well-written article from that interview. We also like ideas from freelancers."

#STANDARD, 6401 The Paseo, Kansas City MO 64131. (816)333-7000x2555. Fax: (816)333-4439. Nazarene. Everett Leadingham, ed. Examples of Christianity in everyday life for adults college-age through retirement. Weekly take-home paper; 8 pgs; circ. 165,000. Subscription $6.75. 95% freelance. Complete ms/cover letter; no phone query. Pays .035/wd (.02/wd for reprints), on acceptance, for one-time rts. Articles (400/yr) & fiction (30-50/yr); 300-1,700 wds. Reports in 2-3 mos. Seasonal year-round. Accepts simultaneous submissions & reprints (indicate). Guidelines/copy for #10 SAE/2 stamps.
Poetry: Buys 50/yr. Free verse, haiku, light verse, traditional; to 50 lines. Pays $5. Submit max. 5 poems.
Fillers: Buys 52/yr. Anecdotes, jokes, short humor; to 300 wds.
** This periodical was #3 on the 1993 Top 50 Plus Christian Publishers list.

STARLIGHT, 408 Pearson St., Wilson NC 27893-1850. (919)237-1591. Allen W. Harrell, pres. For real Christian women, their families and friends; content is personal rather than doctrinal. Quarterly digest; 64-70 pgs; circ 1,000. Subscription $15. 90% freelance. Complete ms only/cover letter; no phone query. **PAYS IN COPIES** for 1st rts. Articles & fiction, short. Reports in 1-4 mos. Seasonal 4 mos ahead. Guidelines; copy $4.
Special Needs: Material for Kid's Korner.
Poetry: Accepts 200/yr. Any type; shorter preferred. Submit max. 12 poems.
Fillers: Cartoons, prose, prayers, and short humor. Short.
Tips: "We cater to unpublished writers. Don't preach. Write as to your diary or God. Show, don't tell. We like brevity, clarity and memorableness."

+THE STAR OF ZION, 401 E. 2nd St., Charlotte NC 28231. (704)377-4329. African Methodist Episcopal Zion Church. Dr. Morgan W. Tann, ed. Ethnic publication; moderate; conservative. Weekly tabloid; 12-16 pgs; circ. 8,000. 10% freelance. Query or complete ms. **PAYS 5 COPIES**. Articles & fiction to 600 wds. Reports in 2 mos. No guidelines or copy.
Poetry: African-American themes.
Fillers: Cartoons and short humor.

SUNDAY DIGEST, 850 N. Grove, Elgin IL 60120. (708)741-0800. Fax: (708)741-0595. David C. Cook Publishing Co. Christine Dallman, ed. To encourage Christian adults (mostly women 30-55) of various denominations in their faith. Weekly take-home paper; 8 pgs; circ 100,000. Subscription $9.95. 60-70% freelance. Complete ms/brief

cover letter; no phone query. Pays $50-220, on acceptance, for 1st or reprint rts. Articles 400-1,800 wds (100/yr) & fiction (5-10/yr), 1,200-1,800 wds. Reports in 4-12 wks. Seasonal 15 mos ahead. Accepts reprints (less payment). Guidelines/theme list; copy for 6x9 SAE/2 stamps.
Special Needs: Articles on senior adult issues.
Poetry: Buys 10-15/yr. Free verse, light verse; 5-20 lines; $50-60. Submit max. 5 poems.
Fillers: Buys 30/yr. Anecdotes, ideas, quizzes; companion sidebars for articles; 100-300 wds; $30-50.
Columns/Departments: Buys 12/yr. Thinking Out Loud (anecdotal—from life—teaches a truth or lesson with a fresh slant), 400 wds. Pays $5-60.
Tips: "Avoid preachy tone, controversial or sensitive topics, or denominational differences. Include a cover letter and briefly introduce yourself. Keep trying; don't give up. We're most open to inspirational/personal experience stories."
** This periodical was #10 on the 1993 Top 50 Plus Christian Publishers list.

+TABLE TALK, 6401 The Paseo, Kansas City MO 64131. (816)333-7000. Fax: (816)333-4439. Nazarene. Bill Rolfe, ed., submit to Amy Loftin, edit. asst. A devotional guide for parents to use with their elementary age children. Quarterly mag; circ. 15,000. Subscription $6.75. 65% freelance. Complete ms/cover letter; no phone query. Pays .05/wd, on publication, for multi-use rts. Articles 750-1,500 wds. Reports in 4-6 wks. Seasonal 1 yr ahead. Accepts simultaneous submissions & reprints. Guidelines; no copy.
Fillers: Buys 5-10/yr. Cartoons, games, ideas, prose; 25-300 wds. Pays .05/wd.
Tips: "Our main need is parenting articles of all types, activity ideas for families, and occasional craft ideas." Margins should be 1.5" all around.

+THE TEACHING HOME, P.O. Box 20219, Portland OR 97220-0219. (503)253-9633. Fax: (503)253-7345. Christian. Sue Welch, ed. Help for parents involved in home schooling. Bimonthly mag; circ. 42,000. Subscription $15. Accepts freelance. Query. Not included in topical listings.

+THEMA, Box 74109, Metairie LA 70002. (504)568-6268. Virginia Howard, ed. Theme-oriented publication for those who like poetry and short stories. Journal published 3X/yr; circ. 300. Subscription $16. 100% freelance. Complete ms/cover letter specifying theme; no phone query. Pays $10-25, on acceptance, for 1st rts. Short stories 300-6,000 wds (34-44/yr). Reports in 1 week or more. Accepts simultaneous submissions & reprints. Guidelines/theme list; copy $5/6x9 SAE/$1.05 postage.
Poetry: Buys 24-32/yr. Any type, including experimental; to two pgs. Pays $10. Submit max. 3 poems.
Tips: "Let the theme roll around in your head and give it time to develop. Don't try to fit a previously-written piece to the theme—write something to fit."

***THIRTEEN POETRY MAGAZINE**, Box 392, Portlandville NY 13834. (607)286-7500. Independent. Ken Stone, ed. Specializes in 13-line poetry describing the beauty of this life. Quarterly mag; circ 350. 100% freelance. Query. **PAYS IN COPIES**, for 1st rts. Not copyrighted. Book reviews to 2 pgs. Reports in 2 wks. Guidelines; copy $2.50.
Poetry: Accepts 200/yr. Free verse; 13 lines ONLY.
Tips: "Send poetry that has something to say besides using up words and space."

#TIME OF SINGING, A Magazine of Christian Poetry, Box 211, Cambridge Springs PA 16403. (814)382-5911. Charles A. Waugaman, ed. We try to appeal to all poets and lovers of poetry. Journal published 3 times/yr; 40 pgs; circ 300. 95% freelance. Complete ms. **PAYS 1 COPY** for 1st rts (may reprint). Poetry only. Reports in 3 mos. Seasonal 3 mos ahead. Accepts simultaneous submissions & some reprints. Guidelines/theme list; copy $4 (current) or $2.50 (back issue).
Poetry: Buys 120-150/yr. Free verse, haiku, light verse (rarely), traditional; any length (prefers short). Submit max. 5 poems.
Contest: Sponsors an annual poetry contest (send SASE for rules).
Tips: "We only review books by our poets."

+TODAY'S BETTER LIFE, 5301 Wisconsin Ave. NW #620, Washington DC 20015. (202)364-8000. Fax: (202)364-8910. Nondenominational. Laura Barker, mng. ed. For Christian adults seeking spiritual, physical and emotional health. Quarterly mag; 112 pgs; circ. 100,000. Subscription $19.80. Est. 1991. 25% freelance. Query; no phone query. Pays .10/wd, on acceptance, for 1st rts. Articles 1,500-2,000 wds. Reports in 8-10 wks. Seasonal 8-10 mos ahead. Guidelines; no copy.
Tips: "Read back issues."

TODAY'S SINGLE, 1933 W. Wisconsin Ave., Milwaukee WI 53233. (414)344-7300. National Association of Christian Singles. John M. Fisco, Jr., pub.; submit to Rita Bertolas, ed. For Christian single adults: never married, divorced, widowed, or separated. Quarterly newspaper; circ 10,000. 85% freelance. Complete ms. **PAYS IN COPIES**, for one-time or reprint rts. Not copyrighted. Articles 300-2,000 wds (12-15/yr). Reports in 2-4 wks. Seasonal 4-5 mos ahead. Guidelines; free copy.
Poetry: Buys 15-20/yr. Free verse, haiku; 4-30 lines. Submit max. 5 poems.
Tips: Deadlines: January 1, April 1, July 1, and October 1.

#TOGETHER, Rt 2 Box 656, Grottoes VA 24441. (703)249-3900. Fax: (703)249-3177. Shalom Foundation, Inc. Eugene K. Souder, ed. Sent in a mass mailing to every home in a community by a sponsoring congregation. Bimonthly tabloid; 8 pgs; circ. 200,000. 50% freelance. Complete ms; no cover letter or phone query. Pays $25-50, on publication, for all, 1st, one-time, reprint or simultaneous rts. Articles 200-1,000 wds (20/yr). Reports in 1 mo. Seasonal 4-6 mos ahead. Accepts simultaneous submissions & reprints. Guidelines; copy for 9x12 SAE/2 stamps.
Fillers: Buys 5/yr. Cartoons, quizzes, quotes, word puzzles, word-search puzzles; 25-100 wds. pays $10-25.
Tips: "Need first-person stories of faith in Christ—how I became a believer."

+TOTAL HEALTH, 6001 Topanga Cyn Blvd. #300, Woodland Hills CA 91367. (818)887-6484. Fax: (818)887-7960. Robert L. Smith, ed. A family health magazine. Bimonthly mag; 70 pgs; circ. 90,000. Subscription $13. 70% freelance. Pays $50-75, on publication, for all rts. Articles 1,200-1,600 wds. Seasonal 3 mos ahead. Accepts simultaneous submissions. Complete ms/cover letter; no phone query. No guidelines; copy $1/9x12 SAE/$1.21.
Columns/Departments: Contemporary Herbal, 1,000 wds. Pays $50.
Tips: "Most open to inspirational and healing articles."

#TOUCHSTONE, A Journal of Ecumenical Orthodoxy, 3300 W. Cullom Ave., Chicago IL 60618. (312)267-1440. Fellowship of St. James. James Kushiner, ed. News and opinion devoted to a thoughtful appreciation of orthodox Christian faith. Quarterly

journal; 44 pgs; circ. 1,500. 25% freelance. Query/clips or complete ms/cover letter. **PAYS IN COPIES** for one-time rts. Articles 2,500 wds; little fiction 3,000 wds. Reports in 3 mos. Accepts simultaneous submissions. Guidelines; copy for 10x13 SAE/7 stamps.
Poetry: Accepts.
Fillers: Cartoons.

***TREE OF LIFE**, 363 Oakland Ave SE, Atlanta GA 30312-2232. (404)624-1442. Eastern Orthodox Christianity. Sr. Gail Cramer, ed. Bimonthly mag; circ 550. Query or complete ms. **PAYS IN COPIES**. Articles 900 wds or more; fillers 150 wds; book reviews 600-900 wds. Seasonal 4 mos ahead. Guidelines; copy for 9x12 SAE/4 stamps. **Tips:** "Whatever religious articles we print should not contradict Orthodox theology and, hopefully, would enhance it."

#THE UNITED CHURCH OBSERVER, 84 Pleasant Blvd., Toronto, ON M4T 2Z8 Canada. (416)960-8500. Fax: (416)960-8477. United Church of Canada. Muriel Duncan, ed. Denominational news. Monthly newsmag; 52 pgs; circ 185,000. 20% freelance. Query or complete ms/cover letter; no phone query. Pays varying rates, on publication, for 1st or all rts. News articles to 1,200 wds (8/yr). Reports in 12-16 wks. Seasonal 3 mos ahead. Accepts reprints. Kill fee. Guidelines; copy $2.
Fillers: Buys 24 cartoons/yr; $20.
Columns/Departments: Buys 12/yr. Front Page (church-related opinion pc.), 800 wds.

#UNITED METHODIST REPORTER, Box 660275, Dallas TX 75266. (214)630-6495. Fax:(214)630-0079. United Methodist. John A. Lovelace, ed; submit to Diane Balay, assoc. ed. Denominational. Weekly newspaper; 4-6 pgs; circ 450,000. 5% freelance. Complete ms/cover letter; phone query ok. Pays .04/wd, on publication, for 1st rts. Articles 200-700 wds (12-15/yr). Reports in 2-3 wks. Seasonal 6 mos ahead. Accepts simultaneous submissions. Free guidelines/copy.
Poetry: Buys 12-15/yr. Any type; 4-16 lines; $2 on acceptance. Submit max. 5 poems.
Columns/Departments: Buys 6-8/yr. Features (people who put faith into practice), 500-700 wds; Arts & Entertainment (how faith reflected in modern culture), 500-700 wds.
Tips: "Avoid being too doctrinal. We like to hear about the 'unsung heroes/heroines' found in every church. Holiday pcs. based on fact and accompanied by good art is a good way to break in."

+U.S. CATHOLIC, 205 W. Monroe St., Chicago IL 60606. (312)236-7782. (312)236-7230. Catholic. Patrick Tuohy, mng. ed. Monthly mag; 52 pgs; circ 50,000. Subscription $18. 95% freelance. Query. Pays $250-500 (fiction $300-400), on acceptance, for 1st rts. Articles 2,500-4,000 wds; fiction 2,500-3,500 wds. Reports in 2 wks. Guidelines; free copy.
Columns/Departments: (See guidelines first.) Sounding Board, 1,100-1,300 wds; pays $250. Gray Matter and A Modest Proposal, 1,100-1,800 wds; pays $250. Actual grace (humor), to 1,300 wds' pays $250.
Tips: "All articles should have an explicit religious dimension, enabling readers to see the interaction between their faith and the issue at hand."

VIBRANT LIFE, 55 W. Oak Ridge Dr., Hagerstown MD 21740. (301)791-7000. Fax: (301)791-7012. Seventh-day Adventist. Barbara Jackson-Hall, ed-in-chief. Total health

publication (physical, mental and spiritual); plus articles on family and marriage improvement; ages 25-45. Bimonthly mag; 32 pgs; circ 50,000. Subscription $12.97. 50% freelance. Query; no phone query. Pays $50-200, on acceptance, for 1st, reprint or world rts. Articles 500-2,000 wds. Reports in 3-4 wks. Seasonal 6 mos ahead. Accepts reprints. Guidelines; copy $1/9x12 SAE/3 stamps.
Special Needs: Cancer prevention, alcoholism, men's health issues, and mental health (fear, depression, and how the brain works).
Tips: "Health articles should be current, include quotes from experts in the field, medically accurate, and written for the lay public. They should not have a heavy Christian slant, but where appropriate mention God and prayer." Most open to feature articles.

***VISION**, 3150 Bear St., Costa Mesa CA 92626. (714)754-1400. Full Gospel Business Men's Fellowship. Dr. Jerry Jensen, ed.; submit to Kay Mangio. For members only (men). Quarterly mag; circ 70,000. Query. Pays .10/wd, on acceptance, for various rts. Articles. Reports in 6 wks. Seasonal 6 mos ahead. Kill fee. Accepts reprints. Free guidelines/copy.
Columns/Departments: 1st Person Male Testimonies (spirit-filled); 2,200 wds.
Tips: "We accept material on an assignment basis, which we delegate."

***VISION**, 8855 Dunn Rd., Hazelwood MO 63042. (314)837-7304. United Pentecostal Church. R.M. Davis, ed. Denominational. Weekly take-home paper. 90% freelance. Complete ms. Pays $8-25, on publication, for all rts. Articles 800-1,800 wds (to 120/yr); fiction 1,200-1,800 wds (up to 120/yr). Seasonal 9 months ahead. Accepts simultaneous submissions & reprints. Guidelines; free copy.
Poetry: Buys 30/yr. Pays $3-12.
Tips: "Most open to good stories and articles for a traditional, fundamental, conservative church."

VISTA, Box 50434, Indianapolis IN 46250. (317)576-8144. Fax: (317)577-4397. The Wesleyan Church. Kelly Trennepohl, ed. Reinforces Sunday school lessons; addresses family concerns and current issues. Weekly take-home paper; 8 pgs; circ 80,000. Subscription $7.80. 60% freelance. Complete ms/cover letter; no phone query. Pays .02-.04/wd; on acceptance; for 1st, simultaneous or reprint rts. Articles 500-700 wds (175/yr); fiction (for senior adults only) 1,000-1,200 wds (15/yr). Reports in 4-10 wks. Seasonal 10 mos ahead. Accepts simultaneous submissions & reprints. Guidelines; copy for 9x12 SAE/2 stamps.
Special Needs: Articles on Sunday school and small groups; discipleship, commitment and family. Nothing on AIDS, abortion, or homosexuality.
Fillers: Buys 25/yr. Cartoons, facts. Pays $25-50 for cartoons; $5-25 for facts.
Columns/Departments: Family, 500-625 wds; Prime Time (fiction/testimonials for seniors), 1,000-1,200 wds; Perspective (insights, opinions, editorials), 500-625 wds; Discipleship (help for discipleship groups), 500-625 wds; Commitment (help for individuals in Christian walk), 500-625 wds.
Tips: "Request guidelines and follow them closely. All departments are open."

VITAL CHRISTIANITY, Box 2499, Anderson IN 46018. (317)644-7721. Fax: (317)622-9511. Church of God. Kathleen Buehler, mng. ed. Denominational. Monthly mag; 64 pgs; circ 22,000. Subscription $19.95. 20% freelance. Complete ms/cover letter. Pays by the pg., on acceptance, for 1st or one-time rts. Articles 850-1,200 wds (20-30/yr), fiction 1,200-1,500 wds (10-12/yr). Reports in 4-6 wks. Seasonal 4 mos ahead. Some

reprints. Guidelines/theme list; copy for 9x12 SAE/7 stamps.
Note: "We will be making possible major changes in the magazine that will begin to be implemented sometime in 1994."

VOICE, 3150 Bear St., Costa Mesa CA 92626. (714)754-1400. Fax: (714)557-9916. Full Gospel Business Men's Fellowship Intl. Submit to The Editor. An evangelistic outreach to the business men in the marketplace. Monthly mag; 40 pgs; circ 250,000. Subscription $7.95. 20% freelance. Query/clips or complete ms/cover letter; no phone query. Pays .10/wd, within 60 days, for 1st & reprint rts. First Person Male Testimonies (spirit-filled) 1,000-2,500 wds (15/yr). Reports in 6-8 wks. Guidelines; copy for 6x9 SAE/2 stamps.

THE VOICE, 2917 S. Holly St., Seattle WA 98108. A & A Evangelistic Assn. Rev. Daniel Ashcraft, ed. Christ-honoring poetry and devotionals for street people and everyday folks. Weekly newsletter. 100% freelance. Complete ms/cover letter; no phone query. **PAYS IN COPIES** for all rts. Devotionals 25-50 wds. Reports in 4 wks. Seasonal 6 mos ahead. Accepts simultaneous submissions & reprints. Guidelines/theme list; copy for $1/#10 SAE/1 stamp.
Poetry: Accepts 50/yr. Free verse, traditional; 5-10 lines. Submit max. 5 poems.
Tips: "Poetry and devotionals only. Avoid preaching."

WAR CRY, 615 Slaters Ln., Alexandria VA 22313. (703)684-5500. Fax: (703)684-5539. The Salvation Army. Colonel Henry Gariepy, ed-in-chief; submit to Lesa Davis, ms ed. Pluralistic readership reaching all socioeconomic strata and including distribution in institutions. Biweekly mag; 24 pgs; circ 500,000+. Subscription $7.50. 10% freelance. Complete ms/brief cover letter. Pays .15/wd, on acceptance, for 1st rts. Articles 500-1,200 wds (30/yr). Reports in 6 wks. Seasonal 6 mos ahead. Guidelines; free copy.
Special Needs: "Looking for 'Year of the Family' features."
Tips: "Most open to current issues, devotional, personality profiles, holiday, and issue-related material."
** This periodical was #50 on the 1993 Top 50 Plus Christian Publishers list.

WESLEYAN ADVOCATE, Box 50434, Indianapolis IN 46250-0434. (317)576-8156. Fax: (317)577-4397. The Wesleyan Church. Jerry Brecheisen, mng. ed. A full salvation family mag; denominational. Monthly mag; 36 pgs; circ 20,000. Subscription $12.50. 50% freelance. Complete ms/cover letter; phone query ok. Pays $10-40 for assigned, $5-25 for unsolicited, .01-.02/wd for reprints; on publication; for 1st rts. Not copyrighted. Articles 700 (some longer) wds (75/yr). Reports in 2 wks. Seasonal 6 mos ahead. Guidelines; copy for $2.
Poetry: Buys 30/yr. Free verse or traditional; pays $5-10. Send max. 6 poems.
Fillers: Prose, 100-300 wds. Pays $2-6.
Columns/Departments: Personal Experiences, 700 wds; Ministry Tips, 600 wds. Pays $10.

+THE WITNESS, 1249 Washington Blvd., Detroit MI 48226-1868. (313)962-2650. Fax: (313)962-1012. Episcopal Church Publishing Co. Jeanie Wylie-Kellermann, ed. Seeks to examine society in light of faith and conscience, with clear advocacy for the poor, women, people of color, and other minority groups. Monthly (10X) mag; 28 pgs; circ. 3,000. Subscription $20. 10% freelance. Complete ms/cover letter (on first submission). Pays $50-150, on publication, for all rts. Articles to 1,500 wds (10/yr).

Reports in 6 wks on accepted mss, no response to unaccepted. Accepts simultaneous submissions. Kill fee. Guidelines; copy for 10x13 SAE/4 stamps.
Poetry: Buys 4/yr. Pays $30.
Tips: "We like brevity, wit and humor. Anything long-winded gets dismissed quickly—so it's worth editing your material ruthlessly before you send it."

#WORLD, Box 2330, Asheville NC 28802. (704)253-8063. Fax: (704)253-1556. God's World Publications Inc. Joel Belz, ed. Current news from a Christian perspective. Weekly newspaper; circ 29,000. Subscription $27.95. 20% freelance. Query; phone query ok. Pays .15/wd, on publication, for 1st rts. Articles 400-1,000 wds. Reports in 1 month. Guidelines/copy.

CHILDREN'S MARKETS

+BIBLE TIME 4's AND 5's, P.O. Box 632, Glen Ellyn IL 60138. (708)668-6000. Scripture Press. Joanne Willanger, ed. To help 4 and 5 year olds apply Scripture to everyday life; correlates with curriculum. Weekly take-home paper; 4 pgs. 50-70% freelance. Complete ms/cover letter. Pays $20-30, on acceptance, for all rts. Articles & fiction 220-225 wds. Reports in 4-6 wks. Guidelines; copy for #10 SAE/1 stamp.

BREAD FOR GOD'S CHILDREN, Box 1017, Arcadia FL 33821. (813)494-6214. Fax: (813)993-0154. Interdenominational. Judith M. Gibbs, ed. A family magazine for serious Christians who are concerned about their children or grandchildren (ages 6-18). Monthly mag; 28 pgs; circ 10,000. Free subscription. 20% freelance. Complete ms/no cover letter; phone query ok. Pays $10-40; on publication; for 1st rts. Not copyrighted. Articles 500-900 wds (3-4/yr); fiction & true stories 600-900 wds for 4-10 yrs, 900-1,500 wds for youth, (10/yr). Reports in 3 wks to several mos. Accepts simultaneous submissions & reprints. Guidelines; 3 copies for 9x12 SAE/5 stamps.
Tips: "Read the sample copies. We want stories that teach without being overly sweet and without preaching or moralizing. Must be true to life with believable characters."

#CHILDREN'S STORY SCRIPTS, Baymax Productions, 2219 W. Olive Ave., Ste. 130, Burbank CA 91506. (818)563-6105. Fax: (818)563-2968. Deedra Bebout, ed. Readers Theater-style scripts for children kindergarten - 8th gd; publishes 5-15/yr. Estab. 1990. Scripts 1,300-2,000 wds (or whatever it takes to tell the story), (20-30/yr). Complete ms. Buys all rts to stories in script form. Pays graduated royalty based on sales. Reports in 1 month. Accepts simultaneous submissions. Guidelines/sample for #10 SAE/2 stamps.
Tips: "Keep in mind that these are not theatrical scripts. Readers are stationary and scripts are read, not memorized."

CLUBHOUSE, Box 15, Berrien Springs MI 49103. (616)471-9009. Fax: (616)471-4661. Non-denominational. Elaine Trumbo, ed. To help young people (9-14) feel good about themselves. Monthly mag; 32 pgs; circ. 8,000. Subscription $5. 80% freelance. Complete ms/no cover letter; no phone query. Pays $10-12 ($25-35 for fiction), 6 mos after acceptance, for any rights. Articles 200-600 wds (10/yr); fiction 600-1,200 wds (30/yr). Reports in 8 wks. Submit all material in March & April. Accepts simultaneous submissions & reprints. Guidelines; copy for 6x9 SAE/3 stamps.
Poetry: Boys 5/yr. Free verse, light verse, traditional; to 12 lines. Pays $12. Submit max. 6 poems.
Fillers: Buys 8-12/yr. Cartoons, games, word puzzles; 50-100 wds. Pays $12.

COUNSELOR, Box 632, Glen Ellyn IL 60138. (708)668-6000. Fax: (708)668-3806. Scripture Press. Janice K. Burton, ed. Presents the way spiritual truths in the weekly lesson can be worked out in everyday life—a correlated teaching tool for 8-12 yr olds.

Weekly take-home paper; 4 pgs. Subscription $9.45. 50% freelance. Complete ms/cover letter; phone query ok. Pays .05-.10/wd; on acceptance; for all, 1st, one-time, or reprint rts. Articles (10-15/yr) 300-600 wds; fiction/true stories (10-15/yr), 900-1,100 wds. Reports in 4-6 wks. Seasonal 9 mos ahead. Reluctantly accepts reprints. Guidelines/theme list; copy for #10 SAE/1 stamp.
Fillers: Buys 15-20/yr. Cartoons, facts, games, jokes, quizzes, word puzzles; 100-200 wds; $8-20.
Tips: "No topic is of interest unless it is addressed to need of 8-12 yr. olds, and primarily dealt with in story form. Prefer true stories (always indicate if story is true)."
** This periodical was #35 on the 1993 Top 50 Plus Christian Publishers list.

CRUSADER, Box 7259, Grand Rapids MI 49510. (616)241-5616. Fax: (616)241-5558. Calvinist Cadet Corp. G. Richard Broene, ed. To show cadets and their friends, boys 9-14, how God is at work in their lives and in the world around them. Mag published 7X/yr; 24 pgs; circ 13,000. Subscription $7.70. 50% freelance. Complete ms/cover letter; no phone query. Pays .02-.05/wd; on acceptance; for 1st, one-time, or reprint rts. Articles (6/yr) & fiction (12/yr), 800-1,500 wds. Reports in 4-6 wks. Seasonal 10 mos ahead. Accepts simultaneous submissions & reprints. Guidelines/theme list; copy for 9x12 SAE/3 stamps.
Fillers: Robert DeJonge. Buys 7-10/yr. Cartoons, games, word puzzles; 20-200 wds; $5-20.
Tips: "Fiction tied to themes; request new theme list after January of each year."

DISCOVERIES, 6401 The Paseo, Kansas City MO 64131. (816)333-7000x2250. Fax: (816)333-4439. Nazarene/Wesleyan Churches. Latta Jo Knapp, ed. For 8-10 yr olds, emphasizing Christian values and holy living. Weekly take-home paper; 4 pgs; circ 30,000. 100% freelance. Complete ms/cover letter; phone query ok. Pays .05/wd, on production, for multi-use rts. Articles (2/yr) & fiction (52/yr), 500-700 wds. Reports in 4 wks. Seasonal 5 mos ahead. Accepts reprints. Guidelines/theme list; copy for #10 SAE/1 stamp.
Fillers: Buys 52 word puzzles/yr; $15.
Tips: " Follow guidelines and theme list. Most open to stories and puzzles; tips with age-level appropriateness."

FAITH 'N STUFF, 16 E 34th St., New York NY 10016. (212)251-8100. Fax: (212)684-0679. Guideposts Inc. Mary Lou Carney, ed; Wallis Metts, articles editor; Lurlene McDaniel, fiction editor. For kids 7-12 yrs. Bimonthly mag; 132 pgs; circ 100,000+. Subscription $15.95. 25% freelance. Query; complete ms for fiction; no phone query. Pays $200-300 for features, $125-300 for fiction; on acceptance; for all rts. Features 1,500 wds., secondary features 1,000 wds., one-pagers 500 wds., kid profiles 200-500 wds. (10/yr); fiction 1,400-1,600 wds (6-8/yr). Reports in 4-8 wks. Seasonal 6 mos ahead. Accepts simultaneous submissions. Kill fee. Guidelines; copy $3.25.
Special Needs: Historical fiction, fun trivia, news leads involving kids.
Poetry: Buys 4/yr. Light verse. Pays $10-50.
Fillers: Buys 12-14/yr. Facts, games, newsbreaks, quizzes & word puzzles; 25-300 wds. Negotiable rates. "No Bible word searches or unscrambling disciples names."
Tips: "Think like a kid. Most open to fiction (no biblical fiction); seasonal pieces. Looking for mini-mysteries."

FOCUS ON THE FAMILY CLUBHOUSE, 8605 Explorer Dr., Colorado Springs CO 80920. (719)531-3400. Fax: (719)531-3499. Focus on the Family. Linda Piepenbrink, ed. For children 8-12 yrs in Christian homes. Monthly mag; 16 pgs; circ 100,000. Subscription $12. 25% freelance. Complete ms/cover letter; no phone query. Pays $75-425 for assigned (less for unsolicited), on acceptance, for 1st rts. Articles 200-1,000 wds (4/yr); fiction 500-1,400 wds (20/yr). Reports in 2-4 wks. Seasonal 6-8 mos ahead. Kill fee. Guidelines; copy for 10x13 SAE/2 stamps.
Poetry: Buys 1/yr. Free verse, light verse, traditional: to 1/2 pg; $5-25.
Fillers: Buys 2/yr. Games, party ideas, quizzes, short humor, word puzzles.
Tips: "Most open to children's fiction."

FOCUS ON THE FAMILY CLUBHOUSE JR. Lisa Brock, ed. For ages 4-8 yrs. Circ 90,000. Articles 200-1,000 wds; fiction 250-650 (beginning reader) or 500-1,100 (read-aloud). See **FOCUS ON THE FAMILY CLUBHOUSE** for additional details.
Tips: "Most open to short, non-preachy fiction, beginning reader stories, and read-to-me."

#GOD'S WORLD TODAY (formerly **IT'S GOD'S WORLD**), P.O. Box 2330, Asheville NC 28803. (704)253-8063. Christian. Norman W. Bomer, ed. Current events, published in 5 editions, for kindergarten through jr. high students, mostly in Christian & home schools. Weekly newsletter (during school yr); 8 pgs; circ. 260,000. 15-20% freelance. Complete ms/cover letter. Pays $75, on acceptance, for one-time rts. Articles 600-900 wds. Reports in 2 mos. Guidelines; free copy.
Tips: "Keep vocabulary simple. Must present a distinctly Christian world view without being moralistic."

***GOOD NEWS**, 1884 Randolph St., St. Paul MN 55105. Catholic. Joan Mitchell CSJ, ed. For 2nd and 3rd graders. Not in topical listings.

GUIDE MAGAZINE, 55 W. Oak Ridge Dr., Hagerstown MD 21740. (301)796-3373. Fax: (301)791-7012. Seventh-day Adventist. Jeannette Johnson, ed. A Christian journal for 10-14 yr olds, presenting true stories relevant to their needs. Weekly mag; 32 pgs; circ 40,000. Subscription $34.97/yr. 20% freelance. Complete ms/no cover letter; phone query ok. Pays .04-.05/wd, on acceptance, for 1st, one-time, simultaneous or reprint rts. Articles or fiction/true stories 500-1,200 wds (100/yr). Reports in 2 wks. Seasonal 6 mos ahead. Accepts simultaneous submissions & reprints (no tear sheets). Kill fee. Guidelines/story schedule; copy for #10 SAE/2 stamps.
Special Needs: "Always need adventure and humor stories—full of mystery, action, discovery, dialogue."
Fillers: Buys 40/yr. Various; to 300 wds; $15-30.
** This periodical was #29 on the 1993 Top 50 Plus Christian Publishers list.

#HIGH ADVENTURE, 1445 Boonville Ave., Springfield MO 65802-1894. (417)862-2781x4178. Fax: (417)862-8558. Assemblies of God. Marshall Bruner, ed. For the Royal Rangers (boys), 5-17 yrs; slanted toward teens. Quarterly mag; 16 pgs; circ 60,000. Subscription $1.75. 75% freelance. Query or complete ms/cover letter; no

phone query. Pays .03/wd; on acceptance; for one-time or reprint rts. Articles 800-1,200 wds (25-30/yr); fiction (25-50/yr) 500-1,000 wds; book reviews 100-200 wds. Reports in 1-2 mos. Seasonal 6 mos ahead. Accepts simultaneous submissions & reprints. Guidelines/theme list; copy for 9x12 SAE/3 stamps.
Fillers: Buys 30/yr. Cartoons, jokes, short humor; 50 wds. Pays $2-20.

JUNIOR TRAILS, 1445 Boonville Ave., Springfield MO 65802. (417)862-2781. Assemblies of God. Sinda S. Zinn, ed. Teaching of Christian principles through fiction stories about children (10-12 yrs). Weekly take-home paper; 8 pgs; circ 65,000. 98% freelance. Complete ms. Pays .02-.03/wd, on acceptance; for one-times. Not copyrighted. Articles 300-1,000 wds (50/yr); fiction 1,200-1,800 wds (50-60/yr). Reports in 2-4 wks. Seasonal 12-15 mos ahead. Accepts simultaneous submissions & reprints. Guidelines; copy for #10 SAE/1 stamp.
Poetry: Buys 20-30/yr. Light verse, traditional; $5.
Fillers: Cartoons, short humor, word puzzles; 300-500 wds. Pays .02-.03/wd.
Tips: "Most open to fiction based on relevant problem for today's kids. Submit well-written, believable stories in which character overcomes real problem based on Bible principles."
** This periodical was #25 on the 1993 Top 50 Plus Christian Publishers list.

KEYS FOR KIDS, Box 1, Grand Rapids MI 49501. (616)451-2009. Hazel Marett, ed. A daily devotional booklet for children (8-14) or for family devotions. Bimonthly booklet; 96 pgs; circ 40,000. 100% freelance. Complete ms; no cover letter; phone query ok. Pays $12-16; on acceptance; for 1st or simultaneous rts. Not copyrighted. Devotionals (includes short fiction story) 400-450 wds (50/yr). Reports in 2-3 wks. Seasonal 4-5 mos ahead. Accepts simultaneous submissions & reprints. Guidelines; copy for 6x9 SAE/$1.05 postage.
** This periodical was #39 on the 1993 Top 50 Plus Christian Publishers list.

LISTEN, 6401 The Paseo, Kansas City MO 64131. (816)333-7000x2359. Fax: (816)333-4439. Nazarene/Wesleyan. Janet R. Reeves, ed.; fiction, poetry & fillers to Amy Lofton, ed. asst. Weekly activity/story paper for 5 yr olds & early 6's; 4 pgs; circ 47,500. Subscription $8. 50% freelance. Complete ms/cover letter; no phone query. Pays .05/wd, on publication, for all or multi-use rts. No articles; contemporary fiction & true stories 300-400 wds. Reports in 4-6 wks. No seasonal. Kill fee. Guidelines/theme list; copy for 9x12 SAE/2 stamps
Special Needs: Exciting, age-appropriate activities for back page.
Poetry: Buys 30-40/yr. Traditional; 4-12 lines; $3 or .05/wd.
Fillers: Buys 30/yr. Games, ideas/activities (age-appropriate); pays $5-15.
Tips: "We need activities and poems that apply to our themes."

MY FRIEND, The Catholic Magazine for Kids. 50 St. Paul's Ave., Boston MA 02130. Sr. Anne Joan Flanagan, mng. ed. Christian values and basic Catholic doctrines for children, ages 6-12. Monthly (10X) mag; 32 pgs; circ 12,000. Subscription $10. 70% freelance. Complete ms/no cover letter; no phone query. Pays $20-150, on acceptance, for all rts. Articles 150-500 wds (10/yr) & fiction (30+/yr), 150-500 wds. Reports in 3-8 wks. Seasonal 1 yr ahead. Occasionally accepts reprints. Kill fee.

Guidelines/theme list; copy $1/9x12 SAE/4 stamps.
Special Needs: Media literacy articles and activities; articles on saints.
Fillers: Accepts 50/yr. Facts, jokes, party ideas; 10-100 wds. Pays $5-25.
Columns/Departments: Buys up to 20/yr. Wonders of God's Creation, 500 wds; Bible Facts (filler), 100 wds. Pays $20-75.
Tips: "Most open to fiction."

#NATURE FRIEND MAGAZINE, 22777 State Rd. 119, Goshen IN 46526. (219)534-2245. Pilgrim Publishers/fundamental creationist. Stanley K. Brubaker, ed. For children's (ages 4-14); about God's wonderful world of nature and wildlife. Monthly mag; 36 pgs; circ 10,000. 40% freelance. Complete ms/cover letter. Pays .05/wd, on publication, for one-time rts. Articles 300-1,500 wds; true stories 300-1200 wds. Reports in 3-6 mos. Seasonal 3 mos ahead. Accepts simultaneous submissions & reprints. Guidelines and 2 copies for $5/6x9 SAE.
Poetry: Buys 10-20/yr. Traditional; $8-20. Submit max. 5 poems.
Tips: "Don't bother submitting to us unless you have seen our guidelines and a sample copy. We are very conservative in our approach."

ON THE LINE, 616 Walnut Ave., Scottdale PA 15683. (412)887-8500. Fax: (412)887-3111. Mennonite. Mary Meyer, ed. Reinforces Christian values in 10-14 yr olds. Weekly take-home paper; 8 pgs; circ 8,500. Subscription $17.10. 80% freelance. Complete ms only/no cover letter; no phone query. Pays .02-.05/wd ($20-60 for fiction), on acceptance, for one-time, reprint, or simultaneous rts. Articles 300-500 wds (35/yr); fiction 1,000-1,500 wds (55/yr). Reports in 4 wks. Seasonal 4-6 mos ahead. Accepts simultaneous submissions & reprints. Guidelines; copy for 7x10 SAE/2 stamps.
Poetry: Buys 10-15/yr. Free verse, haiku, light verse; 3-12 lines; $10-30. Submit any number.
Fillers: Buys 100+/yr. Cartoons, games, jokes, quizzes, word puzzles; 50-300 wds; $10-15.
Ethnic: Targets all ethnic groups involved in the Mennonite religion.
Tips: "Every section open. Please put yourself in a kid's shoes. How do they think? How do they talk? Don't be moralistic or sound like a pious preacher."
** This periodical was #30 on the 1993 Top 50 Plus Christian Publishers list.

#OUR LITTLE FRIEND, Box 7000, Boise ID 83707. (208)465-2500. Seventh-day Adventist. Aileen Andres Sox, ed. For theme and comments, see **Primary Treasure**, below. Weekly take-home paper for 1-6 yr olds (through 1st grade); 8 pgs; circ 45,000-50,000. 75% freelance. Complete ms/cover letter. Pays $25-50; on acceptance; for one-time or reprint rts. True stories 650-900 wds. Reports in 3 mos. Seasonal 7 mos ahead. Accepts simultaneous submissions & reprints. Guidelines/theme list; copy for 9x12 SAE/2 stamps.
Poetry: 12 lines; $1/line.
Tips: "Stories need to be crafted for this age reader in plot and vocabulary."

#PARTNERS, Christian Light Publications, Inc., Box 1126, Harrisonburg VA 22801. (703)434-0768. Mennonite. Crystal Shank, ed. For 9-14 yr olds. Weekly take-home

paper; 4 pgs; circ 5,300. 100% freelance. Complete ms. Pays to .02/wd (1st rts), .03/wd (all rts), or .015/wd (reprints); on acceptance; for all, 1st or reprint rts. Articles 200-800 wds; fiction & true stories to 1,600 wds (or 1,600 wd installments);short fiction to 400 wds. Reports in 4-6 wks. Seasonal 6-7 mos ahead. Accepts simultaneous submissions; serials 2-13 parts (2-4 parts preferred). Guidelines/theme list; copy for 9x12 SAE/2 stamps.
Poetry: Traditional; any length; .20-.30/line. Small batches.
Fillers: Quizzes, word puzzles. Payment varies.

POCKETS, Box 189, Nashville TN 37202. (615)340-7333. Fax: (615)340-7006. United Methodist. Janet R. McNish, ed; submit to Lynn W. Gilliam, assoc. ed. Devotional magazine for children (6-11 yrs). Monthly (11X) mag; 32 pgs; circ 82,000. 50% freelance. Complete ms/no cover letter; no phone query. Pays .12/wd, on acceptance, for 1st rts. Articles 200-1,600 wds (1/yr) & fiction to 1,600 wds (22/yr). Reports in 4 wks. Seasonal 1 yr ahead. Accepts reprints. Kill fee 50%. Guidelines/theme list (new each fall); copy for 8x10 SAE/$1.05 postage.
Poetry: Buys 22/yr. Free verse, haiku, light verse, traditional; to 24 lines; $25 or $2/line. Submit max. 7 poems.
Fillers: Buys 22/yr. Games, ideas, riddles, word puzzles. Pays $25.
Columns/Departments: Buys 20/yr. Peacemakers at Work (examples of environmental peace/justice), 250-600 wds; Kids Cook; Pocketsful of Love (ways to show love), 250 wds; Pocketful of Prayer (prayer activities), 250-600 wds; Someone You'd Like to Know (children doing unusual things).
Contest: Fiction-writing contest, deadline 10/1 every yr. Prize $1,000. Length 1,000-1,700 wds. Send to Pockets Fiction Contest at above address.
Tips: "Get our theme list first. Most open to fiction, Someone You'd Like to Know and Pocketsful of Love."
** This periodical was #20 on the 1993 Top 50 Plus Christian Publishers list.

POWER AND LIGHT, 6401 The Paseo, Kansas City MO 64131. (816)333-7000. Nazarene. Beula Postelwait, ed. For pre-teens, 11-12 year old. Weekly take-home paper; 8 pgs; circ 39,000. Subscription $6.40. Estab. 1993. 40% freelance. Query (complete ms for fiction); no phone query. Pays .05/wd, on publication, for multiple use rts (writer retains right to reuse). Articles 400-700 wds (10/yr); fiction 550-800 wds (36/yr). Reports in 12 wks. Seasonal 1 yr ahead. Accepts simultaneous submissions & reprints. Kill fee 5%. Guidelines/theme list; copy for 5x7 SAE/2 stamps.
Fillers: Buys 52/yr. Cartoons, games, jokes, quizzes, word puzzles; to 200 wds. Pays $15.
Tips: "Most open to fiction, puzzles and cartoons. Request a theme list. Write about preteens from a preteen perspective."

PRIMARY DAYS, Box 632, Glen Ellyn IL 60138. (708)668-6000. Scripture Press. Janice K. Burton, ed. To show children, 6-8, how Bible truths can work out in everyday life. Weekly take-home paper; 4 pgs. 50% freelance. Complete ms/cover letter; phone query ok. Pays .05-.10/wd; on acceptance; for all, 1st, one-time or reprint rts. Articles (10-15/yr) 300-600 wds; fiction (10-15/yr), 900-1100 wds. Reports in 4-6 wks. Seasonal 9 mos ahead. Reluctantly accepts reprints. Guidelines/theme list/copy for

#10 SAE/1 stamp.
Fillers: Buys 15-20/yr. Quizzes, word puzzles; 30-100 wds; $7-10.

***PRIMARY PAL,** 1300 N. Meacham, Schaumburg IL 60173. Regular Baptist. Joan Alexander, ed. For ages 6-8; fundamental, conservative. Weekly take-home paper. Query. Pays on acceptance, for all or 1st rts. Articles 100-500 wds; fiction 500-1,000 wds. Reports in 2-8 wks. Seasonal 1 yr ahead. Guidelines; copy for #10 SAE/2 stamps.
Fillers: Games, word puzzles.
Tips: "Most open to fiction, features, puzzles, activities, and devotionals."

#PRIMARY TREASURE, Box 7000, Boise ID 83707. (208)465-2500. Seventh-day Adventist. Aileen Andres Sox, ed. To teach children Christian belief, values, and practice. God's loving us and our loving Him makes a difference in every facet of life, from how we think and act to how we feel. Weekly take-home paper for 7-9 yr olds (2nd-4th grades); 16 pgs; circ 35,000. 75% freelance. Complete ms/cover letter. Pays $25-50; on acceptance; for one-time or reprint rts. True stories to 1,200 wds; articles used rarely (query). Reports in 3 mos. Seasonal 7 mos ahead. Accepts simultaneous submissions; serials to 10 parts (query). Guidelines; copy for 9x12 SAE/2 stamps.
Poetry: 12 lines; $1/line.
Tips: "We need positive, lively stories about children facing modern problems and making good choices. We always need strong stories about boys. We need a spiritual element that frequently is missing from submissions. We're changing; refer to guidelines."

***PROMISE**, 1884 Randolph St., St. Paul MN 55105. Catholic. Joan Mitchell CSJ, ed. For preschoolers. Not in topical listings.

R-A-D-A-R, 8121 Hamilton Ave., Cincinnati OH 45231. (513)931-4050. Standard Publishing. Margaret Williams, ed. For 8-11 yr olds; correlates with Sunday-school lesson themes. Weekly take-home paper; 12 pgs; circ 110,000. 75-80% freelance. Complete ms; no cover letter or phone query. Pays .03-.07/wd, on acceptance, for 1st or one-time rts. Articles (50/yr) & fiction (150-175/yr), 500-1,000 wds. Reports in 4-8 wks. Seasonal 1 yr ahead. Accepts reprints. Guidelines/theme list/copy for SAE/1 stamp.
Poetry: Buys 25-40/yr. Light verse, traditional; $.40-.50/line.
Fillers: Buys 20/yr. Cartoons ($17.50), jokes, short humor.
Tips: "We mail theme list automatically if you request to be put on list. Keep abreast with the times and where kids are. The issues they are dealing with in personal lives should be a part of their reading."
** This periodical was #8 on the 1993 Top 50 Plus Christian Publishers list.

+SKIPPING STONES, A Multicultural Children's Quarterly, P.O. Box 3939, Eugene OR 97403. (503)342-4956. Not specifically Christian. Arun Narayan Toke', ed. Multi-cultural and multi-ethnic writings for children 7-14. Quarterly mag; 36 pgs; circ. 2,500. 80% freelance. Query or complete ms/cover letter. **PAYS 2 COPIES** for 1st rts. Articles and fiction (usually by children), 500-700 wds. Reports in 3-5 mos. Accepts

simultaneous submissions. Guidelines; copy $4/9x12 SAE/4 stamps. Themes are listed in sample copy.
Poetry: By children only.

STORY FRIENDS, 616 Walnut St., Scottdale PA 15683. (412)887-8500. Fax: (412)887-3111. Mennonite. Marjorie Waybill, ed. For children 4-9 yrs. Weekly take-home paper; 4 pgs; circ 8,000. Subscription $12.35. 50% freelance. Complete ms only; no cover letter or phone query. Pays .03-.05/wd, on acceptance, for one-time, and reprint rts. Not copyrighted. Fiction (30/yr), 500-800 wds. Reports in 3 wks. Seasonal 6 mos ahead. Accepts simultaneous submissions & reprints. Guidelines; copy for 9x12 SAE/2 stamps.
Poetry: Buys 10/yr. Light verse, traditional; to 8 lines (unless story poem); pays $10.
Ethnic: Targets all ethnic groups involved in the Mennonite religion.
Tips: "I like stories that relate to kids and everyday joys and sorrows. No stories about children needing money, or not enough money for toys, etc. Write about things kids experience in real life."
** This periodical was #49 on the 1993 Top 50 Plus Christian Publishers list.

#STORY MATES, Christian Light Publications, Inc., Box 1126, Harrisonburg VA 22801. (703)434-0768. Mennonite. Miriam Shank, ed. For 4-8 yr olds. Weekly take-home paper; 4 pgs; circ 5,200. 95% freelance. Complete ms/cover letter. Pays .02/wd (1st rts), .03/wd (all rts), .015/wd (reprint rts); on acceptance; for all, 1st, & reprint rts. Realistic or true stories to 800 wds. Reports in 2 mos. Seasonal 7 mos ahead. Guidelines/theme list; copy for 6x9 SAE/2 stamps.
Poetry: Traditional, any length.
Fillers: Quizzes, word puzzles. "Need fillers that correlate with theme list."
Tips: "No fantasy, child evangelism, Valentine's Day, Halloween, secular Christmas or Easter material." Very conservative.

TOGETHER TIME, 6401 The Paseo, Kansas City MO 64131. (816)333-7000. Fax: (816)333-4439. Church of the Nazarene. Lynda Boardman, ed. For 3-4 yr olds and parents. Weekly take-home paper; 4 pgs; circ. 7,500. 50% freelance. Complete ms; no cover letter; phone query ok. Pays .05/wd, on production, for all rts. Reports in 10-12 wks. Seasonal 6 mos ahead. Accepts simultaneous submissions & reprints. Kill fee. Not in topical listings. Guidelines/theme list; free copy.
Poetry: Buys 52/yr. Traditional; 4-8 lines; .25/line, $2 minimum. Submit max. 5 poems.
Fillers: Buys 52/yr. Activities; 25-100 wds; $10.
Tips: "We accept freelance for poems and activities only. Keep poems simple and activities easy—3-4-year-old level."

#TOUCH, Box 7259, Grand Rapids MI 49510. (616)241-5616. Fax: (616)241-5558. Para-church (Christian Reformed, Reformed, and Presbyterian). Joanne Ilbrink, ed. To show girls, ages 7-14, that God is at work in their lives and the world around them. Monthly (10X) mag; 24 pgs; circ 15,500. Subscription $9. 75% freelance. Complete ms/cover letter. Pays .025-.05/wd; on acceptance; for 1st & reprint rts. Articles 400-800 wds (36-45/yr); fiction (50/yr) 900-1,200 wds. Reports in 2 mos. Seasonal 9 mos ahead. Accepts simultaneous submissions & reprints. Guidelines/theme list; copy for

9x12 SAE/3 stamps.
Poetry: Buys 20-30/yr. Free verse, Haiku, light verse, traditional; 4-30 lines; $15-20. Poetry fits themes. Submit max. 2 poems.
Fillers: Buys 30/yr. Party ideas, quizzes, word puzzles; 20-200 wds; $15-20.
Tips: "No pat solutions to stories; have believable conflict and solution. Send for biannual updates (February & June) and write to the themes."

***VENTURE**, 1884 Randolph Ave., St. Paul MN 55105. (612)690-7010. Editorial Development Associates. Submit to mng. ed. Connects young people's real life experiences—successes and conflicts in family, neighborhood, classroom, playground—with the Sunday gospels; for intermediate-age children. Weekly take-home paper; circ 140,000. 40% freelance. Query. Pays $75-125, on publication, for all rts. Articles (6-8/yr) & fiction (8-10/yr), 800-900 wds. Reports in 2-8 wks. Seasonal 4-6 mos ahead. Accepts simultaneous query. Guidelines; copy $1.85.
Tips: "We want realistic fiction and nonfiction that raises current ethical religious questions and conflicts in multi-racial settings, believable and detailed, to which intermediate-age children can relate.

WONDER TIME, 6401 The Paseo, Kansas City MO 64131. (816)333-7000. Fax: (816)333-4439. Church of the Nazarene. Teresa Gillihan, ed. asst. For 6-8 yr olds (1st & 2nd graders); emphasis on principles, character-building, and brotherhood. Weekly take-home paper; 4 pgs; circ 45,000. 100% freelance. Complete ms/cover letter; phone query ok. Pays $25, on publication, for multi-use rts. Articles 250-350 wds (52/yr); fiction 250-350 wds (40/yr). Reports in 2 wks. Seasonal 6 mos ahead. Kill fee. Guidelines/theme list; copy for 6x9 SAE/2 stamps.
Poetry: Light verse; 4-12 lines; $3.
Fillers: Buys 52/yr. Games, word puzzles; pays $3-15.
Tips: "Our stories relate to our Sunday school lessons. We try to use it as a Bible-in-action story."

#THE YOUNG CRUSADER, 1730 Chicago Ave., Evanston IL 60201. (708)864-1396. National Woman's Christian Temperance Union. Michael C. Vitucci, mng. ed. Stresses high morals, good character, high values, and abstinence from alcohol, drugs, and tobacco, for 6-12 yr olds. Monthly mag; 12 pgs; circ 3,000. 100% freelance. Complete ms. Pays .005/wd, on publication, for one-time, simultaneous or reprint rts. Not copyrighted. Articles (60/yr) & fiction, 600-700 wds. Reports in 6 wks. Seasonal 6 mos ahead. Guidelines; copy for 6x9 SAE/2 stamps.
Poetry: Buys 30/yr. Light verse; 6-10 lines; $.10/line.
Fillers: Facts, games, ideas, quizzes, short humor, word puzzles.
Tips: "We do not want to see any articles that do not build solid character. Send only copies of your stories as they will be destroyed if not accepted."

CHRISTIAN EDUCATION/LIBRARY MARKETS

BAPTIST LEADER, Box 851, Valley Forge PA 19482-0851. (215)768-2153. Fax: (215)768-2056. American Baptist. Linda Isham, ed. Practical "how-to" or thought provoking articles for local church Christian education lay leaders and teachers. Quarterly mag; 32 pgs; circ 6,000. Subscription $8. 5% freelance. Complete ms/cover letter; no phone query. Pays $10-50, on acceptance, for 1st rts. Articles 1,300-2,000 wds (4/yr). Reports in 2-12 wks. Seasonal 1 yr ahead. Guidelines; copy $1.50.
Poetry: John Pipe. Accepts 2-3/yr. Haiku, light verse.
Fillers: John Pipe. Buys 4-8/yr. Cartoons, jokes, prayers; 25-100 wds; $10-20.
Tips: "Read the magazine. Most open to features—watch the length, make it practical, meet our specs."

BRIGADE LEADER, Box 150, Wheaton IL 60189. (708)665-0630. Fax: (708)665-0372. Christian Service Brigade. Deborah Christensen, mng. ed. For men leading boy's clubs; emphasis on fathering issues. Quarterly mag; 24-32 pgs; circ 9,000. Subscription $6. 10% freelance. Complete ms/cover letter; no phone query. Pays .05-.10/wd; on publication; for 1st or reprint rts. Articles 1,000-1,500 wds (2/yr). Reports in 1 wk. Seasonal 4 mos ahead. Accepts reprints. Kill fee $35. Guidelines; copy $1.50/9x12 SAE/4 stamps.
Tips: "Be familiar with Christian Service Brigade and the issues men are dealing with. We rarely accept freelance mss. We do theme issues and assign specific articles."

#CATECHIST, 2451 E. River Rd., Dayton OH 45439. (513)294-5785. Catholic. Patricia Fischer, ed. For Catholic school teachers. Mag. published 7x/yr; 52 pgs; circ. 45,000. Query (preferred) or complete ms. Pays $25-75, on publication, for all rts. Articles 1,200-1,800 wds. Not in topical listings. Reports in 2-4 mos. Guidelines; copy $2.50.

***CE CONNECTION**, Box 12609, Oklahoma City OK 73157. (405)787-7110. General Christian Education Dept./IPHC. Talmage Garoner, asst to dir. Targets pastors, local Christian education workers/leader for training/how-to. Quarterly mag/newsletter; circ. 6,600. 100% freelance. Cover letter; no phone query. **NO PAYMENT.** Not copyrighted. Articles. Seasonal 4 mos ahead. Accepts reprints. No guidelines; free copy.

CHANGING LIVES & CALLING LEADERS (CLCL), Box 50434, Indianapolis IN 46250. (317)595-4187. Fax: (317)577-4397. The Wesleyan Church. Russ Gunsalus, ed. For church leadership (children, youth, young adult leaders). Quarterly mag; circ. 1,800. Est. 1992. 1% freelance. Complete ms/cover letter; no phone query. Pays to $50, on publication, for one-time rts. Not copyrighted. Articles 500-700 wds (6-12/yr). Reports in 4-6 wks. Seasonal 4 mos ahead. Guidelines/theme list; no copy.

CHILDREN'S MINISTRY, 2890 N. Monroe Ave., Loveland CO 80526. (303)669-3836. Fax: (303)669-3269. Group Publishing. Barbara Beach, dept. ed. For those who work with kids from birth to 6th grade. Bimonthly mag; 48-52 pgs; circ. 30,000. Estab. 1991.

Subscription $24.95. 90% freelance. Query/clips; no phone query. Pays $25-100, on acceptance, for all rts. Articles 150-1,200 wds (30/yr). Reports in 4 wks. Seasonal 6 mos ahead. Kill fee. Guidelines; copy for 9x12 SAE/4 stamps.
Special Needs: Working with volunteers, discipling children, morals, money, friends, grades, and Sunday school programming that works.
Columns/Departments: Buys 30/yr. Teacher Telegram (practical teacher tips); For Parents Only (practical parenting tips); 150 wds. Pays $25-100.
Tips: "Most open to departments. Need 'ah-ha' ideas—practical. Lots of ideas for teachers of children."

CHRISTIAN EDUCATION COUNSELOR (formerly **SUNDAY SCHOOL COUNSELOR**), 1445 Boonville Ave., Springfield MO 65802-1894. (417)862-2781 x4005. Fax: (417)862-0503. Assemblies of God. Sylvia Lee, ed. Presents teaching and administrative helps to lay leaders in local churches. Monthly mag; 28 pgs; circ 30,000. Subscription $8 (leader edition $12). 40% freelance. Complete ms/cover letter; no phone query. Pays .05-.10/wd; on acceptance; for 1st, one-time, or reprint rts. Articles 250-1,500 wds (75/yr). Reports in 2-4 wks. Seasonal 9 mos ahead. Accepts simultaneous submissions & reprints. Kill fee. Guidelines; copy $1/9x12 SAE/2 stamps.
Fillers: Buys cartoons 10/yr. Pay $35-85.
Tips: "Most open to general articles. You need to know Christian education from first-hand experience."
** This periodical was #45 on the 1993 Top 50 Plus Christian Publishers list.

#CHRISTIAN EDUCATORS JOURNAL, Dordt College English Dept., Sioux Center IA 51250-1697. (712)722-6252. Lorna Van Gilst, mng. ed. For educators in Christian day schools at the elementary, secondary, and college levels. Quarterly journal; 36 pgs; circ 4,200. Subscription $7.50. 50% freelance. Complete ms/cover letter; phone query ok. Pays $30, on publication, for one-time rts. Articles 600-1,200 wds (20/yr); fiction 600-1,200 wds. Reports in 1 mo. Seasonal 4 mos ahead. Accepts simultaneous submissions & reprints. Guidelines/theme list; copy $1 or 9x12 SAE/4 stamps.
Poetry: Buys 6/yr. On teaching day school; 4-30 lines; $10. Submit max. 5 poems.
Tips: "No articles on Sunday school, only Christian day school. Most open to theme topics and features."

THE CHRISTIAN LIBRARIAN, Box 4000, Three Hills, AB T0M 2N0 Canada. U.S. address: Box 4, Cedarville OH 45314. (403)443-5511x3343. Fax: (403)443-5540. Assn. of Christian Librarians. Ron Jordahl, ed. Christian librarianship. Quarterly journal; 32 pgs; circ 450. Subscription $20. 25% freelance. Query; phone query ok. **NO PAYMENT**, for 1st, one-time, or simultaneous rts. Not copyrighted. Articles to 1,000-5,000 wds (6/yr). Reports in 2-6 wks. Accepts simultaneous query & reprints. Guidelines; copy $5.
Special Needs: Articles on libraries, books and reading.
Fillers: Anecdotes, cartoons, newsbreaks, short humor; 25-300 wds.

#CHRISTIAN SCHOOL, 1308 Santa Rosa, Wheaton IL 60187. (708)653-4588. Phil Landrum, pub. A publication for Christian school educators and parents. Quarterly mag; 48 pgs; circ 3,000 schools. 2% freelance. Query; phone query ok. **NO**

PAYMENT. Articles 500-1,500 wds (1/yr); fiction (1/yr) 1,000-1,500. Reports in 2-4 wks. Free guidelines/copy.
Special Needs: Education how-to; youth trends; training techniques; children's books.
Poetry: Accepts 1/yr. Traditional. Submit max. 5 poems.
Fillers: Accepts 1/yr. Anecdotes.

CHURCH EDUCATOR, 165 Plaza Dr., Prescott AZ 86303. (602)771-8601. Fax: (602)771-8621. Linda Davidson, ed. Supplementary resources for Christian educators. Monthly journal; 28 pgs; circ 5,200. Subscription $24. 75% freelance. Complete ms/cover letter; phone query ok. Pays .03/wd, on publication, for 1st rts. Articles (100/yr) & fiction (15/yr), 200-1,500 wds. Reports in 2-12 wks. Seasonal 4 mos ahead. Accepts reprints. Guidelines; copy for 9x12 SAE/3 stamps.
Fillers: Bible games and Bible puzzles.
Tips: "Always interested in new writers. Big need is for ideas/programs that have worked in church programming."

CHURCH MEDIA LIBRARY MAGAZINE, 127 9th Ave. N., Nashville TN 37234. (615)251-2752. Southern Baptist. Floyd B. Simpson, ed. Supports the establishment and development of church media libraries; provides how-to articles and articles of inspiration and encouragement to media library workers. Quarterly mag; 52 pgs; circ 36,000. Query. Pays .055/wd; on publication; for all, 1st, or reprint rts. Articles 600-1,500 wds (10-15/issue). Reports in 1 month. Seasonal 14 mos ahead. Free guidelines/copy.

CHURCH RECREATION, 127 9th Ave. N, Nashville TN 37234. (615)251-3841. Fax: (615)251-3879. Southern Baptist. Lisa Wilson, ed. To minister to those with staff responsibilities in church recreation, and to the Southern Baptist layperson, through practical, how-to articles. Quarterly mag; 60 pgs; circ 13,000. Subscription $16.31. 35% freelance. Query; phone query ok. Pays .055/wd ($25-225), on publication, for all, 1st, one-time, or reprint rts. Articles 800-2,000 wds; skits, puppet scripts, dramatic interpretations (music & drama) (20/yr). Reports in 2-3 wks. Seasonal 5-6 mos. ahead. Accepts reprints. Guidelines; copy $3.61/9x12 SAE/4 stamps.
Special Needs: Activities/recreation; crafts - how-to; game ideas for all ages; senior adult devotional material.
Fillers: Buys 50/yr. Cartoons, games, party ideas, quizzes, word puzzles; 50-200 wds. Pays $25-100.
Columns/Departments: Games (groups), 50-400 wds; Social Recreation (group events/activities) 500-1,200 wds; Family Recreation, 500-1,200 wds; Sports (for groups), 500-1,200 wds; Drama (sketches, puppets, monologues), 500-1,200 wds. Complete ms.
Tips: "Need games: concise, how-to instructions; variations; age group; number to participate; materials needed; time involved."

CHURCH TEACHERS - Acquired by **CHURCH EDUCATOR** (see that listing).

CHURCH WORSHIP, 165 Plaza Dr., Prescott AZ 86303. (602)771-8601. Fax: (602)771-8621. Henry R. Rust, ed. Supplementary resources for church worship

leaders. Monthly journal; 24 pgs; circ 1,000. Subscription $20. Estab. 1990. 85% freelance. Complete ms/cover letter; phone query ok. Pays .03/wd, on publication, for 1st rts. Articles to 100-1,500 wds; fiction 100-1,500 wds. Reports in 2-6 wks. Seasonal 4 mos ahead. Guidelines/theme list; copy for 9x12 SAE/3 stamps.
Special Needs: Complete worship services.
Poetry: Submit max. 5 poems.
Tips: "Call editor any Wednesday and discuss any topic. Most open to creative worship services."

#CORNERSTONE CONNECTIONS, 55 W. Oak Ridge Dr., Hagerstown MD 21740. (301)791-7000x2547. Seventh-day Adventist. Mark Ford, ed. Resources for leaders of youth groups. Quarterly mag; 48 pgs; circ 2,400. 20% freelance. Complete ms/cover letter; no phone query. Pays $35-100, on acceptance, for one-time rts. Articles 600-800 wds (30/yr); plays/skits 800 wds; book reports $15/pg.. Reports in 4 wks. Seasonal 6 mos ahead. Accepts simultaneous submissions & reprints. Guidelines; free copy.
Columns/Departments: Buys 30/yr. Outreach Activities (witnessing, caring) 200 wds; Social Activities (games) 200 wds; AY Programs (Programs teens can put on) 800 wds.
Tips: "Most open to plays or programs for use with Adventist youth."
** This periodical was #44 on the 1993 Top 50 Plus Christian Publishers list.

EVANGELIZING TODAY'S CHILD, Box 348, Warrenton MO 63383. (314)456-4321. Child Evangelism Fellowship. Elsie C. Lippy, ed. To equip Christians to win the world's children (4-12) to Christ and disciple them. Bimonthly mag; 64 pgs; circ 22,000. Subscription $17.95. 40% freelance. Query/clips, or complete ms/no cover letter; no phone query. Pays .08-.10/wd, on acceptance, for all & 1st rts, some reprints. Articles 1,200-1,500 wds (20-25/yr); fiction 800-1,000 wds (6/yr), pays .06/wd. Reports in 2-6 wks. Seasonal 1 yr ahead. Accepts simultaneous submissions. Kill fee. Guidelines; copy for $1/9x12 SAE/2 stamps.
Resource Center: Buys 40-60/yr. Complete ms, 200-250 wds. Pays .06-.08/wd for teaching hints, bulletin board ideas, object lessons, missions incentives, etc.
Special Needs: Salvation testimonies of adults saved before age 12, 700-900 wds; 6/yr. Fresh programs to reach unchurched kids.
Tips: "Study the publication. Know children and/or children's workers."
** This periodical was #33 on the 1993 Top 50 Plus Christian Publishers list.

***FOUNDATIONS,** Resource Guide for Church Educators and Youth Workers, 5300 Patterson Ave., Grand Rapids MI 49530-0001. Zondervan. Noel Calhoun, mng. ed. Advertising resource guide to link Christian products and services with specialized audiences (1/2 editorial content). Biannual mag; circ 70,000. 50% freelance. Query or complete ms. Pays .10/wd, on publication, for 1st rts. Articles 2,000 wds; book reviews 700 wds. Accepts simultaneous submissions. Guidelines; free copy.

GROUP MAGAZINE, Box 481, Loveland CO 80539. (303)669-3836. Barbara Beach, dept. ed. Aimed at leaders of high-school-age, Christian youth groups. Mag published 8 times/yr; 56 pgs; circ 50,000. Subscription $25.95. 50% freelance. Query/clips; no phone query. Pays $25-125, on acceptance, for all rts. Articles 500-2,000 wds (64/yr).

Reports in 4 wks. Seasonal 6 mos ahead. Kill fee. Guidelines; copy for $1/9x12 SAE/4 stamps.
Special Needs: Time management; successful youth group stories.
Columns/Departments: Buys 160/yr. Try This One (youth group activities), 125 wds; Strange But True (strange youth-ministry stories), 600 wds; Hands-on Help (Tips for leaders), 125 wds; $15-25. Complete ms.
Tips: "All areas open; new slant; not preachy."

#INSIGHT INTO CHRISTIAN EDUCATION, Box 23152, Charlotte NC 28212. (704)545-6161. Fax: (704)573-0712. Advent Christian. Millie Griswold, ed. For local church Christian education volunteers. Quarterly mag; 8-12 pgs; circ 2,200. Subscription $3.50. 20% freelance. Query or complete ms. Pays $25, on publication. Articles 600-1,500 wds. Reports in 4 wks. Accepts reprints. Seasonal 6 mos ahead. Free copy.

THE JOURNAL OF ADVENTIST EDUCATION, 12501 Old Columbia Pike, Silver Springs MD 20904-6600. (301)680-5075. Fax: (301)622-9627. Seventh-day Adventist. Beverly J. Rumble, ed. For Seventh-day teachers teaching in the church's school system, K-University. Bimonthly journal; circ 10,000. Subscription $15.75. Variable freelance. Query; phone query ok. Pays $50-100, on publication, for 1st rts. Articles 2-8 ms pgs. Reports in 2-6 wks. Seasonal 4-6 mos ahead. Kill fee. Accepts reprints. Guidelines; copy $1.
Special Needs: "All articles in the context of denominational schools (**not** Sunday school tips); professional enrichment & teaching tips for Christian teachers. Need feature articles."
Fillers: Pays $20 for cartoons only.

KEY TO CHRISTIAN EDUCATION, 8121 Hamilton Ave., Cincinnati OH 45231. (513)931-4050. Standard Publishing. Lowellette Lauderdale, ed. For teachers and Christian education leaders. Quarterly mag; 16 pgs; circ 67,000. Subscription $6.95. 97% freelance. Complete ms/cover letter; no phone query. Pays .03-.05/wd, on acceptance, for 1st, one-time & reprint rts. Articles 700-1,200 wds (28/yr). Reports in 6-8 wks. Seasonal 3 mos ahead. Accepts reprints. Guidelines/theme list; copy for 9x12 SAE/3 stamps.
Tips: "Request theme list; if it doesn't fit theme we'll reject it. Write what you know about."

***LEAD**, CYC, Box 50434, Indianapolis IN 46280. Christian Youth Crusaders of the Wesleyan Church. Tom Arminger, ed. To supply ideas, inspiration, and information to CYC leaders, parents, pastors, and persons interested in children's ministries. Bimonthly newspaper; circ 3,600. Query. Pays .02/wd, on publication. Short articles, feature articles, and short ideas that relate to children's ministries; 500 wds. Not in topical listings.

LEADER, Box 2458, Anderson IN 46018. (317)642-0255. Fax: (317)642-0255x299. Church of God (Anderson, IN). Joseph L. Cookston, ed. For teachers, leaders, volunteer workers in local congregations. Bimonthly mag; 16 pgs; circ 4,000. 75%

freelance. Complete ms. Pays $10-30, on publication, for one-time rts. Articles 300-800 wds or 5,000-8,000 wds (50/yr). Reports in 8 wks. Seasonal 2-3 mos ahead. Accepts reprints. Guidelines; free copy.
Fillers: Buys 12/yr. Ideas, quizzes, short humor, word puzzles; 50-300 wds; $10.
Tips: "Ask yourself: How will what I'm saying improve the effectiveness of local church workers? How will the concern expressed foster personal growth through challenges in thinking related to key issues in Christian education today?"

+LEADER IN THE CHURCH SCHOOL TODAY, P.O. Box 801, Nashville TN 37202. (615)749-6474. Fax: (615)749-6079. United Methodist. Keith H. Kendall, ed. For pastors and Christian education leaders in the church. Quarterly mag; 64 pgs; circ. 10,000. Subscription $14. 25% freelance. Complete ms/cover letter; no phone query. Pays .05/wd, on acceptance, for all or 1st rts. Articles to 1,225 wds (20/yr). Reports in 10-12 wks. Seasonal 14 mos ahead. Guidelines; copy for 9x12 SAE/3 stamps.
Fillers: Buys 4/yr. Cartoons, facts, games, ideas; to 250 wds. Pays $20.
Columns/Departments: Buys 20/yr. Idea Exchange (new reports on specific programs and events that are working in local churches), 300 wds. Pays $20.

LEVEL C TEACHER - EARLY CHILDHOOD, 6401 The Paseo, Kansas City MO 64131. (816)333-7000. Nazarene. Lynda T. Boardman, ed. Lessons & guidelines for Sunday school teachers of 3-4 yr. olds. Quarterly; 64 pgs; circ. 1,800. 5% freelance. Complete ms/cover letter; phone query ok. Pays .035/wd, on publication, for all rts. Accepts simultaneous submissions & reprints. Kill fee. No guidelines; copy for 6x9 SAE/2 stamps.
Poetry: Traditional; 4-8 lines; .25/line ($2 min.). Submit max. 5 poems.
Tips: "Mostly assigned. If interested in writing for us, give editor a call. We do accept poems periodically."

***LEVEL D TEACHER**, 6401 The Paseo, Kansas City MO 64131. (816)333-7000x2359. Nazarene. Janet R. Reeves, ed. Kindergarten Sunday school teacher's manual. Quarterly; 64 pgs. 2% freelance. Complete ms/cover letter. Pays .035/wd; on publication; for multi-use rts. Articles 500-700 wds. Reports in 3-5 wks. Kill fee. Not in topical listings.
Special Needs: Training articles.
Tips: "This is a teacher's manual. Therefore, all lessons are written in-house or on assignment."

#LIBRARIANS WORLD, Box 353, Glen Ellyn IL 60138. (708)668-0519. Evangelical Church Library Assn. Nancy Dick, ed. To assist church librarians in setting up, maintaining, and promoting church libraries and media centers. Quarterly mag; 52 pgs; circ 700. Subscription $15. 80% freelance. Query. Pays $20-25/pg, on publication, for one-time or reprint rts. Articles 1-3 pgs (3-4/yr); book reviews, 2 pgs. Reports in 1-2 mos. Accepts simultaneous submissions. No guidelines; free copy.
Tips: "Talk to church librarians or get involved in library or reading programs. Most open to technical and promotional helps."

#LOLLIPOPS, The Magazine for Early Childhood Educators, Good Apple, Inc., Box 299, Carthage IL 62321-0299. (217)357-3981. Fax: (217)357-3987. Donna Borst, ed. Easy-to-use, hands-on, practical teaching ideas and suggestions for early childhood educators. Mag published 5 times/yr; circ 20,000. 20% freelance. Query or complete ms. Pays $10-100, on publication, for all rts. Articles 200-1,000 wds; fiction (for young children) 500-1,200 wds. Seasonal 6 mos ahead. Guidelines (2 stamps); copy for 9x12 SAE/3 stamps.
Poetry: Light verse.
Tips: "Looking for something new and different for teachers of young children; seasonal material."

LUTHERAN EDUCATION, Concordia University, 7400 Augusta, River Forest IL 60305. (708)209-3073. Lutheran Church-Missouri Synod. Wayne Lucht, ed. For Lutheran educators, many who teach on elementary level in Lutheran parochial schools. Bimonthly journal; 64 pgs; circ 4,000. Query. **PAYS IN COPIES**. Not copyrighted. Articles 1,500-3,000 wds (6/yr). Reports in 4 wks. Seasonal 4 mos ahead. Free guidelines/copy.
Fillers: Anecdotes, facts, ideas, jokes, short humor; 50-100 wds.

MEMOS, 1445 Boonville Ave., Springfield MO 65802. (417)862-2781. Fax: (417)862-8558. Assemblies of God. Linda Upton, ed. Leadership magazine for girl's program (ages 3-teens), called Missionettes. Quarterly mag; circ 15,000. Subscription $5.50. 30% freelance. Complete ms/cover letter; phone query ok. Pays $10-50, on acceptance, for 1st rts. Articles 600-1,500 wds; book reviews 50-75 wds. Reports in 4 wks. Seasonal 1 yr ahead. Accepts reprints. Free guidelines/copy.
Special Needs: Children & divorce; children & self image.
Tips: "Most writers are involved as a coordinator/sponsor in Missionettes. Most open to articles on how to work with children; age-level crafts and projects."

PARISH TEACHER, 426 S. 5th St., Box 1209, Minneapolis MN 55440. (612)330-3423. Fax: (612)330-3455. ELCA/Augsburg Fortress Publishers. Carol A. Burk, ed. Articles and ideas for Lutheran church school teachers. Monthly newsletter; 12 pgs; circ 50,000. 60% freelance. Complete ms/cover letter; phone query ok. Pays $15-50, on publication, for 1st rts. Articles 700-1,000 wds (25-30/yr); plays 400-800 wds (3-4/yr). Reports in 4-6 wks. Seasonal 3-4 mos ahead. Accepts simultaneous submissions & reprints. Guidelines; copy for $1/ 9x12 SAE/2 stamps.
Special Needs: Education methods and religious craft ideas.
Tips: "We prefer articles offering practical advice to Sunday school teachers. Most open to unique ideas (100-200 wds) that use interesting but inexpensive materials."

PERSPECTIVE, Box 788, Wheaton IL 60189. (708)293-1600x340. Fax: (708)293-3053. Pioneer Clubs. Rebecca Powell Parat, ed. To help and encourage Pioneer Club leaders (for children ages 2-18). Mag (3X/yr); circ 24,000. Subscription $5. 10-30% freelance. Query; no phone query. Pays $40-90; on acceptance; for 1st, one-time, or reprint rts. Articles 900-1,500 wds (2-3 unsolicited/yr). Reports in 2-4 wks. Seasonal 9 mos ahead. Accepts simultaneous query & reprints. Guidelines; copy $1.75/9x12 SAE.
Fillers: Buys 1-2/yr. Games, party ideas.

Columns/Departments: Buys 2-3/yr. Storehouse (ideas for crafts, games,service projects, tips for leaders, etc.); 100-200 wds; $7-15. Complete ms. Most open to.
Tips: "Most articles done on assignment. We'd like to hear from freelancers interested in working on assignment who have experience with, or access to, a Pioneer Clubs program or Camp Cherith. They should send samples of their work along with a letter introducing themselves."

***PRESCHOOL PLAYHOUSE**, 1350 W. 103rd St., Chicago IL 60643. (219)465-1825. Judith St. Clair Hull, ed. For African-American children, 2-5 yrs. Weekly Sunday school paper; circ. 20,000. 25% freelance. Query; phone query ok. Pays on publication, for all rts. Seasonal 9 mos ahead. Not in topical listings. Free guidelines/copy.
Tips: Open to assigned Sunday school lessons only.

***PRIMARY STREET**, 1350 W. 103rd St., Chicago IL 60643. (219)465-1825. Judith St. Clair Hull, ed. For African-American children, 6-8 yrs. Weekly Sunday school paper; circ. 20,000. 25% freelance. Query; phone query ok. Pays on publication, for all rts. Seasonal 9 mos ahead. Not in topical listings. Free guidelines/copy.
Tips: Open to assigned Sunday school lessons only.

RELIGION TEACHER'S JOURNAL, Box 180, Mystic CT 06355. (203)536-2611. Fax: (203)572-0788. Catholic. Gwen Costello, ed. For volunteer religion teachers who need practical, hands-on information as well as theological background for teaching religion to K through high school. 7X yearly mag; 40 pgs; circ 36,000. Subscription $17.95. 100% freelance. Query or complete ms/cover letter; phone query ok. Pays $5-100, on publication, for 1st rts. Not copyrighted. Articles to 6 pgs (40/yr). Reports in 2-4 wks. Seasonal 3 mos ahead. Guidelines; copy for 9x12 SAE/4 stamps.
Fillers: Buys 20-30/yr. Anecdotes (about teaching), games, ideas, prayers; to 2 pgs; $5-25.
Tips: "Write about projects for children that you have tried."

#RESOURCE, 6401 The Paseo, Kansas City MO 64131. (816)333-7000x344. Fax: (816)333-1683. Church of the Nazarene. Jeanette D. Gardner, ed. To provide information, training, and inspiration to those who are involved in ministering within the Christian Life and Sunday school department of the local church. Quarterly newsletter; circ 12,000. Subscription $6.25. Little freelance. Complete ms or query. Pays .02-.035/wd; on acceptance; for 1st, one-time, or reprint rts. Articles 750 wds (30-50/yr); book reviews 300 wds. Reports in 2-6 wks. Seasonal 5 mos ahead. Accepts simultaneous query. Not in topical listings. Copy for 9x12 SAE/2 stamps.
Poetry: Buys 4/yr. Seasonal or on outreach/Sunday school; to 30 lines; $.25/line, $5 minimum. Submit max. 1 poem.
Fillers: Buys 4 cartoons/yr; $10-25.
Tips: "We use few unsolicited mss, but might be interested in a well-researched topic of major interest. Most open to local Church of the Nazarene ideas that work in the Sunday school."

#SHINING STAR MAGAZINE, Box 299, Carthage IL 62321. (800)435-7234. Becky Daniel, ed. Christian education for K-8th grades. Quarterly mag; 80 pgs; circ 20,000.

99% freelance. Complete ms/cover letter. Pays $10-50; on publication; for all rts. Articles 100-500 wds (8/yr); fiction 100-500 wds (8/yr). Reports in 1-2 mos. Seasonal 9 mos ahead. Accepts simultaneous submissions; serials 4 parts. Guidelines/theme list; copy $4/9x12 SAE/2 stamps (send requests to Box 299, Carthage IL 62321).
Special Needs: Work sheets, puzzles, songs.

SUNDAY SCHOOL COUNSELOR - See **CHRISTIAN EDUCATION COUNSELOR.**

TEACHERS IN FOCUS, 8605 Explorer Dr., Colorado Springs CO 80920. (719)548-4578. Fax: (719)531-3499. Focus on the Family. Charles W. Johnson, ed. To encourage, inform and support Christian teachers in public and private education (K-12). Monthly mag; 16 pgs; circ. 47,000. Subscription $20 donation. Estab. 1992. 60% freelance. Complete ms/cover letter; phone query ok. Pays $150 & up, on acceptance, for 1st rts. Articles 1,200-1,800 wds (10/yr). Reports in 3-4 wks. Seasonal 5 mos ahead. Kill fee 50%. Guidelines/theme list; copy for 9x12 SAE/2 stamps.
Fillers: Buys 20/yr. Cartoons, teacher short humor; 50-150 wds. Pays $25.
Tips: Uses articles of interest to teachers trying to cope in the classroom situation.
** This periodical was #34 on the 1993 Top 50 Plus Christian Publishers list.

#TEACHERS INTERACTION, 3558 S. Jefferson Ave., St. Louis MO 63118-3968. (314)268-1000. Lutheran Church-Missouri Synod. Jane Haas, ed. A magazine church-school workers grow by. Quarterly mag (newsletter 7X/yr); 32 pgs; circ 20,000. 20% freelance. Complete ms/cover letter. Pays $10-75/printed pg, on publication, for all or 1st rts. Articles 750-1,200 wds (6/yr); fiction 750-1,200 wds. Reports in 3 mos. Seasonal 7 mos ahead. Guidelines; copy $1.
Poetry: 12 lines.
Fillers: Cartoons (14/yr); puzzles; teacher tips, 100 wds (40/yr); $10.

***TEAM**, Box 7259, Grand Rapids MI 49510. (616)241-5616. Young Calvinist Federation. Dale Dieleman, ed. Geared to leaders of youth programs, not Sunday school. Quarterly mag; circ 2,000. 10% freelance. Complete ms. Pays $30, on publication, for 1st, simultaneous or reprint rts. Articles 700-2,000 wds (6/yr). Reports in 1 month. Seasonal 6 mos ahead. Kill fee 50%. Accepts simultaneous submissions & reprints. Guidelines; copy $1/9x12 SAE/2 stamps.
Fillers: Cartoons, ideas, party ideas, short humor.
Columns/Departments: Street Beat (issues in urban youth ministry).

TODAY'S CATHOLIC TEACHER, 330 Progress Rd., Dayton OH 45449. (513)847-5900. Fax: (513)847-5910. Catholic. Stephen Brittan, ed. Directed to personal and professional concerns of teachers and administrators in K-12 Catholic schools. Monthly mag (8X during school yr); 55 pgs; circ 60,000. Subscription $14. 80% freelance. Query; phone query ok. Pays $50-200, on publication, for all or 1st rts. Articles (100/yr) 800-2,500 wds. Reports in 7-8 wks. Seasonal 3 mos ahead. Occasionally takes reprints. Kill fee 1-2%. Guidelines/editorial calendar; copy $3.
Special Needs: Activity pages teachers can copy and pass out to students to work on. Try to provide classroom-ready material teachers can use to supplement curriculum.
Poetry: Uses little, unless for teachers or it includes material they can use to teach it.

Fillers: Buys 10-12/yr. Cartoons, facts, games, word puzzles. Pays $5-35.
Tips: "We emphasize material for teachers in grades 3-9."

VISION MAGAZINE, Box 50025, Pasadena CA 91115. (818)798-1124. Fax: (818)798-2346. Christian Educators Assn.,Intl. Judy Turpen, contrib. ed. To encourage and equip Christian educators and parents in public education; inserted in Teachers in Focus. Monthly newsletter; 20 pgs; circ 2,600. 50% freelance. Complete ms/cover letter; no phone query. **PAYS IN COPIES**, for 1st & reprint rts. Articles 350-1,000 wds (2/yr); book reviews, 75-100 wds. Reports in 6 wks. Seasonal 4 mos ahead. Accepts simultaneous submissions & reprints. Guidelines/theme list; copy for 9x12 SAE/3-4 stamps.
Poetry: Uses 2/yr. Light verse, traditional; 4-40 lines.
Fillers: Uses 2-6/yr. Anecdotes, facts, newsbreaks; 300-500 wds.
Tips: "How-to's for teachers on living out one's faith in public education."

YOUTH AND CHRISTIAN EDUCATION LEADERSHIP, P.O. Box 2250, Cleveland TN 37323. (615)476-4512. Fax: (615)478-7521. Pentecostal Church of God/Pathway Press. Lance Colkmire, ed. For church workers. Quarterly mag; 32 pgs; circ 9,000. Subscription $6.80. 10% freelance. Complete ms/cover letter; no phone query. Pays $20-50; on publication; for 1st, one-time, or reprint rts. Articles 300-1,000 wds. Reports in 4 wks. Seasonal 6 mos ahead. Accepts reprints. Guidelines; copy $1/9x12 SAE.
Special Needs: Articles on children's ministry and Sunday school.

THE YOUTH LEADER, 1445 Boonville Ave., Springfield MO 65802. (417)862-2781x4041. Fax: (417)862-1693. Assemblies of God. Rich Percifield, ed.; submit to Chuck Goldberg, mng. ed. To provide help for people working with teenagers. Mag published 8 times/yr; 24 pgs; circ 2,800. Subscription $14.95. 75% freelance. Query or complete ms/cover letter; no phone query. Pays .04/wd, on publication, for 1st rts. Articles 1,000-2,500 wds. Reports in 8 wks. Seasonal 3 mos ahead. Accepts simultaneous submissions & reprints. Guidelines/theme list; copy for 9x12 SAE/3 stamps.
Fillers: Youth facts, newsbreaks, quotes; sermon outlines, 25-250 wds.
Columns/Departments: Brainstorms (ideas for games, fund-raisers, crowd breakers, etc.), 100-250 wds; For Starters (anecdotes, sermon starters, etc., 100-250 wds; Program Plans, 500-750 wds; Spotlight (interview/profile of successful youth leader), 1,000-2,000 wds.
Tips: "Keep material focused on practics of youth ministry—not theoretical but something they can actually use and/or apply."

DAILY DEVOTIONAL MARKETS

Due to the nature of the daily devotional market, the following market listings will include only the name, address, phone number (if available) and editor's name. Because most of these markets assign all material, they do not wish to be listed in the usual way, if at all.

If you are interested in writing daily devotionals, send to the following markets for guidelines and sample copies, write up sample devotionals to fit each one's particular format, and send to the editor with a request for an assignment. **DO NOT** submit any other type of material to these markets unless indicated.

CHRIST IN OUR HOME, 426 S. 5th St., Minneapolis MN 55440. (612)330-3423. Carol A. Burk, ed.

#COME YE APART, Box 419527, Kansas City MO 64131. Paul Martin, ed.

DAILY DEVOTIONS FOR THE DEAF, RR 2 Box 26, Council Bluffs IA 51503. (712)322-5493. Duane King, ed. No payment.

#DEVOTION, 8121 Hamilton Ave., Cincinnati OH 45231. Eileen Wilmoth, ed.

FORWARD DAY BY DAY, 412 Sycamore St., Cincinnati OH 45202. (513)721-6659. Charles H. Long, ed. Pays honorarium.

THE HOME ALTAR, 426 S. 5th St., Minneapolis MN 55440. (612)330-3423. Carol A. Burk, ed. 64 pgs. Pays $15/devotion.

LIGHT FROM THE WORD, Box 50434, Indianapolis IN 46250-0434. (317)576-8144. Carl W. Pierce, sr. ed.

#LIVING FAITH, 10300 Watson Rd., St. Louis MO 63127. (314)821-1363. Catholic. James E. Adams, ed.

MOMENTS WITH GOD, 1 S. 210 Summit Ave., Oakbrook Terrace IL 60181-3994. (708)495-2000. Dorothy Ganoung, ed. Suitable for family devotions.

PATHWAYS TO GOD, Box 2499, Anderson IN 46018-2499. (317)644-7721x245. Dan Harman, ed. Buys B & W photos. Pays $7.50-10/devotion.

#THE QUIET HOUR, 850 N. Grove Ave., Elgin IL 60120. (708)741-0800. Gary Wilde, ed. Pays $15. Send resume and list of credits, rather than a sample.

#REJOICE!, 836 Amidon, Wichita KS 67203. Mennonite. Katie Funk Wiebe, ed. 100 pgs. Pays .04-.05/wd.

THE SECRET PLACE, Box 851, Valley Forge PA 19482-0851. (215)768-2240. Kathleen Hayes, ed. Prefers to see completed devotionals. Uses poetry and photos. 64 pgs. Payment depends on usage (usually $15).

THE UPPER ROOM, P.O. Box 189, Nashville TN 38202-0189. (615)340-7252. Mary Lou Redding, mng. ed. Pays $15 per 250-word devotional. 72 pgs. Note: This publication DOES accept freelance submissions and does not make assignments. Send devotionals up to 250 wds.

THE WORD IN SEASON, 426 S. 5th St., Minneapolis MN 55440. (612)330-3423. Carol A. Burk, ed. 96 pgs. Pays $15.

MISSIONS MARKETS

+AMERICAN HORIZON, 1445 Boonville Ave., Springfield MO 65802. (417)862-2781. Fax: (417)863-7276. Assemblies of God. Traci L. Countryman, ed. Denominational magazine of home missions/mostly on assignment. Bimonthly mag; circ. 34,000. Subscription for contribution. 50% freelance. Est. 1992. Query; phone query ok. Pay .03/wd, on publication, for 1st rts. Articles 700-1,200 wds (17/yr). Reports in 2-3 wks. Seasonal 5 mos ahead. Accepts simultaneous submissions and reprints. Free guidelines/copy.

+AREOPAGUS MAGAZINE, P.O. Box 33, Shatin, New Territories, Hong Kong. (852)691-1904. Fax: (852)695-9885. Tao Fong Shan Christian Centre. John G. LeMond, ed. Provides a forum for dialogue between the good news of Jesus Christ and people of faith both in major world religions and new religious movements. Quarterly mag; 50 pgs; circ. 1,000. Subscription $24/US. 75% freelance. Query; phone query ok. Pays $25-50, on publication, for 1st rts. Articles 1,000-5,000 wds (20/yr); book reviews, 500-750 wds, $25. Reports in 6-12 wks. Seasonal 3 mos ahead. Accepts simultaneous submissions and reprints. Kill fee 50%. Guidelines; copy $4.
Special Needs: Interreligious dialogue.
Poetry: Buys 2/yr. Avant-garde, free verse, haiku, traditional; 3-30 lines. Pays $25. Submit max. 5 poems.
Columns/Departments: Query.
Tips: "We look for compassionate, direct, and unselfconscious prose that reflects a writer who is firmly rooted in his/her own tradition but is unafraid to encounter other religions."

CATHOLIC NEAR EAST, 1011 First Ave., New York NY 10022-4195. (212)826-1480. Fax: (212)838-1344. Catholic (Eastern). Michael La Civita, ed. Interest in cultural, religious, human rights development in Middle East, India, Ethiopia, E. Europe, and parts of U.S.S.R. Bimonthly mag; 32 pgs; circ 90,000. Subscription $10. 70% freelance. Query/clips; phone query ok. Pays .20/wd (edited), on publication, for 1st rts. Articles to 1,500 wds (15/yr). Reports in 4 wks. Guidelines; copy for 7x10 SAE/2 stamps.
Tips: "We strive to educate our readers about the culture, faith, history, issues and people who form the Eastern Christian churches. Material should not be academic."

#CHILDLIFE, 919 W. Huntington Dr., Monrovia CA 91016. (818)357-7979. Fax: (818)357-0915. World Vision, Inc. Terry Madison, ed.; Larry Wilson, articles ed. Child/family life in poverty areas, disaster areas of the Third World; success stories of sponsored children. Quarterly mag; 16 pgs; circ 229,000. 50% freelance. Query only. Pays $100-350 for assigned (otherwise **PAYS IN COPIES**), on publication, for 1st NA & 1st world rts. Articles 800-2,800 wds (50/yr). Guidelines; free copy.
Tips: "Send a letter with resume of past work experience. Most open to personality

profiles, testimonies of children, families whose lives have been enriched through World Vision child sponsorship. Third World `issue' pieces dealing with children and families, i.e., hunger, poverty, child exploitation, etc."

#COMPASSION MAGAZINE, Box 7000, Colorado Springs CO 80933. (719)594-9900. Fax: (719)594-6189. Compassion Intl. Steven J. Wamberg, ed. Covering Compassion's worldwide Christian child development activities. Bimonthly (5X) mag; 16 pgs; circ 155,000. Subscription free to donors. 5% freelance. Query/clips. Pays .09-.15/wd, on publication, for all rts (releases reprint rts). Articles 150-900 wds (12/yr). Reports in 2-3 mos. Seasonal 6 mos ahead. Guidelines; copy .25/9x12 SAE/2 stamps. **Tips:** "Go to Haiti or Uganda and see the difference sponsors can make in the life of one needy child. That's what we're doing with 120,000 children worldwide."

#HEARTBEAT, Box 5002, Antioch TN 37011-5002. (615)731-6812. Fax: (615)731-0049. Free Will Baptist. Don Robirds, ed. To inform and challenge church members with mission needs. Bimonthly mag; 16 pgs; circ 40,000. Subscription free. 3% freelance. Query. Pays .03/wd, on publication, for one-time rts. Articles 1,000 wds (2/yr). Reports in 4-8 wks. Accepts reprints. Guidelines; free copy.

#IMPACT, Box 5, Wheaton IL 60189. (708)665-1200. Fax: (708)665-1418. Conservative Baptist Foreign Mission Society. Art Heerwagen, ed. To inform, stimulate, and educate individuals and churches concerning activities of CBMFS missionaries and Christian nationals. Quarterly mag; circ 42,000. Subscription $4.50. 10% freelance. Query. Pays $50-150, by arrangement, for all rts. Articles 650-1,500 wds. Reports in 2-4 wks. Seasonal 6 mos ahead. Free guidelines/copy.

+INTERNATIONAL JOURNAL OF FRONTIER MISSIONS, 7665 Wenda Way, El Paso TX 79915. (915)779-5655. Fax: (915)778-6440. Interdenominational. Hans Weerstra, ed. Dedicated to frontier missions in places where there are no missionaries. Quarterly Journal; Circ. 1,000. 100% freelance. Complete ms/cover letter; phone query ok. **NO PAYMENT**. Articles 6-7 pgs. Accepts simultaneous submissions & reprints. Guidelines/theme list; copy for 9x12 SAE/2 stamps.

#LATIN AMERICA EVANGELIST, Box 52-7900, Miami FL 33152. (305)884-8400. Fax: (305)885-8649. Latin America Mission. John Maust, ed. To present God's work through the churches and missionaries in Latin America. Quarterly mag; 22 pgs; circ 21,000. Subscription $6. 10% freelance. Query only. Pays variable rates, on publication, for 1st rts. Articles 1,000 wds. Reporting time varies. Accepts simultaneous submissions. Not in topical listings. No guidelines; free copy.
Tips: " Looking for news and analysis of the religious climate and social conditions in Latin America."

THE MAP INTERNATIONAL REPORT, MAP International, Box 50, Brunswick GA 31521-5000. (912)265-6010. Phil Craven, ed. Deals with health care in developing countries. Bimonthly newsletter; 8-12 pgs; circ 13,500. 5% freelance. Prefers query. **NO MENTION OF PAYMENT.** Articles 500 wds. Seasonal 4 mos ahead. Not in topical listings. Free guidelines/theme list/copy.

MARYKNOLL MAGAZINE, Box 308, Maryknoll NY 10545-0308. (914)941-7590. Fax: (914)945-0670. Catholic Foreign Mission Society of America. Frank Maurovich, ed. Monthly (10X) mag; 66 pgs; circ 650,000. Subscription for donation. 10% freelance. Complete ms/cover letter. Pays $150, on publication, for one-time rts. Not copyrighted. Articles 800-1,000 wds (12/yr). Reports in 1 month. Seasonal 4 mos ahead. Guidelines/theme list; copy for 7x10 SAE.
Poetry: Buys 2/yr. Light verse; $25-75.
Tips: "Write about your own experience in a Third World country or anything to do with missions or missionaries, especially if you know or have known one of our Maryknoll missionaries. Also, justice and peace issues are of particular interest."

MISSIOLOGY, Asbury Theological Seminary, Wilmore KY 40390. (606)858-2215. Fax: (606)858-2375. American Society of Missiology; Mennonite. Darrell L. Whiteman, ed. A professional organization for mission studies. Quarterly journal; 128 pgs; circ 2,000. Subscription $18. 80% freelance. Complete ms/cover letter; phone query ok. **PAYS 20 COPIES**, for all and reprint rts. Articles to 20 typed pgs (20-25/yr); book reviews, 200 wds. Reports in 2-6 wks. Free guidelines/copy.
Tips: "Whole journal is open to freelancers as long as they write from a missiological perspective and have adequate documentation."

NEW WORLD OUTLOOK, 475 Riverside Dr., Room 1351, New York NY 10115. (212)870-3765. Fax: (212)870-3940. United Methodist. Alma Graham, ed. or Christie House, assoc. ed. Denominational missions. Bimonthly mag; 48 pgs; circ 33,000. Subscription $12. 1% freelance. Query; phone query ok. Pays $150-250, on publication, for all rts. Articles 500-2,000 wds; book reviews 200-500 wds. No guaranteed response time. Seasonal 5 mos ahead. Kill fee 50%. Guidelines; copy $2.50/9x12 SASE.
Special Needs: Ecumenical mission study issues. 1994-95 mission study: Africa Churches Speak.
Poetry: Buys 1-2/yr. Free verse; no more than a pg. Pay varies. Submit max. 3 poems.
Tips: "Ask for a list of United Methodist mission workers and projects in your area. Investigate them, propose a story, and consult with the editors before writing. Most open to articles and/or photos of U.S. or foreign mission sites visited as a stringer, after consultation with the editor."

***THE OBLATE WORLD AND VOICE OF HOPE**, Box 680, 486 Chandler St., Tewksbury MA 01876. Missionary Society of the Oblate Fathers of Texas. Thomas J. Reddy, ed. Missions publication for Catholic clergy and laity. Bimonthly newsletter; circ 140,000. Pays .01-.02/wd, on acceptance. Missions stories 1,000-1,600 wds. Reports in 3 wks. Not in topical listings. Copy.

P.I.M.E. WORLD, 17330 Quincy Ave., Detroit MI 48221-2765. (313)342-4066. Fax: (313)342-6816. Pontifical Inst. for Foreign Missions/Catholic. Paul Witte, mng. ed. For those interested in and supportive of foreign missions, worldwide scope. Monthly (10X) mag; 32 pgs; circ 30,000. Subscription $3. 10% freelance. Complete ms/cover letter; no phone query. Pays .06/wd, on publication, for 1st rts. Not copyrighted. Articles 800-

1,200 wds (10/yr). Reports in 2-4 wks. Seasonal 2 mos ahead. Accepts reprints. Guidelines; copy for 9x12 SAE/2 stamps.
Tips: "Most open to popular-style writing about missionaries, their work, the countries they work in. Concentrate on interesting details of mission life and what motivates missionaries, lay and clerical. Send feature articles about missionaries."

+THE RAILROAD EVANGELIST, P.O. Box 3846, Vancouver WA 98662. (206)699-7208. Joe Spooner, ed. For railroad and transportation employees and their families. Quarterly mag; circ. 2,500. Subscription $6. 100% freelance. Complete ms/no cover letter; phone query ok. **NO PAYMENT.** Articles 100-700 wds (10-15/yr). Seasonal 4 months ahead. Accepts simultaneous submissions and reprints. Guidelines; copy for 9x12 SAE/2 stamps.
Poetry: Accepts 4-8/yr. Traditional, any length. Send any number.
Fillers: Accepts many. Anecdotes, cartoons, quotes; to 100 wds.
Tips: "We need 400-700 word salvation testimonies."

#URBAN MISSION, Box 27009, Philadelphia PA 19118. (215)887-5511. Fax: (215)884-5404. Westminster Theological Seminary. H.M. Conn, ed. Dedicated to advancement of Christ in cities throughout the world. Quarterly journal; circ. 1,300. Subscription $16. 100% freelance. Complete ms/cover letter; no phone query. **PAYS 3 COPIES.** Articles 2,100-6,000 wds (40/yr). Reports in 1-2 wks. Accepts reprints. No guidelines/copy.

WHEREVER, Box 969, Wheaton IL 60189. (708)653-5300. Fax: (708)653-1826. The Evangelical Alliance Mission/interdenominational. Dana Felmly, ed. coord. For yg. adults interested in overseas missions, short or long term. Mag. published 3X/yr; 16 pgs; circ. 14,000. Free subscription. 90% freelance. Query; no phone query. Pays $75-150, on publication, for 1st rts. Articles (25/yr), length is assigned; considers fiction if it fits theme (0-2/yr), 500-1,000 wds. Reports in 2-4 wks. Guidelines/theme list; copy for 9x12 SAE/3 stamps.
Tips: "Write and ask to be put on mailing list for themes, then query. No first-mission-trip stories unless it has dramatic conflict. You need some kind of experience with overseas missions."

***WORLD CHRISTIAN**, Box 25, Colfax WA 99111. Independent. Submit to Gordon Aeschliman, ed.; June Mears, mng. ed. Missions slant. Monthly mag; circ 40,000. Query. **NO PAYMENT FOR NOW.** Reports in 6-8 wks. Accepts reprints. Articles 1,500-4,500 wds. Accepts simultaneous query. Guidelines/theme list; copy for SASE.

WORLD VISION MAGAZINE, 919 W. Huntington Dr., Monrovia CA 91016. (818)357-1111x3420. Fax: (818)357-0915. World Vision Inc. Larry Wilson, mng. ed. Relevant issues pertaining to the U.S. and the Third World, as well as poverty. Bimonthly mag; 24 pgs; circ 80,000. Subscription free. 60% freelance. Query/clips; no phone query. Pays .20/wd & up, on publication, for 1st rts. Articles 1,000-2,000 wds (40/yr). Reports in 4-8 wks. Seasonal 9 mos ahead. Accepts reprints. Kill fee 2%. Guidelines; copy for 9x12 SAE/$2 postage.
Columns/Departments: Tamera Marko. Buys 6/yr. Turning Points (personal

experience relating to poor), 450-700 wds; pays .20/wd. Most open to.
Tips: "Send us copies of anything written previously. Have experience in nonfiction writing for publications. Be fairly knowledgeable about the Third World."
** This periodical was #23 on the 1993 Top 50 Plus Christian Publishers list.

WORLDWIDE CHALLENGE, 100 Sunport Ln., Dept. 1600, Orlando FL 32809. (407)826-2390. Fax: (407)826-2374. Campus Crusade for Christ. Diane McDougall, ed; submit to Tisha Gentry, asst. ed. For financial supporters of Campus Crusade. Bimonthly mag; 52 pgs; circ 94,000. Subscription $12.95. 10% freelance. Query/clips; no phone query. Pays $25-50 (.10/wd + $100 for assigned), on acceptance, for 1st rts. Articles 300-1,200 wds. Reports in 2-4 wks. Seasonal 4-5 mos ahead. Accepts reprints. Kill fee. Guidelines; copy $2/9x12 SAE/5 stamps.
Special Needs: News reports.
Columns/Departments: Buys 2-5/yr. Upfront (personal experience/commentary); 300-1,000 wds. Most open area. People (with unique ministry of evangelism or discipleship), 1,900 wds; History's Hero, 1,350 wds. Complete ms.
Tips: "Give the human face behind a topic or story. Show how the topic relates to evangelism and/or discipleship."

MUSIC MARKETS

THE CHURCH MUSICIAN, 127 9th Ave. N., Nashville TN 37234. (615)251-2961. Southern Baptist. William M. Anderson, ed. For church music leaders. Quarterly; 16 pages (music), 98 pgs total; circ 16,000. 20% freelance. Complete ms. Pays to .055/wd, on acceptance, for all rts. Articles & fiction (related to church music), to 1,300 wds. Reports in 2 mos. Accepts reprints (pays 50%). Copy for 9x12 SAE/3 stamps.
Poetry: Church music slant/inspirational, 8-24 lines; $5-15.
Fillers: Short humor (with a musical slant); $5-15.
Note: Planning to change format.

#THE CHURCH MUSIC REPORT/CHURCH MUSIC WORLD, Box 1179, Grapevine TX 76099. (817)488-0141. Bill Rayborn, ed. For church music leaders. Monthly newsletter; 8-12 pgs. Ideas, tips, how-tos, and the like. Articles; interviews.

***CHURCH PIANIST/SAB CHOIR/THE CHOIR HERALD**, Box 268, Alcoa TN 37701. (615)982-5669. Hugh S. Livingston Jr., ed. Each of these music magazines has one page devoted to articles that deal with problems/solutions of choirs and accompanists. Bimonthly mags; circ 25,000. 45% freelance. Complete ms/cover letter; no phone query. Pay $15-150, on publication, for all rts. Articles 250-1,250 wds (10-20/yr). Seasonal 1 yr ahead. Reports in 3-6 wks. Guidelines; copy for 9x12 SAE/3 stamps.
Special Needs: Choir experiences; pianist/ organist articles.
Poetry: Accepts 25/yr. Free verse, light verse, traditional, or poetry suitable for song lyrics. Pays $10. Submit max. 5 poems.
Fillers: Accepts 5-10/yr. Anecdotes, cartoons.
Tips: "Best approach is from direct experience in music with the small church."

#CREATOR MAGAZINE, 4631 Cutwater Ln., Hilliard OH 43026. (614)777-7774. Marshall Sanders, pub. For interdenominational music ministry; promoting quality, diverse music programs in the church. Bimonthly mag; 52 pgs; circ 5,500. 20% freelance. Query or complete ms/cover letter. Pays $35-60, on publication, for negotiable rts. Articles 1,000-4,000 wds (6-8/yr). Reports in 3-5 mos. Seasonal 6 mos ahead. Accepts simultaneous submissions. Guidelines; copy for 9x12 SAE/6 stamps.
Special Needs: Music; the Arts in church.
Fillers: Buys 12-15/yr. Cartoons, short humor; 200-800 wds; $10-30.

#GLORY SONGS, 127 9th Ave. N, Nashville TN 37234. (615)251-2913. Southern Baptist. Jere V. Adams, ed. Easy choral music for church choirs; practical how-to articles for small church music programs. Quarterly mag; 26 pgs; circ 85,000. 100% freelance. Complete ms. Pays .055/wd, on acceptance, for 1st rts. Articles 550-1,000 wds (6-7/yr). Reports in 2-4 wks. Seasonal 1 yr ahead. Accepts simultaneous submissions & reprints. Guidelines; free copy.

***Due to printing considerations blank page 250 has been eliminated.**

Special Needs: Vocal techniques, choir etiquette, mission/outreach ideas, music training, etc.
Poetry: Buys 2-3/yr. Free verse, traditional.
Fillers: Cartoons, ideas, party ideas, musical quizzes, short humor.

THE HYMN, Box 30854, Texas Christian University, Ft. Worth TX 76129. (817)921-7608. Fax: (817)921-7333. Hymn Society. W. Thomas Smith, exec. dir.; articles to David W. Music. For church musicians, hymnologists, scholars; articles related to hymnology. Quarterly journal; 56 pgs; circ 3,500. Subscription $40. 100% freelance. Complete ms/cover letter; phone query ok. **NO PAYMENT** for all rts. Articles of variable length (10/yr); book and music reviews to 500 wds. Reports in 4 wks. Seasonal 6 mos ahead. Guidelines; copy $6/9x12 SAE.
Special Needs: Hymns and articles on history of hymns.

#THE MUSIC LEADER, 127 9th Ave. N., Nashville TN 37234. (615)251-2513. Southern Baptist. Anne Trudel, coordinating ed. How-to material for leaders of preschool and children's choirs. Quarterly mag; 92 pgs; circ 35,000. 5% freelance. Query or complete ms/cover letter. Pays .055/wd, on acceptance, for all or one-time rts. Articles 75-80 lines, or 150-170 lines typed 40 characters/line; 250 line max. Seasonal dramas, 7-8 pgs. Reports in 1-2 mos. Guidelines; copy for 9x12 SASE.
Poetry: For choir leaders.

#MUSIC MAKERS, 127 9th Ave. N., Nashville TN 37234. (615)251-2961. Southern Baptist. Darrell Billingsley, ed. For children ages 6-11. Quarterly mag; circ 105,000. Pays .06/wd, on acceptance, for all rts. Articles & fiction 250-500 wds. Reports in 4 wks. Not in topical listings. Guidelines/copy.

#MUSIC TIME, 127 9th Ave. N., Nashville TN 37234. (615)251-2000. Southern Baptist. Derrell Billingsley, literary design ed. For 4 & 5 yr olds; directly related to unit material found in The Music Leader. Quarterly mag; circ 60,000. Complete ms. Pays .05/wd for stories. Pays $9-12, on acceptance, for all rts. Stories for 4 & 5 yr olds. Reports in 15-30 days. Not in topical listings. Guidelines; free copy.
Poetry: 1-7 lines; $5-9.
***RENAISSANCE,** The Resource Publication for the Christian Musician, Box 2134, Lynnwood WA 98036. Renaissance Artists Group/Christian Artists International. Nathan L. Csakany, ed. Issues of interest to Christian musicians. Not in topical listings. Copy.

#THE SENIOR MUSICIAN, 127 9th Ave. N, Nashville TN 37234. (615)251-2913. Southern Baptist. Jere V. Adams, ed. For music directors and choir members of senior adult choirs. Quarterly mag; 26 pgs; circ 32,000. 100% freelance. Complete ms. Pays .055/wd, on acceptance, for 1st rts. Articles 500-900 wds (6-7/yr). Reports in 2-4 wks. Seasonal 1 yr ahead. Some simultaneous submissions; reprints. Guidelines; free copy.
Special Needs: Senior adult's testimonials, inspirational stories, personal growth and development, music training, and choir projects.
Poetry: Buys 2-3/yr. Traditional.
Fillers: Buys 3-4/yr. Cartoons, ideas, party ideas, musical quizzes, short humor.

Tips: "All topics must relate to senior adult musicians and senior choirs—anything else will be returned."

#TRADITION MAGAZINE, Box 438, Walnut IA 51577. (712)366-1136. Prairie Press Ltd. Robert Everhart, ed. Devoted to acoustic traditional music with an over-35 audience. Bimonthly mag; circ 2,500. 20% freelance. Query. Pays $10-15, on publication, for one-time rts. Not copyrighted. Articles 800-1,200 wds (2/yr). Reports in 1 month. Seasonal 6 mos ahead. Accepts simultaneous query & reprints. Copy $1.
Special Needs: Articles on gospel music.
Poetry: Buys 4/yr. Free verse, traditional; 5-20 lines; $2-5. Submit max. 2 poems.
Fillers: Buys 5/yr. Anecdotes, clippings, jokes; 15-50 wds; $5-10.

+WORSHIP TODAY, 756 Munich St. NW, Palm Bay FL 32907. (407)724-2999. Fax: (407)729-8707. Evangelical. Barbie Eslin, mng. ed. For worship leaders, chief musicians, pastors or lay leaders. Bimonthly mag; circ. 50,000. 10-20% freelance. Query or complete ms/cover letter; phone query ok. Pays $200-400, on publication, for all, one-time or reprint rights. Articles 1,500-2,500 wds (4-8/yr); book review, 150-250 wds, $20; music review, 150-250 wds, $10. Reports in 3-6 wks. Seasonal 6 mos ahead. Accepts reprints. Pays kill fee. Guidelines; copy for $1.50/9x12 SAE/4 stamps.
Special Needs: News in worship leadership, new technology in music, spiritual warfare.
Fillers: Newsbreaks.
Columns/Departments: Buys 8/yr. Women in Worship (how women worship leaders see things); Worship & Warfare (how worship warfare affects communities/churches, etc); Kids' Worship; 800 or 1050 wds. Pays $100.
Tips: "Most open to features and columns."

#YOUNG MUSICIANS, 127 9th Ave. N., Nashville TN 37234. (615)251-2944. Southern Baptist. Clinton Flowers, ed. For children 9-11 yrs. Quarterly mag.; 52 pgs; circ 85,000. Query. Pays .05/wd, on acceptance, for 1st rts. Music and music-related articles, stories 400-800 wds. Reports in 1 mo. Free guidelines/copy.
Fillers: Prose, word puzzles (music-related).

***Due to printing considerations blank page 254 has been eliminated.**

PASTOR/LEADERSHIP MARKETS

#ADVANCE, 1445 Boonville Ave., Springfield MO 65802. (417)862-2781x4095. Fax: (417)862-8558. Assemblies of God. Harris Jansen, ed. Directed to denominational ministers and church leaders. Monthly mag; 40-44 pgs; circ 32,000. Subscription $14.75. 5% freelance. Complete ms/cover letter. Pays .06/wd, on acceptance, for 1st or reprint rts. Articles 1,000-1,500 wds. Reports in 2 mos. Seasonal 6-8 mos ahead. Accepts reprints. Guidelines; copy for SAE/1 stamp.
Special Needs: Accepts sermon ideas; sermon illustrations; articles on preaching, doctrine, practice, etc.; and how-to-do-it features (for ministers and leaders).

ART+ REPRO RESOURCE, For Christian Communicators, Box 4710, Sarasota FL 34230-4710. (813)925-7754. Mission Media Inc. Wayne Hepburn, pub. Reproducible illustrations and verse for church bulletins and newsletters. Quarterly mag; circ 2,000. 100% freelance. Complete ms/no cover letter; no phone query. Pays $5-50, on acceptance, for all rts only. Reports in 6-8 wks. Seasonal any time. Accepts simultaneous submissions. Guidelines/theme list; copy for 9x12 SAE/8 stamps.
Poetry: Buys 12-20/yr. Traditional (no unrhymed); 8-24 lines; $15-35.
Fillers: Buys 100/yr. Anecdotes, cartoons, jokes; 5-50 wds; $5-25.
Tips: "Our publication is always seasonally oriented. More open to art than writing."

+THE BETHANY CHOICE, 901 Eastern Ave. NE, Grand Rapids MI 49503-1295. (616)459-6273. Fax: (616)459-0215. Bethany Christian Services. Kathy Adams, mng. ed. For professionals in medicine, legal and counseling who deal with pregnancy and adoption issues, including infertility. Quarterly newsletter; circ. 7,300. Subscription free. 20% freelance. Complete ms/cover letter; no phone query. Pays $15-60, on acceptance, for one-time rts. Articles 250-1,250 wds (4-6/yr); book reviews, $15. Reports in 2-4 wks. Accepts reprints. Guidelines/theme list; copy $1/6x9 SAE.
Tips: Keep professional audience in mind. Most open to personal experience with out-of-wedlock pregnancy, abortion, adoption (as birth parent); infertility and adoption (as adoptive parent).

#BIBLE-SCIENCE NEWSLETTER, Box 32457, Minneapolis MN 55432. (612)755-8606. Bible-Science Assn. Paul A. Bartz, ed. Covers all areas of Bible and science from origins to bio ethics. Mag published every 6 wks; 20 pgs; circ 8,000. 15% freelance. Query. Pays $25-200 ($100/published page), on publication, for all or 1st rts. Articles 500-1,200 wds (4/yr). Reports in 1 mo. Seasonal 6 mos ahead. Accepts reprints. Guidelines/theme list; copy for 9x12 SAE/4 stamps.
Columns/Departments: Buys 10/yr. World View, to 1,700 wds; Cover Feature, to 1,500 wds. Most open to these.

#CHICAGO STUDIES, Box 665, Mundelein IL 60060. (708)566-1462. Catholic. Rev. George Dyer, ed. For the continuing theological development of priests and other

religious educators. Triannual mag; circ 8,200. 50% freelance. Complete ms. Pays $35-100, on acceptance, for all rts. Articles 3,000-4,000 wds (30/yr). Reports in 2 mos. Seasonal 6 mos ahead. Guidelines; copy $5.
Tips: "Include cover letter with information about yourself."

CHRISTIAN MANAGEMENT REPORT, 22632 Golden Springs Dr. #390, Diamond Bar CA 91765. (909)861-8861. Fax: (909)860-8247. Church Management Association. Sandy Scruggs, dir. For Christian managers of nonprofit organizations and people from ministries in general. Bimonthly mag; circ. 3,500. 50% freelance. Complete ms/cover letter; phone query ok. **NO PAYMENT**, for 1st rts. Articles 500-800 wds (20/yr); book reviews 200-500 wds. Reports in 4-8 wks. Seasonal 5 mos ahead. Accepts simultaneous submissions & reprints. Guidelines/theme list; copy for 9x12 SAE/4 stamps.
Columns/Departments: Success Secrets (general business helps); Tax Letters; Software/Hardware Reviews; Internal Revenue Bulletin excerpts.

#CHRISTIAN MINISTRY, 407 S. Dearborn St., Ste. 1405, Chicago IL 60605-1150. (312)427-5380. The Christian Century Foundation. Mark R. Halton, mng. ed. For audience of mainline and liberal evangelical pastors. Bimonthly journal; 40-50 pgs; circ 12,000. 80% freelance. Complete ms/cover letter. Pays $40-100, on publication, for all rts. Articles 1,000-3,000 wds (60/yr). Reports in 2 mos. Seasonal 4 mos ahead. Accepts simultaneous submissions. Kill fee $20. Guidelines; copy $2.50/9x12 SAE/4 stamps.
Fillers: Buys 30/yr. Cartoons, facts, newsbreaks; 150-300 wds; $10.
Tips: "Sermons should be recast with a broader audience in mind, rather than a home congregation."

#THE CHRISTIAN SENTINEL, Box 11322, Philadelphia PA 19137. (215)289-7885. Eastern Christian Outreach, Inc. Jackie Alnor, ed. Leaders oriented publication exploring Christian apologetics issues; cults; issues affecting the church. Quarterly booklet; 36 pgs; circ. 8,000. Estab. 1992. 50% freelance. Query/clips; no phone query. Pays $25-50, on publication, for 1st or reprint rts. Articles 500-1,000 wds; book reviews. Reports in 4 wks. Accepts simultaneous query & reprints. No guidelines; free copy.
Tips: "Read Christian apologetics literature."

#CHURCH ADMINISTRATION, MSN 157, 127 9th Ave. N., Nashville TN 37234. (615)251-2062. Fax: (615)251-3866. Southern Baptist. George Clark, ed. Practical pastoral ministry/church administration ideas for pastors and staff. Monthly mag; 50 pgs; circ 12,000. 15% freelance. Query. Pays .055-.065/wd, on acceptance, for all rts. Articles 1,800-2,000 wds (60/yr). Reports in 8 wks. Guidelines/copy for #10 SAE/2 stamps.
Columns/Departments: Buys 60/yr. Weekday Dialogue; Minister's Mate; Secretary's File; all 2,000 wds.

CHURCH BYTES, 562 Brightleaf Sq. #9, 905 W. Main St., Durham NC 27701. (919)490-8927. Neil B. Houk, ed. Everything about church computing. Newsletter

(8X/yr); circ. 1,000. Subscription $18. 10% freelance. Query; phone query ok. Pays $35; on publication; for 1st or reprint rts. Articles 1,000 wds (12-16/yr). Reports in 2 wks. Accepts reprints. Copy for 9x12 SAE/3 stamps. Not in topical listings.
Tips: "Looking for articles on computers and churches, church experience with computers. I have plenty of reviews of church-related/ Bible-related software."

+CHURCH GROWTH NETWORK, 3630 Camellia Dr., San Bernardino CA 92404. (909)882-5386. Fax: the same. Independent. Dr. Gary L. McIntosh, ed. For pastors and church leaders interested in church growth. Bimonthly newsletter; circ. 9,000. Subscription $12. 10% freelance. Query; no phone query. **PAYS A SUBSCRIPTION**, for one-time or reprint rights. Articles 1,000-1,250 wds (2/yr). Reports in 4 wks. No seasonal. No guidelines; copy for #10 SAE/1 stamp.
Tips: "All articles must have a church growth slant. Should be very practical, how-to material; very tightly written with bullets, etc."

#THE CLERGY JOURNAL, 6160 Carmen Ave. E., Inver Grove Heights MN 55076-4420. Manfred Holck, Jr., pub. "How-to" articles on church administration for protestant ministers. Monthly (10X) mag; 48 pgs; circ 15,000. 20% freelance. Query. Pays $25-50, on publication, for all rts. Articles 1,000-1,500 wds (15/yr); book reviews 250 wds/no pay. Reports in 2 wks. Seasonal 4 mos ahead. Kill fee 50%. No guidelines; copy $3.50/9x12 SAE/6 stamps.
Special Needs: How to manage churches.

#CONGREGATIONAL JOURNAL, 298 Fairfax Ave., Ventura CA 93003. (805)644-3397. American Congregational. Dr. Henry David Gray, ed. For denominational leaders in 59 countries. Triannual journal; 72 pgs; circ 1,500. 2% freelance. Complete ms. **PAYS IN COPIES**, for 1st rts. Articles 4-20 pgs. Reports in 3 wks. Seasonal 3 mos ahead. Copy for 6x9 SASE.
Poetry/Prayers: Rev. Raymond A. Waser, 908-A Ronda Sevilla, Laguna Hills CA 92653. Accepts 3-5/yr. Free-verse, haiku; any length. Submit max. 3 poems.
Fillers: Accepts 5-6/yr. Prose.
Tips: "Write hard thinking, tightly knit, lucid, stimulating and fearless articles, poems, prayers and book reviews. Study Strunk & White."

CROSS CURRENTS, College of New Rochelle, New Rochelle NY 10805. (914)654-5425. Fax: (914)654-5925. Association for Religious & Intellectual Life. Nancy Malone, OJU, ed. For thoughtful activists for social justice and church reform. Quarterly journal; 144 pgs; circ 3,500. Subscription $25. 100% freelance. Mostly written by academics. Complete ms/cover letter; no phone query. **NO PAYMENT**, for all rts. Articles 1,000-5,000 wds (20/yr). Reports in 3-10 wks. Seasonal 6 mos ahead. Accepts simultaneous submissions and reprints. Guidelines; copy $2.
Poetry: Benjamin Mariante. Uses 8/yr. Any type, to 56 lines; no payment. Submit max. 1 poem.
Columns/Departments: Perspectives, 1,000 wds; Correspondence (letter to editor), 500 wds.
Tips: "No fiction at present, but possible."

#DIACONALOGUE, 1304 LaPorte Ave., Valparaiso IN 46383. (219)464-0909. Lutheran Deaconess Assn. Dot Nuechterlein, ed. Focus on ministries of Christian service in everyday life. Semiannual (2-3X) newsletter; 4-6 pgs; circ 1,000. 50% freelance. Complete ms/cover letter. Pays $25, on publication, for one-time rts. Not copyrighted. Articles 1,000 wds (3/yr). Reports in 2-4 wks. Seasonal 6 mos ahead. Accepts reprints. Guidelines/copy for #10 SAE/1 stamp.
Poetry: Free verse.
Tips: "Most open to articles or poems that advocate or illustrate service and caregiving."

#DISCIPLESHIP TRAINING, 127 9th Ave. N., Nashville TN 37234. (615)251-2831. Southern Baptist. Richard Ryan, sr. ed. Training Christians for discipleship. Quarterly mag; 64 pgs; circ 30,000. 10% freelance. Query. Pays .05/wd, 30 days after acceptance, for all or 1st rts. Articles 500-1,500 wds (15/yr). Reports in 6 wks. Seasonal 1 yr ahead. Free guidelines/copy.
Tips: "Most open to testimonies regarding discipleship in the lives of growing Christians."

#EUCHARISTIC MINISTER, 115 E. Armour Blvd., Kansas City MO 64111. (816)531-0538. Catholic. Rich Heffern, ed. For eucharistic ministers. Monthly newsletter; 4-8 pgs; circ 63,000. 90% freelance. Complete ms. Pays $20-200, on acceptance, for one-time rts. Articles 200-2,000 wds (30+/yr). Reports in 1-2 wks. Seasonal 4-6 mos ahead. Accepts simultaneous submissions & reprints. Guidelines; free copy.
Fillers: Buys 10-12/yr. Anecdotes, cartoons, short humor.
Tips: "We want articles to be practical, inspirational, or motivational. They need to be simple and direct enough for the average person to read easily—no heavy theology, pious inspiration, or excess verbiage."

EVANGELISM, 12800 N. Lake Shore Dr., Mequon WI 53097-2402. (414)243-4207. Fax: (414)243-4409. Dr. Joel Heck, ed. For pastors and lay people concerned about personal evangelism. Quarterly journal; 48 pgs; circ 900. Subscription $12. 50% freelance. Complete ms/cover letter; no phone query. Sometimes pays for1st or reprint rts. Articles 1,000-5,000 wds (8/yr). Reports in 4-8 wks. Seasonal 3 mos ahead. Accepts simultaneous submissions & reprints. Guidelines/theme list; copy for 6x9 SAE.
Special Needs: Assimilation and church growth.
Columns/Departments: Accepts 10/yr. Idea Bank (evangelism ideas), 50-500 wds; News Bank (evangelism news), 50-500 wds; Conference Bank (evangelism conferences), 50-500 wds; Introducing... (info on outreach organizations), 1,000-5,000 wds.
Tips: "We need articles on evangelism programs, witnessing, and profiles of outreach organizations."

#FAITH & RENEWAL, Box 7353, Ann Arbor MI 48107. (313)761-8505. Fax: (313)761-1577. The Alliance for Faith & Renewal. John Blattner, ed. To serve clergy and lay leaders in the Protestant, Catholic, and orthodox churches involved in renewal. Bimonthly newsletter; 16 pgs; circ 8,000. Subscription $18. 10% freelance. Query/clips, or complete ms/cover letter. Pays to $100, on publication, for 1st rts. Articles to 4,000

wds (2/yr). Reports in 1 mo. Seasonal 8 mos ahead. Accepts some reprints. No guidelines or copy.
Columns/Departments: Buys 6/yr. Hands On! (practical pastoral care how-to), 750-1,500 wds; From My Experience (lessons learned), 750-1,500 wds; Trends, 1,000-2,000 wds. Pays $50-100.
Tips: "Articles must add to the reader's understanding and/or 'bag of tricks' in ways that he can go out and use it tomorrow. Most are experience-based."

***THE FIVE STONES,** Box D-2, Block Island RI 02807. (401)466-5940. Ecumenical-American Baptist. Anthony G. Pappas, ed. Primarily to small church pastors and laity, denominational staff, and seminaries; to equip for service. Quarterly newsletter/journal; circ 550. Query or complete ms. Pays $5, on publication, for one-time rights. Not copyrighted. Articles (16/yr) & fiction, 500-2,500 wds. Reports in 4-12 wks. Seasonal 6 mos ahead. Accepts simultaneous submissions & reprints. Guidelines/theme list; free copy.
Columns/Departments: Buys 4/yr. Seminary Programs for Small Church Pastors, 500-1,000 wds. Complete ms. Pays $5.
Tips: "Good place for unpublished to break in. Best to call and talk."

#GROUP'S JR. HIGH MINISTRY, Box 481, Loveland CO 80539. (303)669-3836. Rick Lawrence (articles); Barbara Beach (columns). For youth ministers who work with the junior-high age group. Mag published 5 times/yr; 40 pgs; circ 30,000. 50% freelance. Query/clips or complete ms/cover letter; no phone query. Pays $75-150, on acceptance, for all rts. Articles 500-2,200 wds (50/yr). Reports in 1 mo. Seasonal 5 mos ahead. Accepts simultaneous submissions. Kill fee $25. Guidelines; copy $1/9x12 SAE/4 stamps.
Columns/Departments: Buys 30/yr. Parents Page (tips for parents of jr. highers); 150 wds. Pays $25.
Tips: "Most open to features and creative programming; practical articles on issues that really mean something to jr. high leaders. Get a copy of the magazine so you can conform to our style."

#GROWING CHURCHES, 127 9th Ave. N., Nashville TN 37234. (615)251-2485. Fax: (615)251-5091. Southern Baptist. David T. Seay, ed. Practical church-growth ideas for pastors and staff ministers. Quarterly mag; 4 pgs; circ 30,000. Estab. 1990. 30% freelance. Query. Pays .055-.06/wd, on acceptance, for all or one-time rts. Articles 1,200-1,800 wds (20/yr). Reports in 8 wks. Guidelines/copy for 9x12 SAE/2 stamps.
Fillers: Buys 15/yr. Sidebars on church growth; 600 wds.

+HOMILETIC AND PASTORAL REVIEW, 86 Riverside Dr., New York NY 10024. Catholic. Kenneth Baker S.J., ed. Promotion of Catholic faith, primarily for priests. Monthly journal; 80 pgs; circ. 15,000. 90% freelance. Complete ms/cover letter. Pays $100, after publication, for all rts. Articles to 6,000 wds. Reports in 1 mo. No guidelines; free copy.

+THE IVY JUNGLE REPORT, 2639 Iron St., Bellingham WA 98225. (206)733-6212. Fax: (206)734-6228. Mike Woodruff, ed. For people who minister to collegians.

Quarterly journal; circ. 150. Subscription $24.50. Est. 1992. 80% freelance. Query; phone query ok. **NO PAYMENT** for one-time rts. Not copyrighted. Articles 500-1,500 wds; book reviews. Reports in 2 wks. Accepts simultaneous submissions and reprints. Guidelines/theme list; copy for 6x9 SAE/3 stamps.
Fillers: Accepts 10/yr. Anecdotes, cartoons, facts, ideas, jokes, newsbreaks, party ideas, quizzes, quotes, short humor; 15-100 wds.
Tips: "We are looking for writers who understand the unique demands and challenges of college ministry, both church and parachurch."

#JOURNAL OF CHRISTIAN CAMPING, Box 646, Wheaton IL 60189-0646. (708)462-0300. Fax: (708)462-0499. Christian Camping Intl. John Ashman, ed. For those involved in organized camps and conference centers. Bimonthly mag; 32 pgs; circ 6,500. Subscription $24.95. 75% freelance. Query only. Pays .10/wd, on publication, for 1st rts. Articles 600-1,200 wds (20-30/yr). Reports in 1 mo. Seasonal 3-4 mos ahead. Accepts reprints. Kill fee 25%. Guidelines/theme list; copy $2.50/9x12 SAE.
Poetry: Buys 1-2/yr. Free verse.
Fillers: Buys 6-10 cartoons/yr; $25-50.

***JOURNAL OF CHRISTIAN HEALING**, 103 Dudley Ave., Narberth PA 19072. (215)667-0460. Christian Interfaith. Douglas Schoeninger, ed.; Robin Caccese, fiction ed. Focuses on the healing power and presence of Jesus Christ, for health and mental health professionals and healing ministries. Quarterly journal; circ. 1,200. 100% freelance. Complete ms/cover letter; phone query ok. **PAYS IN COPIES**, for all rts. Articles 10-20 pgs (12/yr); fiction 2-5 pgs; book reviews, 2-5 pgs. Accepts reprints. Reports in 8 wks. Guidelines; copy $8.
Poetry: Charles Zeiders. Accepts 12/yr. Free verse, haiku, light verse or traditional; to 40 lines. Submit max. 10 poems.
Fillers: Accepts 10/yr. Various; to 250 wds.
Columns/Departments: Accepts 12/yr. Resources, Medical Practices, Nursing, Pastoral Ministry, Psychiatry, Prayer Ministry, Sexuality, Dreams; 2-5 pgs.
Tips: "All articles or short stories must relate to healing."

#LEADERSHIP JOURNAL, 465 Gundersen Dr., Carol Stream IL 60188. (708)260-6200. Fax: (708)260-0114. Christianity Today, Inc. Marshall Shelley, ed. Practical journal for ministers and church leaders reflecting specific, real-life experiences in ministry. Quarterly mag; 148 pgs; circ 70,000. Subscription $22. 75% freelance. Query or complete ms/cover letter; phone query ok. Pays .07-.10/wd, on acceptance, for 1st & reprint rts. Articles 1,200-3,000 wds (50/yr); book reviews 1,500 wds/$100. Reports in 2 mos.
Seasonal 6 mos ahead. Accepts simultaneous submissions & reprints. Kill fee 50%. Guidelines/theme list; copy $3.
Columns/Departments: Ideas That Work, 150-1,500 wds; To Illustrate (sermon illustrations), 100-350 wds; Back Page (opinion), 1,200 wds. Pays $25-100. Complete ms.
** This periodical was #18 on the 1993 Top 50 Plus Christian Publishers list.

+LITURGY, 8750 Georgia Ave., Ste. 123, Silver Spring MD 20910. (301)495-0885. Fax: (301)495-5945. The Liturgical conference. Blair G. Meeks, ed. For clergy, liturgy planners, musicians, and religious educators. Bimonthly journal; 90 pgs; circ. 2,800. Subscription $42. 10% freelance. Query/clips; phone query ok. Pays $35-75, on publication, for all rts. Articles 1,100 wds (8/yr). Reports in 1-3 wks. Seasonal 10 mos ahead. Guidelines/theme list; copy $10.95/9x12 SAE/3 stamps.
Poetry: Buys 10/yr. 8-30 lines. Pays $35-75.

#LUTHERAN FORUM, 29 S. George St., York PA 17401. (717)854-5589. Evangelical Catholic Lutherans. Dr. Leonard R. Klein, ed. For church leadership, clerical and lay. Quarterly journal; 56 pgs; circ 4,000. 90% freelance. Query/clips. **NO PAYMENT** for one-time rts. Articles 1,000-3,000 wds (2-3/yr). Reports in 1-2 mos. Accepts reprints. Guidelines; no copy.

***MEDIA UPDATE**, Box 5008, San Marcos CA 92069. Al Menconi Ministries. Al Menconi, pub/ed. Music and media evaluation for parents and Christian workers. Bimonthly newsletter; circ 7,500. 10% freelance. Query/clips. **NO PAYMENT**. Articles 500-1,500 wds. Reports in 4 wks. Seasonal 3 mos ahead. Accepts simultaneous query & reprints. No guidelines; free copy.
Special Needs: Insight on today's entertainment & music; parent communication with kids.

MINISTRIES TODAY, 3901 Hield Rd., Palm Bay FL 32907. (407)724-2999. Fax: (407)729-8707. Strang Communications. Michelle Buckingham, ed. Helps for pastors and church leaders in charismatic churches. Bimonthly mag; 84 pgs; circ 30,000. Subscription $21.95. 30-40% freelance. Query or complete ms/cover letter; no phone query (Fax: ok). Pays $200-500, on publication, for all, 1st, one-time or reprint rts. Articles 1,800-3,000 wds; book reviews, $20. Reports in 3-6 wks. Seasonal 6 mos ahead. Accepts reprints only if published in non-profit newsletters, newspapers or magazines. Kill fee. Guidelines; copy $4/9x12 SAE.
Columns/Departments: Buys 12/yr. Soap Box (opinion pcs); The Next Generation (youth/children's ministry); 800 or 1,050 wds. Pays $100.
Tips: "Most open to columns. Write for guidelines and study the magazine."

#NATIONAL & INTERNATIONAL RELIGION REPORT, Box 21433, Roanoke VA 24018. (703)989-7500. Fax: (703)989-0189. Mark Henry, mng. ed. Report of religious news around the world. Biweekly newsletter; 8 pgs; circ. 7,500. Subscription $49. 7% freelance. Query by phone/Fax first. Pays $50, on publication, for 1st rts. News articles 150-400 wds. Reports in 1-2 mos. Guidelines/copy for #10 SASE/1 stamp.

#NETWORKS, Box 685, Cocoa FL 32923. (407)632-0130. Fax: (407)631-8207. Christian Council on Persons with Disabilities. Linda G. Howard, ed. For those with specialized ministry to the mentally retarded. Bimonthly newsletter; 8 pgs; circ 1,700. Estab. 1989. 80% freelance. Query or complete ms. **No Payment** for 1st rts. Articles 250-450 wds (12/yr); book reviews 350 wds. Reports in 6 wks. Seasonal 4 mos ahead. Accepts simultaneous submissions & reprints. Guidelines; copy for 9x12 SAE/6 stamps.

Special Needs: Advocacy, normalization/ integration, church/state issues. June 15 deadline for annual issue on the Christian Council on Persons with Disabilities.
Poetry: Uses 4/yr. Any type; to 66 lines. Submit max. 10 poems.
Columns/Departments: Uses 8/yr. Program Highlights, 1,000 wds; Teachers' Tips, 750 wds.

***PARACLETE**, 1445 Boonville Ave., Springfield MO 65890. (417)862-2781. Assemblies of God. David Bundrick, ed. For pastors/leaders concerned with the person and ministry of the Holy Spirit. Quarterly journal; circ. 4,500. 100% freelance. Complete ms/cover letter; phone query ok. Pays .04/wd (to $100), on acceptance, for one-time rts. Articles 2,000-3,000 wds; book reviews 500-750 wds (copy of book or $20). Reports in 2-8 wks. Accepts simultaneous submissions & reprints. Free guidelines/copy.
Tips: "We only print theological nonfiction. When submitting an article, make sure you have identified your sources."

PASTORAL LIFE, Society of St. Paul, Box 595, Canfield OH 44406-0595. (216)533-5503. Fax: (215)533-1076. Catholic. Anthony Chenevey, ed. For priests, deacons, some ministers, and members of pastoral teams. Monthly (11X) booklet; 68 pgs; circ 3,200. 75% freelance. Query; phone query ok. Pays .03/wd and up, on publication, for one-time rts. Not copyrighted. Articles 900-3,500 wds (70/yr). Reports in 2-4 wks. Seasonal 4 mos ahead. Accepts reprints. Guidelines/theme list; copy for 6x9 SAE.

+PASTOR'S TAX & MONEY, P.O. Box 50188, Indianapolis IN 46250. Interdenominational.Daniel D. Busby, ed. Guidance for pastors in management of church and personal finances. Quarterly newsletter; 10 pgs; circ. 6,000. 50% freelance. Complete ms/cover letter. Pays $50, on publication, for one-time rts. Articles 600-800 wds. Reports in 3 mos. No guidelines; copy $1/6x9 SAE/2 stamps.
Special Needs: Minister's taxes; computers; personal finances and church finances.

PREACHER'S ILLUSTRATION SERVICE, Box 3102, Margate NJ 08402. (609)822-9401. James Colaianni, ed. Sermon illustration resource for professional clergy. Bimonthly loose-leaf booklet, 28 pgs. 15% freelance. Complete ms. Pays .15/wd, on publication, for all rts. Illustrations/anecdotes 50-250 wds. Reports in 6 wks. Seasonal 4 mos ahead. Accepts reprints. Guidelines/topical index; copy for 9x12 SASE.
Special Needs: Seasonal sermon illustration collections for: Advent, Christmas, Easter, Mother's/Father's Day, graduation, marriage, Thanksgiving.
Poetry: Light verse, traditional; 50-250 lines; .15/wd. Submit max. 3 poems.
Fillers: Various; sermon illustrations; 50-250 wds; .15/wd.

THE PREACHER'S MAGAZINE, 10814 E. Broadway, Spokane WA 99206. (509)226-3464. Nazarene. Rev. Randal E. Denny, ed. A trade journal for holiness ministers. Quarterly mag; 80 pgs; circ 18,000. 25% freelance. Complete ms/no cover letter; phone query ok. Pays .035/wd, on publication, for one-time rts. Articles 700-2,500 wds (100/yr); book reviews 300-400 wds. Reports in 2-3 wks. Seasonal 9-12 mos ahead. Accepts simultaneous submissions & reprints. Guidelines/theme list; no copy.
Fillers: Buys 50/yr. Cartoons, facts, ideas, jokes, short humor; 150-500 wds.

Tips: "Material must be relevant to pastor's ministry or personal life."

#PREACHING, P.O. Box 7728, Louisville KY 40257-0728. (502)899-3119. Dr. Michael Duduit, ed. Professional magazine for evangelical preachers; focus is on pulpit ministry. Bimonthly mag; 64 pgs; circ 10,000. Subscription $24.95. 80% freelance. Query (articles) or complete ms (sermons)/cover letter; no phone query. Pays $35-50, on publication, for 1st & reprint rts. Articles 1,000-2,000 wds (18-24/yr). Reports in 2-4 mos. Seasonal 1 yr ahead. Guidelines; copy $2.50.
Fillers: Buys 10-15/yr. Cartoons only. Pays $25.
Tips: "Need practical feature articles about preaching—written by preachers or college/seminary faculty (nothing written by laity). We use articles that provide practical insights and skills for strengthening the preaching ministry."

THE PRIEST, 200 Noll Plaza, Huntington IN 46750. (219)356-8400. Fax: (219)356-8472. Catholic. Owen F. Campion, ed. For Catholic priests, deacons and seminarians; to help in all aspects of ministry. Monthly mag; 48 pgs; circ 9,800. Subscription $30. 70-80% freelance. Complete ms/cover letter; phone query ok. Pays $50-300, on acceptance, for 1st rts. Not copyrighted. Articles 1,000-5,000 wds (72/yr). Reports in 4 wks. Seasonal 4-5 mos ahead. Guidelines; copy for 9x12 SAE/5 stamps.
Tips: "Write to the point, with interest, and when you have said your piece, quit. Most open to features. Keep the audience in mind."
** This periodical was #38 on the 1993 Top 50 Plus Christian Publishers list.

PROCLAIM, 127 Ninth Ave. N, Nashville TN 37234. (615)251-2874. Southern Baptist. Bill Chitwood, ed. Sermons, illustrations, & worship materials for pastors. Quarterly mag; circ. 14,000. Subscription $12.10. 50% freelance. Query; phone query ok. Pays .055/wd, on acceptance, for all, 1st or reprint rts. Articles to 5,000 wds (30/yr). Reports in 3-6 wks. Seasonal 1 yr ahead. Accepts reprints. Guidelines; free copy for 9x12 SAE.

#PULPIT & BIBLE STUDY HELPS, Box 22000, Chattanooga TN 37422. (615)894-6060. Fax: (615)894-6863. Dr. Spiros Zodhiates, ed; submit to Mr. Anastasio Ioannidis. Strictly biblical; to help others understand the Bible more clearly. Monthly newspaper; 28 pgs; circ 210,000. Uses freelance. Complete ms/cover letter; no phone query. **NO PAYMENT** for all rts. Not copyrighted. Articles to 1,000-5,000 wds. Seasonal 2 mos ahead. Accepts simultaneous submissions & reprints. Free copy.
Poetry: Traditional.
Fillers: Elmer & Helen Seifert. 10-300 wds.

#QUARTERLY REVIEW, A Journal of Theological Resources for Ministry, Box 871, Nashville TN 37202. (615)340-7383. Fax: (615)340-7048. United Methodist. Dr. Sharon J. Hels, ed. A theological approach to subjects of interest to clergy—scripture study, ethics, and practice of ministry in Wesleyan tradition. Quarterly journal; 112 pgs; circ 3,000. 95% freelance. Complete ms/cover letter; no phone query. **NO PAYMENT** for one-time rts. Articles 15-18 pgs/3,250-5,000 wds (15/yr); book reviews to 1,000 wds. Reports in 3 mos. Seasonal 9 mos ahead. Guidelines; no copy.
Tips: "Emphasis on top-notch scholarship and accessible writing style. Use up-to-date sources and be prepared to rewrite. Most open to theological reflection or pastoral

experiences. Hone essay-writing skills."

#REFORMED WORSHIP, 2850 Kalamazoo SE, Grand Rapids MI 49560. (616)246-0752. Christian Reformed Church in North America. Dr. Emily R. Brink, ed. To provide liturgical and musical resources for pastors, church musicians, and other worship leaders. Quarterly journal; 48 pgs; circ 3,000. 75% freelance. Query or complete ms/cover letter. Pays $30/printed pg, on publication, for all or 1st rts. Articles 250-1,500 wds (4/yr); book reviews 250 wds/$15. Reports in 3 mos. Seasonal 1 yr ahead. Accepts reprints. Kill fee 50%. Guidelines; copy $5/9x12 SASE.
Fillers: Buys 4-6 cartoons/yr; $50.

RESOURCE: The National Leadership Magazine, 6745 Century Ave., Mississauga, ON L5N 6P7 Canada. (905)542-7400. Fax: (905)542-7313. Pentecostal Assemblies of Canada. Rick Hiebert, ed. For church leadership and practical how-to's on leadership issues. Bimonthly mag; circ 10,500. Subscription $15 Can./$20 U.S. 20-30% freelance. Query; phone query ok. Pays $30-100, on publication, for 1st, one-time and reprint rts. Articles 700-2,000 wds (8/yr); book reviews 250 wds, $20. Reports in 6-10 wks. Seasonal 3 mos ahead. Accepts reprints. Guidelines/theme list; copy $2/9x12 SAE/$1 Canadian postage.
Special Needs: Articles on counseling.
Fillers: Buys 15-20/yr. Cartoons, short humor; 200-600 wds; pays $20-30.
Columns/Departments: Buys 5-8/yr. Encounter (social concerns ministry), 600 wds; Culture Watch (analyzing trends and Christian response), 600 wds. Pays $50.
Tips: "Our readers are looking for practical, hands-on ideas and approaches to ministry."

REVIEW FOR RELIGIOUS, 3601 Lindell Blvd., Rm. 428, St. Louis MO 63108-3393. (314)535-3048. Fax: (314)535-0601. Catholic. Rev. David L. Fleming, S.J., ed. For Catholic priests, brothers, and sisters, to deal specifically with the requirements of religious life. Bimonthly journal; 160 pgs; circ 11,000. Subscription $20. 100% freelance. Complete ms/cover letter; phone query ok. Pays $6/printed page, on publication, for all rts. Articles 1,500-5,000 wds (80/yr); book reviews, 300-900 wds (pays 2 copies). Reports in 1-4 wks. Seasonal 6 mos ahead. Guidelines; copy for 24x16.5 SAE/$1.05 postage.
Poetry: Buys 10/yr. Free verse; to 12 lines; $10.
Tips: "Our guidelines give explicit instructions; write for them."

#SEARCH, 127 9th Ave. N., Nashville TN 37234. (615)251-2074. Fax: (615)251-2074. Southern Baptist Sunday School Board. Judith S. Hayes, sr. design ed. Practical theology, Christian education, preaching/worship, and pastoral care for pastors and staff. Quarterly journal; 66 pgs; circ 10,000. 50% freelance. Query. Pays .055-.06/wd, after acceptance, for all rts. Articles 2,500-5,000 wds (20/yr); book reviews 200-800 wds. Reports in 3 mos. Seasonal 15 mos ahead. Guidelines; free copy.

SINGLE ADULT MINISTRIES JOURNAL, Box 60430, Colorado Springs CO 80960. (719)579-6471. Fax: (719)579-9732. David C. Cook Foundation. Jerry Jones, ed. For pastors and lay leaders involved in ministry with single adults. Journal pub. 8X/yr; 24

pgs; circ 4,000-5,000. Subscription $24. 5% freelance. Query; phone query ok. **USUALLY NO PAYMENT** for 1st rts. Articles 200-2,500 wds (0-4/yr); book reviews 50-300 wds/$15-75. Reports in 6-12 wks. Seasonal 4-6 mos ahead. Theme list; copy for 9x12 SAE/4 stamps.
Fillers: Buys 0-5/yr. Facts, newsbreaks, quotes; 25-200 wds/$10-50.
Tips: "Write to the pastor or leader, not to singles themselves. Interview singles or the leaders who work with them."

TODAY'S PARISH, Box 180, Mystic CT 06355. (203)536-2611. Catholic. Daniel Connors, ed. Practical ideas and issues relating to parish life, management and ministry; human interest relevant to parish life. Mag published 7 times/yr; 40-42 pgs; circ 16,000. 25% freelance. Query or complete ms. Pays $50-100, on publication, for 1st rts. Articles 800-1,800 wds (45/yr). Reports in 3 mos. Seasonal 6 mos ahead. Guidelines; copy for 9x12 SASE.
Poetry: Free verse; to 25 lines.

+WORD & WORLD: Theology for Christian Ministry, 2481 Como Ave., St. Paul MN 55108. (612)641-3482. Fax: (612)641-3354. E.L.C.A./Luther Northwestern Theological Seminary. Frederick J. Gaiser, ed. Addresses ecclesiastical and secular issues from a theological perspective and addresses pastors and church leaders with the best fruits of theological research. Quarterly journal; 104 pgs; circ 3,100. Subscription $18. 10% freelance. Complete ms/cover letter; phone query ok. Pays $50, on publication, for all rts. Articles 5,000-6,000 wds. Reports in 2-8 wks. Guidelines/theme list; copy $5.
Special Needs: Themes for 1995: Children; Revelation & Apocalyptic; The Ministry of Women; Why do the Nations Rage?
Tips: "Most open to general articles. We look for serious theology addressed clearly & interestingly to people in the practice of ministry. Creativity and usefulness in ministry are highly valued."

***WORSHIP LEADER**, 107 Kenner Ave., Nashville TN 37205. (615)386-3011. Interdenominational. David Gillaspey, mng. ed. Intellectual tone with practical advice on leading worship. Bimonthly mag; circ. 50,000. Estab. 1991. 100% freelance. Query/clips; no phone query. Pays .09-.10/wd; 45 days after publication; for 1st or one-time rights (rarely reprint rts). Articles 1,200-3,000 wds. Reports in 1 yr. Seasonal 6 mos ahead. Kill fee 50%. No guidelines; copy for 9x12 SAE/6 stamps.
Special Needs: Worship renewal; praise & worship.
Columns/Departments: Buys 6/yr. Profile of worship leader or minister of music (Q & A format), 1,200-2,200 wds.
Tips: "We need writers from all parts of the country to do profiles of churches, worship leaders/ministers of music in their home cities. Also, suggest articles on worship applications outside the church."

YOUR CHURCH, 465 Gundersen Dr., Carol Stream IL 60188. (708)260-6200. Fax: (708)260-0114. Christianity Today Inc. James D. Berkley, ed. Deals only with the business-administration side of Christian ministry. Bimonthly trade journal; 50 pgs; circ 150,000. Subscription $15. 5% freelance. Query; phone query ok. Pays $75-175, on acceptance, for 1st rts. Articles 800-1,500 wds (5/yr). Reports in 4 wks. Seasonal 6

mos ahead. Accepts reprints. Kill fee. Guidelines; copy for 9x12 SAE/4 stamps.
Special Needs: Audio/visual equipment; books/curriculum resources; music equipment.
Fillers: Buys 20 cartoons/yr. Pays $125.
Columns/Departments: Buys 5/yr. Finance & Law, Ministry Tools, Music & Sound, Maintenance & Construction, Church Furnishings, Computers & Office Equipment; all 1,100 wds; pays $100.
Tips: "Need true experts, or those who have access to experts on church purchasing, needs, business administration."

YOUTHWORKER, 1224 Greenfield Dr., El Cajon CA 92021. (619)440-2333. Fax: (619)440-4939. Youth Specialties Inc. Wayne Rice, ed. For youth workers/church and parachurch. Quarterly journal; 120 pgs; circ 10,000. Subscription $25.95. 90% freelance. Query; phone query ok. Pays $100-150; on acceptance; for 1st & reprint rts. Articles 2,000-3,500 wds (30/yr). Reports in 5 wks. Seasonal 10 mos ahead. Accepts reprints. Kill fee $50. Guidelines/theme list; copy $3/10x13 SAE.
Special Needs: Upcoming themes include The Future, sexuality, resources and results.
Columns/Departments: Buys 10/yr. High School Minister; Middle School Minister; Report From the Front Lines (ideas that worked); 2,000-3,000 wds; $100-150.
Tips: "Read Youthworker; imbibe its tone (professional, though not academic; conversational, though not chatty). Query me with specific, focused ideas that conform to our needs. Writer needs to be a youth minister."

TEEN/YOUNG ADULT MARKETS

#BREAKAWAY, 8605 Explorer Dr., Colorado Springs CO 80920. (719)531-3400. Fax: (719)531-3499. Focus on the Family. Greg Johnson, ed. The 14-year-old, unchurched teen (boy) in the public school is our target; boys 12-17 yrs. Monthly mag; 24-32 pgs; circ 81,000. Subscription $15. Estab. 1990. 60-70% freelance. Complete ms/cover letter; phone query ok. Pays .12-.15/wd, on acceptance, for all, 1st, one-time & reprint rts. Articles 400-1,800 wds (40/yr); fiction (15/yr) 1,200-2,200 wds; music reviews, 300 wds, $30-40. Reports in 1 mo. Seasonal 8 mos ahead. Accepts simultaneous submissions & reprints. Kill fee 33-50%. Guidelines/theme list; copy for 9x12 SAE/3 stamps.
Fillers: Buys 50/yr. Cartoons, facts, quizzes, 200-600 wds. Cartoons $75; others .20-.25/wd.
Columns/Departments: Buys 12/yr. Plugged In (devotional); 700-900 wds.
Tips: "Need strong lead. Brevity & levity a must. Have a teen guy or two read it. Make sure the language is up-to-date, but not overly hip."
** This periodical was #9 on the 1993 Top 50 Plus Christian Publishers list.

BRIO, 8605 Explorer Dr., Colorado Springs CO 80920. (719)548-4577. Fax: (719)531-3499. Focus on the Family. Susie Shellenberger, ed. For teen girls, 12-16 yrs. Monthly mag; 32 pgs; circ 150,000. Subscription $15. 30% freelance. Complete ms/cover letter; phone query ok. Pays .08-.15/wd, on acceptance, for 1st rts. Articles 800-1,000 wds (50/yr); fiction 1,000-1,500 wds (40/yr). Reports in 6 wks. Seasonal 6 mos ahead. Sometimes pays kill fee. Guidelines; copy for 9x12 SAE/6 stamps.
Special Needs: All topics of interest to female teens are welcome: boys, make-up, dating, weight, ordinary girls who have the extra-ordinary, female adjustments to puberty, etc. Also teen-related female fiction.
Fillers: Buys 10/yr. Cartoons, facts, ideas, quizzes, short humor; 500 wds.
Tips: "Study at least 3 issues of *Brio* before submitting. We're looking for a certain, fresh, hip-hop conversational style. Most open to fiction, articles and quizzes."

CAMPUS LIFE, 465 Gundersen Dr., Carol Stream IL 60188. (708)260-6200. Fax: (708)260-0114. Christianity Today, Inc. Christopher Lutes, sr. ed. Seeks to help high school students and early college students navigate adolescence with their faith intact; not overtly religious. Monthly (9X) mag; 64 pgs; circ 120,000. Subscription $14.95. 25% freelance. Query/clips. Pays .10-.20/wd, on acceptance, for 1st & one-time rts. Articles 250-2,500 (1/yr); fiction 750-2,500 wds (1/yr). Reports in 4 wks. Seasonal 4 mos ahead. Accepts simultaneous submissions & occasionally reprints. Kill fee 1/2. Guidelines; copy $2/9x12 SAE/2 stamps.
Poetry: Buys 5-10/yr. Free verse; $25-100. Submit max. 5 poems.
Fillers: Buys 10-20/yr. Various (all high-school oriented); 250-500 wds; $25-75.

***CERTAINTY**, 1300 N. Meacham Rd., Box 95500, Schaumburg IL 60173. Regular Baptist Press. Joan E. Alexander, ed., Sunday school papers. For senior high youth; conservative/fundamental. Weekly take-home paper. Query. Pays .03-.05/wd, on acceptance, for all or 1st rts. Articles 400-1,500 wds; fiction 500-1,500 wds (some multi-part). Reports in 2-8 wks. Seasonal 1 yr ahead. Guidelines; copy for #10 SAE/2 stamps.
Fillers: Various; 100-400 wds.
Tips: "Not everything that is Christian is suitable in a publication intended for readers in fundamental Baptist churches."

***CHALLENGE**, 1300 N. Meacham Rd., Box 95500, Schaumburg IL 60173. Regular Baptist Press. Joan E. Alexander, ed., Sunday school papers. For junior high youth; conservative/fundamental. Weekly take-home paper. Query. Pays .03-.05/wd, on acceptance, for all or 1st rts. Articles 100-1,500 wds; fiction 500-1,500 wds (some multi-part). Reports in 2-8 wks. Seasonal 1 yr ahead. Guidelines; copy for #10 SAE/2 stamps.
Fillers: Anecdotes, facts, games, newsbreaks, prose, word puzzles; 100-400 wds.
Tips: "Not everything that is Christian is suitable in a publication intended for readers in fundamental Baptist churches."

CHALLENGE, 1548 Poplar Ave., Memphis TN 38104. (901)272-2461. Fax: (901)726-5540. Southern Baptist. Submit to Challenge Editor. Missions interest articles for youth, grades 7-12. Monthly mag; 24 pgs; circ 35,000. Subscription $11.28. 30% freelance. Complete ms/no cover letter; no phone query. Pays .05/wd, on publication, for one-time rts. Articles 500-1,000 wds (40/yr). Reports in 4 wks. Seasonal 6 mos ahead. Accepts simultaneous submissions & reprints. Guidelines/theme list; copy for 9x12 SAE/2 stamps.
Fillers: Buys 24/yr. Cartoons, games, word puzzles; 25-50 wds. Pays $10-25.
Tips: "Youth issues and interests are of primary importance. Actual case studies, situations, personalities of today's youth appreciated. Most open to profiles of Christian personalities—sports, music, etc., with youth appeal/popularity."

THE CONQUEROR, 8855 Dunn Rd., Hazelwood MO 63042. (314)837-7300. United Pentecostal Church, Intl. Darrell Johns, ed. For teenagers in the denomination. Bi-monthly mag; 16 pgs; circ 6,000. Subscription $7.50. 90% freelance. Complete ms/no cover letter or phone query. Pays $30, on publication, for various rts. Articles & fiction (many/yr) 500-3,000 wds. Reports in 10 wks. Seasonal 4 mos ahead. Accepts simultaneous submissions & reprints. Guidelines; copy for 11x14 SAE/2 stamps.
Fillers: Various.
Tips: "Articles should be written with the idea of strict morals, standards, and ethics in mind."

+THE EDGE, 455 N. Service Rd. E., Oakville ON L6H 1A5 Canada. (905)845-9235. Fax: (905)845-1966. The Salvation Army. Capt. Bruce Power, ed. Official youth publication of the Salvation Army in Canada; contemporary social and moral issues, Christian lifestyle and contemporary Christian music. Monthly mag; 20 pgs; circ. 5,000. Subscription $1. 50% freelance. **NO PAYMENT.** Not copyrighted. Articles 600-1,800

wds. Reports in 3 wks. Seasonal 3 mos ahead. Accepts simultaneous submissions & reprints. Copy available.
Fillers: Accepts 12 cartoons/yr.

***EVENT**, 127 9th Ave. N., Nashville TN 37234. (615)251-2665. Southern Baptist. Wisty Denton, design ed. Thematic topics of interest to Christian youth, 12-17 yrs old. Monthly; circ 80,000. Limited freelance. Query. Pays .055/wd, on publication, for all or one-time rts. Articles & fiction 1,000-2,500 wds. Seasonal 1 yr ahead. Accepts reprints. Guidelines/theme list.
Poetry: Free verse, traditional; 8-20 lines.
Tips: Preparing to go to a larger size.

FREEWAY, Box 632, Glen Ellyn IL 60138. (708)668-6000. Fax: (708)668-3806. Scripture Press. Amy J. Cox, ed. To help teens (15-22) make wise, biblical choices in their lives. Weekly take-home paper; 4 pgs; circ 50,000. Subscription $7. 95% freelance. Complete ms/cover letter; no phone query. Pays $20-120; on acceptance; for one-time rts. Articles 200-1,200 wds (40/yr); fiction 500-1,200 wds (40/yr); pays $30-120. Reports in 8-12 wks. Seasonal 6 mos ahead. Accepts reprints. Guidelines/copy for #10 SAE/1 stamp.
Poetry: Buys 8/yr. Free verse, light verse, traditional; 4-20 lines; $20-40. Submit max. 5 poems.
Fillers: Buys 5/yr. Cartoons, prose, quizzes, prayers, short humor, word puzzles; 100-500 wds; $10-50.
Tips; "Know the age group: What makes high school and college-age young people tick and what issues they're dealing with. Looking for true stories (profiles, as-told-to's, personal experience). Should show real life struggles, not `super-Christians'."
** This periodical was #15 on the 1993 Top 50 Plus Christian Publishers list.

HICALL, 1445 Boonville Ave., Springfield MO 65802. (417)862-2781. Fax: (417)862-6059. Assemblies of God. Tammy Bicket, ed. To emphasize Christian living through biblical principles for Spirit-filled young people ages 15-17. Weekly take-home paper; 8 pgs; circ 60,000. Subscription $5.80. 50-70% freelance. Complete ms/no cover letter; no phone query. Pays $25-50, on acceptance, for all, 1st, one-time, reprint or simultaneous rts. Articles 500-1,000 wds (50/yr); fiction 800-1,200 wds (50/yr). Reports in 24 wks. Seasonal 18 mos ahead. Accepts simultaneous submissions & reprints. Kill fee 100%. Guidelines/theme list; copy for #10 SAE/1 stamp.
Fillers: Buys 50/yr. Anecdotes, cartoons, short humor; to 300 wds. Pay varies.
Tips: "Write in a hard-hitting, youth-oriented style. Present realistic characters teens can relate to. Characters should work out problems according to biblical principles. Most articles done on assignment basis (contact editor if interested). Stick to themes."

HIGH SCHOOL I.D., 850 N. Grove Ave., Elgin IL 60120. (708)741-2400. Fax: (708)741-0595. David C. Cook Publishing Co. Lorraine Triggs, ed. For evangelical Christian senior highs. Weekly take-home paper; 8 pgs; circ 120,000. Subscription $8. 95% freelance. Query/clips; no phone query. Pays .10/wd, on acceptance, for all rts. Articles 500-1,000 wds (39/yr); fiction 500-1,000 wds (7-8/yr). Reports in 8-10 wks. Seasonal 9 mos ahead. Accepts simultaneous submissions and reprints. Kill fee

variable. Free guidelines/copy for 6x9 SAE/2 stamps.
Special Needs: Articles on contemporary Christian music performers. "We follow a well-developed curriculum plan."
Tips: "We work mainly on an assignment basis, so a query/samples and a resume is best. We don't want the typical Sunday school fare—must be realistic and well developed."

INSIGHT, 55 W. Oak Ridge Dr., Hagerstown MD 21740. (301)791-7000. Fax: (301)791-7012. Seventh-day Adventist. Lori Peckham, ed. For Adventist teenagers, 14-19 yrs. Weekly mag; 16 pgs; circ 25,000. Subscription $35.97. 60% freelance. Complete ms/cover letter; phone query ok. Pays $40-125; on acceptance; for 1st, one-time or reprint rts. Articles 500-1,800 wds (100-150/yr); fiction 500-1,500 wds (50/yr); book and music reviews, 500 wds, $25-50. Reports in 2-4 wks. Seasonal 4-5 mos ahead. Accepts reprints. Guidelines; copy for 9x12 SAE/2 stamps.
Poetry: Buys 60/yr. Avant-garde, free verse, haiku, light verse; to 1 pg; $15-40.
Fillers: Buys 5-10/yr. Anecdotes, cartoons, facts, newsbreaks, party ideas, short humor; to 500 wds; $10-25.
Columns/Departments: Buys 100+/yr. Well-Versed (personal story that demonstrates truth of a Bible verse), 1,000-1,500 wds; On the Edge (drama in real life), 1,000-2,000 wds. Pays $50-100.
Tips: "Write in a realistic, teen point of view. True stories about teens are most appreciated, especially with photos. Most open to Drama-in-Real-Life stories (told like in Reader's Digest)."

INSIGHT/OUT, 55 W. Oak Ridge Dr., Hagerstown MD 21740. (301)791-7000. Fax: (301)791-7012. Seventh-day Adventist. Lori Peckham, ed. For teenagers, 15-19 yrs, of all denominations. Monthly mag; 30 pgs; circ 25,000. 60% freelance. Complete ms. Pays $60-100; on acceptance; for 1st, or reprint rts. Articles & fiction (20 ea/yr), 500-1,500 wds. Reports in 4-12 wks. Seasonal 6 mos ahead. Discourages simultaneous submissions. Kill fee. Guidelines/theme list; free copy.
Poetry: Buys 10/yr. Avant-garde, free verse, haiku; 2-45 lines/$15-40
Fillers: Buys 10/yr. Various; $10-40.

#ISSUES & ANSWERS, The Caleb Campaign, Rt. 4 Box 274, West Frankfort IL 62896-9661. (618)937-2348. Fax: (618)937-2405. D. Ivan Rodden IV, ed.; submit to JoAnne Tegtmeyer, mng ed. A newspaper written from a biblical/creationist viewpoint for young people, 12-20 yrs. Monthly (9X) newspaper; 16 pgs; circ 15,000. 20-50% freelance. Query or complete ms. **NO PAYMENT** for all rts. Not copyrighted. Articles 1,000-2,000 wds (25/yr). Reports in 8 wks. Seasonal 3 mos ahead. Accepts simultaneous submissions & reprints. Guidelines/theme list; copy $1.
Tips: "We are eager for new writers. Need history (list available) and sports interviews. Make articles interesting and relevant."

#THE KILN, Box 5763, Vancouver WA 98668. Gregory Zschomler, ed. To encourage teens (13-19) in the Christian faith. Monthly mag; 12-16 pgs. 30% freelance. Query; no phone query. **USUALLY NO PAYMENT**, pays $12-15 for best work in each issue; for 1st or reprint rts. Articles 1,200-3,000 wds (4/yr). Reports in 1 mo. Seasonal 4 mos

ahead. Accepts simultaneous submissions & reprints. Guidelines/theme list; copy $.30.
Special Needs: Missions, evangelism on campus, values.
Fillers: Buys 50/yr. Anecdotes, cartoons, jokes, quotes, short humor; $1-12.
Columns/Departments: Friar Yuk (humor), $1; Whispers of Wisdom (quotes). Open to new column ideas.
Tips: "Most open to articles biblically on target; approach issues that need change; appeal to teens sense of idealism."

LYF LINES, 1333 S. Kirkwood Rd., St. Louis MO 63122. "We are not currently publishing, but will be doing some new pieces in '94 and '95."

#THE MAGAZINE FOR CHRISTIAN YOUTH!, Box 801, Nashville TN 37202. (615)749-6319. Fax: (615)749-6078/6079. United Methodist. Anthony E. Peterson, ed. To help teenagers (11-18 yrs) develop Christian identity and live the Christian faith in their contemporary culture. Monthly mag; 48 pgs; circ 30,000. 50% freelance. Query (complete ms/cover letter for fiction); phone query ok. Pays $20-150 (assigned) or .05/wd (unsolicited), on acceptance, for all or one-time rts. Articles (5/yr) & fiction (12/yr), 700-2,000 wds; book reviews 200-500 wds, .05/wd. Reports in 2-4 wks. Seasonal 8-10 mos ahead. Accepts simultaneous query & reprints. Guidelines; copy for $2 or 9x12 SAE/5 stamps.
Poetry: Buys 60/yr. Avant-garde, free verse, haiku, light verse, traditional; to 50 lines; no payment. From teens only.
Fillers: Buys 6/yr. various; 50-200 wds; .05/wd.
Tips: "Most open to humor, how-to, social issues, and personal experience that is not preachy."
** This periodical was #27 on the 1993 Top 50 Plus Christian Publishers list.

#PATHWAY I.D., Box 2250, Cleveland TN 37320-2250. (615)478-7599. Church of God. Lance Colkmire, ed. Emphasizing victorious, Spirit-filled living in a secular world for senior highs (15-17). Weekly take-home paper; 8 pgs; circ 18,000. 5-10% freelance. Complete ms/ cover letter. Pays $20-45, on acceptance, for 1st, one-time, reprint & simultaneous rts. Articles 400-800 wds (5/yr). Reports in 1 mo. Seasonal 1 yr ahead. Accepts simultaneous submissions & reprints. Guidelines/copy for #10 SASE/1 stamp.
Tips: "Need true stories of how Christ is making a difference in teens' lives." Not accepting fiction for now; query about future issues.

#PIONEER, 1548 Poplar Ave., Memphis TN 38104. (901)272-2461. Fax: (901)726-5540. Southern Baptist/Baptist Brotherhood Commission. Jene C. Smith, ed. For boys 12-14 yrs who are members of Pioneer Royal Ambassadors, a missions education organization. Monthly mag; 24 pgs; circ 25,500. 5% freelance. Complete ms. Pays .045/wd, on publication, for one-time & reprint rts. Articles 100-800 wds. Reports in 1 month. Seasonal 8 mos ahead. Accepts simultaneous submissions. Guidelines/theme list; copy for 9x12 SAE/5 stamps or $1.20.
Tips: "Most open to stories of Christians involved in sports; articles about nature and outdoors; special interest stories. Nothing preachy."

***QUEST**, 475 Riverside Dr., 10th Floor, New York NY 10115. United Church of Christ, Board for Home Ministries. Submit to Editor. For senior highs (15-18 yrs). Theme list available.

THE ROCK, 850 N. Grove Ave., Elgin IL 60120. (708)741-2400. Fax: (708)741-0595. David C. Cook Publishing Co. Sharon Stultz, ed. Accepting no freelance during 1994. Contact editor in early 1995 for an update on their status.

#SHARING THE VICTORY, 8701 Leeds Rd., Kansas City MO 64129. (816)921-0909. Fax: (816)921-8755. Fellowship of Christian Athletes (Protestant and Catholic). John Dodderidge, ed. Equipping and encouraging athletes and coaches to take their faith seriously, in and out of competition. Monthly (Sept-May) mag; 24 pgs; circ 50,000. 60% freelance. Query/clips; no phone query. Pays $100-200, on publication, for 1st rts. Articles 500-1,000 wds (5-20/yr). Reports in 2-4 wks. Seasonal 3 mos ahead. Accepts reprints. Kill fee. Guidelines; copy $1/9x12 SAE/3 stamps.
Poetry: Buys 3/yr. Free verse. Pays $50.
Tips: "Most open to sports personality features including jr. high, high school and college."

#SPIRIT, Lectionary-based Weekly for Catholic Teens, 1884 Randolph Ave., St. Paul MN 55105. (612)690-7012. Catholic. Joan Mitchell, CSJ, mng. ed. For the religious education of high schoolers (14-18 yrs). Biweekly newsletter; 4 pgs; circ 30,000. 50% freelance. Query (complete ms/cover letter for fiction). Pays $135, on publication, for all rts. Articles & fiction 1,000-2,000 wds (12 ea/yr). Reports in 3 mos. Seasonal 4-6 mos ahead. Accepts simultaneous query. Guidelines/copy for #10 SAE/1 stamp.

STRAIGHT, 8121 Hamilton Ave., Cincinnati OH 45231. (513)931-4050. Fax: (513)931-0904. Standard Publishing. Carla J. Crane, ed. For Christian teens (13-19). Weekly take-home paper; 12 pgs; circ 50,000. Subscription $9.50. 100% freelance. Complete ms/no cover letter; no phone query. Pays .03-.07/wd, on acceptance, for all, 1st or reprint rts. Articles to 1,500 wds (40-60/yr); fiction 1,000-1,500 wds (50-70/yr). Reports in 1-8 wks. Seasonal 9-12 mos ahead. Accepts simultaneous submissions & reprints. Guidelines/theme list/copy for #10 SAE/1 stamp.
Poetry: Buys 20-40/yr. Avant-garde, free verse, light verse, traditional; from teens only. Pays $10. Submit max. 10 poems.
Fillers: Buys 10/yr. Short humor, 500 wds.
Tips: "Request to be put on our theme list. Get to know and work with teenagers."
** This periodical was #12 on the 1993 Top 50 Plus Christian Publishers list.

#THE STUDENT, 127 9th Ave. N, Nashville TN 37234. (615)251-2788. Southern Baptist. Cheryl Lewis, acting ed. Helping college students grow in relationship to Jesus Christ by dealing with needs, problems, current issues, and suggestions for personal growth. Monthly mag; 52 pgs; circ 40,000. 10% freelance. Complete ms. Pays .055/wd; on acceptance; for all rts. Articles to 1,000 wds (20/yr); fiction to 1,000 wds (5-6/yr). Reports in 2 mos. Seasonal 1 yr ahead. Accepts simultaneous submissions. Guidelines; copy for 9x12 SAE/3 stamps.

STUDENT LEADERSHIP JOURNAL, Box 7895, Madison WI 53707. (608)274-9001x425/413. Fax: (608)274-7882. InterVarsity Christian Fellowship. Jeff Yourison, ed. Undergraduate college student Christian leaders, single, ages 18-36. Quarterly journal; 32 pgs; circ 8,000. Subscription $16. 20-30% freelance. Query/clips; no phone query. Pays $35-125, on acceptance, for 1st, one-time or reprint rts. Articles to 2,000 wds (5/yr); fiction (0-1/yr) to 1,500 wds ($25-100); book reviews 150-400 wds/$25-50. Reports in 16 wks. Seasonal 8 mos ahead. Accepts reprints. Guidelines/theme list; copy $3/9x12 SAE/4 stamps.
Special Needs: Campus issues/trends; planning/vision-building; multi-ethnic; making committed choices in a world of options; leadership/spiritual growth.
Poetry: Buys 4/yr. Avant-garde, free verse; to 15 lines; $25-50. Submit max. 5 poems.
Fillers: Buys 0-5/yr. Facts, games, party ideas, quizzes; to 200 wds; $10-50.
Columns/Departments: Buys 6-10/yr. Collegiate Trends, 20-100 wds; Student Leadership Network, 500-800 wds; Chapter Strategy (how-to planning strategy for campus groups), 500-800; $10-75. Query.
Tips: "Most open to main features targeted to college-age students. Be upbeat, interesting and fresh."

TAKE FIVE, 1445 Boonville Ave., Springfield MO 65802. (417)862-2781x4359. Fax: (417)862-8558. Assemblies of God. Tammy Bicket, youth ed. A daily devotional for teens, grades 7-12. Quarterly booklet; 112 pgs; circ 23,000. Subscription $6. 10% freelance. Write for assignment. Pays $15/devotion, on acceptance, for all rts (one-time rts for poetry). Reports in 13 wks. Seasonal 15 mos ahead. Accepts simultaneous submissions & reprints on poetry only. Guidelines; no copy.
Special Needs: Photos; photos of ethnic groups are a plus. Poetry from teens.
Poetry: Buys 36/yr. Any type; 8-25 lines; $15. Submit max. 5 poems. "Poetry is held on file unless writer requests its return."
Tips: "All devotional writing is done on assignment to Assemblies of God writers only. Sample devotional or similar writing can be submitted for editors' evaluation and for future consideration when writing assignments are made."

#TEENAGE CHRISTIAN MAGAZINE, Box 1438, Murphreesboro TN 37133. Church of Christ. Marty Dodson, ed. For early teens (13-19 yrs). Bimonthly mag; 32 pgs; circ 15,000. 70% freelance. Complete ms; no cover letter or phone query. Pays $25, on publication, for 1st or one-time rts. Articles 500-1,200 wds (25/yr); fiction 1,000-2,000 wds (5/yr); book reviews 500-750 wds ($25). Reports in 1-2 mos. Seasonal 4-6 mos ahead. Accepts simultaneous submissions & reprints. Guidelines/theme list; copy for 9x12 SAE/2 stamps.
Special Needs: "Fiction must be believable and well written. Must show that you understand teenagers. Need more articles that show teens how the Bible applies to their lives."
Poetry: Buys 5/yr. Free verse, traditional; 8-25 lines; $10-25. Submit max. 5 poems.
Fillers: Buys 20/yr. Various; 25-125 wds; $5-25.
Columns/Departments: Buys 10-15/yr. Music that Matters (reviews), 400-600 wds; Current Trends, 100-250 wds; Bible Study, 100-250 wds. Pays $10-25.
Tips: "Articles that challenge teens to live for Christ and apply God's word to their lives have the best chance to be published."

***TEEN LIFE**, 8855 Dunn Rd., Hazelwood MO 63042. (314)837-7304. United Pentecostal Church. R.M. Davis, ed. For teens 13-15 years. Weekly take-home paper. 90% freelance. Complete ms; no cover letter or phone query. Pays $8-25, on publication, for all rts. Articles 800-1,800 wds (up to 120/yr); fiction 1,200-1,800 wds (up to 120/yr). Seasonal 9 mos ahead. Accepts simultaneous submissions & reprints. Guidelines; free copy.

Poetry: Accepts 30/yr; $3-12.

Tips: "Most open to good stories and articles for a traditional, fundamental audience."

TEEN POWER, Box 632, Glen Ellyn IL 60138. (708)668-6000. Fax: (708)668-3806. Scripture Press. Amy J. Cox, ed. To help young teens (11-16) explore ways Jesus relates to them in everyday life. Weekly take-home paper; 8 pgs. Subscription $7. 90% freelance. Complete ms/cover letter; no phone query. Pays .06-.10/wd, on acceptance, for one-time rts. Articles 200-700 wds (50/yr); fiction 500-1,200 wds (60/yr). Reports in 8-12 wks. Seasonal 6 mos ahead. Accepts reprints. Guidelines/copy for #10 SAE/1 stamp.

Fillers: Buys 10/yr. Cartoons, prose, quizzes, short humor, word puzzles; 200-600 wds; $15-60.

Tips: "We rely heavily on freelance writers, so this is a good place to break in. Study young teens (jr. high). Know what issues they're dealing with and what makes them click. We're always in need of true stories (profiles, as-told-to, personal experience) and short nonfiction."

** This periodical was #31 on the 1993 Top 50 Plus Christian Publishers list.

#TEEN QUEST (TQ), 2845 W. Airport Freeway Ste. 137, Irving TX 75038. (214)570-7599. Shepherd Ministries. Christopher Lyon, ed. To show teens (14-17) why a relationship with Christ is important now and how to grow in this relationship. Monthly mag; 48 pgs; circ 54,000. 40-50% freelance. Query; phone query ok. Pays .08-.15/wd (reprints .03/wd), on acceptance, for 1st rts. Articles 1,000-2,500 wds (15-20/yr); fiction 1,500-2,250 wds (20-25/yr). Reports in 6 wks. Seasonal 6 mos ahead. Accepts simultaneous submissions. Some kill fees. Guidelines; copy for 9x12 SAE/4 stamps.

Poetry: Lisa Thompson. Buys 8-10/yr. Devotional/thought-provoking; teen-written only. Submit max. 3 poems.

Columns/Departments: Buys 5-6/yr. Together (dating/relationships), 1,000-1,200 wds; BreakOut (profiles of outstanding teenagers); 1,000-1,200 wds; .07-.12/wd.

Tips: "Teen language and behavior must be current. Not too preachy in moral—let the story make its own point. Most open to fiction, personal experience. Ask yourself if teens can readily identify with main characters." Only looking for fiction for now.

#TEENS TODAY, 6401 The Paseo, Kansas City MO 64131. (816)333-7000x2209. Fax: (816)333-4315. Church of the Nazarene. Carol Gritton, ed. For junior high and senior high teens (to age 18). Weekly take-home paper; 8 pgs; circ 55,000. Subscription $7. 25% freelance. Complete ms/cover letter; no phone query. Pays .035/wd, on acceptance, for 1st, simultaneous or reprint rts (.03/wd). Fiction 1,000-1,500 wds (52/yr). Reports in 2 mos. Seasonal 10 mos ahead. Accepts simultaneous submissions & reprints. Guidelines/theme list/copy for #10 SAE/2 stamps.

TQ - See **Teen Quest.**

VENTURE, Box 150, Wheaton IL 60189. (708)665-0630. Fax: (708)665-0372. Christian Service Brigade. Deborah Christiansen, ed. Slanted to boys (10-15) involved in Brigade programs in their churches. Bimonthly mag; 32 pgs; circ 18,000. Subscription $10. 50% freelance. Complete ms/cover letter; no phone query. Pays .05-.10/wd; on publication; for 1st or reprint rts. Articles (6/yr) & fiction (18/yr), 500-1,000 wds. Reports in 1 wk. Seasonal 4 mos ahead. Accepts reprints. Kill fee $35. Guidelines/theme list; copy $1.85/9x12 SAE/4 stamps.
Fillers: Buys 6/yr. Prose (Christian living), short humor; to 500 wds.
Tips: "Get to know boys. They're different from girls. They want to be able to see what you're writing. Know their humor."

***VISIONS**, Lectionary-based Weekly for Catholic Junior Highs, 1884 Randolph Ave., St. Paul MN 55434. (612)690-7010. Editorial Development Associates. Joan Mitchell, CSJ, mng. ed. Connects young people's real life experiences—successes and conflicts in family, neighborhood, classroom—with the Sunday gospel; for junior-high-age young people. Weekly take-home paper; circ 140,000. 40% freelance. Query. Pays $75-125, on publication, for all rts. Articles (6-8/yr) & fiction (8-10/yr), 900-1,000 wds. Reports in 2-8 wks. Seasonal 4-6 mos ahead. Accepts simultaneous query. Guidelines; copy $1.85.

WITH, Box 347, Newton KS 67053. (316)283-5100. Fax: (316)283-0454. Mennonite. Carol Duerksen (fillers & poetry) & Eddy Hall (articles & fiction), co-eds. For high-school teens (15-18 yrs), Christian and non-Christian. Monthly (8X) mag; 32 pgs; circ 5,800. Subscription $16.95. 80% freelance. Query (on first-person and how-to articles); complete ms on everything else/short cover letter; no phone query. Pays .04/wd for unsolicited, .05-.10/wd (.05-.07/wd for fiction) for assignments, .02-.03/wd for reprints; on acceptance; for first, simultaneous or reprint rts. Articles 500-2,100 wds (20/yr); fiction 800-2,000 wds (16-20/yr). Reports in 1-3 wks. Seasonal 6-8 mos. ahead. Accepts simultaneous submissions & reprints. Kill fee 30-50%. Guidelines/theme list; copy for 9x12 SAE/4 stamps. Separate guidelines for 1st-person & how-to articles sent only when requested.
Poetry: Buys 4/yr. All types; 4-50 lines; $10-35. Submit any number.
Fillers: Buys cartoons, 24/yr; $20-35 ($50 for cover).
Tips: "The how-to article is a good place to break in. Study special guidelines and send a query at least 8 months before appropriate theme issue. Fiction to match upcoming theme also good way to break in."
** This periodical was #24 on the 1993 Top 50 Plus Christian Publishers list.

#YOU! MAGAZINE, 29800 Agoura Rd. #102, Agoura Hills CA 91301. (818)991-1813. Fax: (818)991-2024. Catholic. Tom Ehart, mng. ed. An alternative teen magazine (13-18 yrs) aimed at bridging the gap between religion and pop culture. Monthly (10X) tabloid; 28 pgs; circ 35,000. 50% freelance. Query/clips or complete ms/cover letter. Pays .05-.075/wd ($10-105), on publication, for one-time & reprint rts. Articles 100-1,600 wds (25-50/yr); book reviews, 500 wds, .07/wd. Reports in 2 mos. Seasonal 4 mos ahead. Accepts simultaneous query & reprints. Guidelines; copy for 10x15 SAE/5

stamps.
Fillers: Anecdotes, cartoons, facts, ideas, jokes, short humor; 75-250 wds.
Tips: "Write in the language of teens. Must be 'hip'."

#YOUNG ADULT TODAY, 1350 W. 103rd St., Chicago IL 60643. (312)233-4499. Urban Ministries, Inc. Dr. Colleen Birchett, ed. Young adult curriculum for ages 18-24 (student and teacher manuals). Quarterly booklet; 72 pgs; circ 7,500. 60% freelance. Complete ms. Pays $35-50, on publication, for all rts. Articles (24/yr) & fiction (12/yr); 2,900-3,500 characters. Reports in 1-2 wks. Seasonal 3 mos ahead. Free guidelines/theme list/copy.
Tips: "Send resume and writing sample. Writer must be able to relate the writing to the outline given and the Biblical material."

#YOUNG AND ALIVE, Box 6097, Lincoln NE 68506. (402)488-0981. Christian Record Services. Richard Kaiser, ed. For sight impaired young adults, 16-20; for interdenominational Christian audience. Quarterly mag; 65-70 pgs; circ 26,000. 90% freelance. Query or complete ms/cover letter; phone query ok. Pays .03-.05/wd, on acceptance, for one-time rts. Articles & true stories 800-1,400 wds (30/yr). Reports in 2-3 mos. Seasonal 1 yr ahead. Accepts simultaneous query & reprints. Guidelines; copy for 9-12 SAE/6 stamps.
Special Needs: Adventure and relationships for the handicapped.
Tips: "Although many blind and visually impaired yg. adults have the same interests as their sighted counterparts, the material should meet their needs specifically."

YOUNG SALVATIONIST, 615 Slaters Ln., Box 269, Alexandria VA 22313. (703)684-5519. Fax: (703)684-5539. The Salvation Army. Lt. Deborah R. Sedlar, youth ed. For high-school and early college teens in The Salvation Army. Monthly (10X) mag; 16 pgs; circ 50,000. Subscription $4. 75% freelance. Query or complete ms/no cover letter; phone query ok. Pays .10/wd; on acceptance; for 1st, one-time, and reprint rts. Articles 750-1,200 wds (30/yr); fiction 750-1,200 wds (30/yr); book & music review 750-1,200 wds. Reports in 2-4 wks. Seasonal 3 mos ahead. Accepts simultaneous submissions & reprints. Guidelines/theme list; copy for 9x12 SAE/3 stamps.
Poetry: Buys 4/yr. Free verse, traditional; pays $10-20. Submit max. 10 poems.
Fillers: Buys 5/yr. Anecdotes, cartoons, facts, games, quizzes, prayers, short humor, word puzzles. Pays $10-20.
Tips:"We encourage submissions from beginners as well as accomplished and sometimes send suggestions for improvement. Please aim at high schoolers from all different backgrounds and make it relative to the needs of today's teens."
** This periodical was #7 on the 1993 Top 50 Plus Christian Publishers list.

***YOUTH FOCUS**, Paywoods Communications, 4 Daniels Farm Rd., Ste. 134, Trumbull CT 06611. (203)372-1745. For African-American youth, ages 12-17. Quentin Plair, ed. Monthly newsletter; circ 10,000. 75% freelance. Complete ms. Pays $15-100, on publication, for 1st or one-time rts. Articles 10-3,000 wds (2/yr). Reports in 2 mos. Seasonal 5 mos ahead. Accepts simultaneous submissions & reprints. Guidelines; copy $1.
Poetry: Buys 7/yr. Any type; 1-200 lines; $10-30.

#YOUTH UPDATE, 1615 Republic St., Cincinnati OH 45210-1289. (513)241-5615. St. Anthony Messenger Press/Catholic. Carol Ann Morrow, ed. For high-school teens, to support their growth in a life of faith. Monthly newsletter; 4 pgs; circ 35,000. 90% freelance. Query. Pays $350-400 (.14/wd), on acceptance, for 1st rts. Articles 2,200-2,300 wds (12/yr). Reports in 2-3 mos. Guidelines/theme list/copy for #10 SAE/1 stamp.

***YOUTH WORLD**, 8855 Dunn Rd., Hazelwood MO 63042. (314)837-7304. United Pentecostal Church. R.M. Davis, ed. For teens 13-15 years. Weekly take-home paper. 90% freelance. Complete ms; no cover letter or phone query. Pays $8-25, on publication, for all rts. Articles 800-1,800 wds (up to 120/yr); fiction 1,200-1,800 wds (up to 120/yr). Seasonal 9 mos ahead. Accepts simultaneous submissions & reprints. Guidelines; free copy.
Poetry: Accepts 30/yr; $3-12.
Tips: "Most open to good stories and articles for a traditional, fundamental audience."

WOMEN'S MARKETS

ANNA'S JOURNAL, Rt 8 Box 655, Ellijay GA 30540. (706)276-2307. Catherine Ward-Long, ed. Spiritual support for childless couples who for the most part have decided to stay that way. Quarterly newsletter. Subscription $30. Est. 1994. 90% freelance. Complete ms/cover letter; no phone query. **PAYS IN COPIES**, for one-time or reprint rts. Not copyrighted. Articles 500-1,500 wds. Reports in 4-8 wks. Seasonal 3 months ahead. Accepts reprints. Guidelines/theme list; copy $7/#10 SAE/2 stamps.
Poetry: Accepts 3/yr. Any type. Submit max. 3 poems.
Fillers: Anecdotes, ideas (on how church can meet our needs), prose, prayers, letters; 50-250 wds.
Tips: "Looking for innovative ways to improve the child-free lifestyle and self-esteem. No articles on adoption or infertility. It helps if writer is childless or knows someone who is."

#THE CHURCH WOMAN, 475 Riverside Dr., Room 812, New York NY 10115. (212)870-2347. Fax: (212)870-2338. Church Women United. Margaret Schiffert, ed. Highlights women's, peace and justice issues. Quarterly mag; 24 pgs; circ 10,000. Little freelance. Query. **PAYS IN COPIES**. Articles to 3 pgs. Guidelines; copy $1.

CO-LABORER, Box 5002, Antioch TN 37011-5002. (615)731-6812. Fax: (615)731-0049. Free Will Baptist/Women Nationally Active for Christ. Melissa Riddle, ed. For members of WNAC; emphasizes missions, Christian issues, and spiritual development resources. Bimonthly mag; 32 pgs; circ 14,000. Subscription $5.75. 90% freelance. Query/clips; no phone query. **PAYS IN COPIES** for one-time rts. Articles 200-1,000 wds (6/yr); book reviews, 800 wds. Reports in 3-6 wks. Seasonal 6 mos ahead. Accepts reprints. Guidelines; copy $2.
Poetry: Free verse, haiku, traditional; 1-21 lines; on missions only. Submit max. 6 poems.
Fillers: Anecdotes, facts, ideas, prose, prayers, quotes, short humor; 300-500 wds.
Columns/Departments: Crosswinds (overcoming obstacles), 800-1,000 wds.
Tips: "Intelligent queries get attention. Most open to feature columns."

#CONSCIENCE, A Newsjournal of Prochoice Catholic Opinion and Analysis, 1436 U St. NW, Ste. 301, Washington DC 20009-3997. (202)986-6093. Catholic. Maggie Hume, ed. For laypeople, theologians, policymakers, and clergy. Quarterly newsjournal; 48 pgs; circ 12,000. 80% freelance. Query or complete ms/cover letter; no phone query. Pays $25-150, on publication, for 1st rts. Articles 1,000-3,500 wds (8-12/yr); book reviews 600-1,200 wds/$25-50. Reports in 2 mos. Seasonal 6 mos ahead. Accepts simultaneous submissions & reprints. Kill fee. Guidelines; copy for 9x12 SAE/4 stamps.
Poetry: Buys 16/yr. Any type, on subject, to 50 lines; $10 + copies. Submit max. 5 poems.

Columns/Departments: Buys 6/yr. Newsbreaks, 100-300 wds. Pays $25-35.
Tips: "Focus on issues of reproductive choice. Raise serious ethical questions within a generally prochoice framework. Most open to feature articles and book reviews."

+CONTEMPO, P.O. Box 830010, Birmingham AL 35283-0010. (205)991-8100. Southern Baptist. Cindy L. Dake, ed. A young women's (18-34 yrs) publication focusing on missions education and women's/family issues. Monthly mag; 48 pgs; circ. 65,000. 95% freelance. Complete ms/cover letter. Pays .055/wd, on publication, for all rts. Articles to 600 wds. Reports in 12-18 mos.

#DAUGHTERS OF SARAH, 2121 Sheridan Rd., Evanston IL 60201. Ecumenical. Sandra Valentine, mng. ed. Christian feminism magazine with a biblical emphasis, using inclusive language. Quarterly mag; 64 pgs; circ 5,000. 85% freelance. Query (complete ms for fiction). Pays $15/published pg, on publication, for 1st & one-time rts. Articles (40/yr) & fiction (4-6/yr), 500-2,100 wds; book reviews 300-500 wds/pays in copies. Reports in 2 mos. Seasonal 3 mos ahead. Accepts simultaneous query & reprints. Kill fee. Guidelines/theme list; copy $3.
Poetry: Buys 15/yr.
Fillers: Buys 5-10/yr. Cartoons, short humor.
Columns/Departments: Buys 6/yr. Segue (evangelical women), 800 wds. Pay $15-80.
Tips: "Thematic; write for themes."

ESPRIT, Evangelical Lutheran Women, 1512 St. James St., Winnipeg, MB R3H 0L2 Canada. (204)775-8591. Fax: (204)783-7548. Evangelical Lutheran Church in Canada. Anne Beretta, ed. For women in organization/denomination. Bimonthly mag; 52 pgs; circ 7,200. Subscription $15.50, $25 US. 50% freelance. Query; phone query ok. Pays $12.50-50 Canadian (fiction $12.50-37.50), on publication, for 1st rts. Articles 350-1,500 wds (60/yr); fiction 350-1,000 wds (6/yr); book reviews, 1/2 page, $6.75. Reports in 4-8 wks. Seasonal 3 mos ahead. Accepts reprints. Guidelines/theme list; copy for 6x9 SAE/.86 Canadian postage or $1 for non-Canadians.
Poetry: Accepts 10/yr. Free verse, haiku, light verse, traditional; 5-100 lines; $12.50-25. Submit max. 3 poems.
Fillers: Buys 20-30/yr. Anecdotes, cartoons, prose, prayers, quotes, word puzzles; 50-350 wds. Pays $3.25-12.50.
Tips: "Be a Lutheran living in Canada. Use inclusive language, NRSV as reference Bible, focus on women and spiritual/faith issues."

HELPING HAND, Box 12609, Oklahoma City OK 73157. (405)787-7110. Fax: 405-789-3957. Pentecostal Holiness Church/Women's Ministries. Doris L. Moore, ed. Denominational; for women. Bimonthly mag; 20 pgs; circ 4,000. Subscription $6.50. 50% freelance. Complete ms/cover letter; no phone query. Pays $20, on publication, for reprint & simultaneous rts. Articles 600-1,400 wds (30/yr); fiction 600-1,400 wds (10/yr). Reports in 2 wks. Seasonal 4 mos ahead. Accepts simultaneous submissions & reprints. Guidelines; copy for 9x12 SAE/2 stamps.
Poetry: Buys 5/yr. Traditional; $10-20. Submit max. 4 poems.

#HORIZONS, 100 Witherspoon St., Louisville KY 40202. (502)569-5379. Fax: (502)569-8085. Presbyterian Church (USA). Barbara Roche, ed. Justice issues and spiritual life for Presbyterian women. Bimonthly mag.; 40 pgs; circ 30,000. 10% freelance. Complete ms. Pays $50/pg., on publication, for all rts. Articles & fiction 1,500-2,000 wds. Reports in 4 wks. Seasonal 6 mos ahead. Accepts reprints. Guidelines/theme list; copy $2.
Poetry: Buys 4/yr. All types; $25.
Tips: "Know our audience—mostly women in their 40's and up who are interested in social concerns." Most open to fiction and poetry.

+JOURNAL OF WOMEN'S MINISTRIES, 46 Olive St., Methuen MA 01844. (800)334-7626. Episcopal/Council for Women's Ministries. Marcy Darin, ed. Deals with issues of interest to women from a liberal perspective. Biannual mag; 36 pgs; circ. 10,000. Query. Pays $50, on publication, for 1st rts. Articles 1,200-1,500 wds. Reports in 1 mo. Seasonal 3 mos ahead. Guidelines; copy for 9x12 SAE/3 stamps.
Poetry: Free verse, traditional. Submit max. 2 poems.

THE JOYFUL WOMAN, Skates Bldg., 3335 Ringgold Rd., P.O. Box 90038, Chattanooga TN 37412. (615)698-7318. Joy Rice Martin, Ed. To encourage, stimulate, teach, and develop the Christian woman to reach the full potential of her womanhood. Bimonthly mag; 24 pgs; circ 13,000. Subscription $15. 50% freelance. Complete ms. Pays .02/wd & up, on publication, for 1st or reprint rts. Articles 800-2,500 wds (60/yr). Reports in 1-6 wks. Seasonal 4 mos ahead. Accepts simultaneous submissions & reprints. Guidelines; copy $3/9x12 SAE/4 stamps.

#JUST BETWEEN US, Jill Briscoe's Newsletter for Ministry Wives, P.O. Box 7728, Louisville KY 40257. (502)899-3119. Submit to Managing ed. Ideas, encouragement and resources for wives of evangelical ministers. Quarterly mag; 20 pgs; circ 5,000. Estab. 1990. 90% freelance. Query. **NO PAYMENT** for one-time rts. Any length. Reporting time varies. Accepts simultaneous submissions. Guidelines; copy for 9x12 SAE/3 stamps.
Tips: "Virtually all material is written by ministry wives. Always include bio notes."

THE LINK & VISITOR, 30 Arlington Ave., Toronto, ON M6G 3K8 Canada. (416)651-7192. Baptist Women's Missionary Society. Esther Barnes, ed. A positive, practical magazine for Canadian Baptist women who want to make a difference in our world. Monthly (9X) mag; 16 pgs; circ 5,500. Subscription $10 Canada, $14 U.S. 30% freelance. Complete ms/cover letter; phone query ok. Pays to $10-60 Canadian, on publication, for 1st, one-time, or simultaneous rts. Articles 800-1,600. Reports in 4-36 wks. Seasonal 6 mos ahead. Accepts simultaneous submissions & reprints. Copy for 9x12 SAE/.86 Canadian postage.
Special Needs: Articles on courage; stories on a single Beatitude.
Poetry: Buys 6/yr. Free verse, 12-32 lines. Pays $25. Submit max. 4 poems.
Tips: "Canadian writers preferred. If U.S. writers send U.S. postage for returns, they will be rejected. Too many writers seem too focused on themselves and their own experiences."

#LUTHERAN WOMAN TODAY, 8765 W. Higgins Ave., Chicago IL 60631-4189. (312)380-2743. Evangelical Lutheran Church in America. Nancy J. Stelling, ed. For women in the denomination. Monthly (11X) mag: 48 pgs; circ 250,000. 25% freelance. Complete ms/cover letter or query. Pays $60-280, on publication, for 1st rts. Articles (24/yr) & fiction (5/yr), to 1,250 wds. Reports in 1-2 mos. Seasonal 7 mos ahead. Guidelines; free copy.
Poetry: Buys 5/yr. Free verse, haiku, light verse, traditional; to 60 lines; $15-60. Submit max. 3 poems. Poetry must have a spiritual and women's focus.
Columns/Departments: Buys 5/yr. Devotion, 350 wds; Season's Best (reflection on the church yr), 350-700 wds; About Women; Forum (essay); $50-250.
Tips: "Submit a short, well-written article using inclusive language and offering a women's and spiritual focus."

PARENT CARE, Box 12624, Roanoke VA 24027. (703)342-7511. Betty Robertson, mng. ed. For adult children providing care for aging parents. Monthly newsletter; 16 pgs; circ 100+. Subscription $19.95. Estab. 1991. 95% freelance. Complete ms/no cover letter; no phone query. Pays $3-5, on acceptance, for one-time, reprint or simultaneous rts. Articles 750-1,200 wds (40-50/yr). Reports in 2-6 wks. Seasonal 3 mos ahead. Accepts simultaneous submissions & reprints. Guidelines/theme list; copy $2.50.
Poetry: Avant-garde, free verse, haiku, traditional. No payment.
Fillers: Recipes, care-giving tips & ideas; 25-200 wds; no payment.
Tips: "Creative approach to any of the issues facing adult children of aging parents. If you're not a caregiver, talk to some."

+PROBE, 529 S. Wabash, Ste. 404, Chicago IL 60605. (312)663-1980. National Assembly of Religious Women/Catholic/Ecumenical. Cecelia Lavan, ed. Networking tool for members with a progressive, social justice and feminist thrust. Bimonthly newspaper; 12 pgs; circ. 1,800. 90% freelance. Query. **PAYS A SUBSCRIPTION** for one-time rts. Articles to 2,000 wds; fiction to 2,000 wds. Accepts simultaneous submissions. No guidelines; copy $1.
Poetry: Must be theme-related.

#RESPONSE, 475 Riverside Dr., Rm. 1344, New York NY 10115. (212)870-3755. United Methodist. Dana E. Jones, ed. Program journal of United Methodist Women. Monthly (11X) mag; 48 pgs; circ 75,000. 50% freelance. Query. Pays variable rates, on publication, for all rts. Articles 1,000 wds; book reviews 1,000 wds. Seasonal 5 mos ahead. Kill fee. No guidelines; free copy.
Tips: "Send us something that focuses on the concerns of women, youth or children."

+ROYAL SERVICE, P.O. Box 830010, Birmingham AL 35283-0010. (205)991-8100. Southern Baptist/ Women's Missionary Union. Cindy Lewis Dake, mng. ed.; Laura Savage, prod. ed. Focuses on missions; women and family issues. Monthly mag; 48 pgs; circ. 290,000. 95% freelance. Complete ms/cover letter. Pays .055/wd, on publication, for all rts. Articles to 600 wds. Reports in 12-18 mos. No guidelines or copy.

#SALT AND LIGHT, Christian Career Women, Box 531152, Indianapolis IN 46253-1152. (317)328-8714. Mary Reynolds Williams, ed. For Christian working women (25-60); conservative. Bimonthly newsletter; 10-12 pgs; circ 250-275. 80% freelance. Complete ms/no cover letter or phone query. **PAYS IN COPIES.** Not copyrighted. Articles 800-1,500 wds (10-20/yr). Reports in 3-12 wks. Seasonal 6-8 mos ahead. Accepts reprints. Guidelines; copy .75 or 9x12 SAE/3 stamps.
Poetry: Free verse, light verse, traditional. Submit max. 3 poems.

#SISTERS TODAY, The Liturgical Press, St. John's Abbey, Collegeville MN 56321-2099. (612)363-7065. Fax: (612)363-3299. Catholic. Sr. Mary Anthony Wagner, O.S.B., ed. To explore the role of women and the Church in our time. Bimonthly mag; 80 pgs; circ 8,000. 80% freelance. Query or complete ms/cover letter. Pays $5/printed page, on publication, for 1st rts. Articles 8-10 pgs (50-60/yr). Reports in 3 mos. Seasonal 1 yr ahead. Occasionally uses reprints. Guidelines (from various editors); copy $3.50.
Poetry: Buys 18/yr. Free verse, haiku, light verse, traditional; to one-page (prefers 16-20 lines). Pays $10. Submit max. 4 poems.

TODAY'S CHRISTIAN WOMAN, 445 Gundersen Dr., Carol Stream IL 60188. (708)260-6200. Fax: (708)260-0114. Julie Talerico, mng. ed; submit to Jan Senn, asst. ed. To help Christian women grow in their relationship to God by providing practical, biblical perspectives on marriage, sex, parenting, work, health, friendship, and self. Bimonthly mag; 80 pgs; circ 300,000. Subscription $14.95. 25% freelance. Query; no phone query. Pays .15/wd, on acceptance, for 1st rts. Articles 1,200-1,800 wds (6/yr); fiction (0-1/yr) 1,500-1,800/yr. Reports in 4-6 wks. Seasonal 6 mos ahead. Guidelines/theme list; copy $3.50.
Fillers: Buys 24/yr. Anecdotes, short humor; 50-200 wds; $20.
Columns/Departments: Buys 4/yr. One Woman's Story (dramatic story of overcoming a difficult situation), 1,500-2,000 wds, $150; Heart to Heart (true humorous or inspirational anecdotes), 50-200 wds, $20; Issues (first-person perspective on current issues), 1,000-1,500 wds.
Tips: "Articles should be personal in tone and full of real-life anecdotes as well as quotes/advice from noted Christian professionals. Articles should be practical and have a distinct Christian perspective. Most open to One Woman's Story."

VIRTUE, Box 850, 548 Sisters Pkwy., Sisters OR 97759. (503)549-8261. Fax: (503)549-0153. Marlee Alex, ed. Bimonthly mag; 80 pgs; circ 150,000. Subscription $16.95. 50% freelance. Query/clips (complete ms for fiction, poetry or departments); no phone query. Pays .15-.25/wd, on acceptance, for 1st rts (pays on publication for unassigned articles). Articles 1,000-1,500 wds (12/yr) & fiction (6/yr), 1,000-2,000 wds. Reports in 8 wks. Seasonal 6 mos ahead. Accepts simultaneous query & reprints. Kill fee. Guidelines; copy for 9x12 SAE/5 stamps.
Poetry: Buys 6/yr. Free verse, haiku, light verse; any length. Pays $25-45. Submit max. 3 poems.
Departments: Buys 15/yr. Equipped for Ministry (how-to), 500 wds; Working Smarter (household hints), 100 wds; Real Men (men's view of women), 1,000 wds; In My Opinion, to 1,200 wds; One Woman's Journal, to 1,200 wds. Pays $50-90.

Tips: "Well-thought, well-written always makes a good impression. 'Soap-box' or pulpit writing is rejected outright. We prefer an implicit, rather than explicit message."
**This periodical was #1 on the 1993 Top 50 Plus Christian Publishers list.

+THE WESLEYAN WOMAN, P.O. Box 50434, Indianapolis IN 46250-0434. (317)576-8164. Fax: (317)577-4397. The Wesleyan Church. Karen Dishroon, ed. Publishes inspirational articles, issues of moral and social concern, programs related to foreign and domestic service, outreach and witness. Quarterly mag; circ. 4,500. Subscription $7. Complete ms. Articles & book reviews.

#WOMAN'S TOUCH, 1445 Boonville Ave., Springfield MO 65802-1894. (417)862-2781. Fax: (417)862-0503. Assemblies of God. Sandra G. Clopine, ed. A general readership magazine committed to providing help and inspiration for Christian women, strengthening family life, and reaching out in witness to others. Bimonthly mag; 28 pgs; circ 21,000. Subscription $6/leader's edition $7.50. 75-90% freelance. Complete ms/cover letter. Pays $10-35 (.03/wd), on acceptance, for one-time rts. Articles 500-1,200 wds (75/yr). Reports in 3 wks. Seasonal 8 mos ahead. Accepts simultaneous submissions & reprints. Guidelines; copy for 9x12 SAE/3 stamps.
Poetry: Buys 10/yr. Free verse, light verse, traditional; 4-50 lines; $5-20. Submit max. 4 poems.
Fillers: Buys 5/yr. Facts; 50-500 wds; $5-15.
Columns/Departments: Buys 10/yr. An Added Touch (special crafts/decorations/activities); A Personal Touch (personal improvement); A Final Touch (short human interest); 500-800 wds; $20-35. Query/clips.

#WOMEN ALIVE!, Box 4683, Overland Park KS 66204. (913)649-8583. Fax: (913)649-8583. Aletha Hinthorn, ed. To encourage holiness women to apply Scripture to their daily lives. Bimonthly mag; 20 pgs; circ 5,000. Subscription $13.95. 50% freelance. Complete ms/cover letter; phone query ok. Pays $15-40, on publication, for one-time rts. Articles 900-2,000 wds (15-25/yr); fiction 900-2,000 wds (0-1/yr). Reports in 1-2 mos. Seasonal 4-6 mos ahead. Accepts simultaneous submissions & reprints. Kill fee. Guidelines/theme list; copy for 9x12 SAE/4 stamps.
Poetry: Buys 0-3/yr. Traditional, $10-40. Submit max. 3.
Fillers: Buys 0-1/yr. Cartoons, jokes, short humor.
Columns/Departments: Buys 6/yr. Senior Savvy (for older women); 900-1,200 wds; $15-40.

WRITER'S MARKETS

#BYLINE MAGAZINE, Box 130596, Edmond OK 73013-0001. (405)348-5591. General publication for freelance writers and poets. Kathryn Fanning, mng. ed. Teaching new writers how to write and sell their work. Monthly mag; 28 pgs; circ 3,000. 80-90% freelance. Query or complete ms; no cover letter or phone query. Pays $50, on acceptance, for 1st rts. Articles 1,500-2,000 wds (72/yr); personal experiences 800 wds; fiction 2,000-3,000 wds (12/yr). Reports in 2 mos. Seasonal 4 mos ahead. Accepts simultaneous submissions. Guidelines; copy $3.50.
Poetry: Marcia Preston. Buys 110/yr. Any type; 4-30 lines. Pays $5-10. Writing themes. Submit max. 3 poems.
Fillers: Buys 55/yr. Various; 300-800 wds/$15-35.
Columns/Departments: End Piece (personal essay on writing theme), 800 wds; First Sale accounts, 300-600 wds; Only When I Laugh (writing humor), 300-800 wds; $15-35.
Tips: "Most open to End Piece essay or First Sale account."

#CANADIAN WRITER'S JOURNAL, Box 6618, Depot 1, Victoria, BC V8P 5N7 Canada. (604)477-8807. Gordon M. Smart, ed. How-to articles for writers. Quarterly mag; circ 350. 75% freelance. Query or complete ms/cover letter; no phone query. Pays $5/published pg (Canadian); on publication; for 1st, one-time or reprint rts. Not copyrighted. Articles 500-1,200 wds (50-55/yr); book reviews 250-500 wds/$5. Reports in 2 mos. Seasonal 3 mos ahead. Accepts reprints. Kill fee. Guidelines; copy $4.
Fiction: "Most fiction requirements filled by annual contest; 500-1,200 wds."
Poetry: Traditional, haiku: on writing. Sponsors annual poetry contest.
Fillers: Anecdotes, cartoons, ideas, short humor; 100-250 wds.

***CHIPS OFF THE WRITER'S BLOCK**, Box 83371, Los Angeles CA 90083. Secular. Wanda Windham, ed. For beginning writers. Bimonthly newsletter; circ 500+. 100% freelance. Complete ms/cover letter; no phone query. **PAYS IN COPIES**, for one-time rts. Articles (100/yr) to 1,500 wds; fiction (50+/yr) to 1,200 wds. Reports in 6 wks. Seasonal 6 mos ahead. Accepts simultaneous submissions & reprints. Guidelines; copy $3.
Poetry: All forms (on writing only); 1-40 lines. Submit max. 5 poems.
Fillers: Anything on writing; to 300 wds.
Tips: "Need more one-page, well-researched, how-to articles. Open to new columns and ideas."

THE CHRISTIAN COMMUNICATOR, Joy Publishing, Box 827, San Juan Capistrano CA 92625. (714)990-1532. Fax: (714)493-6552. Susan Titus Osborn, ed. For Christian writers/speakers who want to polish writing skills, develop public-speaking techniques, and sell their mss. Monthly mag; 24 pgs; circ 5,000. Subscription $20. 50% freelance. Complete ms/cover letter; phone query ok. Pays $5-10; for 1st, one-time or reprint rts. Articles 600-1,200 wds (62/yr). Reports in 2-6 wks. Seasonal 4 mos ahead. Accepts simultaneous submissions & reprints. Free guidelines/copy.

Poetry: Uses 12/yr. Poems on writing. Submit max. 4 poems. Pays $5.
Fillers: Uses 12/yr. Cartoons, quotes. Pays $5.
Columns/Departments: Buys 12/yr. Communicator Interview (published author), 800-1,200 wds; Publisher's Profile, 800-1,200 wds; Speaker's Corner (techniques for speakers), 600-1,000 wds; Book Reviews (writing/speaking books), 300-400 wds. Pays $5-10.
Tips: "Most in need of publisher or author profiles or book reviews (see columns above)."

***CHRISTIAN VISION**, RR 1, Washago, ON L0K 2B0 Canada. Skysong Press. Steve Stanton, ed. For Christian writers, editors, publishers, and artists. Quarterly newsletter; circ 400. 50% freelance. Complete ms. **PAYS IN COPIES** for one-time rts. Articles 500-1,000 wds (8/yr); book reviews 1 pg. Reports in 4 wks. Accepts simultaneous submissions & reprints. Guidelines/copy for 6x9 SASE.
Poetry: Accepts 4/yr. About writing or publishing. To 1 pg.

CROSS & QUILL, Rt 3 Box 1635, Jefferson Davis Rd., Clinton SC 29325. (803)697-6035. Christian Writers Fellowship Intl. Sandy Brooks, ed. For Christian writers, editors, agents, conference directors. Bimonthly newsletter; circ 1,000. Subscription $18; CWFI membership $35. 66% freelance. Complete ms/no cover letter; no phone query. **PAYS IN COPIES**, for 1st, one-time or reprint rts. Articles to 600 wds (30/yr). Reports in 3 wks. Seasonal 6 mos ahead. Accepts reprints. Guidelines; copy $1/9x12 SAE/2 stamps.
Special Needs: "More informational articles; less personal experience; more help for pros."
Poetry: Accepts 12/yr. Any type; to 12 lines. Submit max. 3 poems. Must pertain to writing/ publishing.
Fillers: Accepts 12/yr. Anecdotes, cartoons, facts, newsbreaks, prayers, quotes, short humor (for writers only); to 50 wds.
Columns/Departments: Writing Rainbows! (writing devotional thought), 500-600 wds; Writer to Writer (how-to), 200-800 wds; Editor's Roundtable (interview with editor), 200-800 wds; ComputerWise (tips), 200-800 wds.
Tips: "Most open to columns, fillers or poetry."

EXCHANGE, #104-15 Torrance Rd., Scarborough ON M1J 3K2 Canada. (416) 439-4320. Audrey Dorsch, ed. A forum for Christian writers to share information and ideas. Quarterly newsletter; circ. 250. Subscription $14. 75% freelance. Complete ms/cover letter; phone query ok. Pays $15-30, on publication, for 1st rts. Articles 250-600 wds (20-25/yr). Reports in 4 wks. Accepts reprints. Guidelines/copy for #10 SAE/1 Canadian stamp.
Fillers: Ideas, quotes; 25-100 wds; no payment.
Tips: "Focus on a very specific aspect of writing."

GOTTA WRITE NETWORK LIT MAG, 612 Cobblestone Cr., Glenview IL 60025. (708)296-7631. Fax: (708)296-7631. Secular. Denise Fleischer, ed. A support system for writers, beginner to well established. Semiannual mag; circ 200. Subscription $12.75. 75% freelance. Query or complete ms/cover letter; phone query ok. Pays $5 for assigned, **PAYS IN COPIES** for unsolicited; on publication; for 1st rts. Articles 3 pgs (20+/yr); fiction to 11 pgs (10+/yr) on writing techniques; book reviews 2.5 pgs. Reports in 3-8 wks. Seasonal 6 mos ahead. Guidelines; copy $5/9x12 SAE/6 stamps.
Poetry: Uses 75+/yr. Avant-garde, free verse, haiku (no rhyme); 4 lines to 1 pg.

Submit max. 5 poems.
Fillers: Uses 20/yr. Anecdotes, cartoons, newsbreaks, quizzes, word puzzles; keep short.
Tips: "Most open to articles on writing techniques. Give me something different and in-depth. No I-love-writing, how-I-did-it."

+HOME OFFICE OPPORTUNITIES, P.O. Box 780, Lyman WY 82937. (307)786-4513. Diane Wolverton, ed. Help and support for people who run offices in their homes. Bimonthly mag; circ. 500. Subscription $18. 90% freelance. Query; no phone query. Pays .01/wd, on acceptance, for 1st or reprint rts. Articles 400-1,500 wds (50/yr); fiction to 2,000 wds (6/yr).Reports in 4-8 wks. Seasonal 4 mos ahead. Accepts simultaneous submissions and reprints (tell when & where published). Guidelines; copy $2/9x12 SAE/2 stamps.
Special Needs: All articles must be related to running a home office. How-to business tips. Would like to see some good, business-related fiction.
Fillers: Buys 6 cartoons/yr. Pays $2.
Tips: "Our profiles are designed to show readers how others have become successful or solved problems—lots of nuts and bolts. We are very open to freelancers in all departments."

HOUSEWIFE-WRITER'S FORUM, Box 780, Lyman WY 82937. (307)786-4513. Secular. Diane Wolverton, ed.; Bob Haynie, fiction ed. Publishes the writings of housewife-writers. Bimonthly magazine; 48 pgs; circ 1,300. 80% freelance. Query (complete ms for fiction/cover letter); no phone query. Pays .01-.02/wd, on acceptance, for 1st or one-time rts. Articles (180/yr) & fiction (6-12/yr), 400-2,000 wds (prefers 400-750). Reports in 4-10 wks. Seasonal 6 mos ahead. Accepts simultaneous query & reprints (sometimes). Guidelines; copy $4/7x12 SAE.
Poetry: Buys 50/yr. Free verse, light verse, traditional; to 36 lines; pays $1-2 in stamps. Submit max. 6 poems.
Fillers: Buys 24-30/yr. Anecdotes, cartoons, facts, ideas; hints (on writing/running a home); 25-200 wds; pays $1-4.
Columns/Departments: Buys 40/yr. Confessions of a Housewife-Writer or Domestic Humor, 500-1,000 wds. Complete ms.
Tips: "Write articles that are specific, vivid, and helpful for housewife/writers. Look for different angles."

***MERLYN'S PEN,** The National Magazine of Student Writing, Box 1058, East Greenwich RI 02818. Secular. R. James Stahl, ed. Written by students in grades 7-10 only. Mag. Fiction to 2,500 wds; reviews and travel pieces to 1,000 wds. **PAYS IN COPIES**. Not in topical listings. Students send for guidelines.
Poetry: To 100 lines.

MINNESOTA INK - See Writer's Journal

***TEACHERS & WRITERS**, 5 Union Square W, New York NY 10003. (212)691-6590. Ron Padgett, ed. On teaching creative and imaginative writing. Mag published 5 times/yr; circ 1,500-2,000. Query. **PAYS IN COPIES**. Articles 3,000-6,000 wds. Not in topical listings. Copy $2.50.

#THE WRITER, 120 Boylston St., Boston MA 02116-4615. Secular. Sylvia K. Burack, ed. How-to for writers. Monthly mag; 48 pgs. 20-25% freelance. No phone query. Pays on acceptance, for 1st rts. Articles about 2,000 wds. Reports promptly. Not in topical listings. Copy $3.

WRITERS ANCHOR, 100 Greenwood Rd., York PA 17404. (717)792-0228. York Writers. Rita Atwell Holler, ed. Quarterly newsletter; circ 60. Subscription $2. 100% freelance. Complete ms/no cover letter; phone query ok. **PAYS IN COPIES** for any rts. Not copyrighted. Articles 10-300 wds (12/yr); fiction (1/yr) 10-300 wds; book reviews 150 wds. Reports in 4 wks. Seasonal 3 mos ahead. Deadlines are the 15th of March, June, September, & December. Accepts simultaneous submissions & reprints. Guidelines/copy for #10 SAE/1 stamp.
Poetry: Uses 14/yr. All types; 3-42 lines. Submit max. 3 poems.
Fillers: Uses 6/yr. Various; 6-150 wds.
Columns/Departments: Uses 6/yr. Games (writing only), 150 wds; Q & A (on writing), 35 wds.

WRITERS CONNECTION, 275 Saratoga Ave. #103, Santa Clara CA 95050-6664. (408)554-2090. Fax: (408)554-2099. Jan Stiles, ed. Nuts and bolts information on writing and publishing in all fields (except poetry). Monthly newsletter; circ 1,700. Subscription/membership $45. 50% freelance. Complete ms; query/clips for profiles; no phone query. **PAYS IN COPIES, SUBSCRIPTION, MEMBERSHIPS OR SEMINARS**, on acceptance; or $20-50 on publication; for 1st and reprint rts. Articles 750-1,800 wds (20/yr); book reviews, 200-300 wds (pays 2 copies). Reports in 2-8 wks. Seasonal 6 mos ahead. Accepts some reprints. Guidelines; copy $5.
Special Needs: In-depth articles on how to write or market your writing (technique). No religious slant or tone.
Fillers: Uses 4-10/yr. Facts, newsbreaks, tips, resources; 50-350 wds.
Columns/Departments: Profiles (useful info/insights from professional editors/agents), 725-800 wds; Business & Technical Writing (hard info an how to write), 750-825 wds. Pays $25-50.
Tips: "Most open to short features or columns; shorter articles that offer specific, in-depth help for writers."

#WRITER'S DIGEST, 1507 Dana Ave., Cincinnati OH 45207. (513)531-2222. Secular. Angela Terez, submissions ed. Information on writing and publishing. Monthly mag; 64 pgs; circ 225,000. 90% freelance. Query or complete ms. Pays .10/wd & up, on acceptance, for one-time rts. Articles 500-3,000 wds (90-100/yr). Reports in 2-4 wks. Seasonal 8 mos ahead. Accepts reprints. Kill fee 20%. Guidelines; copy $3.
Poetry: Buys 24-36/yr. Light verse on writing; 2-20 lines; $10-50. Submit max. 8 poems.
Fillers: Buys 48/yr. Anecdotes & short humor on writing; 50-250 wds; .10/wd.

WRITER`S EXCHANGE, Box 394, Society Hill SC 29593. (803)378-4556. Gene Boone, ed. Uses poetry of all types, including religious material. Quarterly mag; circ. 250. Subscription $10. 95% freelance. Complete ms/cover letter; no phone query. **PAYS IN COPIES,** for one-time or reprint rts. Articles 200-1,200 wds (10+/yr). Reports in 3 wks. Seasonal 6 mos ahead. Reports in 2-3 wks. Accepts reprints. Guidelines/theme list; copy $1/9x12 SAE/2 stamps.
Poetry: Uses 300/yr. Any type; 3-24 lines. Submit max. 6 poems.
Fillers: Uses 300/yr. Various; 10-750 wds.

WRITER'S FORUM, 765 McMurray Dr #N-4, Nashville TN 37211. (615)832-6482. Dr. Bob Mulder, ed. To assist writers in selling. Bimonthly newsletter. 50% freelance. Query. Pays on acceptance for one-time rts. Not copyrighted. Articles (20/yr) to 500 wds. Reports in 2 wks. Seasonal 6 mos ahead. Accepts simultaneous submissions & reprints. No guidelines/copy.

WRITER'S GUIDELINES, Box 608, Pittsburg MO 65724. Fax: (417)993-5544. Susan Salaki, ed. A forum for all those involved with writing/publishing. Bimonthly newsletter; 10 pgs; circ. 700. Subscription $18. 90% freelance. Query or complete ms/cover letter; no phone query. Pays to $25, on acceptance, for one-time rts. Articles to 1,000 wds (40/yr); book reviews 100 wds (query). Reports in 2 wks. Seasonal 6 mos ahead. Guidelines; copy $4.
Fillers: Accepts 7/yr. Cartoons, facts, newsbreaks, 50-200 wds. Pays copy only.

WRITERS INFORMATION NETWORK (W.I.N.), Box 11337, Bainbridge Island WA 98110. (206)842-9103. Fax: (206)842-0536. Professional Assn. of Christian Writers. Elaine Wright Colvin, ed. Bimonthly newsletter; 16 pgs; circ. 1,000. Subscription $20. 50% freelance. Complete ms/cover letter; phone query ok. Pays $10 or subscription, for 1st rts. Articles to 300 wds; book reviews (free books). Reports in 4-8 wks. Guidelines; copy for 9x12 SAE/3 stamps.

#WRITER'S JOURNAL, Minnesota Ink Inc., 27 Empire Dr., St. Paul MN 55103. (612)225-1306. Secular. Valerie Hockert, ed. Monthly journal; circ 45,000. 40% freelance. Complete ms. Pays to $50, on publication, for 1st rts. Articles 700-1,000 wds (30-40/yr). Reports in 4-6 wks. Seasonal 6 mos ahead. Accepts simultaneous query. Not in topical listings. Guidelines; copy $4.
Poetry: Esther M. Leiper. Buys 20-30/yr. All types; to 25 lines; .25/line. Submit max. 5 poems.
Contest: Runs 2 poetry contests each year, spring & fall.

#WRITER'S LIFELINE, Box 1641, Cornwall, ON K6H 5V6 Canada. (613)932-2135. Stephen Gill, mng. ed. For professional freelancers and beginning writers. Needs articles of interest to writers, news items of national and international interest, letters to the editor, poetry, interviews. Needs book reviewers; **PAYS IN BOOK REVIEWED & COPIES**. Bimonthly mag; 16-35 pgs; circ 1,500. Not in topical listings.

THE WRITER'S NOOK NEWS, 38114 3rd St. #181, Willoughby OH 44094. (216)762-9128. Secular. Eugene Ortiz, ed./pub. Dedicated to giving freelance writers specific information for their immediate practical use in getting published and staying published. Quarterly newsletter; circ 1,000. 100% freelance. Complete ms. Pays .06/wd, on acceptance, for 1st rts. Not copyrighted. Articles 200-400 wds (75-80/yr); book reviews 50-100 wds (.06/wd). Reports in 6 wks. Guidelines; copy $5/#10 SAE/1 stamp.
Fillers: Buys 10/yr. Anecdotes, cartoons.
Tips: "Most open to tips and suggestions about the process of writing and publishing."
Additional Publications (Guidelines same as above):
THE NOOK NEWS REVIEW OF WRITERS' PUBLICATIONS
THE NOOK NEWS CONTESTS & AWARDS BULLETIN
THE NOOK NEWS CONFERENCES & KLATCHES BULLETIN
THE NOOK NEWS MARKET BULLETIN

***WRITER'S RESOURCE NETWORK**, Box 940335, Maitland FL 32794. (407)260-5150. Jeffrey Atwood, ed. News and resources for writers. Bimonthly newsletter; circ 1500. 25% freelance. Pays .03/wd, on publication, for all rts. Articles 50-650 wds (uses 10/yr). Reports in 2 wks. Seasonal 3 mos ahead. Accepts simultaneous submissions & reprints. Guidelines; free copy.
Poetry: Haiku, light verse, traditional; 4-20 lines. Pays .03/wd.
Fillers: Uses 10-15/yr. Anecdotes, facts, newsbreaks; 10-100 wds; cartoons, $1.
Tips: "Straightforward, tight news, tips, techniques for writers—religious or otherwise. Especially tips and resources that help writers find ideas or write better."

***WRITING RIGHT NEWSLETTER**, Box 35132, Elmwood Park IL 60635. (708)453-5023. John Biardo, ed. Helping writers and poets with their writing career. Monthly newsletter; circ. 500. Estab. 1992. 50% freelance. Complete ms (query for fiction). **PAYS IN COPIES;** for one-time rts. Articles 600-1,000 wds (50/yr); fiction 500-700 wds (10/yr); book reviews 600 wds. Reports in 2-4 wks. Accepts reprints. Guidelines; copy $4.
Fillers: Accepts 10/yr. Ideas, newsbreaks; 200-300 wds.
Tips: "Most open to writer's tips that have worked for you."

MARKET ANALYSIS TOP PERIODICALS IN EACH CATEGORY BY LARGEST CIRCULATION

Note: Only a few of the Christian magazines are sold in Christian bookstores. The top 20 (based on bookstore sales) are indicated with the number symbol following their circulation. CCM (Contemporary Christian Music #1) and Heaven's Metal (#8) are Christian music publications. Marriage Partnership (#14) is not open to freelance and Today's Better Life (#16) is new to the guide this year. The remaining publications not shown below are Sports Spectrum (#9), Christian Research Journal (#17) and Parents of Teenagers (#20).

TOP 56 ADULT/GENERAL MARKETS

1. Guideposts 3,900,000 (#5)
2. Focus on the Family 2,000,000 (#19)
3. Decision 1,700,000
4. Columbia 1,500,000
5. The Lutheran 960,000
6. Home Life 600,000
7. Catholic Digest 550,000
8. War Cry 500,000+
9. Marion Helpers 500,000
10. Oblates 500,000
11. United Methodist Reporter 450,000
12. AFA Journal 400,000
13. Liguorian 360,000
14. Lutheran Witness 350,000
15. Mature Living 350,000
16. Miraculous Medal 340,000
17. St. Anthony Messenger 325,000
18. Pentecostal Evangel 280,000
20. American Bible Society Record 275,000
21. Anglican Journal 272,000
22. Signs of the Times 270,000
23. Class 250,000
24. Christian Parenting Today 250,000 (#7)
25. Liberty 250,000
26. Voice (CA) 250,000
27. Power for Living 250,000
28. Charisma & Christian Life 200,000 (#3)
29. Christian Reader 200,000 (#13)
30. Christianity Today 200,000 (#6)
31. Messenger of St. Anthony 200,000
32. A Positive Approach 200,000
33. Together 200,000
34. United Church Observer 185,000
35. Ideals 180,000
36. Episcopal Life 170,000
37. Standard 165,000
38. The Family Digest 150,000
39. Live 150,000
40. Lutheran Digest 150,000
41. Moody 142,000 (#12)
42. Lutheran Journal 136,000
43. Our Sunday Visitor 125,000
44. The Lookout 118,000
45. Presbyterian Survey 105,000
46. All About Issues 100,000
47. A Better Tomorrow 100,000
48. Living 100,000
49. Sunday Digest 100,000
50. Today's Better Life 100,000
51. Foursquare World Advance 95,000
52. Discipleship Journal 90,000 (#4)
53. Total Health 90,000
54. Herald of Holiness 81,000
55. Lutheran Layman 80,000
56. Vista 80,000

TOP 20 CHILDREN'S MARKETS

1. God's World Today 260,000
2. Venture 140,000
3. Faith 'n Stuff 100,000+
4. Focus on Fam Clubhouse 100,000
5. FOF Clubhouse Jr 90,000
6. Pockets 82,000
7. Junior Trails 65,000
8. High Adventure 60,000
9. Our Little Friend 45-50,000
10. Guide 40,000
11. Power & Light 39,000
12. Primary Treasure 35,000
13. Touch 15,500
14. Crusader (MI) 13,000
15. My Friend 12,000
16. BREAD for God's Children 10,000
17. Nature Friend 10,000
18. On the Line 8,500
19. CLUBHOUSE 8,000
20. Story Friends 8,000

TOP 15 CHRISTIAN EDUCATION/LIBRARY MARKETS

1. Today's Catholic Teacher 60,000
2. GROUP 50,000
3. Parish Teacher 50,000
4. Teachers in Focus 47,000
5. Catechist 45,000
6. Religion Teacher's Journal 36,000
7. Children's Ministry 30,000
8. CE Counselor 30,000
9. Perspective 24,000
10. Evangelizing Today's Child 22,000
11. Lollipops 20,000
12. Preschool Playhouse 20,000
13. Primary Street 20,000
14. Shining Star 20,000
15. Teacher's Interaction 20,000

TOP 10 MISSIONS MARKETS

1. Maryknoll 650,000
2. Childlife 229,000
3. Compassion 155,000
4. Oblate World 140,000
5. Worldwide Challenge 94,000
6. Catholic Near East 90,000
7. World Vision 80,000
8. Impact 42,000
9. Heartbeat 40,000
10. World Christian 40,000

TOP 5 MUSIC MARKETS

1. Music Makers 105,000
2. Glory Songs 85,000
3. Young Musicians 85,000
4. Music Time 60,000
5. Worship Today 50,000

TOP 10 PASTOR/LEADER MARKETS

1. Pulpit/Bible Study Helps 210,000
2. Your Church 150,000
3. Leadership Journal 70,000
4. Eucaharistic Minister 63,000
5. Worship Leader 50,000
6. Advance 32,000
7. Discipleship Training 30,000
8. Group's Jr High Ministry 30,000
9. Growing Churches 30,000
10. Ministries Today 30,000

TOP 14 TEEN/YOUNG ADULT MARKETS

1. Brio 150,000
2. Visions (MN) 140,000
3. Campus Life 120,000
4. High School I.D. 120,000
5. Breakaway 81,000
6. event 80,000
7. HiCall 60,000
8. Teens Today 55,000
9. Teen Quest 54,000
10. Freeway 50,000
11. Sharing the Victory 50,000
12. Straight 50,000
13. Young Salvationist 50,000
14. The Student 40,000

TOP 8 WOMEN'S MARKETS

1. Today's Christian Woman 300,000
2. Royal Service 290,000
3. Lutheran Woman Today 250,000
4. Virtue 150,000
5. Response 75,000
6. Contempo 65,000
7. Horizons 30,000
8. Woman's Touch 21,000

TOP 4 WRITERS' MARKETS

1. Writer's Digest 225,000
2. Writer's Journal 45,000
3. Christian Communicator 5,000
4. Byline 3,000

ALL PERIODICALS IN ORDER OF LARGEST CIRCULATION

Adult/General

Guideposts 3,900,000
Focus on the Family 2,000,000
Decision 1,700,000
Columbia 1,500,000
The Lutheran 960,000
Home Life 600,000
Catholic Digest 550,000
War Cry 500,000+
Marion Helpers 500,000
Oblates 500,000
United Methodist Reporter 450,000
AFA Journal 400,000
Liguorian 360,000
Lutheran Witness 350,000
Mature Living 350,000
Miraculous Medal 340,000
St. Anthony Messenger325,000
Pentecostal Evangel 280,000
American Bible Society Record 275,000
Anglican Journal 272,000
Signs of the Times 270,000
Class 250,000
Christian Parenting Today 250,000
Liberty 250,000
Voice (CA) 250,000
Power for Living 250,000
Charisma & Christian Life 200,000
Christian Reader 200,000
Christianity Today 200,000
Messenger of St. Anthony 200,000
A Positive Approach 200,000
Together 200,000
United Church Observer 185,000
Ideals 180,000
Episcopal Life 170,000
Standard 165,000
The Family Digest 150,000
Live 150,000
Lutheran Digest 150,000
Moody 142,000
Lutheran Journal 136,000

Our Sunday Visitor 125,000
The Lookout 118,000
Presbyterian Survey 105,000
All About Issues 100,000
A Better Tomorrow 100,000
Living 100,000
Sunday Digest 100,000
Today's Better Life 100,000
Foursquare World Advance 95,000
Discipleship Journal 90,000
Total Health 90,000
Herald of Holiness 81,000
Lutheran Layman 80,000
Vista 80,000
Mature Years 77,000
Vision (CA) 70,000
alive now! 65,000
Christian Single 65,000
Christian Standard 62,000
Presbyterian Record 60,300
Catholic Answer 60,000
Christian History 60,000
Acts 29 55,000
Christian Home & School 52,000
Sports Spectrum 52,000
Annals of St. Anne 50,000
Cornerstone 50,000
Good News Journal 50,000
InterVarsity 50,000
Message 50,000
Parents of Teenagers 50,000
U.S. Catholic 50,000
Vibrant Life 50,000
Church of God Evangel 45,000
Seek 45,000
New Covenant 42,000
The Teaching Home 42,000
Bible Review 40,000
Christmas 40,000
Church Herald 40,000
America 36,000
Cathedral Age 35,000
Christian Century 35,000
Evangelical Beacon 35,000
Pursuit 35,000
Indian Life 34,000
Church & State 33,000
Light and Life 33,000
Catholic Twin Circle 30,000
Progress 30,000
World 29,000
At Ease 28,000
Lifeglow 28,000
Pentecostal Testimony 27,000
Common Boundary 26,000
Canada Lutheran 25,500
African-American Heritage 25,000
Evangel 25,000
Interim 25,000
Christian Research Journal 24,000
Indian Life 24,000
Covenant Companion 22,500
Vital Christianity 22,000
God's Revivalist 21,000
B.C. Catholic 20,000
Discovery 20,000
El Orador 20,000
St. Joseph's Messenger 20,000
Wesleyan Advocate 20,000
Catholic Parent 18,500
Commonweal 18,000
Faith Today 18,000
Good News (KY) 18,000
Messenger/Sacred Heart 18,000
SCP Journal 18,000
Servant 17,500
Purpose 17,100
John Milton 16,400
AXIOS 15,672
Interest 15,000
National Christian Reporter 15,000
Network 15,000
The Shantyman 15,000
Smart Dads 15,000
TableTalk 15,000
Mennonite Brethren Herald 14,800
New Oxford Review 14,000
Psychology for Living 14,000
Emphasis on Faith & Living 13,000
Interchange 12,800
Bible Advocate 12,000
Spiritual Life 12,000
Presbyterian Outlook 11,500
Review for Religious 11,000
Salt 11,000
Evangelical Friend 10,500
Baptist Informer 10,000
Bookstore Journal 10,000
The Door 10,000
Journal of Christian Nursing 10,000
Our Family 10,000
Religious Broadcasting 10,000

Sharing 10,000
Today's Single 10,000
Christian Retailing 9,500
Friends Journal 9,500
International Report 9,500
The Other Side 9,500
Prairie Messenger 9,200
Celebration 9,000
Living Church 9,000
Mennonite, The 9,000
The Bible Today 8,500
Companions 8,000
The Gem 8,000
Home Times 8,000
Pentecostal Messenger 8,000
Star of Zion 8,000
Minnesota Chronicle 7,500
Christian Observer 7,200
The Family 7,000
Church Advocate 6,660
Associate Reformed Presbyterian 6,300
Christian Living 6,100
Alive! 6,000
Christian Courier (Canada) 6,000
Hallelujah! 6,000
Impact 6,000
Jour/Religious Gerontology 6,000
Jour/Relig Psychotherapy 6,000
Pentecostal Homelife 6,000
Evangelical Visitor 5,500
Life Advocate 5,500
Evangelical Baptist 5,000
Maranatha 5,000
Ministry Today 5,000
A New Heart 5,000
Christian Civic League/ME 4,600
AGAIN 4,500
Fellowship Today 4,500
AGAIN Magazine 4,500
Christian Renewal 4,500
Queen of All Hearts 4,500
Companion 4,200
Advent Christian Witness 4,000
Compass 4,000
Cresset 4,000
Message of the Open Bible 4,000
Mountain Laurel 4,000
The Witness 4,000
The Prayer Line 3,800
Messenger, The (Canada) 3,700
Cross Currents 3,500
Perspectives on Science 3,500
ADVOCATE 3,000
Christian Social Action 3,000
The Messenger (NC) 3,000
North American Voice 3,000
Quiet Revolution 3,000
Religious Education 3,000
The Witness 3,000
Church Herald/Holiness Banner 2,500
Railroad Evangelist 2,500
Gospel Tidings 2,200
Prism 2,100
Answers in Action 2,000
Baptist History & Heritage 2,000
The Critic 2,000
The Inspirer 2,000
Journal/Church & State 1,700
Congregational Journal 1,500
Christian Edge 1,500
Comments From the Friends 1,500
The Plowman 1,500
Touchstone 1,500
Social Justice Review 1,250
Methodist History 1,200
Canadian Catholic Review 1,100
Connecting Point 1,000
Starlight Magazine 1,000
Evangelism 900
Morning Glory 800
Creation Social Science 600
New Thought Journal 600
Tree of Life 550
Broken Streets 500
Poetry Forum Short Stories 500
St. Willibrord Journal 500
God's Special People 400
Parenting Treasures 400
Thirteen Poetry 350
Lighthouse Fiction Collection 300+
Baptist Beacon 300
Christian Drama 300
Thema 300
Time of Singing 300
Manna 250
Explorer 200+
Burning Light 200
Dreams & Visions 200
Junebugs Knocking 100
Pegasus Review 100
Ratio 100

Children

God's World Today 260,000
Venture 140,000
Faith 'n Stuff 100,000+
Focus on Fam Clubhouse 100,000
FOF Clubhouse Jr 90,000
Pockets 82,000
Junior Trails 65,000
High Adventure 60,000
Our Little Friend 45-50,000
Guide 40,000
Power & Light 39,000
Primary Treasure 35,000
Touch 15,500
Crusader (MI) 13,000
My Friend 12,000
BREAD for God's Children 10,000
Nature Friend 10,000
On the Line 8,500
CLUBHOUSE 8,000
Story Friends 8,000
Together Time 7,500
Partners 5,300
Story Mates 5,200
Young Crusader 3,000
Skipping Stones 2,500

Christian Education/Library

Today's Catholic Teacher 60,000
GROUP 50,000
Parish Teacher 50,000
Teachers in Focus 47,000
Catechist 45,000
Religion Teacher's Journal 36,000
Children's Ministry 30,000
CE Counselor 30,000
Perspective 24,000
Evangelizing Today's Child 22,000
Lollipops 20,000
Preschool Playhouse 20,000
Primary Street 20,000
Shining Star 20,000
Teacher's Interaction 20,000
Memos 15,000
Church Recreation 13,000
Resource 12,000
Journal/Adventist Education 10,000
Leader/Church School Today 10,000
Youth & CE Leadership 9,000
CE Connection 6,600
Christian Educator's Journal 4,200
Leader 4,000
Lead 3,600
The Youth Leader 2,800
Vision (CA) 2,600
Cornerstone Connections 2,400
Insight into CE 2,200
Team 2,000
Changing Lives 1,800
Librarian's World 700
Christian Librarian 450

Missions

Maryknoll 650,000
Childlife 229,000
Compassion 155,000
Oblate World 140,000
Worldwide Challenge 94,000
Catholic Near East 90,000
World Vision 80,000
Impact 42,000
Heartbeat 40,000
World Christian 40,000
American Horizon 34,000
New World Outlook 33,000
P.I.M.E. World 30,000
Latin America Evangelist 21,000
Wherever 14,000
Missiology 2,000
Urban Mission 1,300
Areopagus 1,000
Intl. Journal/Frontier 1,000

Music

Music Makers 105,000
Glory Songs 85,000
Young Musicians 85,000
Music Time 60,000
Worship Today 50,000
Music Leader 35,000
Senior Musician 32,000
Church Pianist 35,000
Church Musician 16,000
Creation 5,500
The Hymn 3,500
Tradition 2,500

Newspapers

United Methodist Reporter 450,000
Anglican Journal 272,000
Pastor/Bible Study Helps 210,000
Episcopal Life 170,000

Catholic New York 130,000
Our Sunday Visitor 125,000
Christian Chronicle 112,000
Good News Journal 50,000
Catholic Accent 48,000
Catholic Courier 48,000
National Catholic Reporter 48,000
Arlington Catholic Herald 45,000
Good News Etc. 44,000
Spokane/Inland NW Christian 42,000
Catholic Telegraph 40,000
Catholic Exponent 37,000
Beacon Christian News 35,000
Kansas City Christian 35,000
Catholic Twin Circle 30,000
World 29,000
NW Christian Journal 27,000
Christian Crusade 25,000
The Interim 25,000
Discovery 20,000
Catholic Sentinel 16,500
Messenger (KY) 16,000
Expression Christian Newspaper 15,000
Issues & Answers (teen) 15,000
Interchange 12,800
ChristianWeek 11,000
Mennonite Reporter 11,000
Mennonite Weekly Review 11,000
Christian Courier (WI) 10,000
Today's Single 10,000
Montana Catholic 8,300
Home Times 8,000
Minnesota Chronicle 7,500
Arkansas Catholic 7,000
Christian Courier (Canada) 6,000
Maranatha 5,000
Christian Renewal 4,500
Lead (CE) 3,600
Probe (women) 1,800
Christian Edge 1,500

Pastors/Leaders

Preacher's Magazine 18,000
Today's Parish 16,000
Clergy Journal 15,000
Homiletic/Pastoral Review 15,000
Proclaim 14,000
Christian Ministry 12,000
Church Administration 12,000
Review for Religious 11,000
Resource 10,500
Preaching 10,000
Search 10,000
Youthworker 10,000
Celebration 9,000
The Priest 9,800
Brigade Leader 9,000
Christian Growth Network 9,000
Chicago Studies 8,200
Bible-Science Newsletter 8,000
Christian Sentinel 8,000
Faith & Renewal 8,000
Student Leadership Journal 8,000
Media Update 7,500
National/Intl Religion Report 7,500
The Bethany Choice 7,300
Journal/Christian Camping 6,500
Baptist Leader 6,000
Journal/Christian Camping 6,000
Pastor's Tax & Money 6,000
Single Adult Ministries Journal 4-5,000
Lutheran Forum 4,000
Paraclete 4,500
Church Management Report 3,500
Cross Currents 3,500
Word & World 3,100
Quarterly Review 3,000
Reformed Worship 3,000
Liturgy 2,800
Art + Repro 2,000
Networks 1,700
Congregational Journal 1,500
Journal/Christian Healing 1,200
Church Bytes 1,000
Church Worship 1,000
Diaconalogue 1,000
Evangelism 900
Five Stones 550
Ivy Jungle Report 150

Teen/Young Adult

Brio 150,000
Visions (MN) 140,000
Campus Life 120,000
High School I.D. 120,000
Breakaway 81,000
event 80,000
HiCall 60,000
Teens Today 55,000
Teen Quest 54,000
Freeway 50,000
Sharing the Victory 50,000

Straight 50,000
Young Salvationist 50,000
The Student 40,000
Challenge (TN) 35,000
You! 35,000
Youth Update 35,000
Mag/Christian Youth! 30,000
Spirit 30,000
Young & Alive 26,000
Pioneer 25,500
Insight 25,000
Insight/Out 25,000
Take Five 23,000
Pathway I.D. 18,000
Venture 18,000
Issues & Answers 15,000
Teenage Christian 15,000
Youth Focus 10,000
Student Leadership Journal 8,000
Young Adult Today 7,500
The Conqueror 6,000
With 5,800
The Edge 5,000

Women

Today's Christian Woman 300,000
Royal Service 290,000
Lutheran Woman Today 250,000
Virtue 150,000
Response 75,000
Contempo 65,000
Horizons 30,000
Woman's Touch 21,000
Co-Laborer 14,000
Joyful Woman 13,000
Conscience 12,000
Church Woman 10,000
Journal/Women's Ministries 10,000
Sisters Today 8,000
Esprit 7,200
Link & Visitor 5,500
Daughters of Sarah 5,000
Just Between Us 5,000
Women Alive! 5,000
Wesleyan Woman 4,500
Helping Hand 4,000
Probe 1,800
Salt & Light 500
Parent Care 100+

Writers

Writer's Digest 225,000
Writer's Journal 45,000
Christian Communicator 5,000
Byline 3,000
Writers Connection 1,700
Teachers & Writers 1,500-2,000
Writer's Lifeline 1,500
Writer's Resource Network 1,500
Housewife-Writer's Forum 1,300
Cross & Quill 1,000
Writer's Information Network 1,000
Writer's Nook News 1,000
Writer's Guidelines 700
Chips off Writer's Block 500+
Home Office Opportunities 500
Writing Right Newsletter 500
Christian Vision 400
Canadian Writer's Journal 350
Exchange 275
Writer's Exchange 250
Gotta Write Network 200
Writers Anchor 60

Notes:

* If you are a short story writer, the biggest market is for adult fiction (95 markets), then juvenile (43 markets), then teen (37 markets). This division is about the same as last year. The most popular genres (in order) are humorous, contemporary, parables, biblical, adventure and historical. The least desirable are the genre romances.

* If you are a poet, you should be encouraged by the fact that poetry is number four on the list of interest. That's down two places from last year, but still playing as significant a role. Not all poetry markets said how many poems they bought per year, but those who did added up to 4185 poems. There is almost no market for poetry books (16 markets this year), but the serious poet can certainly sell regularly to periodicals if care is taken to target your poetry to fit the needs of the specific markets.

* In comparison to last year, the first 12 topics are the same, with poetry and humor dropping a couple of places, and Family Life and Christian Living moving up slightly. Most genre fiction dropped in popularity, with the exception of Contemporary Fiction, which gained several places in the ratings.

* Following is a list of topics that either increased or decreased in demand since last year. The number following the topic indicates how many positions that particular topic moved up or down in the ratings.

Decreased in interest:

Short Story: Adventure - down 16
Fillers: Ideas - down 14
Fillers: Anecdotes - down 12
Fillers: Short Humor - down 10
Cults/Occult - down 8
Salvation Testimonies - down 8
Short Story: Humorous - down 8
Christian Business: down 8
Sshsort Story: Mystery - down 8
Short Story: Biblical - down 7
Short Story: Historical - down 6
Short Story: Frontier - down 6
Environmental Issues - down 5
Money Management - down 5
Short Story: Science Fiction - down 5
Missions - down 5
Science - down 5
How-To/Self-Help - down 4
Fillers: Cartoons - Down 4
Fillers: Jokes - down 4
Short Story: Skits - down 4

Increased in interest:

Short Story: Contemporary - up 13
Leadership - up 12
Opinion Pieces - up 9
Miracles - up 7
Political - up 7
Fillers: Quotes - up 7
Sermons - up 7
Book Excerpts - up 6
Short Story: Plays - up 6
Book Reviews - up 5
Healing - up 5
Liturgical - up 5
Senior Adult Issues - up 5
Spirituality - up 4
Worship - up 4
Women's Issues - up 4
Controversial Issues - up 4
Short Stories: Parables - up 4
Short Story: Allegory - up 4

PERIODICAL TOPICS IN ORDER OF POPULARITY

NOTE: Following is a list of topics in order by popularity. The numbers indicate how many periodical editors said they were interested in seeing something of that type or topic.

Photographs 288

1. Current/Social Issues 232
2. Family Life 215
3. Christian Living 210
4. Personal Experience 207
5. Poetry 207
6. Interviews/Profiles 206
7. Inspirational 187
8. Prayer 182
9. Holiday Themes 171
10. True Stories 162
11. Marriage 158
12. Christian Education 156
13. Humor 151
14. Spirituality 151
15. Youth Issues 151
16. Church Outreach 147
17. Worship 140
18. Devotions/Meditations 134
19. Missions 134
20. Theological 134

21. Parenting 131
22. Evangelistic 130
23. How-To/Self-Help 126
24. Fillers: Cartoons 125
25. Women's Issues 125
26. Controversial Issues 124
27. World Issues 123
28. Witnessing 122
29. Bible Studies 117
30. Book Reviews 117
31. Discipleship 108
32. Think pieces 108
33. Environmental Issues 104
34. Historical 103
35. Ethics 95
36. Short Story: Adult 95
37. Opinion Pieces 90
38. Health 88
39. Money Management 88
40. Religious Freedom 88
41. Short Story: Humorous 88
42. Singles Issues 88
43. Book Excerpts 87
44. Leadership 87
45. Senior Adult Issues 87
46. Divorce 86
47. Fillers: Short Humor 86
48. Doctrinal 85
49. Salvation Testimonies 85
50. Celebrity Pieces 84
51. Cults/Occult 79
52. Fillers: Anecdotes 79
53. Essays 69
54. Healing 68
55. Liturgical 65
56. Relationships 65
57. Short Story: Contemporary 65
58. Miracles 64
59. Political 63
60. Sports 63
61. Economics 61
62. Fillers: Facts 60
63. Christian Business 57
64. Short Story: Parables 56
65. Short Story: Biblical 55
66. Fillers: Word Puzzles 54
67. Short Story: Adventure 54
68. Fillers: Ideas 53
69. Psychology 53
70. Short Story: Historical 52
71. Men's Issues 50
72. Home Schooling 49
73. Sociology 46
74. Fillers: Quizzes 45
75. How-to Activities (juv.) 43
76. Newspapers 43
77. Short Story: Juvenile 43
78. Church Management 40
79. Prophecy 40
80. Fillers: Games 38
81. Fillers: Prose 37
82. Short Story: Teen/YA 37
83. Science 36
84. Travel 34
85. Fillers: Jokes 31
86. Fillers: Quotes 30
87. Sermons 30
88. Short Story: Mystery 30
89. Short Story: Literary 27
90. Short Story: Fantasy 26
91. Ethnic Markets 25
92. Short Story: Allegory 25
93. Food/Recipes 22
94. Short Story: Frontier 20
95. Plays 19
96. Short Story: Science Fiction 19
97. Fillers: Prayers 18
98. Short Story: Romance 16
99. Skits 13
100. Fillers: Party Ideas 12
101. Music Reviews 12
102. Short Story: Frontier/Romance 9
103. Short Story: Historical/Romance 8
104. Short Story: Mystery/Romance 8

PERIODICALS NOT INTERESTED IN FREELANCE SUBISSIONS OR WHO ASKED NOT TO BE LISTED

Absolute Sound (NY)
Action Tracks
Acorn, The
Action Information (DC)
Adolescence (CA)
Adult Focus (TN)
Adult Teacher (MO)
Alliance Life (CO)
The A.M.E. Church Review (GA)
Anglican Theological Review (IL)
Atlantic Baptist (Canada)
Australian Evangel
The Banner (MI)
Baptist Bulletin (IL)
Baptist Herald (IL)
Baptist World VA)
Berean Statesman (MN)
Bible-in-Life Friends (IL)
Bible-in-Life Pix (IL)
Bible-in-Life Stories (IL)
Bible World (NJ)
Biblical Illustrator (TN)
Bodywise (AR)
Books & Religion (NC)
Bookviews (WI)
Brethren Evangelist (OH)
Brethren Missionary Herald (IN)
Builder (PA)
Catholic Health World (MO)
Catholic Library World (PA)
CBMC Contact (TN)
Challenge (IL)
Children's Church Exchange (MO)
The Chosen People (NC)
Christ For the Nations (TX)
Christian Conquest (AL)
Christian Education Journal (IL)
Christian Example
Christianity & Crisis (IL)
Christian Info (Canada)
Christian Life (OH)
Christian Living (TN)
Christian Medical Society Journal (TX)
Christ in Our Home (MN)
Christopher News Notes (NY)
CHURCHFACTS From Western NY
Church of God MISSIONS (IN)
Church Programs/ Middlers/Jrs (MO)
Church Programs/ Preschoolers (MO)
Church Programs/Primaries (MO
Circuit Rider (TN)
Columban Mission (NE)
Command (CO)
Compassion Today (Canada)
The Congregationalist (WY)
Contact (TN)
Contemporary Christian Music (TN)
COSMET Newsletter (CA)
Courage (IL)
Covenanter Witness (PA)
Daily Blessing (OK)
Daily Meditation (TX)
Dialog (MN)
Directions In Faith (TN)
Disciple, The (MO)
Door of Hope (CA)
Doorways (CO)
Elmbrook (WI)
Epiphany Journal (CA)
Eurovision Advance (CA)
Evangelical Missions Quarterly (IL)
Exodus Standard (CA)
Faith at Work, Inc. (Canada)
FaithQuest (IL)
Family Forum (MO)
Family Therapy (CA)
Family Walk (GA)
Festivals (CA)
Firm Foundation (TX)
Focus Magazine (TN)
The Forerunner (FL) - no response
Forward Day By Day (OH)
Four and Five (OH)
The Free Methodist Pastor (IN)
Fulness Magazine (TX)
God's Word for Today (MO)
Gospel Herald (PA)
Gospel Message (MO)
Greater Europe Report (IL)
Growing Together (IL)

The Herald (KY)
Heritage Herald (NC)
High School Teaching Guide (IL)
The Home Altar (MN)
Image (KS)
IMAGE (VA)
Insight (NC)
Insights (CA)
Interchange (OH)
Interlit (IL)
Invitation (TN)
It's Our World (DC)
Jubilee (DC)
Kindred Spirit (TX)
Last Day Messenger (OR)
Light for Today (MN)
Listen Magazine (DC)
Living Light (DC)
Living Values (IL)
Living With Children (TN)
Living with Preschoolers (TN)
Living with Teenagers (TN)
Look and Listen (TN)
The Lookout (NY)
Luke Society News (MS)
Lutheran Libraries (MN)
Maranatha Manna (MD)
Marriage & Family (IN)
Marriage Partnership (IL)
Men's Ministries (MO)
Messenger (IL)
Ministry (MD)
Miracle Living (AZ)
Mission (MD)
Missionary Monthly (MI)
Missionary Tidings (IN)
Mission Frontiers (CA)
Missions Today (TN)
Modern Liturgy (CA)
Momentum (DC)
Money Matters (GA)
Musicline (CA)
My Daily Visitor
My Delight (OH)
My Devotions (MO)
My Jewels (OH)
My Pleasure (OH)
Neighborly Good News (Canada - now Relationships)
New Catholic World (NJ)
New Jerusalem Music (NJ)
Nor'Easter (NY)
OC International (CA)
Open Doors News Briefs (CA)
Opening the Word (KS)
Open Windows (TN)
PCA Messenger (GA)
People of Destiny (MD)
The Plough (PA)
Plus (NY)
Poet & Writers (NY)
Portals of Prayer (MO)
Preteen Teacher (MO)
Quaker Life (IN)
Reflections (MD)
Reformed Journal (MI)
Religion Teacher's Journal (CT)
Sally Ann (Canada)
Single Adult Ministry Information (MO)
Sojourners (DC)
Sower, The (IL)
Spiritual Women's Times (WA)
The Standard (IL)
Student Venture Newsletter (CA)
Sunday School Illustrator (TN)
The Sunday School Times & Gospel Herald (OH)
Tabletalk (FL)
Teacheraid (PA)
Teen Triumph (TN)
These Days (GA)
Today's Better Life (TX)
The Trim Tab (GA)
The United Brethren (IN)
United Evangelical ACTION (IL)
U.S. Catholic (IL)
Veritas (CA)- no response
Weavings (TN)
Weekly Bible Reader (OH)
Wee Lambs (PA)
Wesleyan World (IN)
Wheaton Alumni (IL)
The Winner (DC)
The Witness (PA)
Word & Way (MO)
Word in Season (MN)
Word of Faith (OK)
Words of Hope (MI)
World Encounter (IL)
Worldorama (OK)
World Pulse (IL)
Worldwide THRUST (PA)

Young Life (CO)
Young Missionary (IN)
Youth Alive (MO)
YouthGuide (KS)
Youth Illustrated (IL)
Youth Walk (GA

PERIODICALS THAT HAVE CHANGED NAMES OR CEASED PUBLICATION

Action (IN)
Aglow Magazine (WA)
Anglican Magazine (Canada)
Believers News (MI)
Bread (MO)
Calvinist Contact (Canada - see Christian Courier)
Campus Leaders Fellowscrip (MO)
Canticle of Mary (IA)
Caring Connection (CO)
Cathedral Voice
Cherith (MN)
Choosing (MN)
Christian College Handbook (IL)
Christian Education Today (CO)
Christian Herald (NY)
Christian Living for Senior Highs (see I.D.)
Christian Outdoorsman (TX)
Christian Outlook (ID)
Chris. Singles
Communicator, The (OR)
Companion of St. Francis & St. Anthony (see Companion Magazine)
Connection (CA/UT)
Choralation (IN)
Christianity & Crisis (NY)
Church Business (Canada)
Church Ministries WORKER (MD)
Church Teachers - See Church Educator
Confident Living (NE)
Cottage Cheese (MN)
Crystal Rainbow (FL)
Dads Only - See Smart Dads
Family Forum (MO)
Family Resources (IL)
Final Draft, The (AZ)
For Parents (NY)
Free Spirit (CA)
Friend (IN)
Gospel Truth (MA)
Happenings (TN)
High School I.D. (see Pathway I.D.)
IDEASheet (IL)
Inner Horizons (MA)
Insights... (GA)
In Touch (IN)
It's God's World - see God's World Today
Journey (MO)
Journey (TN)
Junior Publications (IN)
Kindergarten Teacher (MO - See Level D Teacher)
Lighted Pathway (TN - See Pathway I.D.)
Light...For the Christian Walk (KY)
Light for Today (MN)
Literary Markets (Canada)
Living Words (MO - see Living Faith)
Living Streams (IN)
Moody Monthly (IL - see Moody Magazine)
New England Christian (MA)
New Heaven/New Earth (IN)
Newsletter (FL)
Opus One/Opus Two (TN)
Overcomer, The (IA)
Pavilion/CNF Perspective (CA)
Phoenix Rising (VA) - no current address
Pocket Inspirations (CA)
Primary Teacher (see Wonder Time)
Progressions (IL)
Pulpit Helps (TN - See Pulpit & Bible Study Helps)
Scoreboard Publications (UT)
Shoe Tree (NM)
Spirituality Today (MO)
Sunday School Counselor - See Christian Education Counselor
Trumpet Sounds, The (TX)
Tyro Magazine Canada)
Vision (MI)
Voice of Sarah (KS) - Bad address
Voices in the Wilderness (MA) -can't contact
World Mission Journal - see Missions Today
Writer's Info (ID)
Writers Newsletter (IL)
Zoomer & Co. (OR)

ADDITIONAL NOTES:

* Of those periodicals that indicated a preferrance, 65% will accept a complete manuscript, and 48% will accept a query. (Because some periodicals will accept either, the total percentage is greater than 100%.)

* Fifty-nine percent say no phone queries, with 41% accepting them.

* Forty-four percent of the publishers pay on acceptance, while 56% pay on publication.

GREETING CARD/GIFT MARKETS

(*) Indicates that publisher did not return questionnaire.

(#) Indicates that listing was updated from guidelines or other sources.

(+) Indicates new listing.

Note: See the end of this listing for specialty product lists.

ARGUS COMMUNICATIONS, 200 E. Bethany, Allen TX 75002. (214)390-6300. Lori Potter, ed. Publisher of social expression products for a variety of markets. 80% freelance. Query. Pays $50-125, on acceptance, for all rts. Pays negotiable royalty. Reports in 60-90 days. Produces postcards, posters and Pass It Ons. Needs humorous, informal, sensitive, and relationships. Prefers humorous sentiments. Holiday/seasonal 1 yr ahead. Submit maximum 20 ideas. Guidelines; catalog for 9x12 SAE/4 stamps.
Tips: "We prefer to receive editorial for posters, postcards and Pass It Ons. We update our freelance writers as new needs arise."

BARTON-COTTON INC., 1405 Parker Rd., Baltimore MD 21227. (410)247-4800. Does half general and half religious cards. Submit to Creative Art Dept. Open to illustrations only; buys 150-200 illustrations/yr. Query with resume and photocopies. Pays $150-500/illustration, on acceptance.

RUSS BERRIE & CO., Inc., 111 Bauer Dr., Oakland NJ 07436. (201)337-9000. Angelica Urra, dir. A general card publisher/inspirational line. 25% freelance; buys 100-300 ideas/yr. Outright submission. Pays on acceptance, for all rts. Reports in 4-8 wks. Uses rhymed, unrhymed, traditional, light verse; various lengths. Produces conventional, humorous, informal, inspirational, juvenile, novelty, religious, sensitivity, soft line. Needs card verse for anniversary, birthday, friendship, get well, keep in touch, love, miss you, new baby, please write, sympathy, thank you, wedding. Needs verses for other products for Christmas, Easter, graduation, Halloween, relatives, mother's Day, St. Patrick's Day, Thanksgiving, Valentine's Day. Holiday/seasonal 18-24 mos. ahead. Open to new card lines. Prefers 10 (long) to 20 (short) ideas/submission. Open to ideas for perpetual and undated calendars, gift books, greeting books, plaques, postcards, novelty products/copy, mugs, magnets, picture frames, gift bags, diaries, address books, stationary and gift items. No guidelines or catalog.

BLUE MOUNTAIN ARTS, INC., Box 1007, Dept. CWM Boulder CO 80306. (303)449-0536. Patricia Wayant, poetry ed.. General card publisher/a few inspirational/religious cards. Open to freelance; 50-75 freelance ideas/yr. Query or outright submission. Pays $200 for use on card, $25 for use in gift anthology; on publication; for anthology or exclusive rts. No royalties. Reports in 24-36 wks. Uses any type of poetry, any length. Produces inspirational, young adult/students, and sensitivity. Needs anniversary, birthday, Christmas, congratulations, Easter, friendship, get well, graduation, keep in touch, love, miss you, new baby, please write, relative, sympathy, thank you, Valentines, wedding; Mother's Day, Father's Day, philosophies about life and

achieving one's dreams. Holiday/seasonal 3-4 months ahead. Not open to ideas for new card lines. No limit on number sent (one per page). Guidelines/needs list; no catalog.
Tips: "Should not be overly religious."

#THE CALLIGRAPHY COLLECTION, 2604 NW 74th Pl., Gainesville FL 32606-1237. (904)375-8530. Fax: ((904)374-9957. Katy Fischer, ed. General card publisher/ inspirational cards. Pays $50-100/framed print idea, on publication, for all rts. Reports in 6 months. Uses rhymed and unrhymed (preferred). Produces conventional, humorous, informal, inspirational, sensitivity, and soft line. Unrhymed (preferred) or rhymed. Holiday/seasonal 6 months ahead. Prefers 3 ideas/submission. Also produces gift books, greeting books and plaques.
Tips: Especially needs friendship greetings.

***CARING CARD COMPANY,** Box 90278, Long Beach CA 90809. Shirley Hassell, ed. A specialty card publisher/inspirational and religious cards. 45% freelance. Outright submissions. Pays $10-25, on publication, for all rts. Reports in 8-16 wks. Uses rhymed, unrhymed and traditional; length open. Produces inspirational, religious, sensitivity and soft line. Needs Christmas, friendship, get well, keep in touch, love, miss you, please write, Valentines, significant loss/sympathy (bereavement, hospice environment, life/death transitions). Holiday/seasonal 6-12 months ahead. Prefers 1-12 ideas/submission. Also open to ideas for calendars, posters, plaques, postcards, and T-shirts. Guidelines.

CELEBRATION GREETINGS (A div. of Leanin' Tree), Box 9500, Boulder CO 80301. (303)530-1442. Fax: (303)581-2152. Sheryl Lear, Art & Verse Administrator. Christian/religious card publisher. 75% freelance. Buys 40 ideas/yr. Query. Pays $100/idea, on acceptance, for exclusive rts. No royalties. Reports in 4-12 wks. Rhymed/unrhymed (preferred)/traditional/light verse; to 4 lines. Produces humorous, informal, inspirational, religious, and sensitivity. Needs anniversary, birthday, Christmas, congratulations, friendship, get well, keep in touch, love, miss you, new baby, sympathy, thank you, wedding, and encouragement. Holiday/seasonal 8 mos ahead. Not open to new card lines. Prefers 25 or less ideas/submission. Open to ideas for posters, T-shirts, mugs. Guidelines; no catalog.
Tips: "No special occasion or narrow categories."

CREATIVE GRAPHICS, 785 Grant, Eugene OR 97402. (503)484-2726. Submit to Terry Dusseault, corp. sec. General card publisher/religious lines. Open only to photographs/artwork. Query. Pays $50/card. Guidelines; catalog for $1.50.

#CURRENT, INC., Box 2559, Colorado Springs CO 80901-2559. (719)594-4100. Nan Stine, Supervisor, creative writing. General card publisher/religious line. 5-10% freelance. Buys 150 ideas/yr. Outright submissions. Buys 150 ideas/yr. Outright submission. Pays $50, on acceptance, for all rights. No royalty. Reports in 2 mos. Prefers rhymed, unrhymed, traditional, light verse, original/tasteful humor; short. Produces announcements, conventional, humorous, informal, inspirational, juvenile, novelty, religious, sensitivity, soft line, studio. Needs anniversary, birthday, Christmas, congratulations, Easter, friendship, get well, graduation, Halloween, keep in touch, love, miss you, new baby, please write, sympathy, Thanksgiving, thank you, Valentines, wedding; also terminal illness and coping. Holiday/seasonal 18 months ahead. 12-15 ideas/submission. Open to new card lines, calendars, coloring books, gift books, greeting books, plaques, postcards, posters, puzzles. Guidelines; catalog (call 1-800-525-7170).

#DAYSPRING GREETING CARDS/OUTREACH PUBLICATIONS INC., Box 1010, Siloam Springs AR 72761. (501)524-9301. David Taylor, mng. ed. Christian/religious card publisher. 50% freelance; buys 750-1,000 ideas/yr. Outright submission. Pays from $30-50/idea, on acceptance, for all rts. No royalty. Reports in 2 mos. Uses rhymed, unrhymed (preferred), traditional and light verse; various lengths. Produces conventional, humorous, inspirational, juvenile, religious. Needs anniversary, birthday, Christmas, Easter, friendship, get well, graduation, new baby, relatives, sympathy, Thanksgiving, thank you, Valentines, wedding, and all major sending seasons and everyday occasions. Holiday/seasonal 1 yr ahead. Not open to new card lines and calendar ideas. Prefers 10 ideas/submission. Guidelines; no catalog.
Note: Will not be buying freelance material until the first or middle of 1994.

FREEDOM GREETING CARDS, Box 715, Bristol PA 19007. (215)945-3300. J. Levitt, pres. General card publisher/religious & inspirational lines. Currently has all the freelancers they need. Let them know the kind of work you can do and they will put your name in their file.

***GALLANT GREETINGS**, 2654 W. Medill, Chicago, IL 60647. (312)489-2000. General card publisher/a few inspirational/religious cards. Carolyn McDilda, ed. coord. 90% freelance; buys 500 ideas/yr. Query. Reports in 1 month. Pays 60-90 days after acceptance, for world greeting card rts. Pays royalties. Uses rhymed, unrhymed, traditional and light verse; 4-6 lines. Produces announcements, conventional, humorous, informal, inspirational, invitations, juvenile, religious, studio. Needs all types of greetings. Holiday/seasonal 6 months ahead. Open to new card lines. Prefers 6-10 ideas/submission. Guidelines/needs list; no catalog.

***THE C.R. GIBSON CO.**, 32 Knight St., Norwalk CT 06856. (203)847-4543. John Carroll, product mgr. General card publisher that does a few inspirational and religious cards. Open to freelance. Query. Pays variable amounts, on publication, for greeting card rts. Sometimes pays variable royalties. Reports in 8-12 wks. Uses rhymed, unrhymed and traditional. Produces announcements, conventional, humorous, informal, inspirational, invitations, juvenile, novelty, and religious. Needs anniversary, birthday, Christmas, Easter, friendship, get well, keep in touch, love, miss you, please write, and Valentines; 12 months ahead. Open to ideas for new card lines. Also open to ideas for gift books, greeting books and postcards. Guidelines.

LIFE GREETINGS, Box 468, Little Compton RI 02837. (401)635-8535. Overstocked; not accepting any material this year.

+MAILAWAYS, P.O. Box 782, Tavares FL 32778. (908)742-8196. General card publisher that does a few inspirational & religious cards. Gene Chambers, ed. 100% freelance. Outright submission. Buys variable rights. Variable payment, on acceptance; no royalties. Reports in 1-2 wks. Uses rhymed, unrhymed, traditional, light verse, fables or anecdotes; the shorter the better. Produces conventional, humorous, inspirational, religious and sensitivity. Poetic or humorous verses only; no cards for holidays or special events. Seasonal 3 mos ahead. Not open to new card lines. Send a handful of ideas at a time. May be open to ideas for gift books. Guidelines; no catalog.

***MANHATTAN GREETING CARD CO.**, 150 E 52 St. c/o Platzer/Fineberg, New York

NY 10022. (718)894-7600. General card publisher/inspirational line. Paula Haley, ed. 100% freelance. Reports in 3 wks. Holiday/seasonal 18 months ahead. Produces announcements, conventional, humorous, informal, inspirational, invitations, juvenile, sensitivity, soft line, studio, Christmas (85% of the line). Also open to ideas for bumper stickers, calendars, gift books, greeting books, postcards, and promotions. Pays $5-250. Free guidelines.

***NEW BOUNDARY DESIGNS, INC**, 1453 Park Rd., Chanhassen MN 55317. (612)474-0924. Ronald Olson, marketing mngr. General card publisher/religious line. 5% freelance; 9 ideas/yr. Pays $240/camera-ready design, on publication. Royalties 2-5%. Reports in 6 mos. Prefers unrhymed. Produces traditional, inspirational, juvenile and sensitivity. Holiday/seasonal 1 yr ahead. Open to ideas for greeting books, plaques, postcards, mugs, coaster magnets, bookmarks. Catalog.

+NOVO CARD PUBLISHERS, INC., 4513 N Lincoln Ave., Chicago IL 60625. (312)769-6000. Fax: (312)769-6769. Julia Chae, gen. mgr. General card publisher that does a few inspirational and religious cards. 40% freelance; buys 50-100 ideas/yr. Outright submissions. Pays $15-30, on acceptance, for all rts. No royalties. Reports in 4 wks. Seasonal 9 mos ahead. Uses rhymed, unrhymed, traditional and light verse. Produces announcements, conventional, humorous, informal, inspirational, invitations, juvenile, novelty, religious, sensitivity, soft line and studio. Needs anniversary, birthday, Christmas, congratulations, Easter, friendship, get well, graduation, Halloween, keep in touch, love, miss you, new baby, relatives (all occasions), sympathy, thank you, Valentines, and wedding. No new card lines. Submit 5-10 ideas max. Guidelines; no catalog.
Special Needs: "We would like to do a line of inspirational cards, 24 designs, either with one writer or several writers."

***PACIFIC PAPER GREETINGS, INC**, Box 2249, Sidney, BC V8L 3S8 Canada. (604)656-0504. Inspirational cards. Louise Rytter, ed. 50% freelance; buys 20 ideas/yr. Pays on acceptance, for all rts. Reports in 3 wks. Produces conventional, inspirational, romantic, sensitivity, soft line. Holiday/seasonal 12 months ahead. Guidelines for SAE/1 IRC.

+PAINTED HEARTS & FRIENDS, 1222 N. Fair Oaks Ave., Pasadena CA 91103. (818)798-7633, Fax: (818)798-7385. David Mekelburg, art dir. General card publisher with an inspirational line. Buys 20-30 ideas/yr. Outright submission. Pays $75-100/idea, on acceptance; 5% royalty. Reports in 1-2 wks. Uses unrhymed, traditional, light verse; short and to the point. No guidelines or catalog.

+PAPER MAGIC GROUP, INC, 347 Congress St., Boston MA 02210. (617)357-0254. Anne Leaf, VP/Creative. Secular card company specializing in Christmas cards; also does inspirational cards. 50% freelance. Outright submission on 8 1/2X11 paper. Pays negotiable rates ($20-150), within 30 days, for all rts. Does Christmas, seasonal, inspirational, cute and humorous.
Tip: "MUST be original."

***PARAMOUNT CARDS INC.**, Box 6546, Providence RI 02940. (401)726-0800. Tammy O'Keefe, ed.; submit to Editorial Freelance. General card publisher that does a few inspirational/religious cards. 10% freelance; humor only (no religious humor). Outright submission. Pays $100, on acceptance, for complete world rts. No royalty.

Reports in 3 wks. Prefers 10-15 ideas/submission. Guidelines for SASE; no catalog.

+**C.M. PAULA COMPANY**, 7773 School Rd., Cincinnati OH 45249. Submit to Editorial Supervisor. General gift-line items with inspirational verse; no greeting cards. 10% freelance. Pays on acceptance, for all rts. Reports in 4-6 wks. Holiday/seasonal 1 yr head. Open to verse and prose for plaques, key rings, magnets, stationary pads, mugs, plates, awards and statues. Guidelines.

#**RED FARM STUDIO**, Box 347, Pawtucket RI 02862-0347. (401)728-9300. Lisa Harter Saunders, creative dir. General card publisher with a religious line. 100% freelance. Query or outright submission (get guidelines first). Pays $3/line, on acceptance, for exclusive rts. No royalties. Reports in 2 mos. Use traditional and light verse; 1-4 lines. Produces announcements, invitations, religious. Needs anniversary, birthday, Christmas, friendship, get well, new baby, sympathy, wedding. Holiday 6 months ahead. Not open to ideas for new card lines. Submit any number of ideas. Guidelines/needs list for SASE.

***ROSERICH DESIGNS LTD.**, 79 5th Ave. 4th Fl, New York NY 10003-3034. Buys inspirational cards. 40% freelance. Pays on publication. Reports in 1 month. Produces humorous, inspirational, juvenile, sensitivity, soft lines, and studio. Holiday/seasonal 12 months ahead. Also open to ideas for calendars, gift books, greeting books. Guidelines and market sheet.

***MARCEL SCHURMAN CO., INC.**, 2500 N. Watney Way, Fairfield CA 94533. General card publisher that does soft religious and inspirational cards. Lynnea Washburn, ed. 20% freelance; buys 50 ideas/yr. Pays on acceptance. Reports in 1 month. Uses mostly unrhymed (rhymed ok for juvenile). Produces conventional, light humor, informal, invitations, juvenile, sensitivity, soft religious and inspirational; plus seasonal and everyday. Prefers 10-15 ideas/submission. Guidelines.

SUNRISE PUBLICATIONS, INC, 1145 Sunrise Greeting Ct., Box 4699, Bloomington IN 47402. (812)336-9900. Fax: (812)336-8712. Sheila Gerber, Editorial Coordinator. General card publisher that does inspirational cards. 10% freelance; buys 100 ideas/yr. Outright submission. Pays $50, on acceptance, for exclusive rts in all commercial formats. No royalties. Reports in 6 wks. Prefers unrhymed, traditional, contemporary; 1-4 lines. Produces announcements, conventional, informal, inspirational, invitations. Needs anniversary, birthday, belated birthday, Christmas, congratulations, Easter, friendship, get well, graduation, Halloween, love, miss you, new baby, St. Patrick's Day, sympathy, Thanksgiving, thank you, Valentines, wedding; also baptism, confirmation, bar & bat mitzvah. Holiday/seasonal any time. Not open to ideas for new card lines. Up to 20 ideas/submission. Guidelines; no catalog.

WARNER PRESS INC., 1200 E 5th St, Anderson IN 46018. (317)644-7721. Fax: (317)649-3664. Robin Fogle, product ed. Christian/religious card publisher. 35-40% freelance. Buys 150-200 ideas/yr. Query. Pays $20 and up, on acceptance, for full rts. No royalties. Reports in 4-6 wks. Uses rhymed, unrhymed, traditional; 4-8 lines rhymed, 2-3 lines prose. Produces inspirational, religious. Needs anniversary, birthday, Christmas (needs a good amount for boxed cards), Easter, friendship, get well, graduation, new baby, sympathy, thank you, Valentines, wedding, secret pal. Holiday/seasonal 6 months ahead. Accepts Christmas material in September for next year. Open to new card lines. Accepts 10-15 ideas/submission. Also open to ideas for

calendars, coloring books, postcards, posters and Sunday bulletins. Guidelines; no catalog.
Special Needs: "We purchase for boxed greeting cards. Verses should be warm and personal, but general enough to be sent by a group."
Tips: "We prefer submissions be typed on 3x5 cards with name, address, telephone #, and freelance identification number on the back."

ADDITIONAL CARD PUBLISHERS

The following greeting card publishers do not use freelance material, or did not complete a questionnaire, but are included for reference or to contact on your own. Do not submit to them before you send for guidelines or ascertain their needs.

ABBEY PRESS, St. Meinrad IN 47577. No freelance.
APPALACHIAN BIBLE CO INC., 506 Princeton Rd, Johnson City TN 37601.
BERG CHRISTIAN ENTERPRISES, 4525 SE 63rd Ave, Portland OR 97206.
BOB SIEMON DESIGNS INC., 11609 Martens River Cir., Fountain Valley CA 92708.
+CAROLYN BEAN PUBLISHING, 1129 N McDowell Blvd., Petaluma CA 94954.
CONCORDIA PUBLISHING HOUSE, 3558 S. Jefferson, St. Louis MO 63118.
EISNER ADVERTISING STUDIO (OH) - No freelance.
+EVERGREEN PUBLICATIONS, 422 Larkfield Ctr #252, Santa Rosa CA 95403-1408.
FAYE'S SPECIALTY CARDS (NY) - No freelance.
+FULL MOON CREATIONS, 74 S. Hamilton St., Doylestown PA 18901 - Inspirational cards.
GUERNICA EDITIONS (Canada) - No freelance.
THE HERMITAGE ART COMPANY INC., 5151 N. Ravenwood Ave., Chicago IL 60640.
HIGHER HORIZONS, Box 78399, Los Angeles CA 90016.
J-MAR ASSOCIATES, P.O. Box 23149, Waco TX 76702-3149. Not open to freelance at this time.
JONATHAN & DAVID INC, Box 1194, Grand Rapids MI 49501.
+KIMBERLY ENTERPRISES INC., 15029 S. Figueroa St., Gardena CA 90248 - Inspirational cards.
THE LORENZ COMPANY, 1208 Cimmaron Dr., Waco TX 76712-8174.
MAGIC MOMENTS, 10 Deanna Ct., Deer Park NY 11729.
MAINE LINE CO. - See **RUSS BERRIE AND CO.**
+MALENA PRODUCTIONS INC., Box 14483, Ft. Lauderdale FL 33302 - Inspirational cards.
MANUSCRIPTURES (WI) - No freelance.
MARIAN HEATH GREETING CARDS, (MA) - No freelance.
NORTHWESTERN PRODUCTS INC.(MN) - No freelance.
OAKSPRINGS IMPRESSIONS, Box 572, Woodacre CA 94973.
PRINTERY HOUSE (MO) - No freelance.
QUADRIGA ART (NY) - No freelance.
+QUALITY ARTWORKS, 2262 N. Penn Rd., Hatfield PA 19440 - Inspirational cards.
RAINFALL, INC. (MI) - No freelance.
RENAISSANCE GREETING CARDS (ME) - No freelance.
SANGAMON INC. (IL) - No freelance.
JOSEPH E. SCHULTZ ART STUDIO (IN) - No freelance.

SECOND NATURE LTD. (England) - No freelance.
SEEDS EVANGELICAL GREETING CARDS (NC) - No freelance.
WIZWORKS, Box 240, Masonville CO 80541 -Overstocked.

PUBLISHERS PRODUCING SPECIALTY PRODUCTS

Note: Most of the following publishers are greeting card publishers, but some will be found in the book publisher listings.

ACTIVITY/COLORING BOOKS
Current
Shining Star
Standard
Warner Press

BOARD GAMES
Chariot (Rainfall Inc.)
Master Books
Shining Star
Standard Publishing
Tyndale House
Warner Press (maybe)

CALENDARS
Russ Berrie
Caring Card Co.
Current
Group Publishing
Manhattan Greeting Card
Neibauer Press
Roserich Designs
Tyndale House
Warner Press

COMIC BOOKS
Thomas Nelson

GIFT BOOKS
See listing under Book Topics

GIFT/NOVELTY ITEMS
Argus Communications
Russ Berrie
Manhattan Greeting Card
New Boundry Designs
C.M. Paula Co. (key rings)

GREETING BOOKS
Russ Berrie
Calligraphy Collection
Current
C.R. Gibson
Manhattan Greeting Card
New Boundary Designs
Roserich Designs

MAGNETS
Russ Berrie
New Boundary Designs
C.M. Paula Co.

MUGS
Russ Berrie
Celebration Greetings
New Boundary Designs
C.M. Paul Co.

PLAQUES
Russ Berrie
Calligraphy Collection
Caring Card Company
Current
New Boundary Designs
C.M. Paula Co.

POSTCARDS
Argus Communications
Russ Berrie
Caring Card Co.
Current
C.R. Gibson
Manhattan Greeting Card
New Boundary Designs
Warner Press

POSTERS
Argus Communications
Caring Card Co.
Celebration Greetings
Current
Warner Press

PUZZLES
Current

T-SHIRTS
Caring Card Co.
Celebration Greetings

SECULAR NEWSPAPERS WITH RELIGION EDITORS

Following is a listing of about 234 secular newspapers or news magazines with the names of their religion editors. If you have broad interest religious pieces appropriate for a secular newspaper, send them to these editors, keeping in mind that most of them will want articles written in a journalistic style. In addition, you are encouraged to send Op-Ed (Opinion/Editorial) pieces to these same publications. Address them to the Op-Ed Editor at the newspaper. Remember that if you have a opinion piece (with a religious slant and Scripture quotation) published in a secular publication, you may be eligible for one of several Amy Awards, including the $10,000 grand prize. Writing such pieces is also an excellent way to make an impact on society with your Christian principles.

The names given below are all religion editors. The number at the end of each listing indicates circulation.

Abilene Reporter-News, Roy Jones, 101 Cypress St, Box 30, Abilene TX 79604. 915-673-4271. 40,000.

The Advocate, Ed Pratt, 525 Lafayette St, Box 588, Baton Rouge LA 70821. 504-383-1111. 30,000.

#Akron Beacon Journal, Laura Haferd, 44 E Exchange St, Box 640, Akron OH 44309. 216-375-8111. 159,000.

Albuquerque Journal, Bruce Daniels, 7777 Jefferson St NE, Drawer J, Albuquerque NM 87103. 505-823-3912. 121,000.

Albuquerque Tribune, Jim Wagner, Drawer T, Albuquerque NM 87103. 505-823-3665. 35,000.

+Amarillo Globe-News, Dora Dominguez, Box 2091, Amarillo TX 79166. 806-376-1488.

+Anniston Star, Sean Reilly, Box 189, Anniston AL 36202. 205-236-1551.

Arizona Daily Star, Tom Turner, 4850 S Park Ave, Box 26807, Tucson AZ 85726. 602-573-4132. 90,000.

#Arizona Republic, Kim Sue Lia Perkes, 120 E Van Buren, Box 1950, Phoenix AZ 85001. 602-271-8487. 400,000.

#Atlanta Journal & Constitution, Gayle White, 72 Mariette St NW, Box 4689, Atlanta GA 30303. 404-526-5151. 282,000.

#Augusta Chronicle & Herald, James Dotson, 725 Broad St, Box 1928, Augusta GA 30909. 404-724-0851. 83,000.

+Aurora Beacon-News, Mary Fran Fulton, 101 River St., Aurora IL 60504. 708-844-5585.

#Austin American-Statesman, Carlos Vidal Greth, 305 S Congress, Box 670, Austin TX 78764. 512-445-3604. 180,000.

Bakersfield Californian, Ed King, 1707 Eye St, Box 440, Bakersfield CA 93302. 805-395-7384. 83,000.

#Baltimore Sun, Jay Merwin or Frank Somerville, 501 N Calvert St, Baltimore MD 21278. 410-332-6000. 238,000.

Bay City Times, Bob Carrier, 311 Fifth St, Bay City MI 48708. 517-895-8551. 42,000.

+Beacon News, Steven D. Freeman, 101 S. River St., Aurora IL 60506. 312-232-7000.

+Bergen Record, David Gibson, 150 River St., Hackensack NJ 07602. 201-646-4100.

+Berkshire Eagle, William Bell, 75 S. Church St., Pittsfield MA 04005. 413-447-7311.

Billings Gazette, Sue Olt, 401 North Broadway, Billings MT 59101. 406-657-1200. 54,000.

#Birmingham News, Greg Garrison, 2200 4th Ave N, Box 2553, Birmingham AL 35202. 205-325-2222. 215,000.

Bismarck Tribune, Julie Fredericksen, Seventh and Front Sts, Box 1498, Bismarck ND 58502. 701-223-2500. 32,000.

Boca Raton News, Mary Lou Simms, 33 SE Third St, Box 580, Boca Raton FL 33429. 407-338-4920. 38,000.

#Boston Globe, Jim Franklin, 135 Morrissey Blvd, Box 2378, Boston MA 02107. 617-929-2000. 500,000.

Boston Herald, (no religion editor at this time), One Herald Sq, Box 2096, Boston MA 02106. 617-426-3000. 356,000.

Bozeman Daily Chronicle, Barb Smith, 32 S Rouse St, Box 1188, Bozeman MT 59771. 406-587-4491. 14,000.

+Bridgeport Post, Frank M. Szivos, 410 State St., Bridgeport CT 06604. 203-333-0161. 90,000.

#Calgary Herald, Gordon Legge, 215 - 16th St SE, Box 2400, Station M, Calgary AB T2P 0W8 Canada. 403-235-7560. 123,000.

Camden Courier-Post, Karen Morgan, 301 Cuthbert Blvd, Box 530, Cherry Hill NJ 08034. 609-663-6000. 101,000.

Canton Repository, Charita Goshay, 500 Market Ave S, Canton OH 44702. 216-454-5611. 84,000.

+Casper Star Tribune, G. Thomas Morgan, Box 80, Casper WY 82602-0080. 307-266-0592.

Cedar Rapids Gazette, Bev Duffy, 500 Third Ave SE, Cedar Rapids IA 52401. 319-398-8211. 71,000.

Chattanooga News-Free Press, Jim Ashley, 400 East 11th St, Chattanooga TN 37402. 615-756-6900. 104,000.

#Chattanooga Times, Ruth Robinson, 117 E Tenth St, Box 951, Chattanooga TN 37401. 615-756-1234. 45,000.

#Chicago Sun-Times, Daniel J. Lehmann, 401 N Wabash, Chicago IL 60611. 312-321-3000. 531,000.

#Chicago Tribune, Michael Hirsley or Monique Parsons, 435 N Michigan Ave, Chicago IL 60611. 312-222-3405. 723,000.

#Cincinnati Enquirer, Ben Kaufman or Christiane Wolff, 312 Elm St, Cincinnati OH 45202. 513-768-8370/369-1925. 348,000.

Cincinnati Post, Carmen Carter, 125 East Court St, Cincinnati OH 45202. 513-352-2000. 114,000.

Cleveland Plain Dealer, Darryl Holland, 1801 Superior Ave NE, Cleveland OH 44114. 216-344-4500. 414,000.

+Columbia State, Jennifer Nicholson, Box 1333, Columbia SC 29202. 803-

771-8507. 180,000.

#**Columbus Dispatch**, Derris Blackford, 34 S Third St, Columbus OH 43215. 614-461-8521. 263,000.

+**Commercial Appeal,** David Waters, 495 Union, Memphis TN 38103. 901-529-2399.

+**Contra Costa Times**, Diane Weddington, Walnut Creek CA 94596. 415-935-2525. 100,000.

+**Courier Journal**, Bill Wolfe, 525 W Broadway, Louisville KY 40202. 502-582-4248.

Daily Gleaner, Sterling Kneebone, Box 3370, Fredericton NB E3B 5A2 Canada. 506-452-6671. 31,000.

+**Daily Intelligencer**, Louise Heath, 333 N Broad St., Doylestown PA 18901. 215-345-3000.

+**Daily Mail**, Robert N. Mitchell, Box 484 - 30 Church, Catskill NY 12414. 518-943-2100.

+**Daily Press**, Lisa Daniels, 7505 Warwick, Newport News VA 23601. 804-247-4793. 124,000.

#**Dallas Morning News**, Daniel J. Cattau, Box 655237, Dallas TX 75265. 214-977-8222. 800,000.

#**Dayton Daily News,** Dave Kepple, 45 S Ludlow St, Box 1287, Dayton OH 45402. 513-225-2223. 185,000.

#**Denver Post**, Virginia Culver, Box 1709, Denver CO 80201. 303-820-1223. 262,000.

+**Detroit Free Press,** David M. Crumm, 321 W. Lafayette, Detroit MI 48226. 313-223-4526. 575,000.

#**Detroit News,** Kate DeSmet, 615 W Lafayette Blvd, Detroit MI 48231. 313-222-2245. 434,000.

+**Duluth News Tribune**, Sue Hogan-Albach, 424 W 1st St., Duluth MN 55816. 218-723-5281.

+**Elkhart Truth**, Tom Price, 421 S 2nd, Elkhart IN 46515. 219-294-1661.

+**El Nuevo Herald**, Ivonne Gomez, 3191 Coral Way, Miami FL 33145. 305-447-6817.

+**Fayetteville Observer & Times**, James Pharr or Earl M. Vaughan, 2702 Huntington Rd., Fayetteville NC 28303. 919-323-4848. 82,000.

#**Flint Journal**, Betty Brenner, 200 E First St, Flint MI 48502. 313-767-0660. 120,000.

#**Florida Times Union**, Barbara White, 1 Riverside Ave, Box 1949, Jacksonville FL 32231. 904-359-4111. 186,000.

+**Fort Lauderdale News**, James Davis or Earl Maucker, 101 N. River Dr. E., Ft. Lauderdale FL 33301. 305-761-4000.

#**Fort Lauderdale Sun-Sentinel**, Damon Adams, 3 SW 129th Ave. Ste. 101, Pembroke Pines FL 33027. 305-436-7157. 240,000.

+**Fort Worth Star Telegram**, Jim W. Jones, 400 W 7th St., Fort Worth TX 76102. 817-390-7707. 255,000.

Fremont Argus, Chris O'Connell, 3850 Decoto Road, Fremont CA 94536. 510-794-0111. 33,000.

+**Fresno Bee**, Dee Anne Finken or John G. Taylor, 1626 E. St., Fresno CA 93786. 209-441-6375.

+**Galveston Daily News,** Robert Frelow, Box 628, Galveston TX 77553. 409-744-3611. 409-744-3611.

+Gazette Telegraph, Steve Rabey, Box 1779, Colorado Springs CO 80901. 719-636-9276. 107,000.

Grand Forks Herald, Steve Lee, 120 N Fourth St, Box 6008, Grand Forks ND 58203. 701-780-1114. 40,000.

+Grand Rapids Press, Ed Golder, 155 Michigan St. NW, Grand Rapids MI 49503. 150,000.

Grass Valley Union, Susan Genovese, Box 1025, Grass Valley CA 95945. 916-273-9561. 20,000.

+Greensboro Daily News & Record, Andrew Barron, 200 E. Market St., Greensboro NC 27420. 919-373-7000. 116,000.

+**Extra News Bureau**, Celia Sibley, 6455 Best Friend Rd., Norcross GA 30071. 404-263-3858.

Hamilton Spectator, Ray Brown, 44 Frid St, Hamilton ON L8N 3G3 Canada. 416-526-3333. 134,000.

Harrisburg Patriot-News, Tony Perry, 812 Market St, Box 2265, Harrisburg PA 17105. 717-255-8100. 170,000.

+Hartford Courant, Gerald Renner, 285 Broad St., Hartford CT 06115. 203-241-6200. 228,000.

+The Herald, Richard Jackson, Box 930, Everett WA 98206. 206-339-3423.

+Herald & Review, Theresa Churchill, 601 E. William St., Decatur IL 62525. 217-429-5151.

+Herald Sun, Flo Johnston, Box 2092, Durham NC 27702. 919-419-6638.

+Hillsdale Daily News, Janet Lee, 4300 W Bacon Rd., Hillsdale MI 49242. 517-431-7351.

Honolulu Star-Bulletin, City Desk (for now), 605 Kapiolani Blvd, Box 3080, Honolulu HI 96802. 808-525-8640. 100,000.

+Houston Chronicle, Richard Vara or Cecile Holmes White, Box 4260, Houston TX 77210. 713-220-7659/7562. 440,000.

#Houston Post, Steve Brunsman, 4747 SW Freeway, Box 4747, Houston TX 77001. 713-840-5600. 297,000.

+Huntsville Times, Yvonne T. White, Box 1487 West Station, Huntsville AL 35807. 205-532-4419. 74,000.

Hutchinson News, Joyce Hall, Box 190, Hutchinson KS 67504. 316-662-3311. 42,000.

Imperial Valley Press, Peggy Dale, 205 N 8th St, El Centro CA 92244. 619-352-2211. 19,000.

+Independence Examiner, Richard LeComte, Box 458, Independence MO 64051. 816-254-8600.

+Indianapolis Star, Carol Elrod, 608 E. New York St., Indianapolis IN 46202. 317-663-9471. 229,000.

Inland Valley Daily Bulletin, Nan Cretens, Box 4000, Ontario CA 91761. 909-987-6397. 80,000.

Jackson Sun, Tonya Smith, Box 1059, Jackson TN 38301. 901-427-3333. 36,000.

#Jersey Journal, Elizabeth A. Foley, 30 Journal Sq, Jersey City NJ 07306. 201-653-1000. 70,000.

Johnson City Press-Chronicle, Robert Pierce, 204 W Main St, (37601), Box 1717, Johnson City TN 37605. 615-929-3111. 32,000.

+Journal Tribune, Donna Landry, Box 627, Biddeford ME 04005. 207-282-1535.

#Kansas City Star, Helen Gray, 1729 Grand Ave, Kansas City MO 64108. 816-234-4300. 282,000.

+Keene Sentinel, Diane Nix, 60 West St., Keene NH 03431. 603-352-1234.

Kentucky New Era, Tonya Smith, Box 729, Hopkinsville KY 42240. 502-886-4444. 16,000.

Kingston Whig-Standard, Mr. Rosalind Malcolm, 306 King St, Kingston ON K7L 4Z7 Canada. 613-544-5000. 36,000.

Kitchener Waterloo Record, Donna Shea, 225 Fairway Road S, Kitchener ON N2G 4E5 Canada. 519-894-2231. 83,000.

+Lacrosse Tribune, Gayda Hollnagel, 401 N. Third St., Lacrosse WI 54601. 608-782-9710.

Lafayette Journal & Courier, Byron Parvis, 217 N Sixth St, Lafayette IN 47901. 317-423-5511. 40,000.

Lake County News Herald, Kathy Baur, 38879 Mentor Road, Willoughby OH 44094. 216-951-0000. 46,000.

Lakeland Ledger, Maryalice Quinn, Lime & Missouri Sts, Box 408, Lakeland FL 33802. 813-687-7000. 50,000.

+Lansing State Journal, Sheila Schimpf, 120 E. Lenawee, Lansong MI 48919. 517-377-1000. 92,000.

Las Vegas Review-Journal, Sandy Varvel, 1111 W Bonanza Road, Box 70, Las Vegas NV 89125. 702-385-4241. 129,000.

Lewiston Daily Sun, Jean Lachance, 104 Park St, Lewiston ME 04240. 207-784-5411. 43,000.

Lewistown Tribune, Jeannie DePaul, 505 C St, Box 957, Lewiston ID 83501. 208-743-9411. 26,000.

+Lexington Herald Leader, Paul Prather, 100 Midland Ave., Lexington KY 40508. 606-231-3342. 120,000.

Long Beach Press Telegram, Joy Thompson, 604 Pine Ave, Box 230, Long Beach CA 90844. 310-435-1161. 131,000.

+Los Angeles Sentinel, Virgie W. Murray, 1112 E. 43rd, Los Angeles CA 90011. 213-232-3261. 40,000.

+Los Angeles Times, John S. Dart, 20000 Prairie, Chatsworth CA 91311. 818-772-3342. 1,177,000.

+Lowell Sun, Virginia Kimball, 4 Wayne Rd., Westford MA 01886. 508-458-7100. 57,000.

+Lubbock Avalanche Journal, Beth Pratt, P.O. Box 491, Lubbock TX 79408. 806-762-8844. 70,000.

Lufkin Daily News, Beverly Johnson, Box 1089, Lufkin TX 75902. 409-632-6631. 9,000.

Macomb Daily, Bill Fleming, 67 Cass Ave, Mount Clemens MI 48043. 313-469-4510. 48,000.

Macon Telegraph & News, Rosalan Thompson, 120 Broadway, Box 4167, Macon GA 31213. 912-744-4200. 75,000.

Medford Mail Tribune, Gary Nelson, 33 N First St, Box 1108, Medford OR 97501. 503-776-4411. 35,000.

+Merced Sun-Star, Jeffery Williams, Box 739, 3033 North C St, Merced CA 95341. 209-722-1511. 23,000.

Meriden Record-Journal, Marjorie Fay, 11 Crown St, Box 915, Meriden CT 06450. 203-235-1661. 31,000.

+Mesa Tribune, Lawn R. Griffiths, 120 W 1st Ave., Mesa AZ 85201. 602-898-6514.

#Miami Herald, Bea Hines or Adon Taft, One Herald Plaza, Miami FL 33132. 305-376-3470/3463. 433,000.

#Milwaukee Journal, Marie Rohde, 333 W State St, Box 661, Milwaukee WI 53201. 414-224-2000. 260,000.

Milwaukee Sentinel, Ernie Franzen, 918 N Fourth St, Box 371, Milwaukee WI 53203. 414-224-2151. 179,000.

+Mineral Daily News-Tribune, Ed Bernard, Box 1266, Keyser WV 26726-1266.

+Minneapolis Star-Tribune, Neal M. Gendler, 425 Portland Ave., Minneapolis MN 55488. 612-673-4138. 400,000.

Missoulian, The, Lynn Schwanke, religion reporter, Box 8029, Missoula MT 59807. 406-523-5240. 31,000.

#Mobile Press-Register, Parker Holmes, 304 Government St, Box 2488, Mobile AL 36630. 205-434-8696. 117,000.

Modesto Bee, Dennis Roberts, 1325 H St, Box 3928, Modesto CA 95352. 209-578-2000. 80,000.

Monterey Herald, Mariann Zambo, Monterey Peninsula Herald Co., Box 271, Monterey CA 93942. 408-372-3311. 39,000.

Montgomery Advertiser, Lynn Williamson, 200 Washington Ave, Box 1000, Montgomery AL 36101-1000. 205-262-1611. 60,000.

+Montgomery Journal, Jane Dumont, 11131 Dewey Rd., Kensington MD 20895. 301-942-0103.

+Montreal Gazette, Harvey L. Shepherd, 250 St. Antoine St., Montreal QB H2Y 3R7 Canada. 514-987-2847. 276,000.

Morning News Tribune, Steve Maynard, 1950 S State St, Box 11000, Tacoma WA 98411. 206-597-8649. 110,000.

+Mt. Carmel Register, Larry Reynolds, 115 E 4th, Mt Carmel IL 62863. 618-262-5144.

Muncie Evening Press, Renee Jennings, 125 S High St, Box 2408, Muncie IN 47302. 317-747-5700. 14,000.

#Nashville Banner, Frances Meeker, 1100 Broadway, Nashville TN 37203. 615-259-8270. 67,000.

#Nashville Tennessean, Ray Waddle, 1100 Broadway, Nashville TN 37203. 615-259-8077. 130,000.

New Orleans Times-Picayune, Religion Editor, 3800 Howard Ave, New Orleans LA 70140. 504-826-3448. 279,000.

New York Daily News, Bill Bell, 220 East 42nd St, New York NY 10017. 212-210-2100. 800,000.

New York Newsday, Paul Moses, 2 Park Ave, New York NY 10016. 212-251-6850. 271,000.

+New York Times, Ari Goldman or Peter Steinfels, 229 W 43rd, New York NY 10036. 212-556-1234. 1,115,000.

+Newark Star Ledger, Monica Maske, Star Ledger Plaza, Newark NJ 07101. 201-877-4040. 471,000.

+News & Daily Advance, Jan Vertefeuille, 101 Wyndale Dr., Lynchburg VA 24506. 804-385-5543.

NC

+News & Observer, Erin Kelly or Donna Seese, 215 S McDowell St., Raleigh NC 27604. 919-829-4860.

News Chronicle, John Mitchell, 2595 Thousand Oaks Blvd, Box 3129, Thousand Oaks CA 91359. 805-496-3211. 22,000.

News Journal, The, Janet Applegren, 901 Sixth St, Box 2831, Daytona Beach FL 32117. 904-252-1511. 100,000.

News Press, The, Glenda Anderson, 2442 Dr Martin Luther King Blvd, Box 10, Fort Myers FL 33902. 813-335-0200. 90,000.

+News Tribune, Steven Maynard, P.O. Box 11000, Tacoma WA 98411. 206-597-8738.

+Newsweek, Kenneth L. Woodward, 444 Madison Ave., New york NY 10022.

Oceanside Blade-Tribune, Debbie Rosen, 1722 S Hill, Box 90, Oceanside CA 92054. 619-433-7333. 45,000.

Omaha World Herald, Julia McCord, World Herald Sq, Omaha NE 68102. 402-444-1000. 222,000.

#Orange County Register, Ms. Tracy Weber, 625 N Grand Ave, Box 11626, Santa Ana CA 92701. 714-664-5029. 348,000.

+Oregonian, Sura Rubenstein, 1320 SW Broadway, Portland OR 97201. 503-221-8327. 337,000.

+Oregon Statesman, Lewis H. Ahrends, Jr., P.O. Box 13009, Salem OR 97309. 503-339-6611.

#Orlando Sentinel, Adelle Banks, 633 N Orange Ave, Box 2833, Orlando FL 32802. 407-420-5459. 273,000.

+Ottawa Citizen, Bob Harvey, 1101 Boxter Rd., Ottawa ON K2C 3P4 Canada. 613-596-3689. 500,000.

+Palm Beach Post, Lois Kaplan, Box 24700, West Palm Beach FL 33416. 407-820-4100. 182,000.

+Patriot Ledger, Ann Doyle or Dot Newell, George W. Prescott Publishing, Quincy MA 02169. 617-786-7000/7026. 189,000.

Philadelphia Daily News, no religion editor, 400 N Broad St, Box 7788, Philadelphia PA 19101. 215-854-5900. 225,000.

#Philadelphia Inquirer, Michael Schaffer, 400 N Broad St, Box 8263, Philadelphia PA 19130. 215-854-2000. 500,000.

+Phoenix Gazette, Ben Winton, 120 E Van Buren St., Phoenix AZ 85004. 800-331-9270. 115,000.

+Pittsburgh Press, Ann Rogers-Melnick, 34 Blvd of the Allies, Pittsburgh PA 15230. 412-263-1416. 168,000.

Placerville Mountain Democrat, Joy Haessler, Box 1088, Placerville CA 95667. 916-622-1255. 14,000.

+Post and Courier, Marsha B. Guerard, 134 Columbus St., Charleston SC 29403. 803-745-4151.

+Post Herald, William Singleton, Box 2553, Birmingham AL 35202. 205-325-2370.

+Post Standard, Alva James, Box 4818, Syracuse NY 13211. 315-470-2166.

+Providence Journal & Ledger, Richard Dujardin, 75 Fountain St.,

Providence RI 02902. 202,000.

+Publishers Weekly (magazine), Henry William Griffin, 5120 Prytania St., New Orleans LA 70115. 504-899-5889.

+Pueblo Chieftan, Ada Brownell, 33550 Hwy 96 East, Pueblo CO 81001. 719-544-3520. 50,000.

+Reading Eagle Times, John Smith, Box 582, Reading PA 19603. 215-371-5007. 78,000.

Record, The, David Gibson, Bergen Record Co., 150 River St, Hackensack NJ 07601. 201-646-4182. 700,000.

+Religious News Service, Tom Roberts, 475 Riverside Dr. - 1902, New York NY 10115. 212-870-3311.

Reno Gazette Journal, Sharon Genung, 955 Kuenzli, Box 22000, Reno NV 89520. 702-788-6397. 85,000.

+Reuters, Richard L. Walker, 233 Peachtree St. NE, Atlanta GA 30303. 404-523-3505.

+Richmond County Journal, Jeffrey D. Holland, P.O. Box 1888, Rockingham NC 28379. 919-997-3111.

+Richmond News Leader, Tom Mullen, PO Box C-32333, Richmond VA 23293. 804-649-6000.

#Richmond Times Dispatch, Ed Briggs, Box 85333, Richmond VA 23293-0001. 804-649-6754. 220,000.

Riverside Press Enterprise, Cindy Friday, 3512 14th St, Box 792, Riverside CA 92502. 909-684-1200. 160,000.

+Roanoke Times & World News, Stephen D. Haner & Cody Lowe, Box 2491, Roanoke VA 24010. 703-981-3100. 125,000.

Rocky Mountain News, Gary Massaro, 400 West Colfax Ave, Box 719, Denver CO 80201. 303-892-5000. 356,000.

Rutland Daily Herald, Charlene Tenney, 27 Wales St, Norwich VT 05701. 802-775-5511. 23,000.

Sacramento Bee, Janet Vitt, 2100 Q St, Box 15779, Sacramento CA 95852. 916-321-1000. 263,000.

San Antonio Express News, Michael Parker, Ave E & 3rd St, Box 2171, San Antonio TX 78297. 210-225-7411. 187,000.

San Bernardino Sun, Rosemary McClure, 399 N D St, San Bernardino CA 92401. 909-889-9666. 94,000.

+San Diego Evening Tribune, Bob Diveroli, 350 Camino de la Reina, Box 191, San Diego CA 92108. 619-299-3131. 385,000.

#San Diego Union Tribune, Sandi Dolbee, 350 Camino de la Reina, Box 191, San Diego CA 92112. 619-293-2082. 458,000.

#San Francisco Chronicle, Don Lattin, 901 Mission St, San Francisco CA 94119. 415-777-8479. 600,000.

+San Jose Mercury News. Jill Wolfson, 450 Ridder Park Dr., San Jose CA 95190. 408-920-5974. 279,000.

+San Mateo Times, Tom Krogstad or Steven Shelby, 359 Glenwood, San Carlos CA 94070. 415-348-4321. 47,000.

Santa Barbara News Press, Mr. Willie Mears, Box 1359, Santa Barbara CA 93102. 805-564-5200. 58,000.

Santa Rosa Press Democrat, Suzanne Boynton, 427 Mendocino Ave, Santa Rosa CA 95401. 707-546-2020. 95,000.

Santa Ynez Valley News, Bart Ortberg, 423 Second St, Box 647, Solvang CA 93463. 805-688-5522. 8,000.

#Seattle Times, Lee Mosciwal or Carol M. Ostrom, Box 70, Seattle WA 98111. 206-464-2111. 239,000.

Shreveport Times, David Westerfield, 222 Lake St, Shreveport LA 71101. 318-459-3200. 110,000.

Sioux City Journal, Glenn Olson, Sixth and Pavonia Sts, Sioux City IA 51102. 712-279-5075. 60,000.

Sonora Union Democrat, Lenore Rutherford, 84 S Washington St, Sonora CA 95370. 209-532-7151. 19,000.

#St Joseph News Press, Tim Janulewicz, 825 Edmond St, Box 29, Saint Joseph MO 64502. 816-271-8595. 40,000.

#St Louis Post-Dispatch, Kathy Rogers or Pamela Schaefer, 900 N Tucker Blvd, Saint Louis MO 63101. 314-340-8000. 340,000.

#St Paul Pioneer Press Dispatch, Clark Morphew, 345 Cedar St, Saint Paul MN 55101. 612-222-5011. 209,000.

#St Petersburg Times, Tom Billitteri, 490 First Ave S, Box 1121, St Petersburg FL 33731. 813-893-8410. 352,000.

+Southern Illinoisan, Sharon A. Gibson, 710 N. Illinois Ave., Carbondale IL 62902. 618-529-5454.

+Spartanburg Herald-Journal, Debra Lester, P.O. Box 1657, Spartanburg SC 29304. 803-582-4511.

+Star and Tribune, Martha Allen, 425 Portland Ave., Minneapolis MN 55488. 612-372-4141.

+Standard Examiner, John DeVilbiss, 455 23rd St, Ogden UT 84302. 801-625-4237.

#Staten Island Advance, Julia Martin, 950 Fingerboard Road, Staten Island NY 10305. 718-981-1234. 77,000.

+Sun-Sentinel, Carol Brzozowski or Ken Swart, 3333 S. Congress Ave., Delray Beach FL 33445.

Syracuse Herald-Journal, Jim Reilly, 1 Clinton Sq, Box 4915, Syracuse NY 13221. 315-470-2265. 89,000.

Syracuse Post Standard, Tom Boll, Clinton Sq, Box 4818, Syracuse NY 13221. 315-470-0011. 90,000.

#Tampa Tribune, Karen Long, 202 S Parker St, Box 191, Tampa FL 33601. 813-272-7711. 286,000.

+Telegraph Herald, Lyn C. Jerde, Box 688, Dubuque IA 52001. 319-588-5660.

Telegram Tribune, Mike Stover, 1321 Johnson, Box 112, San Luis Obispo CA 93406. 805-781-7800. 33,000.

+Time Magazine, Richard N. Ostling, Rm 2344, Time-Life Bldg, New York NY 10020. 212-522-3040.

Times-Advocate, Ann Moss, 207 E Pennsylvania Ave, Escondido CA 92025. 619-745-6611. 45,000.

#Times, The, Debbie Kovach, 500 Perry St, Box 847, Trenton NJ 08605. 609-396-3232. 79,000.

+Times Herald, James Ketchum, 911 Military St., Port Huron MI 48060. 313-985-7171.

#Toledo Blade, Judy Tarjanyi, 541 Superior St, Toledo OH 43660. 419-245-6153. 147,000.

Topeka Capital-Journal, Jim Baker, Stauffer Communications, 616 Jefferson, Topeka KS 66607. 913-295-1111. 70,000.

Torrence Daily Breeze, Thom Meade, 5215 Torrence Blvd, Torrence CA 90503. 310-540-5511. 131,000.

Trentonian, no religion editor, Southarn & Perry Sts., Trenton NJ 08602. 609-989-7800.

Tribune-Herald, Chris Hall, Box 2588, Waco TX 76702. 817-757-5757.

+Tribune Star, Madonna Yates, Box 149, Terre Haute IN 47808. 812-231-4200.

Tucson Citizen, Religion Editor, 4850 S Park Ave, Box 26767, Tucson AZ 85726. 602-573-4560. 52,000.

Tulsa World, Carolyn Jenkins, 318 South Main Mall, Box 1770, Tulsa OK 74102. 918-581-8300. 175,000.

+Tyler Morning Telegraph, Tom Pratt, P.O. Box 2030, Tyler TX 75710. 214-597-8111.

Union Leader, The, John Tucker, 100 William Loeb Dr, Box 9555, Manchester NH 03108. 603-668-4321. 72,000.

USA Today, Cathy Grossman, 1000 Wilson Blvd, Arlington VA 22229. 703-276-3400. 6,600,000.

+US News & World Report, Jeffery Sheler, 2400 North St. NW, Washington DC 20037. 202-955-2383.

+Vancouver Sun, Douglas Todd, 2250 Granville St., Vancouver BC V6H 3G2 Canada. 604-732-2159. 491,000.

#Virginian Pilot/Ledger-Star, Marjorie M. Mayfield or Mark O'Keefe, 150 W Brambleton Ave, Norfolk VA 23510. 804-446-2332. 750,000.

#Waco Tribune Herald, Douglas Wong, 900 Franklin Ave, Box 2588, Waco TX 76702. 817-757-5757. 47,000.

#Wall Street Journal, Mr. R Gustav Neibhur, 200 Liberty St, New York NY 10281. 212-416-2500 or 404-233-2831. 2,000,000.

#Washington Post, Laura Sessions Stepp, 1150 15th St NW, Washington DC 20071. 202-334-7228. 814,000.

Washington Post Magazine, Yvonne Lamb, 1150 15th St NW, Washington DC 20071. 202-334-6000. 791,000.

Wisconsin State Journal, William Wineke, 1901 Fish Hatchery Rd, Box 8058, Madison WI 53708. 608-252-6100. 85,000.

+Wichita Eagle Beacon, Tom Schaefer, PO Box 820, Wichita KS 67201. 316-268-6586. 185,000.

Youngstown Vindicator, Marie Shellock, Vindicator Sq, Box 780, Youngstown OH 44501. 216-747-1471. 90,000.

GLOSSARY OF TERMS

Note: *This is not intended to be an exhaustive glossary of terms. It includes primarily those terms you will find within the context of this market guide.*

Advance. Amount of money a publisher pays to an author up front, against future royalties.

All rights. An outright sale of your material. Author has no further control over it.

Anecdote. A short, poignant, real-life story, usually used to illustrate a single thought.

Assignment. When an editor asks a writer to write a specific piece for an agreed-upon price.

Avant-garde. Experimental; ahead of the times.

Bimonthly. Every two months.

Biweekly. Every two weeks.

Book proposal. Submission of a book idea to an editor, usually includes a cover letter, thesis statement, chapter-by-chapter synopsis, market survey, and 1-3 sample chapters.

Byline. Author's name printed just below the title of a story, article, etc.

Circulation. The number of copies sold or distributed of each issue of a publication.

Clips. See "Published Clips."

Column. A regularly appearing feature, section, or department in a periodical using the same heading; written by the same person or a different freelancer each time.

Contributor's copy. Copy of an issue of a periodical sent to the author whose work appears in it.

Copyright. Legal protection of an author's work.

Cover letter. A letter that accompanies some manuscript

submissions. Usually needed only if you have to tell the editor something specific, or to give your credentials for writing a piece of a technical nature.

Critique. An evaluation of a piece of writing.

Devotional. A short piece which shares a personal spiritual discovery, inspires to worship, challenges to commitment or action, or encourages.

Editorial guidelines. See "Writer's guidelines."

Essay. A short composition usually expressing the author's opinion on a specific subject.

Evangelical. A person who believes that one receives God's forgiveness for sins through Jesus Christ, and believes the Bible is an authoritative guide for daily living.

Feature article. In-depth coverage of a subject, usually focusing on a person, event, process, organization, movement, trend or issue; written to explain, encourage, help, analyze, challenge, motivate, warn, or entertain—as well as to inform.

Filler. A short item used to "fill" out the page of a periodical. It could be a timeless news item, joke, anecdote, light verse, short humor, puzzle, game, etc.

First NA serial rights. First North American Serial Rights: the right to publish a written piece for the first time in North America.

First rights. Editor buys the right to publish your piece for the first time.

Freelance. As in 50% freelance: means that 50% of the material printed in the publication is supplied by freelance writers.

Freelancer or freelance writer. A writer who is not on salary, but sells his material to a number of different publishers.

Free verse. Poetry that flows without any set pattern.

Genre. Refers to type or classification, as in fiction or poetry. In fiction, such types as westerns, romances, mysteries, etc., are referred to as genre fiction.

Glossy. A black and white photo with a shiny, rather than matte finish.

Go-ahead. When a publisher tells you to go ahead and write up or send your article idea.

Haiku. A Japanese lyric poem of a fixed 17-syllable form.

Holiday/seasonal. A story, article, filler, etc. that has to do with a specific holiday or season. This material must reach the publisher the stated number of months prior to the holiday/season.

Humor. The amusing or comical aspects of life that add warmth and color to an article or story.

Interdenominational. Distributed to a number of different denominations.

International Postal Reply Coupon. See "IRC."

Interview article. An article based on an interview with a person of interest to a specific readership.

IRC or IPRC. International Postal Reply Coupon: can be purchased at your local post office and should be enclosed with a manuscript sent to a foreign publisher.

Journal. A periodical presenting news in a particular area.

Kill fee. A fee paid for a completed article done on assignment that is subsequently not published.

Light verse. Simple, light-hearted poetry.

Mainstream fiction. Other than genre fiction, such as romance, mystery or science fiction. Stories of people and their conflicts handled on a deeper level.

Ms. Abbreviation for manuscript.

Mss. Abbreviation for more than one manuscript.

Newsbreak. A newsworthy event or item sent to a publisher who might be interested in publishing it because it would be of interest to his particular readership.

Nondenominational. Not associated with a particular denomination.

Not copyrighted. Publication of your piece in such a publication will put it into public domain and it is not then protected. Ask that the publisher carry your copyright notice on your piece when it is printed.

On acceptance. Periodical pays a writer at the time an article is accepted for publication.

On assignment. Writing something at the specific request of an editor.

On publication. Periodical pays a writer at the time an article is published.

On speculation. Writing something for an editor with the agreement that he will buy it only if he likes it.

One-time rights. Selling the right to publish a story one-time to any number of publications (usually refers to publishing for a non-overlapping readership).

Payment on acceptance. See "On acceptance."

Payment on publication. See "On publication."

Pen Name. Using a name other than your legal name on an article in order to protect your identity or the identity of people included in the article. Put the pen name in the byline under the title, and your real name in the upper, left-hand corner.

Personal experience story. A story based on a real-life experience.

Personality profile. A feature article that highlights a specific person's life or accomplishments.

Photocopied submission. Sending an editor a photocopy of your manuscript, rather than an original. Some editors prefer an original.

Published clips. Copies of actual articles you have had published.

Quarterly. Every three months.

Query letter. A letter sent to an editor telling him about an article you propose to write and asking if he is interested in seeing it.

Reporting time. The number of weeks or months it takes an editor to get back to you about a query or manuscript you have sent him.

Reprint rights. Selling the right to reprint an article that has already been published elsewhere. You must have sold only first or one-time rights originally, and wait until it has been published the first time.

Royalty. The percentage an author is paid by a publisher on the sale of each copy of a book.

SAE. Self-addressed envelope (without stamps).

SASE. Self-addressed, stamped envelope. Should always be sent with a manuscript or query letter.

Satire. Ridicule that aims at reform.

Second serial rights. See "Reprint rights."

Semiannual. Issued twice a year.

Serial. Refers to publication in a periodical (such as first serial rights) or a story in several parts published in concurrent issues.

Simultaneous rights. Selling the rights to the same piece to several publishers simultaneously. Be sure everyone is aware that you are doing so.

Simultaneous submissions. Sending the same manuscript to more than one publisher at the same time. Usually done with non-overlapping markets (such as denominational) or when you are writing on a timely subject. Be sure to state in a cover letter that it is a simultaneous submission and why.

Speculation. See "On speculation."

Staff-written material. Material written by the members of a magazine staff.

Subsidiary rights. All those rights, other than book rights, included in a book contract—such as paperback, book club, movie, etc.

Subsidy publisher. A book publisher who charges the author to publish his book, as opposed to a royalty publisher who pays the author.

Tabloid. A newspaper-format publication about half the size of a regular newspaper.

Take-home paper. A periodical sent home from Sunday school each week (usually) with Sunday school students, children through adults.

Think piece. A magazine article that has an intellectual, philosophical, or provocative approach to a subject.

Third world. Reference to underdeveloped countries of Asia and Africa.

Transparencies. Positive color slides, not color prints.

Trade magazine. A magazine whose audience is in a particular trade or business.

Traditional verse. One or more verses with an established pattern that is repeated throughout the poem.

Unsolicited manuscript. A manuscript an editor did not specifically ask to see.

Vanity publisher. See "Subsidy publisher."

Vitae/Vita. An outline of one's personal history and experience.

Work-for-hire assignment. Signing a written contract with a publisher stating that a particular piece of writing you are doing for him is "work for hire." In the agreement you give the publisher full control of the material.

Writers' guidelines. An information sheet provided by a publisher in which he gives specific guidelines for writing for his publication. Send an SASE with your request for guidelines.

CHRISTIAN WRITERS' CONFERENCES AND WORKSHOPS

ALABAMA

+SOUTHERN CHRISTIAN WRITERS CONFERENCE. Samford University/Birmingham, June 10-11, 1994. Contact: Joanne Sloan, 3230 Mystic Lake Way, Northport AL 35476. (205)333-8603.

ARIZONA

ARIZONA CHRISTIAN WRITERS CONFERENCE. Phoenix, November 10-12, 1994. Contact: Reg A. Forder, Box 5168, Phoenix AZ 85010. (602)838-4919. Attendance: 200. This group is offering additional seminars across the country. Send SASE for complete list.

CENTRAL ARIZONA CHRISTIAN WRITERS WORKSHOP. Cottonwood, February 19, 1994. Contact: Mona Gansberg Hodgson, Box 999, Cottonwood AZ 86326-0999. (602)634-0384. Attendance: 60.

MINI WRITING WORKSHOPS. Held in various U.S. locations, throughout the year. Contact and speaker: Donna Goodrich, 648 S. Pima St., Mesa AZ 85210. (602)962-6694. Two-hour to day-long workshops on various topics. Attendance: 10-20.

***PRESCOTT CHRISTIAN WRITERS SEMINAR.** Prescott, September 1994. Contact: Barbara Spangler, Box 26449, Prescott Valley AZ 86312. (602)772-6263 or Pauline Dunn, 1840 Iron Springs Rd. #A2F, Prescott AZ 86301. (601)778-7342.

CALIFORNIA

+CHRISTIAN COMMUNICATORS CONFERENCE AT THE MASTER'S COLLEGE. Santa Clarita, July 14-17, 1994. Keynote speaker: John MacArthur. Contact: Susan Titus Osborn, 3133 Puente Blvd., Fullerton CA 92635-1952. (800)-95 WORDS. New conference; estimated attendance 200.

CHRISTIAN LEADERS AND SPEAKERS SEMINARS (C.L.A.S.S.). Arrowhead Springs CA, February 7-9, 1994; Sandy Cove MD, April 18-20, 1994; San Antonio TX, June 6-8, 1994; San Diego CA, August 15-17, 1994; Cincinnati OH, October 3-5, 1994; Colorado Springs CO, November 7-9, 1994. Speakers: Florence Littauer, Marita Littauer, and Marilyn Heavilin. Contact: Marita Littauer, 1645 S. Rancho Santa Fe #102, San Marcos CA 92069. (619)471-1722. Attendance: 100.

***CHRISTIAN WRITERS FELLOWSHIP OF ORANGE COUNTY.** Huntington Beach, March and October 1994. Contact: Marian Bray, 2420 N. Bristol St., Santa Ana CA 92706. Attendance: 60.

EVANGELICAL PRESS ASSOCIATION CONVENTION. Costa Mesa, CA, May 9-11, 1994 (held in different location each year). Contact: Ron Wilson, dir., Rt 2 Box 83, Earlysville VA 22936. (804)973-5941. Attendance: 300-400. Annual convention; freelance communicators welcome.

INLAND EMPIRE CHRISTIAN WRITERS SEMINARS. Moreno Valley, February 26 and September 24, 1994; February 25 & September 30, 1995. Contact: Bill Page, Box 8154, Moreno Valley CA 92552. (909)924-0610. Attendance: 50-60

***LODI ALL-DAY WRITERS SEMINAR.** Stockton, no date set for 1994. Contact: Dee Porter, Box 1863, Lodi CA 95241. (209)334-0603. Write and ask to be put on mailing list.

MOUNT HERMON CHRISTIAN WRITERS CONFERENCE. Mount Hermon (near Santa Cruz), March 25-29, 1994, April 7-11, 1995. Keynote speaker '94: Jerry B. Jenkins. Offers advanced track. Contact: David R. Talbott, Box 413, Mount Hermon CA 95041-0413. (408)335-4466. Attendance: 175-250.

***NARRAMORE CHRISTIAN WRITERS CONFERENCE.** Narramore Christian Foundation/Rosemead, April 1994. Contact: Dr. Clyde M. Narramore, 1409 N Walnut Grove Ave., Rosemead CA 91770. (818)288-7000. Attendance: 30.

SAN DIEGO CHRISTIAN WRITERS GUILD ONE-DAY SEMINAR. San Diego, September 24, 1994. Keynote speaker: Jerry Jenkins. Contact: Dr. Sherwood Wirt, 14140 Mazatlan Ct., Poway CA 92064. (619)748-0565. Attendance: 115.

SAN DIEGO STATE UNIVERSITY WRITERS CONFERENCE. San Diego campus, January 22-23, 1994. Contact: Jan Wahl, College of Extended Studies, SDSU, 5630 Hardy St., San Diego CA 92182-0723. (619)594-2514. Attendance: 400.

***SOUTH BAY CHRISTIAN WRITERS SEMINARS.** Hermosa, contact for dates. Contact: Diane Shober, 14100 S. Mariposa, Gardena CA 90247. (310)323-6847. Attendance: 75. Also has critique groups and writing classes.

+VENTURA COUNTY WRITERS SEMINAR. Ventura, February 5, 1994. Speaker: Wes Haystead. Contact: Julie Carobine, 10142 Fallen Leaf Ct., Ventura CA 93004. (805)647-4566.

***WEST CONTRA COSTA COUNTY CHRISTIAN WRITERS CONFERENCE.** Oakland, September 1994. Contact: Tammy Nichols, 4839 State Crt., Richmond CA 94804. (510)237-9890.

***WRITE TO BE READ WORKSHOPS.** Hume Lake, contact for dates. Speaker & contact: Norman B. Rohrer, 260 Fern Ln., Hume Lake CA 93628. (209)335-2333. Attendance: 45

YWAM CHRISTIAN WRITERS SEMINARS. Various states, (OR, HI & TX); various dates. Contact: Registrar, YWAM Writer's Seminars, Box 3464, Orange CA 92665. (714)637-1733. Fax: (714)282-0496.

COLORADO

+CHRISTIAN ARTISTS' SEMINAR IN THE ROCKIES. Estes Park, July 31-August 6, 1994; July 30-August 5, 1995. For anyone interested in Christian music industry and ministry. Has classes in song writing and sketch writing. Contact: Jim Chaffee, 425 W 115th Ave., Denver CO 80234. (800)755-7464. Attendance: 1,000.

CHRISTIAN BOOKSELLERS ASSN. CONVENTION. Denver, June 25-30, 1994. Contact: CBA, Box 200, Colorado Springs CO 80901. (719)576-7880. Entrance badges available through book publishers.

COLORADO CHRISTIAN COMMUNICATORS RETREAT. Colorado Springs, Adults: June 24-25, 1994; Children & Teens, June 25, 1994. Contact: Scoti Domeij, 5209 Del Paz Dr., Colorado Springs CO 80918-2001. Conference attendance: 100.

COLORADO CHRISTIAN WRITERS CONFERENCE. Boulder; March 4-5, 1994; March 3-4, 1995. Keynote speaker 1994: Dr. Gene Edward Veith. Contact: Debbie Barker, 67 Seminole St., Lyons CO 80540. (303)823-5718. Attendance: 225.

GLEN EYRIE WRITERS' WORKSHOPS. Glen Eyrie Conference Center, Colorado Springs; March 26-31, 1994 (contact for other dates). Speaker: Monte Unger. Contact: Judith Weins, Box 6000, Colorado Springs CO 80934. (800)944-4536. Attendance: 20 maximum in each.

OBSERVATION SKILLS WORKSHOP. Denver, June 1994. Contact: Chris Adams, 2573 Benton St., Edgewater CO 80214. (303)232-9470. Attendance: 50.

***WRITING FOR THE LOCAL CHURCH...AND SOMETIMES BEYOND.** Nazarene Bible College/Colorado Springs, April 1996 (held every three years). Instructor: Betty B. Robertson. Contact: Verla Lambert, NBC, Box 15749, Colorado Springs CO 80935. (719)596-5110.

***THE WRITING INSTITUTE.** Workshops on article writing for Christian publications. Held around U.S. throughout year. Contact and speaker: Monte Unger, 1228 N. Custer Ave., Colorado Springs CO 80903. (719)471-8194. Fax:(719)471-0711. One-day to three-day workshops. Attendance: 10-25.

CONNECTICUT

WESLEYAN WRITERS CONFERENCE. Middletown, June 26-July 1, 1994. Contact: Anne Green, c/o Wesleyan University, Middletown CT 06459. (203)347-9411, ext. 2448. Attendance: 100.

FLORIDA

+CATHOLIC PRESS ASSOCIATION ANNUAL CONVENTION. Tampa, 1994. Contact: Owen McGovern, exec. dir., 119 N Park Ave., Rockville Centre NY 11570. (516)766-3400. Attendance: 350.

+CHARISMA/CREATION HOUSE SCHOOL OF WRITING. Orlando; February 24-27, 1994. Speakers: Elizabeth Sherrill, and others. Contact: Christian Writers Institute, 177 E. Crystal Lake Ave., Lake Mary FL 32746. (407)324-5465, Fax: (407)324-0209. New conference.

FLORIDA CHRISTIAN WRITERS CONFERENCE. Park Avenue Retreat Center/Titusville; January 27-31, 1994. January 26-30, 1995; Calvin Miller, keynote speaker. Contact: Billie Wilson, 2600 Park Avenue, Titusville FL 32780. (407)269-6702x202. Attendance: 150-200.

FLORIDA CHRISTIAN WRITERS CONFERENCE. Miami. October 20-22, 1994. Contact Reg A. Forder, American Christian Writers, Box 5168, Phoenix AZ 85010. (800) 21-WRITE.

WRITING STRATEGIES FOR THE CHRISTIAN MARKET. Classes for beginning, intermediate & advanced writers. Also material available for an independent studies program by mail. Contact: Rosemary J. Upton, 1420 N Atlantic Ave. #801, Daytona Beach FL 32118. (904)253-6666. Write to be put on mailing list.

GEORGIA

GEORGIA CHRISTIAN WIRITERS CONFERENCE. Atlanta. September 22-24, 1994. Contact: Reg A. Forder, American Christian Writers, Box 5168, Phoenix AZ 85010. (800) 21-WRITE.

***NORTHEAST GEORGIA WRITERS CONFERENCE.** Gainesville, October 1995 (biennial). Contact: Elouise Whitten, 660 Crestview Terrace, Gainesville GA 30501. (404)532-3007.

HAWAII

YWAM WRITERS SEMINAR. Kona, July 17-30, 1994. Speakers: Janice Rogers & Beverly Caruso. Contact: Beverly Caruso, 1621 Baldwin Ave., Orange CA 92665. (714)637-1733. Fax: (714)282-0496. Attendance: 30-40.

IDAHO

NORTHWEST CHRISTIAN WRITERS CONFERENCE. Post Falls; September 15-17, 1994. Contact: Sheri Stone, Box 1754, Post Falls ID 83854-1754. (208)667-9730. Attendance: 125.

ILLINOIS

+AFRICAN-AMERICAN CHRISTIAN WRITERS' CONFERENCE. Chicago, May 26-28, 1994. Contact: Dr. Stanley B. Long, c/o American Tract Society, P.O. Box 462008, Garland TX 75046. New conference.

CHRISTIAN WRITERS INSTITUTE CONFERENCE. Wheaton College, May 28-June 1, 1994. Teens invited. Contact: Dottie McBroom, 177 E Crystal Lake Ave., Lake Mary FL 32746. (407)324-5465. Attendance: 200.

***MISSISSIPPI VALLEY WRITERS CONFERENCE.** Augustana College/Rock Island, June 1994. Contact: David R. Collins, 3403 45th St., Moline IL 61265. (309)762-8985. Attendance: 80.

THE SALVATION ARMY CHRISTIAN WRITERS' CONFERENCE. Des Plaines IL, March or April 1995 (held every other year). Contact: Major Marlene Chase, 10 W. Algonquin Rd., Des Plaines IL 60016-6006. (708)294-2050. Attendance: 60. For S.A. officers, laymen, and employee staff.

WRITE-TO-PUBLISH CONFERENCE. Chicago, June 20-24, 1994. Contact: Lin Johnson, director, 9731 N. Fox Glen Dr. # 6F, Niles IL 60714. (800)95-WORDS. Attendance: 200. May 15 deadline for registration.

INDIANA

***CHARLENE FARRIS WRITING CLASSES.** Indiana University/Continuing Education; contact for dates. Also, Christian Cruises for Christian Writers, to the Bahamas and Caribbean, are tentatively planned for August and November 1994. Contact: Charlene Farris, 9524 Guilford Dr. #A, Indianapolis IN 46240. (317)848-2634, or call school at (317)274-5051.

MIDWEST WRITERS WORKSHOP. Muncie, July 27-30, 1994. Speakers: Robin Rue, agent; Linda Tomblin, editor; Alice Friman, poetry; Dennis Hensley, writer. Contact: Dr. Earl Conn, Dept. of Journalism, Ball State University, Muncie IN 47306. (317)285-8200. Attendance: 120.

IOWA

THE WRITING ACADEMY SEMINAR. Des Moines IA; August 7-12, 1994. Speaker: Thomas Boogaart & Shirley Stevens. Contact: Ann Poppen, 6512 Colby, Des Moines IA 50311-1713. (515)274-5026. Attendance: 50.

***WRITING THAT MAKES A DIFFERENCE.** Cedar Rapids, October 1994. Contact: Rev. Marvin Ceynar, 104 Meadow Ln., Tipton IA 52772. (319)396-2732. Attendance: 15-25.

KANSAS

***BCCC CREATIVE WRITING WORKSHOP.** Butler County Community College, El Dorado; Fall 1994. Contact: Vivien Minshull-Ford, 901 S. Haverhill Rd., El Dorado KS 67042. (316)321-5083, ext. 233. Attendance: 200.

+NAZARENE WRITERS CONFERENCE. Olathe, July 27-30, 1994. Contact: Bonnie Perry, 6401 The Paseo, Kansas City MO 64131. (816)233-7000.
Attendance: They expect 200+ at their first conference in 8 yrs.

KENTUCKY

THE PRESBYTERIAN WRITERS GUILD SEMINAR. Louisville, April 22-26, 1994. Speakers: Ann Weems, Perry Biddle, Jane Huber, Jim Gittings, Vic Jameson, & Jack Purdy. Contact: Ann Barr Weems, 6900 Kingsbury Blvd., St. Louis MO 63130. (314)725-6290.

LOUISIANA

***LOUISIANA BAPTIST CHRISTIAN WRITERS CONFERENCE.** Tall Timbers, April 1994. Contact: Louisiana Baptist Convention, Box 311, Alexandria LA 71309.

LOUISIANA CHRISTIAN WRITERS GUILD WORKSHOP. Shreveport; July 1994. Contact: Dr. Don M. Aycock, Box 12765, Lake Charles LA 70612-2765. (318)855-6280. Attendance: 50+.

MARYLAND

SANDY COVE CHRISTIAN WRITERS CONFERENCE. Sandy Cove/North East, October 2-6, 1994. Speakers: Don Wyrtzen, Col. Henry Gariepy, and Les Stobbe. Contact: Gayle Roper, RD 6 Box 112, Coatesville PA 19320. (215)384-8125. Attendance: 125.

REVIEW AND HERALD WRITERS' WEEK. Review & Herald Publishing Assn., Hagerstown; July 1994. Contact: Penny E. Wheeler, 55 W. Oak Ridge Dr., Hagerstown MD 21740. (301)790-9731. Attendance: 50.

MASSACHUSETTS

***CAPE COD WRITERS' CONFERENCE.** Craigville Conference Center, August 21-26, 1994. Contact: Marion Vuilleumier, c/o Cape Cod Conservatory, Rt. 132, West Barnstable MA 02668. (508)775-4811 or 362-2772. Attendance: 150. Also offers **CAPE LITERARY ARTS WORKSHOPS**: 6 simultaneous week-long workshops (poetry, romance novels, juvenile writing, children's book illustrating, and play writing), August 1994. Limited to 10 in each workshop.

MICHIGAN

ANDREWS UNIVERSITY CHRISTIAN WRITER'S AND COMMUNICATOR'S CONFERENCE. Berrien Springs, June 13-17, 1994. Contact: Dr. Kermit Netteburg, Communications Dept., Andrews University, Berrien Springs MI 49104. (616)471-3618. Attendance: 85.

INDIAN LAKE CHRISTIAN WRITERS SEMINAR. Nazarene Campgrounds (near Kalamazoo). July 7-8, 1994. Contact Donna Clark Goodrich, 648 S. Pima St., Mesa AZ 85210. (602) 962-6694. Expected attendance: 500.

MARANATHA CHRISTIAN WRITERS SEMINAR. Maranatha Bible & Missionary Conference/Muskegon, August 22-26, 1994. Speakers: Jack Metzler, Paul Tell Jr., Nellie Pickard, and Leona Hertel. Contact: Leona Hertel, 4759 Lake Harbor Rd., Muskegon MI 49441. (616)798-2161. Attendance: 50.

MICHIGAN CHRISTIAN WRITERS CONFERENCE. Detroit. August 11-13, 1994. Contact:: Reg A. Forder, American Christian Writers, Box 5168, Phoenix AZ 85010. (800) 21-WRITE.

***MICHIGAN NORTHWOODS WRITERS CONFERENCE.** Glen Arbor, July 1994. Contact: Robert Karner, 1 Old Homestead Rd., Glen Arbor MI 49636. (616)334-3072.

***"SPEAK UP WITH CONFIDENCE" SEMINARS.** Hillsdale, contact for dates. Contact: Carol Kent, 4184 Quaker Hill Dr., Port Huron MI 48060. (313)982-0898. Speaking seminar. Attendance: 125.

MINNESOTA

MINNESOTA CHRISTIAN WRITERS CONFERENCE. Minneapolis. June 16-18, 1994. Contact:: Reg A. Forder, American Christian Writers, Box 5168, Phoenix AZ 85010. (800) 21-WRITE.

MINNESOTA WRITERS GUILD CONFERENCE. Wayzata, April 29-30, 1994. Speaker: Charette Barta. Contact: Joan Martin, 15535 Holdridge Dr., Wayzata MN 55391. (612)475-1466. Attendance: 50.

MISSOURI

***CENTRAL MISSOURI WRITER'S RETREAT**. Warrensburg. July 1994. Contact: Central Missouri State University, Office of Extended Campus, 402 Humphreys Bldg., Warrensburg MO 64093. 1-800-SAY-CMSU. Secular.

***GREATER ST. LOUIS INSPIRATIONAL WRITERS WORKSHOP.** St. Louis metro area. Contact: Lila Wold Shelburne, 23 Blackberry, St. Charles MO 63301. (314)946-8533.

MISSOURI CHRISTIAN WRITERS CONFERENCE. St. Louis. July 21-23, 1994. Contact:: Reg A. Forder, American Christian Writers, Box 5168, Phoenix AZ 85010. (800) 21-WRITE.

MARK TWAIN WRITERS CONFERENCE (10th annual). Hannibal-LaGrange College, June 13-17, 1994. Speakers include Gene Perret and Kathryn Fanning. Contact: Dr. James C. Hefley, 921 Center St., Hannibal MO 63401. (314)221-2462. Attendance: 100.

***RIGHT WRITING CHRISTIAN WRITERS' WORKSHOP.** Columbia, October 1994. Contact: Teresa Parker/Linda Ordway/Mike Kateman, 237 E. Clearview Dr., Columbia MO 65202. (314)875-1141/449-2465. Attendance: 100.

NEW JERSEY

+NEW JERSEY SOCIETY OF CHRISTIAN WRITERS ANNUAL FALL SEMINAR. Fairton, October or November 1994. Contact: Dr. Mary Ann Diorio, P.O. Box 748, Millville NJ 08332-0748. (609)327-1231. Attendance: 20-25.

NEW MEXICO

LAS CRUCES CHRISTIAN WRITERS SEMINAR (3rd). Las Cruces, May 7, 1994. Speakers: Donna Goodrich, Bea Carlton, and others. 8 workshops. Contact: Jewel Johnson, 2050 Thomas Dr., Las Cruces NM 88001. (505) 521-0316. Attendence: 25-30.

SOUTHWEST CHRISTIAN WRITERS SEMINAR. Farmington, September 17, 1994, September 16, 1995. Keynote speaker: Joy Gage (94). Contact: Kathy Cordell, 91 - Rd. 3450, Flora Vista NM 87415. (505)334-0617. Attendance: 25.

WRITERS' CONFERENCE AT SANTA FE. Santa Fe, February 19-20, 1994. Keynote speaker: Lois Duncan. Contact: Ruth Crowley, Program Coordinator, Santa Fe Community College, Box 4187, Santa Fe NM 87502-4187. (505)438-1251. Attendance: 150.

NEW YORK

***GREATER SYRACUSE CHRISTIAN WRITER'S CONFERENCE.** Liverpool, May 1994. Contact: Janice Wise, 2178 Slussun Rd., West Monroe NY 13167. (315)668-2874. Attendance: 60-75.

NORTH CAROLINA

STAR BOOKS WRITERS' WORKSHOP. Star Books, 408 Pearson St., Wilson NC 27893-1850. Not being held for now.

OHIO

+ANTIOCH WRITERS WORKSHOP. Secular. Antioch College/Yellow Springs; July 23-30, 1994. Keynote speaker: John Jakes. Contact: Susan Carpenter, P.O. Box 494, Yellow Springs OH 45387. (513)767-7068.

***CINCINNATI BIBLE COLLEGE CHRISTIAN WRITERS WORKSHOP.** Cincinnati, September 1994. Contact: Dana Eynon, 2700 Glenway Ave., Cincinnati OH 45204. (513)244-8181. Attendance: 100.

COLUMBUS CHRISTIAN WRITERS FALL CONFERENCE. Columbus, October 1, 1994. Speaker: Jim Hostetler. Contact: Brenda Custodio, 3732 Shoreline Dr., Columbus OH 43232. (614)837-8825. Attendance: 75.

MARION AREA CHRISTIAN WRITERS SEMINAR. Marion, April 1994 (tentative). Contact: Irene M. Sprague, 603 Henry St., Marion OH 43302

NORTHWEST OHIO CHRISTIAN WRITERS SEMINAR. Fostoria; September 24, 1994 (tentative date). Contact: Nancy Kintner, 4235 Lyman, Toledo OH 43612-1584. (419)478-1055. Attendance: 80.

***WRITER`S WORLD CONFERENCE.** Akron, May 1994. Contact: Tom Raber, Box 966, Cuyahoga Falls OH 44223. Attendance: 100-200.

OKLAHOMA

WRITING WORKSHOPS. Various locations and dates. Contact: Kathryn Fanning, 1016 NW 39th, Oklahoma City OK 73118.

PROFESSIONALISM IN WRITING SCHOOL (12th annual). Tulsa, March 25-26, 1994; March 31-April 1, 1995. Keynote speaker: Clifton Taulbert. Contact: Norma Jean Lutz, 4308 S. Peoria #701, Tulsa OK 74105. (918)PIW-5588. Attendance: 180.

OREGON

***CASCADE EAST CHRISTIAN WRITERS SEMINAR.** Redmond, April 1994. Contact: Lois Brenchley, 4773 NE Vaughn, Terrebonne OR 97760. (503)548-5773. Attendance: 35-50.

OREGON ASSN. OF CHRISTIAN WRITERS COACHING CONFERENCE. Aldersgate (near Salem), August 1-4, 1994. Keynote speaker: Dr. Maxine Hancock. Contact: Pat Rushford, 3600 Edgewood Dr., Vancouver WA 98661. (206)695-2263. Attendance: 125.

***WRITER'S BREW, A SCHOOL FOR CREATIVE WRITING.** Portland, classes ongoing throughout the year. Eight week course; one day a week; 2 hours a session; $10/hr. Day or evening. Contact: Beverly Reed, 5160 NE Holman, Portland OR 97218. (503)282-8962. Limit: 10/class.

PENNSYLVANIA

***CHRISTIAN WRITERS WORKSHOP.** Northeastern Christian Junior College, Villanova; mid-October 1994. Contact: Eva Walker Myer, 1860 Montgomery Ave., Villanova PA 19085. (215)525-6780. Attendance: 100.

GREATER PHILADELPHIA CHRISTIAN WRITERS' CONFERENCE. Downingtown, April 29-30, 1994. Contact: Marlene Bagnull, 316 Blanchard Rd., Drexel Hill PA 19026. (215)626-6833. Attendance: 250.

MONTROSE BIBLE CONFERENCE CHRISTIAN WRITERS CONFERENCE. Montrose, July 11-15, 1994. Speakers: Col. Henry Gariepy, Jonathan Graf. Contact: Jill Renich Meyers, 204 Asbury Dr., Mechanicsburg PA 17055. (712)278-4815. Attendance: 50.

ST. DAVIDS CHRISTIAN WRITERS' CONFERENCE. St. Davids, June 19-24, 1994. Contact: Carol Wedeven, 1 Old Covered Bridge Rd., Newtown Square PA 19073. (215)356-8159 or 8208. Attendance: 80+.

+"WRITE HIS ANSWER" SEMINARS. Various locations around U.S.; dates throughout the year. Contact: Marlene Bagnull, 316 Blanchard Rd., Drexel Hill PA 19026. (215)626-6833. Attendance: 40-100. Day or day-and-a-half seminars by the author of Write His Answer—Encouragement for Christian Writers.

WRITING FOR PUBLICATION. Pittsburgh Theological Seminary, April 20-21, 1994. Speaker: Dr. Roland Tapp. Contact: Rev. Mary Lee Talbot, 616 N. Highland Ave., Pittsburgh PA 15206. (412)362-5610x296. Attendance: 25.

YWCA WRITER'S CONFERENCE. Penn State/York Campus; January 21-22, 1994. Offers business panel for published authors. Contact: Rita Atwell Holler, 100 Greenwood Rd., York PA 17404-5766. (717)792-0228. Attendance: 125-150.

TENNESSEE

***RELIGIOUS COMMUNICATIONS CONGRESS.** Nashville, April 1994. Contact: RCC, Mail Stop 192, 127 Ninth Ave. N., Nashville TN 37234.

***SOUTHERN BAPTIST WRITERS WORKSHOP.** Nashville, July 1994. Contact: Director, 127 Ninth Ave. N., Nashville TN 37234. (615)251-2939. Attendance: 50.

THE WRITING ACADEMY SEMINAR. Nashville; August (2nd week), 1995. Contact: Ann Poppen, 6512 Colby, Des Moines IA 50311-1713. (515)274-5026. Attendance: 50.

TEXAS

***THE ART OF WRITING, THE ACT OF WRITING.** Longview, March 1994. Contact: Ernestine Finigan, Box 8513, Marshall TX 75670. (214)935-3047 or 938-0756 (days). Attendance: 50+.

TEXAS CHRISTIAN WRITERS CONFERENCE. Irving. May 12-14, 1994. Contact:: Reg A. Forder, American Christian Writers, Box 5168, Phoenix AZ 85010. (800) 21-WRITE.

TEXAS CHRISTIAN WRITERS CONFERENCE. Houston. January 19-21, 1995. Contact:: Reg A. Forder, American Christian Writers, Box 5168, Phoenix AZ 85010. (800) 21-WRITE.

***FRONTIERS IN WRITING.** Amarillo College, August 1994. Contact: Doris R. Meredith, Box 19303, Amarillo TX 79114. (806)352-3889. Attendance: 150

SOUTHWEST CHRISTIAN WRITERS GUILD CONFERENCE. Dallas, early October 1994. Contact: Debra Frazier, 1809 Waterford Ln., Richardson TX 75082. (214)783-6319.

TEXAS CHRISTIAN WRITERS FORUM. Pasadena TX; August 13, 1994. Contact: Maxine E. Holder, 3606 Longwood Dr., Pasadena TX 77503. (713)477-3716. Attendance: 60.

VIRGINIA

+WRITING FOR CHRISTIAN PUBLISHERS. Regent University/Virginia Beach; August 1994 (tentative). Contact: Dr. Doug Tarpley, chairman, School of Journalism, Regent University, Virginia Beach VA 23464. (804)532-7091/436-2926. New—projected attendance: 100-200.

WRITING FOR THE LOCAL CHURCH...and Sometimes Beyond. Held in various locations by invitation. Contact: Betty B. Robertson, P.O. Box 12624, Roanoke VA 24027-2624. (703)342-4003.

WASHINGTON

SDA CAMP MEETING WRITING CLASS. Auburn, June 20-24, 1994. Open to non-Adventists. Contact: Marion Forschler, 18115 - 116th Ave. SE, Renton WA 98058-6562. (206)235-1435. Attendance: 65.

***NORTHWEST CHRISTIAN WRITERS ASSN. SEMINARS.** Seattle area, date to be announced. Contact: Margaret Sampson, 8227 NE 115th Way, Kirkland WA 98034.

***SEATTLE PACIFIC CHRISTIAN WRITERS CONFERENCE.** Seattle, June 1994. Contact: Linda Wagner, Humanities Dept., Seattle Pacific University, Seattle WA 98119. (206)281-2109. Attendance: 160.

+WASHINGTON CHRISTIAN WRITERS FELLOWSHIP SEMINAR. Seattle, February 1994. Speakers: Elaine Colvin, Myrtlemay Crane, Marilou Flinkman & others. Contact: Elaine Colvin, P.O. Box 11337, Bainbridge Island WA 98110. (206)842-9103.

+WENATCHEE CHRISTIAN WRITERS MINI-SEMINAR. Wenatchee, May 1994 (tentative). Contact: Shirley Pease, 1818 Skyline Dr. #31, Wenatchee WA 98801. (509)662-8392.

+WRITERS HELPING WRITERS. Spokane; 2nd or 3rd weekend in March. This is not a conference, but a booth offering manuscript evaluation and help to writers during the annual Christian Workers Conference. Contact: Pat Pfeiffer, P.O. Box 104, Otis Orchards WA 97027-0140. (509)927-7671 or 226-3532 (evenings).

WRITERS INFORMATION NETWORK (W.I.N.) SEMINARS. Various locations/dates. Contact: Elaine Colvin, Box 11337, Bainbridge Island WA 98110. (206)842-9103. Attendance: 75-150.

+WRITER'S WEEKEND AT THE BEACH. Ocean Park, February 25-27, 1994. Contact: Pat Rushford, 3600 Edgewood Dr., Vancouver WA 98661. (206)695-2263 or Birdie Etchison, P.O. Box 877, Ocean Park WA 98640. (206)665-6576.

+WRITERS WORKSHOP: FROM PEN TO PUBLISHER, Walla Walla Community College, March 5, 1994. Save $10 if you register before February 25. Speakers include: Sandy Dengler, Pat Rushford and Colleen Reece. Contact: Marcia Mitchell, 835 Valencia, Walla Walla WA 99362.

WISCONSIN

GREEN LAKE CHRISTIAN WRITER'S CONFERENCE. Green Lake, July 9-16, 1994. Contact: Jan DeWitt, Program Dept., American Baptist Assembly, Green Lake WI 54941. (800)558-8898 or (414)294-3323. Attendance: 75+.

+SWORD & LIGHT WRITERS' SEMINAR. Milwaukee, no date set. Contact: Andrea Kuhn-Boeshar, 10605 W. Wabash, Milwaukee WI (414)355-8915.

THE WRITER'S TOUGHEST JOB - MARKETING. Menasha; May & November 1994. Instructor: Margaret Houk. Contact: Eugene Gibas, Dir. of Continuing Education, University of Wisconsin-Fox Valley, 1478 Midway Rd., Menasha WI 54952. (414)832-2636. Also classes in nonfiction writing and selling for the religious marketplace. Write for catalog.

***TIMBER-LEE CHRISTIAN WRITER'S CONFERENCE.** Timber-Lee Christian Center/East Troy, February 1994. Contact: Gene Schroeppel, 2381 Scout Rd., East Troy WI 53120. (414)642-7345. Attendance: 30-40.

CANADA

GOD USES INK WRITERS CONFERENCE/ON. Ancaster, Ontario; June 9-11,1994. Speakers: John White & Luci Shaw. Contact: Audrey Dorsch, Box 8800, Sta. B, Willowdale ON M2K 2R6 Canada. (905)479-5885. Attendance: 110.

GOD USES INK WRITERS AT BRIERCREST SCHOOLS. Caronport, Saskatchewan, Briercrest Bible College; May 12-14, 1994. Contact: Donna Lynn Erickson, 510 College Dr., Caronport SK S0H 0S0 Canada. (306)756-3214. Attendance: 100.

***ALBERTA CHRISTIAN WRITERS FELLOWSHIP CONFERENCE.** St. Albert, Alberta; October 1994. President: Dr. Gerald Hankins, 229-1489. Write: Lela Ball, RR 3, Wetaskiwin AB T9A 1X1 Canada. Attendance: 60-70.

+WORDPOWER. Winnipeg, November 1995. Contact: MB Herald, 3-169 Riverton Ave., Winnipeg MB R2L 2E5 Canada. (204)669-6575. Attendance: 100-150.

FOREIGN COUNTRIES

***BEST NEWS WRITERS SEMINAR.** Santa Cruz, Trinidad; no date set. Contact: Peter Lee Sam, 52 Tenth St., Barataria, Trinidad/Tobago, West Indies. 675-1515.

YWAM WRITING SEMINARS. Seminars scheduled in Autralia 1995 and Peru 1994. Open to invitations. Contact: Beverly Caruso, 1621 Baldwin Ave., Orange CA 92665. (714)282-0496. Attendance 15-50.

AREA CHRISTIAN WRITERS' CLUBS, FELLOWSHIP GROUPS, AND CRITIQUE GROUPS

(*) Asterisk before a listing means the information was not verified or updated by the group leader.

(+) A plus sign before a listing indicates a new listing.

ALABAMA

+CHRISTIAN WRITERS CLUB OF WEST ALABAMA, Birmingham/Northport area. Contact: C. Joanne Sloan, 3230 Mystic Lake Way, Northport AL 35476. (205)333-8603. Membership open.

ARIZONA

BETHANY CHRISTIAN WRITERS' CLUB. Phoenix. Contact: Rod Hugen, 2140 W. Nicolet, Phoenix AZ 85021. (602) 995-1857. Membership (25+) open.

FOUNTAIN HILLS CHRISTIAN WRITERS. Contact: Rosemarie D. Malroy, 10413 N. Demaret Dr., Fountain Hills AZ 85268-5742. (602)837-8494. Membership (12) open.

MESA CHRISTIAN WRITERS CLUB. Contact: Donna Goodrich, 648 S. Pima St., Mesa AZ 85210. (602)962-6694. Membership (20) open.

PHOENIX CHRISTIAN WRITERS CLUB. Contact: Vic Kelly, 2135 W. Cactus Wren Dr., Phoenix AZ 85021. (602) 864-1390. Membership (20) open.

***PRESCOTT CHRISTIAN WRITERS FELLOWSHIP.** Contact: Barbara Spangler, Box 26449, Prescott Valley AZ 86312. (602)772-6263/778-7342. Membership (10-15) open. Sponsors one-day seminar (usually 4th Saturday in September).

S.E. ARIZONA CHRISTIAN WRITERS. Benson. Contact: Neta M. Warawa, HC2 Box 2828, Benson AZ 85602. (602) 586-7704. Attendance open.

SWEETWATER CHRISTIAN WRITERS GROUP. Phoenix. Contact: Carla Bruce, PO Box 5640, Glendale AZ 85306. (602)486-1720/247-0174. Membership (12) open.

TEMPE CHRISTIAN WRITERS GROUP. Contact: Marsha Crockett, 1604 W. Barrow Dr., Chandler AZ 85224. (602) 963-5637. Membership (20) open.

ARKANSAS

***NORTHEAST ARKANSAS CHRISTIAN WRITERS CLUB.** Horseshoe Bend. Contact: Thelma McMillon, 1307 Park Lane, Horseshoe Bend AR 72512. (501)670-4477. Membership (3) open.

CALIFORNIA

***CHRISTIAN WRITERS FELLOWSHIP OF ORANGE COUNTY.** Huntington Beach. Contact: Marian Bray, 2420 N. Bristol St., Santa Ana CA 92706. (714)543-2430. Membership (100) open. Monthly newsletter. Sponsors critique groups in Costa Mesa, Fullerton, Fountain Valley, Huntington Beach, Santa Ana, and Long Beach (contact critique group coordinator, Dorothea Nyberg at (714)543-6922). Sponsors two Writers' Days: March and October 1994.

***CHRISTIAN WRITERS GROUP.** Contact: Judy Bacchetti, 3665 Dolbeer, Eureka CA 95501.

CHRISTIAN WRITERS OF VENTURA COUNTY. Ventura. Contact: Karen Weldin, 851 Camelia Dr., Port Hueneme CA 93041. (805)486-0635. Sponsors February seminar. Membership (15+) Open.

DIABLO VALLEY CHRISTIAN WRITERS GROUP. Danville. Contact: Peggy Parker, 2275 Trotter Way, Walnut Creek CA 94596. (510)934-3221. Membership (8-12) open.

GLENDALE CHRISTIAN SCRIBES. Contact: Stephanie Smedley, 10413 Oro Vista, Sunland CA 91040. (818)352-7017. Membership (8) open.

HAYWARD CHRISTIAN WRITERS GROUP. Hayward. Contact: Wesley Sharpe, 29416 Providence Wy, Hayward CA 94544. (510)785-2049. Membership (8) open.

INLAND EMPIRE CHRISTIAN WRITERS GUILD. Moreno Valley. Contact: Bill and Carole Gift Page, Box 8154, Moreno Valley CA 92552-8154. (909)924-0610. Membership (46) open. Sponsors twice-yearly seminars in February & September.

***LODI WRITERS ASSOCIATION.** Contact: Dee Porter, Box 1863, Lodi CA 95241. (209)334-0603. Membership (75) open. Sponsors one-day workshop in the spring.

LONG BEACH CHRISTIAN WRITERS. Contact: Jessica Shaver, 186 E. Cameron Pl., Long Beach CA 90807-3851. (310)595-4162. Membership (5-6) open.

SACRAMENTO CHRISTIAN WRITER'S CLUB. Fair Oaks. Contact: Jeri Honberger, 405 Dawnridge Rd., Roseville CA 95678. (916)783-5888. Membership (50+) open. Is working on putting a seminar together.

SAN DIEGO COUNTY CHRISTIAN WRITERS' GUILD. Contact: Sherwood E. Wirt, 14140 Mazatlan Ct., Poway CA 92064. (619)748-0565. Membership (240) open. Sponsors fall seminar (September 24, 1994) and spring awards banquet (March 4, 1994).

***WEST CONTRA COSTA COUNTY CHRISTIAN WRITERS GROUP.** Richmond area. Contact: Bill Edmunds, 535 - 38th St., Richmond CA 94805. (510)232-1493. Membership (12) open. Sponsors annual seminar.

***WORDSMITHS.** Contact: Pam Price, Box 25883, Santa Ana CA 92799.

THE WRITE BUNCH. Stockton. Contact: Shirley Cook, 3123 Sheridan, Stockton CA 95219. (209)477-8375. Audrey Seitelman, secretary, (209)477-3734. Membership (6-7) open.

COLORADO

CHRISTIAN WRITERS' CLUB. Ft. Collins. Contact: Martie McNeil, 6801 N. County Rd. 15., Fort Collins CO 80524. (303)490-2764. Membership (8) open.

***COLORADO CHRISTIAN COMMUNICATORS.** Colorado Springs. Contact: Madalene Harris, 810 Crystal Park Rd. 23, Manitou Springs CO, 80829. (719)685-9432. Membership (30+) open. Sponsors fall seminar.

COLORADO CHRISTIAN WRITERS. Longmont or Lyons. Contact: Debbie Barker, Box 3303, Lyons CO 80540. (303)823-5718. Membership (10+) open. Sponsors an annual seminar and several critique groups.

CHRISTIAN WRITERS IN TOUCH. Edgewater. Contact: Chris Adams, 2573 Benton St., Edgewater CO 80214. (303)232-9470. Membership (70+) open.

FLORIDA

+ADVENTURES IN CHRISTIAN WRITING. Orlando. Contact: Mary Shaw, 350 E. Jackson St., Orlando FL 32801. (407)841-4866. Membership open.

***CHRISTIAN WRITERS GROUP.** Contact: Patricia J. Birkhead, 940 Douglas Ave., Apt. 140, Altamonte Springs FL 32714. Membership open.

SUNCOAST CHRISTIAN WRITERS GROUP. Largo. Contact: Elaine Creasman, 13014 - 106th Ave. N., Largo FL 34644-5602. (813)595-8963. Membership (20) open.

TITUSVILLE CHRISTIAN WRITERS' FELLOWSHIP. Titusville. Contact: Nancy Otto Boffo, 2625 Riviera Dr., Titusville FL 32780-5144. (407)267-7604. Membership (12) open.

WRITING STRATEGIES CRITIQUESHOP. Daytona Beach. Contact: Rosemary J. Upton, 1420 N. Atlantic Ave. #801, Daytona Beach FL 32118. (904)253-6666. Membership open.

GEORGIA

***NORTHEAST GEORGIA WRITERS.** Contact: Elouise Whitten, 660 Crestview Terr., Gainesville GA 30501. (404)532-3007. Membership (26) open. Sponsors day and night groups, contests, critique groups, two all-day workshops, and a biennial writers' conference.

IDAHO

CHRISTIAN WRITERS OF IDAHO. Post Falls. Contact: Sheri Stone, Box 1754, Post Falls ID 83854-1754. (208)667-9730. Membership (25) open. Sponsors an annual fall seminar.

ILLINOIS

***CHRISTIAN WRITERS GROUP.** Contact: Diane Skinner, Route 3, Shelbyville IL 62565.

DECATUR BRANCH OF AMERICAN PEN WOMEN. Around Decatur. Contact: Martha B. Query, Rte. 1 Box 379, Maroa IL 61756-9503. (217)794-3796. Membership (10) open. Working group.

***JUVENILE FORUM.** Moline. Contact: David R. Collins, 3403 45th St., Moline IL 61265. (309)762-8985. Membership (8-15) open to those writing for children or youth.

***QUAD-CITY CHRISTIAN WRITERS CLUB.** Treasurer: Enid Rebenar, 545 - 42nd Ave. #813, East Moline IL 61244.

+TRUE VINE CHRISTIAN FELLOWSHIP, Faith Logan, 813 S. 13th St., Springfield IL 62702. Membership (8) open.

INDIANA

CHRISTIAN WRITERS GUILD. Crawfordsville. Contact: Aileen Karg, 1004 Cottage Ave., Crawfordsville IN 47933. (317)362-9186. Membership (10) open.

***CREATIVE WRITERS.** Marion. Contact: Mary M. Cain, 631 Candlewood Dr., Marion IN 46952. (317)662-6222. Membership (14) open.

FORT WAYNE CHRISTIAN WRITERS CLUB. Fort Wayne. Contact: Linda R. Wade, 739 W. Fourth St., Fort Wayne IN 46808-2613. (219)422-2772. Membership (25) open.

***SEYMOUR CHRISTIAN WRITER'S CLUB.** Contact: Anna Belle Stewart, Route 2 Box 29, Seymour IN 47274. (812)523-8178. Membership open.

THE WRITING ACADEMY. Contact: Rev. Benny Boling, PO Box 10783, Springfield MO 65808-0783. Membership (56) open. Sponsors year-round correspondence writing program and annual seminar in August (held in IN).

IOWA

CEDAR RAPIDS CHRISTIAN WRITER'S CRITIQUE GROUP. Contact: Helen Hunter, 1132-21st St. SE, Cedar Rapids IA 52403. (319)362-4777. Membership (12-18) open.

***RIVER CITY WRITERS.** Council Bluffs. Contact: Dee Barrett, 16 Susan Lane, Council Bluffs IA 51503. (712)322-7692. Membership (4-6) open.

KANSAS

***CHRISTIAN WRITERS GROUP.** Contact: Shirley Burr, 506 Hampton Rd., Wichita KS 67206.

***CHRISTIAN WRITERS GROUP OF TOPEKA** Contact: Charles White, 4102 NW Dondee Ln., Topeka KS 66618. (913)286-0388. Membership (14) open.

CREATIVE WRITERS FELLOWSHIP. Newton, Halsted, Hesston. Contact: Chester Osborne, 429 N Weaver, Hesston, KS 67062. Membership (15) open.

***LAMPLIGHTERS CHRISTIAN WRITERS CLUB.** Andover. Contact: Sharon Stanhope, Box 415, Benton KS 67017. (316)778-1043. Membership (20) open.

LEARNERS CHRISTIAN WRITING CLUB. Medicine Lodge. Contact: Dorothy Reed, 317 W Kansas, Medicine Lodge KS 67104-1438. (316)886-5709. Membership (10) open. Sponsors fall workshop.

PITTSBURG CHRISTIAN WRITERS FELLOWSHIP. Pittsburg. Contact: Anita Heistand, Route 2, Box 484, Gelena KS 66739-9445. (316)856-5157. Membership (12) open.

PRAIRIE WRITERS. Larned. Contact: Marilyn Phemister, 206 E 10th St., Larned KS 67550. (316)285-6217. Membership (3-4) open.

KENTUCKY

***CHRISTIAN WRITERS GROUP.** Contact: Jerry Hopkins, Box 121, Mount Vernon KY 40456.

JACKSON CHRISTIAN WRITERS' CLUB. Jackson or Vancleve. Contact: Donna J. Woodring, Box 10, Vancleve KY 41385-0010. (606)666-5000. Membership (10) open.

***OHIO VALLEY FELLOWSHIP OF CHRISTIAN WRITERS.** Contact: Irmgard L. Williams, Rt. 6 Box 108, 1280 Adams Ln., Henderson KY 42420. (502)826-4144. Membership open.

THE PRESBYTERIAN WRITERS GUILD. No regular meetings. National writers organization with a quarterly newsletter. Dues $15 per year. Contact: Ann Barr Weems, 6900 Kingsbury Blvd., St. Louis MO 63130. (314)725-6290. Sponsoring an April 22-26, 1994 seminar in Louisville KY.

LOUISIANA

+LOUISIANA CHRISTIAN WRITERS GUILD. Various locations. Contact: Dr. Donald M. Aycock, P.O. Box 12765, Lake Charles LA 70612-2765. (318)855-6280. Membership (50+) open.

MARYLAND

ANNAPOLIS FELLOWSHIP OF CHRISTIAN WRITERS. Annapolis. Leader is Mark Littleton. Contact: Jeri Sweany, Box 411, Annapolis MD 21404. (410)267-0924. Membership (11-15) open.

MASSACHUSETTS

***CHRISTIANS IN THE ARTS NETWORKING INC.** No meetings. Networking, newsletter and data base. Address: Box 1941, Cambridge MA 02238.

WESTERN MASSACHUSETTS CHRISTIAN WRITERS FELLOWSHIP. Springfield. Contact: Barbara A. Robidoux, 127 Gelinas Dr., Chicopee MA 01020. (413)594-6567. Membership (50) open. Monthly newsletter.

MICHIGAN

***CHRISTIAN WRITERS FELLOWSHIP.** Royal Oak. Contact: Audrey Perry, 255 W 14 Mile #1518, Clawson MI 48017. (313)288-0913. Membership (75) open.

***CHRISTIAN WRITERS GROUP.** Contact: Shirley J. Ruder, 5515 Gun Lake Rd., Hastings MI 49058.

MINNESOTA

MINNESOTA CHRISTIAN WRITERS GUILD. Edina. Contact: Joan C. Webb, 7749 Cayenne Plaza W., Woodbury MN 55125. (612)738-8745. Membership (95+) open. Sponsors two writers' seminars each year (spring & fall).

MISSOURI

***CHRISTIAN WRITERS GROUP.** Contact: Reba Fitz, 202 Ballman, Ferguson MO 63135.

***CHRISTIAN WRITERS GROUP.** Contact: Carol Patterson, Rt. 1 Box 77, Osawatomie KS 66064.

***CHRISTIAN WRITERS GROUP.** Contact: Earl A. Vansickle, 417 W. Halsey St., Maryville MO 64468. (816)582-3440.

***CHRISTIAN WRITERS GROUP.** Contact: Marjorie Bellavia, 5102 Mulberry Terrace, St. Joseph MO 64506.

***INSPIRATIONAL WRITERS WORKSHOP OF GREATER ST. LOUIS.** St. Charles. Contact: Lila Wold Shelburne, 23 Blackberry, St. Louis MO 63301. (314)946-8533. Membership (2-3) open to writers.

***CHRISTIAN WRITERS WORKSHOP.** St. Louis. Contact: Celeste Rhea, 7527 Flora Ave., Maplewood MO 63143. (314)645-5460. Membership (8) open.

***NORTHLAND CHRISTIAN WRITERS.** Kansas City. Contact: Margaret Owen, 207 NW 67th St., Gladstone MO 64118. (816)436-5240.

SPRINGFIELD CHRISTIAN WRITERS CLUB. Contact: Eleanor G. Syler, RR 3 Box 255, Strafford MO 65757. (417)736-2565. Membership (20) open.

***UMC CHRISTIAN WRITERS GUILD**. Columbia. Contact: Mike Kademan, 3401 Crestview, Columbia MO 65201. (314)445-6533. Membership open.

MONTANA

HELENA CHRISTIAN WRITERS. Contact: Lenore Puhek, 1215 Hudson, Helena MT 59601. (406)443-2552. Membership (12) open as space allows. Has one-day writers retreat for members.

***MONTANA CHRISTIAN WRITERS**. Contact: Margaret Wilkison, 2007 Sweet Grass Rd., Helena MT 59061. (406)442-9939.

NEBRASKA

***LINCOLN WORD WEAVERS.** Contact: Frenchy Dennis, 2212 Hanover Ct., Lincoln NE 68512. (402)421-3670. Membership (10) open.

NEW HAMPSHIRE

THE WORDSMITHS. Nashua. Contact: Cynthia Vlatas, 5 Jeremy Ln., Hudson NH 03051. (603)882-2851. Membership (15) open.

NEW JERSEY

NEW JERSEY CHRISTIAN WRITERS FELLOWSHIP OF SCOTCH PLAINS. Scotch Plains. Contact: Fran Pasch, 165 Norwood Ave., North Plainfield NJ 07060. (908)755-2075. Membership (10) open.

NEW JERSEY SOCIETY OF CHRISTIAN WRITERS. Fairton. Contact: Dr. Mary Ann Diorio, Box 748, Millville NJ 08332-0748. (609)327-1231. Membership (49) open. Sponsors fall seminar.

RAINBOW WRITERS. Bridgewater. Contact: Dr. Megan D. Simpson, 9 Iroquois Trail, Branchburg NJ 08876-5451. (908)231-9437. Membership (8) open.

***SOUTH JERSEY CHRISTIAN WRITERS FELLOWSHIP.** Atlantic City. Contact: Sandi Cleary, 308 Clark Pl., Northfield NJ 08225. (609)646-5694.

NEW MEXICO

MESILLA VALLEY CHRISTIAN WRITERS CLUB. Las Cruces. Contact: Jewel Johnson, 2050 Thomas Dr., Las Cruces NM 88001. (505 521-0316. Membership open. Sponsors annual seminar (May 7, 1994).

SOUTHWEST CHRISTIAN WRITERS ASSOCIATION. Farmington. Contact: Kathy Cordell, 91 - Rd 3450, Flora Vista NM 87415. (505)334-0617. Membership (14) open. Sponsors annual one-day seminar in September.

NEW YORK

***BROOKLYN WRITER'S CLUB.** Contact: Ann Dellarocco, Box 184, Bath Beach Station, Brooklyn NY 11214. (718)837-3484. Membership (500+) open.

+NEW YORK CHRISTIAN WRITERS GROUP. New York. Contact: Sharita Hunt, c/o Calvary Baptist Church, 123 W. 57th St., New York NY 10019. (212)975-0170. Membership (20) open.

***SYRACUSE CHRISTIAN WRITERS' GUILD.** Liverpool. Contact: Janice Wise, 2178 Slussun Rd., West Monroe NY 13167. (315)668-2874. Membership (25-60) open. Sponsors annual seminar.

NORTH CAROLINA

***CHRISTIAN WRITERS CLUB.** Contact: David F. Browning, Box 4311, Rocky Mount NC 27801. (919)442-7119.

FORSYTHE FELLOWSHIP OF CHRISTIAN WRITERS. Winston-Salem. Contact: Catherine Jackson, 113D Westgate Circle, Winston-Salem NC 27106. (919)765-3028. Membership (10) open.

OHIO

***AKRON MANUSCRIPT CLUB.** Contact: Tom Raber, Box 966, Cuyahoga Falls OH 44223. (216)928-7268. Membership open. Sponsors annual writers' conference in May.

COLUMBUS CHRISTIAN WRITERS. Contact: Brenda Custodio, 3732 Shoreline Dr., Columbus OH 43232. (614)837-8825. Membership (50) open. Sponsors a fall workshop.

DAYTON CHRISTIAN SCRIBES. Kettering. Contact: Lois Pecce, Box 613, Dayton OH 45459-0613. (513)433-6470. Membership (42) open.

GREATER CINCINNATI CHRISTIAN WRITERS' FELLOWSHIP. Contact: Teresa Cleary, 895 Garnoa St., Cincinnati OH 45231-2618. (513)521-1913. Membership (15) open.

***LEBANON CHRISTIAN WRITERS GROUP.** Contact: Jayne Schooler, 506 S. Elm St., W. Carrollton OH 45449. Membership (20-25) open.

MARION AREA CHRISTIAN WRITERS. Marion. Contact: Irene M. Sprague, 603 Henry St., Marion OH 43302. (614)387-3047. Membership (12) open. May sponsor an April seminar.

NORTHWEST OHIO CHRISTIAN WRITERS. Bowling Green. Contact: Nancy Kintner, 4235 Lyman, Toledo OH 43612-1584. (419)478-1055. Membership (30) open. Sponsors a Saturday seminar in September.

***OHIO FELLOWSHIP OF CHRISTIAN WRITERS.** Contact: John G. Hoffman, 233 W. Church St., Marion OH 43302. (614)387-6683. Membership open. Sponsors annual writers' conference.

STATELINE CHRISTIAN WRITER'S CLUB. Celina. Contact: Shirley Knox, 54106 Club Island Rd., Celina OH 45822. (419)268-2040. Membership (10) open.

+WESTERN OHIO CHRISTIAN WRITERS. Sidney. Contact: Alice Linsley, 231 N. Miami Ave, Sidney OH 45365. (513)663-4131. Membership (28) open.

OKLAHOMA

***THE KING'S SCRIBES.** Contact: Shirlene Braswell, 4501 N. College, Bethany OK 73008.

***TULSA CHRISTIAN WRITERS.** Contact: Vicki Musser, 14801 E. 111th St., Broken Arrow OK 74011-3904. (918)251-2706. Membership (65) open. Sponsors annual spring writers' conference.

OREGON

***CHRISTIAN SCRIBES.** Contact: Shirley Cody, 9340 SE Morrison, Portland OR 97216.

OREGON ASSOCIATION OF CHRISTIAN WRITERS. Contact: Marcia Mitchell, pres., 4400 Bren Loop NE, Salem OR 97305. (503)588-0372. Meets three times annually: February in Salem, May in Eugene, and October in Portland. All-day Saturday meetings. Membership (250) open. Sponsors annual conference in August (near Salem).

THE RIGHT TO WRITE CRITIQUE GROUP. Salem. Contact: Marcia Mitchell, 4400 Bren Loop N.E., Salem OR 97305. (503)588-0372. Membership (7) not open.

SMITH ROCK CHRISTIAN WRITERS. Redmond area. Contact: Josephine Manes, 2135 NE O'Neil Way, Redmond OR 97756. (503)548-8872. Sponsors Saturday seminars in April & September. Membership (5) open.

WORDSMITHS. Gresham/East Multnomah County. Contact: Susan Thogerson Maas, 27526 SE Carl St., Gresham OR 97080-8215. (503)663-7834. Membership (6) open. Christian and secular writers.

PENNSYLVANIA

***CHRISTIAN WRITERS GROUP.** Contact: Linda Brickajlik, RR 4 Box 389, Perkasie PA 18944.

***THE FIRST WORD.** Sewickley. Contact: Shirley Stevens, 326 B Glaser Ave., Pittsburgh PA 15202. (412)761-2618. Membership (12) open.

GREATER PHILADELPHIA CHRISTIAN WRITERS' FELLOWSHIP. Broomall. Contact: Marlene Bagnull, 316 Blanchard Rd., Drexel Hill PA 19026. (215)626-6833. Membership (50) open. Sponsors annual writers` conference.

HARRISBURG AREA CHRISTIAN WRITERS' FELLOWSHIP. Mechanicsburg. Contact: Georgia Burkett, 220 Dock St., Middletown PA 17057. (717)944-4427. Membership (60) open.

MONTROSE CHRISTIAN WRITERS FELLOWSHIP. Contact: Patti Souder, 35 Lake Ave, Montrose PA 18801. (717)278-4815. Membership (15) open.

YORK WRITERS. Contact: Rita Atwell-Holler, 100 Greenwood Rd., York PA 17404-5766. (717)792-0228. Membership (30) open. Sponsors January seminar.

SOUTH CAROLINA

CHRISTIAN WRITERS FELLOWSHIP INTL. Contact: Sandy Brooks, Rt. 3 Box 1635, Jefferson Davis Rd, Clinton SC 29325. (803)697-6035. No meetings, but offers bimonthly newsletter (Cross & Quill), prayer fellowship, writing instruction, and consultations. Membership open.

+CHRISTIAN WRITERS GROUP. Greenville. Contact: Nancy Parker, 150-12C Oak Ridge Place, Greenville SC 29615. (803)281-0876. Membership (6) open.

+SPARTANBURG WRITERS GROUP. Contact: Linda Gilden, 105 Pheasant Rd., Spartanburg SC 20302. Membership (6) open.

TENNESSEE

***CHATTANOOGA BIBLE INSTITUTE CHRISTIAN WRITERS WORKSHOP**. Chattanooga. Contact: Barbara Tucker, 1902 Duncan Ave., Chattanooga TN 37404. (615)624-1346. Membership (10) open.

TEXAS

***CHRISTIAN WRITERS LEAGUE OF AMERICA.** Contact: Dr. Noel Dudley, RR 2 Box 505, San Benito TX 78586.

***GOSPEL ARTISTS AND MUSICIANS ASSOCIATION.** Contact: Lena Nelson Dooley, 1913 Sage Trail, Hurst TX 76054. (817)281-1599. Monthly meetings and workshops.

INSPIRATIONAL WRITERS ALIVE! Pasadena/ Houston/Amarillo. Contact: Maxine E. Holder, 3606 Longwood Dr., Pasadena TX 77503-2221. (713)477-3716. Membership (103) open. Sponsors summer seminar. Monthly newsletter.

INSPIRATIONAL WRITERS ALIVE!/AMARILLO CHAPTER. Contact: Helen Luecke, 2921 S. Dallas, Amarillo TX 79103-6713. (806)376-9671. Membership (30) open.

+INSPIRATIONAL WRITERS ALIVE!/DAYTON CHAPTER. Dayton, TX. Contact: Mary Ann Evans, (409)267-3284 or Shelia Shook, (409)258-7961. Membership open.

***INSPIRATIONAL WRITERS ALIVE!/SECOND BAPTIST CHAPTER.** NW Houston. Contact: Kay Carpenter, (713)667-9607. Membership (30) open.

SOUTHWEST CHRISTIAN WRITERS GUILD. Dallas. Contact: Jan Winebrenner, 2709 Winding Hollow, Plano TX 75093. (214)783-6319. Membership (60) open. Sponsors early October seminar.

***RED CLAY WRITERS.** Marshall. Contact: Ernestine Finigan, P.O. Box 8513, Marshall TX 75670.

UTAH

UTAH CHRISTIAN WRITERS FELLOWSHIP. Salt Lake City. Contact: Kimberly Malkogannis, 117 W Park St., Copperton UT 84006-1134. (801)568-0939. Or Kate Mauch, (801)942-1803. Membership (20+) open. Monthly newsletter $12.

VIRGINIA

***CHRISTIAN WRITERS GROUP.** Contact: Mrs. Reeford Chaney, 3910 Monza Dr., Richmond VA 23234.

***CHRISTIAN WRITERS GROUP.** Contact: LaVera Murray, 5003 Treetop Ln., Alexandria VA 22310.

S.O.N. WRITERS. Alexandria. Contact: Susan Lyttek, 2434 Temple Ct., Alexandria VA 23307. (703)768-5582 (after 6 p.m.). Membership (10) open.

WASHINGTON

ADVENTIST WRITERS ASSOCIATION OF WESTERN WASHINGTON. Seattle area. Contact: Marion Forschler, 18115 - 116th Ave. SE, Renton WA 98058-6562. (206)235-1435. Membership (25) open. Newsletter $10/yr. Sponsors annual writers` conference.

+CHILDREN'S WRITING CRITIQUE GROUP. Spokane. Contact: Pat Pfeiffer, P.O. Box 104, Otis Orchards WA 99027-0104. (509)927-7671 or 226-3532 (evenings). Or call Christian at (509)448-0593. Membership open.

CHRISTIAN WRITERS. Walla Walla. Contact: Dolores Walker, 904 Ankeny, Walla Walla WA 99362-3705. (509)529-2974. Membership (8) open.

***CHRISTIAN WRITERS GROUP.** Contact: Arlie Hull, 166 Summerside Dr., Centralia WA 98531.

KITSAP COUNTY CHRISTIAN WRITERS SUPPORT GROUP. Bainbridge Island. Contact: Kay Stewart, 7584 Meadowmeer Ln., Bainbridge Island WA 98110. (206)842-4269.

NORTHWEST CHRISTIAN WRITERS ASSN. Bellevue. Contact: Agnes Lawless, 17462 NE 11th St., Bellevue WA 98008-3814. (206)644-5012. Meets monthly. Membership (90) open.

+NOVELIST CRITIQUE GROUP. Spokane. Contact: Pat Pfeiffer, P.O. Box 104, Otis Orchards WA 99027-0104. (509)927-7671 or 226-3532 (evenings). Membership open.

SOUTH KING COUNTY CHRISTIAN WRITERS. Des Moines. Contact: Carolyn Bishop Robinett, 1717 S. 268th St., Kent WA 98032-1414. (206)839-4732. Membership (10) open.
***SPOKANE CHRISTIAN WRITERS.** Contact: Niki Anderson. (509)448-6622. Membership open.

WASHINGTON CHRISTIAN WRITERS FELLOWSHIP. Seattle. Contact: Elaine Wright Colvin, Box 11337, Bainbridge Island WA 98110. (206)842-9103. Membership (300) open. Dues $15. Plans a February 1994 seminar.

WENATCHEE CHRISTIAN WRITERS` FELLOWSHIP. East Wenatchee. Contact: Shirley R. Pease, 1818 Skyline Dr. #31, Wenatchee WA 98801. (509)662-8392. Membership (35) open. Plans mini seminar in May 1994 (tentative).

***WHATCOM CHRISTIAN WRITERS CLUB.** Group does not meet regularly. Area contact: Judy Slotemaker, 840 E Pole Rd., Lynden WA 98264. (206)354-2636.

WRITERS INFORMATION NETWORK (W.I.N.). Meetings held in various states as announced. Contact: Elaine Wright Colvin, Box 11337, Bainbridge Island WA 98110. (206)842-9103. Resource and referral/marketing newsletter. Membership open. Seminar date to be announced.

WISCONSIN

***THE PRESBYTERIAN WRITERS GUILD.** (Meets once a year where PCUSA General Assembly is held.) Dr. Dale Robb, president. Contact: Jeanne Giles, 625 Illinois Pl., Box 160, Palmyra NE 68418. Gives two annual awards, one to a seminary senior and one to a Presbyterian writer. Membership (140) open.

SWORD & LIGHT/GREATER MILWAUKEE CHRISTIAN WRITERS' GUILD. Milwaukee. Contact: Andrea Kuhn-Boeshaar, 10605 W. Wabash Ave., Milwaukee WI 53224-2315. (414)355-8915. Membership (5) open. Sponsors a seminar.

WISCONSIN FELLOWSHIP OF CHRISTIAN WRITERS. Janesville. Contact: Jean Marie Wuttke, 1710 Randolph Rd., Janesville WI 53545. (608)752-1323. Membership (6) open.

WORD & PEN CHRISTIAN WRITERS CLUB. Menasha. Contact: Beth Grosek, 529 E. Cecil St., Neenah WI 54956-3818. (414)727-4753. Membership (18) open.

CANADA

CHRISTIAN WRITERS CLUB. Waterloo, Ontario. Contact: Pat Breithaupt, 33 Scott St., Waterloo ON Canada. (519)886-4509.

CHRISTIAN WRITERS CLUB OF SOUTHERN MANITOBA. Winkler, Morden or Roland. Contact: Isabel Allison, Box 208, Roland MB, R0G 1T0 Canada. (204)343-2119. Membership (5) open.

FRASER VALLEY CHRISTIAN WRITERS. Clearbrook/ Abbotsford. Contact: Ingrid Shelton, 2082 Geneva Ct., Clearbrook, B C V2T 3Z2 Canada (Box 783, Sumas WA 98295). (604)859-7530. Membership (30) open.

***MANITOBA CHRISTIAN WRITERS ASSN.** Winnipeg. Contact: Eleanor Bilsland, 201 - 177 Watson St., Winnipeg MB R2P 2P8 Canada. Membership (15) open.

***SPIRITWOOD SCRIBES.** Meets 19X/yr. Contact: Richard W. Unger, Box 212, Spiritwood SK, S0J 2M0. (306)883-2462. Annual dues $5. Membership open.

+STRATHROY WRITERS CLUB. Contact: Jean Thompson, 498 Saulsbury St., Strathroy ON N7G 2B6 Canada. Membership (9) open.

+SWAN VALLEY WRITERS GUILD. Manitoba. Contact: Marlene Hohne, Box 273, Minitonas MB R0L 1G0 Canada. (204)525-4652. Membership (8) open.

+WRITERS CHALLENGE & SUPPORT GROUP. Langley, BC. Contact: K. Christy Bowler, Box 56040, Valley Center PO, Langley BC V3A 8B3 Canada. (604)857-2696. Membership (20-25) open.

TRINIDAD/TOBAGO

***BEST NEWS WRITERS CLUB**. San Juan. Contact: Peter Lee Sam, 52 Tenth St., Barataria, Trinidad, West Indies. 675-1515. Membership (10) open. Sponsoring 1994 seminar.

Note: If your group is not listed here, please send information to: Sally Stuart, 17768 SW Pointe Forest Ct., Aloha OR 97006. December 15 is deadline for the next year's edition.

EDITORIAL SERVICES

The following listing is included because so many writers contact me looking for experienced/qualified editors who can critique or evaluate their manuscripts. These people from all over the country offer this kind of service. I cannot personally guarantee the work of any of those listed, so you may want to ask for references or samples of work.

The following abbreviations indicate what kinds of work they are qualified to do: GE indicates they do general editing/manuscript evaluation; LC indicates line editing or copy editing; GH - Ghostwriting; CA - co-authoring; B - brochures; NL - newsletters; SP - special projects; and BC - book contract evaluation. The following abbreviations indicate the types of material they evaluate: A - articles, SS - short stories, P - poetry, F - fillers, N - novels, NB - nonfiction books, BP - book proposals, JN - juvenile novels, PB- picture books, BS - Bible studies, T - technical material, E - essays, D - devotionals, S-scripts.

Always send a copy they can write on and an SASE for return of your material.

ARIZONA

DONNA GOODRICH, 648 S Pima St., Mesa AZ 85210. (602)962-6694. Call/write. GE/LC. Does A/SS/P/F/N/NB/BP/JD. $1.50/pg.

KAREN MARTELL, 5829 N. 81sr St., Scottsdale AZ 85250. (602)991-1134. Fax: (602)949-1041. Call/write. GE/LC. Does A/SS/F/N/NB/JN/BS/T/D. Charges $15/hr-$1.50/pg.

'LEEN POLLINGER, 12610 Westgate Dr, Sun City West AZ 85375-5137. (602)546-4757. Call/write. GE/LC. Does SS/F/N/NB/BP/JN/BS/D. Charges $12-35/hr depending on work done. Fee schedule available for SASE.

CALIFORNIA

CHRISTIAN COMMUNICATOR MANUSCRIPT CRITIQUE SERVICE, 3133 Puente St., Fullerton CA 92635-1952. Phone & Fax: (714)990-1532. Call/write/send material with $60 deposit. Staff of 7 editors. GE/LC/book contract evaluation. Does A/SS/P/F/N/NB/BP/JN/PB/BS/TM/E/D/S. Articles & stories $45. Three-chapter book proposal $60. Additional editing $15/hr.

DINA DONOHUE, 1633 Diamond St. #9, San Diego CA 92109-3161. (619)272-2890. Write. GE. Does A/SS/F/D. Articles/1,500 wds/$20, short stories/3,000 wds/$25; $5 ea, additional 1,000 wds; fillers/to 750 wds/$10.

DIANE FILLMORE PUBLISHING SERVICES, 13776 Starhill Ln., LaPuente CA 91746-2733. (818)336-5899. Call/write. GE/LC/GH/CA/B/NL/SP. Does A/SS/F/N/NB/BS/D/small group or SS curriculum. Charges $15/hr.

JOY P. GAGE, 99 Yosemite Rd., San Raphael CA 94903. (415)499-8027. Send material with $25 deposit. GE. Does A/N/NB/BP/BS/E/D. Charges $25/hr.

+VICKI HESTERMAN, PhD, P.O. Box 6788, San Diego CA 92166. (619)224-4549. Call/Write. GE/LC/CA/SP. Does A/NB/BP/TM/E/D. Specializes in helping people tell their personal stories. Charges standard rates.

DARLENE HOFFA, 512 Juniper St., Brea CA 92621. (714)990-5980. Write. GE. Does A/F/NB/BP/BS/D. Charges $35/article or short piece.; $65 for book ms up to 52 pgs, plus $1.25/pg.; or $15/hr.

DENELLA KIMURA, 1000 Cottonwood Dr., Roseville CA 95661-4724. (916)783-7866. GE/LC. P/F/D. Send $10/poem; $45 for poetry book evaluation. Produces chapbooks.

***LIGHTHOUSE EDITING/DR. LON ACKELSON**, 13326 Community Rd., #11, Poway CA 92064. (619)748-9258. Write. GE/LC/revision. Does A/SS/BP/BS. Charges $25 for article/short story critique; $35 for book proposal; $25 + $3/pg for critique and revision.

MARY CARPENTER REID, 925 Larchwood Dr., Brea CA 92621. (714)529-3755. Write. GE. Does A/SS/N/BP/JN/PB/E. Charges $35/article or short piece; $65 for book ms up to 52 pgs, plus $1.25/pg.

JANE RUMPH, 1130 Leonard Ave., Pasadena CA 91107-1746. (818)351-8703. Write. GE/LC. Does A/F/NB/BS/T/E/D/theses/dissertations. Charges $15-20/hr.

+DR. WESLEY SHARPE, 29416 Providence Way, Hayward CA 94544-6416. (510)785-2049. Call/write/send material with $25. GE/LC/B/NL. Does A/F/NB/BP/D. Charges $30/hr. Contact for estimate.

LAURAINE SNELLING, 952 Marie Ave., Martinez CA 94553-3519. (510)372-9047. Call/write. GE/GH/CA/N/SP. Does A/SS/N/NB/BP/JN. Charges $40/hr, or by the project after discussion with client.

COLORADO

COLORADO CHRISTIAN WRITERS CONFERENCE/ DEBBIE BARKER, Box 3303, Lyons CO 80540. Phone & Fax: (303)823-5718. Call. GE/LC/book contract evaluation. Does A/SS/N/NB/BP/JN/BS/T/E/D/queries. Negotiable rates on a project basis.

***BEVERLY M. LEWIS**, 4265 Dream Ln., Colorado Springs CO 80917. (719)596-6965. Send with $1/pg. GE. Does A/SS/F/BP/JN/PB. Charges $1/pg.

***EDITH QUINLAN**, 9030 W. 3rd Pl., Lakewood CO 80226. (303)237-8358. Write. GE/LC. Does A/F/NB. Charges $10/hr.

***THE WRITING INSTITUTE/MONTE UNGER**, 1228 N. Custer Ave., Colorado Springs CO 80903. (719)471-8194. Fax:(719)471-0711. Call/write. GE. Does A/NB/BP. Rate sheet for SASE.

FLORIDA

***JULIA LEE DULFER**, 705 Hibiscus Trail, Melbourne Beach FL 32951. (407)727-8192. Write or call for information.

***KISTLER LONDON**, 325 Wilder Blvd. #302A, Daytona Beach FL 32114. (904)255-8585. Call/write. GE/LC/GH/CA/B/SP. Does A/SS/P/F/N/ NB/BP/BS/TM/medical. Also organizes, transcribes, writes, rewrites, produces camera-ready copy. Send for rate sheet.

LESLIE SANTAMARIA, 4019 Cardinal Blvd., Daytona Beach FL 32127. (904)788-7720. Call/write. GE/LC/GH/CA/SP. Does A/SS/N/NB/ BP/JN/T. Charges $1/page for GE; $2/page for LC; $15 minimum.

IDAHO

***PAGE ONE COMMUNICATIONS/KEN MCFARLAND**, 15580 Cantrice Ln., Caldwell ID 83605. (208)459-4200. Writing/editing/publishing.

ILLINOIS

+EDITECH/DOUGLAS C. SCHMIDT, 836 Benridge, Mundelein IL 60060. (708)949-5303. Write. GE/LC. Does A/SS/F/BS/T/E/D. Charges $25/hr or negotiated flat fee.

VIRGINIA J. MUIR, 130 Windsor Park Dr. #C205, Carol Stream IL 60188. (708)665-2994. Write. GE/LC/CA/SP. Does A/SS/F/N/NB/BP/JN/PB/BS/E/D. Charges $30/hr; $30 minimum, plus telephone, research expenses and postage.

***JIM RIORDAN**, 4207 W. Josephine Dr., Kankakee IL 60901. Write. GE. Does N/NB/BP/T. Book proposal $250; books under 200 pgs. $400; books over 200 pgs. $400 + $50/100 pgs.

***WIGHTMAN WEESE**, 1114 E. Wakeman, Wheaton IL 60187. (708)665-9064. Write. GE. Charges $18-20/hr.

+THE WRITER'S EDGE, P.O. Box 1266, Wheaton IL 60189. A subsidiary of Harold Shaw Publishers.
Charges $35 to evaluate a book proposal and if publishable, they will send it to editors who might be interested. If not publishable they will tell how to improve it. If interested, send an SASE for guidelines and a Book Information Form.

INDIANA

DENEHEN, INC./DR. DENNIS E. HENSLEY, 6824 Kanata Ct., Fort Wayne IN 46815-6388. (219)485-9891. Send/full payment. GE/LC/GH/CA/SP. Does A/SS/N/NB/BP/E/D/ editorials. Rate sheet for SASE.

MICHIANA EDITORIAL SERVICES/GRACE PETTIFOR, Box 356, Granger IN 46530. (219)272-7595. Write/call. GE/LC/SP/typesetting. Does A/SS/N/NB/JN/PB/BS/E/D. Rate sheet for SASE.

***PMN PUBLISHING/GEORGE ALLEN**, Box 47024, Indianapolis IN 46247. (317) 888-7156. Various editorial services. Call or write for services available and charges.

KANSAS

***ESTHER L. VOGT**, 113 S. Ash, Hillsboro KS 67063. (316)947-3796. Send/$25 deposit. GE/LC/GH. Does N/JN. $15 for first 1,200 wds; $12 for ea. 1,200 wds thereafter.

LOUISIANA

BLUE-PENCIL SPECIALISTS/JOHN M. CUNNINGHAM, JR., Box 640908, Kenner LA 70064. (504)467-2722. Write. GE/LC/B. Does A/SS/F/BS/D. Charges according to word count; rate sheet for SASE.

+GLORY ARTS/BARBARA NAUER, P.O. Box 82510, Baton Rogue LA 70884. (504)673-6481. Fax: (504)673-6330. Does editing, re-writing, ghosting, graphics, radio promo, and author advising. Charges by the hour. Send SASE for price list.

MARYLAND

NEE EDITORIAL SERVICE/KATHIE NEE, 7115 Varnum St., Landover Hills MD 20784. (301)577-9072. Call/write. GE/LC/GH/CA/B/SP. Does A/F/NB/BP/E/D/tracts/pamphlets/resumes/job application letters/ biographical sketches. Charges $10/hr and up. Brochure available for SASE.

MASSACHUSETTS

MARION VUILLEUMIER, 579 Buck Island Rd., West Yarmouth MA 02673. (508)775-4811. Call. GE (readies mss for presentation to publishers). Does NB/BP. $60 for initial reading & consultation; $30/hr. thereafter. Also has an information service: Writers' Helpline, (900)988-1838x549. $2/minute (3 minute max.). Gives up-to-date market news and writing tips.

WORD PRO/BARBARA ROBIDOUX, 127 Gelinas Dr., Chicopee MA 01020. (413)594-6567. Call/write. GE/LC/B/NL. Does A/SS/F/NB/BP/T/D. Fee negotiable.

MISSOURI

DEBI STACK, Box 11805, Kansas City MO 64138. (816)763-5743. Send #10 SASE for brochure. GE/LC/GH/B/NL/SP. Does A/SS/F/NB/BP/JN/PB/BS/customized marketing analyses. Charges $1-$2.50/pg. Consulting $15/hr. Market analysis $40/hr.

NEW HAMPSHIRE

SALLY WILKINS, Box 393, Amherst NH 03031-0393. (603)673-9331. Write. GE/LC. Does A/F/JN/PB/BS/T. Rate sheet for SASE.

NEW JERSEY

DAYSTAR COMMUNICATIONS/DR. MARY ANN DIORIO, Box 748, Millville NJ 08332. (609)327-1231. Fax: (609)327-0291. Write. GE/LC/B/NL/SP. Does A/SS/P/F/NB/BP/E/D/S/copy for ads and PR material/resumes/business letters. Rate sheet for SASE.

NEW MEXICO

***K.C. MASON**, 1882 Conejo Dr., Santa Fe NM 87501. Write for information, fees, and availability.

NEW YORK

WILLIAM H. GENTZ, 300 E. 34th St. (9C), New York NY 10016. (212)686-5737. Call/write. GE of book mss/contract evaluation. Charges by the project after consultation.

OHIO

+BOB HOSTETLER, 6687 Baker Rd., Somerville OH 45064. (513)726-6618. Call/write. GE/LC/CA/GH. Does A/SS/P/F/N/NB/BP/JN/PB/BS. Rate sheet available for SASE.

OREGON

***BEST SELLER CONSULTANTS/THORN & URSULA BACON**, Box 922, Wilsonville OR 97070. (503)682-3235. Helps author refine manuscript, then matches book with literary agent to sell it. Secular, but handles Christian books.

***CHRISTIAN WRITING SERVICES/ED STEWART**, 3540 SE Spring Dr., Hillsboro OR 97123. (503)640-2522. Call. LC/GH/CA. Does NB/BP. Charges by the project based on $35/hr.

GAIL DENHAM, Box 89, Newberg OR 97132. (503)538-4691. Call. GE. Does A/SS/P/F/JN/PB/E/D/brochures/newsletters. Has photos to go with articles or books. Charges $20/hour; $25 minimum.

MARION DUCKWORTH, 2495 Maple NE, Salem OR 97303. (503)364-9570. Call/write. GE. Does A/F/NB/BP/BS/D. Charges $10.00 for 1st 1,000 wds; $5 for each additional 1,000 or fraction. Contact for terms on other. Consultations or private lessons, $15/hr.

***NANCY HENDERSON**, Box 1472, Coos Bay OR 97420. (503)267-6692. Write. GE/LC. Does A/SS/P/N/NB/BP/TM. Usually charges a negotiated flat fee.

***LYON'S LITERARY SERVICES/ELIZABETH LYON**, 2123 Marlow Ln., Eugene OR 97401. (503)344-9118. Call/write. GE/LC. Does A/SS/N/NB/BP/JN/T. Variable rates, roughly $30/hr.

THE WRITE TOUCH/SALLY PETERSEN, 14815 SW 141st Ave., Tigard OR 97224. (503)639-9610. Fax: (503)590-0692. Call. GE/LC/B/N/SP. Does A/F/NB/BP/T. Will guide through self-publishing process. Makes bid based on hourly rate and estimate of job length (roughly $50/hr) for brochures, newsletters, etc; less for editing manuscripts.

***PRIMA FACIE PUBLISHERS/BEN RIGALL**, 534 NE 71st Ave., Portland OR 97213. (503)255-2199. Write or call. GE/LC. Contact for information and fees.

CONNIE SOTH, 4890 SW Menlo Dr., Beaverton OR 97005. (503)644-4972. Call/Write. GE/LC. Does A/N/NB. Negotiable rates.

SALLY STUART, 17768 SW Pointe Forest Ct., Aloha OR 97006. (503)642-9844. Call/write. GE. Does A/SS/N/NB/BP/JN/PB/E. Charges $20/hr. for critique/$25/hr. for consultations. Publishing contract evaluation $35-50.

PENNSYLVANIA

MARLENE BAGNULL, 316 Blanchard Rd., Drexel Hill PA 19026. (215)626-6833. Call/write. GE/LC. Does A/SS/N/NB/BP/JN/BS/D. Charges $20/hr.

+IMPACT COMMUNICATIONS/DEBRA PETROSKY, 11331 Tioga Rd., N. Huntingdon PA 15642-2445. (412)863-5906. Call. GE/LC/B/NL/SP. Does A/SS/F/N/NB/BP/BS/TM. Typesetting available. Charges $20/hr. Per page rates also available.

GAYLE ROPER, RD 6 Box 112, Coatesville PA 19320. (215)384-8125. Call. GE. Does A/SS/N/NB/BP/JN. Charges $25/hr.

SOUTH CAROLINA

CHRISTIAN WRITERS FELLOWSHIP INTL./SANDY BROOKS, Rt. 3 Box 1635, Clinton SC 29325. (803)697-6035. Send/$25 deposit. GE/LC. Does A/F/N/NB/JN/D. Charges $1/pg ($25 min.)for general editing; $2/pg ($30 min.) for line editing. Enclose payment.

TEXAS

NEW WRITER'S ADVISOR SERVICE/DEBORAH COX, 4950 FM1960 W. Ste. C348, Houston TX 77069. (713)583-2845. Always call first. GE/LC/GH/B/NL/SP. Does A/SS/P/F/N/NB/BP/JN/ PB/BS/TM/E/D/S. Call for quote on price. Also suggests publishers for books.

VIRGINIA

***HCI EDITORIAL SERVICES/DAVID HAZARD**, Box 71, Lincoln VA 22078. (703)338-7032. Write or call. GE. Does N/NB & BP. Works with agents and self-publishers. Fees on request.

TEXAS

SYLVIA BRISKEY, P.O. Box 9053, Dallas TX 75209-9053. (214)521-7507. Call/send ms/full payment. GE/LC. Does SS/P/N/JN/PB/children's stories/secular articles. Poetry, charges $5.60 plus $1/line; fiction $30 to 2,000 wds, $2.50/page thereafter.

WASHINGTON

***BIRDIE ETCHISON**, Box 877, Ocean Park WA 98640. (206)665-6576. Write. GE/LC. Does A/SS/F/N/BP/PB. Charges according to length, $15 minimum.

KALEIDOSCOPE PRESS/PENNY LENT, 2507 - 94th Ave. E., Puyallup WA 98371-2203. (206)848-1116 (phone & Fax:). Call/write/send material. GE/LC/G/CA/B/NL/SP. Does A/SS/F/N/NB/BP/JN/PB/BS/T/E/D. Line item editing $3/pg; other projects negotiated individually.

AGNES C. LAWLESS, 17462 NE 11th St., Bellevue WA 98008-3814. (206)644-5012. Write. GE/LC/CA. Does A/SS/P/F/N/NB/BP/JN/BS/E/D. Send SASE for rate sheet. $15/hr.

THE LITERARY (SERVICE) AGENCY/BRENDA WILBEE, 4514 Fir Tree Way, Bellingham WA 98226. (206)733-2774. GE/LC. Does N/NB. Charges $100 handling fee to determine if she can take on project. Various services from $1,000-$5,000. Rate sheet for SASE. Specialties include adult fiction, in-depth psychology, spirituality, and recovery issues.

***VIRGINIA A. MOODY**, 17402 - 114th Pl. NE, Granite Falls WA 98252. (206)691-5402. Call/write. GE/CA/B/NL/SP. Does A/SS/F/N/NB/BP/JN/PB/ BS/TM. Charges $1/pg. Very interested in co-authoring.

PAULINE SHEEHAN, Box 801, Lake Stevens WA 98258. (206)334-7049. Write/$20 deposit. GE/LC. Does A/N/NB/BP/JN/S. Charges $20 minimum, plus $2/pg after first 10 pages; $50 for a book proposal.

***SHIRLEY POPE WAITE**, 1604 Pleasant, Walla Walla WA 99362. (509)525-5592. Write. GE. Does A/F/Devotions/meditations. Charges $5-25 according to word count.

CHRISTIAN LITERARY AGENTS

+ALIVE COMMUNICATIONS, P.O. Box 49068, Colorado Springs CO 80949. (719)260-7080. Agent: Rick Christian. Well known in the industry. Est. 1989. Represents 40 clients. Open to unpublished authors (but most clients come from referrals). Handles novels for all ages, picture books, and adult nonfiction; short stories & articles. Deals in both Christian and general market.
Contact: Query with synopsis, author bio, and sample chapters/SASE.
Commission: 15%
Fees: Only extraordinary costs with client's pre-approval.
Comments: "We handle whatever our clients write. We pick clients carefully, then stick by them."
Tips: "Be original. There's too much 'me-too' publishing going on."

+BK NELSON LITERARY AGENCY, 84 Woodland Rd., Pleasantville NY 10570. (914)741-1322. Fax: (914)741-1324. Agent: John Benson. Recognized in the industry. Est. 1979. Represents 2 clients. Open to unpublished authors. Handles adult fiction and nonfiction, motion picture and television scripts.
Contact: Send inquiry and SASE with reading fee of $320.
Commission: 15%
Fees: The $320 reading fee also covers expenses.

BRANDENBURGH & ASSOCIATES LITERARY AGENCY, 24555 Corte Jaramillo, Murrieta CA 92562. (909)698-5200. Agent: Don Brandenburgh. Recognized in industry. Est. 1986. Represents 23 clients. Open to some unpublished authors. Handles adult novels and nonfiction (also adult nonfiction for general market if related to education and/or psychology). Books only.
Contact: Send letter of inquiry/SASE.
Commission: 10%; 20% for foreign or dramatic rights.
Fees: $35 for mailing/materials when contract is signed.

PEMA BROWNE LTD., Pine Rd. HCR Box 104B, Neversink NY 12765. (914)985-2936. Fax: (914)985-7635. Agents: Perry or Pima Browne.
Recognized in industry. Est. 1966. Open to unpublished authors. Handles adult/teen children novels; adult/teen nonfiction; picture books; movie scripts from published books. Book authors & illustrators only.
Contact: Query with credentials & SASE.
Commission: 15%.
Fees: No reading fees for Christian mss, juvenile or romance mss.

LOIS CURLEY ENTERPRISES, 18755 W. Bernardo Dr., Suite 1039, San Diego CA 92127-3010. (619)675-2031. Fax: (619)675-2026. Agents: Lois L. Curley or Eva DeLos. Recognized in industry. Est. 1979. Represents 57 clients. Open to unpublished authors. Rarely handles adult fiction; handles children's fiction & picture books, nonfiction for all ages; also academic topics. Books only. Currently has a waiting list of new clients.
Contact: Query, Fax: or call. If interested, they'll send submissions guidelines.
Commission: 15%

Fees: Also offers various consulting/ evaluation services at $40/hr. or by the number of pages. See submission guidelines.

THE CURTIS BRUCE AGENCY, P.O. Box 967, Plover WI 54467-0967. (715)341-3096. Fax: (715)341-3296. President: Bruce W. Zabel. Contact: Curtis H.C. Lundgren. Recognized in industry. Est. 1990. Represents 80 clients. 10% unpublished authors. Handles child/teen/adult novels; child/teen/adult nonfiction; picture books. Specializes in novels.
Contact: Query with brief synopsis, sample chapter, resume, and return postage mailer. Reports in 3-5 weeks on query; 18-24 wks on mss.
Commission: 15% on domestic fiction, nonfiction, dramatic & film sales; 20% on foreign sales. Offers a written contract.
Fees: Related office costs. Also offers marketability evaluation service, $100-200; critique service, $500-$1,000.

+DEERING LITERARY AGENCY, 1507 Oakmont Dr., Ste. B, Acworth GA 30102. (404)591-2051. Fax: (404)591-0369. Agent: Charles Deering. Recognized in the industry. Est. 1989. Represents 23 clients. Open to unpublished authors. Handles novels and nonfiction for all ages, picture books, scripts, and poetry books. Book length material only.
Contact: Query letter and synopsis.
Commission: 12%
Fees: Reading fee, plus expenses. i.e., postage, phone calls, Faxing, etc.
Tips: "I see so many mss that are not in the appropriate format. Please edit for spelling, tense, sentence structure, etc. Good religious material is so needed in our society today. Write uplifting material."

+JOYCE FARRELL AND ASSOCIATES, 669 Grove St., Upper Montclair NJ 07043. Phone/Fax: (201)746-6248. Agent: Joyce Farrell. Recognized in the industry. Est. 1985. Represents 15-20 clients. Open to new authors. Handles fiction and nonfiction for all ages, picture books, electronic books, issue books, scientific/psychological/theological books for a general audience.

GOOD NEWS LITERARY SERVICE, Box 4498, Visalia CA 93278. (209)636-0232 (also Fax:). Agent: Cynthia Wachner. Recognized by some in industry. Est. 1986. Represents 12 clients. No unpublished authors. Handles novels and nonfiction for all ages; picture books; scripts; stories, articles, plays.
Contact: Phone, Fax: or mail. Send proposal/chapter synopses/3 chapters; resume and tearsheets.
Commission: 15%; 20% foreign. Sliding percentage scale for magazine-length material.
Fees: $100 deposit toward out-of-pocket expenses. Charges a $1/pg reading fee.
Comments: "Interested in those fully committed to the work and time required to successfully market manuscripts."

+HARTLINE MARKETING, 123 Queenston Dr., Pittsburgh PA 14235. (412)829-2483. Fax: (412)829-2450. Agent: Joyce Hart. Recognized in industry. Est. 1990. Open to unpublished authors (with certain qualifications). Handles adult novels and nonfiction, especially health, motivational, financial, and self-help. Also provides marketing services for self-published books.

***HOLUB & ASSOCIATES**, 24 Old Colony Rd., North Stonington CT 06359. (203)535-0689. Agent: William Holub. Recognized by Catholic publishers. Est. 1966. Open to unpublished authors. Handles adult nonfiction; possibly picture books; Christian living in secular society.
Contact: Query with outline, 2 sample chapters, intended audience, and bio.
Commission: 15%.
Fees: Postage and photocopying.

***THE LITERARY (SERVICE) AGENCY**, 4514 Fir Tree Way. (206)733-2774. Agent: Brenda Wilbee.

MILLS HOUSE, 443 Pinehurst Ave., Unit 1, Los Gatos CA 95032. (408)371-7196. Agent: Roy M. Carlisle. Recognized in industry. Est. 1987. Represents 11 clients. Open to unpublished authors if PhD in psychology. Handles adult nonfiction; professional Christian psychology. Specializes in professional level books in psychology, recovery, and spirituality. Books only. Also sells Christian books to secular publishers.
Contact: Write.
Commission: 15%
Fees: Expenses for post, phone, copying. Also works as an editorial consultant and charges by the hour.

***JEAN V. NAGGAR LITERARY AGENCY**, 216 E. 75TH St., New York NY 11201. (212)794-1082. Agent; Jean Naggar. Not recognized in industry. Est. 1978. Represents 5 clients. Open to unpublished authors. Handles adult/teen/children novels and nonfiction, picture books. Handles articles/short stories only if handling book-length as well.
Contact: Query letter/1-2 pg. synopsis.
Commission: 15%; 20% foreign.
Fees: No reading fee, but copying, telephone & overseas mailing for clients.

+PEN & INK LITERARY AGENCY, 2867 Silvercliff Dr., Dayton OH 45449. (513)434-0686. Agent: Theresa Freed. Recognized in industry. Est. 1993. Building client list. Open to unpublished authors. Handles fiction and nonfiction for all ages, picture books, scripts, poetry books; informational, motivational and how-to. Books only.
Contact: Send SASE for information.
Commission: 15%; 20% foreign.
Fees: Charges a $90 reading fee that is refunded on receipt of advance from publisher; also office expenses and marketing fee.
Tips: "Please submit ms in proper form. This will save everyone time and money."

+PUBLISHING IDEAS UNLIMITED, 804 Howard St., Wheaton IL 60187. (708)668-4017. Fax: (708)668-4017. Agent: Mr. Leslie H. Stobbe. Recognized in the industry. Est. 1992. Represents 6 clients. Handles adult novels and adult nonfiction.

A RISING SUN LITERARY GROUP, 8010 Stonewood Dr, Kennesaw GA 30144. (404)514-0380. Agent; Lynn Watson. Recognized in the industry. Est. 1989. Represents 30 clients. Open to unpublished authors. Handles fiction and nonfiction for all ages, picture books, scripts and poetry books.
Contact: By phone or mail. Then send manuscript with a 1-3 page synopsis.
Commission; 13%.
Fees: Reading fee $125. Contract fee varies depending on manuscript.

+DICK SLEEPER, 18680 B Langensand Rd., Sandy OR 97055. (503)668-3454. Fax: (503)668-5314. Recognized in the industry (35 yrs). Est. 1993. Represents 12 clients. Open to unpublished authors. Handles children/teen/adult nonfiction and fiction; picture books.
Contact: Phone, Fax: or letter.
Commission: 15%
Fees: Copying/postage expenses. In some cases, a retainer.
Comments: "Not looking for new clients but will talk to anybody. I'm primarily a marketer doing agenting because I've been asked."

+WILLIAM PENS, 342 Alden Cove Dr., Smyrna TN 37167. (615)355-4455. Fax: (615)355-9977. Agent: William D. Watkins. Recognized in the industry. Est. 1993. Represents 8 clients. Open to unpublished authors. Handles adult novels and nonfiction. Books only.
Contact: Phone, Fax or mail.
Commission: 10% to negotiate contracts only; 15% for full literary services.
Fees: Charges for telephone, copying, mai,l and travel expenses.
Tips: "Unlike most other agents, I provide writing and editing services as well as consulting services for authors, publishers, and ministries."

+WOLGEMUTH & HYATT, INC., 330 Franklin Rd., Ste. 120, Brentwood TN 37024-0897. (615)370-9937. Fax: (615)370-9939. Agents: Michael S. Hyatt and Robert D. Wolgemuth. Well recognized in the industry. Est. 1992. Represents 25 clients. Open to unpublished authors. Handles only adult or teen/young adult nonfiction.
Contact: By letter.
Commission: 15%
Fees: No reading fees.
Other Services: Speaker's bureau. Manuscript Review Service (for a fee).
Comments: "We work with authors who are either best-selling authors or potentially best-selling authors. Consequently, we want to represent clients with broad market appeal."

ADDITIONAL AGENTS

NOTE: The following agents did not return a questionnaire, but have been identified as agents who handle religious manuscripts. Be sure to send queries first if you wish to submit to them.
(*) Indicates they are known in the industry.

Julian Bach Literary Agency
22 E. 71st St
New York NY 10021
(212)753-2605
nonfiction/fiction

Elizabeth H. Backman
Box 536
Johnnycake Hollow Rd
Pine Plains NY 12567
(518)398-6408
nonfiction/fiction

Michele Glance Serwach
Creative Concepts
LiteraryAgency
PO Box 10261
Harrisonburg VA 17105
(717)432-5054
nonfiction/fiction

Bonnie Crown
B R Crown Intl Literary & Arts Agency
50 E. 10th St
New York NY 10003
(212)475-1999
nonfiction/fiction

Carol Atwell
Diamond Literary Agency
3063 S Kearney St
Denver CO 80222
(303)759-0291
nonfiction/fiction

Janet Dight
Janet Dight Literary Agency
3075 Inspiration Dr
Colorado Springs CO 80917
(719)597-7675
nonfiction/fiction

Ethan Ellenberg
Ethan Ellenberg Liter Agency
#5-E 548 Broadway
New York NY 10012
(212)431-4554
nonfiction/fiction

Al Hart
Fox Chase Agency Inc
Rm 930/Public Ledger Bldg
Independence Square
Philadelphia PA 19106
(215)625-2450
nonfiction

Maia Gregory
Maia Gregory Assoc
311 E 72nd St
New York NY 10021
(212)288-0310
nonfiction

*Stephen Griffith
PO Box 3439
Boone NC 28707-0739
(704)262-3345

Nikki Cane
Gary L Hegler Literary Agency
Box 890751
Houston TX 77289
(713)486-8478
nonfiction/fiction

Lawrence Jordan
Lawrence Jordan Literary Agency
250 W 57th St Ste 1527
New York NY 10107
(212)690-2748
nonfiction/fiction

Ned Leavitt
The Ned Leavitt Agency
70 Wooster St #4F
New York NY 10012
(212)334-0999
nonfiction/fiction

K. Allman
Literary Marketing Consultant
One Hallidie Plaza #701
San Francisco CA 94102
(415)979-8170
nonfiction/fiction

*Etta G. Wilson
March Media
7003 Chadwick Dr. Ste. 256
Brentwood TN 37027
(615)370-3148
Children's books

Pamela G. Ahearn
Southern Writers
635 Gravier St #1020
New Orleans LA 70130
(504)525-6390
nonfiction/fiction

DENOMINATIONAL INDEX OF BOOK PUBLISHERS AND PERIODICALS

An attempt has been made to divide publishers into appropriate denominational groups. However, due to the extensive number of denominations included, and sometimes incomplete denominational information, some publishers may have inadvertently been included in the wrong list. **Additions and corrections are welcome.**

ASSEMBLIES OF GOD
Periodicals:
American Horizon
Advance
At Ease
CE Counselor
HiCall
High Adventure
Junior Trails
Live
Maranatha
Memos
Paraclete
Pentecostal Evangel
Pentecostal Testimony (Canada)
Resource (Canada)
Take Five
Woman's Touch
Youth Leader

BAPTIST, SOUTHERN
Book Publishers:
Broadman Press
Holman Bible
New Hope Publishers
Renewal Press
Southern Baptist Press
Women's Missionary Union

Periodicals:
Baptist History & Heritage
Challenge
Christian Single
Church Administration
Church Media Library
Church Musician
Church Recreation
Discipleship Training
event
Glory Songs
Growing Churches
Home Life
Mature Living
Music Leader
Music Makers
Music Time
Pioneer
Proclaim
Search
Senior Musician
Student, The
Young Musicians

BAPTIST, OTHER
Book Publishers:
Judson Press (American)
National Baptist (Missionary)

Periodicals:
American Baptist
Baptist Beacon
Baptist Informer (General)
Baptist Leader (American)
Certainty (Regular)
Challenge (Regular)
Co-Laborer (Free Will)
Conquest
Contact (Free Will)
The Five Stones (American)
Fundamentalist Journal
God's Special People (Independent)
Heartbeat (Free Will)
Impact (Conservative)
LIGHT...For/Christian Walk

***Due to printing considerations blank page 364 has been eliminated.**

(Independent)
Link & Visitor
Messenger, The
(Pentecostal Free Will)
Moments with God (North American)
Primary Pal (Regular)
Secret Place (American)
Standard, The
Writer's Forum

CATHOLIC
Book Publishers:
ACTA Publications
Alba House
American Catholic Press
Ave Maria Press
Don Bosco Publications
Brown Publishing
Catholic University of America Press
Center for Learning
Christian Classics
Cistercian Publications
Dimension Books
Franciscan Herald Press
Franciscan Univ. Press
Harper SF (Cath. bks)
ICS Publications
Liguori Publications
Liturgical Press
Loyola University Press
Thomas More Press
Orbis Books
Our Sunday Visitor
Pastoral Press
Paulist Press
Regina Press
Regnery Gateway
Resurrection Press
St. Anthony Messenger
St. Bede's Publications
St. Paul Books
Sheed & Ward
Tabor Publishing

Periodicals:
America
Annals of St. Anne
Arkansas Catholic
Arlington Catholic Herald
Bible Today
Canadian Catholic Review
Catechist
Catholic Accent
Catholic Courier
Catholic Digest
Catholic Exponent
Catholic Health World
Catholic Heritage
Catholic Life
Catholic Near East
Catholic New York
Catholic Parent
Catholic Sentinel
Catholic Telegraph
Catholic Twin Circle
Chicago Studies
Columbia
Commonweal
Companion of St. Francis
Compass
Conscience
The Critic
Eucharistic Minister
Family, The
Family Digest, The
Homiletic & Pastoral Review
Interim, The
Liguorian
Living Words
Marian Helpers Bulletin
Maryknoll
Messenger/Sacred Heart
Messenger (KY)
Messenger/St. Anthony
Miraculous Medal
Montana Catholic
My Friend
National Catholic Reporter
New Covenant
New Oxford Review
N.A. Voice of Fatima
Oblates
Oblate World
Our Family
Our Sunday Visitor
Pastoral Life
Prairie Messenger
Priest, The
Queen of All Hearts
Religion Teacher's Journal
Review for Religious
St. Anthony Messenger
St. Joseph`s Messenger
St. Willibrord Journal

Sisters Today
Social Justice Review
Spirit
Spiritual Life
Today's Catholic Teacher
Today's Parish
U.S. Catholic
YOU! Magazine
Youth Update

CHRISTIAN CHURCH/ CHURCH OF CHRIST
Book Publishers:
CBP Press (Disciples of Christ)
Chalice Press (Disciples of Christ)
College Press (Church of Christ)
Friendship Press (Church of Christ)
Pilgrim Press, The (United Church of Christ)

Periodicals:
Christian Chronicle
Christian Standard
Disciple, The (Disciples of Christ)
Four and Five
Lookout, The
R-A-D-A-R
Straight
Teenage Christian (Church of Christ)
Weekly Bible Reader

CHURCH OF GOD (Anderson, IN)
Book Publisher:
Warner Press
Periodicals:
Christian Leadership
Church of God MISSIONS
Pathways to God
Vital Christianity

CHURCH OF GOD (Cleveland, TN)
Periodicals:
Church of God EVANGEL
Lighted Pathway
Youth and CE Leadership

CHURCH OF GOD, OTHERS
Periodicals:
Bible Advocate (Seventh Day)
Church Advocate
Church Herald and Holiness Banner (Holiness)
Gem, The
Pentecostal Messenger

CHURCH OF THE NAZARENE
Book Publishers:
Lillenas (music)
Beacon Hill Press

Periodicals:
Children's Church Exch.
Discoveries
Herald of Holiness
Level C Teacher
Level D Teacher
Listen
Power and Light
Preacher's Magazine
Resource
Standard
Table Talk
Teens Today
Together Time
Wonder Time

EPISCOPAL/ANGLICAN
Book Publishers:
Alban Institute
Forward Movement
Morehouse Publishing

Periodicals:
Acts 29
Cathedral Age
Episcopal Life
Interchange
Living Church
The Witness

FREE WILL BAPTIST
Periodicals:
Co-Laborer
Heartbeat

FREE METHODIST
Periodicals:
Evangel
Light and Life
Light From the Word
Response (SPU)

LUTHERAN
Book Publishers:
Augsburg Press (ELCA)
Concordia
Langmarc Publishing

Periodicals:
Canada Lutheran (ELC - Canada)
Christmas (ELCA)
Cresset
Diaconalogue
Esprit (ELCC)
Evangelism (MO Synod)
Lutheran, The (ELCA)
Lutheran Digest
Lutheran Educ. (MO Synod)
Lutheran Forum
Lutheran Journal
Lutheran Laymen (MO Synod)
Lutheran Witness (MO Synod)
Lutheran Woman Today(ELCA)
Morning Glory
Northwestern Lutheran
Parenting Treasures (MO Synod)
Parish Teacher (ELCA)
Word & World (ELCA)
Teachers Inter. (MO Synod)

MENNONITE
Book Publishers:
Herald Press
Kindred Press

Periodicals:
Christian Living
Companions
Mennonite, The
Mennonite Brethren Herald
Mennonite Reporter
Mennonite Weekly Review
The Messenger
Missiology
On the Line
Partners
Provident Book Finder
Purpose
Story Friends
Story Mates
With

MISSIONARY CHURCH
Book Publisher:
Bethel Publishing

Periodicals:
Emphasis/Faith & Living
Ministry Today

PENTECOSTAL HOLINESS CHURCH
Periodicals:
ADVOCATE
CE Connection
Helping Hand, The
Worldorama

PRESBYTERIAN
Book Publishers:
John Knox Press
Presbyterian & Reformed
Westminster Press

Periodicals:
Assoc. Ref. Presbyterian
Covenanter Witness
Horizons (USA)
PCA Messenger
Presbyterian Outlook (USA)
Presbyterian Record
Presbyterian Survey

QUAKER/FRIENDS
Book Publishers:
Barclay Press
Friends United Press

Periodicals:
Evangelical Friend
Friends Journal

REFORMED CHURCHES
Periodicals:
Church Herald
Reformed Worship
Vision (MI)

SEVENTH-DAY ADVENTIST
Book Publishers:
Pacific Press
Remnant Publications
Review and Herald

Periodicals:
Cornerstone Connections
GUIDE Magazine
Insight (MD)
Insight/Out
Journal/Adventist Ed

Liberty
Message
Ministry
Our Little Friend
Primary Treasure
Signs of the Times
Vibrant Life
Young and Alive

UNITED METHODIST
Book Publishers:
United Methodist Publishing House
Imprints: Abingdon Press
Cokesbury
Dimensions Press
Discipleship Resources
Upper Room Books

Periodicals:
alive now!
Christian Social Action
Good News
Leader/Church School Today
Magazine/Christian Youth!
Mature Years
Methodist History
Nat. Christian Reporter
New World Outlook
Pockets
Quarterly Review
Response
United Methodist Reporter
Upper Room

UNITED PENTECOSTAL
Periodicals:
Conqueror, The
Pentecostal Homelife
Teen Life
Vision
Youth World

WESLEYAN CHURCH
Periodicals:
Changing Lives
Friend
In Touch
Vista (IN)
Wesleyan Advocate
Wesleyan World

MISCELLANEOUS DENOMINATIONS

Brethren Church
Brethren Evangelist

Christian Missionary & Alliance
Christian Publications

Christian (Plymouth) Brethren
Interest Magazine

Congregational
Congregational Journal

Evangelical Covenant Church
Cornerstone
Covenant Companion

Evangelical Free Church
Evangelical Beacon

Fellowship of Christian Assemblies
Fellowship Today

Fellowship of Evangelical Bible Churches
Gospel Tidings

Foursquare Gospel Church
Foursquare World Advance

Open Bible Standard Churches
MESSAGE of the Open Bible

United Brethren in Christ
The United Brethren

United Church of Canada
United Church Publishing House
United Church Observer

United Church of Christ
United Church Press

GENERAL INDEX

- A -

- B -

*Due to printing considerations blank page 370 has been eliminated.

- C -

- D -

- E -

- F -

- N -

- O -

- P -

- Q -

- R -

- S -

- T -

- U -